AME

publication of this book is supported by a grant from

JEWISH FEDERATION OF GREATER HARTFORD

For a complete list of books that are available in the series, visit brandeisuniversitypress.com

Gary Phillip Zola and Marc Dollinger, editors
  American Jewish History: A Primary Source Reader
Vincent Brook and Marat Grinberg, editors
  Woody on Rye: Jewishness in the Films and Plays of Woody Allen
Mark Cohen
  Overweight Sensation: The Life and Comedy of Allan Sherman
David E. Kaufman
  Jewhooing the Sixties: American Celebrity and Jewish Identity—Sandy Koufax, Lenny Bruce, Bob Dylan, and Barbra Streisand
Jack Wertheimer, editor
  The New Jewish Leaders: Reshaping the American Jewish Landscape
Eitan P. Fishbane and Jonathan D. Sarna, editors
  Jewish Renaissance and Revival in America
Jonathan B. Krasner
  The Benderly Boys and American Jewish Education
Derek Rubin, editor
  Promised Lands: New Jewish American Fiction on Longing and Belonging
Susan G. Solomon
  Louis I. Kahn's Jewish Architecture: Mikveh Israel and the Midcentury American Synagogue
Amy Neustein, editor
  Tempest in the Temple: Jewish Communities and Child Sex Scandals

Jack Wertheimer, editor
  Learning and Community: Jewish Supplementary Schools in the Twenty-first Century
Carole S. Kessner
  Marie Syrkin: Values beyond the Self
Leonard Saxe and Barry Chazan
  Ten Days of Birthright Israel: A Journey in Young Adult Identity
Jack Wertheimer, editor
  Imagining the American Jewish Community
Murray Zimiles
  Gilded Lions and Jeweled Horses: The Synagogue to the Carousel
Marianne R. Sanua
  Be of Good Courage: The American Jewish Committee, 1945-2006
Hollace Ava Weiner and Kenneth D. Roseman, editors
  Lone Stars of David: The Jews of Texas
Jack Wertheimer, editor
  Jewish Education in an Age of Choice
Edward S. Shapiro
  Crown Heights: Blacks, Jews, and the 1991 Brooklyn Riot
Marcie Cohen Ferris and Mark I. Greenberg, editors
  Jewish Roots in Southern Soil: A New History
Kirsten Fermaglich
  American Dreams and Nazi Nightmares: Early Holocaust Consciousness and Liberal America, 1957-1965
Andrea Greenbaum, editor
  Jews of South Florida
Sylvia Barack Fishman
  Double or Nothing? Jewish Families and Mixed Marriage

American Jewish History

A PRIMARY SOURCE READER

Edited by

GARY PHILLIP ZOLA

and

MARC DOLLINGER

BRANDEIS UNIVERSITY PRESS

Waltham, Massachusetts

BRANDEIS UNIVERSITY PRESS
© 2014 Brandeis University
All rights reserved
Manufactured in the United States of America
Designed by Richard Hendel
Typeset in Utopia by Integrated Publishing Solutions

For permission to reproduce any of the material
in this book, contact Brandeis University Press,
415 South Street, Waltham, MA 02453,
or visit brandeisuniversitypress.com

Library of Congress Cataloging-in-Publication Data
American Jewish history: a primary source reader /
edited by Gary Phillip Zola and Marc Dollinger.
    p. cm.—(Brandeis Series in American Jewish History,
Culture, and Life)
ISBN 978-1-61168-509-1 (cloth: alk. paper)—
ISBN 978-1-61168-510-7 (pbk.: alk. paper)—
ISBN 978-1-61168-511-4 (ebook)
1. Jews—United States—History. 2. Jew—United
States—History. I. Zola, Gary Phillip, editor.
II. Dollinger, Marc, 1964- editor.

E184.35.A45 2014
973'.04924—dc23
                        2014022377

To our students

CONTENTS

Preface *xxi*

List of Abbreviations *xxv*

Introduction *1*

CHAPTER 1.
Creating Community:
The American Jewish Experience during
the Colonial Period, 1654–1776 *7*

BEGINNINGS

1.01. Rabbi Isaac Aboab de Fonseca, Recife, Brazil, n.d. *9*

1.02. Recife, Brazil, by Zacharias Wagenaer, n.d. *10*

1.03. Peter Stuyvesant, Manhattan, to the Amsterdam Chamber of Directors, September 22, 1654 *10*

1.04. Amsterdam Jewry's Successful Intercession for the Jewish Immigrants, January 1655 *11*

1.05. Extract from Reply by the Amsterdam Chamber of the West India Company to Stuyvesant's Letter, April 26, 1655 *12*

1.06. Moses Lopez Becomes a Naturalized Citizen, 1741 *12*

1.07. Barnard Gratz to Michael Gratz, Giving Advice on Immigrating to Philadelphia, November 20, 1758 *13*

GOVERNMENT, POLITICS, AND CIVIC STATUS

1.08. Description by a Non-Jew of the Jews of New York City, November 2, 1748 *15*

1.09. Why the Court Refused to Naturalize Aaron Lopez, Superior Court of Rhode Island, Newport, SS. March Term, 1762 *16*

BUSINESS AND LABOR

1.10. Petition from Abraham Haim DeLucena and Justus Bosch to Governor Robert Hunter, Requesting Permission to Ship Provisions to Jamaica, June 3, 1713 *17*

1.11. Newspaper Business Advertisement against Emanuel Abrams, by Allan Melville, October 21, 1754 *18*

1.12. Reply Advertisement by Emanuel Abrams against Alan Melville, 1754 *18*

1.13. Isaac Elizer and Samuel Moses to Captain John Peck, Giving Instructions for a Journey to Purchase Slaves, October 29, 1762 *19*

RELIGION

1.14. Touro Synagogue, Exterior, n.d. *20*

1.15. Touro Synagogue, Interior, Front View, n.d. *21*

1.16. Constitution of Shearith Israel, New York, the Oldest Extant Constitution of a North American Jewish Community, September 15, 1728 *22*

1.17. The Prosecutor's Summary of the Evidence from the Trial of Solomon Hays, 1755–1756 *24*

FAMILY LIFE AND PHILANTHROPY

1.18. Abigaill Franks, in New York, to Her Son, Heartsey, in London, June 7, 1743 *26*

1.19. Meir Josephson to Michael Gratz concerning a Female Domestic, July 25, 1762 *27*

1.20. Hannah Paysaddon to Aaron Lopez, Requesting Charity, July 26, 1770 *28*

1.21. Congregation Gate of Heaven (London) to American Jews, Requesting Support for the Jews of Hebron, Palestine, May 5, 1773 *29*

CHAPTER 2.
Forging a Nation: The American Jewish
Experience during the Revolution and the
Early National Period, 1776–1820 *31*

IMMIGRATION AND ADAPTATION

2.01. Joseph Salvador to His Cousin Emanuel Mendes da Costa, Describing America, January 22, 1785 *33*

2.02. Rebecca Samuel to Her Parents in Hamburg, Germany, Describing Her Experiences in Virginia, January 12, 1791 *34*

GOVERNMENT, POLITICS, AND CIVIC STATUS

2.03. Francis Salvador to South Carolina Chief Justice William H. Drayton, Reporting Local Militia Activity against Native Americans and Loyalists, July 18 and 19, 1776 *36*

2.04. Maryland Constitution, Articles 33, 35, and 55, Restricting Officeholders to Christians, November 11, 1776 *37*

2.05. New York Constitution, Articles 35, 38, and 39, Making New York the First State to Emancipate Jews, April 20, 1777 *38*

2.06. Isaac Touro, a Loyalist, to British General Guy Carleton, Requesting Funds to Relocate to Jamaica, December 12, 1782 *39*

2.07. Jonas Phillips, Asking the Constitutional Convention to Emancipate Pennsylvania's Jews, September 7, 1787 *40*

2.08. Address of the Newport Congregation to the President of the United States of America, August 17, 1790 *41*

2.09. President George Washington to the Newport Congregation, 1790 *42*

2.10. Anonymous Reply to James Rivington's Antisemitic Preface in *The Democrat*, December 17, 1795 *43*

2.11. Sampson Simson's Hebrew Oration at Columbia College, 1800 *44*

2.12. Isaac Harby to James Monroe on Religious Freedom and the Recall of Mordecai Noah from the U.S. Consulate in Tunis, 1816 *45*

2.13. Thomas Jefferson to Mordecai Noah on Religious Tolerance, May 28, 1818 *48*

2.14. Thomas Jefferson to Jacob de la Motta, September 1, 1820 *48*

2.15. The First Form of the "Jew Bill," 1819 *49*

2.16. J. I. Cohen to E. S. Thomas on the Maryland Jew Bill, 1818 *50*

BUSINESS AND LABOR

2.17. Haym Salomon, Business Advertisement, *Freeman's Journal*, 1782 *52*

2.18. Will of Charleston's Jacob Jacobs, Which Included Slaves, 1797 *52*

2.19. A. H. Cohen to Thomas Jefferson, regarding the Health Benefits of Mineral Water, December 21, 1807 *53*

2.20. Reply of Thomas Jefferson to A. H. Cohen, February 10, 1808 *54*

RELIGION

2.21. Congregationalist Minister Ezra Stiles to His Friend Rabbi Haim Isaac Carigal, July 7, 1775 *56*

2.22. Appeal to the Citizens of Philadelphia for Donations to Save Their Synagogue from Foreclosure, Mikve Israel Congregation, Philadelphia, April 30, 1788 *57*

2.23. Hannah Adams, Reporting on Gershom Seixas's Survey of American Jewry, 1812 *58*

2.24. Address by Phillip Milledoler on Evangelizing the Jews, 1817 *61*

FAMILY LIFE

2.25. Frances Sheftall to Her Husband, July 20, 1780 *64*

2.26. Samuel Jones, Last Will and Testament, Including Information on His African American Slave, Jenny, and Their Son, Emanuel, January 20, 1809 *65*

CHAPTER 3.
Migrations across America: Jews in the Antebellum Period, 1820–1860 *67*

IMMIGRATION AND ADAPTATION

3.01. Penina Moïse, Poem, "To Persecuted Foreigners," 1820 *69*

3.02. Charles L. Mailert to August Mailert, on His Reservations about Immigrating to the United States, 1835 *69*

3.03. Reasons for Emigration from Bavaria to the United States, *Leipziger Zeitung*, 1839 *70*

3.04. Joseph Jonas to Rev. Isaac Leeser, Describing Life in Ohio, December 25, 1843 *71*

GOVERNMENT, POLITICS, AND CIVIC STATUS

3.05. Letter from Jacob Ezekiel to President
John Tyler, Arguing That America Is Not a
"Christian Nation," 1841—with Tyler's
Reply 73

BUSINESS AND LABOR

3.06. Lt. Col. Aaron Levy, "On Land Promoting,"
1821 75

3.07. Abraham Kohn, Reflections of a New
England Peddler, ca. 1842–1843 76

3.08. Henry J. Labatt, Newspaper Article on
Jews and Business in the Gold Rush, *True
Pacific Messenger*, 1861 77

RELIGION

3.09. Memorial to the President and Members
of the Adjunta of Kahal Kadosh Beth
Elohim of Charleston, South Carolina,
Demanding Religious Reform, December
23, 1824 79

3.10. Abraham Rice to Isaac Leeser, regarding
Religious Reform, December 15, 1848 81

3.11. Rosa Mordecai, Memoir Describing
Hebrew School Education in Antebellum
America, 1850s 82

3.12. Isaac Jalonick to Isaac Leeser on Jewish
Life in Texas, May 28, 1853 84

3.13. I. J. Benjamin, "The Education of Jewish
Women in America, 1859–1862" 85

SOCIAL LIFE

3.14. Mordecai Manuel Noah, Address at
Ararat, a Proposed Refuge for Jews,
1825 87

3.15. Review of *Harrington*, a Fictional
Account Describing Intermarriage,
1833 89

ANTI-JEWISH ATTITUDES

3.16. Newspaper Account, Cohen-Chisolm
Duel, July 25, 1827 91

3.17. Israel B. Kursheedt and Theodore J.
Seixas to President Martin Van Buren,
on the Damascus Blood Libel, August 24,
1840 91

CHAPTER 4.

*Slavery and Freedom: American Jews
during the Civil War and Reconstruction,
1861–1879* 93

CHOOSING SIDES

4.01. Letter from Alfred Mordecai to His Brother
G. W. Mordecai, March 17, 1861 94

4.02. Private Letter from Alfred Mordecai to
Lt. Col. James W. Ripley, on His Resignation
from the U.S. Army, May 2, 1861 96

4.03. "The Jews and Slavery," by Bernhard
Felsenthal, *Sinai*, July 1862 97

4.04. Eleanor H. Cohen, Journal Entries
Detailing the Author's Love for Both the
North and the South, *Champion of the Lost
Cause*, February 28, 1865 100

JEWS AND THE UNION

4.05. Abram J. Dittenhoefer, Excerpt regarding
Lincoln's Election, from *How We Elected
Lincoln—Personal Recollections of Lincoln
and Men of His Time*, 1860 102

4.06. Grant's General Orders Number 11,
1862 103

4.07. Gen. H. W. Halleck's Revocation of Grant's
Orders Number 11, January 4, 1863 104

4.08. Letter from B'nai B'rith Missouri Lodge,
Protesting Grant's Orders Number 11,
January 5, 1863 104

4.09. Isaac M. Wise, "The Revolutionary Object
of Extremists," Editorial Opposing
Abolitionism, the *Israelite*, February 27,
1863 104

4.10. Myer S. Isaacs to Abraham Lincoln on the
Jewish Vote in the 1864 Election, October 26,
1864 107

JEWS AND THE CONFEDERACY

4.11. Resolution of the Hebrew Congregation in
Support of the Confederacy, Shreveport,
Louisiana, May 1861 109

4.12. Eugenia Levy Phillips, Diary Reporting the
Author's Experiences as a Confederate,
1861 110

4.13. Twenty-Year Bond Issued by the
Confederacy in Honor of Judah P. Benjamin,
1861 *111*

4.14. Confederate Two-Dollar Bill Showing
Judah P. Benjamin, 1864 *112*

4.15. Isaac Levy to His Sister, Leonora, Detailing
the Celebration of Passover at a Confederate
Encampment in Adam's Run, South
Carolina, April 24, 1864 *112*

JEWS AND RECONSTRUCTION

4.16. Isaac M. Wise, "On to Richmond,"
Describing Conditions in the
Reconstruction South, the *Israelite*, June 28,
1867 *113*

4.17. Double Lynching of a Jew and a Negro,
the *Israelite*, August 28, 1868 *114*

4.18. Benjamin F. Peixotto, U.S. Consul in
Romania, to President Ulysses S. Grant,
Denying Accusations "of a Scandalous
Character" Leveled against His Person,
November 6, 1871 *116*

RELIGION

4.19. Morris Raphall, "The Bible View of
Slavery: A Discourse," a Defense of Slavery
by a Northern Rabbi, January 4, 1861 *118*

4.20. David Einhorn's Response to Raphall,
Offering a Baltimore Rabbi's Opposition to
Slavery, *Sinai,* 1861 *121*

4.21. Petition from American Jews to the U.S.
Senate and House, on the Chaplaincy Issue,
1861 or 1862 *122*

4.22. Rabbi Kalisch to U.S. Congress, regarding
the Chaplaincy Issue, December 9,
1861 *124*

4.23. Rev. Arnold Fischel to Mr. Henry I. Hart,
President of the Board of Delegates of
American Israelites, December 11, 1861 *125*

4.24. Isaac Leeser to Abraham Lincoln,
Requesting the Commissioning of Jewish
Chaplains, August 21, 1862 *126*

4.25. Letter from the U.S. Surgeon General
Opposing the Commissioning of Jewish
Chaplains in Washington, D.C., October 27,
1862 *127*

4.26. Excerpt from Isidor Straus's Memoirs,
1862–1863 *127*

CHAPTER 5.
*The Gilded Age and Progressive Era:
American Jewish Life, 1880–1918* *129*

IMMIGRANT LIFE IN THE OLD AND
THE NEW COUNTRY

5.01. Letter to the Editor, Urging Eastern
European Jews Not to Emigrate, *Ha-Magid*,
May 3, 1882 *131*

5.02. Abraham Cahan's Impressions upon
Arrival in the United States, "Imaginary
America," 1882 *131*

5.03. Emma Lazarus, "The New Colossus,"
1883 *132*

5.04. H. L. Sabsovich, "The Woodbine
Settlement of the Baron de Hirsch Fund,"
Describing the Creation of a Jewish
Agricultural Settlement in New Jersey,
1891 *133*

5.05. Constitution of the United States and
Declaration of Independence; cover, in
English and Yiddish, 1892 *134*

5.06. Mary Antin, Selection Describing the
Author's Journey to the United States,
From Plotzk to Boston, 1899 *135*

5.07. Baseball, *Forward*, August 27, 1909 *138*

5.08. Hebrew Immigrant Aid Society, Cover of
the *Jewish Immigrant*, January 1909 *139*

5.09. Creation of the New York Jewish
Federation by the State of New York,
May 15, 1917 *139*

GOVERNMENT, POLITICS, AND CIVIC STATUS

5.10. Revised Words to Lincoln's Gettysburg
Address, Written by HIAS for an Event
Honoring the Election of Moses Alexander
as Governor of Idaho, 1915 *141*

BUSINESS AND LABOR

5.11. Julia Richman, Selection from "New York's
East European Working Women," 1893 *142*

5.12. Morris Winchevsky, "A Socialist Parodies
the Ten Commandments," 1895 *144*

5.13. "Women as Wage Earners," *Ordens Echo*, 1897 *145*

5.14. The Protocol of Peace, Ending the 1910 Cloak Makers' Strike, New York City, 1910 *146*

5.15. Triangle Shirtwaist Company Fire, March 1911 *149*

5.16. "The Big Stick," regarding the Triangle Shirtwaist Company Fire, April 7, 1911 *150*

5.17. Rose Schneiderman, Selection regarding Labor Relations in the Early Twentieth Century and the Shirtwaist Fire, *All for One*, 1967 *150*

RELIGION

5.18. Menu, "Trefa Banquet," July 11, 1883 *153*

5.19. The Pittsburgh Platform, 1885 *153*

5.20. The Preamble and Article II of the Constitution of the Jewish Theological Seminary, May 9, 1886 *154*

5.21. Ray Frank, "What a Jewish Girl Would Not Do If She Were a Rabbi," May 23, 1890 *155*

5.22. Cyrus Adler, Selection from "A Jewish Renaissance," the *American Hebrew*, November 9, 1894 *156*

5.23. Principles Adopted by the [Orthodox] Jewish Congregational Union of America, June 8, 1898 *158*

5.24. Elkan C. Voorsanger, "Passover Services in France," *Emanu-El*, May 3, 1918 *158*

FAMILY LIFE

5.25. Martha Thal, Selections from *Early Days: The Story of Sarah Thal*, on Life in a Pioneer Farmer Family in North Dakota, ca. 1880 *160*

5.26. "Bintel Brief," on Intermarriage, *Forward*, 1906 *161*

5.27. Emma Goldman to Margaret Sanger on Birth Control, December 7, 1915 *162*

5.28. "A New Supplication for a Woman Whose Husband Has Deserted Her," 1916 *163*

ZIONISM

5.29. Selection regarding American Zionism from Zvi Hirsch Masliansky's Memoirs, ca. 1895 *165*

5.30. Isaac Mayer Wise's Rejection of Zionism, Central Conference of American Rabbis, July 6, 1897 *166*

5.31. Moses Descending with the Ten Commandments into Yosemite Valley, Congregation Sherith Israel, San Francisco, 1905 *167*

5.32. Louis Brandeis, "The Jewish Problem: How to Solve It" (Excerpt), April 25, 1915 *168*

ANTISEMITISM

5.33. Simon Wolf, "Kishineff—An Appeal," *Jewish Criterion*, May 22, 1903 *170*

5.34. "The Mass Meeting," Pertaining to the Kishinev Pogrom, *Jewish Criterion*, June 12, 1903 *172*

5.35. "Bintel Brief," Letter from an Immigrant Experiencing Antisemitism, *Forward*, 1907 *172*

5.36. Police Commissioner Theodore A. Bingham, Selection from "Foreign Criminals in New York," September 1908 *173*

5.37. Leo Frank to C. P. Connolly, Discussing the Murder Notes and How These Might Demonstrate His Innocence, March 11, 1915 *174*

5.38. Leo Frank, August 1915 *176*

5.39. Leo Frank, n.d. *176*

JEWISH AID, RELIEF, AND PHILANTHROPY

5.40. Resolution Founding the National Council of Jewish Women, September 7, 1893 *177*

5.41. Louis Marshall to Joseph Stolz, Organizing the American Jewish Committee, January 12, 1906 *178*

5.42. Jacob Schiff to President Taft on the Mistreatment of Jews in Russia, February 20, 1911 *179*

CHAPTER 6.
American Jews between the World Wars, 1918–1941 *181*

GOVERNMENT, POLITICS, AND CIVIC STATUS

6.01. Relief Expenditures of Fifty-Two Jewish Family Welfare Agencies, 1929–1935 *183*

6.02. Isaac Rubinow, "What Do We Owe Peter Stuyvesant?" 1930 *183*

6.03. "New NRA Compliance Director Blends Efficiency and Beauty," Jewish Telegraphic Agency, December 9, 1934 *185*

BUSINESS AND LABOR

6.04. Judah L. Magnes, Address Delivered at the Opening Session of the First Jewish Labor Congress, January 16, 1919 *187*

6.05. Rabbi Stephen S. Wise, Statement Supporting Organized Labor, September 1, 1919 *189*

RELIGION

6.06. Louis Marshall to Elias A. Cohen, January 25, 1923 *191*

6.07. "Yeshiva to Erect Modern College Buildings," *Jewish Tribune*, September 26, 1924 *193*

6.08. Bernard Revel, "The Vision of Yeshiva College," 1926 *195*

6.09. Conference for the Discussion of the Problem of Judaism, Chicago, February 21–22, 1928 *196*

6.10. Rabbi Israel H. Levinthal to Jacob Rader Marcus on the Rabbinic Training of Helen Hadassah Levinthal, 1939 *200*

POPULAR CULTURE

6.11. Edgar A. Guest, "Speaking of Greenberg," 1934 *202*

INTERFAITH AND INTERGROUP RELATIONS

6.12. Constitution and By-Laws of the Synagogue Council of America, 1926 *203*

6.13. The Story of the National Conference of Christians and Jews, 1928 *204*

ZIONISM

6.14. Broadside, Zionist Organization of America, Early 1920s *207*

6.15. Henrietta Szold, Familiar Letters from Palestine, December 21, 1921 *208*

6.16. Statement Acknowledging Increasing Support for Zionism, Central Conference of American Rabbis, June 1935 *211*

6.17. Excerpts from the "Guiding Principles of Reform Judaism," Central Conference of American Rabbis, Forty-Eighth Annual Convention, May 27, 1937, Columbus, Ohio *211*

6.18. "Official Declaration of the Rabbinical Assembly," June 7–9, 1937 *212*

6.19. Labor Zionist Handbook, Poale Zion/ Zeire Zion of America, 1939 *215*

ANTISEMITISM

6.20. Rabbi Stephen S. Wise, "Henry Ford's Challenge and a Jew's Reply," October 10, 1920 *217*

6.21. "The Scope of Jewish Dictatorship in the U.S.," *Dearborn Independent*, December 11, 1920 *218*

6.22. A. Lawrence Lowell to Judge Julian Mack, on Jewish Quotas at Harvard College, March 29, 1922 *219*

6.23. "Kaplan" Page in *The Lucky Bag* Yearbook, United States Naval Academy, 1922 *220*

6.24. Letter from West Virginia Senator Howard Sutherland to President Harding, June 1922 *221*

6.25. "The Declaration of Independence Addressed the World," *Der Tog*, July 4, 1924 *222*

6.26. Arthur M. Kaplan, "Are Medical Colleges Unfair to Jewish Students?" *Jewish Tribune*, August 1, 1930 *223*

6.27. "Memorandum on Nazi Activities in the United States," Non-Sectarian Anti-Nazi League to Champion Human Rights, 1936 *224*

6.28. American Nazi Parade, New York City, 1937 *225*

6.29. Excerpts from the Speech of Rep. Samuel L. Dickstein, Delivered before the National Convention of the Anti-Nazi League, May 22, 1938 *226*

6.30. "Persecution—Jewish and Christian," Broadcast by Rev. Charles E. Coughlin, November 20, 1938 *228*

6.31. Stephen S. Wise, "Coughlinism, Jews and America," December 4, 1938 *229*

6.32. Charles Lindbergh, Des Moines Speech, September 11, 1941 *230*

JEWISH AID, RELIEF, AND PHILANTHROPY

6.33. Louis Marshall to President Woodrow Wilson, Requesting Support for European Jews after World War I, August 6, 1919 *232*

6.34. President Wilson to Marshall, Rejecting the Request, August 14, 1919 *233*

6.35. Report on the Joint Distribution Committee's Efforts to Purchase Farmland for Russian Jews, Dr. Joseph A. Rosen, 1925 *234*

6.36. "$67,000,000 Spent in 40 Countries by the JDC since 1914 to Rebuild Lives and Souls of Stricken Jews," 1927 *235*

6.37. Stephen S. Wise, Addressing a Mass Meeting Held at Madison Square Garden, March 27, 1933 *238*

6.38. Abba Hillel Silver to Samuel Wohl, Opposing a Proposal to Bring German-Jewish Children to Palestine, November 26, 1934 *239*

6.39. Jewish War Veterans Ladies' Auxiliaries, "Naziism Is Spreading and So Must Our Boycott Activities," ca. 1938 *239*

6.40. Letter from Abraham Joshua Heschel to Dr. Julian Morgenstern, April 30, 1939 *240*

6.41. Letter from Morgenstern to Heschel, July 5, 1939 *241*

CHAPTER 7.

Waging War: American Jews, World War II, and the Shoah, 1941–1945 *243*

GOVERNMENT, POLITICS, AND CIVIC STATUS

7.01. Hitler Poster, "Wanted for Murder," 1941 *245*

7.02. Distribution of Jewish Servicemen by Branches and Activities, 1941–1945 *246*

7.03. Irving Berlin, Lyrics, "This Is the Army, Mr. Jones," 1942 *247*

7.04. Passover Observed by Armed Forces, 1943 *247*

7.05. Lt. Dick Gottlieb, Affidavit, Recounting His Experience Liberating the Dachau Concentration Camp near Landsberg, Germany, April 1945 *248*

INTERFAITH AND INTERGROUP RELATIONS

7.06. John J. Mahoney to Chaplain S. Joshua Kohn, regarding the February 3, 1943, Sinking of the USS *Dorchester*, December 7, 1944 *251*

7.07. U.S. Postage Stamp Commemorating Clergy Who Died in the Sinking of the USS *Dorchester*, 1948 *252*

THE HOLOCAUST AND ZIONISM

7.08. "Statement of Principles by Non-Zionist Rabbis," American Council for Judaism, August 12, 1942 *253*

7.09. Telegram from Gerhart Riegner (via Samuel Silverman) to Stephen S. Wise, August 29, 1942 *254*

7.10. Letter from Stephen S. Wise to Franklin D. Roosevelt, December 2, 1942 *255*

7.11. Sumner Welles to Stephen S. Wise, February 9, 1943 *256*

7.12. *We Will Never Die* Program, Memorializing the Slaughtered Jews in Europe and Commemorating Jewish Contributions to Civilization, March 9, 1943 *256*

7.13. Report on Attempts to Stage *We Will Never Die*, Early 1944 *257*

7.14. Max Lerner, "What about the Jews, FDR?" July 22, 1943 *259*

7.15. Rabbi Abba Hillel Silver, Selection from "Zionism: What It Is—What It Is Not," ca. 1944 *260*

7.16. "Report to the Secretary on the Acquiescence of This Government in the Murder of the Jews," Treasury Department, January 13, 1944 *262*

7.17. Franklin Roosevelt Establishes a War Refugee Board, January 22, 1944 *267*

7.18. Jewish Refugees at Emergency Shelter, Fort Ontario, August 4, 1944 *269*

7.19. Leland Robinson et al. to President Harry Truman, Requesting U.S. Citizenship for Refugees Housed at Fort Ontario, Oswego, New York, October 22, 1945 *269*

7.20. Poster Urging American Jews to Support the United Jewish Appeal Campaign, n.d. *271*

ANTISEMITISM

7.21. Chart, Domestic Antisemitism, 1940–1946 *272*

7.22. Activities of Antisemitic and Antidemocratic Groups in the United States, American Jewish Congress, April 2, 1943 *272*

7.23. Chart, World Jewry before and after the War, 1939–1945 *274*

CHAPTER 8.
American Jewish Life, 1945–1965 *275*

IMMIGRATION AND ADAPTATION

8.01. Levittown (Pa.) Resident Reflects on His Community, 1950s *277*

8.02. Income Levels and Religious Affiliation in Levittown, 1950s *279*

8.03. "NCRAC Discusses Decline in Jewish Population in Cities," Jewish Telegraphic Agency, June 22, 1955 *279*

GOVERNMENT, POLITICS, AND CIVIC STATUS

8.04. Phineas J. Biron, "Portrait of an Informer," *Israel Light*, December 31, 1947 *281*

8.05. Preface to the Transcript of Record (June 7, 1952) Provided by the National Committee to Secure Justice in the Rosenberg Case *283*

8.06. Flyer for Clemency, Rosenberg Case, May 30, 1953 *284*

8.07. "Meaning of the [Rosenberg] Execution," *Jewish Life*, August 1953 *285*

8.08. Soviet Cable Incriminating Julius Rosenberg, September 21, 1944 *286*

RELIGION

8.09. Maurice L. Zigmond, Selection from "Brandeis University Is One Year Old," 1949 *288*

8.10. Rabbi Abba Hillel Silver, Selection from "Living Judaism," Delivered at the Dedication of the New UAHC Headquarters, October 27, 1951 *289*

8.11. Beth Sholom Synagogue, Designed by Frank Lloyd Wright, Elkins Park, Pennsylvania, 1953 *293*

8.12. Image from the American Jewish Tercentenary Filmstrip, Union of American Hebrew Congregations, 1954 *294*

8.13. Menachem Schneerson, "In Orthodoxy the Woman Is Not Inferior," May 27, 1957 *294*

8.14. "Ufaratzta!" A Programmatic Statement Delivered by the Lubavitcher Rebbe, Menachem M. Schneerson, 1959 *296*

8.15. Rabbi Menachem M. Schneerson, "Letter on the Question of Prayer in the Public Schools," 1964 *298*

FAMILY LIFE

8.16. Mrs. Allen I. Edles, Selection from "The American Jewish Woman of Tomorrow," 1958 *302*

POPULAR CULTURE

8.17. Bess Myerson, "Miss America Speaks to Young America," *Jewish Veteran*, 1945 *304*

INTERFAITH AND INTERGROUP RELATIONS

8.18. Selection from "A Statement by Stephen S. Wise to a U.S. Senate Education Sub-Committee," April 1947 *306*

8.19. Rabbi Julian B. Feibelman, "Petition to the Orleans Parish School Board," September 12, 1955 *306*

8.20. Rabbi Jacob Rothschild, "No Place to Hide," *Southern Israelite*, August 1963 *308*

8.21. Rabbi William Malev, "The Jew of the South in the Conflict on Segregation," *Conservative Judaism*, 1958 *310*

8.22. Selection from an Address by South Carolina Speaker of the House Solomon Blatt to the Hebrew Benevolent Society of Charleston, April 6, 1959 *314*

8.23. Selection from an Open Letter from Rabbi Richard W. Winograd to the National Director of B'nai B'rith, 1963 *315*

8.24. Selection from a Speech Delivered by Rabbi Joachim Prinz at the March on Washington, August 28, 1963 *317*

8.25. March on Washington, August 28, 1963 *318*

8.26. Search for Civil Rights Workers James Chaney, Andrew Goodman, and Michael Schwerner, 1964 *319*

8.27. Selection from Oral History Interview with Kivie Kaplan, regarding His Entrance into Civil Rights Work and His Election as President of the NAACP, 1970 *319*

ZIONISM

8.28. President Harry S. Truman, Recognition of the State of Israel, May 14, 1948 *322*

8.29. Exchange between David Ben-Gurion and Jacob Blaustein on the Relationship between American Jews and the State of Israel, August 1950 *322*

JEWISH AID, RELIEF, AND PHILANTHROPY

8.30. "Major U.S. Jewish Groups Appeal for Equal Rights for Soviet Jews," Jewish Telegraphic Agency, September 29, 1960 *327*

8.31. "UN Told Russia Denies Universal Declaration of Human Rights to Jews," *Jewish Criterion*, November 18, 1960 *328*

8.32. "Khrushchev Talks about Soviet Jews," *Jewish Criterion*, March 31, 1961 *329*

8.33. "Soviet Mistreatment of Jews Attacked in Both Houses of U.S. Congress," Jewish Telegraphic Agency, January 25, 1962 *331*

ANTISEMITISM

8.34. American Jewish Committee, 1945, 1950–1959, Chart, Antisemitism in the United States during the 1940s and 1950s *332*

8.35. "No Anti-Jewish Bias Exists in New York College Admission Study Shows," Jewish Telegraphic Agency, July 27, 1959 *333*

CHAPTER 9.

Turning Inward: Jews and American Life, 1965–1980 335

GOVERNMENT, POLITICS, AND CIVIC STATUS

9.01. Betty Friedan, "A Comfortable Concentration Camp?" 1963 *337*

9.02. Norman Podhoretz, "My Negro Problem—and Ours," *Commentary*, February 1963 *339*

9.03. Michael Wyschogrod, Selection from "The Jewish Interest in Vietnam," *Tradition*, Winter 1966 *341*

9.04. Rabbi Abraham Joshua Heschel, Selection from "The Moral Outrage of Vietnam," January 31, 1967 *343*

9.05. "Radical Saul Alinsky: Prophet of Power to the People," *Time*, March 2, 1970 *345*

9.06. Jewish Defense League Ten-Point Program, n.d. *347*

9.07. Zvi Lowenthal and Jonathan Braun, "An Interview with Meir Kahane," 1971 *348*

9.08. Jewish Defense League Flyer, n.d. *350*

9.09. Jo Ann Levine, "A Woman's Place Is in the House," *Christian Science Monitor*, June 28, 1972 *350*

9.10. Arthur Hertzberg and David G. Epstein, "Jewish Political Trend . . . ," *Los Angeles Times*, May 24, 1984 *352*

9.11. Proposed Mission Statement of New Jewish Agenda, 1987 *354*

9.12. New Jewish Agenda Promotional Flyer: Some Examples of Our Work, n.d. *355*

RELIGION

9.13. "Depaul University, a Catholic Institution, Opens Full Department of Jewish Studies," Jewish Telegraphic Agency, September 4, 1968 *358*

9.14. "Jewish Students Launch Drive for Judaic Studies Departments in City University System," Jewish Telegraphic Agency, December 9, 1970 *358*

9.15. Sylvia Rothchild, "Havurat Shalom: Community without Conformity," *Hadassah*, June 1970 *359*

9.16. Bernard Reisman, "The Impact of the Havurah," *Jewish Digest*, Summer 1978 *361*

9.17. Ezrat Nashim, "Jewish Women Call for Change," 1972 *363*

9.18. "The First American Woman Rabbi," Reflections by Rabbi Sally Priesand, 1972–1975 *364*

9.19. "Jewish Women's Mag *Lilith* Hits the Stands," *Jewish Chronicle*, July 15, 1976 *366*

INTERFAITH AND INTERGROUP RELATIONS

9.20. "Sharp Decline Reported in Anti-Jewish Bias in Winter Resorts," Jewish Telegraphic Agency, August 6, 1965 *368*

9.21. Statement for Release by Black and Jewish Organizations, August 28, 1979 *369*

9.22. NAACP Head Benjamin Hooks, Speech on Civil Rights, American Jews, and the Palestine Liberation Organization, 1979 *371*

9.23. Advertisement, "Jews against Jackson," *New York Times*, November 11, 1983 *373*

POPULAR CULTURE

9.24. Philip Roth, Selection from "Writing about Jews," 1963 *375*

9.25. Robert Alter, "Malamud as Jewish Writer," *Commentary*, September 1966 *377*

9.26. Saul Bellow, "I Said That I Was an American, a Jew, a Writer by Trade," November 14, 1976 *379*

9.27. Allan Sherman, Lyrics, "If I Were a Tishman," 1967 *381*

ZIONISM

9.28. "Half of All Americans Register Support for Israel; No American Backs Arabs," Jewish Telegraphic Agency, June 12, 1967 *383*

9.29. Milton K. Susman, "As I See It," *Jewish Chronicle*, June 16, 1967 *384*

9.30. "The Portrait of Courage: The People Made Israel Victorious," *Jewish Chronicle*, June 16, 1967 *385*

9.31. "The Week That Rocked the World," June 5–11, *Jewish Chronicle*, June 16, 1967 *385*

9.32. Breira's National Platform, February 21, 1977 *385*

JEWISH AID, RELIEF, AND PHILANTHROPY

9.33. Jackson-Vanik Amendment, 1974 *387*

9.34. Poster of Anatoly Sharansky, n.d. *388*

CHAPTER 10.

Contemporary America: Jewish Life since 1980 389

IMMIGRATION AND ADAPTATION

10.01. Kevin West, "The Persian Conquest," *W*, July 2009 *390*

10.02. Saba Soomekh, American Jewish University, "The Political Emergence of the Los Angeles Persian Community," 2010 *392*

GOVERNMENT, POLITICS, AND CIVIC STATUS

10.03. Vision and Mission Statements, United States Holocaust Memorial Museum, 1993 *394*

10.04. "Gore's Choice for Veep Electrifies American Jews," *Forward*, August 11, 2000 *395*

10.05. "Remarks as Prepared for Delivery by Senator Joseph Lieberman," Democratic National Convention, August 16, 2000 *396*

10.06. Global Anti-Semitism Review Act, October 8, 2004 *399*

RELIGION

10.07. Selections, Mandell L. Berman Institute—North American Jewish Data Bank, n.d. *401*

10.08. Rabbi Alexander M. Schindler, "To the Board of Directors of the New York Federation of Reform Synagogues," March 3, 1983 *403*

10.09. Report of the Committee on Patrilineal Descent, Central Conference of American Rabbis, March 15, 1983 *405*

10.10. Rabbis Joel Roth and Akiba Lubow, A Standard of Rabbinic Practice regarding Determination of Jewish Identity, 1986 *407*

10.11. Press Release, Ezrat Nashim, October 24, 1983 *408*

10.12. Rabbi David Weiss Halivni, Letter to the Faculty Assembly of the Jewish Theological Seminary, 1983 *409*

10.13. Judith S. Antonelli, "Jewish Feminisms Explore Torah, God, and Sexuality," *Jewish Advocate*, January 25, 1991 *410*

10.14. Mission Statement of the Society for Humanistic Judaism, October 8, 1999 *412*

10.15. Charles Passy, "Debbie Friedman Is a Troubadour of Faith; Synagogues Ring with Folk," *Palm Beach Post*, December 6, 2004 *413*

10.16. Oren Lee-Parritz, "Synaplex: A Creative Response to a Decline in Synagogue Identification," *Jewish Post*, ca. 2007 *414*

10.17. Haviva Ner-David, "Breaking the Glass Mehitza," *Hadassah*, May 2004 *416*

10.18. Josh Nathan-Kazis, "In Dispute over Using 'Rabba,' Supporters Find Reason for Optimism," *Forward*, March 10, 2010 *418*

10.19. Tamar Snyder, "Beyond the Rabba-Rousing," *Jewish Week*, March 24, 2010 *419*

10.20. Camille Shira Angel, "Rabbi's Welcome" and Selections from *Siddur Sha'ar Zahav*, 2009 *422*

ZIONISM

10.21. Amanda Carpenter, "J Street Pro-Israel Lobby Takes on AIPAC, Alienates Backers," *Washington Times*, October 21, 2009 *424*

10.22. Alan M. Dershowitz, "Boycotting Israeli Universities: A Victory for Bigotry," *Haaretz*, December 17, 2013 *425*

POPULAR CULTURE

10.23. Mission Statement, JDate, 1997 *427*

10.24. Paulette Kouffman Sherman, "Eight Love Lessons from the Festival of Light," December 8, 2013 *427*

10.25. Jonathan Miller, "How Adam Sandler's 'Chanukah Song' Helped Save the Jews," *Huffington Post*, December 23, 2011 *428*

AMERICAN JEWISH LIFE: TWENTY-FIRST-CENTURY DEVELOPMENTS

10.26. Tri-Faith Initiative of Omaha, Nebraska, May 2010 *431*

10.27. The Adventure Rabbi Program, 2012 *432*

10.28. "Moishe House a Place to Call Home," March 20, 2013 *434*

10.29. Presidential Proclamation—Jewish American Heritage Month, May 2013 *435*

Index *437*

In 1950, Morris U. Schappes (1907–2004) published the first documentary history of the Jews in the United States. In his "Introduction" to that pioneering volume, Schappes offered some noteworthy observations about "the form of a documentary history": "The document has unquestionable authenticity; this is the record, in its original appearance and language, strained by no intervening 'interpretation.' This is how the Jews themselves spoke and lived and thought of themselves for two centuries in our country, and how their contemporary non-Jews thought and wrote of them."[1]

This documentary volume is essentially predicated on the same convictions. The editors of this volume were motivated to produce a readable collection of source materials that would enable American Jews to speak for themselves. *American Jewish History: A Primary Source Reader* contains a diverse array of historical documents and other primary source materials that illuminate the story of the Jewish experience in North America from its communal beginnings to the present. Some of the documents in this volume relate to the careers of prominent American Jews who distinguished themselves in their respective fields of endeavor. Most of the materials, however, shed light on those whose lives and professional careers were outside the public eye. The editors sought to include a comprehensive cross-section of primary source materials that would broaden a reader's understanding of the Jewish experience in America across a variety of perspectives. Working people as well as the so-called elites, religious as well as secular Jews, women and men from across the nation's regions and local communities, both urban and rural, are all included.

This primary source reader strives to give voice to historical figures who have not yet enjoyed the attention of scholars. We have also sought, in each chapter, to include documents that highlight an era's major thematic questions and tell stories about what it was like to immigrate and acculturate to American life, practice different forms of Judaism, engage the larger political, economic, and social cultures that surrounded American Jews, and offer assistance to Jews in need around the world.

Students engaged in the study of the American Jewish experience at the undergraduate level will certainly benefit from this volume. It complements general textbooks in both American and American Jewish history by making original documents and significant source materials available for exploration, analysis, and critique. By tracing the experience of Jews in America through their own words and actions, students will have an opportunity to interact with the materials in this volume and thereby gain a deeper appreciation for their subjects of study.

The benefit of a published volume containing primary source readings extends beyond its applicability to the American Jewish history survey course. Graduate students in the fields of American history, American religion, American Jewish history, American Judaism, and even ethnic history in general will find a trove of documents that illuminate a wide range of historical issues. This collection will also serve as a valuable resource for adult education programs seeking to enrich students' understanding and knowledge of the American Jewish experience.

In order to enhance this book's readability, we have elected not to include an elaborate apparatus of footnotes, extensive bibliographic annotations, or expansive historical contextualization. Instead, each historical document or source reading is preceded by a headnote that strives to orient the reader to the document and briefly explain the resource's historical significance. In other words, we have attempted to provide the requisite historical background and contextualization so that the reader will be able to understand the document itself and appreciate the ways in which it brings historical themes or trends into bold relief.

This primary source reader attempts to provide useful source materials that highlight significant themes covering the entire arc of the American Jewish experience, from 1654 to the second decade of the twenty-first century. We have deliberately tried to enlarge the canon of documents from that used in other documentary histories, and many of the documents in this source reader have never before appeared in print. At the same time, in an effort to provide access to a range of preeminent sources that are so well known they could not be excluded, this volume also includes a number of previously published documents. To be sure, a few of these cardinal documents have been published numerous times. If a given document in this reader has previously appeared in print, we take care to identify the publication source we have chosen to use for this volume. It is beyond the scope of this project, however, to assure readers that the published sources we have used were themselves faithful transcriptions of the original document. Indeed, we discovered that many documents that have previously appeared in print betray interesting and oftentimes inexplicable variants. We have done our level best to produce an accurate transcription of the documentary source we have selected, but more than this we cannot promise.

At the beginning of each chapter, we provide a brief historical overview highlighting some of the most important developments in both American and American Jewish history of that particular era. We have employed a two-column-per-page typesetting style in order to maximize the number of documents published in a single volume, reflecting our ambition to compile a comprehensive, unified, and accessible resource.

In his exemplary and pioneering source reader *The Jew in the Medieval World*, Jacob Rader Marcus (1896–1995) noted that the selection process for a documentary history is a challenging, even Sisyphean task. How does one select a representative array of source documents for a reasonably sized volume while, as Marcus wrote, "omitting nothing of prime importance"? We can surely identify with Marcus's frank confession: "We are not sure that we have always succeeded." In this volume, we sought to bring as many new items to our readers as possible and attempted to select primary source documents on the basis of the same criteria that Marcus employed seventy-five years ago: "importance, interest, clarity, and diversification."[2]

Jacob Rader Marcus customarily began his scholarly volumes by reminding readers that "no book writes itself."[3] How true! It is no exaggeration to say that this primary source reader might never have appeared had it not been for the selfless support proffered by dozens of colleagues and institutions over the past several years. We are grateful for this opportunity to express our sincere gratitude to those who helped bring this volume to completion.

In a certain sense, this volume owes its very existence to the Jacob Rader Marcus Center of the American Jewish Archives (AJA), the distinguished research center located on the historic Cincinnati campus of Hebrew Union College–Jewish Institute of Religion (HUC-JIR). Although the credits that follow will show that dozens of primary source documents have been culled from a wide range of archival centers, libraries, and valuable publications, the leading role played by the AJA's holdings in shaping the contents of this volume is evident from the credits. In so many ways, this primary source reader sheds a bright light on the AJA's exceptionally diverse and rich holdings. We are deeply indebted to the AJA and its extraordinary staff for the unstinting help they have offered over the years when this project was incubating.

It is literally impossible for us to express a full measure of our gratitude for the help and support we have received from so many distinguished scholars of the American Jewish experience. Professor Jonathan D. Sarna has served as a primary reviewer and wise counselor from the inception of this project through to the final publication. Professor Sarna has graciously read and reread numerous iterations of this manuscript, and the entire enterprise has benefited significantly from his storehouse of knowledge. He has been unfailingly generous with his time and his expertise, and we are deeply grateful for his steadfast encouragement. Earlier versions of this manuscript were also read by Professor Eric Goldstein, whose keen insights unquestionably resulted in an improved manuscript. We also received many helpful suggestions from an array of learned reviewers, including Professors Dianne Ashton, Mark Bauman, Hasia Diner, Eli Faber, Ari Kelman, Pam Nadell, and Holly Snyder. These scholars did their very best to help us produce a useful and historically accurate documentary reader. While acknowledging their generous efforts, we, the editors, hasten to assume full responsibility for any factual errors or infelicities in this volume that may have eluded us.

We are deeply grateful for the editorial contributions of Dana Herman, the Marcus Center's academic associate and managing editor of the *American Jewish Archives Journal*. Dana invariably subjects herself to the highest standards of excellence in every project she undertakes, and her work at the Marcus Center testifies to this assertion. Without exaggeration, she has played a supporting role in every facet of this project from its very beginning. She has served as researcher, editor, strategist, and wise academic counselor. We wish to express our heartfelt gratitude for her invaluable assistance and scholarly support every step of the way.

Sonja Rethy has checked and rechecked each and every document in this volume in an effort to ensure the highest accuracy of transcription from the original source. In addition, Sonja adroitly repaired inaccuracies and corrected numerous inconsistencies in both the chapter introductions and document headnotes. We gratefully acknowledge that without Sonja's skillful editorial contributions, the contents of this reader would not have achieved their present levels of cogency and editorial style.

Those who have had the opportunity to conduct research at the AJA, or who have ever had an occasion to ask one of the AJA's archival professionals for scholarly assistance, will confirm that it sets an extremely high bar for being "research friendly." We have received the same outstanding archival assistance, and we are profoundly grateful to the following members of the AJA archival staff for their commitment to the highest standards of their profession: Kevin Proffitt, senior archivist for research and collections, Dorothy Smith, archivist, Nathan Tallman and Elisa Ho, associate archivists, and Camille Servizzi, assistant to the archivists. The Marcus Center's administrative staffers also deserve recognition for their contributions to our work on this volume: Stacey Roper, Nancy Dowlin, Al Simandl, as well as those who retired from the AJA before this volume was ready for publication: Eleanor Lawhorn, Jennifer Cole, Ruth Kreimer, and Elise Nienaber. Phil Reekers, the AJA's talented digitization and graphic design staffer, originally keystroked many of the documents in this volume. His contributions to this project have consistently gone above and beyond the call of duty. Last but surely not least, we are grateful to Lisa B. Frankel, director of programs and administration at the Marcus Center. This project would have been infinitely more difficult to complete without her loyal support and valuable administrative insight.

We also wish to express our sincere gratitude for the generous support we have received from our academic homes: San Francisco State University (SFSU) and HUC-JIR. Marc Dollinger received a sabbatical leave from SFSU enabling him to complete his work on this volume, and Gary P. Zola has benefited from the support of David Ellenson, president and now chancellor of HUC-JIR. We both wish to acknowledge the support provided through HUC-JIR's renowned Klau Library, and we are particularly grateful to David Gilner, director of libraries, Laurel Wolfson, administrative librarian, and the Klau Library staff for their assistance. Thanks are also due to HUC-JIR graduate student Matthew Semler, who served as an academic research assistant on this volume. Matt played a very important role in helping us locate and organize the hundreds of documents that needed to be reviewed as this source reader took shape. Over the years, a number of research assistants have contributed to the development of this volume, including Emma Burgin, Sherry Kingston, Jason Mellman, Kortney Sanders, and Lizzie Spicehandler. We are also grateful to Howard Simon for his helpful editorial comments and to the staff of Brandeis Hillel Day School, Marin, California, and its librarian, Elizabeth Atterman, for providing Marc Dollinger with the study space wherein this manuscript was completed.

The editor in chief of the University Press of New England/Brandeis University Press, Phyllis Deutsch, has been a loyal supporter of this project since the idea was first proposed a number of years ago. She has pushed and prodded—and she has demonstrated extraordinary forbearance and patience as the manuscript slowly made its way to completion. We express our sincere gratitude to Phyllis for helping us navigate the turbulent publication waters that a large documentary reader such as this inevitably encounters. We would also like to acknowledge the following members of UPNE's editorial team who invested countless hours in this project: Susan Abel, Bronwyn Becker, and Jason Warshof. This volume would not have appeared without their dedicated efforts. We would also like to thank the volume's indexer, Joanne Sprott, for her work.

Finally, we wish to thank our spouses, Marci Dollinger and Stefi Zola, as well as our children, Rebecca and Shayna Dollinger, and Mandi, Jory, Jeremy, and Samantha Zola. Their contributions to this project—the many hours of family time they donated—were involuntary and incalculable. No words, no matter how eloquently phrased or strikingly polished, can adequately express the extent or depth of our gratitude for their encouragement, support, and love.

NOTES

1. Morris U. Schappes, *A Documentary History of the Jews in the United States, 1654–1855* (New York: Citadel Press, 1950), xiv.

2. Jacob Rader Marcus, *The Jew in the Medieval World: A Source Book, 315–1791* (Cincinnati: Union of American Hebrew Congregations, 1938), xv.

3. Jacob Rader Marcus, *The American Jew, 1585–1990: A History* (New York: Carlson Publishing, Inc., 1995), vii.

AJ
  Jacob R. Marcus. *American Jewry: Documents, Eighteenth Century*. Cincinnati: Hebrew Union College Press, 1959.

AJA
  The Jacob Rader Marcus Center of the American Jewish Archives

AJAJ
  American Jewish Archives Journal

AJHS
  American Jewish Historical Society

AJW
  Jacob R. Marcus. *The American Jewish Woman: A Documentary History*. New York and Cincinnati: Ktav and American Jewish Archives, 1981.

CAJS
  Herbert D. Katz Center for Advanced Judaic Studies, University of Pennsylvania

DHJ
  Morris U. Schappes, ed. *A Documentary History of the Jews in the United States, 1654–1875*. New York: Citadel Press, 1950; rev. 1952.

HUC-JIR
  Hebrew Union College–Jewish Institute of Religion

JAW
  Jacob R. Marcus, ed. *The Jew in the American World: A Sourcebook*. Detroit: Wayne State University Press, 1996.

JUS
  Joseph L. Blau and Salo W. Baron. *The Jews of the United States, 1790–1840: A Documentary History*. 3 vols. New York: Columbia University Press, 1963.

PAJHS
  Publications of the American Jewish Historical Society

American Jewish History: A Primary Source Reader contains ten chapters, covering the history of Jews in Dutch and British colonial America and the United States from 1654 to the present. The first chapter explores the Dutch and British colonial periods, from the original permanent settlement in North America by Jewish immigrants in 1654 until the outbreak of revolution in 1776. It investigates the significance of the immigration and acculturation process, exploring the ways early American Jews negotiated their lives in the midst of a varied, and often changing, colonial experience.

Chapter 2 examines the profound impact of the Revolution on American Jewish history. From the creation of the United States in 1776 until 1820, when westward expansion and the rise of Jacksonian America brought dramatic change to the new nation, American Jews debated the merits and risks of joining the patriots, first in their civil protests against the British crown and eventually in armed conflict. This chapter also explores how American Jews responded to debate over the concentration of power in a central government, whether in the Confederation period between 1776 and 1787 or in the Constitution-based early national period between 1787 and 1820.

The antebellum period, between 1820 and 1860, is the focus of chapter 3. During this era, more than a hundred thousand new Jewish immigrants from Central Europe settled in the United States, changing the demographic profile of American Jewry. Some of these newcomers settled in the Northeast, but many struck roots in the Midwest and the South. Others rushed westward to California after 1849 together with the masses of Americans who flooded into the Sacramento Valley in the hope of finding gold. The enormous influx of Central European Jewish immigrants also influenced the character of the American synagogue, which slowly adapted itself to its American setting. The liturgical dominance of the Spanish-Portuguese rite used in all the synagogues established during the eighteenth century was superseded by the Ashkenazi ritual carried to U.S. shores by Jewish immigrants mainly from Central Europe. These new trends included a diversity of ideological approaches to the practice of Judaism in America. Many advocated the ideals of Reform Judaism, while others vehemently insisted that a traditional albeit Americanized ritual was the best way to safeguard the future of Jewish life in the American nation.

Chapter 3 notes the regional influences that culminated in the "irrepressible conflict"—the Civil War. Regional differences among Jews emerged as northerners and southerners debated the questions of slavery and states' rights. American Jews on both sides of the Mason-Dixon Line weighed the attitudes of their neighbors against their own perspectives as Jews. At the same time, the massive westward migration had spawned new Jewish communities in locales such as San Francisco, Portland, and Denver, thereby creating new generations of American Jews with historical experiences that were notably different from their coreligionists' experiences in the East, Midwest, and South.

Chapter 4 focuses on American Jewry and the Civil War, the bloodiest military conflict in all U.S. history, presenting primary source documents that pertain to Union loyalists and Jewish Confederates alike—including government leaders as well as ordinary citizens. This chapter also explores the topic of Jews who resided in the border states, where the question of firm allegiance to the North or the South often proved difficult. Finally, it includes some materials that examine the relationship between African Americans and Jews in this period.

Chapter 5 explores the immigration and acculturation of Eastern European Jews to the

United States between 1880 and 1924. This chapter begins with life in the Old Country and then details the experiences of first-generation American Jews as they encountered both opportunities and challenges. Within the religious sphere, rabbis adapted Judaism to their new surroundings. Leftist Jewish immigrants created and joined labor unions, adjusting their views to the realities of the nation's larger political culture. Intracommunal tensions also surfaced as established American Jews of Central European origin sought to Americanize new arrivals in their own image. An Americanized form of Zionism emerged in this period, as did a growing American eugenics movement that surprisingly enjoyed the support of a number of Jewish leaders. Finally, this chapter includes some documents concerning American Jewry and World War I. These materials shed light on how a new generation of American Jews—immigrants or children of immigrants—responded to their nation's call to arms.

Chapter 6 covers American Jewish life in the 1920s and 1930s. The 1920s at once reflected the enormous successes of a Jewish community on the heels of a massive two-million-strong migration from Eastern Europe just as it revealed the depth of anti-Jewish sentiment in a nation recoiling from the dramatic social and economic changes of the late nineteenth and early twentieth centuries. For American Jewry, the post–World War I years were filled with conflicting experiences of social acceptance and rejection. Men like Louis Brandeis (1856–1941), Benjamin Cardozo (1870–1938), and Bernard Baruch (1870–1965) assumed prominent positions in the nation's government. Theatergoers were enthralled by Edna Ferber's (1885–1968) play *Showboat*, which in 1927 became a musical hit thanks to the collaborative efforts of Jerome Kern (1885–1945) and Oscar Hammerstein (1895–1960). At this same time, however, the famed automaker Henry Ford (1863–1947) was publishing his own twisted version of *The Protocols of the Elders of Zion* in his newspaper, the *Dearborn Independent*, while nativism across America's

heartland inspired the U.S. Congress to establish a national origins quota system that all but ended Jewish immigration.

The same contrasting circumstances continued into the 1930s, when many American Jews enjoyed unprecedented access to the corridors of power through Franklin Delano Roosevelt's New Deal. Jewish thinkers helped the Roosevelt administration formulate its policies, while Jewish government workers led the charge for innovation in government. At the same time, Hitler's popularity in Germany inspired American antisemites to step up their campaigns against Jews. Boycotts of Jewish-owned businesses by the Nazis in Germany were met with attempts by American Jews to boycott German goods in the United States. The popularity of antisemites such as Father Charles Coughlin (1891–1979) and growing nativist sentiment, stirring opposition to U.S. participation in the European war, worried American Jews, who feared a backlash should they advocate the overthrow of Hitler. Of course, all these developments took place in the context of the Great Depression, which cast a pall of anxiety and uncertainty over American Jews, just as it did over the nation as a whole.

Chapter 7 investigates American Jewish life during World War II. The chapter details American Jewish responses to the U.S. entry into the war and focuses especially on how wartime Jews reacted as word of the Shoah (Holocaust) reached American shores. As conditions for European Jewry deteriorated in the 1930s and early 1940s, American Jews began to realize that no other Jewish community in the world was in so strong a position to exert itself on behalf of the embattled Jews of Europe. Suddenly, American Jewry, which had never been viewed as a great spiritual center of Jewish life, found itself thrust into a leading role on the world Jewish stage. Yet as the documents in this chapter illustrate, American Jews were not of one mind as to how best to respond to the unfolding calamity in Europe. The community was fragmented, uncertain, and completely inexperienced in responding to a crisis of this magnitude. Some felt constrained by the war itself and were fearful that too specific a push for European Jews could be viewed by their neighbors as dual loyalty and by the U.S. government as an attempt to compromise Allied war aims.

Chapter 8 looks at American Jewish life in the early postwar years. Throughout American history, Jews have tended to congregate in cities and urban areas. Although some farming communities did exist from the early years of Jewish settlement in America, most Jews flocked to the business and commerce centers of the East Coast. In the post–World War II era, though, American Jews moved, en masse, to the suburbs, reinventing Jewish life while they took advantage of the economic growth, declining antisemitism, and educational opportunities of the 1950s. Whereas the 1930s brought grave economic depression and the 1940s a world war and the Shoah, the 1950s launched a new generation of college-educated, home-owning American Jewish professionals who joined the anticommunist Cold War consensus and celebrated their social acceptance into mainstream America.

At the same time that many American Jews were themselves enjoying increased acceptance into the broader surrounding culture, they stepped up their engagement in the civil rights movement in the South. A hallmark in American Jewish history, the disproportionate participation of Jews in the African American movement for racial equality has emerged in the historical literature as an exemplar of American Jewish commitment to justice and compassion, and as evidence of a continuing commitment to Judaism's prophetic impulse. Yet a close examination of the primary sources reveals a more layered and complex story that undermines earlier filiopietistic analyses. Most southern Jews did not join their northern coreligionists in the high-profile public protests of the movement, and although some took heroic action on behalf of racial equality, most preferred to express themselves with what historians have referred to as "quiet voices." Similarly, while most northern Jews were generally more widely embracing than southern

Jews of the Supreme Court's famous 1954 ruling that rendered segregation unconstitutional, only a small percentage of the community was actively involved in the civil rights movement. When the civil rights movement shifted to America's urban centers a decade later and the focus turned to economic justice and opportunity, many northern Jews remained on the sidelines in a manner that paralleled some of the earlier southern Jewish responses.

Chapter 9 examines the impact of the social protest movements of the late 1960s and early 1970s on American Jewish life. In just a ten-year span, the high-profile civil rights and free speech social protest movements gave way to more militant, and occasionally violent, actions against the Vietnam War. The Black Power movement inspired a host of ethnic, racial, and gender groups to organize. For Jews, these changes seemed to betoken a sad end to a once-optimistic time of interfaith and interracial cooperation. By the 1970s, though, American Jews enjoyed an ethnic and religious renewal informed by an intensity similar to that which characterized the social protest movements of the time. The second-wave feminist movement, too, inspired Jewish women to press for equality in American society as well as within Jewish life. The primary source materials documenting this era reflect the complex, and sometimes paradoxical, relationship between American Jews and their historic partners in other racial and ethnic groups. This chapter also highlights a number of documents that shed light on American Jewry's influence on popular culture in the 1960s.

Chapter 10 looks at American Jewish life in the contemporary period. Since the 1960s, profound demographic changes in American Jewry have launched a fierce debate over the current state of Jewish life. As Jews have enjoyed greater and greater integration into the mainstream of American life, intermarriage rates have increased, while levels of Jewish education and religious observance have diminished. Even though the data from community and national surveys all tend to affirm these assimilationist trends, scholars, as well as Jewish communal leaders, often disagree over their meaning and import. To some, the increased numbers of non-Jewish spouses signal detachment from Jewish life and a generation of children and grandchildren without the basic knowledge necessary for Jewish continuity. Others, though, are opportunistic, pressing for greater outreach to intermarried families in a larger bid to increase and strengthen American Jewry.

As these chapters unfold, readers will begin to discern several broader themes that characterize the entirety of the American Jewish experience. Although each chapter tackles a specific era, the documents concomitantly contribute to the telling of a larger narrative. Jonathan D. Sarna articulated four overarching characteristics that not only help readers frame the past but also remind us of a central idea informing the study of the Jew in the American world: American Jewish history *is* American history. Collectively, the documents in this book illuminate the four characteristics that Sarna delineated. Over the course of their history, American Jews have exhibited (1) a belief in the promise of American life; (2) a faith in pluralism; (3) a quest for success; and (4) a commitment to Jewish survival.[1]

🔖 In their research, scholars employ a wide variety of primary source materials that collectively contribute to their overall ability to reconstruct the past. Traditional primary source documents include letters, newspaper articles, government records, and personal diaries. Social historians, those interested in studying the lives of everyday people, look as well toward material culture—objects that document the day-to-day patterns of human existence in various times and places. These might include a person's home furnishings, clothing, and work tools, or even his or her favorite books, magazine subscriptions, or art. In recent times, new technologies have created even more source materials for scholars. Still and motion picture cameras, for example, have captured graphic images of people, events, and places, while the personal computer has enabled scholars to identify, analyze, and even recreate data in ways that earlier generations of academics could not begin to envision.

Within the academic world, historians debate one another over the primary sources they choose to employ as well as the conclusions they draw from them. Some gravitate toward political documents that tell the story of established leaders, while others prefer to explore primary sources that reveal insights into the larger populace. Still others choose subjects of inquiry focused on particular themes such as class, race, gender, or religion. The monographs and books these researchers produce reflect these variegated methodological approaches, and these works differ from one another in scope, focus, and interpretation. Over time, we can observe trends in both the subjects historians engage and the conclusions they draw from their research. Rather than simply retelling a single historical narrative, scholars use primary sources to fashion new interpretative frameworks for different historical events and eras. Historiography, the study of the way history is written, develops fields of inquiry and guides scholars as they determine new directions for their continuing research.

This reader employs a variety of primary source documents, and it is important to bear in mind that all genres of primary source material must be analyzed judiciously and prudently. *Letters* and various forms of correspondence enable a researcher to eavesdrop on conversations that occurred between two or more correspondents. Social historians utilize letters as a lens into the lives of individuals whose experiences largely have been ignored by scholars more interested in reading public documents issued by national leaders. Political historians employ letters, especially those private in nature, as an important source in understanding the thoughts and ideas behind a leader's policies. But letters contain predilections that can mislead the unsuspecting scholar. Oftentimes, for example, letters are informed by the inter-personal relationship between the writer and the recipient as well as by the biases of the letter writer. The subjects engaged in letters, the style in which subjects are described, and the various points made (and ignored) also can reflect more about the mind-set of the letter writer than about the events he or she is addressing.

Similar to letters, *journals* and *diaries* offer historians an insider's view into the private thoughts and attitudes of their subjects. These documents reveal background information and perspectives that frequently never reach the public record. Journals and diaries provide re-searchers with a remarkably personal window into the private ruminations of the writer on a range of subjects that have historical signifi-cance. Yet the very private nature of these docu-ments can sometimes lead to misapprehension. Some journal writers knew that their reflections would one day be read by others. In these in-stances, the author may have been writing for posterity and not to record unfiltered personal impressions.

Government records are important sources because they show the position of one of the most significant historical actors, broadly speak-ing, in U.S. history—the government itself. Scholars of the American Jewish experience, interested in understanding the development of Jewish life, often rely on proclamations, laws, and written documents emanating from various government officials. Yet as with other primary sources, government records must be read care-fully. These sources frequently provide little background information, and the final docu-ment reveals little of the internal debates and the eventual compromises often associated with democratic government processes.

This reader also makes use of many other types of primary sources, including *Jewish com-munal records*, *newspaper articles*, *petitions*, *me-morials*, *maps*, *quantitative data*, and *topical sermons*, that shed light on how various issues and concerns were discussed in their own era. We, the editors, have also inserted a select num-ber of documentary *images* that function as pri-mary source material and not as illustrations or illuminations. In other words, these documen-tary images offer useful information or visual data that enrich our understanding of the past.

Ultimately, it is our hope that this new source reader will reinforce an appreciation of the sym-biotic relationship that has typified the Ameri-can Jewish experience for more than 350 years. In presenting primary source materials that focus on Jews living in America, we have si-multaneously presented a documentary history that contributes to a fuller appreciation of life in America as a whole. We thus begin this new source reader with a slightly amended version of the words Joseph L. Blau (1909–1986) and Salo W. Baron (1895–1989) used to introduce the noteworthy documentary history they au-thored fifty years ago: "Here, then, are collected a number of documents illustrating all phases of Jewish life in the United States" from 1654 to 2013.[2]

NOTES

1. Jonathan D. Sarna, *The American Jewish Experi-ence*, 2nd ed. (New York: Holmes & Meier, 1997), xiv–xv.

2. Joseph L. Blau and Salo W. Baron, *The Jews of the United States, 1790–1840: A Documentary History*, vol. 1 of the Jacob R. Schiff Library of Jewish Contributions to American Democracy (New York: Columbia University Press, 1963), xxiv.

1.01—RABBI ISAAC ABOAB DE FONSECA, RECIFE, BRAZIL, N.D.

Rabbi Isaac Aboab de Fonseca (1605–1693) served as the spiritual leader of Recife's Jews from 1642 until 1654. Portuguese-born, Aboab was raised in France and Amsterdam. He became a rabbi while in Amsterdam and later served the community's Congregation Bet Israel. His first years in Recife witnessed a flourishing Jewish community aided by Dutch colonial authorities who respected religious pluralism. Beginning in 1646, though, a series of Portuguese raids on Recife unsettled its Jewish community. When Portuguese forces recaptured their onetime colony in 1654, they evicted its Jewish residents, who fled to Amsterdam, the Caribbean, as well as the Dutch colony of New Amsterdam in North America. The second image is a painting of Recife by Zacharias Wagenaer (1614–1668). Wagenaer (also spelled Wagener, Wagenaar, or Wagner) was the son of a German illustrator who lived in the Dutch colony during the late 1630s.

Source: PC-11, AJA.

Source: PC-3616, AJA.

1.03—PETER STUYVESANT, MANHATTAN, TO THE AMSTERDAM
CHAMBER OF DIRECTORS, SEPTEMBER 22, 1654

In the letters that follow, Dutch colonial governor Peter Stuyvesant (1612–1672) communicates with the Dutch West India Company on the status of New Amsterdam's recent Jewish arrivals. While Stuyvesant opposed a permanent Jewish community in his jurisdiction, owners of the West India Company, which included some Jews, rallied behind the Jewish immigrants. In April of 1665, the directors informed Stuyvesant of their decision. The Jewish refugees would be allowed to "travel and trade" and to "live and remain" in New Netherland "provided the poor among them shall not become a burden to the company or to the community . . . [and] be supported by their own nation."

The Jews who have arrived would nearly all like to remain here, but learning that they (with their customary usury and deceitful trading with the Christians) were very repugnant to the inferior magistrates, as also to the people having the most affection for you; the Deaconry [which takes care of the poor] also fearing that owing to their present indigence [due to the fact that they had been captured and robbed by privateers or pirates] they might become a charge in the coming winter, we have, for the benefit of this weak and newly developing place and the land in general, deemed it useful to require them in a friendly way to depart; praying also most seriously in this connection, for ourselves as also for the general community of your worships, that the deceitful race,—such hateful enemies and blasphemers of the name of Christ,—be not allowed further to infect and trouble this new colony, to the detraction of your worships and the dissatisfaction of your worships' most affectionate subjects.

Source: As printed in *JAW*, 29–30. Reprinted with permission of the AJHS, from *PAJHS* 18 (1909): 4–5, 19–21.

1.04—AMSTERDAM JEWRY'S SUCCESSFUL INTERCESSION FOR THE JEWISH IMMIGRANTS, JANUARY 1655

To the Honorable Lords,
Directors of the Chartered West India Company,
Chamber of the City of Amsterdam

The merchants of the Portuguese nation [the Sephardic Jewish community] residing in the City [of Amsterdam] respectfully remonstrate to your Honors that it has come to their knowledge that your Honors raise obstacles to the giving of permits or passports to the Portuguese [Sephardic] Jews to travel and to go to reside in New Netherland, which if persisted in will result to the great disadvantage of the Jewish nation. It can also be of no advantage to the general Company but rather damaging.

There are many of the nation who have lost their possessions at Pernambuco and have arrived from there in great poverty, and part of them have been dispersed here and there. [Pernambuco, or Recife, the stronghold of Dutch Brazil, was captured by the Portuguese, January 1654.] So that your petitioners had to expend large sums of money for their necessaries of life, and through lack of opportunity all cannot remain here [in Holland] to live. And as they cannot go to Spain or Portugal because of the Inquisition, a great part of the aforesaid people must in time be obliged to depart for other territories of their High Mightinesses the States-General [the Dutch government] and their Companies, in order there, through their labor and efforts, to be able to exist under the protection of the administrators of your Honorable Directors,

observing and obeying your Honors' orders and commands. [The West India Company owned the young Dutch colony of New Netherland.] It is well known to your Honors that the Jewish nation in Brazil have at all times been faithful and have striven to guard and maintain that place, risking for that purpose their possessions and their blood. . . .

Your Honors should also consider that the Honorable Lords, the Burgomasters of the City and the Honorable High Illustrious Mighty Lords, the States-General, have in political matters always protected and considered the Jewish nation as upon the same footing as all the inhabitants and burghers. Also it is conditioned in the treaty of perpetual peace with the King of Spain [the treaty of Muenster, 1648] that the Jewish nation shall also enjoy the same liberty as all other inhabitants of these lands.

Your Honors should also please consider that many of the Jewish nation are principal shareholders in the [West India] Company. They having always striven their best for the Company, and many of their nation have lost immense and great capital in its shares and obligations. . . .

Therefore the petitioners request, for the reasons given above (as also others which they omit to avoid prolixity), that your Honors be pleased not to exclude but to grant the Jewish nation passage to and residence in that country; otherwise this would result in a great prejudice to their reputation. Also that by an Apostille [marginal notation] and Act the Jewish nation be permitted, together with other inhabitants, to travel, live, and traffic there, and with them enjoy liberty on condition of contributing like others. . . .

Source: As printed in *JAW*, 30–31. Reprinted with permission of AJHS, from *PAJHS* 18 (1909): 4–5, 9–11.

1.05 — EXTRACT FROM REPLY BY THE AMSTERDAM CHAMBER OF THE WEST INDIA COMPANY TO STUYVESANT'S LETTER, APRIL 26, 1655

Honorable, Prudent, Pious, Dear, Faithful [Stuyvesant] . . .

We would have liked to effectuate and fulfill your wishes and request that the new territories should no more be allowed to be infected by people of the Jewish nation, for we foresee therefrom the same difficulties which you fear. But after having further weighed and considered the matter, we observe that this would be somewhat unreasonable and unfair, especially because of the considerable loss sustained by this nation, with others, in the taking of Brazil, as also because of the large amount of capital which they still have invested in the shares of this company. Therefore, after many deliberations we have finally decided and resolved to apostille . . . upon a certain petition presented by said Portuguese Jews that these people may travel and trade to and in New Netherland and live and remain there, provided the poor among them shall not become a burden to the company or to the community, but be supported by their own nation. You will now govern yourself accordingly.

Source: As printed in *JAW*, 32–33. Reprinted with permission of AJHS, from *PAJHS* 18 (1909): 4–5, 8.

1.06 — MOSES LOPEZ BECOMES A NATURALIZED CITIZEN, 1741

Moses Lopez (1706–1767), like his younger and better-known half-brother, Aaron (1731–1782), was born in Portugal to a wealthy converso family. Moses immigrated to New York in 1740–1741 before he and his brother settled in Newport, Rhode Island. The following document demonstrates that Moses enjoyed distinction as one of the first American Jews to become a British citizen under the 1740 British Naturalization Act, which eased the process for gaining citizenship and created avenues for both Jews and Catholics to enjoy full civil equality.

George the Second, by the Grace of God of Great Britain, France, and Ireland, King, Defender of the Faith, etc. To all to whom these presents shall come or may concern, greeting:

Know ye that it appears unto us by good testimony that Moses Lopez, of the city of New York, merchant, being a person professing the Jewish religion, hath resided and inhabited for the space of seven years and upwards within some of our colonies in America, and that the said Moses Lopez, on the twenty third day of October last, betwixt the hours of nine and twelve in the forenoon of the same day, in our Suprem[e] Court of Judicature of our Province of New York, before our judges of our said court, did take and subscribe the oaths of allegiance and supremacy and the abjuration oath, pursuant to the directions of an act of our Parliament of Great Britain, made and passed in the thirteenth year of our reign, entitled "An Act for Naturalizing Such Foreign Protestants and Others therein Mentioned as Are Settled or Shall Settle in Any of His Majesty's Colonies in America," and that the said Moses Lopez's name is registred as a natural born subject of Great Britain, both in our said Supreme Court and in our Secretarie's office of our said province, in books for that purpose severally and particularly kept, pursuant to the directions of the aforesaid act.

In testimony whereof we have caused the great seal of our said Province of New York to be hereunto affixed. Witness our trusty and well beloved George Clarke, Esq., our Lieutenant Governor and Commander in Chief of our Province of New York and the territories thereon depending in America, etc., the thirteenth day of April, *Anno Domini* 1741, and in the fourteenth year of our reign.

George Joseph Moore, deputy secretary

Source: As printed in *AJ*, 201. MS-107, Nathan/Kraus Family Collection, 1738-1939, AJA.

1.07—BARNARD GRATZ TO MICHAEL GRATZ, GIVING ADVICE ON IMMIGRATING TO PHILADELPHIA, NOVEMBER 20, 1758

Barnard Gratz (1738-1801), born in Langendorf, Upper Silesia (which would become part of Germany), immigrated to Philadelphia in 1754, where he became a merchant. By 1758, he was prepared to enter business with his brother, Michael (1740-1811), who had already immigrated to London from Langendorf. In 1759, the brothers reunited in Philadelphia, where they eventually won contracts to supply the colonial government with goods traded from various American Indian tribes.

Greetings to my dearly beloved brother who is as dear to me as my own life, the young man, Yehiel [Michael]—long may he live—that princely, scholarly, and incomparable person:

I report that I am in good health, and I hope you are too.

I learn, dear brother, from the letter of our relative Solomon [Henry] to our relative Koppel [Jacob Henry] that you have returned from India. I am very much surprised, but I cannot say much because I do not know the reason [for your return].

Only if you are satisfied to live in the country and keep a shop—if you are at all able to do that—or to live with my employer, Mr. David Franks, would I advise you to come here in the spring by the first boat. But you must agree to follow our advice while you are here. In that case I hope everything will turn out satisfactorily to you. My plan would be that you come here and stay with my employer two or three years until you learn the business. Meanwhile you will get the same wages that I got.

[In that case] [y]ou might turn your money over to Mr. Moses Franks and take an order on Mr. David Franks [his brother], to be paid here when you arrive. I think this would be better than keeping a shop in the country. Mr. David Franks is a very good man, and you will be able to make some money with your capital here. Otherwise, "do as is good in thine own eyes," do what you want, but do let me know through someone what you have in mind. And don't be too proud. From me,

Your brother,

Issachar Ber [Barnard].

Remember me to everybody in our family.

P.S. Dear brother, if you intend to come here and live with Mr. Franks, you should not bring with you any merchandise whatsoever. You will be able to earn more with your money here. Will you please, therefore, do me the favor of paying our relative Solomon [Henry] nineteen pounds, i.e. £19 ster. on my account. When you arrive, I shall return the sum at once. The rest you ought to give to Moses Franks, and have him issue an order on Mr. David Franks here. Come over by the first boat, as I have already spoken to my employer about you, and he will wait for you until the month of Nisan or Iyyar [April/May]. However, you may do as you please.

I have just reconsidered the matter with our relative Jacob. If you have some money, you might bring with you about eighteen or twenty silver watches, worth from forty-five to fifty-five dinars [shillings?] a piece, some new-fashioned watchchains, about twenty dozen of women's shoes made of calamanco and worsted damask of all colors, a few dozen of women's mittens of black worsted, and a few other articles. In this case you can invest your money [in these articles] and not turn it over to Moses Franks. You might ask him what he thinks you ought to bring here, if you have more money than you need for the articles mentioned above. Let them be insured.

Source: As printed in *JAW*, 53–54. Reprinted with permission of AJHS. Translation, except for minor changes, taken from Joshua N. Neumann, "Some Eighteenth-Century American Jewish Letters," *PAJHS* 34 (1937): 79–80.

1.08—DESCRIPTION BY A NON-JEW OF THE JEWS OF NEW YORK CITY, NOVEMBER 2, 1748

Peter Kalm (1716-1779), a Swedish non-Jew, visited New York City in the mid-eighteenth century. In the following document, he reflects on insights he gained from his interactions with the city's Jews as well as his experience attending a Jewish worship service.

November the 2d. Besides the different sects of Christians, there are many Jews settled in New York, who possess great privileges. They have a synagogue and houses, and great country-seats of their own property, and are allowed to keep shops in town. They have likewise several ships, which they freight and send out with their own goods. In fine, they enjoy all the privileges common to the other inhabitants of this town and province.

During my residence at New York, this time, and in the next two years, I was frequently in company with Jews. I was informed, among other things, that these people never boiled any meat for themselves on Saturday, but that they always did it the day before; and that in winter they kept a fire [going continuously] during the whole Saturday [for kindling fire anew on the Sabbath is prohibited by Jewish law]. They commonly eat no pork; yet I have been told by several men of credit, that many of them (especially among the young Jews), when traveling, did not make the least difficulty about eating this, or any other meat that was put before them; even though they were in company with Christians.

I was in their synagogue last evening for the first time, and this day at noon I visited it again, and each time I was put into a particular seat, which was set apart for strangers or Christians. [This synagogue, Shearith Israel, was then on Mill (South William) Street.] A young rabbi [Benjamin Pereira] read the divine service, which was partly in Hebrew, and partly in the rabbinical dialect [Aramaic]. Both men and women were dressed entirely in the English fashion; the former had all of them their hats on, and did not once take them off during service. The galleries, I observed, were appropriated to the ladies, while the men sat below. During prayers, the men spread a white cloth [the prayer shawl, the talit] over their heads, which perhaps is to represent sackcloth. But I observed that the wealthier sort of people had a much richer sort of cloth than the poorer ones. Many of the men had Hebrew books, in which they sang and read alternately. The rabbi stood in the middle of the synagogue, and read with his face turned towards the east; he spoke, however, so fast, as to make it almost impossible for any one to understand what he said.

Source: As printed in *JAW*, 47–48. From Francis Newton Thorpe, comp. and ed., *The Federal and State Constitutions, etc.* (Washington, D.C.: Government Printing Office, 1909), 3:1870, 1881; 5:2722, 2783–85, 3052, 3062–63.

1.09—WHY THE COURT REFUSED TO NATURALIZE AARON LOPEZ, SUPERIOR COURT OF RHODE ISLAND, NEWPORT, SS. MARCH TERM, 1762

In this document, two Jewish residents of Newport, Rhode Island, Aaron Lopez (1731–1782) and Isaac Eliezer (1720?–1807), seek citizenship rights under the 1740 British Naturalization Act. According to the edict, individuals of any faith community, as long as they had resided for at least seven years in one of the British colonies, could become citizens. After their petition for citizenship was denied by the Rhode Island Superior Court, the two appealed their case to the Rhode Island General Assembly. In the lower house of the General Assembly, lawmakers approved their call for citizenship, though with the stipulation that their citizenship rights excluded the ability to vote and serve in government. Members of the General Assembly's upper house, by contrast, refused the request, arguing that they lacked proper jurisdiction. Lopez and Eliezer (also spelled Elizer—see document 1.13, to follow) were instructed to seek resolution with the Rhode Island Supreme Court. On March 11, 1762, the court considered and then denied the citizenship request, reasoning that since the 1740 British Naturalization Act's intended goal of increasing the colony's population had already been achieved, the act did not here apply. The court also cited an earlier 1663 Rhode Island law barring citizenship to non-Christians.

The petition of Messrs. Aaron Lopez & Isaac Eliezer, persons professing the Jewish Religion, praying that they may be naturalized on an act of Parliament made in the 13th year of His Majesty's reign George the Second, having been duly considered, and also the act of Parliament therein referred to, this court are unanimously of opinion that the said act of Parliament was wisely designed for increasing the number of inhabitants in the plantations, but this colony being already so full of people that many of [H]is Majesty's good subjects born within the same have removed and settled in Nova Scotia and other places, [the petition] cannot come within the intention of the said act. . . .

Further, by the charter granted to this colony, it appears that the full and quiet enjoyment of the Christian religion and a desire of propagating the same were the principal views with which the colony was settled; and by a law made and passed in the year 1663, no person who does not profess the Christian religion can be admitted free of this colony. [This proviso is not found in the original charter of 1663, but was added about 1699.] This court therefore unanimously dismiss the said petition as absolutely inconsistent with the first principle upon which the colony was founded and [inconsistent with] a law now of the same in full force.

Source: As printed in *JAW*, 38–39. From Franklin Bowditch Dexter, ed., *Extracts from the Itineraries and Other Miscellanies of Ezra Stiles, E.E., LL.D., 1755–1794* (New Haven, Conn.: Yale University Press, 1916), 16.

1.10—PETITION FROM ABRAHAM HAIM DELUCENA AND JUSTUS BOSCH TO GOVERNOR ROBERT HUNTER, REQUESTING PERMISSION TO SHIP PROVISIONS TO JAMAICA, JUNE 3, 1713

Between 1702 and 1713, European colonial powers engaged one another in a war over control of the New World. Called the War of Spanish Succession in Europe, it was known as Queen Anne's War in British colonial North America. As part of its war effort, Britain imposed an embargo on exports, complicating businesses such as that of Abraham Haim DeLucena (d. 1725), a Jewish New York merchant, and his non-Jewish partner, Justus Bosch (1674–1739). In the petition that follows, DeLucena and Bosch make their case for an exception to the trade embargo.

To His Excellency, Robert Hunter, Esq., Capt. Generall and Governor in Cheife of the Provinces of New York, New Jersey, and territories thereon depending in America, and Vice-Admirall of the same, etc., in Councill:

The humble petition of Abraham De Lucena and Justus Bosch, owners of the sloop, *Mary and Abigall*, John Smith, master, sheweth:

That before the order made by Your Excellency and councill the 7th of May last, that the collector should not cleare any vessell in which there was any quantity of provisions, nor take any entry for any provisions to be exported,

Your petitioners had actually cleared and entred their said sloop at the custom house for Jamaica, with twenty tons of flower [flour], bread, and bacon which your petitioners had long before purchased for that purpose, and had then actually shipped on board twenty-six barrels of flower, part of the said provisions, the rest remaineing in your petitioners' warehouse, ready to be shipt on board.

That after the order for the embargo as aforesaid, your petitioners applyed themselves to the collector of the customes for leave to take the remainder of their said provisions on board, who declared his opinion that seeing they were entred and cleared before the said embargoe, your petitioners might ship the same on board; and accordingly, your petitioners proceeded [to] ship the same on board. The ____ of May last obtained Your Excellencie's let pass [permit] for their said vessell to proceed on her said intended voyage, but some obstructions hitherto have retarded your petitioners' said vessell from saileing.

And now, by vertue of Your Excellencie's further order in Councill of the second of June instant, your petitioners' said vessell (being just ready to sayle) was stopt from proceeding on her said intended voyage.

Wherefore, and for that your petitioners will be very great sufferors, and their designed voyage wholly ruined in case your petitioners' said vessell be now stopt, and some other vessells, under the like circumstances with your petitioners, haveing since beene permitted to proceed on their voyage,

Your petitioners most humbly pray Your Excellencey will be pleased to take the premisses into Your Excellencie's consideration and permitt your petitioners' said sloop to proceed on her said intended voyage with the aforesaid loading soe entred and cleared as aforesaid.

And your petitioners shall pray, etc.

Abraham De Lucena, Justus Bosch
New York, 3d June, 1713

Source: As printed in *AJ*, 311–12. New York Colonial Manuscripts, LVIII, 125, New York State Library.

1.11—NEWSPAPER BUSINESS ADVERTISEMENT AGAINST EMANUEL ABRAMS, BY ALLAN MELVILLE, OCTOBER 21, 1754

In the preceding document, two New York colonists—a Jew and a non-Jew—collaborated as business partners. In the following exchange of newspaper ads that appeared in 1754, we find two rival Boston merchants, Emanuel Abrams (1718–1802), a Jew, and Alan Melville, a non-Jewish competitor, hurling accusations at each other in an attempt to convince consumers that they offer the highest quality goods. This sort of exchange, conducted in the public sphere of the newspaper, reveals the limits of Jewish communal support as it offers perspective on the everyday lives of Jewish merchants.

Whereas Emanuel Abrams, a Jew, has of late had the notorious impudence to go thro' the town imposing on the inhabitants, to the disadvantage of all honest traders and sellers of snuff, a certain kind of trash of his own making; which in order to make it sell quick, he is pleased to give in the name of Kippen's. And as he has had the front to say he bought it of me, the subscriber, I would therefore inform the publick that I never sold that person snuff of any kind to my knowledge, nor so much as know such a fellow existing.

Allan Melville.

N.B. This may also serve to inform the above-named snuff merchant, that if he does not leave off his villainous practice of fathering of his musty trash upon me, I will certainly make it turn out the dearest snuff that ever he bought.

Boston, October 21, 1754.

Source: Boston Weekly Gazette, Oct. 22, 1754. As printed in *JAW*, 51. Reprinted by permission of the publishers from *Early American Jews* by Lee M. Friedman, pp. 11–12, Cambridge, Mass.: Harvard University Press, copyright © 1934 by the President and Fellows of Harvard College. Copyright © renewed 1961 by Elsie Friedman and Sophie Friedman.

1.12—REPLY ADVERTISEMENT BY EMANUEL ABRAMS AGAINST ALAN MELVILLE, 1754

Whereas Mr. Allan Melville, merchant, has made free with my character in last Tuesday's paper; and I value my credit and reputation, equal as he himself, or any other gentleman; therefore notify the publick that said advertisement is without foundation, and as I always treated my customers with the utmost civility and the best of goods, hope they'll continue their favours, and shall always be as ready to receive their command.

Ema. Abrahams.

N.B. As Mr. Melville is pleased to give my goods the character of trash and musty trash, with an intent to hurt the sale of my goods, this may serve to acquaint him, as also the publick, I have as good snuff as he, or any imported, and customers may have samples on trial.

E. A.

Source: As printed in *JAW*, 51–52. *Boston Weekly Gazette*, Nov. 5, 1754. Reprinted by permission of the publishers from *Early American Jews* by Lee M. Friedman, p. 12, Cambridge, Mass.: Harvard University Press, Copyright © 1934 by the President and Fellows of Harvard College. Copyright © renewed 1961 by Elsie Friedman and Sophie Friedman. Emanuel Abrams's name appears variously as "Abrams" and "Abrahams."

1.13—ISAAC ELIZER AND SAMUEL MOSES TO CAPTAIN JOHN PECK, GIVING INSTRUCTIONS FOR A JOURNEY TO PURCHASE SLAVES, OCTOBER 29, 1762

When slavery was instituted in North America in the early seventeenth century, almost no one objected. In its early years, Africans earned their freedom after a period of service akin to indentured servitude. By the eighteenth century, though, the institution of slavery formalized, depriving Africans and, most important, their African American descendants, of ever attaining their liberty. The forced importation of Africans into North American slavery proved a critical part of the colonial economy. While historians have learned that Jews were underrepresented in the colonial slave trade, Jewish merchants did participate in what became known as "the peculiar institution."

Captain John Peck,

As you are at present master of the sloop *Prince George* with her Cargo on board and ready to sale you are to observe the following orders:

That you Imbrace the first fair wind and proceed to sea and make the best of your way to the windward part of the Coast of Affrica, and at your arrival there dispose of your Cargo for the most possible can be gotten, and Invest the neat proceeds into as many good merchantable young slaves as you can, and make all the Dispatch you possibly can. As soon as your Business there is Compleated, make the best of your way from thence to the Island of New Providence [Bahamas] and there dispose of your Slaves for Cash, if the Markets are not too dull: but if they should [be], make the Best of your

way home to this port, take pilates and make proper protest [before the authorities as to the state of your cargo of vessel] where ever you find it necessary. You are further to observe that all the Rum on board your Sloop shall come upon an average in case of any Misfortune, and also all the slaves in general shall come upon an Average in case any Casualty or Misfortune happens, and that no Slaves shall be brought upon freight for any person, neither Direct nor Indirect.

And also we allow you for your Commission four Slaves upon the purchase of one hundred and four, and the privilege of bringing home three slaves and your mate one.

Observe not neglect writing us by all opportunitys of every Transaction of your Voyage. Lastly be particular Carefull of your Vessell and Slaves, and be as frugal as possible in every expense relating to the voyage. So wish you a Good Voyage and are your Owners and humble Servants.

[No firm signature]

But further observe if you dispose of your Slaves in Providence lay out as much of your neat proceeds as will Load your Vessel in any Commodity of that Island that will be best for our advantage and the remainder of your Effects bring home in money.

Isaac Elizer
Samuel Moses

Source: *DHJ*, 37–38. Massachusetts Historical Society Collections, 7 ser., 9, Commerce of Rhode Island, 1726–1774, 1, 96–97.

1.14—TOURO SYNAGOGUE, EXTERIOR, N.D.

Designed by the highly regarded colonial architect Peter Harrison (1716–1775), Yeshuat Israel (later known as Touro Synagogue) holds the distinction of being the oldest synagogue building in the United States. Completed in 1763, the synagogue was named in the nineteenth century after the congregation's first spiritual leader, Isaac Touro (1738–1783). It achieved particular note in 1790 when synagogue leaders exchanged a series of letters on religious freedom with President George Washington.

Source: PC-3304, AJA.

Source: PC-3304, AJA.

The 1728 constitution of Shearith Israel in New York organized the administrative structure of one of the most important centers of Jewish life in colonial America. In this document, the synagogue articulates the roles, responsibilities, and salaries of its officers as well as expectations for its lay leaders. Responding to experiences since the congregation's founding in 1706, leaders of Shearith Israel established rules of conduct for its membership as well as punishment, in the form of fines, for those who violated its provisions.

In the Name of the Blessed God, Amen [In Hebrew]

Whereas, on or about the year 5466 [1706], certain wholesome rules and restrictions have been made by the then elders of our holy congregation, to preserve peace, tranquility, and good government amongst th'm, and those after them; and as they have been neglected to be put in due force for some time past, wee now meet with common consent and resolve to revive the same with some amendments and additions, which are as follows:

F[ir]stly There shall be elected a parnaz [president] and two *hatanim* [officers], w'ch shall like wise serve as assistants [board members] for the good government of our holy congregation, and in order to w'ch we have now, this year of 5489 [1728-29] elected Mr. Mosses Gomez for parnaz, to whom we gave power that he might elect two *hatanims* and as assistants for this present year. And accordingly, he did elect Mr. Daniel Gomez for *hatan torah* and first assistant, and Mr. Binj[ami]n Mendez Pacheco as *hatan bereshit* and second assistant, and for the future, the parnaz and his assistants, then in being, has power to chuse another parnaz and assistants in their roome yearly.

2ndly We give authority to the gent'[le]m[en] that shall be elected yearly, as is customary in the Jewish congregations, that with the fear of God they may act as their conscience shall dictate [to] them for the well governing of our said congregation.

3rdly If any person or persons whatsoever shall offer to give any affront or abuse, either by words or action to any person or persons within the said sinagog, he or they so offending shall be obliged to pay to the parnaz, then in being, the sum of twenty shillings, if it be adjudged by the said parnaz and assistants that he or they have offended, which money shall be applyd for the use of the sinagog. And if refus'd to pay the said fine, the whole congregation shall assist the said parnaz and assistants to recover the same.

4thly Whoever shall be elected parnaz and refuse to serve shall pay the sum of three pounds. Alsoe those *hatanims* that shall be elected and refuse to act in the s'd post shall pay a fine of foarty shillings, each one [of] which sums shall be apply'd as in the 3d article is specified.

5thly In case any disputes may arise so that the parnaz and his assistants cannot agree, an indifferent [impartial] person whom they shall chuse shall decide the difference between them.

6thly No unmarried man shall be elected parnaz, nor a married man before he has served [either] for *hatan torah* or *hatan bereshith.*

7thly If any poor person should happen to come to this place and should want the assistance of the sinagog, the parnaz is hereby impowerd to allow every poor person for his maintainance the sum of eight shillings p'r week, and no more, not exceeding the term of twelve weeks. And the parnaz is also to use his utmost endeavours to dispatch them to sum othere place as soon as possible, assisting them with necessarys for their voyage, that is, for a single person fourty shillings. But if it be a family, then the parnaz shall call his assistance [assistants] and consult with them, both for their maintainance whilst ashore and also for their necessarys when they depart. Those poor of this congregation that shall apply for *sedaca* [charity] shall be assisted with as much as the parnaz and his assistants shall think fitt.

8thly The offerings [donations] shall be gather'd every three months by the parnaz. As likewise, it not being convenient the selling of misvots [religious honors], it's resolved for the future that in lieu thereof the parnaz w'th his assistants shall tax the men's seats in the sinagog, as they are now seated, but not exceeding fifteen shillings each seat p'r annum, nor less than five shillings. And the misvots shall be given out by the parnaz as the whole year.

9thly We, now prezent, and those that shall hereafter be admitted as yechidims [first-class members] into this congregation, do and shall submit to the foregoing articles.

10thly The parnaz shall be oblidged twice a year to cause these articles to be read in the sinagog both in Portugues and English. Sign'd. In New Yorck in the *Kl Ks* [*Kahal Kodesh* or Holy Congregation] of Sheerit Israell, the 12 of [Tishrei] [in the year] 5489 [September 15, 1728].

Here fallows the articles for the officers, vizt.:

And that the officers of this holly congregation may not at any time pretend ygnorance of what is at their charge to observe, we have with concorde [resolved] *that*

1stly The hazan [minister], Mosses Lopez de Fonseca, shall be oblidged to atend at the sinagog at the custumary hours twice every week day, and three times on the Sabath and feasts, to preform prayers, and what more belongs to his function, as is custumary in othere congregation[s] and that he also, in case the *bodeck* [meat inspector] be indispos'd, shall assist in his room, for the which he shall have his selary of fifety pounds and six cords of wallnut wood [for fuel] per annum, also Passover cakes [matzos] for his family, all which shall be payd him out of the *tsedaca* [treasury].

2ndly That Benjamin Elias shall have twinty pounds salary per annum, in concideration of his haven [having] served as *bodeck*, and his age and circumstance requiring assistance. And we give authority unto the parnaz that he may receive such sums w'ch divers persons perticulerly have subscrive for that perpose. He shall also have two cords of wood and [P]assover cakes.

3rdly That Semuel Bar Meyr [H]aCohen, *bodeck* of this *kahall* [congregation], shall be oblidged to kill at severall places [for different butchers], and sufficiently for the whole congregation, and that every six months he shall submit to be exameend in the dinimz [ritual laws] by the hazen and any other *bodeck* said hazan shall choose, for which he shall have twenty pounds salary per annum.

4thly That Valentin Campanall *shamaz* [beadle], shall be oblidged to atend at the sinagog and shall call the yechidimz that they may assemble togeathere at the usuall hours; and he likewise be oblidged to call to *selichot* [penitential prayers] such persons as shall be given him by the parnaz in [a] list. That he shall keep the synagog candlesticks and lamp clean, and make the candles; also shall keep the sestern [cistern, for washing hands] supplyed with watter, for which he shall have sixteen pound[s], two cords of wood, and masot [matzos] p'r annum.

5thly If any whatsoever of the officers, above said, shall neglect in not doeing what he ought, and what is aforesaid, the parnaz and his assistants have power to fine him or them in the sum they shall judge fitt, not exceeding three pounds, and in case the offence shall be great, the parnaz and assistants shall not discharge any of said officers out of their place without first call'g all the yechidimz for to give their vote, and the major part shall carry it, the parnaz haveing two votes.

6thly That the afores'd salarys are to be understood for this present year of 5489 [1728–29], and that on the begining of the year 5490 [1729–30] the parnaz and assistants that shall then be named they are to declare if they confirm or anull these articules, so farr as concerns the officers and their salarys or any part of them. And if confirmed they shall subscribe their names on foot of this, and the same shall be done by those that then shall follow.

Moseh Gomez, parnas, et al.

Source: As printed in *JAW*, 58–61. Reprinted with permission of AJHS, from *PAJHS* 21 (1913): 1–5, 74–75, 90, 93–94, 96–97, 100–101.

1.17—THE PROSECUTOR'S SUMMARY OF THE EVIDENCE FROM THE TRIAL OF SOLOMON HAYS, 1755–1756

On a very hot and muggy September 14, 1755, women seated on the balcony of New York City's Congregation Shearith Israel for services on Kol Nidre, the evening of Yom Kippur, opened a window to increase air circulation. After a storm passed over the synagogue, one of the female congregants—Gitlah Hays—who was seated closest to the open window was drenched by the sudden downpour. The following morning, Gitlah's husband, Solomon Hays, climbed up to the balcony—intruding upon the women's space—to ensure that the window remained closed for the duration of the Yom Kippur morning service. A tussle thereupon ensued between Solomon Hays and various members of the congregation's leadership who insisted that the other women sitting in the balcony wanted the window to remain open. Members of the congregation were already impatient with Hays, who had a history of alienating himself from his coreligionists. Hays refused to accommodate the demands of the other women, and therefore several members of the congregation's board of elders (including Moses, Daniel, and Isaac Gomez, Hayman Levi, Nepthali Hayman, and Asher Myers) forcibly removed him from the synagogue's yard. The synagogue's leadership levied a fine on Hays, who, in turn, brought the matter to New York's civil court, where he charged the congregation's entire board of elders with assault. After a protracted legal battle, and despite the prosecutor noting that the board of elders had itself been guilty in the past of "outrages and indecencies," the court ruled against Hays, who was formally excommunicated from the synagogue. Many years would pass before the Hays family would be readmitted to synagogue membership.

The King

ag.

Moses Gomez & others

The 14th September 1755 as Mrs. Hayes the wife of Solomon Hayes, was in the Synagogue, and her seat being put before one of the windows there, where she sat with a Neighbour, one Mrs. Still who went to the Synagogue with her out of Curiosity, a Thunderstorm arose of the sudden, and the windows being carried away by the order of Mr. Nepthali Hart Myers as he himself told Mrs. Hayes, she and her Neighbour was exposed to the Hurricane. She went home in the evening and complained of this Usage to her Husband, who the next morning went before the Synagogue convened, searched, found where they were hid and hung them up in their places, and when Mrs. Hayes came to the Synagogue again the same day she found the windows in their places, in the Afternoon of the same day as Mr. Hayes was in the yard of the Synagogue, he saw Moses Gomez, who pretended [claimed] to be one of the Rulers of the Synagogue walking across the yard looking indignantly at the windows in their places again—and run up stairs and pulled off one of the Windows which was— behind to Mrs. Hayes and brought it into the

Yard, and Mr. Hayes seeing him said to him, "So you show your Authority that you are an elder," upon which without any other provocation he struck Mr. Hayes in the Face so that the Blood flew from his Mouth, saying at the same time "Damn you, I'll send you to Goal [sic], and upon Mr. Hayes replying "it don't lye in your power nor any of Your Family to do it," and young Gomez speaking loud and making a great Noise, Daniel Gomez his Father, Isaac Gomez his Father in Law, Nepthali Hart Myers, Hayman Myers, a Jew, Butcher, Asher Myers a Coppersmith and Hayman Levi who pretended [claimed] to be a Jew Constable came out and all of them together laid violent Hands on Mr. Hayes, some grasping his Throat, others seizing him by several other parts of his Body and forcing him out of the Yard and after they got him a little way from the Yard left him.

[. . .]

Note the Jews have for sometime since taken a great dislike to Mr. Hayes, it seems he once accused old Gomez Daniel [sic] of taking Usury of him, and since that it seems he has given them farther offence with regard to two strange Jews one Ephraim Chapman the other named Levi who offered to set up shops at Albany as natural born Subjects of the King, but the Corporation of Albany mistrusting that they were Aliens and not born at Plymouth as they pretended, they sent for Mr. Hayes and examined him and he declaring that he always understood that they were born in Holland they were obliged afterwards to apply for an Act of Assembly to naturalize them, and upon this it seems the Jews were very angry, and in particular the Defendant Mr. Nepthali Hart Myers who called Mr. Hayes

an Informer in the Synagogue. Another Reason it seems which has given the Jews an offence against Mr. Hayes, is his discovery that the Jews did prevail upon one Frances the wife of one Isaac Isaacs, a Christian woman, to renounce her Saviour, and become a proselite to the Jewish Religion, and upon these Accounts they have taken a most inveterate Hatred to Mr. Hayes, and have taken all manner of Opportunities to put indignities upon him, and hurt his Credit, and in particular have refused to his Children their Right which they claim when arrived at a certain Age of reading the Law in the Synagogue, and further have presumed to read a paper in the Synagogue representing him as a Disturber of their peace and quiet, and of scandalizing them among the Christians and therefore by such paper did publickly prohibit all Jews to have any correspondence or communication with him, and that concluded with a terrible Injunction that all Israel should hear and Fear, but in order to obviate this Calumny Mr. Hayes can prove by innumerable Number of witnesses, that he never was a Disturber of them, nor Guilty of any Scandal towards them, except what is Matter of Fact. But on the contrary it can be plainly made appear, that these very Defenders, or most of them, have been guilty of the greatest Outrages and Indecencies in the Synagogue, and in particular young Moses Gomez held up his Cane at Mr. Franks and threatened him in the Synagogue.

Source: Sheldon and Judith Godfrey, "The King vs. Moses Gomez et al.: Opening the Prosecutor's File, over 200 Years Later," *American Jewish History* 80, no. 3 (Spring 1991): 403–5.

1.18—ABIGAILL FRANKS, IN NEW YORK, TO HER SON, HEARTSEY, IN LONDON, JUNE 7, 1743

Bilhah Abigaill Franks, known as Abigaill Franks (1696–1776), was the wife of the successful merchant Jacob Franks (1687–1769). She enjoyed a high level of education and maintained an observant Jewish lifestyle. One of her children, Naphtali (whom she called Heartsey), was sent to London, as was often the case with the male children of wealthy Jewish colonial merchants. London provided these youths with an opportunity to advance their education and to increase the likelihood that they would meet, and later marry, Jewish women. Abigaill's letter to Heartsey, written in 1743, reveals a mother's reaction to the upsetting discovery that one of her other children, a daughter named Phila, had eloped and secretly married outside the Jewish faith.

Dear Heartsey:

My wishes for your felicity are as great as the joy I have to hear you are happyly married. May the smiles of Providence waite allways on y'r inclinations and your dear [wife] Phila's whome I salute with tender affections, pray'g kind Heaven to be propitious to your wishes in makeing her a happy mother. I shall think the time teadious untill I shall have that happy information, for I don't expect to hear it by the return of these ships, and therefore must injoyn your care in writing by the first opportunity (after the birth of wathever it shall please God to bless you with) either by via Carrolina, Barbadoz, or any other.

I am now retired from town and would from my self (if it where possiable to have some peace of mind) from the severe affliction I am under on the conduct of that unhappy girle [your sister Phila]. Good God, wath a shock it was when they acquainted me she had left the house and had bin married six months. I can hardly hold my pen whilst I am a writting it. Itt's wath I never could have imagined, especialy affter wath I heard her soe often say, that noe consideration in life should ever induce her to disoblige such good parents.

I had heard the report of her goeing to be married to Oliver Delancey, but as such reports had offten bin off either off your sisters [Phila and Richa], I gave noe heed to it further than a generall caution of her conduct wich has allways bin unblemish'd, and is soe still in the eye of the Christians whoe allow she had disobliged us but has in noe way bin dishonorable, being married to a man of worth and charector.

My spirits was for some time soe depresst that it was a pain to me to speak or see any one. I have over come it soe far as not to make my concern soe conspicuous but I shall never have that serenity nor peace within I have soe happyly had hittherto. My house has bin my prisson ever since. I had not heart enough to goe near the street door. Its a pain to me to think off goeing again to town, and if your father's buissness would permit him to live out of it I never would goe near it again. I wish it was in my power to leave this part of the world, I would come away in the first man of war that went to London.

Oliver has sent many times to beg leave to see me, but I never would tho' now he sent word that he will come here [to Flatbush]. I dread seeing him and how to avoid I know noe way, neither if he comes can I use him rudly. I may make him some reproaches but I know my self soe well that I shall at last be civill, tho' I never will give him leave to come to my house in town, and as for his wife, I am determined I never will see nor lett none of the family goe near her.

He intends to write to you and my brother Isaac [Levy] to endeavour a reconciliation. I would have you answer his letter, if you don't hers, for I must be soe ingenious to conffess nature is very strong and it would give me a great concern if she should live unhappy, tho' its a concern she does not meritt. . . .

Wath you say abouth y'r sister's [Richa] comeing to England, I shall very readly agree to it, and the sooner the better if it was only a means of her not seeing the other [Phila], wich she will hardly be able to avoid unless she intirely excludes her self from all company, wich she has don for this three months past, tho' Phila has not bin in town since she left us but has (wathever I have forbid) found means to send messages, for as they lived very affectionately it subsists still, and I am sure she will find all the means she can to see Richa. . . .

My spirets is too depresst to write. It is with reluctancy I doe write to any one at pr'st, therefore whoever I omit you must excuse me to them. I think I've spun this to a considerable length and shall conclude with the repetition of my prayers for your health and happyness. I am, my dear son,

Your affectionate mother,
Abigaill Franks. . . .

Source: As printed in *AJW*, 3–5. Reprinted from Leo Hershkowitz and Isidore S. Meyer, eds., *The Lee Max Friedman Collection of American Jewish Colonial Correspondence: Letters of the Franks Family, 1733–1748* (Waltham, Mass.: American Jewish Historical Society, 1968), 57ff., 116ff. "Heartsey" appears in some printed versions of this document with the "s" capitalized ("HeartSey").

1.19—MEIR JOSEPHSON TO MICHAEL GRATZ CONCERNING A FEMALE DOMESTIC, JULY 25, 1762

In a 1762 correspondence between Meir (also spelled Meyer and Myer) Josephson, a German Jewish immigrant living in Reading, Pennsylvania, and Philadelphia merchant Michael Gratz (1740–1811), Josephson reflects on his own level of religious observance and the strong communal bonds among the colony's Jews. In rather candid language (the letter was written originally in Yiddish and has been translated), Josephson comments about his African American slave, testifying to the fact that many Jews were fully acclimated to the prevailing attitudes about slavery and women servants.

Reading (with the help of God, may God protect it herein),
Sunday, 5 Ab, 5522 [July 25, 1762].

Peace to my beloved friend, the honorable Mr. Yehiel [Michael Gratz]. May the Lord protect him, and may this letter find his entire household at peace.

Your letter came at a propitious moment, also the books and bills of exchange [?] and one jar [?] of anchovies which was very important and which my wife, may she live long, has already eaten. Of course, I helped her somewhat. So if I could obtain another jar of this kind, will you send it to me, because it is the best I ever saw.

Also, I was very sorry to see from your letter that you, my special good patron, intend to leave Philadelphia, which I had not expected at this time. However, if you think that it is not to your best interest to remain, I cannot blame you. One must do many things for the sake of a livelihood. I wish it were in my power to advise you what is best for you to do and arrange that you would not leave Philadelphia, because your brother, may he be blessed, intends at present to go to London, and you, sir, will leave also, and I'll be a stranger when I come to Philadelphia. I really don't know where I can go!

If you come here for the coming Sabbath Nachmu [the Sabbath of Consolation]—may it come at an auspicious moment!—it would please me very much, because we are presently very lonesome on the Sabbath. And if you could stay here with us for eight days, it would be still better.

I also inform you that I may again sell my nigger wench at a profit. So if a ship with niggers should arrive, or a ship with [indentured] Germans, you will let me know, because I cannot manage without a servant. The wench I now have has two virtues, both bad ones. First, she is drunk all day, when she can get it, and second, she is mean, so that my wife cannot say a word to her. She is afraid of her. How did all this happen? A free nigger here wants to court her and to buy her from me. I don't want to give her away for less than 110 pounds, with her bastard, be-cause I bought the bastard too. At present she costs me 90 pounds. So if I can make out with her, I think it is best to let her go and get another. So if you should have occasion to hear of a good nigger wench, or of a good servant, you will inform me.

I am,

Your affectionate friend, the humble
Meir, son of Joseph from Yever,
scholar, of blessed memory

[Postscript in English]

My spouse gives hear [her] complements to you and very much oblige to you for your coucumers.

Source: As printed in *AJW*, 7–8. MS-451, Henry Joseph Collection of Gratz Papers, AJA.

1.20—HANNAH PAYSADDON TO AARON LOPEZ, REQUESTING CHARITY, JULY 26, 1770

Newport Jewish merchant Aaron Lopez (1731–1782) distinguished himself through his philanthropic work as well as his business successes. In colonial America, Jewish leaders such as Lopez often received requests from needy Jews and Christians, as well as from civil entities. In the appeal that follows, Hannah Paysaddon of New York, aware of Lopez's reputation as a generous benefactor, appeals to him for aid.

New York, July 26, 1770

Dear Sir:

I take the liberty once moor of troubling you in the letter way, which I hope you'l pardon. Necesseaity drives me to it. I am now in years and unable to do anny thing for my self. It's comeing to quarter [rent] day, and I am affraid I shall be troubled. I am helpt by my friends, but it is not sufficient to keep me from disstress. So, dear sir, I hope your heart, which is naturly tender, will be moved with kind compassion for a poor fellow creature who is laboring under greater distress then it's possible to express. What ever you do for me, I hope God will doubly return.

So, remain with great respect,

Your obedient servant,
Hannah Paysaddon

Source: As printed in *AJ*, 16. Champlin Collection, New York State Library, Albany, New York.

Colonial American Jews maintained communal ties to Jews in the Holy Land as well as other places abroad. Eighteenth-century Palestine, then under Ottoman rule, offered pious Jews the opportunity to live in several of Judaism's most sacred cities, including Jerusalem. Most Palestinian Jews in this era lived in poverty, relying on the support of Jews from elsewhere in the world. In May 1773, members of London's Congregation Saar Asamaim (Gate of Heaven) sent an "open letter" to congregations in colonial British America asking them to sponsor an appeal by Hebron's rabbi, Samuel Cohen, in support of destitute Jews living in his city, sacred for Jews because it is the site of the tomb of the biblical patriarchs and matriarchs.

Most worthy gentlemen, parnessim [presidents], gabaim [treasurers] of the holy kehilot [congregations] of America:

Having seen the contents of the letter which was signed by the gentlemen, hahamim [rabbis] of the city of Hebron in the Holy Land and addressed to us, and since it is clear to us that the wretchedness and misery are true which are happening to our brothers in Palestine, caused by the civil wars, which, also for those regions, as also for their safety.

Now you will please take note that we have granted the request which the same gentlemen made of us in the above-mentioned letter, and we recommend to all our brothers, the gentlemen parnassim deputes [officers] and *yehidim* [members] of the various kehilot of America, that the Great God have mercy on the misfortunes and miseries of our brothers of Hebron, and that they respond to this call for aid with their generous assistance to their messenger, the gentleman R.[abbi] Samuel Cohen, bearer of this letter, for the relief and refuge of the said people of Hebron. And may He [God] reward this pious work with an increase in His good gifts as the culmination of His goodness bestowed upon this *K. K.* of Saar Asamaim [Holy Congregation, Gate of Heaven] in London, the 5 of May, of Sivan 5533 [1773].

Signed by the following gentlemen:
Abraham Aboab Osorio, President,
Isaac Israel Nunes
David Abarbanel
Charles Serra
Isaac Serra, Gabay [treasurer]

Source: As printed in *JAW*, 87–88. Petition, May 5 Siran 5533 (1733), minute book, archives of Congregation Shaar Hashamaim (Bevis marks), London, England.

2 Forging a Nation

THE AMERICAN JEWISH EXPERIENCE DURING THE REVOLUTION AND THE EARLY NATIONAL PERIOD, 1776–1820

Throughout premodern Jewish history, powerful autocratic governments—especially those with an established religion or national church—often treated Jews poorly, relegating them to status as second-class citizens, scapegoating them, insisting they were instigators of various social ills, and, in many cases, evoking antisemitic imagery that led to occupational restrictions, special "Jew taxes," ghettoization, and violent oppression.

In the newly formed United States of America, unlike in many parts of the Old World, Jews benefited from the European Enlightenment ideal of natural right, upon which the Declaration of Independence was based. According to natural right theory, each and every individual, regardless of his (less often her) religious beliefs or group status, enjoyed "certain inalienable rights" that government could not deny. With the founding of the United States, American Jews looked forward to protections for their life and liberty, however these would eventually be defined by the government.

Yet American Jews at the time of independence still wrestled with competing political allegiances. Although most joined the Revolution and backed the new experiment in democracy, others remained loyal to the British Crown, supporting the colonies' chief trading partner, Great Britain, in the hope that war could be avoided. These Jewish loyalists wanted to protect their livelihoods. They believed that through negotiation and compromise on the tax issues that triggered the conflict a peaceful resolution could ultimately be obtained. When the war ended with a patriot victory, many such loyalists fled the United States for England or one of its other colonies.

When the Continental Congress's first attempt to create a federal government contract, the Articles of Confederation, failed to provide the nation with the political might necessary for effective governance, many of the Founding Fathers gathered in Philadelphia, in 1787, to draft a more comprehensive constitution. The Constitutional Convention, conducted in secret over a nine-month period, produced a document aimed at strengthening the federal government and safeguarding the rights of the states while protecting citizens from the threat of governmental tyranny. The framers of the U.S. Constitution resolved the question of excessive federal authority by creating an elaborate system of governmental checks and balances. They divided the federal government into three distinct branches, apportioned authority among them, limited the power of the federal government by granting wide discretion to state governments, and encouraged state governments, in turn, to transfer power to the local level. Most important for American Jews, the Constitution promised explicit protection of religious freedom.

As citizens, Jews adapted to life in the new United States. In their workplaces, still dominated by jobs focused on trade and commerce, Jews forged business relationships that recognized the nation's new political independence and the end of British colonial rule. Within their religious worlds, Jews reached out to their Christian neighbors to support Jewish institutions. And, as European Jews contemplated immigration to the new nation, they learned about what adaptations would be necessary for them to experience a meaningful Jewish life.

2.01—JOSEPH SALVADOR TO HIS COUSIN EMANUEL MENDES DA COSTA, DESCRIBING AMERICA, JANUARY 22, 1785

In a letter to Emanuel Mendes da Costa (1717-1791), Joseph Salvador (1716-1786) recounted vivid details about life in America. Salvador, who immigrated to the United States at age sixty-eight in 1784, was the father-in-law and uncle of Francis Salvador (1747-1776), the first Jewish casualty in the American Revolution. His experience in his new home proved quite trying, as his letter indicates. For Salvador, an accomplished scientist who was reared as an aristocratic British subject, life in the fledgling United States of America was difficult. Writing to da Costa, a scientist of note in Great Britain, Salvador described how living in South Carolina affected his everyday experiences, his social status, as well as his interest in the sciences.

My dear friend and Cousin,
Sir,

I have long since desired to write to you, but have been so distressed and ill that I could not do it.

I have suffer[e]d every want and, having no one till within this month to write for me, have been forc[e]d to write too much myself; my eyes and hands are very much impair[e]d, and I am entirely depriv[e]d of doing anything by night as candles are not in use in this country, nor does anyone know how to make a pen; few write or read.

I am now in a wild country, have but one servant, and, tho they speak English, we frequently don[']t understand each other. The inhabitants are descendants of the wild Irish and their ignorance [is] amazing; they have all the bad Spanish customs but none of that nation[']s good qualities. They are as poor as rats, proud as dons. They will not work nor permit their families to serve;

They are naked and famish[e]d and immensely lazy. They have no religion or morals, the few that have any adopt the patriarchal sistem. They have no belief in Christ, little in Judaism or a future state. Their minds are wholly bent on their horses whom they prize more than their wives and families. They hate society and pass their days in the woods or, loitering about, they drink hard. Rum is their deity; they ruin their healths and are short livers, always happy when they can do any ill natur[e]d thing and molest their neighbours. The better sort of people are here very docile and tractable and don[']t want [for] good sense, but [are] totally unimproved. They wish good government, but dare not oppose the others. In short there is no power in government; all goes by chance and time must bring amendment. They now are like a set of Tartars; there are above 50,000 whites in the district. Scarce fifty houses, the rest are cabins or huts. They are daily extending backwards in the country and always moving; not a village and scarce two houses together.

[. . .]

The soil is excellent and would produce anything, but the inhabitants will cultivate nothing. They have all fruits, but bad—peaches, pears, mulberryes, plums, grapes, but none good, they being ungrafted, bad strawberries, some water melons, gourds and pumpkins, and middling melons, some other southern fruits, and greens, pineapples, oranges, and limes from abroad, but not good; they have apples from the north but no cherries or currants. They are very scarce of greens, mostly kidney beans, cabbage and lettuce, some pease, but rare and bad; small greens in general are all wanting, some bad asparagus and artichokes. Their wheat is good and Indian corn plenty. I hope to get some hops and beer;

we have deer skins and bear skins. Tobacco and indigo maintain this country, the first is grown common and is as good as Virginia, the indigo is ordinary but will mend. In the low land vast quantities of fine rice is made. There is little or no credit or money in the country. I would continue my narrative, but have no time. The waggons are upon departure and there is no other conveyance. I will beg you to wait on the president of our society, wishing my compliments. Tell him I have met with nothing worthy his attention in my passage, and have been very ill, but hope to be soon able to communicate some matters of these inland countries which are little known in Europe; that about this date last year, being ill att Cross Creek, I saw a small bearded comet. Having no instrument in the place, all I could do was to observe her course with the eye. She seem[e]d to me to be about eighteen degrees to the southward of Capricorn; I don[']t know the name of the constellation, knowing little astronomy and particularly of the southern heavens. Her course seem[e]d to me near W. S. W., going to the sun. The [comet] every day gain[e]d that way, set sooner, and about the thirty was not visible to the eye, setting nearly with the sun, but more to the southward. Per-

haps she grew visible att sun rise; I doubt it as she declin[e]d so much to the southward. In June we had the hottest day known here; it is said the thermometer reached 107 in the shadow. I went into the air and felt as if warm water was thrown on me, and all agreed in the coolest places our blood and pulses were above fever heat for three hours; in eight hours after it was cold. There was frost last winter and this has been very cold, frequently freezing all liquids in my room but spirits, and close by large wood fires. Few such days are in Eng[lan]d.

I can [write] no more on these subjects. . . .

On natural history, I hope soon to write to you; there seems to be less than one would expect.

My love to Jos[hua] and Judy [presumably the author's son-in-law and daughter] and communicate this to them, my service to all friends. I am

dear sir
Y[ou]r. cousin and humble servant
Joseph Salvador

Coroneka 22 Jan[uar]y 1785

Source: Cecil Roth, "A Description of America," in Jacob R. Marcus, ed., *American Jewish Archives* 17, no. 1 (April 1965): 29–32.

2.02—REBECCA SAMUEL TO HER PARENTS IN HAMBURG, GERMANY, DESCRIBING HER EXPERIENCES IN VIRGINIA, JANUARY 12, 1791

Rebecca Alexander Samuel, a young mother who immigrated with her husband to Petersburg, Virginia, from Hamburg, Germany, had many experiences similar to those of Joseph Salvador. According to Samuel, there was no real Jewish life in Virginia. Yiddish speaking, and traditional in her religious observance, she laments these circumstances in a letter to her parents in Hamburg. Yet Samuel also details aspects of American life that she enjoyed, such as the possibility of earning a good living and her community's lack of a rabbi, an absence of

authority that actually allowed Jews in America to practice their religion without fear of excommunication.

Petersburg, January 12, 1791, Wednesday, 8th [7th?] Shebat, 5551.

Dear and Worthy Parents:

I received your dear letter with much pleasure and therefrom understand that you are in good health, thank God, and that made us especially happy. The same is not lacking with us—may we live to be a hundred years. Amen.

[. . .]

You write me that Mr. Jacob Renner's son Reuben is in Philadelphia and that he will come to us. People will not advise him to come to Virginia. When the Jews of Philadelphia or New York hear the name Virginia, they get nasty. And they are not wrong! It won't do for a Jew. In the first place it is an unhealthful district, and we are only human. God forbid, if anything should happen to us, where would we be thrown? There is no cemetery in the whole of Virginia. In Richmond, which is twenty-two miles from here, there is a Jewish community consisting of two quorums [twenty men], and the two cannot muster a quarter [quorum when needed?].

You cannot imagine what kind of Jews they have here [in Virginia]. They were all German itinerants who made a living by begging in Germany. They came to America during the war, as soldiers, and now they can't recognize themselves.

One can make a good living here, and all live at peace. Anyone can do what he wants. There is no rabbi in all of America to excommunicate anyone. This is a blessing here; Jew and Gentile are as one. There is no *galut* ["exile," rejection of Jews] here. In New York and Philadelphia there is more *galut*. The reason is that there are too many German Gentiles and Jews there. The German Gentiles cannot forsake their anti-Jewish prejudice; and the German Jews cannot forsake their disgraceful conduct; and that's what makes the *galut*.

[Rebecca Samuel]

Source: As printed in *AJ*, 51–52. MS-451, Henry Joseph Collection of Gratz Papers, AJA.

2.03—FRANCIS SALVADOR TO SOUTH CAROLINA CHIEF JUSTICE WILLIAM H. DRAYTON, REPORTING LOCAL MILITIA ACTIVITY AGAINST NATIVE AMERICANS AND LOYALISTS, JULY 18 AND 19, 1776

In a July 18, 1776, letter to South Carolina's Chief Justice William H. Drayton (1742–1779), American Jewish revolutionary soldier Francis Salvador recounted vivid and dramatic details of a frontline battle between South Carolina troops and a group of Cherokees aligned with the British. This document captures the depth of American Jewish commitment to the Revolution and the degree to which Jews were welcomed into military service. While Salvador, raised in an affluent and well-known Spanish-Portuguese family in England, represented an American Jewish elite, responses to him in life and death reveal a profound willingness by senior revolutionary leaders to embrace Jews as fellow patriots.

Dear Sir:

. . . . You would have been surprised to have seen the change in this country two days after you left me [June 29th, at my plantation, Coronaca]. On Monday morning one of Capt. [Aaron] Smith's sons came to my house with two of his fingers shot off and gave an account of the shocking catastrophe at his father's. . . .

I immediately galloped [twenty-eight miles] to Major [Andrew] Williamson's to inform him but found another of Smith's sons there, who had made his escape and alarmed that settlement. The whole country was flying—some to make forts, others as low as Orangeburgh [over halfway to Charlestown].

Williamson was employed night and day sending expresses [couriers] to raise the militia, but the panic was so great that the Wednesday following, the Major and myself marched to the late Capt. Smith's with only forty men. The next day we were joined by forty more and have been

gradually increasing ever since, tho' all the men in the country were loth to turn out till they had procured some kind of fancied security for their families. However, we had last night 500 men, but have not been joined by any from the other side of the [Saluda] River. I rode there last Saturday and found Col. Williams and Lisles [Lisle] and two companies from Col. Richardson's regiment, amounting to 430 men.

They were attacked on [early] Monday morning, July 15th, by Indians and Scopholites [Tories and partisans], but repulsed them, taking thirteen white men prisoners. The Indians fled the moment day appeared.

I will not trouble you with more particulars, as Major Williamson will send a circumstantial account to his Excellency [John Rutledge, President of South Carolina].

I am afraid the burthen of the war will fall on this regiment, and that the people over the [Saluda] River [to the north] will do nothing. They grumble at being commanded by a Major; and, I fear, if they join us at all, which I doubt, they will be very apt to prejudice the service by altercations about command. I cannot help saying that if Williamson is fit to conduct such an expedition, he certainly ought to have a much higher rank than any of these chaps, who don't object to his person but his rank. I likewise think it an omission that the colonels on the other side the River have no written orders to put themselves, or their men, under his command.

On the last accounts from town [Charlestown]—that [Robert] Cuningham and his companions [suspected Tories] were set at liberty—we were very near having a mutiny in camp. And it [this release] is really a measure which, though certainly intended for the best, [is] very alarming to all ranks of people. The ignorant look upon it as turning their enemies loose on their backs in the day of their distress. And the sensible part consider it as a dangerous exercise of a dispensing power, assumed contrary to the express determination of [the Provincial] Congress and a corroborating resolve of the succeeding House of Assembly. . . .

Our men seem spirited and very much exasperated against our enemies. They are all displeased with the people over the River for granting quarter to their prisoners, and declare they will grant none either to Indians or white men who join them. We have just received an account that two of the Cherokees' head warriors were killed in the late skirmish at Lindley's Fort.

19th July.

. . . . We have just heard from over the River that the white people in general [the Tories] had quitted the Indians after the repulse at Lindley's and were delivering themselves up to Col. Liles [Lisle]. He has sent all these to Ninety Six jail [a trade outpost at "location marker ninety-six"] against whom there is proof of having been in the action.

I hope you will pardon the freedom with which I express my sentiments, but I look upon it as an advantage to men in power to be truly informed of the people's situation and disposition. This must plead my excuse, and believe me to be, with great respect, dear sir,

> *Your most obedient humble servant,*
> *Francis Salvador*

P.S. We, this day, increased to 600, all from the same regiment. Capt. [James] McCall, with twenty men, was sent by Major Williamson to the Cherokees at Seneca [Essenecca] to make prisoners of some white men [Tories], by the encouragement of some Indians who had been at the Major's. When the detachment got near, the Indians came out to meet them, spoke friendly to them, and invited the captain, lieutenant, and another man to sup with them, leaving three of their own people in their room. And, in a few hours after, in the night, the Indians returned and suddenly attacked the detachment which fled as fast as possible. They are all returned but the captain and six men.

This happened immediately [before July 1st] before Smith's family was cut off, who lost five negro men, himself, wife, and five children [Three of these five were later found alive]. . . .

Source: "Jews and the American Revolution: A Bicentennial Documentary," in Jacob R. Marcus, ed., *American Jewish Archives* 27, no. 2 (Nov. 1975): 125–28.

2.04—MARYLAND CONSTITUTION, ARTICLES 33, 35, AND 55, RESTRICTING OFFICEHOLDERS TO CHRISTIANS, NOVEMBER 11, 1776

The issuance of the Declaration of Independence on July 4, 1776, did not lead to the immediate political enfranchisement of American Jews. Just as various colonies offered differing levels of civil equality to Jews in the prerevolutionary period, the newly organized states worked independently, and at their own pace, toward achieving the new nation's promise of "life, liberty, and the pursuit of happiness." In Maryland, delegates to a November 1776 state constitutional convention in Annapolis issued a Declaration of Rights that removed the privileged position of the Church of England as well as granted Roman Catholics the right to worship as their faith required. Yet Maryland's framers did not permit the state's Jewish citizens to hold public office; this right only came after the legislature passed its "Jew Bill" in 1826. In the state of New York, where Jews were both more numerous and engaged in the important economies of trade and commerce, delegates to the July 1776 and April 1777 state constitutional conventions offered full civil equality to their Jewish residents—the first of the original thirteen states to do so.

XXXIII. That, as it is the duty of every man to worship God in such manner as he thinks most acceptable to him; all persons, professing the Christian religion, are equally entitled to protection in their religious liberty; wherefore no person ought by any law to be molested in his person or estate on account of his religious persuasion or profession, or for his religious practice; unless, under colour of religion, any man shall disturb the good order, peace or safety of the State, or shall infringe the laws of morality, or injure others, in their natural, civil, or religious rights; nor ought any person to be compelled to frequent or maintain, or contribute, unless on contract, to maintain any particular place of worship, or any particular ministry; yet the legislature may, in their discretion, lay a general and equal tax, for the support of the Christian religion; leaving to each individual the power of appointing the payment over of the money,

collected from him, to the support of any particular place of worship or minister, or for the benefit of the poor of his own denomination, or the poor in general of any particular country. . . .

XXXV. That no other test or qualification ought to be required, on admission to any office of trust or profit, than such oath of support and fidelity to this State, and such oath of office, as shall be directed by this convention, or the legislature of this State, and a declaration of a belief in the Christian religion. . . .

LV. That every person, appointed to any office of profit or trust, shall, before he enters on the execution thereof, take the following oath, to wit: "I[,] A. B. [generic initials, equivalent to "John Doe"], do swear, that I do not hold myself bound in allegiance to the King of Great Britain, and that I will be faithful and bear true allegiance to the State of Maryland"; and shall also subscribe a declaration of his belief in the Christian religion.

Source: As printed in *JAW*, 95–96. From Francis Newton Thorpe, comp. and ed., *The Federal and State Constitutions, etc.* (Washington, D.C.: Government Printing Office, 1909), 3:1686, 1689–90, 1700.

2.05—NEW YORK CONSTITUTION, ARTICLES 35, 38, AND 39, MAKING NEW YORK THE FIRST STATE TO EMANCIPATE JEWS, APRIL 20, 1777

XXXV . . . That all such parts of the said common law, and all such of the said statutes and acts aforesaid, or parts thereof, as may be construed to establish or maintain any particular denomination of Christians or their ministers, or concern the allegiance heretofore yielded to, and the supremacy, sovereignty, government, or prerogatives claimed or exercised by the King of Great Britain and his predecessors, over the colony of New York and its inhabitants, or are repugnant to this constitution, be, and they hereby are, abrogated and rejected. . . .

XXXVIII. And whereas we are required, by the benevolent principles of rational liberty, not only to expel civil tyranny, but also to guard against that spiritual oppression and intolerance wherewith the bigotry and ambition of weak and wicked priests and princes have scourged mankind, this convention doth further, in the name and by the authority of the good people of this State, ordain, determine, and declare, that the free exercise and enjoyment of religious profession and worship, without discrimination or preference, shall forever hereafter be allowed, within this State, to all mankind: *Provided*, that the liberty of conscience, hereby granted, shall not be so construed as to excuse acts of licentiousness, or justify practices inconsistent with the peace or safety of this State.

XXXIX. And whereas the ministers of the gospel are, by their profession, dedicated to the service of God and the care of souls, and ought not to be diverted from the great duties of their function; therefore, no minister of the gospel, or priest of any denomination whatsoever, shall, at any time hereafter, under any pretence or description whatever, be eligible to, or capable of holding, any civil or military office or place within this State.

Source: As printed in *JAW*, 96–97. From Francis Newton Thorpe, comp. and ed., *The Federal and State Constitutions, etc.* (Washington, D.C.: Government Printing Office, 1909), 5:2635–37.

2.06—ISAAC TOURO, A LOYALIST, TO BRITISH GENERAL GUY CARLETON, REQUESTING FUNDS TO RELOCATE TO JAMAICA, DECEMBER 12, 1782

For American Jews loyal to the British, political opposition to the American Revolution often wrought physical dislocation as patriot troops advanced. For the Dutch-born Isaac Touro (1738–1783), the retreat of British troops first forced a move from his home in Providence, Rhode Island, where Touro served as religious leader of the renowned congregation Yeshuat Israel (later known as the Touro Synagogue), to British-held New York City. In 1782, Touro, unable to support himself, appealed to the British government for financial help through Gen. Guy Carleton so that he could return with his family to the British-ruled island of Jamaica, where he had resided prior to his immigration to Newport.

To His Excellency, Sir Guy Carleton, K. B. [Knight of the Bath], General and Commander in Chief, etc., etc., etc.:

The petition of Isaac Touro, late rector of the Jewish synagogue at Rhode Island, humbly sheweth:

That from the distresses which your petitioner sufferd from persecution for his attachment to [His Majesty's] government, and coming with [H]is Majesty's troops from Rhode Island to this city [New York], he was so reduced in his circumstances, that had it not been for the humane interference of General [William] Tryon, General [John] Marsh, and other respectable persons, he must have sunk under the weight of his affliction and distress;

That from their kind patronage, the bounty of government has been extended to him, and he has made shift to support himself and family;

That the petitioner is now anxiously desirous of removing himself and family to the island of Jamaica, but is incompetent to defray the expences of his passage, etc.:

That the only resource he has left him is Your Excellency's humanity and benevolince, in the hope that you will grant him an advance of one twelvemonth's allowance, which would effectually enable him to accomplish his wishes.

Your petitioner therefore humbly prays that Your Excellency will be favorably pleased to order a twelve months' allowance to be paid to him, to enable him to remove with his family to the island of Jamaica.

And, as in duty bound, he will every pray, etc., etc.

Isaac Touro

New York, the 12th December, 1782.

Source: "Jews and the American Revolution: A Bicentennial Documentary," in Jacob R. Marcus, ed., *American Jewish Archives* 27, no. 2 (Nov. 1975): 189–90.

2.07—JONAS PHILLIPS, ASKING THE CONSTITUTIONAL CONVENTION TO EMANCIPATE PENNSYLVANIA'S JEWS, SEPTEMBER 7, 1787

In 1781, all thirteen states had ratified the Articles of Confederation, but many citizens found this agreement inadequate. Those leaders who favored a stronger national government began meeting in Philadelphia in February 1787 to frame a new constitution for the young nation. As this new constitution took shape, Americans wondered how the document would treat a range of controversial issues.

Many American Jews hoped the new constitution would safeguard the right of religious liberty in the republic. In a famous letter addressed to the delegates of the convention, Jonas Phillips (1736–1803) of Philadelphia urged the framers to maintain respect for freedom of conscience and to confer "equal footing" under the law to all religions, including Judaism.

Phillips, no doubt, was pleased with the proposed constitution that emerged from the convention. In Article VI, the document forbade the use of "a religious test as a requirement for holding a governmental position." Those who feared a strong centralized government still worried that the new constitution granted too much authority to the federal government, so ten amendments, known as the Bill of Rights, were proposed by Congress in 1789 and ratified by the states in 1791. These amendments guaranteed the rights of individuals to liberty and property. The First Amendment prohibited the government from establishing a state religion and from interfering with the free exercise of religion.

Sires:

With leave and submission I address myself to those in whom there is wisdom, understanding, and knowledge; they are the honourable personages appointed and made overseers of a part of the terrestrial globe of the earth, namely the 13 United States of America in convention assembled, the Lord preserve them, amen.

I, the subscriber, being one of the people called Jews, of the city of Philadelphia, a people scattered and dispersed among all nations do behold with concern that among the laws in the constitution of Pennsylvania, there is a clause, sect. 10 to viz., "I do believe in one God the creatur and governor of the universe and rewarder of the good and the punisher of the wicked and I do acknowledge the Scriptures of the Old and New Testament to be given by divine inspiration." To swear and believe that the New Testiment was given by divine inspiration is absolutely against the religious principle of a Jew, and is against his conscience to take any such oath. By the above law a Jew is deprived of holding any publick office or place of government which is a contradictory to the [Pennsylvania] Bill of Right, sect. 2 viz.:

That all men have a natural and unalienable right to worship Almighty God according to the dictates of their own conscience and understanding, and that no man ought or of right can be compelled to attend any religious worship or [accept a] creed, or [erect or] support any place of worship, or maintain any minister, contrary to, or against his own free will and consent. Nor can any man who acknowledges the being of a God be justly deprived or abridged of any civil right as a citizen on account of his religious sentiments or peculiar mode of religious worship. And that no authority can or ought to be vested in or assumed by any power whatever that shall in any case interfere, or in any manner controul the right of conscience in the free exercise of religious worship. . . .

It is well known among all the citizens of the 13 United States that the Jews have been true and faithful Whigs, and during the late contest with England they have been foremost in aiding and assisting the states with their lifes and fortunes. They have supported the cause, have bravely fought and bled for liberty which they can not enjoy.

Therefore if the honourable convention shall in their wisdom think fit and alter the said oath and leave out the words to viz.: "and I do acknowledge the Scripture of the New Testiment to be given by divine inspiration," then the Israelites will think themself happy to live under a government where all religious societys are on an equal footing. I solicit this favour for myself, my children, and posterity, and for the benefit of all the Israelites through the 13 United States of America.

My prayers is unto the Lord. May the people of this states rise up as a great and young lion; may they prevail against their enemies; may the degrees of honour of his Excellency, the president of the convention, George Washington, be exhalted and raise up. May everyone speak of his glorious exploits.

May God prolong his days among us in this land of liberty. May he lead the armies against his enemys as he has done hereuntofore. May God extend peace unto the United States. May they get up to the highest prosperitys. May God extend peace to them and their seed after them so long as the sun and moon endureth; and may the almighty God of our father Abraham, Isaac and Jacob indue [sic] this noble assembly with wisdom, judgment and unanimity in their counsells; and may they have the satisfaction to see that their present toil and labour for the wellfair of the United States may be approved of through all the world and particular by the United States of America, is the ardent prayer of sires.

Your most devoted obed. servant,

Jonas Phillips

Philadelphia, 24th Ellul, 5547, or Sep'r 7th 1787.

Source: As printed in *JAW*, 99–100. Reprinted with permission of AJHS, from *PAJHS* 2 (1894): 108–10.

2.08—ADDRESS OF THE NEWPORT CONGREGATION TO THE PRESIDENT OF THE UNITED STATES OF AMERICA, AUGUST 17, 1790

In one of the most important and famous exchanges in American Jewish history, the leadership of Newport, Rhode Island's congregation wrote a letter to President George Washington on the occasion of his visit to their city. Washington's reply, in which he repeats the Newport congregation's call for "a government which to bigotry gives no sanction, to persecution no assistance," solidified the civic standing of the nation's Jewish community as the president assured his readers that "All possess alike liberty of conscience and immunities of citizenship." The free exercise of religion is not a national indulgence, Washington proclaims, but an "inherent natural right."

Sir, Permit the Children of the Stock of Abraham to approach you with the most cordial af-

fection and esteem for your person and merits—and to join with our fellow-citizens in welcoming you to New Port.

With pleasure we reflect on those days—those days of difficulty and danger, when the God of Israel, who delivered David from the peril of the sword—shielded your head in the day of battle:—and we rejoice to think that the same Spirit, who rested in the bosom of the greatly beloved Daniel, enabling him to preside over the Provinces of the Babylonish Empire, rests, and ever will rest upon you, enabling you to discharge the arduous duties of Chief Magistrate in these States.

Deprived as we have hitherto been of the invaluable rights of free citizens, we now, (with a deep sense of gratitude to the Almighty Disposer of all events) behold a Government (erected by the Majesty of the People) a Government which to bigotry gives no sanction, to persecution no assistance—but generously affording to All liberty of conscience, and immunities of citizenship—deeming every one, of whatever nation, tongue, or language equal parts of the great governmental machine. This so ample and extensive federal union whose basis is Philanthropy, mutual confidence, and public virtue, we cannot but acknowledge to be the work of the Great God, who ruleth in the armies of Heaven, and among the inhabitants of the Earth, doing whatsoever seemeth him good.

For all the blessings of civil and religious liberty which we enjoy under an equal and benign administration we desire to send up our thanks to the Antient of days, the great Preserver of Men—beseeching him that the Angel who conducted our forefathers through the wilderness into the promised land, may graciously conduct you through all the dangers and difficulties of this mortal life—and when like Joshua full of days, and full of honor, you are gathered to your Fathers, may you be admitted into the heavenly Paradise to partake of the water of life and the tree of immortality.

Done and signed by order of the Hebrew Congregation in New Port, Rhode Island, August 17th, 1790.

Moses Sexias [*sic*] Warden.

Source: As printed in *DHJ*, 79–80. *Washington Papers*, 17–18; Library of Congress, Washington, D.C.

2.09—PRESIDENT GEORGE WASHINGTON TO THE NEWPORT CONGREGATION, 1790

Gentlemen:

While I receive with much satisfaction your address replete with expressions of affection and esteem, I rejoice in the opportunity of assuring you that I shall always retain a grateful remembrance of the cordial welcome I experienced in my visit to New Port from all classes of Citizens.

The reflection on the days of difficulty and danger which are past is rendered the more sweet from a consciousness that they are succeeded by days of uncommon prosperity and security.

If we have wisdom to make the best use of the advantages with which we are now favored, we cannot fail, under the just administration of a good government to become a great and happy people.

The Citizens of the United States of America have a right to applaud themselves for having given to mankind examples of an enlarged and liberal policy, a policy worthy of imitation. All possess alike liberty of conscience and immunities of citizenship.

It is now no more that toleration is spoken of, as if it was by the indulgence of one class of people, that another enjoyed the exercise of their inherent natural rights. For happily the government of the United States, which gives to bigotry no sanction, to persecution no assistance, requires only that they who live under its protection should demean themselves as good citizens, in giving it on all occasions their effectual support.

It would be inconsistent with the frankness of my character not to avow that I am pleased with your favorable opinion of my administration, and fervent wishes for my felicity.

May the children of the Stock of Abraham, who dwell in this land, continue to merit and enjoy the good will of the other inhabitants, while every one shall sit in safety under his own vine and fig-tree and there shall be none to make him afraid.

May the Father of all mercies scatter light and not darkness in our paths, and make us all in our several vocations useful here, and in his own due time and way everlastingly happy.

G. Washington.

Source: As printed in *DHJ*, 80–81. *Washington Papers,* 19–20; Library of Congress, Washington, D.C.

2.10—ANONYMOUS REPLY TO JAMES RIVINGTON'S ANTISEMITIC PREFACE IN *The Democrat,* DECEMBER 17, 1795

In 1795, newspaper publisher James Rivington (1724-1802) wrote an antisemitic preface to Henry James Pye's (1745-1813) novel The Democrat. *Rivington, a staunch loyalist who elected to remain in New York after the defeat of the British, called Jews "the tribe of Shylock" and blamed them for what he considered the failings of the new nation. In response, Thomas Greenleaf (1755-1798), publisher of the* New York Journal, *printed two replies that challenged Rivington's prejudiced views. An abbreviated version of one of these replies, with the anonymous signature "Slow and Easy," is included here.*

a. To the WRITER of the PREFACE to DEMOCRAT

It is a good maxim not to ridicule religion, or the natural defects of the human body. The first shews the depravity of the head, the latter the malignity of the heart. If this observation is just, we may conclude from the extraordinary preface, lately published by J-m-s R-v--gt-n to a novel entitled [*The*] *Democrat*, that the writer's head is as destitute of every liberal sentiment, as his heart is deficient in charity and compassion for the defects of his fellow-creatures, had such defects really existed.

I shall endeavour, in the course of a few observations, to place the preface in its proper point of view, but being unaccustomed to writing, the public are not to expect well-turned periods or elegance of diction, but in lieu thereof, I will endeavour to give them facts in plain and unadorned language; in doing this, I am in some measure under the disagreeable necessity of using a mode similar to that of the author of the preface, not indeed with a view of wounding the feelings of any person whatever, but merely to expose the absurdity of the practice itself. I shall only take notice of such part of the preface as respects the Democrats, of whose Society I am a member, and leave those whom it concerns to notice the rest.

Speaking of the Democratic Society, it has the following words—"*This itinerant gang will be easily known by their phisiognomy,*" &c. The public will doubtless admire your sagacity, in discovering the Democrats to be a wandering *gang*. An abusive stile, Sir, is ever a very bad one; the word gang is made use of to denote ruffians and highway men.—Let us try how those elegant expressions will sound, when applied to other Societies—For instance, to the St. George's, St. Andrew's, St. Patrick, Tammany, Black Friars, or any other in this city. I believe, Sir, they will not be in a hurry to erect a statue to your memory, for the politeness of the expression, or the honour you meant to confer on them—"*They all seem, like their Vice-President, of the tribe of Shylock.*"—Really, Sir, this is extremely sarcastic; the wits of the age ought to have your name wrote in letter of gold, for this brilliant proof of your satire. Perhaps some readers of your preface may be ignorant of the source from whence this pretty story took its rise; you ought to have the goodness to inform them, that by turning to [Ellis] Farneworth['s *The Life of*] *Pope Sixtus the Vth*, page 401, they would find it recorded at large; but this story, as erroneously represented by Shakespeare, could not be applied to the Vice-President, as it would not by any means suit his liberality of sentiment and general character.... If, by the word Shylock, you mean a Jew, from my knowledge of the Vice-President, I dare say he would think himself honoured by the appellation, Judaism being his religious profession, as Democracy is his political creed.

It is an old remark, that the great Author of the Universe has so beautifully variegated his works, that scarce any two things appear alike. To your inventive genius it was left to discover, that all the members of the largest Society in the state, look exactly like their Vice-President—Go on, Sir, and convince the Philosophers of the age, that you have no equal.

With your permission I will make use of an old adage—It must be a bad rule that won't work both ways—let us try it. Your most gracious sovereign, for instance, was unfortunately inflicted with insanity; by a parity of reasoning, all his liege subjects must be mad men....

Your enemies, as well as your friends, do you justice, and say you are no changeling; that you have acted, and still do act, consistently from your appointment of printer to his most gracious majesty to the present time. Courtier like, you have feared and flattered your superiors, and represented all those in the most ludicrous and false colouring, from whom you supposed you had nothing to fear.—While the British fleets

and armies were wantonly burning our towns, and committing scenes that will scarcely at this day be believed, did not your zeal then, and does it not still continue to represent them as the bravest and most gallant people on the globe terrestrial? Did you not, on every occasion, represent the worthy and brave General Washington, and his army of heroes, as banditti, that could never stand before British troops? Did you not turn their well fought battles into so many defeats, and represent them as retreating with dismay over the Alleghany Mountains? . . .—I am bold to say, Sir, that the whole of the Democratic Society, from the President to the Door Keeper individually, would be pleased with an opportunity to serve you precisely in the same way: but rest assured, merit like yours will never fail to meet its due reward.

If I had a thousand mouths of brass, they would be inadequate to trumpet forth the many exploits you have made the bravest and most magnanimous people on the globe terrestrial perform, and it would require as many more to represent the dastardly and dreadful situation in which you have uniformly placed the Americans, and do still some of their best friends.

To conclude, Sir, I deny the allegations as set forth in your preface, respecting the Democratic Society and their Vice-President, as untrue, but say the facts contained herein are true, and leave the decision to the impartial public.

Slow and Easy.

Source: As printed in *DHJ*, 86–88. From the *Argus, or Greenleaf's New Daily Advertiser*, December 17, 1795.

2.11—SAMPSON SIMSON'S HEBREW ORATION AT COLUMBIA COLLEGE, 1800

As early as the eighteenth century, Columbia College offered courses in Hebrew so that students could properly understand the Holy Scriptures in their original language. For

Sampson Simson (1781–1857), generally believed to be Columbia's first Jewish graduate, the school's interest in the study of this classical language translated into an opportunity to offer a commencement address in Hebrew. Simson's speech, delivered in 1800, and reputedly written on his behalf by Gershom Seixas, a cantor and a trustee of Columbia College, depicted the Jew as an American patriot and concomitantly provided his listeners with a formal attempt to reconstruct the history of American Jewry.

Although not accustomed to speak in public, I rise with perfect confidence that you will kindly consent to listen to me and I earnestly crave your indulgence for any error I may commit in the course of my address. And if I have found grace in your eyes I shall essay to speak concerning my brethren residing in this land. It is now more than 150 years, since Israelites first came to this country, at the time when this province was under the dominion of Holland, but until now no one of them or their children has on a similar occasion been permitted thus to address a word in public, and I am a descendant of one of those who were among the first settlers here. It is known to you, that at the time when this province, then called New Amsterdam, was exchanged for the colony of Surinam, all the inhabitants remaining here came under the dominion of England. Among them were the Jews who until then could only congregate for worship in private rooms in their own dwellings until the year 5490 [1730] (according as we reckon in this city of New York). It was then that our regular Synagogue was built, where we have been serving Almighty God unmolested for upwards of seventy years. During this long period the Jews have not been as numerous as the other sects, for only few in number they came hither; but now, behold the Lord has enlarged and increased in this and in all the other provinces of these United States the descendants of those few families that came from Holland in the year 5420 [1660], one hundred and forty years ago. Among these was one man with his wife, one son and four daughters. The father and son died soon after they had reached this place, leaving the wife with her four daughters and behold they have exalted themselves in this city, and from them sprang forth many of the Congregation now known as "Shearith Israel." Afterwards, in the year 1696, there came from France some families by the way of England, who brought with them letters of denization from the king, constituting them freemen throughout all the provinces under his dominion. And in the year 1776 at the time when the people of this country stood up like one man in the cause of liberty and independence every Israelite that was among them rose up likewise and united in their efforts to promote the Country's peace & prosperity. And even now we endeavor to sustain the government of these provinces, free of any allegiance to any other whatsoever, monarchial or republican, and we exclaim in the language of King David, "Rid us, (O Lord!) from the hand of the children of the stranger, whose mouth speaketh vanity and whose right hand is the right hand of falsehood."

Source: PAJHS 27 (1920): 373–75.

2.12—ISAAC HARBY TO JAMES MONROE ON RELIGIOUS FREEDOM AND THE RECALL OF MORDECAI NOAH FROM THE U.S. CONSULATE IN TUNIS, 1816

Mordecai Manuel Noah (1785–1851) gained widespread attention when he was appointed U.S. consul to the Kingdom of Tunis in 1813. In this role, Noah was charged with a secret mission of ransoming Americans held hostage in nearby Algeria. When he was unable to free all the prisoners and accused of overpaying ransom for the two he did free, President James Madison

and Secretary of State James Monroe decided to
relieve him of his duties. Since they did not want
to expose the undercover operation, Madison
and Monroe argued instead that Noah's work
on behalf of Morocco's Jewish community
compromised his diplomatic professionalism.
Monroe's letter of discharge pointed out that
had the U.S. government realized Noah was a
Jew, he would never have been appointed
because a Jewish diplomat could not effectively
serve in a Muslim country. Noah shared his
correspondence and documents concerning
the secret Algiers mission with his friend and
colleague Isaac Harby (1788-1828), a Jewish
resident of Charleston, who promptly composed
a letter of complaint to Monroe. Harby was
appalled to read that an American Jew had
been disqualified from representing his country
on account of his religion, and minced no words
in reminding Secretary Monroe that freedom of
religion was, for all Americans, a "principle of
equal inalienable, constitutional Rights."

Office of the Southern Patriot
Charleston May 13th 1816
Honble James Monroe
Dr. Sir

I have just finished the perusal of a pamphlet, submitted to my inspection and *impartial Judgment*, by Mr. Noah, our late consul at Tunis. To say that the explanation & documents exhibited in this pamphlet, were Satisfactory, *to my mind*, of the zeal & ability with which Mr. Noah discharged his official duties, might possibly be attributed to the friendship contracted between us, during a long acquaintance. But You, Sir, who can look upon him from higher and more impartial ground; you, whose *candour* as a man blends so happily with that strict *justice* which should guide your public actions, can judge of Mr. Noah's conduct with cooler and steadier calculation, than myself. On this impartiallity, this purity of mind that has ever distinguished your official life, Mr. Noah must rely for a full justification. His friends are also willing to rely upon it.

When this gentleman was first recommended to the regard of government, he was supported by many worthy & influencial men. These men must think it due to themselves, to know how he has realized the expectations of his friends. May I add, Sir, that I think it due to *yourself*, to the *Country*, to the *Constitution*, to enquire into the nature of the *cause* why he has been so abruptly recalled?

. . . But, I do think, that the successful termination of Mr. Noah's negociation, generally; his zeal and industry for the interests of his countrymen; his *manners* so well adapted to win his way among strangers; these, taken together, should at least have entitled him to a full and impartial hearing, before your sudden fiat had issued, to his injury & to the astonishment of his friends.

. . . The first sentence in your letter of recal to Mr. Noah, contains these words: "It was not known at the time of your appointment as consul for Tunis, that the *religion* which you professed would form any *obstacle* to the exercise of your functions:"!! It was this sentiment, Sir, which immediately fixed and rivetted my attention, my astonishment. I would ask, since it was not *then* known, whether it has been *since* discovered, that *Religion* disqualifies a man from the exercise of his political functions? Or has this doctrine *ever* been known, since the first hour of the establishment of our invaluable Constitution? Had such a sentiment proceeded from an *intollerant* mind, had it been uttered by the minister of any other cabinet than that of America, we should not have wondered. But, proceeding from *You*, from a component part of the Executive of the United States, from you, one of the soundest constitutional lawyers in the country, surely we *might* wonder; and in respect for you, attribute the expression to haste and inconsiderateness rather than to principle. To *principle!* God forbid. When, in the convention of Virginia (a theatre filled with talents) You and other true and liberal statesmen, guarranty'd *perfect freedom of Religion*, then it was you acted upon *principle*. When the constitution of the United States declares that Liberty shall be *secured to every citizen*, this is *principle*. The principle of *equality of rights*, is inherent in every letter, and breathes its spirit throughout the whole mass of our laws. This salutary principle, which forever destroys the union of Church & State, that bane of political happiness, that insult to Heaven, mingles with the feelings, and morals, and education of the American people. An objection, on the score of Religion, would sound to them "most monstrous and unnatural." They Know no Religious distinctions. One great character of *Citizenship* alone prevails.

> "spiritus intus alit, totamque infusa per artus,
> mens agitat molem, et magno se corpore miscet."
> [the spirit within nourishes, and the mind that is diffused throughout the living parts of nature activates the whole mass and mingles with the vast body of the universe (Virgil)]

It is upon the principle, not of *toleration* (for man has no *power* to tolerate Religion, that is a concern between Man and his maker) but upon the principle of equal inalienable, *constitutional Rights*, that we see Jews appointed to offices, that we see them elected in our State Representation, & that, in proportion as their talents and their influence can bear them through, we see their mingling in the honours of their country. They are by no means to be considered as a *Religious sect*, tolerated by the government; they constitute a portion of *the People*. They are, in every respect, woven in and compacted with the citizens of the Republic. Quakers and Catholics; Episcopalians and Presbyterians, Baptists and Jews, all constitute one great political family. "Simplex duntaxat et unum" [each as good and

as much intended as another (Horace)]. In this light, every wise Statesman must regard them. I do therefore appeal to you, not only as a Philanthropist, but as a politician; not only as a *just man*, but as the Secretary of State to this free government, to erase the sentence in your letter above alluded to, strike it from the records of your office. It can only remain to your own injury, and to the reproach of the liberal character of our institutions.

[. . .]

With respect to any *reparation* (not on account of Mr. Noah, he is only *secondary* in the affair) for the sake of a large portion of the American people, from whom such a transaction should be for ever buried, for the sake of Justice, of the constitution, of your own cause, I certainly must leave every thing remedial, to your well known candour and your better Judgement: suggesting, however, at the same time, that an appointment to an equal rank, or at least some public and honourable mention of Mr. Noah, would be highly satisfactory to his feelings, to the feelings of all his co-religionaires and, I doubt not, to the feelings of your bosom.

What I have written, I trust you will regard (as I sincerely assure you it is meant to be) moderate, friendly and respectful. No Government, no officer of government, however highly endowed, but in the course of a long political carreer *may* commit an error. To remedy it, is in this case, left to *your* liberallity and justice.

Believe me Sir, to be with the highest respect,

Your obt. Servant
Isaac Harby

Source: RG 59, General Records of the Department of State, U.S. National Archives and Records Administration.

After Mordecai Noah's diplomatic career ended, he was invited to deliver a speech dedicating New York's Shearith Israel synagogue building. His 1818 address was widely published, earning a response from Thomas Jefferson, who emphasized his unswerving commitment to religious toleration. Two years later, Jacob de la Motta (1789–1845), a physician in South Carolina and then Georgia and a Jewish communal leader, delivered a dedicatory address at the consecration of Mikvah Israel's new synagogue building in Savannah, Georgia. De la Motta sent copies of his address to both James Madison and Thomas Jefferson. In his reply, printed here, Jefferson reaffirmed his commitment to religious pluralism.

Sir,—

I thank you for the Discourse on the consecration of the Synagogue in your city, with which you have been pleased to favor me. I have read it with pleasure and instruction, having learnt from it some valuable facts in Jewish history which I did not know before. Your sect, by its sufferings, has furnished a remarkable proof of the universal spirit of religious intolerance inherent in every sect, disclaimed by all while feeble, and practised by all when in power. Our laws have applied the only antidote to this vice, protecting our religious, as they do our civil rights, by putting all on an equal footing. But more remains to be done. For although we are free by the law, we are not so in practice. Public opinion erects itself into an Inquisition, and exercises its office with as much fanaticism as fans the flames of an *Auto da fé*. The prejudice still scowling on your section of our religion, altho' the elder one, cannot be unfelt by yourselves. It is to be hoped that individual dispositions will at length mould themselves to the model of the law, and consider the moral basis on which all our religions rest, as the rallying point which unites them in a common interest; while the peculiar dogmas branching from it are the exclusive concern of the respective sects embracing them, and no rightful subject of notice to any other. Public opinion needs reformation on this point, which would have the further happy effect of doing away the hypocritical maxim of "intus ut lubet, foris ut moris" ["inside as it pleases, outside as maintained according to custom"]. Nothing I think would be so likely to effect this as to your sect particularly as the more careful attention to education, which you recommend, and which placing it's [*sic*] members on the equal and commanding benches of science, will exhibit them as equal objects of respect and favor. I should not do full justice to the merits of your discourse, were I not, in addition to that of its matter, to express my consideration of it as a fine specimen of style and composition. I salute you with great respect and esteem.

Th. Jefferson

Source: Library of Congress, Washington, D.C.

2.14—THOMAS JEFFERSON TO JACOB DE LA MOTTA, SEPTEMBER 1, 1820

Monticello

Th. Jefferson returns his thanks to Dr. de la Motta for the eloquent discourse on the Consecration of the Synagogue of Savannah which he has been so kind as to send him. It excites in him the gratifying reflection that his own country has been the first to prove to the world two truths, the most salutary to human society, that man can govern himself, and that religious freedom is the most effectual anodyne against religious dissension: the maxim of civil government being reversed in that of religion, where it's [*sic*] true form is "divided we stand, united we fall." He is happy in the restoration, of the Jews particularly, to their social rights, & hopes they will be seen taking their seats on the benches of science, as preparatory to their doing the same at the board of government. He salutes Dr. de la Motta with sentiments of great respect.

Source: Library of Congress, Washington, D.C.

2.15—THE FIRST FORM OF THE "JEW BILL," 1819

With the adoption of the U.S. Constitution in 1787 and formal passage of the Bill of Rights in 1791, Congress was forbidden from passing any law that infringed on religious liberties. Yet that rule did not apply to state governments, which were free to limit the rights of religious minorities. For many Jews in America, civil restrictions continued long after the U.S. Constitution and the Bill of Rights were ratified. A number of the original thirteen states continued to administer a religious test, or oath, which effectively prohibited Jews from holding state office or participating in the state's governmental machine. Thus, Jews obtained political equality through a protracted effort—a struggle that had to be fought on a state-by-state basis. Perhaps the best-known example of this fight for equality took place in Maryland in the legislative battle over the adoption of a "Jew Bill."

WHEREAS, It is the acknowledged right of all men to worship God according to the dictates of their own consciences. And whereas, it is declared by the thirty-sixth section of the bill of rights of this state, "That the manner of administering an oath to any person ought to be such as those of the religious persuasion, profession, or denomination of which such person is one, generally esteem the most effectual confirmation by the attestation of the divine Being. And whereas, religious tests for civil employment, though intended as a barrier against the depraved, frequently operate as a restraint upon the conscientious; and as the constitution of the United States requires no religious qualifications for civil office, Therefore,

Sec. 1. *Be it enacted, By the General Assembly of Maryland,* That no religious test, declaration or subscription of opinion as to religion, shall be required from any person of the sect called Jews, as a qualification to hold or exercise any office or employment of profit or trust in this state.

Sec. 2. *And be it enacted,* That every oath to be administered to any person of the sect of people called Jews, shall be administered on the five books of Moses, agreeably to the religious education of that people, and not otherwise.

Sec. 3. *And be it enacted,* That if this act shall be confirmed by the General Assembly, after the next election of delegates, in the first session after such new election, as the constitution and form of government direct; that in such case, this act and the alterations and amendments of the constitution and form of government therein contained, shall be taken and considered, and shall constitute and be valid as part of the said constitution and form of government, to all intents and purposes, any thing in the declaration of rights, constitution and form of government contained, to the contrary notwithstanding.

Sec. 4. *And be it enacted,* That the several clauses and sections of the declaration of rights, constitution and form of government, and every part of any law of this state, contrary to the provisions of this act, so far as respects the sect of people aforesaid, shall be, and the same is hereby declared to be repealed and annulled on the confirmation hereof.

Source: As printed in *JUS,* vol. 1, 39–40. Reprinted from *Sketch of Proceedings in the Legislature of Maryland, December Session, 1818, on What Is Commonly Called the Jew Bill* (Baltimore: James Robinson, 1819), 12–13.

E. S. Thomas, Esq.,
Annapolis, Md.

Dear Sir:

Noticing the proceedings of the present legislature of Md., I observe a committee has been appointed in the house of Delegates to bring in a Bill "to extend to persons professing the Jewish Religion the same civil privileges that are enjoyed by other religious sects" and that yourself with Mr. Kennedy by whom the motion was made and Mr. Breckenridge compose that committee.

Having the pleasure of a personal acquaintance with you I am induced from the importance of the subject to address you.

You cannot be aware Sir from not having felt the pressure of religious intolerance, of the emotions excited in the breast of an Israelite whenever the theme of liberty of conscience is canvassed. The subject of religion being the nearest and most vital to the soul of every sectarian it awakens every spark of feeling in support of those unalienable rights which the very nature of man forbids a transfer. On the question of the extension of religious freedom to any sect or denomination, the Jew feels with solicitude for a Brother sufferer and with the anxiety of him for whom the subject is intended particularly to operate, exults in his success or sinks deeper than before with the pangs which oppression have thrown over him, and in a tenfold degree bends him below his former station.

[...]

The motion of Mr. Kennedy at the same time that it reminds us of the indignity of our situation in the States also brings to mind the many blessings our profession enjoys in this country of liberty—that by the Constitution of the United States an Israelite is placed on the same footing with any other citizen of the Union and can be elevated to the highest station in the gift of the government or in the people such toleration is duly appreciated. On the other hand we are not insensible of the protection in our persons and property even under the laws of Maryland still as those obnoxious parts of its Constitution were produced only in times of darkness and prejudice why are they continued as blots on the present enlightened period and on the honor of the State in direct opposition also to the feature and principles in the Constitution of the United States.

I can scarcely admit a doubt that on a moment's consideration and reflection a change will be made as the Prayer of Justice and reason.

The grievance complained of and for which *redress* is asked is that part of the Constitution of Maryland, which requiring a declaration of belief in the Christian Religion prevents a Jew accepting any office his fellowmen might elect him to or think him deserving the enjoyment of. He is thus incapacitated because he cannot *abjure* the principles instilled in him of worshipping the Almighty according to the dictates of his own conscience and take an oath of belief in other tenets as if such declaration of Belief made him a better man or one more capable of exercising the duties of the office which the want of that declaration would deprive him of because he maintains his unalienable rights with a steadfast and upright hand. Because he cannot consent to act hypocritically he is deemed unworthy to be trusted and to be as it were disfranchised, thus incapacitating on the very grounds that ought to entitle him to confidence in the discharge of any duty he might be called upon to perform *viz*: a complete independence and unbiased judgment formed on the broad foundation of moral *rectitude*.

[...]

In times of peril and war the Jews have borne the privations incident to such times and their best exertions have been given to their utmost, in defense of the common cause. See the Israelite in the ranks of danger, exposing his life in the defense of the Country of his adoption or of his nativity and then ask the views of the man in such exposure—the cause alone—he bears the brunt of the battle and the toils of the day with the knowledge of having discharged his duty; he retires with the pleasing consolation of mental correctness and the silent approbation of his own conscience. Here he rests, having attained the summit of his expectations. Sensible of his worth, his Commander would offer him promotion the honorable and only boon a Soldier aspires to. He cannot, vain are his wishes. The State under whose banners he has fought and bled debars him its acceptance. Here Sir, is an evidence of the injustice of the act of the Constitution, and the effect perhaps of that inaction which I have noticed above.

Still stranger tho are the cases requiring the decision of a Jury, look there at the situation of a man professing the Jewish Religion. I wish not to be understood that he could not obtain justice, such is not my meaning, but he is to be judged by men whom perhaps prejudice might influence in their verdict and the very course of justice be *impeded* by mere caprice incident to strong individual feeling.

By the present system a Jew is deprived of a seat in that body where by a liberal construction of matters and circumstances and a free interchange of sentiment on the broad basis of both Jewish and Christian doctrine to "do unto others as you would have others do unto you" might those prejudices be combatted and justice satis-

fied in its strictest sense. I cannot name the unworthy equality a Jew is placed on trial by Jury. On this great question of right, the guarantee of Freedom and political liberty I will leave you to judge as a legislator and an American Freeman.

Your attention I need not solicit on this occasion, being satisfied of the liberality of your views and the pleasure it would afford you in the opportunity of *redressing* the grievances of your Constituents. A bill relating to an equality of rights intended for the present purposes was reported in the Senate of Maryland during the Session of 1816 and was not acted upon. I do not know why. I confidently trust however that the present legislature will take up the subject with the consideration it merits.

Whatever may be the fate of the proposed bill permit me to request, if not improper that the Ayes and Nays be taken and placed on record on the general question as well as on any previous one, which might involve such general question or be indicative of its final result.

[. . .]

I am, Dear Sir, Yours with great Respect, (*signed*)

J. I. Cohen.

Source: As printed in *JUS,* vol. 1, 33–37. Draft in the Mendes Cohen Collection, Maryland Historical Society, Folder II.

2.17—HAYM SALOMON, BUSINESS ADVERTISEMENT, *Freeman's Journal*, 1782

Haym Salomon (1740–1785), a Polish-born Jew, immigrated to New York City in 1775, where he became quite involved in pro-revolutionary work as a member of the Sons of Liberty. Enduring two arrests by the British for his activism, Salomon managed to escape his captivity and settle in patriot-held Philadelphia, where he emerged as an important financier aiding the revolutionary cause. With the war's conclusion, Solomon took up business in Philadelphia. He described his services in a 1782 advertisement.

Haym Salomon, Broker to the Office of Finance, to the Consul General of France, and to the Treasurer of the French Army, at his office in Front Street, between Market & Arch streets. *Buys* and sells on commission *bank stock, bills of exchange* on France, Spain, Holland, and other parts of Europe, the West-Indies, and inland bills, at the usual commissions.

He buys & sells *loan office certificates, continental and state money,* of this or any other state, paymaster and quartermaster generals notes; these, and every other kind of paper transactions (bills of exchange excepted) he will charge his employers no more than *one half per cent,* for his commission.

He procures *money on loan* for a short time and gets notes and bills discounted.

Gentlemen and others, residing in this state, or any of the United States, by sending their orders to the office, may depend on having their business transacted with as much fidelity and expedition as if they were themselves present.

He receives tobacco, sugars, tea, and every other sort of goods, to sell on commission, for which purpose he has provided proper stores.

He flatters himself his assiduity, punctuality, and extensive connection in his business, as a broker, is well established in various parts of Europe, and in the United States in particular.

All persons who shall please to favour him with their business may depend upon his utmost exertion for their interest, and part of the *money advanced,* if desired.

Source: As printed in *JAW*, 124–25. From *Freeman's Journal, or North-American Intelligencer,* Nov. 6, 1782.

2.18—WILL OF CHARLESTON'S JACOB JACOBS, WHICH INCLUDED SLAVES, 1797

South Carolina auctioneer Jacob Jacobs (1742–1797) typified the status and position of more prosperous southern Jews in the early national period. His will, included as follows, offers details of his net worth, his possessions, as well as his network of family and friends, both in the United States and overseas. Jacobs also included his synagogue in his will, reflecting his engagement with local Jewish life. As was the case with other southern Jews in this period, Jacobs owned slaves, whom he left to his wife.

While some slave owners chose to free their slaves upon their death or that of a surviving spouse, Jacobs ordered his charges to be sold after his wife's death so that the proceeds could go to friends in Charleston.

In the Name of God, Amen. I Jacob Jacobs of the City of Charleston, in the State of South Carolina Vendue Master, being of sound and disposing Mind, Memory and Understanding do this twenty fourth day of June in the Year of our Lord One thousand seven hundred and Ninety-Six, Make, publish and declare this my last Will and Testament in manner and form following, that is to say: First, I will that all my just Debts and Funeral charges be fully paid, as soon as may be after my decease, by my Executors herein after named. Item I give unto the Synagogue in Charleston of which I am a Member the Sum of Ten Pounds. Item I give unto my Sister Rachael Jacobs the Sum of Twenty five Pounds to be remitted to her in Great Britain free of all deductions by my Executors herein after named, as soon as may be after my decease. Item I give unto my Brother Samuel Jacobs the Sum of Ten pounds, To my Sister in law Phila Nunes I give the Sum of Twenty Pounds, And my Will is that the said several pecuniary Legacies shall be paid free from all deduction whatever. Item my Will is, and I do hereby give unto my Friend Gershon Cohen of the City of Charleston aforesaid, my gold Stock Buckle, Silver Shoe Buckles and Stone Knee Buckles. Item I give and bequeath unto my dearly beloved Wife Katey Jacobs all my Household and Kitchen Furniture, Plate, China, Stock of Liquors, Horses, Carriages, Monies, Bonds, Notes, and Book Debts whatsoever and wheresoever absolutely for ever, subject nevertheless to the several Devises and Bequests herein before by me made and given. Item I give and devise unto my said dearly beloved Wife Katey Jacobs during her Widowhood and no longer all

those my Negro and other Slaves named Toby, Scipio, Jack, Jenny with her three Children Peter, John and Eve, and Flora with her two Children Rachael and Lucy and all the other Slaves that I may be possessed of, at the time of my death. And from and immediately after the death or Marriage of her my said Wife, which may first happen, then my Will further is, and I do hereby direct, enjoin, authorize and empower my Executors herein after named, or such of them as shall take upon themselves the burden and execution of this my Will, to expose to Sale and sell either at public or private Sale, each, every, and all of the said Negro, and other Slaves, with the Issue of the Females, herein before given unto my said Wife, and the money arising from the Sale of the said Slaves, to be placed out at Interest, and secured with a Mortgage of real Estate, and also good and Sufficient personal Security. And the Proceeds arising from the Sale of the said Slaves to be equally divided share and share alike between each and every of the Children (if more than one) of my Friends Gershom and Rebecca Cohen of Charleston . . . In Witness Whereof I have hereunto set my Hand and Seal, the day and Year first above written.

Jacob Jacobs Ls

Source: As printed in *JUS,* vol. 1, 104–5; 107. Recorded in Charleston *Will Book,* 26 (1793–1800), 640–44. "Friend Cohen" appears as "Gershon" and "Gershom" in the original.

2.19—A. H. COHEN TO THOMAS JEFFERSON, REGARDING THE HEALTH BENEFITS OF MINERAL WATER, DECEMBER 21, 1807

Abraham Hyam Cohen (1779–1841)—son of Jacob Raphael Cohen (1738–1811), spiritual leader of Philadelphia's Mikve Israel congregation—was a merchant interested in marketing the health benefits of mineral water. In writing to Thomas Jefferson in 1807, Cohen hoped to persuade one of the nation's Founding Fathers to provide a public endorsement of his

product. In a courteous but firm reply, Jefferson declined Cohen's request.

His Excellency Thos. Jefferson
Honoured Sir
Regarding you as the Patron of Arts & Sciences in our Infant Country. I am Led to Take the Liberty of offering to your Notice an Institu-

tion which If favoured with your Approbation will I flatter myself produce a Publick Good. as Such am Confident it will Need no other Commendation to Merit your Patronage. The Beneficial Effects derived from the Use of Mineral Waters which have become Celebrated by affording Relief in Cases where most other Remedies have failed has Induced the most Celebrated Chemists to Ascertain by a Correct Annalysis these Beneficial properties & by Chemically combining those Traits to produce by Art what Nature hath so bountifully bestowed and so far have they Succeeded. as to Merit a decided preferrence of the Artificial to the Natural Waters by Increasing their Active properties and Excluding foreign particles not Necessary but Rather detrimental to Health. . . . The Happy Effects derived from their Use have been already Evinced by an approving Publick & Testimonies of the most Celebrated & Eminent Chemists & Medical Characters in this City. Yet in order to Give it all the Advantages that Might Result It Requires the aid of a Larger Capital than in my power to afford. to Render it of that Extensive Utility. to prove a Publick Benefit the aid of a Capital from 10 to 15000 doll. would Accomplish the Object of Erecting a Suitable Building in which foun-

tains would be Placed as the Waters are now delivered and would be Sufficient to furnish a Supply to the United States or also to furnish them Gratuitously to the Poor, to whom the Physicians Might deem it Necessary.

. . . I now Submit an Outline of the Plans for [your] Approval, the above Sum to be divided into Shares of 50 dol. cash payable in Installments, the Subscribers to be Entitled to Exclusive privilige & receive the amount to themselves or order in Mineral Waters at a deduction of 20 [per ct.(?)] from the Selling price. your Approval & patronage Joined to the Respectable characters in this city will fully Enable me to accomplish this object and dedicate an Institution to you Whose Virtues an Applauding Mind will Never cease to Emulate and which the Voice of Envy cannot Tarnish. Nor Shall any Exertions on my Part be wanting to Render the Establishment Worthy of this Honour & prove the Gratitude of Yr Respectfull & Obt Serv.

Abraham Cohen

Phil: Dec. 21 1807.

No 31 So. 2d Street

Source: As printed in *JUS,* vol. 1, 481–82. U.S. National Archives and Records Administration.

2.20—REPLY OF THOMAS JEFFERSON TO A. H. COHEN, FEBRUARY 10, 1808

Sir

I have not been able sooner to acknolege the receipt of your letter of Dec. 21 which did not come to hand till Jan. 27 nor to return you my thanks for the mineral waters which came with it. I am happy to learn that these productions of nature can be successfully imitated by art, and that something may thereby be added useful to mankind. of the degree of that utility I acknolege myself not a judge, being little acquainted with the composition of these waters, and still less with their effects on the human body, a consciousness of this would make it too presump-

tuous in me to suppose that any connection of my name with an establishment for their preparation would be a recommendation of them to the public. they would be sensible that it is out of my line and would view it as neither favorable to myself or the medecine. the names of the celebrated Physicians of Philadelphia are those which would give a just reputation to these waters, and present them with authority to the notice of the public giving every just praise therefore to the efforts you have so meritoriously exerted in perfecting a preparation which may relieve the afflicted from some of their sufferings. I feel it a duty to leave it's [*sic*] fortunes & it's direction in the hands of those so much better qualified to promote it's success: and I pray you to accept my best wishes for that, & my respectful salutations.

Th. Jefferson

Mr: Cohen.

Source: As printed in *JUS,* vol. 1, 482–83. U.S. National Archives and Records Administration.

2.21—CONGREGATIONALIST MINISTER EZRA STILES TO HIS FRIEND RABBI HAIM ISAAC CARIGAL, JULY 7, 1775

The strong personal friendship between Ezra Stiles (1727–1795), a Congregationalist minister in Newport, Rhode Island (who later would become president of Yale College), and Haim Isaac Carigal (1733–1777), a Hebron-born rabbi, began in 1773, when Stiles met Carigal at the Newport synagogue. As the letter to follow demonstrates, these two men respected each other and developed a warm personal association. Carigal tutored Stiles during his brief sojourn in North America, and the two began exchanging letters in Hebrew. After Carigal left for the Caribbean in September of 1773, the two men maintained a correspondence that continued until Carigal's death in 1777. In this interesting communication written in 1775, Stiles sadly informs Carigal about the death of his wife. He also provides the rabbi with a detailed description of the American Revolution.

Newport July 7, 1775

Reverend Sir

A few days ago Mr Ribera [probably the Newport merchant Jacob Rodriguez Rivera (1717–1789)] informed me that you complained in a Letter to him of your not havg recd. my Answer to your several kind Letters. Be assured, dear Sir, it has not proceeded from Want of Affection & Respect to my very worthy friend. Your Letters of 17[?] Sept. 1773, May 27 1774 July 5 1774 and Oct. 11 1774 are now before me—the last tho' written last October I did not receive till this day. They all gave me the great pleasure & Satisfaction that you was in health & that you was agreeably settled at Barbados to your Mind, being Installed & estabd the Rabbi and Hocham of the Synagogue there & that you hoped & waited the Arrival of your Lady & Children from the holy Land to settle down in Tranqy with you for the rest of Life. I pray Gd soon to give you a sight of your dear Famy & long continue you with them. Whatever shall contribute to your happs in Time & Eterny I shall sincerely rejoice in. You have my best Wishes in whatever may concern your Welfare.

I myself am in Tears & Sorrow. It has pleased the Most High in whose hand are all our Changes, to take to himself my dear Wife who died 29th May last. I trust & hope She is now at rest *b'gan eden* [in Paradise] with Abraham, Sarah, Isaac, Rebecca and Jacob, Rachel. She had a great Esteem & Respect for you, & often enquired after you & spake of you with pleasure. The tenderest of all Sorrows is that of parting with a bosom Friend. Oh! the last—last—Silence of a Friend. May it be long before you, dear Sir, shall be called to experience so tender a Grief. But one Condition of our comg together in the married Life is, that, sooner or later one shall mourn the death of the other. May we live the Life of Holiness & Virtue on Earth thro' the Intercession of the Angel of the Cov[enan]t, we may meet & rejoyce in that better World where all Tears shall be wiped away, & sighing & sorrow shall be no more. . . .

You will joyn with me in lamentg that Great Britian [*sic*] & the Engsh Colonies in America are involved in a most unnatural *Civil War*; which rages with unbounded Fury Horrors & Desolation especially in New Engld. The Kings Troops in & about Boston with the last Recruits come over are nearest *Eight-Thousd*. The Continental American Army at Cambridge & around Boston were *Twenty Thousd & upwards* last Week under a continual Increase. Last week Connecticutt voted an Addition of 2000, N York 3000 and Pensylva. 4500: so that you may rely upon it that the

American Army this summer consists of *Thirty Thousd* in actual service. Hostilities were commenced at Lexington 15 miles from Boston 19th April last. A second considerable Action was at Noddle Isld [East Boston] on 27 May. But a third & far the greatest was at Charlesto. on 17th June. You will see & hear very various & differing accounts of them all. With all the Candor I can, I will give you an Estimate of the losses on both sides—tho' it is difficult to obtain the exact Truth. In that of 19th April the Americans lost exactly *fourty two killed & twenty two*, a much smaller proportion wounded than usual in Battles, owing probably, under God, to their scattered hussar [?] manner of Fighting. The [British] Regulars lost accordg to the Return of a Major Brigadr [?] of their own *sixty one* killed 157 wounded 23 missing privates, besides one officer killed & inclusive of him 17 Officers wounded & Captives. So that they were damaged 258, while the Americans were damaged scarcely one Quarter of that Number. . . .

. . . The Continental Congress have constituted *Mr. Washington* of Virginia Generalissimo of all the American Continental forces, & 5 others Major Generals, viz, [Artemas] *Ward*, [Charles] *Lee*, [Philip] *Schuyler* [,] [Israel] *Putnam*, & [John] *Sullivan*. Mr Lee has been an English Officer & a General in the Service of the King of Poland. Gens Washg & Lee arrived at Head Qurs in Cambridge 2d. Instant. We are in constant Expecta of a bloody Battle. The Americans have made their Appeal to Heaven—and the Event is with the Ld of Hosts.

Ezra Stiles

To Rabbi Carigal
Hocham of Barbados
Sent by Mr Miller of Barbados who sailed July 24 1775

Source: Stanley Chyet, ed., *The Event Is with the Lord* (Cincinnati: American Jewish Archives, 1976), 1–6. Beinecke Rare Book and Manuscript Library of Yale University.

2.22—APPEAL TO THE CITIZENS OF PHILADELPHIA FOR DONATIONS TO SAVE THEIR SYNAGOGUE FROM FORECLOSURE, MIKVE ISRAEL CONGREGATION, PHILADELPHIA, APRIL 30, 1788

A gesture during a financial crisis at Philadelphia's Congregation Mikve Israel demonstrated the heightened sense of hope and optimism that surrounded interfaith relations in early national America. In 1788, the leadership of Mikve Israel revealed that the synagogue faced a debt of 800 pounds sterling: the congregation's capital campaign appeal had fallen short of its goal after several of its wealthy congregants left Philadelphia to return to their permanent homes in New York City, Newport, and Savannah (all of which had been occupied by British forces until the Revolution's end). Faced with foreclosure, synagogue leaders made an emergency appeal across religious lines to the general Philadelphia community. Some of

the most prominent non-Jewish citizens of Philadelphia, including Benjamin Franklin, Charles Biddle, William Rush, and David Rittenhouse, responded to the April 30, 1788, appeal reprinted as follows.

To the humane, charitable, and well disposed people, the representation and solicitation of the good people of the Hebrew society [community] in the City of Philadelphia, commonly called Israelites.

Whereas, the religious order of men in this city denominated Israelites were without any synagogue or house of worship untill the year 1780 [1782], when, desirous of accommodating themselves and encouraged thereto by a number of respectable and worthy bretheren of the Hebrew society then in this place [who generously contributed to the design], they purchased a lot of ground and erected thereon the buildings necessary and proper for their religious worship.

And whereas many of their number at the close of the late war returned to New York, Charleston, and elsewhere their homes (which they had been exiled from and obliged to leave on account of their attachment to American measures), leaving the remaining few of their religion here burthened with a considerable charge consequent from so great an undertaking;

And whereas the present congregation, after expending all the subscriptions, loans, gifts, etc., made the society by themselves and the generous patrons of their religious intentions, to the amount of at least £2200, were obliged to borrow money to finish the building, and contract other debts that is now not only pressingly claimed, but a judgment will actually be obtained against their house of worship, which must be sold unless they are speedily enabled to pay the sum of about £800; and which, from a variety of delicate and distressing causes they are wholly unable to raise among themselves;

They are therefore under the necessity of earnestly soliciting from their worthy fellow-citizens of every religious denomination their benevolent aid and help, flattering themselves that their worshipping Almighty God in a way and manner different from other religious societies will never deter the enlightened citizens of Philadelphia from generously subscribing towards the preservation of a religious house of worship. The subscription paper will be enrolled in the archives of their congregation, that their posterity may know and gratefully remember the liberal supporters of their religious society.

Philadelphia, April 30th, 1788.

Source: As printed in *JAW*, 107–8. Archives, Mikveh Israel, Philadelphia.

2.23—HANNAH ADAMS, REPORTING ON GERSHOM SEIXAS'S SURVEY OF AMERICAN JEWRY, 1812

In the early nineteenth century, Hannah Adams (1755–1831), a non-Jew, took an interest in the nation's Jewish community. Reflecting on information she gained from two leading American Jews, New York's most distinguished Jewish clergyman, Gershom Mendes Seixas (1745–1816), and a Charleston merchant named Philip Cohen (1781–1866), Adams published a narrative history documenting Jewish life in two of the country's largest and most important Jewish communities.

PREFACE

The history of the Jews since their dispersion has been but little investigated even by the literary part of the world, and is almost entirely unknown to the general mass of mankind. The design of this work, including the introduction, is to give a brief sketch of their situation, after their return from the Babylonian captivity, to the nineteenth century. . . .

. . . The history of the Jews is remarkable, above that of all other nations, for the number and cruelty of the persecutions they have endured. They are venerable for the antiquity of their origin. They are discriminated from the rest of mankind by their wonderful destination, peculiar habits, and religious rites. Since the destruction of Jerusalem, and their universal dispersion, we contemplate the singular phenomenon of a nation subsisting for ages without its civil and religious polity, and thus surviving its political existence.

But the Jews appear in a far more interesting and important light when considered as a standing monument of the truth of the christian religion; as the ancient church of God to whom were committed the sacred oracles; as a people selected from all nations to make and preserve the knowledge of the true God. To them the gospel was first preached, and from them the first christian church in Jerusalem was collected. To them we are indebted for the scriptures of the New, as well as of the Old Testament. . . .

To the intelligent and well informed the difficulty of collecting the history of a people so little known, particularly in this country, during the last and present century, wholly from desultory and unconnected materials, will appear obvious. The compiler can only say, that however deficient and ill arranged her history may be, she has spared no exertions in her power to collect authentic documents, and has used them to the best of her ability. But while she relies on the candour and indulgence of the publick, she cannot forbear to express the warmest gratitude to those respectable gentlemen whose generous patronage has enabled her to devote her time to literary pursuits.

CHAP. XXXIV

The Jews have never been numerous in New England; but among those who settled in the colonies some have been distinguished for the respectability of their characters. Judah Monis, a Jewish convert to the christian religion, was admitted a publick teacher at Harvard University. He is stated to have been a native of Algiers, who probably received his education in Italy, though we know nothing of him till his arrival in this country. But after he came to Boston he seems to have been soon invited to fill the office of Hebrew instructer in the university, where he was settled March 27th, 1722. Before he could be admitted, it was rendered necessary by the statutes, that he should change his religion, which he professes to have done with perfect disinterestedness, though he continued till his death to observe the seventh day as the sabbath. . . .

Previous to the American revolution, while the Jews convened at their synagogue in Rhode Island, the late president [of Yale Ezra] Stiles commenced an acquaintance with Haijim Carigal, a rabbi who had lately arrived in the city. "Having travelled very extensively in the eastern world, and being a man of observation, learning, and intelligence, his conversation was highly entertaining and instructive. He was born at Hebron, and educated there and at Jerusalem. He had travelled all over the Holy Land, and visited many cities in Asia and Europe. The doctor was greatly delighted with his society, and had frequent intercourse with him for the purpose of acquiring the pronunciation of the Hebrew; of ascertaining the meaning of ambiguous expressions in the original of the Old Testament; of learning the usages of the modern Jews; of conversing on past events relating to this extraordinary nation, as recorded in sacred history; and of tracing its future destiny by the light of prophecy. They cultivated a mutual friendship when together, and corresponded in Hebrew when apart."

The rabbi, not long after his arrival, attended his worship by agreement, and heard him discourse in an affectionate manner on the past dispensations of God's providence towards his chosen people; on his promised design of rendering them an exalted nation in the latter day glory of the Messiah's kingdom; and on the duty of Christians, and of all nations, to desire a participation in their future glorious state.

"So catholick was the intercourse between this learned Jew and learned Christian, that they often spent hours together in conversation; and the information which the extensive travels of the Jew enabled him to give, especially concerning the Holy Land, was a rich entertainment to his christian friend. The civilities of the rabbi were more than repaid. The doctor very frequently attended the worship of the synagogue at Newport, not only when rabbi Carigal officiated, but at the ordinary service before his arrival, and after his departure."

With six other rabbis of less eminence he became acquainted, and showed them every civility, while he maintained a friendly communication with the Jews in general in Newport. Such rare and unexpected attentions from a christian minister of distinction could not but afford peculiar gratification to a people, conscious of being a proverb and bye word among nations. To him they accordingly paid every attention in return, and expressed peculiar pleasure in admitting him into their families, and into their synagogues.

Dr. [Abiel] Holmes [father of Oliver Wendell] in concluding this account judiciously remarks, that "this civility and catholicism towards the Jews is worthy of imitation. It is to be feared that Christians do not what ought to be done towards the conversion of this devoted people. While admitted into most countries for the purpose of trade and commerce, instead of being treated with that humanity and tenderness which christianity should inspire, they are often persecuted and condemned as unworthy of notice or regard. Such treatment tends to prejudice them against our holy religion, and to establish them in their infidelity."

A respectable rabbi of New York has given the following account of his brethren in the United States.

"There are about fifty families of Jews in New York, which, with a number of unmarried men, make from seventy to eighty subscribing members to the congregation *Sherith Israel*, which is incorporated by an act of the legislature of the state, empowering all religious societies to hold their property by charter, under the direction of trustees chosen annually by the communicants of the society, according to certain rules prescribed in the act. . . ."

A more particular account of the Jews in South Carolina has been given by one of the principal members of their congregation in the capital of the state, the substance of which is as follows.

"The first emigration of the Jews to Charleston took place long before the revolution. The spirit of commerce can never be extinct in them; and their wealth increased with their numbers, which were augmented from time to time, both by marriages, and acquisitions from Europe. The present number of Jews may be estimated about a thousand. Charleston alone contains about six or seven hundred individuals.

"The present number of Hebrews in the city are chiefly Carolinians, the descendants of German, English, and Portuguese emigrants, who, from the civil and religious tyranny of Europe, sought an asylum in the western world. While the contest for freedom and independence was carried on, the majority distinguished themselves as brave soldiers and gallant defenders of the cause of a country which protected them. This spirit still actuates them; and as it is but natural that a people, who for ages have groaned under the impolitic barbarity and blind fanaticism of Europe, should inhale the breath of freedom with delight, the Hebrews in this city pay their hearty homage to the laws, which guarantee their rights, and consolidate them into the mass of a free people.

"The religious rites, customs, and festivals of the Jews are all strictly observed by those of this nation in Charleston; but ameliorated with that social liberality, which pervades the minds and manners of the inhabitants of civilized countries. Indeed the seats in a Jewish synagogue are often crowded with visitors of every denomination. The episcopal functions are now discharged by the Rev. Ca[r]valho, late professor of the Hebrew language in the college of New York. . . .

"The institutions which the Jews have established in Charleston, are chiefly religious and charitable. They have built an elegant synagogue; and what strongly exhibits the liberality of the city is, that the Roman Catholick church is directly opposite to it. They have also societies for the relief of strangers, for attending the sick, and for administering the rites of humanity, and burial to the dying and the dead. The most modern institution is a society for the relief of orphans. The capital is already considerable, and it is yearly increasing. The children receive every advantage which is necessary to enable them to be well informed and honourable citizens of their country."

... The United States is, perhaps, the only place where the Jews have not suffered persecution, but have, on the contrary, been encouraged and indulged in every right of citizens.

The Jews in all the United States, except Massachusetts, are eligible to offices of trust and honour; and some of them in the southern states are in office. They are generally commercial men, and a number of them considerable merchants.

Source: As printed in *JUS,* vol. 1, 88–93. From Hannah Adams, *History of the Jews* (Boston: n.p., 1812), 1, iii–iv, vi; 2, 210–21.

2.24—ADDRESS BY PHILLIP MILLEDOLER ON EVANGELIZING THE JEWS, 1817

Although American Jews enjoyed constitutional protection of religious expression, they still faced various challenges, among them attempts by private Christian organizations to proselytize. In 1816, a Christian group based in New York City, the American Society for Evangelizing the Jew, established itself with the aim of bringing "the Jews to the acknowledgment of Jesus Christ of Nazareth as the true Messiah." The following year, the group's president, Rev. Dr. Phillip Milledoler (1775–1852), delivered an address in which he expanded on the society's purpose.

Whether we contemplate, dear Brethren, the general signs of the times in which we live, or the particular providences which have recently occurred in this city, and which have marked the case before us, does it not appear that we are called to do something in favour of the Jews?

That we are not destitute of encouragement, nay, that we are in duty bound to make the attempt, will, we think, appear from various and important considerations.

The restoration of that people to the Lord is positively contemplated and predicted in numerous prophecies.

Encouraged by this circumstance, the church of God has never ceased, either before or since the destruction of Jerusalem, to offer prayer for them, and that to an extent which has not yet been, but will most assuredly be answered. They are also certainly included in the general commission, "Go ye into all the world, and preach the Gospel to every creature."

It is also believed, that there is nothing in their political, moral, or religious character at the present day, which presents a more formidable barrier to the spread of the Gospel among them, than when it was first propagated among them by the disciples of the Lord. . . . Their civil relation to the inhabitants of this country is supposed to be favourable to the objects we have in view; so far from being treated amongst us with insult and injury, as in other lands, they have enjoyed equal privileges with their fellow citizens. This circumstance ought to soften, and probably has softened, their prejudices against the Christians of these United States.

Although we recognize with pleasure that the Jews have suffered no immediate or direct persecution at our hands, yet we may not, and dare not assert, that they have never suffered at the hands of our forefathers. For this, so far as we have it in our power, we owe them reparation.

But is it not a fact, brethren, that the Jews have strong claims upon us on the score of gratitude? Were not the oracles of the living God in the first instance committed to that people? Have they not been the honoured instruments of preserving and handing down to us Gentiles those precious and uncontaminated records? To whom pertained "the adoption, and the glory, and the covenants, and the giving of the law, and the service of God, and the promises," but to that people? . . . Is not that nation rendered illustrious above all others, by that single circumstance of the descent from them according to the flesh, of Messiah, that great Prince; that

Almighty conqueror; that eternal Saviour? And who were the first Heralds of the glorious Gospel of the blessed God to the perishing nations? Who were Peter, and James, and John, and Paul, with their noble minded associates? Were they not Jews? . . .

But for their efforts, their intrepidity, their tears, and groans, and blood, we might, humanly speaking, have been to this day, worshipping with horrid rites the gods of our idolatrous ancestors. As, then, the blessings of the Gospel we enjoy are of incalculable worth, we owe an inextinguishable debt of gratitude to the Jews, from whose hands we have received them. . . .

In vain do we look in their religious rites for that warm and devotional spirit which characterized the worship of their pious fathers. It is said, and we believe they have not been slandered, that their religious exercises are scarcely conducted with the form, much less with the spirit, of devotion.

The female character among them holds a station far inferior to that which it was intended to occupy by the God of nature and of providence; and their children, where semblance of regard is still preserved for ancient institutions, are in many instances taught to contemn and to blaspheme that worthy name which is connected with all that is valuable in life or cheering in death. Are the eyes of any of them partially opened to the truth? Do they discover a disposition to fly to the banners of the despised Nazarene? What contempt do they not experience? What opposition do they not encounter from their associates? What strong appeals are made, not to their reason, nor to the Scriptures, but to the love of kindred, to early attachments, and to their fears? These appeals, followed by corresponding acts, are certainly calculated in ordinary cases to arrest further inquiry, and to blast in its first appearance the very germ of hope. In this description of the Jews it will be remembered that we are speaking in general terms. We do not by any means intend to say, that all which is here stated will apply to every individual and family among them:—we still

hope better things of some of them, and especially of that part of the nation which is resident in this country. We believe, however, as a general statement, that what has been said of them is strictly correct. . . .

Can we behold a Jew without emotions of compassion, or contemplate his situation without pain? If so, how can we flatter ourselves that we possess the spirit of our Master, or of the friends of our Master? Do we remember how he, the Lord Jesus, laboured among them? Do we remember his prayer for them on the Cross? Have we buried in oblivion the transactions of the day of Pentecost? Thousands on that memorable day, whose hands were yet reeking with his blood, were made the monument of his mercy. What ardent zeal is manifested by the Apostle Paul in behalf of his brethren, his kinsmen according to the flesh? Did not that zeal pervade the whole college of the Apostles, and where or when has it been extinguished among the Disciples of the Lord?

We hope that none will object to the work of attempting their salvation. What reasonable objection to it can be made? Is it their attachment to their ancient worship? Is it their hatred of Christianity? Is it the hardness of their hearts —their unwillingness to receive instruction—or their malevolence towards those who labour in their cause? Ah, if the Apostles of the Lord had reasoned in this manner, we might have been to this day like the Jews, without hope and without God in the world. No objection of this kind will apply to them which would not have equally applied to the Gentiles of other times, as well as to the Gentiles of the present hour. . . .

With the accomplishment of this object, brethren, is connected the glory of God—the honour of the Redeemer—the prosperity of Zion —and the diffusion and establishment of the faith once delivered to the saints. Let it not be forgotten that the restoration of the Jews is to be a signal for the conversion of the great body of the Gentiles. It is more than probable that through their instrumentality as Missionaries of the Cross, those Scriptures will be fulfilled which relate to the general conversion of the Gentiles. . . .

To conclude—As final prosperity in this measure must depend on the Almighty co-operation of a redeeming Saviour, we entreat all those who have the hope of an interest at the throne of grace, to offer, both in public and in private, more particular, more extensive, and more fervent prayer to God, than has been usual, for that people in general, and for the success of this object in our own city in particular.

By order,
Philip Milledoler,
President.

Source: Religious Intelligencer 1 (Jan. 25, 1817): 555.

2.25—FRANCES SHEFTALL TO HER HUSBAND, JULY 20, 1780

In 1778, Mordecai Sheftall (1735–1797) and his son Sheftall Sheftall (1762–1849) were captured by British soldiers and imprisoned for having served as quartermasters for Georgia's militia during the Revolutionary War. Just before their release on parole in 1780, Mordecai's wife, Frances (1740–1820), wrote a letter that provides insight into the challenges she faced while her husband and son languished in jail.

Charls Town [South Carolina], July 20th, 1780
My dear Sheftall:

I have now the pleasure to inform you that I received your letter on the 19 instn., dated May the 5, and sincerly congratulate you and my dear childe on your enlargement [impending release], hoping that we may once more meet again in a great deal of pleasure, for I can assure you that we have been strangers to that for some time past. But I still hope that our troubles will now be soon at an end.

I make not the least doubt, but ere thise comes to hand that you have herd that thise place [Charleston] was given over to the British troops on May 12th by a caputalation after three longe months sige. During that time I retier'd into the country with my family, and a great many of our people [Jews] ware at the same place. During the sige thare was scarce a woman to be see[n] in the streets. The balls flew like haile during the cannonading.

After the town was given over, I returned to town and have hierd a house in St. Michael's Alley belonging to Mrs. Stephens at the rate of fifty pounds sterlinge a year. And whear the money is to come from God only knows, for their is nothing but hard money goes here, and that, I can assure you, is hard enough to be got.

I am obliged to take in needle worke to make a living for my family, so I leave you to judge what a livinge that must be.

Our Negroes [slaves] have every one been at the point of death, so that they have been of no use to me for thise six weeks past. But, thankes be to God, they are all getting the better of it except poor little Billey; he died with the yellow fever on the 3 of July.

The children have all got safe over the small pox. They had it so favourable that Perla had the most and had but thirty [pockmarks]. How I shall be able to pay the doctor's bill and house rent, God only knowes. But I still trust to Providence knowing that the Almighty never sends trouble but he sends some relife.

As to our Adam [a free servant?], he is so great a gentleman that was it to please God to put it in your power to send for us, I do thinke that he would come with us.

I wrote to you about three weeks agoe by way of St. Austatia [Eustatia] to Antigua [where you were held by the British] whare I mention every particular to you, but must now refer it untill it shall pleas God that we see you again. You[r] brother Levy went out of town during the sige toward the northward and has not returned as yet. Thise day his youngest baby, Isaac, was buried. The poor baby was sicke for about three weeks and then died.

We have had no less than six Jew children buried since the sige, and poor Mrs. Cardosar [Cardozo], Miss Leah Toras that was, died last week with the small pox. Mr. DeLyon has lost his two grand children. Mrs. Mordecai has lost her child. Mrs. Myers Moses had the misfortune to have her youngest daughter, Miss Rachel, killed with the nurse by a cannon ball during the sige.

Perla begs that you will excuse her not writing by thise oppertunity as she has been with her Aunt Sally for several nights and is very much fatigued, and the flag [of truce ship] goes immediately [with my letter], but hopes that she will be the bearer of the next [letter] herselfe. But havinge so favourable an oppertunity as the flag [I] was willing to let you no [know] some little of our family affairs.

I have nothing more at present but wish to hear from you by the first oppertunity.

The children joine me in love to you and their brother, and I remain

Your loving wife,
Frances Sheftall.

Source: As printed in *JAW*, 105–7. Marion Levy Mendel's Sheftall Collection, Savannah, Ga. Reprinted with permission of Marion Levy Mendel.

2.26—SAMUEL JONES, LAST WILL AND TESTAMENT, INCLUDING INFORMATION ON HIS AFRICAN AMERICAN SLAVE, JENNY, AND THEIR SON, EMANUEL, JANUARY 20, 1809

Romantic relationships between Jews and African Americans in the early nineteenth century are difficult to document since they were not sanctioned. Yet historians have identified various instances of de facto marriages. Many scholars have suggested that Samuel Jones (d. 1809)—a Jewish soldier in the War of Independence and a resident of Charleston, South Carolina, for forty-six years—fathered a son, Emanuel, with his slave Jenny. Jones's will, dated January 20, 1809, bequeaths to Jenny and Emanuel the majority of his estate, as well as the right to continue living in his house. Such unusual generosity toward a slave suggests that Jones may very well have fathered Emanuel.

In the Name of God Amen I Samuel Jones of the City of Charleston, South Carolina being at Present sound in Mind Praised be God for it, Do make this my last Will and Testament in manner following. That is to say First and Principally I commend my Soul into the hands of Almighty God, my Creator hoping for Pardon and forgivenefs of all my Sins, as to such of my Worldly Estate with which it has Pleased God to entrust

me with I dispose of in the following Manner, After my Funeral expences and my lawful Debts are Paid, If I should not emancipate My Negro Woman Jenny, and her Son Emanuel during My life time, it is my desire that my Executors Do, emancipate My Negro Woman Jenny, and her Son Emanuel, and give to Jenny My Bed Sheets, Bedstead, Blankets, Tables, Pots, Plates, Chairs, Looking Glafs, allowing to Nanny, such part of them as she may stand in need of and also to Benjamin. My House in which I lived in King Street, two Months after my decease I desire to be sold and the Money arising from the sale thereof I request to be disposed of in Manner following[.] That is to say To Kerin Ka Ye Mot [Keren Kayemet—a charitable fund], One hundred Dollars. To Abi Ye to Men [Avi Yetomim—an orphan society] Fifty Dollars[.] To the Hebrew Benevolent Society Sixty Dollars[.] To the Orphan House One hundred Dollars[.] To My Negro Woman Jenny two hundred Dollars[.] To My Mullatto Woman Nanny One hundred and fifty Dollars. To Samuel Lee, Ben, David, Nathan and Emanuel One Hundred Dollars each[.] The amount of My Clock, Shop Goods and Plate, when sold, and the Legacies Paid the Overplus to be remitted to Great Britain to Abigail Jones, to be equally divided between her and her Children. My Lot up King Street, which is let on Leases, I leave to Nanny and Jenny, during their lives, the income of the same, after the Taxes are Paid, to Jenny I leave of the income of the Leases One hundred Dollars Pr. Year to be Paid to her Quarterly[.] To my Mulatto Woman Nanny[,] Ben, Nathan, David, and Emanuel I leave three hundred Dollars, to be equally divided amongst them, and to be Paid Quarterly[.] If in case of the Death of Either Jenny or Nanny their respective incomes to be divided equally amongst their Children[.] Also after the Death of Jenny and Nanny, the Land is to be sold and to be at their Option to lay it out in Lots, and the Money aris- ing from the Sales, to be remitted to Great Brit- ain to Abigail Jones and her Children. And it is my further desire not to drive Jenny and her Children out of my House in King Street, untill they have time to Procure a Place for their abode.

It is further my desire to give them all Plain de- cent Mourning and a decent Tomb Stone for myself. And Lastly, I do Nominate and appoint My Worthy friends Moses C. Levy and Michael Lazarus My Executors[.] Witnefs My hand and Seal this Sixteen-Day of December in the Year of One thousand eight hundred and eight, and in the thirty second Year of the Independence of the United States of America.

Samuel Jones (Seal)
Signed and Sealed in the presence of
Charles Prince
A. L. Mender
William Forbes
Proved before Charles Lining Esquire O.C.T.D [Old Charles Towne District]. January 20, 1809
    At same time qualified Michael Lazarus oth- erwise called Marks Lazarus Executor
Source: SC-5855, AJA.

3 Migrations across America
JEWS IN THE ANTEBELLUM PERIOD, 1820–1860

During the antebellum period, from 1820 to 1860, the relatively small Jewish population in the United States welcomed a large influx of Jewish immigrants from both Central and Eastern Europe, who, escaping economic hardship, journeyed across the Atlantic to create new homes and communities. While the contemporaneous arrival of Jews from Eastern Europe complicates a simplistic characterization of this era as "the German period," it was those German-speaking Jews who rose to prominence in both American Jewish and general American society in the years before the massive Eastern European Jewish immigration began in the later decades of the century.

The documents in this chapter encompass a wide variety of historical themes reflecting the broad spectrum of American Jewish experiences during the antebellum period. In the colonial and early national periods, most American Jewish history originated in the New York or Eastern Seaboard experience because cities such as New York, and later Philadelphia and Charleston, boasted a disproportionate number of the nation's Jews. In the antebellum period, the larger American policy of Manifest Destiny opened western lands to American settlement for the first time in U.S. history. Jewish arrivals followed that larger migration, first to the old Northwest. Then, in the years after the discovery of gold in northern California, Jewish merchants migrated further westward to ply their wares in San Francisco, Sacramento, and the gold camps in the foothills of the Sierra Nevada mountain range. Along the way, other groups of Jews created communities in both large cities and small towns across the continent. In these new locales, Jews faced the challenges of increased rates of intermarriage as well as stepped-up efforts by Christian evangelical groups to convert them. As they engaged these challenges, antebellum Jews negotiated dynamic new relationships with the non-Jews living around them, developing communities in cities, towns, and outposts that underscored the apothegm that "American Jewish history is *not* New York Jewish history writ large."

With the benefits of a much larger critical mass, the emerging American Jewish communities of the antebellum period expanded their Jewish organizations and identities beyond the synagogue, which had typified organized Jewish life in the colonial and early national periods. Even within the religious lives of antebellum Jews, the new arrivals challenged existing customs and practices, actively supporting the reformation and Americanization of Jewish religious practice. Their novel approaches significantly influenced the evolution of Jewish life in the United States.

The rise of Jacksonian democracy at the beginning of this era encouraged even greater Jewish participation in political life, civic engagement, and the public square. Westward expansion eased the prevailing property restrictions that earlier limited civil equality to only the wealthiest Americans. The last remaining state-initiated limits on Jewish rights disappeared in an industrializing nation growing in both population and landmass. Anti-Jewish sentiment or Judeophobia, a theme much more prominent in Europe than in the United States, also shaped the direction of Jewish life during the antebellum period as the American Jewish community insisted on being viewed as "a portion of the people" and never "a people apart."

The "Impending Conflict," or the factors that impelled the nation toward civil war, also became a dominant theme in the antebellum period. Like other Americans, Jews debated their attitudes toward slavery and took political positions on the conflict that pitted states' rights against the interests of the federal government. While recent scholarly research has demonstrated a limited role of Jews in slavery and the slave trade, some southern Jews did accommodate themselves to the racial status quo, whereby white southerners often used Bible references to defend the "peculiar institution." There were Jews in the North, too, who insisted that the goal of preserving the Union was vastly more important than the abolition of slavery. In short, northern and southern Jews were split on the great political issues that dominated the antebellum era, reflecting the political culture of the nation at large.

3.01—PENINA MOÏSE, POEM, "TO PERSECUTED FOREIGNERS," 1820

Penina Moïse (1797–1880), the Charleston-born daughter of a French-born Sephardic Jew who journeyed to the United States after a stay in the West Indies, emerged early in her life as a prolific poet, enjoying publication in both the Jewish and secular markets. As an adult, she served as Charleston's first Jewish religious school director. The poem that follows, "To Persecuted Foreigners," written in the wake of anti-Jewish riots in Germany, urges Europe's Jews to consider immigration to the United States, where "a Western sun will gild [their] future day."

Fly from the soil whose desolating creed,
Outraging faith, makes human victims bleed.
Welcome! Where every Muse has reared a
    shrine,
The aspect of wild Freedom to refine.

Upon *our* Chieftain's brow no crown appears;
No gems are mingled with his silver hairs,
Enough that Laurels bloom amid its snows,
Enriched with these, the sage all else foregoes.

If thou art one of that oppressed race,
Whose pilgrimage from Palestine we trace,

Brave the Atlantic—Hope's broad anchor
    weigh,
A Western sun will gild your future day.

Zeal is not blind in this our temp'rate soil;
She has no scourge to make the soul recoil.
Her darkness vanished when our stars did
    flash;
Her red arm grasped by Reason dropt the lash.

Our Union, Liberty and Peace imparts,
Stampt on our standards, graven on our hearts,
The first, from crush'd Ambition's ruin rose,
The last, on Victory's field spontaneous grows.

Rise, then, elastic from Oppression's tread,
Come and repose on Plenty's flowery bed.
Oh! Not as Strangers shall your welcome be,
Come to the homes and bosoms of the free!

Source: From Charleston Section, Council of Jewish Women, *Secular and Religious Works of Penina Moïse, etc.* (Charleston, S.C.: N. G. Duffy, 1911), v. 177; Penina Moïse, *Fancy's Sketch Book* (Charleston, S.C.: J. S. Burges, 1833), 97–98.

3.02—CHARLES L. MAILERT TO AUGUST MAILERT, ON HIS RESERVATIONS ABOUT IMMIGRATING TO THE UNITED STATES, 1835

In a series of letters, brothers Charles and August Mailert described the profound human toll taken on a family emigrating from Europe to the United States. While Charles wanted to follow his brother August to the United States, his plans changed when he faced the responsibility and burden of caring for his mother, who was concerned about her sons' ability to do so in the United States. In the letter that follows, Charles explains his situation to his brother and, in the process, sheds light on the many pressures that Central European Jews faced during this time of decision.

Dear brother!

Only too just are the reproaches for my not talking honestly that you made in your last letter. But listen to my excuses: you know Europe, know my situation, and can easily conclude from that that, in the long run, I shall not be able to remain in Europe. Income is no larger than expenditures; there is no hope of improvement, but rather a fear of deterioration, should things continue in this way for some time to come; add to this the tremendous expenses and taxes, etc. This has led me to the desire to emigrate, but mother is afraid, and I did not want to seem, by being openhearted, as if I intended to become a burden to you. You ask what my plan in this world is—by no means to stay in Europe—as long as the good mother is alive, I must remain on European soil, of course, although *here are but a few flowers*. My view of life is that *Life is a frost of cold felicitie, And death the thaw of all vanitie.*

But now to the main point: as was said already, mother is afraid of being in as dire straits, or possibly worse off, in America; this fear would disappear if you were to write definitely that we should come. Of course, this is not too easy for you. You must know whether your circumstances will permit you to care for mother, at least in the beginning. I am not afraid for myself, I hope to obtain a position as clerk or bookkeeper; or, if you should need one yourself, so much the better; I could also travel to buy and sell for you, and this would perhaps help both you and me. Should you not be able to make use of me, I would find a place elsewhere, *having no wife or children to provide for*. Now I have been as honest as a brother, but you, too, dear brother, must now be benevolent and by no means believe that I plan to burden you. Write your definite opinion about it and your advice, if you're able to advise.

In Europe the play will soon be over. [Do not believe] that I want to be an adventurer. What is especially close to mother's heart is that she would have to sell the old chinaware [?]. It was my firm intention not to say another word about America, but your letter demands an answer. Wish we had just one short hour to talk things over face-to-face. *My resolution is taken.* Don't mention anything openly in your next letter, since mother knows nothing of the answer contained in this letter. But speak clearly and definitely. I shall believe what my beloved brother writes me. *Fare well.*

Your ever loving brother.

[. . .]

Charles Lucius Mailert

Source: *JUS,* vol. 1, 812–14. Mailert Family Correspondence, SC-7672–7673, AJA.

3.03—REASONS FOR EMIGRATION FROM BAVARIA TO THE UNITED STATES, *Leipziger Zeitung,* 1839

The German newspaper Leipziger Zeitung *offered an 1839 article explaining the rationale for Jewish emigration from Central Europe. With empathy and understanding, editors recounted how the threat of military conscription faced by Jewish families provided an incentive to leave Europe while also acknowledging the many* *opportunities that awaited Jews on the other side of the Atlantic Ocean.*

Munich, Sept. 3. The *Leipziger Zeitung* contains the following article sent from here concerning the recent emigration of Israelites from Bavaria. . . .

1. "Conscription remains a thorn in the side of the Israelites. Who can blame a father if he sells out and leaves with his family? The parents are then joined by hundreds of engaged couples, candidates for degrees and physicians, commercial clerks, journeymen and every sort of people eager to work. Naturally, there is never any talk about purchases in the North American woods, of agriculture, landed estates, etc. One becomes a merchant[,] i.e., carries on trade in the ever-roaming wagons and steamboats, until one gets a house and established store, or one carries on one, two, three trades, according to what he has derived from others, in addition to what he has, in passing, learned here. A German is gladly accepted as a workingman in America; the German Jew is preferred to any other. Thus hopelessness at home, a secure future overseas, no pressure or persecution of one or another sort lead the Bavarian Israelite to take up the wanderer's staff."

Source: JUS, vol. 1, 804–5. From *Allgemeine Zeitung des Judentums*, September 28, 1839, as translated by Rudolf Glanz, "Source Materials on the History of Jewish Immigration to the United States, 1800–1880," *YIVO Annual of Jewish Social Science* 4 (1950): 93.

3.04—JOSEPH JONAS TO REV. ISAAC LEESER, DESCRIBING LIFE IN OHIO, DECEMBER 25, 1843

In the early decades of the nineteenth century, Cincinnati, Ohio, rested on the western frontier of the United States. For Jews, life in the outreaches of their larger religious community proved especially challenging. They had difficulty securing basic needs such as kosher foods and struggled to achieve a prayer quorum of ten men (minyan) to conduct services, to offer their children a Jewish education, and, subsequently, to find Jewish partners for them to marry. Joseph Jonas (1792–1869) migrated from Great Britain to the United States and, in 1817, settled in Cincinnati. Many years later, in 1843, Jonas published a fascinating first-person account of his experiences as the founder of Jewish communal life in Cincinnati in the pages of Isaac Leeser's (1806–1868) periodical, the Occident.

Rev. Isaac Leeser,

Dear Sir—In accordance with the request to furnish you "with a history of the settlement of the Jews in Ohio," with much pleasure I attend to that subject, and shall probably be more minute than many would consider necessary: you must indulge me in this my weakness, as every thing connected with the settlement of our nation, and the establishment of our holy religion in this city and state renews within me feelings of gratitude and veneration to the great Author of our being, who from a *single* individual, alone adoring his Unity, has in a few years assembled in this noble city two considerable congregations, numbering more than eighteen hundred souls.

It was in the month of October, 1816, that a young man arrived in New York from the shores of Great Britain, to seek a home and a residence in the New World. This individual's name was Joseph Jonas, from Plymouth, in England. He had read considerably concerning America, and was strongly impressed with the descriptions given of the Ohio river, and had therefore determined to settle himself on its banks, at Cincinnati. . . . He . . . became acquainted with the venerable Mr. Levi Philips, who took a great interest in him, using many persuasive arguments not to proceed to Ohio. One of them was frequently brought to his recollection: "In the wilds of America, and entirely amongst gentiles, you will forget your religion and your God."

But the fiat had gone forth, that a new resting place for the scattered sons of Israel should be commenced, and that a sanctuary should be erected in the Great West, dedicated to the Lord of hosts, to resound with praises to the ever-living God. The individual solemnly promised the venerable gentleman never to forget his religion nor forsake his God: he received his blessing, and taking leave of the kind friends with whom he had resided, departed for Pittsburg on the 2d of January, 1817. . . . [H]e arrived [in Cincinnati] on the 8th day of March 1817. The city then contained about six thousand inhabitants, but the only Israelite was himself. With the assistance of the God of his ancestors, he soon became established in a lucrative and respectable business, and his constant prayer was, that he might be a nucleus around whom the first congregation might be formed, to worship the God of Israel in this great western territory. . . . Some time in December, 1818, his heart was delighted with the arrival of his lamented and ever-valued friend, David Israel Johnson, (from Portsmouth, England,) with his wife and infant child. But they were bound for Brookville, Indiana, and again for a while solitude was his portion. . . . In 1820 arrived Solomon Buckingham, Moses Nathan, and Solomon Minken, all from Germany, and the *yomim tovim* [Jewish Holidays] of 1820 were solemnized in due form with the legal number and a Sepher Torah. . . . During the ensuing year, 1823, arrived Simeon Moses, from Barbadoes, and Morris and Joseph Symonds, from Portsmouth, England. We are now arrived on "terra firma," and have official records for reference. On the 4th of January, 1824, a majority of the Israelites in Cincinnati assembled at the residence of Morris Moses, who was called to the chair, and Joseph Jonas appointed secretary, when the following proceedings took place, and the subjoined preamble was adopted: "Whereas,

it is the duty of every member of the Jewish persuasion, when separated from a congregation, to conform as near as possible to the worship and ceremonies of our holy religion, and as soon as a sufficient number can be assembled, to form ourselves into a congregation for the purpose of glorifying our God, and observing the fundamental principles of our faith, as developed in the laws of Moses:—with these impressions, the undernamed persons convened at the residence of Morris Moses, in the city of Cincinnati, state of Ohio, on the 4th day of January, 1824, corresponding to the 4th of Shebat, 5584."

[. . .]

In the month of Heshvan, 5603 [1843], the Hebrew Benevolent Society of Cincinnati was instituted; its first President was Mr. Phineas Moses, under whom it flourished exceedingly; it now consists of seventy members, with every prospect of being much more numerous. Their anniversary dinner was well attended, and the voluntary contributions remarkably liberal. Mr. Joseph Jonas was elected Parnass for 5604 [1844]. The congregations in this city are continually increasing, their character stands high for morality, honesty and sobriety; sorry am I to say that I cannot state the same of many of them in a religious point of view. If only a *few* of the most able and respectable would commence *sincerely* keeping their Sabbaths and Festivals, it would have considerable influence on the minds of their erring brethren. But the "Solitary" is still thankful to the God of Israel, that he has been made the humble instrument in collecting near *two thousand* of his brethren of Israel, to worship the Lord of Hosts in this beautiful metropolis of the Great West.

Source: DHJ, 223–35. From the *Occident*, February 1844, 547–50; April 1844, 29–31; June 1844, 143–47.

3.05—LETTER FROM JACOB EZEKIEL TO PRESIDENT JOHN TYLER, ARGUING
THAT AMERICA IS NOT A "CHRISTIAN NATION," 1841—WITH TYLER'S REPLY

*Jacob Ezekiel (1812-1899), a native of
Philadelphia before moving as an adult to
Richmond, Virginia, was a proud Jew who was
determined to promote political equality in the
United States and to uphold the values
separating church and state as expressed in the
Constitution. Ezekiel would successfully lobby
to repeal excessive fines for violating Sunday
closing laws, and for the Jewish Sabbath,
observed on Saturday, to enjoy the same
protections as the Christian day of rest on
Sunday. He also protested U.S. governmental
support of Switzerland, which discriminated
against its Jewish residents.*

*One of Ezekiel's proudest moments came as a
result of a letter he wrote to President John Tyler
on April 16, 1841. Tyler, originally elected vice
president, ascended to the presidency only a
month after his inauguration when President
William Henry Harrison died of pneumonia.
Tyler promptly issued a proclamation calling
on all Americans to go to their respective houses
of worship and observe "a day of fasting and
prayer by such religious services as may be
suitable on the occasion." Ezekiel had no
objection to Tyler's appeal, but he deeply
resented the new president's decision to begin
his proclamation by noting that "when a
Christian people feel themselves to be overtaken
by a great public calamity . . . etc."*

*Ezekiel thus chastises the president for
labeling all Americans as Christians, and
his letter constitutes a classic example of the
American Jew's insistent reminder that "the wise
framers of our glorious Constitution have
guaranteed unto all who seek its refuge . . ."
freedom of religion and equal footing under
the law.*

Richmond April 16, 1841
   To His Excellency
John Tyler, President of the United States,
Esteemed, and Respected Friend!
   I being by birth an American and one who
loves his country, but by the will of Him who
is the Most High reared up strictly to the observances of the Mosaic dispensations, *and in
Common with our fellow citizens know no distinction of Sect or Creed in the Observances of
any day set apart for a National Thanksgiving to
our Maker* for the manifold blessings he has bestowed on us *as an American People*, in a country like this, famed throughout the known world
for its *liberal toleration* of *Religious Sentiments*,
for the protection of which, the wise framers of
our Glorious constitution *have guaranteed unto
all* who seek its refuge.
   I as well as others were somewhat surprised
to find in the columns of our Journals, as in the
age in which we live, that the Chief Magistrate of
this Union should by an *Official* recommendation to the People of the United States, address a
"Christian People as being overtaken by a general public calamity" no doubt forgetting that
during the Revolution of this Country blood of
all denominations was shed for its freedom, in
those days there was *no distinction*[,] it was not
asked whether it was Christian, Jewish, or Pagan,
blood that flowed freely for the liberty *we all*
now possess.
   I am fully conscious that a denomination of
a "Christian People" exists in this country as in
others, and no doubt you are aware that there
exists a *Jewish People also* "that have been overtaken by this great public calamity" which has
befallen our country, as well as a *People who
neither profess Judaism or Christianity* but be-

leivers in a Supreme Being and Creator of the universe whom they adore.

[Page 2]

The demise of our late chief magistrate William H. Harrisson [sic] is an heavy affliction cast upon us, under the dispensation of an All Wise Providence, for which, we dare not even murmer [sic]. Although it is a duty incumbent *on us as a Nation* to implore a continuance of His Mercy and Gracious favour upon our Government and Country.

Not considering myself as numbering with a "Christian People" in matters of *a National Character* although ever ready to recognize them as Brethren, and Children of One God, beleive [sic], *that all Sectional prejudices should Subside* in an enlightened country like this, *and that most especially in the affairs of our Governments,* under that firm impression respectfully ask (with all due defference [sic] to your own private opinions) in behalf of *our Common Country* that such modification or explanation be made in your late recommendation to the People of the United States, as may meet the views of those *who do not profess Christianity* though beleivers in the Supreme Being of the world and wish to participate in the fast which you have most properly recommended to be observed on the 14th of May next by the People of the United States.

I remain your humble Servant and fellow Citizen
Jacob Ezekiel

Washington April 19, 1841
Sir,

I beg you to be perfectly assured that in writing the language in my recommendation to the people of the United States to observe the 14th of May as a day for religious exercises in consequence of the bereavement which the country has sustained in the death of the late President, I designed in nothing to exclude any portion of my fellow Citizens from a cordial union in the solemnities of that occasion. In speaking, in the first paragraph of the duties of *a Christian people*, I meant in no way to imply that similar duties should not be performed by *all mankind*. The last paragraph is an invitation *to all*, and excludes the idea of any especial invocation. For the people of whom you are one, I can feel none other than profound respect. The wisdom which flowed from the lives of your prophets, has in times past, and will continue for all time to come, to be a refreshing fountain of moral instruction to mankind—while holy records bear witness to the many instances of divine favour and protection of the God of Abraham and of Isaac and of Jacob, God of the Christian and the Israelite, to his chosen people. May I then hope Sir, that this explanation will remove all difficulties, and that your voice and the voices of all your brethren will ascend to our common Father in supplication and prayer on the day which I have suggested.

I tender you assurances of great respect
John Tyler
Source: Rare document, AJA.

3.06—LT. COL. AARON LEVY, "ON LAND PROMOTING," 1821

In his description of an event he staged on July 4, 1821, a former U.S. Army officer and New York real estate speculator named Aaron Levy (1771–1852) combined his own interest in promoting his business with the ideals of American patriotism. Levy gathered together the aging veterans of the American Revolution, invited a local Christian religious leader to offer a prayer, and hosted a dinner for all the invitees. He hoped that by fostering American patriotic ideals he would simultaneously encourage communal support for his real estate ventures.

. . . 4th of July, 1821 was celebrated at Caldwell by the inhabitants of the patent [real estate plot] formerly known as Smith & Mitchell's patent in a style never before witnessed in this northern clime and for simplicity of manners, correct deportment, and true patriotism we can venture to say it was not surpassed in any part of the Union. At 10 o'clock the inhabitants of the patent with a few visitors from the adjacent country began to collect and to the heart of philanthropy a more interesting sight could not be exhibited. Among the number were to be seen a few of our revolutionary patriots whose toil and ardor in defense of our independence were recounted by them with many original anecdotes relative to our struggle both interesting and amusing; also the old and the young of both sexes amounting to nearly three hundred free souls. The exercises of the day commenced with a prayer from Rev. Abm. J. Switz of Schenectady, a hymn suited to the occasion sung by a choir of the inhabitants, the declaration of American Independence together with an address delivered by Lieutt. Colonel Aaron Levy, an oration by Mr.

Switz, a moral and patriotic hymn by the choir. The service concluded with an impressive prayer by the Rev. Mr. Eastwood, resident preacher of the patent, after which at the request of the inhabitants Mr. Eastwood in a complimentary manner named the patent *Mount Levy* with appropriate benedictions to the same. The company then sat down to a dinner prepared under a bower decorated with laurel and evergreen, where the produce of the country was displayed in the greatest profusion. The scene was animated with a number of very handsome young ladies. Several songs were sung, and many patriotic toasts drank. After fully enjoying the refreshments the party formed a procession, of both sexes, and marched around the adjacent hills to music when the company dispersed in the most perfect order and harmony each satisfied with both the service and the repast of the day. The day was uncommonly fine and a stage covered with greens was previously prepared for the orators and deacons of the Mount and it may be with truth asserted, it was the feast of reason and the flow of soul.

Mem'd: I notice here the preceding publication in consequence of my being the principal projector and one of the actors in its scene, and as it is a new settlement under my direction and the day or anything like it never before celebrated, I leave this as a future memorandum for another generation to look at, when I am, as I hope to be, enjoying in another and better world more solid and everlasting blessings. Amen.

Source: JAW, 126–27. Reprinted with permission of AJHS, from *PAJHS* 42 (1952–53): 399–404.

Abraham Kohn (1819–1871) was twenty-three years old when he immigrated to the United States from the Bavarian village of Moenichsroth. Two years later, he became one of the first Jews to strike roots in the fledgling city of Chicago. Prior to this move, Kohn peddled his way through New England. He made note of his thoughts and impressions in his diary, which offers vivid descriptions of his activities. The content of Kohn's personal journal advances our understanding of the social history of Central European immigrants who eked out their livelihoods by working as itinerant peddlers during the mid-nineteenth century.

This week I went, together with my brother Juda, from Boston to Worcester [Massachusetts]. We were both delighted, for the trip was a welcome change from our daily, heavy work. Together we sat in the grass for hours, recalling the wonderful years of our youth. And in bed, too, we spent many hours in talking.

Today, the thirtieth of October, we are here in Northborough, and I feel happier than I have for a fortnight. Moses is in New York, and we will meet him, God willing, at Worcester on Tuesday. . . .

I regret that the people here are so cold to immigrants and that their watchword seems to be "Help yourself; that's the best help." I cannot believe that a man who adapts himself to the language, customs, and character of America can ever quite forget his home in the European countries. Having been here so short a time, I should be very arrogant if I were to set down at this time my judgments on America. The whole country, however, with its extensive domestic and foreign trade, its railroads, canals, and factories, looks to me like an adolescent youth. He is a part of society, talking like a man and pretending to be a man. Yet he is truly only a boy. That is America! Although she appears to know everything, her knowledge of religion, history,

and human nature is, in truth, very elementary. . . . American history is composed of Independence and Washington; that is all! On Sunday the American dresses up and goes to church, but he thinks of God no more than does the horse that carries him there. . . .

Thursday was a day of rest owing to twelve inches of snow. On Friday and Saturday business was very poor, and we did not take in $2 during the two days.

On Sunday we stayed with Mr. Brown, a blacksmith, two miles from Lunenburg. Both of us were in a bitter mood, for during the whole week of driving about in the bitter cold we had earned no money. I long for the beautiful days in my beloved homeland. Will they ever return? Yes, a secret voice tells me that all of us will again find happiness and, although there are many obstacles to be overcome, the old maxim will guide me! . . .

Last week in the vicinity of Plymouth I met two peddlers, Lehman and Marx. Marx knew me from Fürth, and that night we stayed together at a farmer's house. After supper we started singing while I felt melancholy and depressed. O, how I thought of my dear mother while I sang! . . .

Today, Sunday, October 16th, we are here in North Bridgewater [Massachusetts], and I am not so downcast as I was two weeks ago. The devil has settled 20,000 [2,000?] shoemakers here, who do not have a cent of money. Suppose, after all, I were a soldier in Bavaria; that would have been a bad lot. I will accept three years in America instead. But I could not stand it any longer.

As far as the language is concerned, I am getting along pretty well. But I don't like to be alone. . . .

Dear, good mother, how often I recall your letters, your advice against going to America: "Stay at home; you can win success as well in Germany." But I would not listen; I had to come to America. I was drawn by fate and here I am, living a life that is wandering and uncertain. . . .

On Tuesday morning at ten I left Worcester, it being my turn to travel alone for seven weeks. A thousand thanks to God, I felt far stronger than when I first left my brothers in Boston. Now I have become more accustomed to the language, the business, and the American way of life. . . .

It is hard, very hard indeed, to make a living this way. Sweat runs down my body in great drops and my back seems to be breaking, but I cannot stop; I must go on and on, however far my way lies. . . .

Here in the land of the free, where every child, every human being, preaches and enjoys liberty, it is I who am compelled to follow such a trade, to devote myself to so heavy and difficult a life. Each day I must ask and importune some farmer's wife to buy my wares, a few pennies' worth. Accursed desire for money, it is you that has driven the Bavarian immigrants to this wretched kind of trade! No, I must stop this business, the sooner the better. . . .

Source: Abraham J. Karp, *Golden Door to America: The Jewish Immigrant Experience* (New York: Viking Press, 1976), 55–57. Abraham Kohn Diary, 1842–1845, SC-6384, AJA.

3.08 — HENRY J. LABATT, NEWSPAPER ARTICLE ON JEWS AND BUSINESS IN THE GOLD RUSH, *True Pacific Messenger*, 1861

When gold was discovered in the foothills of the Sierra Nevada, Jews from the East Coast as well as Central Europe made the trek to San Francisco, where they often headed east to Sacramento and then to the smaller communities bursting with miners intent on getting rich. Most of the Jewish arrivals opted to work in the mercantile business, providing goods necessary for the miners, instead of seeking gold themselves. This proved a profitable decision for many. The paradigmatic example of this phenomenon was the career of Levi Strauss (1829–1902), who made a fortune during this period in the outfitting business.

In May 1861, Henry J. Labatt (1832–1900), an attorney who traveled to California from New Orleans, penned a newspaper article describing the rise, strategies, and success of Jewish businesses in Gold Rush California.

On a first arrival in our city, it becomes a matter of astonishment to all who see the large number of mercantile houses conducted by Israelites, being much greater, in proportion to the commerce, than in any other city in America. Every line of business is engaged in by them, with credit to themselves and honor to the community.

Among the largest importers, rank foremost many Jewish firms, the prosperity of whose engagements is evident in the large returns which are made on every steamer day.

The influence they command upon the trade in the State, the weight of their transactions, and the generality of their mercantile callings, may well class them among the most useful, beneficial, and respectable merchants.

Each mining town and city has a large representation, and everywhere you hear of their success and prosperity, which in turn they devote to the improvement of the place, by erecting substantial buildings and warehouses for the increase of their business, caused by industry, economy, and attention.

In all the great fires which have devastated the settlements of California, they have been great sufferers. Year after year, have they seen the hard earnings of their labor swept away by the ruthless conflagration, and yet, with the indomitable energy of their race, have they toiled on to regain what they thus were deprived of by misfortune. Often, indeed, would they not only lose what they had accumulated, but become reduced by being brought into debt by the destruction of their stock. Even this would not deter them.—The previous character which prudence and honesty had stamped upon them, created unmistakable confidence and sympathy, and they soon rose above these accidents.

Every where they seemed anxious to guard against this great affliction of our country and, by erecting substantial tenements, avoid another calamity.

In all commercial enterprises they keep pace with the marked improvements of the day, and, as merchants, are courted, admired—nay, even sometimes envied.

The almost universal success of the Jews, as merchants, in California, must be attributed to some peculiar reasons; for while many of all nations have succeeded in this State, yet, as a general thing, no class of people who began with so small a capital, have accumulated the same amount of fortune. Any close observer will find that their individual industry dispenses with the necessity for extra clerks, who, at the exorbitant rates necessary for their support, soon make sad inroads upon the monthly profit. They seldom pay unwarrantable rents, being willing to submit to many inconveniences rather than indulge in extravagance. They eschew all display of brilliant fixtures, or other unnecessary expenses, but study economy in every department of their business. Yet, after years of success, when they are conscious of their ability to display their wares and merchandise, then you may find a few who indulge in such outlays.

Their method of conducting business is also worthy of consideration. They seem anxious to dispose of their stock in a short time, and at little profit, and you will generally find throughout the country, that their stores are known as the "cheap stores." This is a great secret of trade; and when once that reputation is acquired, the custom will seek that store. For the most part, they first seek this enviable notoriety for their establishment, and then, by courtesy and a determination to give satisfaction, success seems inevitable; and what is thereby gained, economy secures.

Their quick perception gives them an insight into the requirements of every branch of trade, and when they once embark in it they are determined to call to their assistance every available faculty; and the natural sympathy of, and connection with, the other members of their faith, incite them to an emulation, the result of which is a high commercial position in the community.

Merchandise, from the time it is freighted on the clipper ships until it is consumed, passes principally through the hands of the Jewish merchants. As importers, jobbers, and retailers, they seem to monopolize most of the trade, and our business streets are thickly studded with their warehouses, shops, and stores. Their commercial position is high indeed, and without them now, trade would almost become stagnated in the State. The Express Companies of the interior depend mainly upon them for support, and the freight and package lists continually abound with their names. This position they have not acquired without great attention, honesty, industry, and personal sacrifice, and by unremitted prudence and civility; and they seem determined to add to it dignity and wealth.

This has had much influence in banishing the shameful prejudices otherwise existing against the Israelites, as a sordid and cunning race. Practice and experience in California have taught our neighbors the falsity of these opinions. Nowhere in America is the Jew so well understood, and so readily appreciated, as in this State; and nowhere does he more deserve the respect and esteem of his fellow citizens. May it always be so. May this abandonment of those prejudices be as lasting as it is just; and the Jew, as he is just and honest, ever merit that esteem and regard which has been so long withheld from his nation, and which always the liberty of America, and the honesty of California, is willing to accord to his enterprise, civility, forbearance, and capability.

Source: DHJ, 441–44. Reprinted from the Jewish Messenger, *July 12, 1861, p. 5, cols. 2–3.*

3.09—MEMORIAL TO THE PRESIDENT AND MEMBERS OF THE ADJUNTA OF KAHAL KADOSH BETH ELOHIM OF CHARLESTON, SOUTH CAROLINA, DEMANDING RELIGIOUS REFORM, DECEMBER 23, 1824

Frustrated by the inability of their religious leadership to keep their community engaged in Jewish religious life, forty-seven members of Charleston, South Carolina's Jewish community, led by Isaac Harby and Abraham Moïse Jr. (1799–1869), composed a document calling for a reformation of Judaism in their synagogue, Congregation Beth Elohim. While the Reform movement in American Judaism would not flourish until the second half of the nineteenth century, historians argue that this document marks the first call for reform in American Jewish history. It argues, among other things, for greater reliance on English within a more abbreviated worship service.

Gentlemen,

The memorial of the undersigned, showeth unto your honourable body, that they have witnessed with deep regret, the apathy and neglect which have been manifested towards our holy religion. As inheritors of the *true faith*, and always proud to be considered by the world as a portion of "God's chosen people," they have been pained to perceive the gradual decay of that system of worship, which, for ages past, *peculiarly* distinguished us from among the nations of the earth. Not unmindful, however, of the various causes which regulate human conduct; and at the same time, unwilling to shield themselves from any censure to which their actions may justly entitle them, they have ingenuously investigated the reasons which may have led them from the Synagogue, and are now seriously impressed with the belief, that certain defects which are apparent in the present system of worship, are the sole causes of the evils complained of.

In pointing out these defects, however, your memorialists seek no other end, than the future welfare and respectability of the nation. As members of the great family of Israel, they cannot consent to place before their children examples which are only calculated to darken the mind, and withhold from the rising generation the more rational means of worshipping the true God.

It is to this, therefore, your memorialists would, in the first place, invite the serious attention of your honourable body. By causing the Hasan, or reader, to repeat in English such part of the Hebrew prayers as may be deemed necessary, it is confidently believed that the congregation generally would be more forcibly impressed with the necessity of Divine Worship, and the moral obligations which they owe to themselves and their Creator; While such a course, would lead to more decency and decorum during the time they are engaged in the performance of religious duties. It is not every one who has the means, and many have not the time, to acquire a knowledge of the Hebrew language, and consequently to become enlightened in the principles of Judaism; What then is the course pursued in all religious societies for the purpose of disseminating the peculiar tenets of their faith among the poor and uninformed? The principles of their religion are expounded to them from the pulpit in the language that they understand; for instance, in the Catholic, the German and the French Protestant Churches: by this means the ignorant part of mankind attend their places of worship with some profit to their morals, and even improvement of their minds; they return from them with hearts turned to piety, and with feelings elevated by their sacred character. In this consists the beauty of religion,—when men are invoked by its divine spirit, to the practice of virtue and morality.

[...]

Your memorialists would next call the particular attention of your honourable body to the absolute necessity of abridging the service generally. They have reflected seriously upon its present length, and are confident that this is one of the principal causes why so much of it is hastily and improperly hurried over. This must be evident to every reflecting mind, when it is seen, that notwithstanding the evil complained of, the service of the Sabbath, for instance, continues until *twelve* o'clock, although usually commencing at *nine*. It is therefore manifest, that, according to the prayer of your memorialists, should the service be in future conducted with due solemnity, and in a slow, distinct, and impressive tone, its length would certainly occupy the attention of the congregation, until two o'clock, if not later.

[...]

It is also worthy of observation, that a number of Israelites, whom it should be the special care of your honourable body to bring back under your immediate protection and influence, are now wandering gradually from the true God, and daily losing those strong ties which bind every pious man to the faith of his fathers! In these individuals, your honourable body have fair subjects for the holy work of reformation; by moulding your present form of worship to suit their comprehensions, you will instantly receive them among you; they will collect under your especial care and guardianship; they will aid in the pecuniary resources of your holy institutions; and if, from among the whole number now scattered about our city and state, either through irreligion, through disabilities imposed, or any other cause, you are enabled to make but

one convert, it will add much to those laudable ends which it should be the principal desire of your honourable body to accomplish. It should also be remembered that while other sects are extending the means of Divine Worship to the remotest quarters of the habitable globe—while they are making the most zealous efforts to bring together the scattered of their flock, offering the most flattering inducements to *all denominations*—we, who may be termed the mere remnant of a great nation, are totally disregarding the fairest opportunities of increasing our own numbers, and at the same time neglecting the brightest prospects of enlarging our resources, and effectually perpetuating our national character.

[...]

Thus . . . it appears, that no climes, nor even tyranny itself, can forever fetter or control the human mind; and that even amidst the intolerance of Europe, our brethren have anticipated the free citizens of America in the glorious work of reformation; Let us then hasten to the task with harmony and good fellowship. We wish not to *overthrow*, but to *rebuild*; we wish not to *destroy*, but to *reform* and *revise* the evils complained of; we wish not to *abandon* the institutions of Moses, but to *understand and observe them*; in fine, we wish to worship God, not as *slaves of bigotry and priestcraft*, but as the enlightened descendants of that chosen race, whose blessings have been scattered throughout the land of Abraham, Isaac and Jacob.

And your memorialists will ever pray.

Signed by forty-seven Israelites of the City of Charleston.

Source: DHJ, 171–77. From L. C. Moise, *Biography of Isaac Harby with an Account of the Reformed Society of Israelites of Charleston, S. C., 1824–1833* (Columbia, S.C.: R. L. Bryan Co., 1931), 52–59.

*The following document introduces two
significant nineteenth-century American Jewish
personalities: Rabbi Abraham Rice (1800–1862)
and Rev. Isaac Leeser. Rice holds the distinction
of being the first ordained rabbi to serve as the
spiritual leader of an American synagogue. Born
near Würzburg, Bavaria, he immigrated to the
United States in 1840 to assume the pulpit of
Congregation Nidche Israel, later known as
Baltimore Hebrew Congregation. In contrast to
Rice, Leeser was not an ordained rabbi, but he
was a very learned pioneer of the American
Jewish pulpit. Born in Westphalia, Prussia,
Leeser immigrated to Richmond, Virginia, in
1824 to work in his uncle's store. In 1828, the
young Leeser became the reader and cantor for
Philadelphia's Congregation Mikve Israel, a
position from which he retired in 1850. In 1857,
he became the spiritual leader of Congregation
Beth-El-Emeth in Philadelphia, where he served
until his death. Over the course of his long
career, Leeser also distinguished himself as
an author, translator, editor, and publisher.*

*Although Rice and Leeser shared a deep
commitment to traditional Jewish practice, they
disagreed over how best to preserve the ancient
traditions of Judaism in America. Rice scorned
any attempt to Americanize Judaism, while
Leeser believed a loyal devotion to Jewish
traditionalism could be preserved by adapting
it to its American context. In 1848, Isaac Mayer
Wise (1819–1900) urged the "ministers and
other Israelites" of the United States to band
together in a conference in hopes of fostering
an ecclesiastical unity among American Jews.
Leeser published and offered his personal
endorsement for Wise's call in the pages of his
newspaper, the* Occident. *As we see in the letter
to follow, Rice, whose written English betrays his
struggle to learn the language, disagreed with
his compatriot and urged him to abandon any
plan that might result in the modernization of
Judaism.*

Baltimore 15th Dec. 48.

My Dear Friend.

I think we are acquainted enough to talk with
you freely, what my humble opinion is about the
convention of Rabbis, spoken of in your last periodical. I know very much that you are sincere in
religious matters as you are the latest [last] who
would make any innovation, but let me tell you
as a friend you have to consider also, that in your
early lives [life] you were mingled with the american life; many of your Ideas will not do for true
Judaismen, though you may think it is no harm in
it. The כוזרי [*Kuzari*] says כונתך רצויה ומעשיך אינם רצוים
[your intentions are acceptable but not so your
acts], what is by many the case now. Further you
know, that we have a certain class, which the
word "Religion" is every moment in their mouth,
but in their hearth is nothing as sellfishness &
the true יראה [reverence] is wanting. What benefit shall arise from this "reunion"? If we all act
according to our שלחן ערוך [*Shulhan Arukh*], one
Jew can live in one corner of the world & yet we
have with him one rule & regulation. Can we establish better rules as we find written down by
our ancient [writers]? Or will we please the spirit
of [the] times? if we would adhere conscientiously to our rules? Will they not say?

מאי אהני לן רבנן, מעולם לא שרי לנו עורב ולא אסר
לנו יונה – [סנהדרין צט:]

[of what use are the Rabbis to us? They have
never permitted us the raven, nor forbidden us
the dove, *Talmud Babli—Sanhedrin* 99:2.]

Is the convention of the German Rabbis lost
from your memory? Are our Rabbis better men?
Have we not some wolves clothed in sheeps-
cover? How is it possible to establish an equal
Reform in our prayers? & if it were possible what
is done for true religion? These are only form
& not [the] essential part of religion. Would or
can this convention establish rules for keeping
the Sabbath strikly? That every married Jewish
lady has to go to מקוה [*mikveh*]? Or will come the
question for them, to abolish the second day of

יו״ט [festivals]? I, for my part, can tell this prophesy, that the latter question will come sooner off.

You must not charge me, that I am too sanguinish, the heaven is my witness, that I deliberate very cool, but I am afraid for such a convention ואתה ! תקוה לגדל ענבים ותקבל באושים

ויקו לעשות ענבים ויעש באושים [ישעיה ה–ב]

["And he looked that it should bring forth grapes, And it brought forth wild grapes." Isaiah 5:2]

The only result will be, we will have more permissiveness and liencies [licentiousness] & no strength at all will derive from it.

I ask you? are we better Jews, if we say not any longer פיוטים [*piyyutim*]? Comes more Devotion in our Synagogues if we have a Choir. I say candidly, no! All is nonsense, we have here a Choir, Our Chasan & the whole Congn dont know what is devotion. This is all spoken of to please the spirit of [the] time[s] & to be like other sects.

In the same manner, I consider such a Convention, we like to be like other sects, they have their convention we must have ours too. Our שלחן ערוך [*Shulhan Arukh*] is our Conference. We have no power to alter one Iod [*yud*—smallest letter in Hebrew alphabet][.] Instead to call חזק ונתחזק בעד עמיך [Be strong and let us be strengthened for the sake of our people] we will call; [ב״מ קז;] קשוט עצמך תחלה ואח״כ קשוט אחרים [justify yourself and then justify others—*Talmud Babli—Baba Metziah* 107:2].

If every Rabbi has a true Jewish spirit & he will act according to our true religion, & keep st[r]ictly to our דין [law], than every one will bring back few to true religion וכל המקיים נפש אחת מישראל כאילו קים עולם מלא [סנהדרין לז׳] [one who saves one Jewish life, is as he preserved an entire world—*Talmud Babli—Sanhedrin* 37:1]. To bring the eyes of the world on our Convention is nothing for a man who will do nothing for the world, only for the good of his faith.

My Dear, I hope you will not find yourself offended by my talking. You know me—for out of the abundance of my complaint and grief have I spoken hitherto. Take therefore the admonition of a true friend & consider well, before you go in, for such a step; on the consequences of introducing such a convention, who will be attended with dangerous consequences[.]

I remain for ever, Your truly friend & humble servant

A Rice

NB. You must not laugh about my language. I write in English only for that reason, to make me more acquainted with the words.

Source: I. Harold Sharfman, *The First Rabbi: Origins of Conflict Between Orthodox and Reform: Jewish Polemic Warfare in Pre-Civil War America: A Biographical History* (Malibu, Calif.: Pangloss Press, 1988), 239–41.

3.11—ROSA MORDECAI, MEMOIR DESCRIBING HEBREW SCHOOL EDUCATION IN ANTEBELLUM AMERICA, 1850S

Rebecca Gratz (1781–1869), the Pennsylvania-born daughter of a successful merchant family, devoted her early adult life to various secular social service causes in Philadelphia. She also helped build Jewish communal life, founding the Female Hebrew Benevolent Society in 1819. By 1838, she had turned her professional attention to Jewish education, founding what is credited as the nation's first Jewish Sunday school— Philadelphia's "Hebrew Sunday School." Gratz served as both superintendent and president of the school, and played a central role in the development of its curriculum. In the 1850s, Rosa Mordecai (1839–1936), Gratz's grandniece, attended the school. In the selection to follow from Mordecai's memoirs, published in 1897,

My first distinct impression of going to the Hebrew Sunday School was some years after it was organized by my great aunt, Miss Rebecca Gratz, and while she was still its moving spirit (sometime I think in the early fifties). The room which the school then occupied was on Zane Street (now Filbert Street) above Seventh Street, over the Phoenix Hose Company. This was prior to the days of the Paid Fire Department. Before mounting the stairs, I would linger, as many of the girls and all the boys did, to admire the beautifully-kept machines, with the gentlemanly loungers, who never wearied of answering our questions. The sons of our most "worthy and respected" citizens ran after the Phoenix in those days. But I catch a glimpse of Miss Gratz approaching, and we all scatter as she says "Time for school, children!"

[...]

Here Miss Gratz presided. A stately commanding figure, always neatly dressed in plain black, with thin white collar and cuffs, close-fitting bonnet over her curled front, which time never touched with grey, giving her, even in her most advanced years, a youthful appearance. Her eyes would pierce every part of the hall and often detect mischief which escaped the notice of the teachers.

The only punishment, I can recall, was for the delinquent to be marched through the school and seated upon the little platform, before mentioned, under the table. Sometimes this stand would be quite full, and I was rather disposed to envy those children who had no lessons to say. But, her duties over, Miss Gratz would call them by name to stand before her for reproof, which, apparently mild, was so soul-stirring that even the most hardened sinner would quail before it. She was extremely particular to instill neatness and cleanliness. A soiled dress, crooked collar, or sticky hands never escaped her penetrating glance and the reproof or remedy was instantaneous.

The benches held about ten children each; they were painted bright yellow, with an arm at each end; on the board across the back were beautiful medallions of mills, streams, farmhouses, etc., etc.

The instruction must have been principally orall in those primitive days. Miss Gratz always began school with the prayer, opening with "Come ye children, hearken unto me, and I will teach you the fear of The Lord." This was followed by a prayer of her own composition, which she read verse by verse, and the whole school repeated after her. Then she read a chapter of the Bible, in a clear and distinct voice, without any elocution, and this could be heard and understood all over the room. The closing exercises were equally simple; a Hebrew hymn sung by the children, then one of Watts' simple verses, whose rhythm the smallest child could easily catch as all repeated "Send me the voice that Samuel heard," etc., etc.

[...]

"Pyke's Catechism" was freely distributed, and instead of being taught, parrot-fashion, by the teacher, the tiny green books went home to many Jewish households, with a penalty of five cents attached if injured or lost; and this fee was strictly exacted by the young librarian, who was a great disciplinarian. Books were not very often allowed by him, to be taken home, but were read, after the lessons were recited by the scholars, or aloud by the teacher, if it so happened that all her class studied in the same book, or the same lesson. Generally, however, owing to private reasons, kinship or popularity, a class would be composed of eight or ten boys and girls of different ages and ability, and consequently these were taught out of several books, or even different parts of the same book.

Both Rev. Isaac Leeser and the Rev. Dr. (then Mr.) [Sabato] Morais were constant visitors. The former with his strongly marked face, gold spectacles and inexhaustible fund of ever-ready information was a most welcome sight to the young teachers, puzzled by the questions of their big, clever scholars. He knew every child and teacher, called each by name, and nothing was too trivial or too intricate to claim his clear explanation.

[. . .]

Simple days of our youth, where are you now?

Source: As printed in *JAW,* 152–56.

3.12—ISAAC JALONICK TO ISAAC LEESER ON JEWISH LIFE IN TEXAS, MAY 28, 1853

Isaac Jalonick (1824–1893), an immigrant from Warsaw, Poland, who arrived in the United States in 1837, would become one of the earliest Jewish residents of Texas. He lived in Mexico and California before arriving in Belton, Texas, located about fifty miles south of Waco. At a time when the Jewish population of Texas numbered fewer than one thousand, Jalonick penned a letter to Isaac Leeser requesting a subscription to his periodical, the Occident, *and seeking copies of Jewish religious texts. Jalonick's interest in maintaining a link with Jewish life amid his frontier isolation is a familiar theme among Jews who settled in remote locations all across the nation during this same period.*

Belton, Bell Co., Texas, May 28th, 1853

Mr. Isaac Leeser.

Dear Sir:

It will surprise you, sir, to hear from such re-moot part on the frontier of Texas. But it is as it shuld be, the prophicing must be full fild [the biblical prophecy that Jews are to be scattered throughout the world]. I am surry to say that I am a poor scolar; I cane not express my feeling with the pen when I accidently came in poses-tion of such valuible inphomation as containing in your valuble [newspaper] *Occident.* May the

leeving God spair you that you may accomplish which you have undertakin to do. I am surry to say that I was igronent what was going on, all though I am in this countiry fifteen years. But nearly all that time was spent heur and in Mex-cico and Califonia. I am happy, wery happy in-deeth, to see that our true riligion has a poblick advocate. I cane not find words to express my feelings. You cane put me on your list of sob-scribers. I would like to send you the pay in ad-vance but hear we cane not obtain paiper muny when we please, and I live a long wais from the coust; as soon as I cane obtain paper muny I will rimit it to you. I find in the *Occident* that you are a bougt [about] to transilait the [Hebrew] Bible. I will all so send for one of them and if you have the transilation of the *machser* [High Holyday prayer book] I would be very glad to get it all so. The expence is not in my way.

I hope you will ansure this, and belive me to be a true Jew and a frend to our cous [cause],

Isaac Jalonick Address Isaac Jalonick . . .

Belton, Bell Co. Texas

Source: As printed in *JAW,* 191–92. CAJS ARC MS 2, Isaac Leeser Collection, box #25 photostatic copy. Original item missing. Courtesy of the Library at the Herbert D. Katz Center for Advanced Judaic Studies, University of Pennsylvania. See also *American Jewish Archives* 8 (1956): 75.

3.13—I. J. BENJAMIN, "THE EDUCATION OF JEWISH WOMEN IN AMERICA, 1859–1862"

Reflecting on his travels in the United States between 1859 and 1862, the peripatetic Moldavian Israel Joseph Benjamin (1818–1864) was frequently critical of the freewheeling behavior he observed among American Jews. In the document to follow, he lambasts the educational experience of American Jewish girls and women, challenging the optimistic appraisal of Jewish life in the United States and giving support to European Jews fearful about the impact of Americanization on Jewish identity.

Of all the inflexible demands which his religion and his duty make on each Israelite, the first and foremost is to give his child a good education; to equip it for the journey through life and give it the means to find its way. The American schools, of which we are about to speak, certainly guarantee this in part; but it is much to be regretted that, because they exclude all religion and confessions of faith—not with an unwise purpose—I must say with the deepest regret that the study of the Holy Scriptures, particularly, is much neglected among the daughters of Israel.

Jewish boys after a fashion—for that is the established way—are instructed in their religion, as is also the case with the sons and daughters of Christians. The Jewish boys attend some Hebrew school or other, or are instructed privately; but in this respect, what does the situation look like for the daughters of Israel? What a great difference! How sad is the provision for the religious instruction of these Jewish housewives and mothers of the future! How little do they learn of their duties towards God and man! What do they know of what our faith requires and of the commandments that they must obey as daughters of Israel? Should not those who are to perform the holiest religious duties be thoroughly prepared for such performance? These duties are indeed many and noble and it is with regret and astonishment that one learns that half of the American Jewesses are at present unable to undertake and fulfil worthily the place in life for which they are intended; nevertheless, it is unfortunately all too true. And why? The reason for this lies in their neglected education.

To throw more light on this statement and confirm the truth of it, let us describe the upbringing that the American Jewish women of today receive, and then let us proceed to show how the evil may, and should be remedied.

The mother of a little girl, a good-hearted, rather well-to-do woman, let us say, will try to impress on the young spirit of her child as much good instruction as ever she can. This private care lasts until the child is five. Then the child, it is obvious, must be sent to a public school or, what is more respectable, to a so-called "institute." Accepted by the "institute," the child begins the usual course of studies, makes the acquaintance of girls of other religions and has friends among them, and may well, without any objection or even realization of its significance, kneel during morning prayers which are arranged for those of other faiths, before classes begin. After school, she studies her lessons for the next day or, like all children, plays. Upon going to bed or arising in the morning, she may very likely recite for her mother some Hebrew or English prayers; but as for Judaism, the child experiences nothing and knows nothing.

In this manner the girl continues to be brought up until she is fifteen, except for the unimportant difference that in time she leaves the institute to attend high-school or college. On her fifteenth birthday a new life begins; the longed-for day arrives at last; Papa and Mamma have promised her that on this day she shall be free and shall leave school, and she "graduates," to her great joy. What useful knowledge has she gained during this time? Extremely little in fact. She has spent ten years of her precious life among all kinds of books, and with all that, she has not advanced in the least; the time is lost, indeed, forever. What she has learned is of no use to her and of no profit. She does not know how to sew, has no knowledge of household affairs, and still less of higher things. Ask her who has created her, who clothes her, who gives her her daily bread; and she may have the correct answer—perhaps, but it is more likely that she will say: "That was not in my book."

Her good parents have increased their wealth during these ten years and have taken the commendable resolution that their daughter should not forget all that she has learnt. Accordingly, they provide her—to complete her education—with a music-teacher, a singing-teacher, a drawing-teacher, and a governess to continue the practice of French; the latter also teaches her how to sew, knit and the like; and to give it all a final touch, they assign a teacher to give her Hebrew lessons. He must make her acquainted with the alphabet of a language in which, as a child, she should have lisped the name of God. She will find this last teacher, as is only to be expected, a bore. She will find Hebrew too dull and also too difficult; she will weep over her lessons so that her yielding parents, who will be touched by her tears and moved to pity, will give the teacher notice—he whom they should have engaged first and dismissed last. But they took the opposite course, out of their own lack of true religious feeling, and so they engaged him last and, again, dismissed him first.

Since, in this manner, the girl has come to the end of her religious upbringing, she continues to recite in English the few prayers which she has learnt from her mother. Should she, quite by accident, attend synagogue, she takes a book in the same language. Her other teachers soon share the same fate as her former Hebrew teacher. Because of the parties, balls, soirees, and so on, which have now become the important questions of the day for her, and at which she remains until the last, the girl becomes full of whims, her mind is distracted. She listens to the chatter of young men and all thought of study and the desire for it is gone. The young lady—she will no longer permit herself to be called a girl—believes that her upbringing is now completed in every respect, considers herself qualified to take her place in the world, able to make a man happy and become a Jewish mother. . . .

Source: As printed in *JAW*, 253–55. Reproduced from *Three Years in America, 1859–1862* by I. J. Benjamin, translated by Charles Reznikoff, by permission of the University of Nebraska Press. Copyright 1956 by the Jewish Publication Society of America, Philadelphia.

3.14—MORDECAI MANUEL NOAH, ADDRESS AT ARARAT, A PROPOSED REFUGE FOR JEWS, 1825

In one of American Jewry's earliest expressions of territorialism, Mordecai Manuel Noah, the well-known Jewish leader and former ambassador to Tunis, sought the creation of Ararat, a city for Jewish refugees, located on Grand Island near Buffalo, New York. For Noah, Ararat would serve as an important center for Jewish refugees to live in anticipation of the Jewish people's eventual creation of their own national homeland. As the following document attests, the dedication ceremonies proved both formal and impressive, as Noah, joined by Seneca Chief Red Jacket (1757–1830) and other dignitaries, offered a robust vision for Jewish life in upstate New York and pointed, by inference, to the great possibilities of American Jewish life in general. Of special interest are the many similarities Noah draws between Jews and Native Americans.

Brothers, Countrymen, and Friends,

Having made known by proclamation the re-establishment of the Hebrew government, having laid the foundations of a city of refuge, an asylum for the oppressed in this free and happy republic, I avail myself of that portion of my beloved brethren here assembled, together with this concourse of my fellow citizens, to unfold the principles, explain the views, and detail the objects contemplated in the great work of re-generation and independence to which it has pleased the Almighty God to direct my attention. Truth and justice demand that I should candidly state the motives that have induced me to aim at higher objects than mere colonization. The world has a right to know what inducements have led to this declaration of independence, and what measures are contemplated to carry the design into successful execution. The peace of mankind,

the security of persons & property, the changes incidental to the revival of the Jewish government, the progress and effect of emigration, and all those vicissitudes arising from change of climate, new laws, new society admonish me to be explicit in my declaration, & candid in my statements. I shall not deceive the expectations of the world.

Two thousand years have nearly elapsed since the dissolution of the Jewish government, and no period has presented itself more auspiciously than the present for its reorganization. Peace exists among civilized powers, the march of learning and science has been rapid and successful, and mankind are at this day better qualified to estimate the blessings of toleration and liberal views, and better disposed and capacitated to encourage and enforce them, than at any former time. Religion generally, though divided and subdivided into various sects, assumes a milder aspect, and feelings of universal love and charity have superseded the darkness and bigotry of former ages. The nations of the old and new world, including the children of Africa, have had their rights acknowledged, and their governments recognized. The oldest of nations, powerful in numbers and great in resources, remains isolated, without a home, a country or a government.

[...]

In calling the Jews together under the protection of the American Constitution and laws and governed by our happy and salutary institutions, it is proper for me to state that this asylum is temporary and provisional. The Jews never should and never will relinquish the just hope of regaining possession of their ancient heritage, and events in the neighborhood of Palestine indicate an extraordinary change of affairs.

[...]

The time has emphatically arrived to do something calculated to benefit our own condition, and excite the admiration of the world, and we must commence the work in a country free from ignoble prejudices and legal disqualifications—a country, in which liberty can be insured to the Jews without the loss of one drop of blood.

[...]

Those who are most conversant with the public and private economy of the Indians, are strongly of the opinion that they are the lineal descendants of the Israelites, and my own researches go far to confirm me in the same belief.

The Indians worship one Supreme Being as the fountain of life, and the author of all creation. Like the Israelites of old, they are divided into tribes having their Chief and distinctive Symbol to each. Some of these tribes it is said are named after the Cherubimical figures that were carried on the four principal standards of Israel. They consider themselves as the select and beloved people of God, and have all the religious pride which our ancestors are known to have possessed. Their words are sonorous and bold, and their language and dialect are evidently of Hebrew origin. They compute the time after the manner of the Israelites, by dividing the year into four seasons, and their subdivisions are the lunar months, or our new Moons, commencing after the ecclesiastical year of Moses, the first Moon after the vernal equinox. They have their prophets, high Priests, and their sanctum sanctorum, in which all their consecrated vessels are deposited, and which are only to be approached by their archimagas or high Priest. They have their towns and cities of refuge—they have sacrifices and fastings—they abstain from unclean things, in short, in their marriages, divorces, punishment of adultery, burial of the dead, and mourning, they bear a striking analogy to our people. How came they on this continent, and if indigenous, when did they acquire the principles and essential forms of the Jews? The Indians are not Savages, they are wild and savage in their habits, but possess great vigour of intellect and native talent—they are a brave and eloquent people, with an Asiatic complexion, and Jewish features. . . .

I recommend the establishment of emigration societies throughout Europe, in order that proper aid may be afforded to those who may be disposed to visit this country, and also to ascertain the character and occupation of each emigrant, and supply them with passports and information. Passage in all cases should be taken for New-York. It should be distinctly understood by emigrants of limited means, that it will be necessary to have at least a sufficiency to support their families for six months, as by that time they may be enabled to realize the fruits of enterprise and industry, and a sufficient sum may at that period be paid into the general Coffers, to aid them in the purchase of land. No mistaken impression should exist, that the Jews must not labour in this country: we all are compelled to work, but with the same portion of industry, exercised in other parts of the world, we realize a greater proportion of happiness, tranquility and personal rights. We shall not be prepared to receive emigrants on Grand Island, until the ensuing summer, and this notice is given to prevent an indiscriminate and hasty emigration, which may defeat many good objects. . . .

Source: New York Evening Post, September 24, 1825.

3.15—REVIEW OF *Harrington*, A FICTIONAL ACCOUNT DESCRIBING INTERMARRIAGE, 1833

In 1817, the Irish author Maria Edgeworth (1768–1849) published a fictional autobiography titled Harrington. *The novel's central character is compelled to confront his anti-Jewish prejudices when he meets an American woman, Bernice. While he assumes that Bernice is Jewish, he later learns that he was mistaken. Mrs. Sarah Hall (1761–1830), an American author from Philadelphia, composed a fascinating critique of Edgeworth's views on intermarriage that subsequently appeared in Reuben Percy's* Relics of Literature *(London: T. Boys, 1823), 171–73. Hall insisted that Edgeworth's fiction underscored the cultural divide between the United States and Great Britain. Among other points, Hall proudly insisted that as far as the United States was concerned, "we know of no uncharitable barriers between Jews and Christians in our happy community."*

The story of "Harrington," by *Miss Edgeworth*, has excited more than common attention, because it is stated to have been written to conciliate a particular description of people; one of whose members, "an American lady," had complained that her society had been harshly treated in the writings of that celebrated author. Harrington, the hero of this tale, is captivated by a young lady of the Hebrew stock. Both himself and his parents entertain violent prejudices against *Jews*. These prejudices, in due time, are removed by concurring circumstances; yet, her religion being an insurmountable bar to their marriage, it is suddenly discovered that she had been educated a Christian! and all concludes happily in the usual way.

One of our critics in the New York Magazine, after commenting with sufficient amplitude on novel-writing in general, and Miss Edgeworth's manner in particular, gives a summary of this fashionable tale, and concludes with the following remarks;

"Miss Mentonero is a lovely, sensitive, interesting girl, but she is no Jewess! and the whole fabric, which the author had raised, falls before this single fact. By doing away this prominent impediment to the union of the lovers, she completely destroys the interest of the reader, and the moral of her tale. The mode adopted to dispose of the difficulty is a tacit admission that it could be got over in no other way. Miss Edgeworth is quite willing to allow the Jews to be very clever, good people, but it is pretty plain that she does not think a Hebrew damsel a proper helpmate for a John Bull."

We readily agree with this writer, that by removing the impediment to the match, she has destroyed the interest of the reader, but not, we hope, the fabric *she meant* to raise, or the "moral of her tale." Her design was simply to concede that Jews are like other men, good and bad, and this she has effected. But had she intended to inculcate that heartless liberality which supposes that conflicting opinions in the most essential articles of a religious creed, should be no impediment to a matrimonial union; she would, indeed, have betrayed an evidence of that indifference to all religions, with which she has sometimes been charged. She was perfectly right in admitting that "the difficulty" must be removed; but there was another, and but one other way, the sacrifice of their love to their religion. Had she finally separated the lovers on this account, our sympathy would have been sustained, and to the virtues intended to be conceded to the still venerated name of Israelite, would have been added, that tenacious adherence to their faith which we know they practise, and so long as they sincerely think it right, they are highly commendable in doing so.

With such laws as could only be performed at Jerusalem, the Jews are now obliged to dispense; but all that are practicable in their dispersed state, they piously obey. Had not this been the case, they would have been long ago amalgamated, like every other ancient people, with the Gentiles, and their very name would have been discovered only in their history. Their absolutely abstaining from intermarriages with any others than those of their own communion, is the principal means by which they are preserved in their separate state; nor can we see how two persons, each conscientiously attached to a creed essentially so different as those of the Jew and the Christian, could live together in that perfect harmony, which ought, at least, to be *anticipated* by every individual who enters into the most important of all engagements.

In the course of her work, Miss Edgeworth has taken occasion to notice the liberality of public sentiment, and the undistinguishing toleration of our laws in America. A recent opportunity would seem, indeed, to show that the former at least, must be very much at variance with the state of feeling in England. In all the conversations to which [the influential Anglo-American painter] Mr. [Benjamin] West's celebrated picture had given rise in the last two or three years, we have never heard it intimated that the English critics had objected to the complexion by which the artist has thought proper to distinguish the High-Priest and his adherents from *their brethren*, the disciples of Christ. With us, it is seen with one universal feeling of surprise and disgust. There is not the shadow of authority for such a liberty in the Scriptures; and if it be adopted in the license of the poet, though it be temerity to differ with Mr. West, we cannot but say there is a gross absurdity in ex-

hibiting in the same picture two groups of persons, all *of the same family*, and the same period of time, of opposite colours—the one white, the other black! *Friends* and *enemies* are very properly discriminated by the expression of their features; but no strength of passion, especially at the moment of its birth, can change the colour of the skin.

Miss Edgeworth has gone beyond the courtesy of either party, and proved too much, when she compliments us so far as to say, that "in America Jews have *frequently* married Christian women, and the wives have continued undisturbed in their faith." Page 137. She has been misinformed in this particular. A few such instances, it is true, have occurred; but in some cases, one of the parties has wholly embraced the opposite creed; and in others they have evinced their total indifference to all religion, by suspending the exercise of their own opinions during the lives of their companions, and returning to it afterwards. In all the various intercourse of social life, we know of no uncharitable barriers between Jews and Christians in our happy community. Talents and virtues are alike honoured in both: but in the view of a more intimate connexion, many a youth enchained by the charms of a lovely Jewess, has breathed the vain aspiration of Paul to Agrippa, "I would thou wert not only almost, but altogether such as I am," *not excepting these bonds!*

Source: JUS, vol. 3, 681–83. From *Selections from the Writings of Mrs. Sarah Hall* (Philadelphia: Harrison Hall, 1833), 57–60.

3.16—NEWSPAPER ACCOUNT, COHEN-CHISOLM DUEL, JULY 25, 1827

In the American South especially, dueling emerged in the colonial period as a dignified approach to recovering a man's honor after he had suffered some form of insult. With its origins in Europe, dueling in the United States typically pitted two white men of high social status against each other in a well-choreographed ritual. An unusual example of this practice was sparked when a Charleston Jew named G. P. Cohen was upset by some blatantly condescending and anti-Jewish remarks that were attributed to a Dr. Edward Chisolm. Cohen challenged Chisolm to a duel, but the doctor ignored the invitation on the grounds that dueling with a Jew was beneath him. Irate and insulted, Cohen felt he had no alternative but to publicize the entire matter in the pages of the local newspaper, the Charleston Mercury.

To the Public.

Having had a dispute with Dr. Edward Chisolm, and feeling myself insulted by an illiberal expression made by him, I applied to a gentleman of respectability and honorable feeling, to call on Dr. Edward Chisolm, and to demand an apology. If this was not promptly given, then to demand the only redress that *Honor* has long established as the practice in these cases. Dr. Chisolm, through his friend, answered that he would give me no satisfaction, and that I was not *on a footing with him!* because I was a Jew, nor did he conceive any Jew to be on a footing with him! As such a subterfuge as this marks the individual, not only with illiberality and ignorance, but with COWARDICE, it therefore becomes my painful duty to intrude these remarks on the public, in order to expose him to the community in which I live, the place of my nativity.

The Constitution of the U. States, and of my native State, give me and every citizen, of every religious denomination, equal rights and equal privileges. Religious distinctions are not known in this country. Members of the same community are valued only according to their conduct in life, and none but a *bigot* and a *Coward*, like Edward Chisolm, would attempt to insult a whole nation, by refusing that satisfaction which every *gentleman* is ready to give and to receive.

G. P. Cohen

Charleston, (S.C.) July 25th, 1827.

Source: "To the Public," *Charleston Courier* 25, no. 8525 (July 26, 1827).

3.17—ISRAEL B. KURSHEEDT AND THEODORE J. SEIXAS TO PRESIDENT MARTIN VAN BUREN, ON THE DAMASCUS BLOOD LIBEL, AUGUST 24, 1840

The blood libel, one of the most horrific and powerful expressions of anti-Jewish fervor and Judeophobia, falsely insisted that Jews killed Christian children around the time of Passover and used the children's blood to make matzo. This cruel canard, devised originally during the medieval period, was repackaged and recycled over the course of centuries. It reemerged in at least a dozen cases during the nineteenth century, including the infamous Damascus Affair of 1840.

When a Franciscan priest, Father Thomas, who served as president of the Catholic Church of Damascus, and his Greek servant went missing, a charge of ritual murder was brought against several prominent Damascus Jews, who had been identified by two tortured "witnesses." The accused were arrested, themselves tortured, and sentenced to death. The situation continued to worsen when local officials seized sixty-three Jewish children and refused to release them until the accused revealed where they had hidden the blood.

Through their respective defense organizations, the Jews of Great Britain and France organized formal protests. The fledgling U.S. Jewish community—numbering approximately 15,000—had no national organization, yet the dimensions of the calamity spurred a disunited American Jewry to act, and in many American cities public rallies, meetings of synagogue congregations, and committees of correspondence sprang into existence. Letters from the Jewish communities in New York, Philadelphia, Richmond, and Cincinnati— among other cities—called on President Martin Van Buren to intervene in Damascus.

On August 14, 1840, Van Buren instructed Secretary of State John Forsyth (1780–1841) to convey his "horror" in a letter to the U.S. consul in Alexandria, John Gliddon. Forsyth informed Gliddon that the president could not refrain from "expressing equal surprise and pain, that in this advanced age, such unnatural practices should be ascribed to any portion of the religious world. . . ." Unaware that the president had already taken some action, a group of protesters in New York resolved to convey their distress over the affair directly to Van Buren. The letter that follows was penned by the chair of the New York rally, Israel Baer Kursheedt (1766–1852), and its secretary, Theodore J. Seixas (1803– 1882). This communication—and others written in various U.S. cities—marks the earliest collective action taken by American Jewry on behalf of their oppressed coreligionists living in the Old World.

To His Excellency Martin Van Buren, *President of the United States.*

Sir:—At a meeting of Israelites of the City of New York, held on the 19th inst., for the purpose of uniting in an expression of sympathy for their brethren at Damascus, and of taking such steps as may be necessary to procure for them equal and impartial justice, the following resolution was unanimously adopted:

Resolved, That a letter be addressed to his Excellency, the President of the United States, respectfully requesting that he will direct the Consuls of the United States, in the Dominions of the Pacha of Egypt, to co-operate with the Consuls or other agents accredited to the Pacha, to obtain a fair and impartial trial for our brethren at Damascus.

In transmitting the same to your Excellency, we beg leave to express what we are persuaded is the unanimous opinion of the Israelites throughout the Union, that you will cheerfully use every possible effort to induce the Pacha of Egypt to manifest more liberal treatment toward his Jewish subjects, not only from the dictates of humanity, but from the obvious policy and justice by which such a course is recommended by the intolerant spirit of the age in which we live. The liberal and enlightened views in relation to matters of faith, which have distinguished our Government from its very inception to the present time, have secured the sincere gratitude and kind regard of the members of all religious denominations, and we trust the efforts of your Excellency in this behalf will only serve to render more grateful and to impress more fully on the minds of the citizens of the United States, the kindness and liberality of that Government under which we live.

With the best wishes of those in whose behalf we address you—for your health and happiness, and for the glory and honor of our Common Country, we have the honor to be,

Your Excellency's obedient servants,

I. B. Kursheedt, Chairman
Theodore J. Seixas, Secretary

Source: MS, RG 59, General Records of the Department of State, U.S. National Archives and Records Administration.

4

Slavery and Freedom

AMERICAN JEWS DURING THE CIVIL WAR
AND RECONSTRUCTION, 1861–1879

The sectional crisis in American history coincided with the height of Central European Jewish immigration to the United States in the 1850s. Northerners and southerners debated the status of new states entering the Union as either free or slave, while political disagreements over the relative power of the federal government versus states' rights brought the nation to the brink of civil war with the election of Abraham Lincoln in 1860.

The Civil War and Reconstruction tested long-established American Jewish families as well as the new Central European arrivals. Arguments over slavery pitted Jews in the North and South against one another, with partisans calling on Jewish sources to defend their respective positions. In the North, most Jews vigorously opposed slavery, though not always on ethical grounds. Echoing the sentiments of President Lincoln, these Jews worried more about a divided Union than the "peculiar institution." Other northern Jews did speak out in opposition to slavery, in ways that were closely aligned to the ideals of the abolitionist movement. The Chicago rabbi Bernhard Felsenthal, for instance, insisted in a newspaper article that Jews had a special obligation to oppose slavery in the American South because of their own historic experience with slavery. Yet northerners, including Jews in the mercantile businesses, even though they lived a thousand miles from the South, profited from slavery through their dependence on the Cotton South for their economic success. And at least one northern rabbi cited Jewish texts to justify the institution of slavery.

In the South, Jews acculturated to the communities around them, aided by their categorization as whites in a binary racial system that placed African Americans in servitude. As owners of commercial businesses, Jews enjoyed economic success. They supported synagogues and other Jewish communal organizations just as they enjoyed a large measure of social acceptance from their white Christian neighbors. While only a few southern Jews owned large numbers of slaves, Jews still sided with their southern friends and neighbors as the debates over slavery and the sectional conflict intensified.

During the war, Jewish soldiers fought on both sides of the conflict as rabbis sought official status as chaplains in the armed forces of both the Union and the Confederacy. During the Reconstruction period, Jews in both the North and the South reflected on the horrendous impact of the Civil War and offered their thoughts, mostly pessimistic, on the future of the nation.

4.01—LETTER FROM ALFRED MORDECAI TO HIS BROTHER G. W. MORDECAI, MARCH 17, 1861

The conflicted loyalty of American Jews reveals itself in the story of the Mordecais, one of the "first families" in American Jewish history. The root of the family's American branch was Moses Mordecai, who lived from 1707 until 1781. One of Moses's sons, Jacob Mordecai (1762–1838), had thirteen children with two wives, all of whom, except his son Alfred (1804–1887), settled in the American South. Alfred left the South to study at the United States Military Academy in West Point, New York. After graduating with distinction in 1823, he remained at West Point as an instructor and enjoyed a brilliant career in the military, eventually becoming one of its most highly regarded weaponry experts. On the brink of the Civil War, Maj. Alfred Mordecai had run some of the country's largest weapons arsenals, including arsenals in Washington, D.C. (1833 and again in 1844–1855); Frankford, Pennsylvania (1836); and Watervliet, New York (1857–1861).

In contrast to Alfred's more nuanced attitude toward the conflict between the states, most of his many brothers and sisters were intensely loyal to the South. As we see from the letters he wrote to his brother George Washington Mordecai (1801–1871) on the eve of the Civil War, one of which is included here, Alfred was repulsed by the senseless extremism that gripped both sides of the debate, and he was convinced that a war between the states would be a complete "calamity." Apart from his own political views, Alfred had no intention of taking up arms against his own family members, who were sure to enlist in the Confederate forces. It is also interesting to note that Alfred's own son, Alfred Jr. (1840–1920), himself a graduate of West Point, did indeed elect to fight for the
Union. Like his father, Alfred Jr. amassed a distinguished career of service in the military.

On the threshold of the war, Mordecai asked his commanding officer, Col. James Wolfe Ripley (1794–1870), to assign him to a post in California, far away from the likely battleground. Ripley denied this request and, as we can see from the ensuing communication, Mordecai then resigned his commission. Subsequently, the Confederacy offered him a commission, but he refused this post too.

Ultimately, Alfred Mordecai concluded that if he was "doomed to witness that calamity" he would do so from the sidelines, and this is what transpired. The conflicted military officer taught mathematics as a private tutor while the war raged.

Watervliet [NY] Arsenal, March 17/61
My dear brother:

In these calamitous times it is well that relatives & friends should understand each other's positions, & as my views may not be fully known by our family, I will devote this leisure Sunday to communicating to you so much of them as best as may influence my own action in relation to public affairs.

I do not think it necessary to begin at the beginning & to give you my opinion on the abstract questions of the moral effect, or the social or political advantages & disadvantages of the institution of African Slavery, which has produced the convulsion that is now rending the Union to pieces. To any common sense appreciation of the subject it appears to be sufficient to know that at the formation of our government slavery existed all over the land & was expressly protected by the Constitution from being interfered with by any authority but the states themselves, that therefore the people who have obtained it are entitled to the enforcement of their constitutional right with regard to it, both in the letter and the spirit.

This being conceded, the whole question is as to the best way of maintaining those rights against communities or persons who are inclined to interfere with them. I confess that if, as indicated by the resolution adopted by the late Peace conference, the state of public feeling at the North is so squeamish on this subject that the very *name* of slavery cannot be used in expressing what are meant to be conciliatory measures towards the South, the continuance of harmony between the sections seems to be well nigh hopeless; but I regard the existence of the Union so essential to the welfare & respectability of our country, at home & abroad, that I am unwilling to give up the hope that both sides may yet see the utter madness of the course on which we are rushing to our ruin. Therefore I have avoided doing anything to encourage the revolutionary ideas which prevail among the extremists of both sections; & I have been unwilling, until very lately, to believe that there is any considerable body of our countrymen so insane as to desire a separation of the states, if it can be avoided without a sacrifice of the most valuable & indeed vital principles. In the North, notwithstanding the prevalent feeling against slavery, there is undoubtably a large party who are willing to sustain the South in all that they ask; which is simply, as Mr. Davis expressed it at Boston, to be let alone. Into the late Presidential contest the South entered with the hope that through the aid of this party they might prevail; & it seems to me that they were bound to abide by the result, until it was shown that the administration [indecipherable] of the party which has attained the ascendancy was incompatible with the enjoyment of their essential rights—with the congress, in both branches, opposed to the republican administration, if the Southern states had remained as presented, it would not have been possible to enact any measures seriously injurious to the latter; & if the executive had evinced,

by his recommendations & appointments to office, a disposition to infringe the rights of the South, & had been supported by the public opinion of his own party, the South would have enjoyed the great advantage of being placed obviously in the right, when resistance became necessary, & no doubt also of being sustained in their opposition by a great body of the Northern people. If therefore they were sincere in their desire to maintain the Union as long as possible, it seems to me that it was evidently the duty of the Southern people to try all constitutional remedies, before resorting to the extreme of revolution; nor can I imagine how, by this extreme measure, they can reasonably expect to place themselves in a better & more secure position as regards the preservation of their slaves, & even of the institution of slavery. But I did not mean to enter so fully into the discussion of this political question; I only intended to express my belief that one people, and I should say, the people of the extreme South, have pursued an injudicious & rash course, & I am glad that the Northern slave states have not suffered themselves to be hurried onwards into the precipitate measures of their Southern neighbors. Under these circumstances I have not felt disposed to join in the cause of the extreme South & I have peremptorily declined the advances made to me to enter the service of the Southern states. I have continued to discharge my duty to the government at Washington faithfully & zealously, without any reservation or arrière-pensée, as to the effect on the Southern states of the measures in which I am called upon to assist; hence the arsenal under my charge has presented a sense of unusual activity during the last month or five weeks, in the preparation & forwarding of warlike stores. I hope it is no dereliction of sincerity to wish, with Mercutio's quarrelsome fellow, that "God may send us no need of them."

You are not to suppose, however, that I mean to deny to the Southern people the right to judge of the injury which they have sustained or with which they are threatened, & of the remedy or redress which they shall seek for. On the contrary, if any great body of them think that their existence or happiness is inconsistent with the maintenance of the Union, let them go in peace. But it is at least reasonable to demand that they shall agree among themselves as to the extent of the evils complained of & the nature of the remedy; & not suffer the country to be split up into incoherent fragments, to become the incoherent foes of each other, & the scorn & contempt of the rest of the world. I have no patience to think of the spectacle which our lately prosperous country would present under such circumstances, & no disposition to join in the miserable strife which will result from the entire rupture of our Union. If I am doomed to witness that calamity, which certainly seems to be impending very nearly, you know that I would not take sides against the South; but I confess that I should be almost equally reluctant to enter the ranks against those with whom I have been so long associated on terms of close intimacy & friendship. In such a case, my first wish would be to retire, at least for a time, to private life, & seek in a civil pursuit the means of supporting my family during (what should expect to be) the miserable remnant of my days. But the whole subject is so utterly distasteful to me, that I try my best to put it out of consideration; in the fond hope that, through some wonderful interposition of providence, the necessity for a decision may be averted. I trust there are many officers of the army, from the North as well as the South, who feel as I do on this unhappy subject.

. . . This is the first time that I have attempted to express my opinions on this subject at any length, in writing, & I scarcely even speak of them. So many considerations crowd on me that I dare say I may not have expressed myself very clearly; but I wish my Southern friends to understand my position & I know they will appreciate my motives for adhering, to the last, to the hope, even the most feeble, of a re-adjustment, which may repair this incredible calamity & restore us to respectability in the family of nations.

Although social bonds cannot restrain, when the ties of nations are severed, my family relations with the North may, almost unconsciously & certainly not inexcusably, exert an influence on the decision which I may find myself compelled to make, as to a change of condition; but in this I know that I shall not be liable to misconstruction on your part.

I trust that nothing may prevent my carrying out the intention of making a visit in April with my dear wife to our good mother & all of you. Besides being the pleasantest season for the journey, that is the time when I can most conveniently leave my business here—as soon as we can determine on the time we will let you know.

. . . May we soon meet you all in peace & health.

Ever truly,
[Illegible] brother,
A. Mordecai
Source: SC-8388, AJA.

4.02—PRIVATE LETTER FROM ALFRED MORDECAI TO LT. COL. JAMES W. RIPLEY, ON HIS RESIGNATION FROM THE U.S. ARMY, MAY 2, 1861

Private.
Watervliet Arsenal.,
May 2nd, 1861.
Lieut. Colonel J. W. Ripley.

My Dear Colonel: I am truly sorry that my first private letter to you, since your return,

should be on so unpleasant a subject. I hoped that some arrangement might be made by which my private feelings could be consulted, without a dereliction of duty on the part of the government, but your answer to my official letter leaves me no room to hope for this consideration, and no alternative therefore but to resign. I shall not make known my resignation here until my successor arrives, or until it is announced from Washington; so everything will go on as usual at the Arsenal. If you can send Thornton to relieve me, and quickly, I shall be glad; I think the position is due to his industry and zeal, as well as to his rank.

I have no hesitation in saying confidentially to you, what I have said to my brother and family, that when I contemplated the possible necessity of resigning, in order to avoid engaging in this unhappy contest against my kindred, I had no intention of joining the Southern army. I hoped to be permitted by both sides to retire quietly to private life. I shall make no preparations now which may indicate the course I have taken, hoping that some way be afforded me to pack up such of my furniture and effects as I may not otherwise dispose of. I shall then take my family to Philadelphia and make arrangements for my future life.

Source: SC-8388, AJA.

4.03 — "THE JEWS AND SLAVERY," BY BERNHARD FELSENTHAL, *Sinai*, JULY 1862

Bernhard Felsenthal (1822–1908), born in Münchweiler, Germany, immigrated to America in 1854. After a brief sojourn in Madison, Indiana, where he served for three years as a rabbi and teacher, Felsenthal moved to Chicago in 1858 and began working in a banking house owned by relatives, the Greenebaum Brothers (Elias and Henry). He also became one of the founders of the Jüdische Reformverein, which soon became Sinai Congregation, Chicago's first Reform synagogue. Felsenthal led Sinai until 1864, when he became rabbi of another newly established Reform synagogue, Zion Congregation, located in West Chicago.

In 1862, one of Felsenthal's sermons appeared in the pages of Rabbi David Einhorn's (1809–1879) German newspaper, Sinai. Felsenthal spoke out against slavery. He told his people that if there is anyone in all of humankind who "should nurture the most simmering and irreconcilable hatred against the 'curious institution of the South,'" it should be the Jew. Although he supposed that most Jews, whether living in the North or South, were in their hearts unsympathetic to slavery, Felsenthal conceded that too many southern Jews defended the practice. As the document to follow demonstrates, he offered readers a fascinating contemporary perspective as to why this is so.

Those Israelites residing in New-Orleans are, man for man, with only a few exceptions, strongly for secession, and many among them, "real Fire-eaters." . . . The reason that these gentlemen are so very interested in secession, was always a mystery to me.

That the Israelites in New-Orleans, and probably in the entire South, are, to a large degree, secessionists, is indeed a fact, which, at first, seems strange. How is it possible, one asks oneself in astonishment, that members of a tribe, which for millennia has been oppressed, persecuted, and enslaved, like few here, in America, where they are afforded full freedom, are defenders of the most shameful institution on earth, slavery, and enemies of the struggle for freedom? People, who, each morning and each night thank God for freeing their fathers from Egypt's enslavement; whose brothers and relatives in many German and non-German states in the Old World, today still have to petition and agitate for their own emancipation, here reveal themselves as fanatic apologetics for Negro slavery! People who themselves learned on the European continent, from the point of view of feudalists and clerics opposed to the emancipation of Jews, that they belonged to a different race, and they would, if emancipated, take the bread away from the Christians, that they were, by divine providence, condemned to eternal ranks of slavery, these people would flood that state which declared them to be equal citizens from everywhere, etc. Those people are narrow-minded and mean enough to bring forward those reasons against the emancipation of the Negroes! If anyone, above everyone, the Jew should nurture the most simmering and irreconcilable hatred against the "curious institution of the South," and make the expression *fiat justitia, pereat mundus* (Let there be justice, though the world perish!) his motto.

If one examines the facts more closely, it soon will come out that the alleged predilection of the Jews for Negro-slavery is not as common as one widely seems to believe. Hundreds of Jews, living in the Southern states, have, partly voluntarily, partly forced, at the outbreak of the rebellion, and during its course, left the homes that they had established, because they did not want to swim with the flowing stream. Hundreds of Jews who are today still living in the South are carrying another, no lesser, martyrdom, the martyrdom of silence, and in their hearts they impatiently yearn for the time when the awful rebellion of the aristocrats of the South, with crushed heads, will be down on the ground. Hundreds of Jews, living in the North, who are openly and with heart and soul for the antislavery movement, side with the upright together with the honorable William Lloyd Garrison, who, living for a high ideal, applies the words of their prophet by referring to the statement "the Union as it was, and the Constitution as it is" as an "alliance with death and a contract with hell," and striving in word and deed to make the Declaration of Independence a truth everywhere. Even in the border states, there are Jews who play prominent roles in the movement for emancipation; we have named, for example, the gentlemen [Charles Louis] Bernays from St. Louis, until a year ago editor of the *Report of the West*, M[eyer] Friede and I[sador] Busch, Republican members of the legislature of the Missouri State Convention, L[ewis Naphtali] Dembitz from Louisville, who, as a delegate attended the Chicago Convention, which nominated President Lincoln, etc.

However, the fact is that many Jews sympathize with slavery and the Southern rebellion. What are the reasons?

We want to refrain from the notion that many of the Jews who came from Europe belong to the large class of people unable and too lazy to think, who like the Bourbons learned nothing and forgot nothing. Such people can't help but be taken along by the stream, in whose midst they find themselves; and there is obviously a power against which the Gods themselves fight in vain. Others cannot elevate themselves to a higher, more moral level of observation, and believe the material well-being of the country as well as their own beloved self is in jeopardy, if this "damn agitation of the question of slavery" continues. Those are the fanatics of silence, and in their eyes there is no worse word than agitator or abolitionist. Without doubt, it was nobles of this sort who during the '40s submitted petitions to the provincial court in Posen and to the ministry in Berlin opposing their own emancipation, because back then there was agitation on behalf of the equality of Jews and Christians.

We can, unfortunately, not refrain from noting another reason, which has contributed to the fact that so many Jews are in the opposing camp. The Germans in America, it must be noted in their undying honor, are largely open enemies of slavery. Between a portion of the German Jews and the rest of the Germans there is now a certain antipathy; therefore, because the rest of the Germans are against slavery, some of the Jewish Germans are for the South and slavery. Although it should happily be acknowledged that for eighty years many of the most noble and celebrated Germans, who were born in the realm of Christianity, were brave to openly be in favor of the rights of Jews (we are naming from earlier times, [Gotthold] Lessing and [Ernst] Dohm, from later times, [Friedrich Wilhelm Heinrich Alexander von] Humboldt and [Jakob Philipp] Fallmerayer). The German people, boasting of their humanism and idealism, have not until today entirely succeeded in being just toward the Jews, and in most of the German states Jews occupy politically and socially lesser status and have to act on behalf of their own rights. Not only from 1815 to 1819 did the Christian-Germanic-Romantic spirit make itself manifest in crude Jew-hatred and the brutal slaughter of innocent old men—whose hundreds of sons had just given their lives, fighting for freedom for the "German fatherland"—which despised them, and against the "foreign Frenchie," who treated the Jews as equal citizens. Almost to this day, many leaders of the so-called liberal party, in the press and in the courts, have not been able to overcome their inexplicable Germanic hatred of Jews. While all around, in France, Belgium, Holland, Denmark, Sardinia, the Jews were emancipated, the free-spirited professor in Heidelberg, Paulus, vehemently wrote against the emancipation of Jews, and free-spirited representatives in Munich spoke and voted with the Jesuit Döllinger and Lassaulr, in Karlsruhe with Councilor Buss and Freiherr. And law, in Prussia with Stahl and Wagener, against the emancipation of the Jews. Although we don't want to offend the men of Rotteck and Itzstein in any way, but rather honor them as men who gave great service and achieved great things for the freedom of Germany, in the case of the Jews they were under the sway of an inherited and inbred prejudice. It is inexplicable, but it is a fact. Is it not at least excusable, under such circumstances, if even among some Jews no elevated, noble disposition develops because of these low insults which would make the rise of an aversion against Christian Germans impossible?

A while ago, we heard from a Jew who emigrated from Schleswig, that back home almost all Jews side with the Danish party. And how is one supposed to be surprised by that? Denmark already has granted its Jewish sons all the freedoms, while the Germans in Schleswig and Holstein and the Lutheran pastors are treating the Jews, who are near them, like pariahs. Therefore,

whoever desires it, be enthusiastic for a German Schleswig! Make sure that the feudal ponytail gets cut off as thoroughly as in Denmark, and the Jews will become good Germans like you. You want the Alsace to be a German province again. However, not only the local Jews, but even 99,000 of the local Christians are not in favor. Should the former, who already have been "French" for seventy years, desire the beloved German circumstances, in which they, at most, are "tolerated"? First make sure of justice and full freedom in your own fatherland, then talk about acquiring Alsace again.

But we veered from our subject and will return to it with a few words.

Some Jewish voices have also been publicly heard in favor of slavery, and these too might have contributed to poisoning the opinion of some Jews. One year ago, newspapers in Richmond, Charleston, New Orleans, etc. featured articles with the headline "The Jews Are for Us," and they did not only refer to Judah P. Benjamin and David Levy Yulee, but also to some northern pro-slavery clerics. People such as these always accumulate followers, and it becomes difficult to open the eyes of an ignorant person, who looks up to them as if it were bright lights, because generally he is too stupid to comprehend the reasons for the contempt which others have for them.

At the end the fact should be stated that despite stupidity and pettiness, and despite the efforts of a few demagogues, the large majority of the American Jews completely understands the meaning of the current brutal struggle and the even greater struggle of ideas, and that they are to be found on the side of freedom.

Source: Sermon translated from German original by Ina Remus for the American Jewish Archives. Special thanks to Dr. Timothy Quinn for pointing out that the phrases "German Fatherland" and "foreign Frenchie" come from "To the German Fatherland," a lyric by the nationalist poet Ernst Moritz Arndt (1769–1860). The document epigraph is from a New Orleans correspondence, announced in the *Illinois Staats-Zeitung*, dated June 6.

*Eleanor H. Cohen (1839–1874), a pharmacist's
daughter from Charleston, South Carolina, was
a diarist from the time she was a young child.
For reasons unknown, she destroyed her
childhood reflections, but on February 28, 1865,
Cohen once again began keeping a personal
journal—excerpts of which have been
reproduced to follow. The diary reveals the
preoccupations of a twenty-six-year-old Jewish
southern belle. In addition to the deep love she
professes for her fiancé, Benjamin Seixas
(1832–1884), Cohen expresses her ardent
patriotic commitment to the Confederacy as
well as her unvarnished views on politics and
slavery. The intensity of her feelings for the South
is manifest in her reaction to the news that
Abraham Lincoln has been murdered.*

February 28, 1865

Dear Journal, I suppose you think, as I am
still Miss Cohen and twenty-six, that I am an old
maid. No, for next month was to have smiled
on my wedding, now *indefinitely* postponed. But
I am betrothed, and to one who loves me truly,
fondly, and with his whole heart, and I return
his love. Yes, my noble, precious, darling, come
what may, my heart is yours. I have been engaged six months to Mr. B. M. Seixas. He is very
good-looking, gentlemanly, good-hearted, liberal, honest, and upright, and devotedly attached
to me. My precious love, what would I not give
for a glance at your dear face! . . .

I was to be married in April [1865], father was
going to housekeeping [for himself], all was
bright before me. Mr. Seixas left here on [the]
seventh of February [for Charleston], promising
to come again in March, and in April to come
to claim his promised bride. Vain hope! When
he left me, I felt a foreboding of evil and begged
him to remain here. I made him reiterate again
and again, and tell me repeatedly of his love,

and vow again and again that nothing should
wean his heart from me. . . .

April 16, 1865

Joy is mine, dear Journal. I have had a letter
from my most precious love. He is well and
doing well, is doing business in Charleston, in
dear old King St. He expects us down, but says if
Pa don't come, he will come for me, and be married. Oh, happy I am to be reassured of his love,
to read his fond letter, and know he loves me as
fondly as ever! And yet there is a sad struggle in
my heart, if [whether] to leave my dear parents
in their time of trouble, our cause and country
in her darkest hours, to follow him, or to allow
him to come for his wife, and find her unwilling
to return with him. I do not yet clearly see my
duty. . . . I fear I don't see clearly, for the path
of duty is seldom adorned with flowers. Father,
mother, and all here think I should go. I am getting ready the few things I have to do. Oh, it is
sad to see what my trusseau now will be and
compare it with what it might have been! But my
love loves me not for fine clothes.

April 20, 1865

A dark, heavy cloud dims the brightness that
has illumed my life since I received Mr. S.'s letters. Father call[ed] me and told me a friend had
told him that there was much bad feeling excited towards Mr. S., owing to his intimacy with
the Yankees, and some even declared he was in
their *pay*, and [that Mr. Seixas] had pointed out
Rebel property, and that his life was not safe if
he came up. Father said he wished to write him
not to come up for the present. Farewell to all
my hopes of a speedy marriage, and, saddest of
all, he may come up and be arrested. Oh, God,
have pity on me! I have suffered *greatly*; spare
me *this*.

April 30, 1865

Politically I have much to say. No peace yet
agreed upon, but negociations are being carried

on, and people generally think peace will follow. Abram Lincoln was assassinated in the Washington theatre by a man [John Wilkes Booth] who exclaimed: "Death to traitors; Virginia is avenged!" So our worst enemy is laid low, and [Secretary of State William H.] Seward, the arch fiend, was also stabbed, and today we hear the glorious tidings that the Yankee Congress had a row, and [Vice President] Andy Jonson [Johnson] was killed. God grant so may all our foes perish! I had a short letter today from Mr. S., but it told me he was well, and loved me; so I am happy.

June 2, 1865

I cannot but blame myself for my long neglect of this dear old book, but really I have lived in such a whirl that I entirely forgot to note events, important as they are. Peace has come, but, oh, God, what a different peace to the one we prayed for! We are conquered by superior numbers. Sherman and Johns[t]on declared an armistice; since then, the war is over, we know not on what terms.

Slavery is done away with. Our noble [Confederate President] Jeff Davis, as well as all of our great men, are prisoners; even the governors of the several states have been arrested. Confederate money is worthless, and greenbacks rule the day. Columbia and all the principal [cities] are garrisoned by Yankees. How it makes my Southern blood boil to see them in our streets! Yes, we are again in the hated Union, and over us again floats the banner that is now a sign of tyranny and oppression. [Andrew] Johnson was not killed and is now President. Sad, sad is the change since the days of [President George] Washington. My brothers are all home after fearful deprivations and hardships. Thank God, they are spared. Poor Josh Moses, the flower of our circle, was killed at Blakely [Alabama, April, 1865]. He was a noble man, another martyr to our glorious cause. . . .

Source: As printed in Jacob R. Marcus, ed., *Memoirs of American Jews*, vol. 3 (Philadelphia: Jewish Publication Society of America, 1955), 359–74. SC-11164, AJA.

4.05—ABRAM J. DITTENHOEFER, EXCERPT REGARDING LINCOLN'S ELECTION, FROM *How We Elected Lincoln—Personal Recollections of Lincoln and Men of His Time*, 1860

Abram J. Dittenhoefer (1836–1919), a native of Charleston, South Carolina, who was raised in New York City, established himself as an attorney and worked to elect Abraham Lincoln in 1860. Many years later, Dittenhoefer wrote a memoir titled How We Elected Lincoln, *in which he describes his political maturation and its relationship to Judaism.*

Circumstances brought to me personal knowledge of Mr. Lincoln for nearly four years. I had frequent interviews with him, and so was able to form a well-considered estimate of the great Emancipator's character and personality.

Born in Charleston, South Carolina, of Democratic pro-slavery parents, I was brought in early youth to New York; and although imbued with the sentiments and antipathies of my Southern environment, I soon became known as a Southerner with Northern principles. At that time there were many Northern men with Southern principles.

The city of New York, as I discovered upon reaching the age of observation, was virtually an annex of the South, the New York merchants having extensive and very profitable business relations with the merchants south of the Mason and Dixon line.

The South was the best customer of New York. I often said in those days, "our merchants have for sale on their shelves their principles, together with their merchandise."

[. . .]

At nineteen I was wavering in my fidelity to the principles of the Democratic party, which, in the city of New York, was largely in favor of slavery.

I had just graduated from Columbia College, which was then situated in what is now known as College Place, between Chambers and Murray streets. At that time many of our prominent and wealthy families lived in Chambers, Murray, and Warren streets, and I frequently attended festivities held by the parents of the college boys in the old-fashioned mansions which lined those thoroughfares.

Soon after leaving college I became a student in the law office of Benedict & Boardman, occupying offices in Dey Street, near Broadway. At that time the late John E. Parsons, a distinguished member of the New York bar, was the managing clerk; and Charles O'Conor, the head of the New York bar in that generation, and who, in later years, ran as an Independent candidate for the Presidency, was connected with that firm as counsel.

Sitting one day at my desk, I took up a newspaper, and the debate between Judah P. Benjamin, the rabid but eloquent pro-slavery Senator from Louisiana, and Benjamin F. Wade, the free-soil Senator from Ohio, attracted my attention.

Benjamin had made a strong address in defense of slavery when Wade arose and replied. He began his reply with some bitter and memorable words, words which completely changed my political views.

"I have listened with intense interest," said he, "as I always do to the eloquent speech of my friend, the Senator from Louisiana—an Israelite with Egyptian principles."

My father, who was a prominent merchant of New York in those days, and very influential with the German population, had urged me to become a Democrat, warning me that a public career, if I joined the Republican party, would be impossible in the city of New York. I felt that he was right in that view, as the party was in a hopeless minority, without apparent prospect of ever being able to elect its candidates.

[. . .]

And yet my convictions were irrevocably changed by the reading of Wade's speech in answer to Benjamin. It struck me with great force that the Israelite Benjamin, whose ancestors were enslaved in Egypt, ought not to uphold slavery in free America, and could not do so without bringing disgrace upon himself.

[. . .]

One can hardly appreciate to-day what it meant to me, a young man beginning his career in New York, to ally myself with the Republican party. By doing so, not only did I cast aside all apparent hope of public preferment, but I also subjected myself to obloquy from and ostracism by my acquaintances, my clients, and even members of my own family. . . .

Source: DHJ, 394.

4.06—GRANT'S GENERAL ORDERS NUMBER 11, 1862

Ulysses S. Grant's General Orders Number 11 represents one of the most odious and confounding documents in all American history. On December 17, 1862, Grant authorized the expulsion of the "Jews as a class" *from territory under his military command—the Military Department of Tennessee, which included Tennessee, Kentucky, and parts of Alabama and Mississippi. One of those actually expelled, Cesar J. Kaskel (1833–1892) of Paducah, Kentucky, went to Washington, D.C., and, on January 3, 1863, personally described the experience to President Lincoln. On the spot, Lincoln ordered General-in-Chief Henry Wager Halleck (1815–1872) to revoke the order. To this day, it is difficult to explain the rationale for summarily banishing Jewish men, women, and children from U.S. territory.*

Following are a number of documents relating to this infamous event. First, we reproduce the text of the order itself (sometimes referred to as General Orders Number 12), issued on December 17, 1862, together with General Halleck's official revocation of the order in accordance with Lincoln's directive. Second, we reproduce one of the many letters of protest composed by Jews once they heard news of the order. The letter from the B'nai B'rith Missouri Lodge (which seems to have been one of the first

Jewish organizations to formally protest the action) is dated two days after Lincoln had already revoked Grant's order in Kaskel's presence.

Headquarters 13th Army Corps
Department of the Tennessee
Oxford, Miss. December 17, 1862

I. The Jews, as a class, violating every regulation of trade established by the Tennessee Department, and also Department orders, are hereby expelled from the Department.

II. Within twenty-four hours from the receipt of this order by Post Commanders, they will see that all of this class of people are furnished with passes and required to leave; and any one returning after such notification will be arrested and held in confinement until an opportunity occurs of sending them out as prisoners, unless furnished with permits from their Headquarters.

III. No passes will be given these people to visit Headquarters for the purposes of making personal application for trade permits.

Source: As printed in *JAW*, 199–200. Reprinted with permission of AJHS and Southern Illinois University Press, from *PAJHS* 17 (1909): 71ff; see also John Y. Simon, ed., *Papers of Ulysses S. Grant* (Carbondale: Southern Illinois University Press, 1977), 7:9n1.

4.07—GEN. H. W. HALLECK'S REVOCATION OF GRANT'S ORDERS NUMBER 11, JANUARY 4, 1863

War Department
Washington, January 4, 1863
Major General Grant,
Holly Springs, Miss.

A paper purporting to be a General Orders, No. 11, issued by you December 17, has been presented here. By its terms it expels all Jews from your department.

If such an order has been issued, it will be immediately revoked.

H. W. Halleck
General-in-Chief

Source: As printed in *JAW*, 201. Reprinted with permission of AJHS and Southern Illinois University Press, from *PAJHS* 17 (1909): 71ff; see also John Y. Simon, ed., *Papers of Ulysses S. Grant* (Carbondale: Southern Illinois University Press, 1977), 7:9n1.

4.08—LETTER FROM B'NAI B'RITH MISSOURI LODGE, PROTESTING GRANT'S ORDERS NUMBER 11, JANUARY 5, 1863

United Order B'ne B'rith Missouri Loge [*sic*]
St. Louis. Jan. 5, 1863
To his Excellency
Abr. Lincoln
President U.S.

Sir:
An Order, Expelling and Ostracizing all Jews as a class has been issued by Maj. Genl. U. S. Grant and has been enforced at Holly Springs, Trenton, Corinth, Paducah, Jackson and other places.

In the name of the class of *loyal* citizens of these U.S. which we in part represent.

In the name of hundreds, who have been driven from their houses, deprived of their lib-erty and injured in their property *without* having violated any law or regulation.

In the name of the thousands of our Brethren and our children who have died and are now willingly sacrificing their lives and fortunes for the Union and the suppression of this rebellion.

In the name of religious liberty, of justice and humanity—we Enter our solemn Protest against this Order, and ask of you—the Defender and Protector of the Constitution—to annull that Order and protect the liberties even of your humblest constituents.

Morris Hoffman   Henry Kuttner
Secy   President

Source: Library of Congress, Washington, D.C.

4.09—ISAAC M. WISE, "THE REVOLUTIONARY OBJECT OF EXTREMISTS," EDITORIAL OPPOSING ABOLITIONISM, THE *Israelite*, FEBRUARY 27, 1863

Rabbi Isaac Mayer Wise's political perspectives shed light on the diversity of opinions among American Jews concerning issues such as slavery, states' rights, abolitionism, and civil war. In a series of editorials that appeared in his weekly journal, the Israelite, *Wise typically claimed what was, in his time, a middle ground. Writing in February of 1863—barely two months after the issuance of the Emancipation Proclamation—Wise defended the institution of slavery, but he simultaneously expressed his opposition to extending slavery into the American West. He insisted that the fraying of the Union was fundamentally a states' rights issue and should not be construed as a fight over whether or not slavery should exist. Wise went on to criticize abolitionists for their own racism and their unwillingness to extend the same empathy they showed African Americans to immigrant (Jewish?) Americans, whom the abolitionists largely considered a liability to American life.*

Every dispassionate man acquainted with the history of the last decennium, at least every one who is capable and willing to trace back effects to the causes thereof, will admit that the present rebellion originated in the fanaticism of extremists. "Slavery is a divine institution," is a phrase no older than the anti-slavery preaching from the pulpit. It is the natural product of re-action. Part of the sectarian clergy of the North, together with the leaders of the atheists, materialists and pantheists, initiated the anti-slavery demonstration which, step by step, worked its way into politics, and resulted finally in the present state of affairs. This can not well be denied, as almost all sectarian organs, proceedings of conferences and synods, as well as the atheistical press from the last ten years prove this proposition satisfactorily. . . .

In this part of the revolutionary object the extremes met; but, the clergy of this class has a second, though to them not secondary object in view, to which the other flank of the camp can not agree; they wish to have the constitution changed into a sectarian instrument. Remember these words, they are literally true, and fraught with terrific consequences; for before this object could be attained no less blood than in the present war would be shed. A religious war is the worst form of civic tragedies. In Europe it is THE clerical party that struggles to maintain its influence and power over the balance of men; here it is a clerical party that attempts to impose its claims on a free people. If one thinks of the

currents of blood shed in Europe in disputing the assumed rights and privileges of the clergy, he may form an idea of the blood it would cost here to impose anew those very claims.

Speculation, however, is not the object of this paper; we only propose to state facts. The letters of Thomas Jefferson to several clergymen in opposition to a state church, were frequently mentioned in this journal. That sage succeeded in proving to the American, that an entire separation of state of church are necessary for the benefit of either. Better than half a century this wise doctrine was religiously regarded by the American people. It was not tolerated, that the preacher meddle in politics, or that politics interfere with the affairs of the church. We lived in peace and concord, "Every man under his vine and every man under his fig tree," precisely as long as this fundamental doctrine of liberty was scrupulously regarded.

Of late, however, some preachers turned politicians in the pulpit and Sunday-school, at the conference and synod, in the religious press and petitions to congress, in every possible form down to vulgar electioneering for the political candidate, who endorsed their views. Exactly as old as this practice among us are feuds of all kinds, discord, fanaticism and bloodshed. Exactly as old as this practice is the frightful increase of infidels, who abandon the church on account of her priests.

The desire to change the constitution of the United States into a sectarian instrument, in the earlier stage of its history, appeared quite modest and bashful; it peeped shyly through the crevices of unguarded words. But gradually the advocates took courage, and after the election of President Lincoln, elated by the victory achieved, the advocates of this innovation grew bolder, and demanded of congress to subscribe to and realize it at once. Our readers remember the resolutions of the Pittsburg convention of Presbyterians, introduced two years ago in congress, in which that clergy prayed for the acknowledgment of God, Jesus and abolition of slavery by the nation. Since then the clash of arms only rendered their voices inaudible; but they never ceased speaking and working in this direction. . . .

. . . Every man of ordinary capacities must see the wrong this should impose on law abiding citizens who love justice and peace, but do not believe all and everything proposed in the amendment *in spe*. Still for the benefit of those who never thought of this novel subject, we propose to make some remarks.

The slavery question being purely political we can not discuss it here, so we must limit our remarks to the religious tenets of the paper under consideration.

The people of the United States consist of all the citizens thereof. Although we decide questions by the voice or vote of the majority, still it is not the people, and its vote to wrong any person is as null and void as if one person should vote to wrong all the rest. In order to maintain intact and inviolable this principle of justice to every individual, constitutions are made and adopted, i.e., people enter into a solemn and reciprocal contract, that those in power, officers or majorities, will respect and protect the rights and privileges of the powerless, the governed, the minority, or the individual. This is the definition of a constitution. Violating *the rights* of minorities or of the individual citizen by an amendment to the constitution signifies to repeal that entire instrument, or in another word, to violate the pledges and the honor of the majority of that people who break a most sacred compact.

After the right of a man to his life and limbs, the one to his belief is the most sacred and inviolable. If there is any form of slavery worse than another, it is the slavery of opinion. To insert a creed into the constitution of the state signifies to compel every person being component part of said state, to discard and renounce his own belief and adopt the constitutional creed.—This is the worst form of slavery. None can take of any person his right of belief, a clause of the constitution to the contrary is no law but a violation of rights. So much in regard to the justice of the matter.

[. . .]

In proposing this species of slavery which is worse than the physical one, those men speak of the Law of God. Is there a Law of God that gives you the right to interfere with my conscience? Where is that law which entitles you to force your opinion upon your neighbor? "The Law of God is perfect," but you know nothing thereof.— The Law of God ordains "One law shall be for all," but you cut men into lunatical factions. The Law of God teaches "Love thy neighbor as thyself," which you misinterpret to loving your church members who pay your salaries. The Law of God teaches "Every righteous man is God's own son" and you disgrace the image of God by your theories of hell and damnation, original sin and universal depravity, devil and demons, to frighten him into your churches and increase your salaries. The law of God teaches religious liberty and you teach slavery in its worst form. You want to free the black and enslave the white man. You are all humanity for the black, and have hearts like rock and flint for the sufferings of the white. If so many Negroes had been injured as were Hebrews by the order of General Grant, the bottomless absurdities of Parson [William Gannaway] Brownlow,[1] and the heartless agent of the Associated Press; you would have cried as loudly as the people of Sodom and Gomorrah; but for the white Hebrew who gave you a God and a religion, you had not a word to say. We know you, priests, we know you thirst after an inquisition and a seat for every bishop in congress, we know you and will always oppose you. So will every liberal man, and we are the majority and shall never allow the minority to enslave us. Onward and not backward, by science, philosophy and true piety and not by sectarian mysticism and fanaticism; onward to light, to the union of mankind and the domination of justice, and not backward to priestly darkness, to factions and the reign of fanaticism the way of Providence leads. This is the law of God, foreign to narrow minds, clear to His servants, "the righteous walk therein, and transgressors stumble thereon."[2]

1. William Gannaway "Parson" Brownlow (1805–1877) was a minister, newspaper editor, and politician. Possessed of uncompromising opinions and inclined toward inflammatory rhetoric, Brownlow had ardent admirers and bitter enemies. He served as governor of Tennessee from 1865 to 1869 and as a U.S. senator from Tennessee from 1869 to 1875.

2. Hosea 14:9.

Source: Isaac Mayer Wise Digital Archive, AJA.

4.10—MYER S. ISAACS TO ABRAHAM LINCOLN ON THE JEWISH VOTE IN THE 1864 ELECTION, OCTOBER 26, 1864

On October 26, 1864, a week before the U.S. presidential election, the young journalist Myer S. Isaacs (1841–1904), the son of Rev. Samuel Myer Isaacs (1804–1878), a religious leader and the editor of New York's Jewish Messenger, *composed a letter of concern to Abraham Lincoln regarding the impending national election. The twenty-three-year-old Isaacs—who was also secretary of the Board of Delegates of American Israelites—had heard that a group of Jewish leaders had recently gone to the White House to assure Lincoln that he would win the "Jewish vote." Although Isaacs shared his belief that the President would indeed most likely win such a majority in the Union, he also wanted Lincoln to know that, in America, Jews voted as individuals and were not mandated to vote as a block or to follow the dictates of their religious leaders.*

Private
Jewish Messenger Office
119 West Houston Street,
New York, October 26th 1864
Your Excellency:

As a firm and earnest Union man, I deem it my duty to add a word to those that have doubtless been communicated to you from other sources, with reference to a recent "visitation" on the part of persons claiming to represent the Israelites of New York or the United States and pledging the "Jewish vote" to your support, and, I am informed, succeeding in a deception that resulted to their pecuniary profit.

Having peculiar facilities for obtaining information as to the Israelites of the United States, from my eight years' connection with the Jewish paper of this city and my position as Secretary of their central organization, the "Board of Delegates"—in which capacity I have had the honor heretofore of communicating with yourself and the Departments—I feel authorized to caution you, Sir, against any such representations as those understood to have been made.

There are a large number of faithful Unionists among our prominent coreligionists—but there are also supporters of the opposition; and, indeed the Israelites are not, as a body, distinctively Union or democratic in their politics. In the conduct of our Journal for example, while, from the first firing upon our national flag, there has been a steady support of the government in its efforts to maintain the integrity of the Union and crush the unhallowed rebellion, there has also been a studied persistence in the expression of what is an implicit belief, that the Jews, as a body, have no *politics*: and while we have earnestly counseled & implored attachment to the Union at whatever cost, we have refrained from interfering with the private political views of individual readers. This is predicated on our direct knowledge of the character and opinions of our coreligionists.

Therefore, Sir, I am pained and mortified to find that you had been imposed upon by irresponsible men, animated, I am sure by mercenary motives; and I wish to inform you with all promptitude, that such acts are discountenanced and condemned most cordially by the community of American Israelites—As an illustration that an influential class of Jewish citizens are warm adherents of the administration, you have the fact that a Hebrew will cast for you the vote of a New York city congressional district. A single Union meeting this week presented these facts: the chairman of the Executive Committee & Committee of Arrangements, the gentlemen who presented the resolutions, two principal speakers and many prominent persons upon the platform, were Jews.—I refer to the German Union Mass Meeting on Monday night.

It is because I sympathize heart and soul with the action of government in using every means to restore the Union and overthrow the machinations of those who seek its disruption, that I the more regret this attempt to deceive you. There is no "Jewish vote"—if there were, it could not be bought. As a body of intelligent men, we are advocates of the cherished principles of liberty & justice, and must inevitably support and advocate those who are the exponents of such a platform—"liberty & Union, now and forever."

Pardon the liberty I take in thus trespassing on your attention, but I pray that you will attribute it to the sole motive I have, that of undeceiving you and assuring you that there is no necessity for "pledging" the Jewish vote which does not exist—but at the same time that the majority of Israelite citizens must concur in attachment for the Union and a determination to leave no means untried to maintain its honor and integrity.

With the expression of high esteem, I am, sir,
Yours Most Respectfully,
Myer S. Isaacs

Source: Library of Congress, Washington, D.C.

4.11—RESOLUTION OF THE HEBREW CONGREGATION IN SUPPORT OF THE CONFEDERACY, SHREVEPORT, LOUISIANA, MAY 1861

Weeks after the outbreak of the Civil War, Samuel Myer Isaacs (1804–1878), editor of the Jewish Messenger, *published an editorial titled "Stand by the Flag!" The paper called upon its readers to remain loyal to the Union. But the leadership of Shreveport, Louisiana's Hebrew Congregation took umbrage at Isaac's editorial. In a strongly worded response, the Jews of Shreveport called on their fellow parishioners to cancel their subscriptions to the northern periodical. Shreveport's editorialists wanted to make it crystal clear that they had every intention of "standing by the flag"—the flag of the Confederacy!*

Whereas, we received the "Jewish Messenger" of the 26th of April, a paper published in New York, in which an appeal has been made to all, whether native or foreign born, Christian or Israelite. An article headed "Stand by the Flag!" in which the editor makes an appeal to support the stars and stripes, and to rally as one man for the Union and the Constitution. Therefore be it

Resolved, That we, the Hebrew congregation of Shreveport, scorn and repel your advice, although we might be called Southern rebels, still, as law-abiding citizens, we solemnly pledge ourselves to stand by, protect, and honor the flag, with its stars and stripes, the Union and Constitution of the Southern Confederacy with our lives, liberty, and all that is dear to us.

Resolved, That we, the members of said congregation, bind ourselves to discontinue the subscription of the "Jewish Messenger," and all Northern papers opposed to our holy cause, and also to use all honorable means in having said paper banished from our beloved country.

Resolved, That while we mistook your paper for a religious one, which ought to be strictly neutral in politics, we shall from this out treat it with scorn, as a black republican paper, and not worthy of Southern patronage; and that, according to our understanding, church and politics ought never to be mingled, as it has been the ruination of any country captivated by the enticing words of preachers.

Resolved, That we, the members of said congregation, have lost all confidence and regard to the Rev. S. M. Isaacs, Editor and Proprietor of the "Jewish Messenger," and see in him an enemy to our interest and welfare, and believe it to be more unjust for one who preaches the Word of God, and to advise us to act as traitors and renegades to our adopted country, and raise hatred and dissatisfaction in our midst, and assisting to start a bloody civil war amongst us.

Resolved, That we believe like the Druids of old, the duties of those who preach the Holy Word to be first in the line of battle, and to cheer up those fighting for liberty against their oppressors, in place of those who are proclaiming now from their pulpits, words to encourage an excited people, and praying for bloody vengeance against us. Brutus, while kissing Caesar, plunged the dagger to his heart.

Resolved, That a copy of these resolutions be sent to the editor of the "Jewish Messenger."

Resolved, That papers friendly to the Southern cause, are politely requested to publish the foregoing resolutions.

M. Baer, *President.*

Ed. Eberstadt, *Secretary, pro tem.*

Source: DHJ, 439–41. From the *Jewish Messenger*, June 7, 1861, p. 172, col. 3.

4.12—EUGENIA LEVY PHILLIPS, DIARY REPORTING THE AUTHOR'S EXPERIENCES AS A CONFEDERATE, 1861

Eugenia Levy Phillips (1820–1902) was a thoroughgoing southern patriot. Born in Charleston, South Carolina, she eventually moved to Mobile, Alabama, with her husband, Philip Phillips (1807–1884), in the 1830s. In 1852, Eugenia moved with Philip, who had been elected to serve as his district's representative in the U.S. House of Representatives, to Washington, D.C. After just one term in office, Philip left Congress, but he and his family remained in the nation's capital, where he pursued his legal career. Although her husband was unquestionably in favor of preserving the Union, Eugenia Phillips was an outspoken partisan of the South. At the onset of the Civil War in 1861, Union forces entered Phillips's home in Washington and arrested her for supporting the Confederacy. During her three weeks of incarceration, Eugenia recorded a diary of her experiences. The values and ideals she professed were similar to those of thousands of southern patriots.

Seated in my parlor, enjoying the company of a quiet but nervous friend, Miss Margaret L., on the morning of the twenty-third [twenty-fourth] August, I was suddenly attracted by a noise in the hall. On turning my head in that direction, I observed two men enter the room, and was immediately accosted with the enquiry: "Are you Madam, Mrs. Phillips"? Replying in the affirmative, I was again asked if the gentleman of the house was in. Comprehending at once the position, and hoping to give P. L. [my husband] time to collect his thoughts and determine his course, I answered evasively, I did not know. I was then informed that my family was arrested in the name of the government. . . .

In Prison

Thursday 28 August 1861

This day has ushered in a new era in the History of the Country, one which marks the ar-

rest and imprisonment of women, for political opinions! At eleven o'clock we were notified by an officer that my sister (a visitor)[,] my two daughters and myself were by the orders of the government to be taken from our house, and conveyed as prisoners to another place of confinement. We immediately prepared with courageous hearts, inspired with the thought that we were suffering in a noble cause, and determined so to bear ourselves, as not to shame our southern countrywomen. My dear husband was my chief sorrow. For ourselves, conscious we had done no wrong, we feared nothing. After a brief interval of preparation, we were borne away from our home, and here we are, confined to two small rooms of the upper story of a house on [an unknown] street, an armed guard placed at the chamber door.

Friday 30 August 1861

. . . Again I ask myself what is my crime?

If an ardent attachment to the land of my birth and the expression of deepest sympathy with my relatives and friends in the South, constitute treason—then I am indeed a traitor. If hostility to Black Republicanism, its sentiments and policy—is a crime—I am self condemned—! If detestation of this unholy war, inaugurated by party lust—is deserving punishment, then am I worthy of its severest penalties—! and thus suffering I would shout Hosannas for the glorious cause of southern independence.

Monday, 9 Sept.

We are again made happy with the glorious intelligence that President Davis *is not dead*! May he long live to vindicate the rights of the South and to place his own name where it properly belongs at the side of Washington's!

One of the letter writers in today's paper suggests that the "lady prisoners" should be punished by depriving them of their *mirrors*. They may probably learn that these "lady prisoners" care for no reflection, but such as they are justified in making upon the infamy of the Government and its minions.

Source: As printed in Marcus, *Memoirs of American Jews,* 3: 163–96. Used with permission of the College of Charleston, Special Collections and Digital Initiatives.

4.13—TWENTY-YEAR BOND ISSUED BY THE CONFEDERACY IN HONOR OF JUDAH P. BENJAMIN, 1861

On August 19, 1861, the Confederate States of America honored its first attorney general, Judah P. Benjamin (1811–1884), by issuing a twenty-year bond bearing his image. Three years later, Benjamin, who had served as the Confederate secretary of war and, subsequently, secretary of state, was feted once again when his *likeness was emblazoned on the Confederate two-dollar bill. Prior to the outbreak of the war, Benjamin served as a U.S. senator from Louisiana. He was one of the first American Jews to serve in the U.S. Senate, and the only Jew whose countenance appeared on currency in the New World.*

Source: Used with permission of the College of Charleston, Special Collections and Digital Initiatives.

Source: Rare document, AJA.

4.15—ISAAC LEVY TO HIS SISTER, LEONORA, DETAILING THE CELEBRATION OF PASSOVER AT A CONFEDERATE ENCAMPMENT IN ADAM'S RUN, SOUTH CAROLINA, APRIL 24, 1864

In 1864, Isaac Levy (1843–1864), a Jewish Confederate soldier from Richmond, Virginia, was stationed with the Forty-sixth Virginia Infantry near Adam's Run, South Carolina. Isaac composed a letter to his younger sister, Leonora (1848–1925), detailing how he and his older brother, Ezekiel (1833–1908), had celebrated the festival of Passover in April of 1864. Tragically, only four short months later, young Isaac would lose his life along with 210 of his compatriots in the bloody battle of Globe Tavern in Petersburg, Virginia.

Adams Run April 24th, 1864

Dear Leonora,

No doubt you were much surprised on receiving a letter from me addressed to our dear parents dated on the 21st inst. which was the first day of Pesach. We were all under the impression in camp that the first day of the festival was the 22nd and if my memory serves me right I think that Ma wrote me that Pesach was on the 22nd inst. Zeke [Isaac's brother Ezekiel J. Levy] was somewhat astonished on arriving in Charleston on Wednesday afternoon, to learn that that was the first Seder night. He purchased *matzot* sufficient to last us for the week. The cost is somewhat less than in Richmond, being but two dollars per pound. We are observing the festival in a truly Orthodox style. On the first day we had a fine vegetable soup. It was made of a bunch of vegetables which Zeke brought from Charleston containing new onions, parsley, carrots[,] turnips and a young cauliflower also a pound and a half of fresh [kosher] beef, the latter article sells for four dollars per pound in Charleston. Zeke E. did not bring us any meat from home. He brought some of his own, smoked meat, which he is sharing with us, he says that he supposes that Pa forgot to deliver it to him.

No news in the section at present. Troops from Florida are passing over the road enroute for Richmond. 'Tis probable that we will remain in this department and were it not for the unhealthy season which is approaching, would be well satisfied to remain here.

We received this morning Sarah's letter of the 18th inst. and are truly sorry to hear that her sight is affected and that in a few days she will have recovered entirely her perfect sight.

Love to all,
Your affectionate Brother
Isaac J. Levy

Source: Rare document, AJA.

4.16—ISAAC M. WISE, "ON TO RICHMOND," DESCRIBING CONDITIONS IN THE RECONSTRUCTION SOUTH, THE *Israelite*, JUNE 28, 1867

Two years after the war's end, Rabbi Isaac Mayer Wise journeyed from his home in Cincinnati to Richmond, Virginia, observing conditions in the war-torn South as he traveled. After his return, he published his reflections on the experience in his newspaper, the Israelite. *Wise offered his readers a grim and pessimistic analysis in which he inaccurately predicted the takeover of the South by its black inhabitants. The aftermath of the war made him "sick," and the rabbi blamed selfish politicians for the havoc wreaked upon the nation. Interestingly, he predicted that the South would never recuperate from the economic devastation it suffered. In ominous tones, Wise prophesied that before the end of the nineteenth century the North would again battle the South, but this time the war would be a racial conflagration wherein whites from the North would fight blacks from the South.*

Richmond being of historical importance—it was that already before the war—I looked upon it with an unusual degree of curiosity. Right at the bridge over the James river I saw the ruins, the terrible witnesses of that awful Sunday night when Lee and his army left, and a band of fanatics, thieves, and ruffians, set the city on fire. I have never been able to see the point in that awkward policy of burning cotton, tobacco, and towns, to punish the Yankees, which actually impoverished the South. This policy is visible in the ruins of Richmond and the poverty of the people. The principal business houses have been rebuilt; but the factories and private houses are still in ruins. Still this is only a small portion of the city, which has not been damaged. The United States Custom House, standing in the midst of the burning houses, as it did, escaped unhurt, not by any particular miracle, but by the nature of its fire-proof structure.

[...]

Posterity will consider us an admirably generous class of people, who not only expunged the disgrace of slavery at an expense of a million of men and three thousand millions of treasure, and now support a standing army at an expense of two hundred millions a year, to protect the freedmen; but also virtually give them eleven States, to be entirely under their control and safe-keeping. As inevitable as fate, the eleven Southern States are to belong to the negroes. The enfranchisement of the negro and the disfranchisement of so many white men, places the destiny of those States entirely in the hands of the negro. The next consequences will be, that as many white men as will possibly be able to sell out, will go to the North. This again is as inevitable as fate; for the Southern man will not submit to negro rule one minute longer than he must. His only alternative is to sell out and go, as tens of thousands would do this day, if property was not now at so low a figure. Besides, the longevity and prolification of the negro in that climate gives him a natural advantage over the white race, and must, in time, press it from those States. The next consequence of the emigration of the white, will be a new imigration [*sic*] of negroes from Africa. Eleven negro legislatures, the representatives of eleven States in Congress, the thinly populated country, the want of labor, the better climate than the African, the good government and the rich country—take all these circumstances together, and you can not deny that the Southern States, in the course of twenty-five years, will be a new Africa, as the North is a New Europe. I do not know whether anybody has calculated these inevitable results; still they are inevitable. Anybody can see that a thousand Africans will emigrate to America, where negroes have the full political power, before one American will go to Africa. Congress, whenever eleven negro States shall be represented therein, will not think more of prohibiting emigration from Africa than from any other part of the world.

[...]

Friday, May 31st, was a great gala day for the garrison—parade and review. Meanwhile the ladies of Richmond visited the graves of confederate soldiers and decorated them. It is a melancholy satisfaction to the poor people to decorate the graves of their sons, brothers, husbands, and fathers, who died in a lost cause. I was also on the Jewish burial ground, where the confederate soldiers, as many as could be ascertained, are buried side by side, the graves decorated in a simple style. I found many a name of persons I have known well in former days, mostly young Germans. The Hebrew congregations of Richmond have done all in their power to preserve the names, &c., of those fallen soldiers. They ought to be published in the Jewish papers, for information of their friends in the old countries. These graves, and the decoration of these mournful and silent mounts, made me feel sick. I felt sick at the manufacturers of politics; most of them are reckless human beings, who care little for the feelings, prosperity, or life of their fellowmen. This war of politicians has inflicted a wound upon our country which this century will not heal.

[...]

If one believes the reconstruction in 1869, after the presidential election—it will not be done before—closes this terrible drama, he is decidedly mistaken. The elements to a new catastrophe are already collecting. Before the close of this century another war with the South is inevitable; but then it will not be necessary to wear different uniforms, the faces will tell. The South will never be what it was, her cotton trade is ruined. The white people will leave as fast as they can. That is the end of it.

Source: Isaac Mayer Wise Digital Archive, AJA.

4.17—DOUBLE LYNCHING OF A JEW AND A NEGRO, THE *Israelite*,
AUGUST 28, 1868

In the years after the Civil War, the federal government sought to "reconstruct" the South— largely against the will of the majority of its white citizens. Southern states were compelled by law to enfranchise the African American, democratize the local government, promote a wider distribution of land among the citizenry, foster the growth of manufacturing, and so on. Under the watchful eye of the U.S. military, many African Americans, together with a minority of whites—some of whom came to the South from the North—actively supported these changes.

Yet many southerners were determined to resist Reconstruction, and some used the threat of physical violence to intimidate those who cooperated in the government's transformational objectives. In 1866, six Confederate veterans organized a vigilante group called the Ku Klux Klan in Pulaski, Tennessee, in order to oppose the program of Reconstruction and reinstate white supremacy in the South. The KKK was actually one of many vigilante groups that arose during this era and used terroristic tactics to restore the South's old social order.

The sad saga of S. A. Bierfield illustrates the cultural war that raged in the South during these years. Bierfield, a Russian Jew who came to Franklin, Tennessee, after the Civil War to open a small dry goods business, hired a black man named Lawrence Bowman to be a clerk in his shop. Local vigilantes branded Bierfield a "Black" Republican—a contemptuous label used by white southerners to describe those who supported giving African Americans equal footing under the law. On August 15, 1868, masked men on horseback broke into Bierfield's store, lynched him and Bowman, and wounded another African American who lived to describe the details of this double murder. The newspaper article that follows is one of a number of contemporary accounts that appeared in the press during the weeks after the brutal murders.

The deliberate and fiendish murder of Mr. Bierfeld, an Israelite, and a gentleman of good standing and character, as also the murder at about the same time a Negro in Bierfeld's [*sic*] employ, has been reported a week ago by telegraph, but so vaguely, that we refrained from mentioning the dark affair until the receipt of a more reliable account. This we find in the Nashville *Republican* of the 19th inst., sent us by a friend, and we reproduce the same below. The hands of the Ku Klux are, doubtless, red with guilt in the sad premises, and their real grounds consisted of but the fact, that Bierfeld was an intelligent advocate of the present reconstruction policy of Congress, and a friend to the freedmen of his neighborhood, among whom—he being a merchant—he commanded quite a trade, and perhaps found it expedient to keep one from among their number in his employ, who shared the fate of his employer at the same hands.

The scarce less detestable creatures who apologized for the hounds in human guise on the surmise that Bierfeld was accessory to the murder of a young man a few days previous, are liars inferentially we are safe to say, since no member of the Jewish race in this country, if in the world, at the present day would be accessory to a foul murder, and that, too, in a locality where he lives in peace, and prospers as a merchant. We let the aforesaid journal speak, display lines and all:

TERRIBLE MURDERS
Two Men Killed in Franklin by a Lot of Armed Horsemen
The *Press and Times* of a late issue contains the following: At eleven or twelve o'clock on

Saturday night, as great crowds of people were going to their homes after leaving Robinson's circus, a troop of horsemen dashed into town, yelling frightfully, and telling the crowd which they passed to get into their houses as quickly as possible. In a few moments every one was in doors, and a dead silence reigned around, save when heavy sounds were borne on the night from the dry-goods store of one Bierfeld, an Israelite, who carried on a little business in that line, and had a Negro man employed selling goods for him. The horsemen were breaking in his house. They dragged the Israelite out. They were about to hang him when he escaped and ran some hundred yards away from his house and took refuge in a livery stable. His enemies were upon him immediately, pistol in hand. They shot four balls into him, from the effects of which he died almost instantly. The colored man remained in the store, where they found and shot him through the body. He died yesterday morning.

The cause of the intense enmity which could ripen into so fearful a crime is not definitely known. Our informants, Dr. Cliffe and N. J. Nichol, said it was thought that Bierfeld had something to do with the murder of young Ezell, some two or three weeks ago. He is the same man that was driven out of Pulaski some months since by the same sort of fellows.

There is no apparent cause for the murder of the colored man. When the fiendish outrage had been committed, the squad of troopers rode furiously out of town, whooping and hallooing frightfully.

Since the above was in type, we have received the following statement from a gentleman from Franklin:

"On Saturday night, the 15th inst., about eleven o'clock, Mr. Bierfeld, an Israelite, who was engaged in trading, fled from his store scared by men in disguise who had entered his place of business and attempted to conceal himself in Mr. Bostick's stable, but was pursued by the said disguised parties, and violently and forcibly dragged into the streets. While pleading for his life, and begging them to spare him for his mother's sake, he was shot four times in the breast. This happened in the streets of Franklin, near Mr. Briggs' store. If any one offered to intercede for him, it is not known. The parties who say they know the reason why he was killed by the men in disguise, alledge [sic] that he was in some way connected with the killing of Ezell, and that the foul deed was done in retaliation. Six or eight witnesses will testify that Mr. Bierfeld, on the night of the killing of Ezell, slept in the house of Mr. Colby. The good citizens condemn the atrocious act, while others attempt to justify the crime by saying that it was done in retaliation. Mr. Bierfeld was an active and prominent Republican, having considerable influence with the colored people."

Our informant says that was his only crime. A clerk of Mr. Bierfeld, whose name we can not learn, was killed at the same time, and by the same parties. Mr. Bierfeld's body was brought to Nashville yesterday for interment.

Source: Isaac Mayer Wise Digital Archive, AJA.

4.18—BENJAMIN F. PEIXOTTO, U.S. CONSUL IN ROMANIA, TO PRESIDENT ULYSSES S. GRANT, DENYING ACCUSATIONS "OF A SCANDALOUS CHARACTER" LEVELED AGAINST HIS PERSON, NOVEMBER 6, 1871

Benjamin Franklin Peixotto (1834–1890) was one of the most prominent Jewish leaders of the nineteenth century. Born in New York, Peixotto moved to Cleveland, Ohio, after his father died in 1843, where he ultimately became an attorney and engaged himself in Jewish communal affairs. Peixotto was involved in the national Jewish fraternal organization B'nai B'rith and, in 1863, at twenty-nine, he became the Grand Master of the Order. After the Civil War, Peixotto moved to San Francisco, where he established a successful law practice. In 1870, President Ulysses S. Grant appointed Peixotto to serve as consul-general to Romania. Grant's appointment of a Jewish American was intended to remind the Romanian government that, in the United States, Jews enjoyed full equality and that Romania should embrace the same policy.

Once in Bucharest, Peixotto hoped to persuade the Romanians to emancipate the Jews, but there was little governmental support for his efforts. His ambitions on behalf of Jewish emancipation were also opposed by a group of wealthy and assimilated French-speaking Romanian Jews. Eventually, Peixotto abandoned his initiative to persuade the Romanians to enfranchise the Jews in favor of encouraging his persecuted coreligionists to immigrate to the United States.

While he was working for the emancipation of his Romanian coreligionists, Peixotto also promoted the idea of secular education for Jewish Romanians. He hoped to raise funds to create schools that would prepare Romanian Jews to be citizens worthy of the same rights that English, German, and French Jews enjoyed. Evidently, President Grant received word that Peixotto was using his post as consul to raise these funds by putting undo pressure on donors and by advocating his cause in the local press. Peixotto forcefully defended himself from these assertions in a letter of explanation to the president, saying "the accusations are wholly devoid of truth."

Bucharest, 6th Nov., 1871

My dear General:

I have today received a despatch from the State Dept. saying information had reached the

Gov. of a scandalous character, i.e.: that I had requested large sums of money from individuals in Europe to support with dignity my consulate, and for influencing the press, and that you had requested to know what explanation I had to offer in response. Such undefined and unqualified charges could have but one reply, and I have returned that answer; viz: that the accusations are wholly devoid of truth.

And this is the fact.

No american would make such charges and if a European alleged such, there must be some reason for this accusing a man who has made every sacrifice to help forward the cause of humanity and justice.

Who is my accuser? who are my maligners? That I have written to Baron Wilhelm Rothschild of Frankfort [Germany] is true, and told him very freely of the actual situation of the Israelites of this country, which is dreadful. But I had his warrant for these letters—as last winter, while in Frankfort on my way hither, he requested me write to him. I have complied and very frankly told him that to effect the civil and political liberty of the Jews of Roumania the only way to secure them from persecution is to furnish means to render my quiet, unostantate [sic] social and diplomatic labors, a success. I do not think any communication has reached the Gov. from that source. If you desire I can obtain from Prince Charles a letter that I have been true in all respects to the outward forms required of any foreign representative, and that my quiet but earnest pleadings made in the social circle of my own home, in his Palace, or among the influential of his Court have always had his sanction and approval.

He is earnestly desirous that my Mission shall be successful and that this laurel—the Emancipation of the Jews of Roumania—may be his to wear and perpetuate.

I think you will believe your countryman before all the liars, maligners or secret foes—the friends of despotism and intolerance—and I have told Mrs. Peixotto, to whom I have shown the State Dept. communication as much. She believes with me and apropos desires me to express the renewal of her thanks joined with my own, for that act of courtesy manifested towards her when on her way to visit her parents in Kentucky before coming hither with her large little brood, she had the honor of meeting your Excellency. An act of courtesy which we shall always cherish with the liveliest remembrance of respect and gratitude.

Dear General don't believe the lies of the enemies and ignorant, but trust to the faith, the honor, the patriotism and devotion of your fellow countryman and friend.

Benj. F. Peixotto

To his Excellency
Ulysses S. Grant
President of U.S. of A.

Source: E. Lifschutz, "Benjamin Peixotto's Mission to Rumania," *Zion: A Quarterly for Research in Jewish History* 26, no. 2 (1961): 98. AJA, nearprint file.

4.19—MORRIS RAPHALL, "THE BIBLE VIEW OF SLAVERY: A DISCOURSE," A DEFENSE OF SLAVERY BY A NORTHERN RABBI, JANUARY 4, 1861

On December 14, 1860, President James Buchanan issued a proclamation calling on the people of the United States to observe a day of "Humiliation, Fasting and Prayer throughout the Union . . . in view of the present distracted and dangerous condition of our country."

To honor Buchanan's proclamation, Rabbi Morris J. Raphall (1798–1868) delivered an address entitled "The Bible View of Slavery" to his congregation, B'nai Jeshurun, of New York City. This sermon—which Raphall also delivered a week later to a largely non-Jewish audience at the New York Historical Society—sparked a firestorm of controversy that spread across the nation.

Despite insisting he was not defending southern slavery, the rabbi argued that, as far as the Hebrew Bible was concerned, "slaveholding [was] not only recognized and sanctioned as an integral part of the social structure . . . [but] the property in slaves [was] placed under the same protection as any other species of lawful property."

Raphall's address—excerpted and printed as follows—was published and circulated throughout the nation. Southerners insisted the rabbi was defending their cause, and those who opposed slavery were appalled by the implications of Raphall's argument.

On January 9, 1861, Rabbi David Einhorn (1809–1879), a leading reformer, put pen to paper and composed a vigorous critique of Raphall's assessment. While granting a moral understanding for slaveholders who were, in Einhorn's mind, simply adopting the dominant values of their surrounding communities, the Reform rabbi challenged the validity of Raphall's assertions. Einhorn's opposition to slavery eventuated in his flight from Baltimore that same year. He moved to Philadelphia,

where he became the rabbi of the Keneseth Israel congregation.

Einhorn's article, excerpted here, first appeared in his German-language periodical, Sinai, *and was subsequently translated into English by his daughter, Johanna Einhorn Kohler (1848?–1932).*

My Friends—We meet here this day under circumstances not unlike those described in my text. Not many weeks ago, on the invitation of the Governor of this State, we joined in thanksgiving for the manifold mercies the Lord had vouchsafed to bestow upon us during the past year. But "coming events cast their shadows before," and our thanks were tinctured by the foreboding of danger impending over our country. The evil we then dreaded has now come home to us. As the cry of the prophet [Jonah 3:4], "Yet forty days and Nineveh shall be overthrown," alarmed that people, so the proclamation [of South Carolina on December 20, 1860], "the Union is dissolved," has startled the inhabitants of the United States. The President—the chief officer placed at the helm to guide the vessel of the commonwealth on its course—stands aghast at the signs of the times. He sees the black clouds gathering overhead, he hears the fierce howl of the tornado, and the hoarse roar of the breakers all around him. An aged man, his great experience has taught him that "man's extremity is God's opportunity"; and conscious of his own inability to weather the storm without help from on high, he calls upon every individual "to feel a personal responsibility towards God," even as the King of Nineveh desired all persons "to cry unto God with all their strength"—and it is in compliance with this call of the Chief Magistrate of these United States that we, like the many millions of our fellow-citizens, devote this day to public prayer and humiliation. . . .

. . . If they truly and honestly desire to save our country, let them believe in God and in His Holy Word; and then when the authority of the Constitution is to be set aside for a higher Law, they will be able to appeal to the highest Law of all, the revealed Law and Word of God, which affords its supreme sanction to the Constitution. There can be no doubt, my friends, that however much of personal ambition, selfishness, pride, and obstinacy, there may enter into the present unhappy quarrel between the two great sections of the Commonwealth—I say it is certain that the origin of the quarrel itself is the difference of opinion respecting slaveholding, which the one section denounces as sinful—aye, as the most heinous of sins—while the other section upholds it as perfectly lawful. It is the province of statesmen to examine the circumstances under which the Constitution of the United States recognizes the legality of slaveholding; and under what circumstances, if any, it becomes a crime against the law of the land. But the question whether slaveholding is a sin before God, is one that belongs to the theologian. I have been requested by prominent citizens of other denominations, that I should on this day examine the Bible view of slavery, as the religious mind of the country requires to be enlightened on the subject.

In compliance with that request, and after humbly praying that the Father of Truth and of Mercy may enlighten my mind, and direct my words for good, I am about to solicit your earnest attention, my friends, to this serious subject. My discourse will, I fear, take up more of your time than I am in the habit of exacting from you; but this is a day of penitence, and the having to listen to a long and sober discourse must be accounted as a penitential infliction.

The subject of my investigation falls into three parts:—

First, How far back can we trace the existence of slavery?

Secondly, Is slaveholding condemned as a sin in sacred Scripture?

Thirdly, What was the condition of the slave in Biblical times, and among the Hebrews; and saying with our Father Jacob, "for Thy help, I hope, O Lord!" I proceed to examine the question, how far back can we trace the existence of slavery?

I. [. . .] If we consult Sacred Scripture, the oldest and most truthful collection of records now or at any time in existence, we find the word *Ngebed*[,] "slave," which the English version renders "servant," first used by Noah, who, in Genesis ix, 25, curses the descendants of his son, Ham, by saying they should be *Ngebed Ngabadim*, the "meanest of slaves," or as the English version has it "servant of servants." The question naturally arises how came Noah to use the expression? How came he to know anything of slavery? There existed not at that time any human being on earth except Noah and his family of three sons, apparently by one mother, born free and equal, with their wives and children. Noah had no slaves. From the time that he quitted the ark he could have none. It therefore becomes evident that Noah's acquaintance with the word slave and the nature of slavery must date from before the Flood, and existed in his memory only until the crime of Ham called it forth. You and I may regret that in his anger Noah should from beneath the waters of wrath again have fished up the idea and practice of slavery; but that he did so is a fact which rests on the authority of Scripture. I am therefore justified when tracing slavery as far back as it can be traced, I arrive at the conclusion, that next to the domestic relations of husband and wife, parents and children, the oldest relation of society with which we are acquainted is that of master and slave.

[. . .]

II. Having thus, on the authority of the sacred Scripture, traced slavery back to the remotest period, I next request your attention to the question, "Is slaveholding condemned as a sin in sacred Scripture?" How this question can at all arise in the mind of any man that has received a religious education, and is acquainted with the history of the Bible, is a phenomenon I cannot explain to myself, and which fifty years ago no man dreamed of. But we live in times when we must not be surprised at anything. . . . Receiving slavery as one of the conditions of society, the New Testament nowhere interferes with or contradicts the slave code of Moses; it even preserves a letter written by one of the most eminent Christian teachers to a slave-owner on sending back to him his runaway slave. And when we next refer to the history and "requirements" of our own sacred Scriptures, we find that on the most solemn occasion therein recorded, when God gave the Ten Commandments on Mount Sinai— . . . slaveholding is not only recognized and sanctioned as an integral part of the social structure, . . . [b]ut the property in slaves is placed under the same protection as any other species of lawful property, when it is said, "Thou shalt not covet thy neighbor's house, or his field, or his male slave, or his female slave, or his ox, or his ass, or aught that belongeth to thy neighbor" (Ibid. xx. 17; v. 21). That the male slave and the female slave here spoken of do not designate the Hebrew bondman, but the heathen slave, I shall presently show you. That the Ten Commandments are the word of God, and as such, of the very highest authority, is acknowledged by Christians as well as by Jews. . . . When you remember that Abraham, Isaac, Jacob, Job— the men with whom the Almighty conversed . . . all these men were slaveholders, does it not strike you that you are guilty of something very little short of blasphemy? . . . My friends, I find, and I am sorry to find, that I am delivering a pro-slavery discourse. I am no friend to slavery in the abstract, and still less friendly to the practical working of slavery. But I stand here as a teacher in Israel; not to place before you my own feelings and opinions, but to propound to you the word of God, the Bible view of slavery. With a due sense of my responsibility, I must state to you the truth and nothing but the truth, however unpalatable or unpopular that truth may be.

III. It remains for me to examine what was the condition of the slave in Biblical times and among the Hebrews. . . .

. . . The slave is a *person* in whom the dignity of human nature is to be respected; *he has rights*. Whereas, the heathen view of slavery which prevailed at Rome, and which, I am sorry to say, is adopted in the South, reduces the slave to a *thing*, and a thing can have no rights.

The result to which the Bible view of slavery leads us, is—1st. That slavery has existed since the earliest time; 2d. That slaveholding is no sin, and that slave property is expressly placed under the protection of the Ten Commandments; 3d. That the slave is a person, and has rights not conflicting with the lawful exercise of the rights of his owner. If our Northern fellow-citizens, content with following the word of God, would not insist on being "righteous overmuch," or denouncing "sin" which the Bible knows not, but which is plainly taught by the precepts of men— they would entertain more equity and less ill feeling towards their Southern brethren. And if our Southern fellow-citizens would adopt the Bible view of slavery, and discard that heathen slave code, which permits a few bad men to indulge in an abuse of power that throws a stigma and disgrace on the whole body of slaveholders— if both North and South would do what is right, then "God would see their works and that they turned from the evil of their ways"; and in their case, as in that of the people of Nineveh, would mercifully avert the impending evil, for with Him alone is the power to do so.

Source: DHJ, 407–18. From a pamphlet published in New York by Rudd and Carleton, with a preface by Morris Raphall, dated January 15, 1861.

This is not the first time that we have had occasion to admire the originality of Dr. Raphall; but we never would have given him credit for the originality displayed in a sermon which he delivered on January 4th, and published in the *New York Herald, and in which he claims for the institution of slavery the sanction of the Bible, in language the most positive and decided.* . . .

The point at issue is certainly not whether the South ought to be, or should be deprived of its slaves, for every truly moral man would look upon such an outrage, in view of its horrible effects, as a grievous sin. Nor is it the question, whether the slaveholder, as such, is or is not a moral monster, with whom no kind of commerce should be had. No considerate person will venture to doubt that slaveholders may be men of honor and character; since they have been raised and educated under the influence of this institution, and find consolation in the consciousness that their slaves are treated with humanity. The moral sentiment, in spite of its absolute authority, is subject to all kinds of modification growing out of time and place, and owing to the variation of habits, customs and youthful impressions. Abraham was a slaveholder, and had Hagar for a concubine, and yet he is for us a model of virtue, when we take into consideration the age in which he lived. . . .

The question restricts itself exclusively to this: "Is the institution of Slavery, *per se*, a moral evil or is it not?" And here it is that Dr. Raphall earned for himself the sorry reputation of declaring, on the authority of the divine law, the legitimacy and moral rectitude of slavery, and inveighed sharply against Christian ministers who happen to differ from him. A Jew, the offspring of a race which daily praises God for deliverance from the bondage of Egypt, and whose fellow-believers are to this hour groaning under the heavy yoke of slavery in most of the cities of the old world and crying to the Almighty for help, undertakes to parade slavery as a perfectly sinless institu-tion, sanctioned by God, and to confront those presumptuous people who will not believe it, with somewhat of an air of moral indignation! A more extraordinary phenomenon could hardly be imagined. But when the speaker, in the midst of his oratorical effort, became himself aware of the grandeur of his undertaking, and from a bosom overflowing with loving kindness, the following words escaped his lips, "I find, and I am sorry to find, that I am delivering a pro-slavery discourse, . . . but I stand here to propound to you the word of God," then surely the crown of martyrdom must have descended upon his head, had not the black skull-cap at the time covered the enviable spot.

[. . .]

In the history of the Creation, of which our pious speaker, engaged in his own creative efforts, takes not the least notice, we read: "So God created man in his own image, in the image of God created He him, male and female created He them. And God blessed them and God said unto them, Be fruitful and multiply and replenish the earth, and subdue it: and have dominion over the fish of the sea, and over the fowl of the air, and over every living thing that moveth upon the earth." This passage at least is devoid of any intimation respecting dominion over negroes, except it be assumed that the latter are included in the class of animals that creep upon the earth.

[. . .]

And now, one word to you, my fellow-believers, and more especially to the members of my congregation! Whilst I write this—January 9th—the threatening clouds are still above our heads, and envelope the future of our beloved country in a thick mist. There may be some among us who will hardly justify the open manner in which I have given expression to my convictions of what Moses taught respecting slavery. The Jew is conservative from principle, and intensely so in a land which, in spiritual and material blessings, offers to him everything that he can desire. He wishes for peace, almost at any price, and trembles, perhaps more than any other, for the perpetuation of the Union—like a son for the life of his mother, sick unto death. I also share your patriotic sentiments with my full heart, and join you in the fervent supplication, that God may answer right speedily our prayers for peace. But, whatever party we may follow, we are not permitted to let the sanctuary of our religion be dragged into the political arena, and made subservient to the interests of this or that party, as has been attempted with such publicity, and from a consecrated place, in the instance stated above. The immaculate virtue of the Mosaic principles has been our pride, and our boast, and our weapon these thousands of years. This weapon we cannot yield without supplying our enemies with formidable means of attack; this pride and this boast we dare not, and will not, suffer to be taken from us. It were unpardonable; the greatest triumph of our opponents, and our certain destruction; too dearly exchanged for the unstable and evanescent favors of the moment. Might it not be said, and with justice, as it has already been said, in reference to the lamentable event which has called forth this disclaimer: Look at these Jews! there, where they are oppressed, they cannot find words enough to boast of the humanity of their religion; but where they are free, their preachers pronounce,

on the authority of that "solemn and most holy occasion," on Sinai, the divine sanction of slavery; whilst Christian ministers in the South, and in the presence of the representatives of the people advise moderation, sometimes openly deprecate or plead the force of circumstances in extenuation of the established institution!

I am not a politician, and have nothing to do with politics. But to proclaim in the name of Judaism, that God has consecrated the institution of slavery! Such a shame and reproach the Jewish religious press is in duty bound to disown and disavow, if both are not to be stigmatized for ever. If a Christian clergyman in Europe had delivered a sermon like that of Dr. Raphall, all the Jewish orthodox and reform pens would have immediately been set to work—heaven and earth been summond for witnesses to prove its fallacies—to repel such a foul charge, and to inveigh against this desecration of God's holy name. Why should we, in America, keep silence when a Jewish preacher plays such pranks? Those Jews only who value the dollar more than their God and their religion, can give it their consent and approval.

Source: D. Einhorn, *The Rev. Dr. M. J. Raphall's Bible View of Slavery* (New York: Thalmessinger, Cahn & Benedicks, 1861), 5–22. Reprinted from *Sinai* 6 (1861): 2–22; translated by Mrs. Kaufmann Kohler.

4.21—PETITION FROM AMERICAN JEWS TO THE U.S. SENATE AND HOUSE, ON THE CHAPLAINCY ISSUE, 1861 OR 1862

The Civil War era focused attention on religious pluralism in the military chaplaincy. While the U.S. military charged its chaplains with tending to the religious needs of all soldiers in their command, it only hired Protestant clergy until the 1850s, when Catholic priests first were permitted to serve.

The right of Jewish clergy to serve as military

chaplains became a salient issue after Confederate forces attacked a U.S. military installation at Fort Sumter in South Carolina on April 12, 1861. Lincoln called on Congress to raise a volunteer army from each state. The ninth section of the "Volunteer Bill" authorized regimental commanders to appoint military chaplains for each regiment's soldiers. However, the bill stipulated that all chaplain appointees must be "regular ordained ministers of some Christian denomination."

As the petitions reprinted to follow demonstrate, the chaplaincy controversy quickly became a high communal priority for Jews. Rabbi Isidor Kalisch (1816–1886), a prominent Reform rabbi who was then serving the Indianapolis Hebrew Congregation, asked U.S. senator Lyman Trumbull (1813–1896) to circulate the petition he composed to members of both chambers of Congress. Rabbis from around the country sent petitions similar to Kalisch's, which is included here. Presidents of Jewish organizations similarly expressed their dissatisfaction with the chaplaincy law. The resolution sent to Abraham Lincoln from the B'nai B'rith lodge in St. Louis, also included, is illustrative of this writing campaign.

In December of 1861, the Board of Delegates of American Israelites asked a New York rabbi who had already applied to serve as a military chaplain, Arnold Fischel (1830–1894), to go to Washington and lobby President Lincoln in person. This meeting took place on December 9, 1861, and Fischel provided the Board's president, Mr. Henry Hart (1811–1901), with a detailed report on the results of his activities. Selections from Fischel's communications with Hart shed light on Lincoln's responsiveness and his personal involvement in the controversy.

On July 17, 1862, Congress passed a law that authorized Jewish ministers to serve as military chaplains. Now the president needed to make an appointment. In a letter that follows, Rabbi Isaac Leeser, writing on behalf of the Board of Ministers of the Hebrew Congregations of Philadelphia, urged President Lincoln to "speedily comply" with the Board's request that a Jewish chaplain be appointed to serve soldiers in military hospitals in and near Philadelphia. On September 18, 1862, Lincoln appointed Rabbi Jacob Frankel (1808–1887) to serve as the first officially commissioned military chaplain.

Finally, it is interesting to note that only a few months later the surgeon general of the U.S. Army, William Alexander Hammond (1828–1900), and Medical Inspector General Thomas F. Perley (1816–1869) concluded that appointing a Jewish chaplain in Washington, D.C., would be superfluous since there were too few wounded Jews in the District's military hospitals.

To the Honorable, the Senate and House of Representatives of the United States of America:

The subscribers, your memorialists, respectfully show: That they are the President and Secretary of the "Board of Delegates of American Israelites," and that they are duly empowered to submit to your honorable body the facts herein set forth, and to crave, at your hands, that attention to the subject, which its importance to American citizens professing the Jewish religion, demands.

Your memorialists respectfully show: That by the 9th Section of the Act of Congress, approved July 22, 1861, and the 7th Section of the Act of Congress, approved August 3, 1861, it is provided that "the Chaplain appointed by the vote of the field officers and company commanders, must be a regular ordained minister of some Christian denomination," and that, as appears by the following letter from the War Department, to which your memorialists beg leave to refer, the said sections have been interpreted to exclude from the office of Chaplain in the service of the United States, "regular ordained ministers" of the *Jewish* faith:

"War Department, October 23, 1861. "Rev. A. Fischel, Rabbi, Jewish Synagogue, New York.

"*Sir.*—Your communication of the 17th inst. . . . has been received.

"In reply, you are respectfully informed that by the 9th section of the Act of Congress, approved July 22, 1861, it is provided that the Chaplain appointed by 'the vote of the field officers and company commanders, must be a regular ordained minister of some Christian denomination.' A like provision, also, is made in the 7th section of the Act of Congress, approved August 3, 1861. Were it not for the impediments thus directly created by the provisions of these two Acts, the Department would have taken your application into its favorable consideration.

> *I have the honor to be,*
> *Very respectfully,*
> *Simon Cameron,*
> *Secretary of War."*

Your memorialists respectfully submit that the body of citizens of the United States whom your memorialists represent, numbering not less than two hundred thousand, are unexcelled by any other class of citizens in loyalty and devotion to the Union, that thousands of them have volunteered into the Army of the United States, and are, by the provisions of the Acts hereinbefore mentioned, excluded from the advantages of spiritual advice and consolation provided by Congress for their fellow-citizens professing Christianity;

That the said Acts are oppressive, inasmuch as they establish a prejudicial discrimination against a particular class of citizens, on account of their religious belief; and further,

That the said Acts, inasmuch as they establish "a religious test as a qualification for an office under the United States," are manifestly in contravention of Section 3, Article VI of the Constitution and Article I of Amendments thereto.

Your memorialists, therefore, respectfully pray that your honorable body will take this, their memorial, into favorable consideration and that you will, in your wisdom, cause the Acts of Congress approved July 22nd and August 3rd, 1861, respectively, to be formally amended, so that there shall be no discrimination as against professors of the Jewish faith, in the several laws affecting the appointment of Chaplains in the service of the United States.

And your memorialists will ever pray, &c.

(Signed)

> *Henry I. Hart, President.*

(L.S.)

Myer S. Isaacs, Secretary.

Source: PAJHS 12 (1904): 128–29.

4.22—RABBI KALISCH TO U.S. CONGRESS, REGARDING THE CHAPLAINCY ISSUE, DECEMBER 9, 1861

To the Honorable members of the Congress
New York Decembr. 9th 1861
Gentlemen,

You have in former session enacted the law, that none but a minister of any Christian denomination shall serve as chaplain in the army of the U. St.

You have probably overlooked, that many of the Jewish creed serve in the army of the U. St., and that these brave patriots are desiring and have the same right, according to the constitution of the U. St. which they endeavor to preserve and defend with all their might and ability

like their Christian fellow soldiers, to enjoy in the hour of danger[,] agony and death the same privilege as the others do.

I appeal therefore to your sense of justice and request you sincerely to repeal the above mentioned law, and to make provisions, that Jewish divines shall also be allowed to serve as chaplains in the army and hospitals of the U. St.

Respectfully Your obedient servant,
Isidor Kalisch D.D.
Care of Mr. Louis Tobias No 248 Grand Str.

Source: Bertram Korn Papers, MS 99, box 5, F.1, AJA.

Having obtained important letters of introduction to Senators, I started for Washington, where I arrived on Tuesday evening, and went at once to work to obtain an interview with the President. All the influential gentlemen with whom I spoke on the subject, assured me that it would be impossible for me to get an audience, as the President's time was altogether taken up with public business. The same opinion was expressed by Mr. [John G.] Nicolay, his private Secretary, who even told me that Mr. Lincoln would not have time to read the letter in which I solicited an interview, and that there would be little chance for me to see him before the adjournment of Congress; that, in fact, none but Cabinet Ministers, Senators and army officers could be admitted. Seeing that I could not obtain admission by the usual process, I had to devise a plan whereby the subject could be at once brought under the notice of the President, and in this I was perfectly successful. I called this morning at ten o'clock at the White House, where hundreds of people were anxiously waiting for admission, some of whom told me that they had been for three days awaiting their turn. I was, nevertheless, at once invited to his room and was received with marked courtesy. After having read the letter of the Board and delivered to him several letters of introduction, he questioned me on various matters connected with this subject and then told me that he fully admitted the justice of my remarks, that he believed the exclusion of Jewish chaplains to have been altogether unintentional on the part of Congress, and agreed that something ought to be done to meet this case. I suggested that he might do for Jewish, what he had done for the Christian volunteers, and take upon himself the responsibility of appointing Jewish chaplains for the hospitals. He replied that he had done that at a time when Congress was not in session, deeming the subject to require immediate attention, but that, after the meeting of Congress, he would not be justified in taking the responsibility upon himself. Finally, he told me that it was the first time this subject had been brought under his notice, that it was altogether new to him, that he would take the subject into serious consideration, that I should call again tomorrow morning, and if he had five minutes to spare he would receive me and let me know his views. I thanked him for his kind reception, and expressed to him my best wishes for his welfare. In the course of my remarks I gave him clearly to understand that I came to him not as an office-seeker but to contend for the principle of religious liberty, for the constitutional rights of the Jewish community, and for the welfare of the Jewish volunteers, which he seemed fully to appreciate. . . .

Rev. Arnold Fischel to Mr. Henry I. Hart, December 13, 1861:

You have no doubt received my first letter in which I gave the substance of my interview with the President. As he wished me to call again on the following day, I readily availed myself of his invitation, but, much to my regret, he was unable to see me, as he had important public business to transact with the Governor of Indiana and foreign ambassadors. He sent me, however, a note in which he stated that "he is not forgetting my case and *will lay it before the Cabinet to-day* (Friday)." It may be that some days will elapse before I know the result of their deliberations. At all events, I have succeeded in obtaining the favorable consideration of the President, which I entirely attribute to the excellent letters of introduction submitted to him. All the public officers, from the President down to the Members of Congress, have too much to occupy their attention, so that unless an extraordinary amount of political influence is brought to bear upon them, you may for weeks solicit an interview without obtaining it. Under these circumstances, I consider myself fortunate in having accomplished so much in a few days.

Rev. Arnold Fischel writes the text of a letter he received from President Lincoln on December 14, 1861:

Rev. Dr. A. Fischel

My Dear Sir.—I find there are several particulars in which the present law in regard to chaplains is supposed to be deficient, all which I now design presenting to the appropriate Committee of Congress. I shall try to have a new law broad enough to cover what is desired by you in behalf of the Israelites.

Yours truly,
A. Lincoln.

Source: Myer S. Isaacs, "A Jewish Army Chaplain," *PAJHS* 12 (1904): 131–33.

4.24—ISAAC LEESER TO ABRAHAM LINCOLN, REQUESTING THE COMMISSIONING OF JEWISH CHAPLAINS, AUGUST 21, 1862

To the Hon. Abraham Lincoln
President of the United States of America
Sir
By order of the Board of Ministers of the Hebrew Congregations of Philadelphia, I take the liberty, as their secretary of addressing you briefly on a subject of great importance to us as a religious body.

Many Israelites are serving in the army of the United States, and this city and vicinity being the locality where numerous hospitals for the sick and wounded soldiers have been established, it is to be expected that not a few persons of our persuasion will be brought hither in a condition to require spiritual no less than bodily care. In fact, two at least of our persuasion have already died in the hospitals, one of these had his religious affinities not made known to us till after he had already been buried without an Israelite being present. From the steps taken by us it is not probable that another Israelite will die under similar circumstances without some one of his fellow believers being made cognizant of his case.

Nevertheless it has at our last meeting been deemed highly expedient to have a Jewish chaplain appointed by the President of the United States, to be invested with the privileges pertaining to ministers of other persuasions holding the same position. The act of the last session of Congress having given you full authority to delegate to Israelites this office of mercy, we trust that you will speedily comply with our request.

The object of this being merely a preliminary step, to bring the matter under your notice, it is useless to enlarge, especially as we are well aware that your time is greatly occupied by public concerns of the gravest importance. Still our request is one which should of right receive the kind attention of the chief magistrate of the Union, mainly because the moral effect of the compliance with our request cannot fail of being manifest to yourself.

If an appointment is made, it is suggested that the district for the operation of the chaplain might conveniently include York, Harrisburg, Chester and other towns at not too great a distance, where U.S. hospital[s] are or may be established.

Please to command my services in whatever way I could convey such information as may be needed by you.

For our trustworthiness, as our board are strangers to you, we may refer to Messrs. Biddle,

Lehman & Kelly, members of the House of Representatives of this city.

Respectfully your obd. Sevt.
Isaac Leeser

Minister, Franklin St. Synagogue
and secry. Board of Heb. Mins. of Phila.

Philadelphia
1229 Market St.
August 21, 1862
Source: Library of Congress, Washington, D.C.

4.25—LETTER FROM THE U.S. SURGEON GENERAL OPPOSING THE COMMISSIONING OF JEWISH CHAPLAINS IN WASHINGTON, D.C., OCTOBER 27, 1862

Surgeon General's Office
Washington City, D.C.
October 27, 1862
Sir,

In conformity with your order of the 10th instant, I sent a circular to all the hospitals in the District, calling for a report of the number of Jews at present in each hospital. The reports have been very slow in coming in, and are at present incomplete. I have however received accounts from 13 hospitals, representing over 5,000 beds, and the result is that in these hospitals there are but 7 Jews, and the same ratio doubtless prevails in the balance. I have therefore no hesitation in expressing an opinion that it is inexpedient to appoint a chaplain of that faith.

There would not be over 25 soldiers, to whom he could administer and they so scattered, that it would be impracticable for a clergyman to find and attend to them.

I have the honor to be sir
Very Respectfully
Your Ob't Servt
Thomas F. Perley Surgeon General USA

Brig. Gen. W. A. Hammond
Surgeon General USA
Source: SC-4610, AJA.

4.26—EXCERPT FROM ISIDOR STRAUS'S MEMOIRS, 1862–1863

Lazarus Straus (1809-1898) immigrated to the United States from Germany in 1852 and began his career as a peddler in Oglethorpe, Georgia. In 1854, Straus relocated to Talbotton, Georgia, and, before long, he was operating three stores in the vicinity. After the Civil War broke out, federal blockades frequently hindered the procurement of goods for merchants to sell. The cost of necessities often skyrocketed. All merchants faced these circumstances, but in

1862 a grand jury in Talbotton singled out Jewish merchants and charged them with speculating. The accusation offended Lazarus, and he relocated his business and family to Columbus, in the same state. Years later, Lazarus's son, Isidor (1845-1912), recollected these events in his memoirs.

The blockading of all Southern ports, which cut off the supplies that the Southern merchants had theretofore procured from the Northern markets, made all the better grades of dry goods, clothing, etc., very scarce, and as the smaller inland cities, towns, and villages were slow in becoming apprized of conditions, the seaport cities and towns sent agents throughout the country and bought up stocks of merchandise which commanded higher prices than the ordinary retail values which these country dealers had placed thereon when first put on sale. In other words, the enhancement of values through scarcity, and the depreciation of the currency from gold values, which made themselves felt in the more important centers, had not penetrated the interior. This, in a few months, resulted in the merchandise stocks finding their way to the larger from the smaller towns, and in due course the rural communities awakened to the realization of what had happened, too late, of course, to check or remedy conditions.

Perhaps the Jewish merchants were represented in these foraging expeditions throughout the country to their full proportion, and there began a tirade in the newspapers against this practice. The men who were engaged in this perfectly legitimate business enterprise were denounced as extortionists, speculating on the necessities of the people while many of their breadwinners were at the front, risking their lives on the altar of their country, and the Jews were singled out as if they alone were the perpetrators of what was termed iniquitous practices. It is so easy, when once a wave of denunciation has been started, for people, without reflection or examination of facts, feeling that the complaint of one community finds echo in its own, to join in attributing deplorable conditions to one and the same cause, and thus a prejudice against the Jewish merchants was inaugurated

that found utterance in official and semi-official quarters. So it occurred that a grand jury of Talbot County, in winding up its session and making its presentments to the court, as was the custom, referred to the evil and unpatriotic conduct of the representatives of Jewish houses who had engaged in this nefarious business.

When my father became aware of the action of the grand jury, he immediately let it be known that he would move away from a community which had cast such a reflection on him, as the only Jew living in their midst, and promptly took steps to carry out his determination, insisting, notwithstanding all protests to the contrary, that he was justified in construing the jury's action as a personal affront to him. Father's action caused such a sensation in the whole county that he was waited upon by every member of the grand jury, also by all the ministers of the different denominations, who assured him that nothing was further from the minds of those who drew the presentment than to reflect on father, and that had anyone had the least suspicion that their action could be construed as they now saw clearly it might be construed, it never would have been permitted to be so worded.

Father, nevertheless, would not be persuaded to change the plans he had determined upon, and consequently removed his business and family to Columbus, Ga. The loyalty and good will of the people towards him was made manifest to him, as he often stated, by the customers from Talbotton who visited his store in Columbus, not a few of them never having traded with him while in Talbotton, but who became regular clients in Columbus.

Source: Marcus, *Memoirs of American Jews,* 3:303–4. SC-12064, AJA.

5 The Gilded Age and Progressive Era

AMERICAN JEWISH LIFE, 1880–1918

During the late nineteenth and early twentieth centuries, the arrival of two million Eastern European Jews brought to the forefront of American Jewish history the themes of immigration and Americanization—the processes by which immigrant Jews and their descendants interacted within the larger society. During this forty-year period of large-scale Jewish immigration to the United States, new arrivals confronted a variety of questions about their emerging identities as Americans and as Jews. Within the religious sphere, Jewish immigrants weighed the value and meaning of Jewish observance in their new surroundings. Oftentimes, greater success in their working lives demanded compromises when it came to Jewish tradition. Raising children as native-born English-speaking American Jews also pressured immigrant parents to adapt Judaism's precepts to new surroundings.

Within the public sphere, Jewish immigrants and their children interacted with local, state, and even federal governments, enjoying full citizenship rights in a nation that offered constitutional protection of free religious expression. At the end of this period, the Great War (later known as World War I) offered American Jews the opportunity to demonstrate their patriotic spirit.

In the Jewish communal world, Eastern European immigration brought the theme of intracommunal relations into sharp focus. With the arrival of the new immigrants, established American Jews of Central European origin began to engage in a complex and ambivalent relationship with their coreligionists. On the one hand, they created a network of social service, educational, and cultural institutions designed to improve the new immigrants' quality of life. On the other, the Eastern Europeans charged the Central Europeans with paternalism and elitism, and with forcing the Eastern European arrivals to emulate a more assimilationist approach to American Jewish life.

Jewish nationalism also emerged as a major theme in this period, a development that offers students of American Jewish history the opportunity to compare and contrast the experiences of those Eastern European Jews who chose immigration to the United States with those who decided to settle in Palestine instead. For the vast majority of Jewish immigrants, the economic opportunities of an expanding American industrial economy trumped ideological calls for the creation of a Jewish homeland. Still, a fledgling American Zionist movement challenged Jews to resolve the tensions between their growing affinity and loyalty to the United States and their support, however it was defined, for the Zionist movement. American Zionism also created a split among American Jews; some rose to great prominence in the Jewish nationalist movement, while others pressed just as hard against calls for Jewish sovereignty.

This period also witnessed a growing anti-immigrant sentiment among native-born Americans concerned that the new arrivals would ruin the nation's social fabric. While they took action against a variety of immigrant groups, nativists advanced classical anti-semitic tropes against Eastern European Jews, whose entry to the nation they eventually sought to restrict. During this era, a movement advocating scientific racialism also emerged. This ideology, based on a type of contemporary pseudoscientific thinking, was called eugenics. In spite of the fact that numerous antisemites would later use this kind of racialism against Jews in America and Europe, in the early decades of the twentieth century many Jews were ardent supporters of movement initiatives such as birth control.

5.01—LETTER TO THE EDITOR, URGING EASTERN EUROPEAN JEWS NOT TO EMIGRATE, *Ha-Magid*, MAY 3, 1882

As early as 1882, when Eastern European Jewish immigration to the United States was still relatively small, the experience of new arrivals proved so challenging that they advised their coreligionists against making the journey. In this letter, published in Ha-Magid, *a Hebrew-language newspaper published in Prussia and distributed throughout the Pale of Settlement, one Eastern European immigrant implored his brethren to stay in the Old Country.*

As a kindness to our oppressed brethren in Russia and for the good of all, I beg of you . . . have mercy on the unfortunates and warn them with all your power of persuasion not to leave their native land to come to America. I see the pain of the afflicted when they come here. My hair stands on end, and I find myself incapable of describing the fate of the poor unfortunates. The "benefactors" who send their poor brethren to America will need to render an account before the Almighty because of the tragedy they inflict upon them. The number of newcomers grows daily at an alarming rate, and our brethren here can care for only a portion of them. The rest suffer hunger and pain, and there is no one here to open their homes to them . . . therefore, every Jew who can must make it his sacred task to warn the unfortunates that they should not rush like cattle into the valley, where they literally put their lives in danger. . . . Only the young, healthy, unmarried men with a trade may be able, after years of hard labor, to make a living. The others will simply languish. They are already a burden and an embarrassment to those already settled here . . .

Source: Abraham J. Karp, *Golden Door to America: The Jewish Immigrant Experience* (New York: Viking Press, 1976), 83–84.

5.02—ABRAHAM CAHAN'S IMPRESSIONS UPON ARRIVAL IN THE UNITED STATES, "IMAGINARY AMERICA," 1882

Abraham Cahan (1860–1951) grew to become one of the most important and influential figures in New York City immigrant Jewish life. Born in Lithuania, Cahan moved to Vilna at the age of six, where he received a traditional Jewish education before embracing socialism. In 1882, he immigrated to New York City, where he joined the Socialist Party of America and worked to translate texts from the leftist press into Yiddish so that they could be read by Jewish immigrants. Although Cahan would devote his career to Yiddish-language writing and lecturing, he mastered English, received training from American journalists, and served as an English-language contributor to the Sun *and* Commercial Advertiser. *In 1903, he rose to the editorship of the Yiddish-language* Forward, *the largest non-English daily newspaper in the United States. In a job he held for forty-three years, Cahan influenced attitudes toward subjects as varied as politics, evidenced in his paper's socialist orientation, and advice on Americanization, as expressed in the "Bintel Brief" advice column. Sixteen years after his 1882 arrival, Cahan reflected on his early days in the United States.*

[1882] I set foot on American soil on a scorching day in July, and the first American I saw was an old customs officer, with a white beard and in the blue uniform of his office. The headless men in gray vanished as if at the stroke of a magic wand, but then, gleaming green, fresh and beautiful, not many hundred yards off, was the shore of Staten Island, and, while I was uttering exclamations of enchantment in chorus with my fellow passengers, I asked myself whether my dreams of a meadow had not come true.

Still, pretty as America was, it somehow did not seem to be genuine, and much as I admired the shore I had a lurking impression that it was not the same sort of grass, trees, flowers, sod as in Europe, that it was more or less artificial, flimsy, ephemeral, as if a good European rainstorm could wipe it all off as a wet sponge would a colored picture made with colored chalk on blackboard.

I remember joking of the seeming unreality of things in my new home. "The ice here is not cold," I would say, "The sugar is not sweet and the water is not wet." And a homesick German thereupon added in the words of a famous poet of his that America was a country where "the birds had no sing [*sic*], the flowers no fragrance and the men no hearts." Why I should have doubted the actuality of things in the New World I do not know. Now that I try to account for that vague, hidden suspicion which the sky and clouds of New York arouse in me, it occurs to me that it may have been due to my deep-rooted notion of America as something so far removed from my world that it must look entirely different from it. If Staten Island had the appearance which its reflections had in the water, if the trees and the cliffs were all upside down, I should have been surprised but satisfied. . . .

When I found myself on the street and my eye fell on an old rickety building, I expressed a feeling akin to surprise. I could only conceive of America as a brand-new country, and everything in it, everything made by man, at least, was to be spick and span, while here was an old house, weatherbeaten and somewhat misshapen with age. How did it get time to get old?

Source: Abraham J. Karp, *Golden Door to America: The Jewish Immigrant Experience* (New York: Viking Press, 1976), 67–68. Originally appeared in the *Advertiser* (August 6, 1898).

5.03—EMMA LAZARUS, "THE NEW COLOSSUS," 1883

In 1875, Edouard René de Laboulaye (1811–1883) announced plans to commission a statue as a gift from the people of France to the United States to mark the following year's American centennial. The statue, formally named Liberty Enlightening the World, was not completed on time; only its right arm and hand were displayed at the 1876 Centennial Exposition in Philadelphia. Meanwhile, fundraisers in the United States began a campaign to build the pedestal that would support the statue. They enlisted Emma Lazarus (1849–1887), a Jewish poet, to help stir the strong emotional responses that organizers knew would encourage people to contribute to the cause. The original version of "The New Colossus" was sold as part of a December 1883 fundraiser, but the effort ultimately failed to attract the funds necessary to build the statue in New York Harbor. With critical support from an 1885 Joseph Pulitzer newspaper campaign that raised $102,000, construction on the statue continued until its opening in 1886. The words of "The New Colossus" lingered in obscurity until 1903, when the poem was placed on a wall inside the pedestal it helped create.

Not like the brazen giant of Greek fame
With conquering limbs astride from land to
   land;

Here at our sea-washed, sunset gates shall
   stand
A mighty woman with a torch, whose flame
Is the imprisoned lightning, and her name
Mother of Exiles. From her beacon-hand
Glows world-wide welcome; her mild eyes
   command
The air-bridged harbor that twin cities frame,
"Keep, ancient lands, your storied pomp!" cries
   she

With silent lips. "Give me your tired, your poor,
Your huddled masses yearning to breathe free,
The wretched refuse of your teeming shore,
Send these, the homeless, tempest-tossed to
   me,
I lift my lamp beside the golden door!"

*Source: AJW, 328. From The Poems of Emma Lazarus
(Boston: Twayne, 1888), 2:14–15.*

5.04—H. L. SABSOVICH, "THE WOODBINE SETTLEMENT OF THE BARON DE HIRSCH FUND," DESCRIBING THE CREATION OF A JEWISH AGRICULTURAL SETTLEMENT IN NEW JERSEY, 1891

*Not all Jewish immigrants flocked to urban
centers. In 1891, the Baron de Hirsch Fund,
based in New York City, created the Woodbine
Colony, a 5,300-acre Jewish agricultural
settlement in New Jersey designed to ease the
suffering of recent Eastern European immigrants
to the United States, divert Jewish immigrants
away from New York City and Philadelphia,
and instill, according to Woodbine
superintendent H. L. Sabsovich (1859–1915),
"the true American spirit."*

The Woodbine Settlement of the Baron de
Hirsch Fund
   By Prof. H. L. Sabsovich, Superintendent
   Introduction.—The Woodbine Colony from a
Social Student's standpoint can be considered
as one of the successful attempts undertaken
in this country to help the needy to help them-
selves, and stands as an example of what can be
done to counteract the cityward tendency of the
rural population.
   The Aims.—The Baron de Hirsch Fund, of
New York City, an organization composed of
most prominent persons of the Jewish faith in
New York and Philadelphia, called to life by
the forced immigration into this country of the
East European Jew—the Russian, Galician and

Roumanian—have founded Woodbine with a
three-fold purpose in view: Firstly, to relieve the
man—the co-religionist suffering from the most
barbarous persecutions; secondly, to prevent the
increase of over-crowdedness in the large cities,
if not to drain the so-called Ghetto of New York
and Philadelphia; and thirdly, to instill in the
immigrant the true American spirit by providing
him, and particularly his children, with the best
American schools, and good, healthy housing
facilities; by giving to the hungry the possibility of earning a decent living, to the homeless a
home.
   The Realization of the Aims.—Did the Trustees of the Baron de Hirsch Fund succeed in their
undertaking? As a sociological experiment, to
be followed by practical philanthropists as well
as by the earnest students of the various problems resulting from the modern urban conditions of life, Woodbine has not disappointed
them. This is best shown by the following figures:
   In 1891, Woodbine represented a tract of 5,300
acres of waste land, covered with scrub-oak,
stunted pine, intermixed with black and white
oak. Three or four tumble-down structures sheltered a population of 10 or 12 railroad employees. Ten years passed. Thanks to the liberality

and wisdom of the Trustees of the De Hirsch Fund, to the beaver-like activity of the population, to its industriousness, frugality and perseverance, Woodbine in 1901 became the manufacturing, agricultural and educational centre of Cape May county.

The maltreated, down-trodden, despised subject of the Russian tyrant, of the haughty nobility of Galicia, and of the ruined Boyars of Roumania, in ten years, under the protective wings of the American Eagle, was redeemed for humanity, became a producing, useful member of society, and thankful, devoted son of the country which has adopted him.

. . . We have at present four public day schools, containing nine rooms, partly graded from kindergarten to high school, with a school population of about 300; there is a night school attended by 50 to 60 boys and girls of school age, who are obliged to work in the factories; and finally, there is an agricultural school, principally for boys, though out of the 110 pupils 15 are girls. In the last school we give not only special instruction in natural science as well as in the applied, which concern farming in its diversified aspects, but also a general English education, as a great majority of the pupils are newcomers not familiar with the language. We give them also a practical training, so that after leaving the school the graduates are able to occupy positions as farm help, assistant managers on farms of a general character, or in dairy, horticultural, poultry establishments, &c.

Source: SC-130, AJA.

5.05 — CONSTITUTION OF THE UNITED STATES AND DECLARATION OF INDEPENDENCE; COVER, IN ENGLISH AND YIDDISH, 1892

In order to help Yiddish-speaking immigrants learn about the American system of government, Kasriel Sarasohn (1835–1905), a Polish-born Jewish journalist who founded several American Jewish newspapers in the 1870s and 1880s, including the first-ever Hebrew paper in the United States, published Yiddish translations of the most important documents in U.S. history. Following is the cover of an 1892 Yiddish version of the U.S. Constitution and the Declaration of Independence. With these translations, immigrant Jews gained immediate access to, and knowledge of, the American democratic system.

Source: Library of Congress, Washington, D.C. From the collections of the Hebraic Section, African and Middle Eastern Division, Library of Congress, Washington, D.C.

Mary Antin (1881–1949), an immigration rights activist and author of the well-known autobiography The Promised Land, *published a lesser known but still important volume,* From Plotzk to Boston, *in 1899. Though she actually emigrated from a different town, named Polotzk, her earlier work (the title of which was accidentally misspelled) offered a powerful narrative of her journey to the United States in 1894 and vividly described what it was like for her mother, herself, and her siblings to reunite with their husband and father, already in the United States.*

From Plotzk to Boston
By
Mary Antin
Second Edition
Boston, Mass
W. B. Clarke & Co., Park Street Church
1899

In the year 1891, a mighty wave of the emigration movement swept over all parts of Russia, carrying with it a vast number of the Jewish population to the distant shores of the New World—from tyranny to democracy, from darkness to light, from bondage and persecution to freedom, justice and equality. But the great mass knew nothing of these things; they were going to the foreign world in hopes only of earning their bread and worshiping their God in peace. The different currents that directed the course of that wave cannot be here enumerated. Suffice it to say that its power was enormous. All over the land homes were broken up, families separated, lives completely altered, for a common end.

The emigration fever was at its height in Polotzk, my native town, in the central western part of Russia, on the Dvina River. "America" was in everybody's mouth. Business men talked of it over their accounts; the market women made up their quarrels that they might discuss it from stall to stall; people who had relatives in the famous land went around reading their letters for the enlightenment of less fortunate folks; the one letter-carrier informed the public how many letters arrived from America, and who were the recipients; children played at emigrating; old folks shook their sage heads over the evening fire, and prophesied no good for those who braved the terrors of the sea and the foreign goal beyond it;—all talked of it, but scarcely anybody knew one true fact about this magic land. For book-knowledge was not for them; and a few persons—they were a dressmaker's daughter, and a merchant with his two sons—who had returned from America after a long visit, happened to be endowed with extraordinary imagination, (a faculty closely related to their knowledge of their old countrymen's ignorance), and their descriptions of life across the ocean, given daily, for some months, to eager audiences, surpassed anything in the Arabian Nights. One sad fact threw a shadow over the splendor of the gold-paved, Paradise-like fairyland. The travelers all agreed that Jews lived there in the most shocking impiety.

Driven by a necessity for bettering the family circumstances, and by certain minor forces which cannot now be named, my father began to think seriously of casting his lot with the great stream of emigrants. Many family councils were held before it was agreed that the plan must be carried out. Then came the parting; for it was impossible for the whole family to go at once. I remember it, though I was only eight. It struck me as rather interesting to stand on the platform before the train, with a crowd of friends weeping in sympathy with us, and father waving his hat for our special benefit, and saying—the last words we heard him speak as the train moved off—

"Good-bye, Polotzk, forever!"

[. . .]

. . . At this time, cholera was raging in Russia, and was spread by emigrants going to America in the countries through which they travelled. To stop this danger, measures were taken to make emigration from Russia more difficult than ever. I believe that at all times the crossing of the boundary between Russia and Germany was a source of trouble to Russians, but with a special passport this was easily overcome. When, however, the traveller could not afford to supply himself with one, the boundary was crossed by stealth, and many amusing anecdotes are told of persons who crossed in some disguise, often that of a mujik who said he was going to the town on the German side to sell some goods, carried for the purpose of ensuring the success of the ruse. When several such tricks had been played on the guards it became very risky, and often, when caught, a traveller resorted to stratagem, which is very diverting when afterwards described, but not so at a time when much depends on its success. Some times a paltry bribe secured one a safe passage, and often emigrants were aided by men who made it their profession to help them cross, often suffering themselves to be paid such sums for the service that it paid best to be provided with a special passport.

[. . .]

We enjoyed everything offered for breakfast, two matzos and two cups of tea apiece—why it was a banquet. After it came the good-byes, as we were going soon. As I told you before, the strangers became fast friends in a short time under the circumstances, so there was real sorrow at the partings, though the joy of the fortunate ones was, in a measure, shared by all.

About one o'clock (we didn't go to dinner—we couldn't eat for excitement) we were called. There were three other families, an old woman, and a young man, among the Jewish passengers, who were going with us, besides some Polish people. We were all hurried through the door we had watched with longing for so long, and were a little way from it when the old woman stopped short and called on the rest to wait.

[. . .]

We got on a little steamer (the name is too big for it) that was managed by our conductor alone.

Before we had recovered from the shock of the shrill whistle so near us, we were landing in front of a large stone building.

Once more we were under the command of the gendarme. We were ordered to go into a big room crowded with people, and wait till the name of our ship was called. Somebody in the little room called a great many queer names, and many passengers answered the call. At last we heard, "Polynesia!"

We passed in and a great many things were done to our tickets before we were directed to go outside, then to a larger steamer than the one we came in. At every step our tickets were either stamped or punched, or a piece torn off of them, till we stepped upon the steamer's deck. Then we were ordered below. It was dark there, and we didn't like it. In a little while we were called up again, and then we saw before us the great ship that was to carry us to America.

[. . .]

. . . And when at last the wheels overhead began to turn and clatter, and the ripples on the water told us that the "Polynesia" had started on her journey, which was not noticeable from any other sign, I felt only a sense of happiness. I mistrusted nothing.

[. . .]

Nobody expected seasickness as soon as it seized us. All slept quietly the whole night, not knowing any difference between being on land or at sea. About five o'clock I woke up, and then I felt and heard the sea. A very disagreeable smell came from it, and I knew it was disturbed by the rocking of the ship. Oh, how wretched it made us! From side to side it went rocking, rocking. Ugh! Many of the passengers are very sick indeed, they suffer terribly. We are all awake now, and wonder if we, too, will be so sick. Some children are crying, at intervals. There is nobody to comfort them—all are so miserable. Oh, I am so sick! I'm dizzy; everything is going round and round before my eyes—Oh-h-h!

I can't even begin to tell of the suffering of the next few hours. Then I thought I would feel better if I could go on deck. Somehow, I got down (we had upper berths) and, supporting myself against the walls, I came on deck. But it was worse. The green water, tossing up the white foam, rocking all around, as far as I dared to look, was frightful to me then. So I crawled back as well as I could, and nobody else tried to go out.

By and by the doctor and the steward came. The doctor asked each passenger if they were well, but only smiled when all begged for some medicine to take away the dreadful suffering. To those who suffered from anything besides seasickness he sent medicine and special food later on. His companion appointed one of the men passengers for every twelve or fifteen to carry the meals from the kitchen, giving them cards to get it with. For our group a young German was appointed, who was making the journey for the second time, with his mother and sister. We were great friends with them during the journey.

The doctor went away soon, leaving the sufferers in the same sad condition. At twelve, a sailor announced that dinner was ready, and the man brought it—large tin pails and basins of soup, meat, cabbage, potatoes, and pudding (the last was allowed only once a week); and almost all of it was thrown away, as only a few men ate. The rest couldn't bear even the smell of food. It was the same with the supper at six o'clock. At three milk had been brought for the babies, and brown bread (a treat) with coffee for the rest. But after supper the daily allowance of fresh water was brought, and this soon disappeared and more called for, which was refused, although we lived on water alone for a week.

[. . .]

Oh, the sad mistake! For six days longer we remain in our berths, miserable and unable to eat. It is a long fast, hardly interrupted, during which we know that the weather is unchanged, the sky dark, the sea stormy.

[. . .]

The morning was glorious. It was the eighth of May, the seventeenth day after we left Hamburg. The sky was clear and blue, the sun shone brightly, as if to congratulate us that we had safely crossed the stormy sea, and to apologize for having kept away from us so long. The sea had lost its fury; it was almost as quiet as it had been at Hamburg before we started, and its color was a beautiful greenish blue. Birds were all the time in the air, and it was worth while to live merely to hear their songs. And soon, oh joyful sight! we saw the tops of two trees!

What a shout there rose! Everyone pointed out the welcome sight to everybody else, as if they did not see it. All eyes were fixed on it as if they saw a miracle. And this was only the beginning of the joys of the day!

What confusion there was! Some were flying up the stairs to the upper deck, some were tearing down to the lower one, others were running in and out of the cabins, some were in all parts of the ship in one minute, and all were talking and laughing and getting in somebody's way. Such excitement, such joy! We had seen two trees!

Then steamers and boats of all kinds passed by, in all directions. We shouted, and the men stood up in the boats and returned the greeting, waving their hats. We were as glad to see them as if they were old friends of ours.

Oh, what a beautiful scene! No corner of the earth is half so fair as the lovely picture before us. It came to view suddenly,—a green field, a real field with grass on it, and large houses, and the dearest hens and little chickens in all the world, and trees, and birds, and people at work. . . .

It was about three hours since we saw the first landmarks, when a number of men came on board, from a little steamer, and examined the passengers to see if they were properly vaccinated (we had been vaccinated on the "Polynesia"), and pronounced everyone all right. Then they went away, except one man who remained. An hour later we saw the wharves.

Before the ship had fully stopped, the climax of our joy was reached. One of us espied the figure and face we had longed to see for three long years. In a moment five passengers on the "Polynesia" were crying, "Papa," and gesticulating, and laughing, and hugging one another, and going wild altogether. All the rest were roused by our excitement, and came to see our father. He recognized us as soon as we him, and stood apart on the wharf not knowing what to do, I thought.

What followed was slow torture. Like mad things we ran about where there was room, unable to stand still as long as we were on the ship and he on shore. To have crossed the ocean only to come within a few yards of him, unable to get nearer till all the fuss was over, was dreadful enough. But to hear other passengers called who had no reason for hurry, while we were left among the last, was unendurable.

Oh, dear! Why can't we get off the hateful ship? Why can't papa come to us? Why so many ceremonies at the landing?

[. . .]

Still the ceremonies went on. Each person was asked a hundred or so stupid questions, and all their answers were written down by a very slow man. The baggage had to be examined, the tickets, and a hundred other things done before anyone was allowed to step ashore, all to keep us back as long as possible.

Now imagine yourself parting with all you love, believing it to be a parting for life; breaking up your home, selling the things that years have made dear to you; starting on a journey without the least experience in travelling, in the face of many inconveniences on account of the want of sufficient money; being met with disappointment where it was not to be expected; with rough treatment everywhere, till you are forced to go and make friends for yourself among strangers; being obliged to sell some of your most necessary things to pay bills you did not willingly incur; being mistrusted and searched, then half starved, and lodged in common with a multitude of strangers; suffering the miseries of seasickness, the disturbances and alarms of a stormy sea for sixteen days; and then stand within a few yards of him for whom you did all this, unable to even speak to him easily. How do you feel?

Oh, it's our turn at last! We are questioned, examined, and dismissed! A rush over the planks on one side, over the ground on the other, six wild beings cling to each other, bound by a common bond of tender joy, and the long parting is at an END.

Source: SC-349, AJA.

5.07—BASEBALL, *Forward*, AUGUST 27, 1909

In a 1909 issue of the Yiddish-language socialist Der Forverts (Forward), *the most important and widest circulating newspaper among American Jews, editors included an image of an American baseball diamond, with each of the fielding positions annotated in Yiddish. By learning the rules of America's pastime, immigrant Jews furthered their acculturation to the United States, strengthening their American identities by rallying around their local sports franchises.*

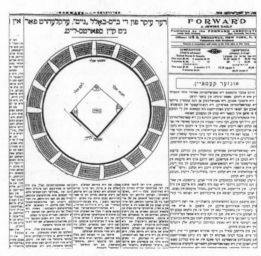

Source: Forward, August 27, 1909. Reprinted courtesy of the publisher.

5.08—HEBREW IMMIGRANT AID SOCIETY, COVER OF THE *Jewish Immigrant*, JANUARY 1909

Growing nativist sentiment in the United States led Congress to establish the Dillingham Commission in 1907, charged with investigating the consequences of increased immigration to the United States. At the same time, Congress considered legislation that would limit the number of immigrants from the "less desirable" locales of Eastern and Southern Europe. In the midst of this larger xenophobic national political culture, the Hebrew Immigrant Aid Society, which assisted Jewish immigrants on their arrival to the United States, published a 1909 journal cover featuring Lady Liberty herself, wearing a hat inscribed with "America" in Yiddish, affirming the value of continued immigration. The key she holds in her right hand symbolizes the opportunities available to new immigrants, while the text at the base of the gate, from the books of Psalms (118:19) and Isaiah (26:2), translates as "Open the gates of righteousness for me" and "Open the gates and let a righteous nation enter."

Source: From the collections of the Hebraic Section, African and Middle Eastern Division, Library of Congress, Washington, D.C.

5.09—CREATION OF THE NEW YORK JEWISH FEDERATION BY THE STATE OF NEW YORK, MAY 15, 1917

Throughout their history, Jews have taken seriously the Torah's injunction to care for the poor: "For the poor shall never cease out of the land; therefore I command you, saying, You shall open your hand wide to your brother, to your poor, and to your needy, in your land (Deuteronomy 15:11)." To address the needs of the poor, Jews over time have developed a range of philanthropic mechanisms. In America, literally thousands of Jewish charitable organizations arose in an effort to provide assistance of one sort or another to the Eastern European masses pouring into the country at

the fin de siècle. American Jewish leaders in major metropolitan areas sought ways to coordinate and streamline their communal welfare efforts. In New York City, for example, some 3,637 different Jewish agencies offered services to the Jewish community at the turn of the twentieth century. In 1916, the influential financier and Jewish communal leader Felix Warburg (1871–1937) spearheaded an effort to create one umbrella fundraising organization that would provide financial support for the hundreds of philanthropic societies then striving to meet the needs of Jews living in Manhattan *and the Bronx. Warburg's initiative led to the establishment of the Federation for the Support of Jewish Philanthropic Societies of New York City, which was incorporated by the State of New York in 1917. The new Federation raised $2.2 million in its first year of operation.*

Laws of New York, 1917.
Chap. 498.

AN ACT to enable any corporation, now or hereafter existing, formed primarily for the benefit of the Jews of New York City, for charitable, benevolent or educational purposes, to affiliate with and to become members of the Federation for the Support of Jewish Philanthropic Societies of New York City and by agreement with the latter to regulate their mutual relations.

Became a Law May 15, 1917, with the approval of the Governor, Passed, three-fifths being present.

The People of the State of New York, represented in Senate and Assembly, do enact as follows:

Section 1. It shall be lawful for any corporation, now or hereafter existing, formed primarily for the benefit of the Jews of New York City, for charitable, benevolent or educational purposes, to affiliate with and to become a member of the corporation known as Federation for the Support of Jewish Philanthropic Societies of New York City, hereinafter referred to as the Feder-

ation, upon such terms and conditions as the Federation may prescribe.

Section 2. Any such affiliating corporation may, with the approval of a majority of the members of its board of directors or trustees, enter into an agreement with the Federation whereby the mutual relations between such corporation and the Federation, shall be defined and regulated. Such agreement may include provisions conferring on any or all of the members or contributors of the Federation, membership in any such affiliating corporation, without liability to the latter for dues or otherwise by reason of such membership, with the right to vote at any election of officers, directors or trustees held by it, and authorizing any such affiliating corporation to designate or participate in the election of such number of trustees and of members of the board of delegates of the Federation as may be stipulated therein or in any instrument amendatory thereof or supplemental thereto, or as may be prescribed by the by-laws of the Federation, with such voting power as shall be permitted by such by-laws. Any such affiliating corporation may also agree that, so long as it shall remain affiliated with the Federation, it will not solicit members or contributors or make any appeals for pecuniary assistance, or any independent collection of funds for its corporate purposes, except with the consent of the Federation.

Section 3. This act shall take effect immediately.

Source: UJA-Federation of New York.

GOVERNMENT, POLITICS, AND CIVIC STATUS

5.10—REVISED WORDS TO LINCOLN'S GETTYSBURG ADDRESS, WRITTEN BY
HIAS FOR AN EVENT HONORING THE ELECTION OF MOSES ALEXANDER AS
GOVERNOR OF IDAHO, 1915

*The following document comes from a public
reception organized by the Hebrew Immigrant
Aid Society (HIAS) honoring Idaho governor
Moses Alexander (1853–1932), the first Jew to
be elected governor of a U.S. state. The reception
was held on Thursday evening August 26, 1915,
in Faneuil Hall, Boston. To bring some humor to
the occasion, the highly regarded Hebrew writer
Abraham Alpert (1871?–1939), whose nom de
plume was Ish Kovna (not to be confused with
the Hebrew poet Isaac Rabinowitz [1843–1939],
who took the same name), contributed an
English parody of the Gettysburg Address to
entertain those immersed in the work of
immigrant aid.*

Four and seven years ago a score of loyal
Jewish citizens brought forth in this community
a new organization conceived in necessity and
dedicated to the proposition that we "aid, Americanize and naturalize the Jewish immigrants."
Now we are engaged in a great civil strife, testing
whether this organization or any organization
so conceived and so dedicated can long endure.
We are met at the crisis of that strife. We have
come to dedicate the Hebrew Immigrant Aid
Society as a monument for those who gave their
energies that this organization might live. It is
altogether fitting and proper that we should do
this. But in a larger sense we cannot dedicate,
we cannot consecrate, we cannot hallow this
body. The willing workers here and elsewhere,
who have worked here, have consecrated it far
above our power to add or detract.

The world will little note or long remember
what we say here, but it can never forget what
they did here. It is for us, the present members,
rather to be dedicated here to the unfinished
task which they who labored here have thus far
so nobly advanced. It is rather for us to be here
dedicated to the great task remaining before
us, that from these willing workers we take increased devotion to that cause for which they
gave the full measure of devotion; that we here
highly resolve that these efforts and sacrifices
shall not have been in vain; that this organization, under God, shall have a new birth of freedom, and that the government of this organization by the Jews, and for the Jews, shall not
perish from the earth. A. A.

(With apologies to Abraham Lincoln.)
Source: SC-1233, AJA.

5.11—JULIA RICHMAN, SELECTION FROM "NEW YORK'S EAST EUROPEAN WORKING WOMEN," 1893

Jewish immigrant women endured particular hardships as they entered the American workforce. Without knowledge of the English language, they piled into factories that too often became sweatshops, instead of filling better-paying and safer jobs such as those in retail sales. As wage laborers, they worked in hazardous conditions for long hours with little pay. As early as 1893, Julia Richman (1855–1912), a New York–born daughter of Central European Jewish immigrants, protested against conditions experienced by her coreligionists. Richman, one of the most important progressive educators of her generation, offered her thoughts in an address given at the founding of the National Council of Jewish Women in Chicago. In the years after her address, she rose to become the first woman to serve as a district superintendent, taking control of schools on the Lower East Side of Manhattan, known for its Jewish immigrant population.

Who are our women wage-workers? . . . Perhaps the simplest classification on practical lines would be in general terms:

Women engaged in professional work.

Women engaged in domestic service.

Women engaged in store or factory work. . . .

And now we come to the third class, "Women engaged in store or factory work." Perhaps this class comprises more grades of work than could be classed under any other general head.

The manager of one large dry-goods house reports to me that he employs women as buyers, forewomen, dressmakers, milliners, saleswomen, cashiers, stock-girls, office-assistants, bundlers, operators, addressers, and scrub-women; while a manufacturer of tin toys uses female help exclusively for painting on tin, cutting tin, packing

toys, making paper boxes, and working foot presses. There are almost as many grades of woman's work as there are branches in every style of factory work. A word, now and again, is all that I can say in reference to these.

Saleswomen in large establishments are, on the whole, fairly well paid; but this avenue is closed to the immigrant, until she shall have mastered the English language to such an extent that there is no room for misunderstanding between herself and her customer.

"Figures" [models] in wholesale cloak and suit houses are well paid; their hours are short, their work never onerous, and "between seasons" they have little or no work to do. But, perhaps, no other class of working women in large cities is so directly placed in the way of temptation, and the mother who lets her daughter, particularly if she be attractive and vain, take a position as a "figure" [a model], has need of all our prayers added to her own to protect her girl. You, who are doing such zealous work among working girls, try to reach this class. God help them! They have need of you. . . .

Probably, the manufacture of clothing and cloaks gives employment to a larger number of immigrant Jewish girls and women than does any other single industry in New York City, and, unfortunately, many, perhaps even most, of these women are compelled to run heavy machines, in badly lighted, worse ventilated dens [sweatshops]. The manufacturer is only indirectly to blame for this, owing to the pernicious "middleman" system; and let me say right here that if *"the kindest proprietor in the world is a Jew of the better class,"* there is no employer of our Jewish working girls who shows less kindheartedness to his employees than these Jews of the other class, call them middlemen, or sweaters, or what you please. They are, with few exceptions, so hard, so harsh, so grasping, so unreasoning, and so unreasonable, that on several occasions, in my capacity as president of a Working Girls' Club, I tried to find better paying positions for some of these girls in order to take them away from shops owned or controlled by their own fathers. I recall one case distinctly—a girl, not over fifteen, whose father runs a shop for the manufacture of ladies' wrappers—over twenty machines in two small rooms lighted by kerosene lamps, the air vile, the language not less so, the employees paid by piece-work, laboring from seven in the morning until after ten at night, and for this, the girl I refer to received three dollars a week, of which she paid her father two dollars and a half for board. I saw her growing hollow-eyed, round-shouldered, narrow-chested, with a never-ceasing pain in the back. It was not until I found a place for her in which she earned six dollars a week, working daily from 8 to 6, that her father would let her leave his shop, and then only upon her promise to pay him four dollars a week for board. . . .

Almost all the female immigrants who come to this shore, through lack of knowledge as to the means by which they can swing themselves above the discouraging conditions which face them, sink down into the moral and intellectual maelstrom of the American ghettos, becoming first household or factory drudges, and then drifting into one of three channels: that of the careless slattern, of the giddy and all-too-frequently sinful gad-about, or of the weary, discontent wife.

We must disentangle the individual from the mass. We must find a way or several ways of leading these girls, one by one, away from the shadows which envelop them, if not into the sunshine of happiness and prosperity, at least, into the softening light of content, born of pleasant surroundings, congenial occupations, and the inward satisfaction of a life well spent.

[. . .]

In this age of materialism, in these days of close inquiry as to the "Why?" of every condition, it has been claimed that the ever-increasing

proportion of unmarried women among the Jews of America is largely due to the independent position women make for themselves, first, by becoming wage-earners, and second, through the development of self-reliance brought about by societies, working girls' clubs, and kindred movements. If marriage always meant happiness, and if celibacy always meant unhappiness, to make women independent and self-reliant would be a calamity. But, in the face of much married unhappiness and so much unmarried contentment, it is hardly pessimistic to wish that there might be fewer marriages consummated until the contracting parties show more discrimination in their selection of mates.

The saddest of many sad conditions that face our poor Jewish girls is the class of husbands that is being selected for them by relatives. It is the rule, not the exception, for the father, elder brother, or some other near relative of a Jewish working girl, to save a few hundred dollars, by which means he purchases some gross, repulsive Pole or Russian as a husband for the girl. That her whole soul revolts against such a marriage, that the man betrays, even before marriage, the brutality of his nature, that he may, perhaps, have left a wife and family in Russia, all this counts for nothing. Marry him she must, and another generation of worthless Jews is the lamentable result.

I wish it distinctly understood that there is no desire on my part to disparage matrimony; indeed, happy wifehood and motherhood are to my mind the highest missions any woman can fulfill; but in leading these girls to see the horror of ill-assorted marriages, I intend to teach them to recognize the fact that many of them may never find suitable husbands; and recognizing this fact, they must fill up their lives with useful, perhaps even noble work. Should the possible husband fail to appear, their lives will not have been barren; should he come, will a girl make a less faithful wife and mother because she has been taught to be faithful in other things?

And so I could go on showing how, in every direction, the harm and the evil grow, until the day will come when charity, even with millions at her disposal, will not be able to do good. It is easier to save from drowning than to resuscitate the drowned. Disentangle the individual from the mass; create a new mass of disentangled individuals, who shall become the leading spirits in helping their benighted sisters, and with God's help, the future will redeem the present and the past.

Source: As printed in *JAW*, 232–25.

5.12—MORRIS WINCHEVSKY, "A SOCIALIST PARODIES THE TEN COMMANDMENTS," 1895

Born in Kovno, Poland, Morris Winchevsky (1856–1932) emerged as one of the leading socialist writers and activists in London, where he first immigrated, and then in New York City. Opposed to organized religion, Winchevsky penned a socialist parody of the Ten Commandments. Two years after its publication, he joined Abraham Cahan as one of the founders of the Forward.

I. *I am the Lord thy god* and Mammon is my name. Heaven and earth, hear my word! Capital, I am thy soul and thy conscience. I cause starvation and I can bring gratification. I can make bitter or I can make sweet every bite you eat. I rule alone down below and up above. I can bring you peace or rivers of blood. I make the sun to rise and the snow to fall. I am the king and I am above all. Mammon is my name and money is my eternal flame.

II. *Thou Shalt Have No Other Gods . . .* Don't dare to set up any other gods in my temple—it will hurt my feelings. I permit no other gods—or goddesses! A goddess makes me uneasy, especially the goddess of liberty—she is an obstacle to the enforcement of my laws, which are needed to protect us against our foes. And the goddess of equality is a troublemaker. Her place is more properly in the graveyard than in my temple! In a word, thou shalt have no other gods before me—and don't you forget it!

III. *Thou Shalt Not Take My Name . . .* Never swear falsely unless by doing so you are adding to your bank account. In your business dealings you may do what the millionaires do so charmingly—tell a lie and then swear to it . . . ;

IV. *Remember the Sabbath Day . . .* One day a week your employees shall do no manner of labor for you—and that includes your horse, your ox, your cow. If they protest, tell them to behave or you'll give them seven days a week rest. Get my meaning?

V. *Honor Thy Father and Mother . . .* Especially if you have inherited all your gold and silver and oriental rugs from them. In this respect, the worker is luckier than you—he does not have the burden of this commandment, because after all, what does he own for which he should be thankful to his mother and father?

VI. *Thou Shalt Not Murder . . .* No matter how vast your treasures, this is too heavy a sin to bear, my son. On the other hand, do not upset yourself if someone brings you the news that one of your workers has had his head split open by a machine in your factory. This is no worse than happens in a war—whether it be for gold or for revenge or even for a medal of honor.

VII. *Thou Shalt Not Commit . . .* Avoid amorous interludes with women of your own kind—it interferes with your ability to augment your fortune. What do you need it for? There are many young women in the labor market who are willing to sell their talents—and some of them can dance and sing too. But don't go boasting about it all over town, lest the world begin to doubt you are the upright and Mammon-fearing citizen you're supposed to be.

VIII. *Thou Shalt Not Steal* . . . Don't stoop to common thievery—it will lead to nothing but prison. And don't get involved with underworld characters—a partnership means your cut is only half. Stick to the big bankruptcies. If you play according to my rules, you'll stay out of trouble. Furthermore, you can swim in gold up to your neck if you set up trusts in the U.S. of A. Free countries let themselves be skinned alive without uttering a peep. They even help you weave the ropes to tie them up. On pain of death I command you: Don't be a petty crook!

IX. *Thou Shalt Not Bear False Witness* . . . Don't bear false witness against your business associate. Don't tell tales out of school. You both have a common interest; to stand united for the status quo. But if you find yourself in court with him don't let him off easy simply because he's your friend. Don't take undue advantage of him either, if you hold the better cards, because you may both want to get together afterward and testify against the socialists who are trying to tear down my temple.

X. *Thou Shalt Not Covet* . . . Do not covet your neighbor's servants, nor his mistress, nor his children. Avoid that like the plague, if you want to be the founder of new temples of Mammon. If you must covet, covet his millions, covet Vanderbilt's estates or Pinkerton's spies, covet Venezuela's oil or the tin of Bolivia. Don't waste such powerful emotions on unprofitable trivia. . . .

Source: As printed in *JAW*, 346–47.

5.13 — "WOMEN AS WAGE EARNERS," *Ordens Echo,* 1897

In 1846, Henrietta Bruckman (1810–1888) and a group of women from New York City's Emanu-El congregation formed the Independent Order of True Sisters. Later renamed the United Order of True Sisters (UOTS), the group emerged as one of the earliest, if not the earliest, women's organizations in the United States. Originally a secret society, created in order to respect the Jewish ethic of anonymity in philanthropy, the UOTS revealed insights into women's social activism as well as gender roles in nineteenth century Jewish America. In an October 1897 Ordens Echo newspaper article, the UOTS focused attention on the deplorable conditions of Jewish working women by engaging a woman identified as Miss Sadie to address "women as wage earners."

Does the employment of women throw men out of work, and why? Without any doubt we all know that there are more women engaged in earning their own living to-day than there were ten years ago, and it is safe to say that the number will go on increasing as the women fit themselves to occupy other fields of labor.

Men complain that women, by working so much cheaper than men, take the employment away from them, and then, in the next breath, say that female help should be cheaper than male.

Why? I ask. If two people do exactly the same work in the same way, and accomplish the same results, should they not receive equal remuneration? If a man and a woman both apply for the same position, it is not going to be a question of superior merit with the employer, but a matter of dollars and cents, and as a matter of course, the cheaper help, that is the woman help, is engaged and a man is kept from a position that he no doubt could fill as well, perhaps better than the woman. For this condition of affairs both men and women are to blame. The men for not considering competence rather than cheapness in engaging their help, for not thinking that a woman is entitled to a living wage as a man. But more than this is the woman to blame. With her rests the question of refusing or accepting lower wages than would be offered to men. If she cheapens her mental power how can she expect men to hold it in high repute. A recent advertisement for a clerk in a publishing house required a "young woman, not over twenty-five, to act as correspondent, must write English, German and French fluently," and offered the munificent sum of eight dollars per week.

While such a state of things lasts, there are bound to be firms who would rather employ women at lower rates than men at even a dollar or two more. But once let woman demand as high a wage as her brother, and the question of employment must necessarily be one of merit. Each stands the same chance; let neither underbid the other, and the race will be to the swiftest, the battle to the strongest.

"But women should not earn as much as men," I hear someone say. "Their needs are not as great, they are not the bread-winners, they are too independent as it is," is the cry. Why do men need more than women? Simply because men have always been banker, cashier, and pay teller of the establishment; the handling of the cash has been man's province, and he has regulated his life in accordance with the old proverb, "To the lion belongs the lion's share"; having generally had the wherewithal to gratify his tastes, certain luxurious habits have become necessaries of life, and accordingly a man needs more than women. The cry that women are not the bread-winners, is, or in most cases ought to be, true, but in nine cases out of ten where a woman earns her own living it is not for the pleasure of work, nor for glory, nor for love of independence, but because stern necessity has driven her to it; because in order to support herself or help keep a home together or to take the burden from an already overburdened father, she was obliged to put her shoulder to the wheel.

And now for the last complaint—the one we hear oftenest: "It makes women too independent; the number of old maids is on the increase." Well, that surely is not the woman's fault, is it? I read once that every old maid is one from choice, but not her own choice. Well, if women ask more nowadays so do men. Men ask more in the way of money; why shouldn't women? Men want more of social position, so should women; and if women ask more in the way of intellect, breeding, manners, and morals, so much the better for future generations. Perhaps after we get through educating women we shall have to form societies for the higher education of men. But if women are more independent perhaps girls will not rush into marriage as an escape from the limitations of girlhood; it may make her more careful to judge for herself, to decide on her own chances of happiness, to learn her own possibilities both of success and f[ail]ure, and through the very fact [word missing] when she does marry she will [word missing] how to appreciate his struggles [word missing] livelihood, how to take care [word missing] money he has earned, since s[he her]self has been through the mill, [word missing] she has learned the value of m[oney] when she herself was one of the [word missing] of "Wage-Earners."

Miss Sadie C [word missing]

Source: MS-638, AJA.

5.14—THE PROTOCOL OF PEACE, ENDING THE 1910 CLOAK MAKERS' STRIKE, NEW YORK CITY, 1910

When Eastern European Jewish immigrants, including a disproportionate number of women, went to work in New York City's textile industry, almost all of them labored under the direction of American Jewish factory owners of Central European origin. While frequent strikes brought attention to the plight of workers, they also cast light on class divisions among American Jews. After a high-profile cloak makers' strike in 1910, representatives from both labor and management agreed to bring their differences to the respected Boston lawyer Louis Brandeis (1856–1941), who, along with famed jurist Louis Marshall (1856–1929), negotiated a settlement known as the "Protocol of Peace," which, among other labor victories, delivered union recognition for the workers.

New York, September, 1910

Louis Marshall, Esq.,
37 Wal[l] Street,
New York City.
Dear Sir:

The undersigned, constituting the General Strike Committee of the Cloak, Suit and Skirt Makers Unions, herewith inform you that at a meeting this day held, the revised Protocol agreed upon between Meyer London, Esq., Julius Henry Cohen, Esq.[,] and yourself, was submitted and was adopted, and the strike heretofore ordered is herewith declared off; provided, however, that before this announcement is to be made and this declaration is to be effective, you shall have received from the Cloak, Suit and Skirt Manufacturers Protective Association a communication directed to you, accepting the terms of said revised Protocol.

Very truly yours,
Abraham Rosenberg, President, et al.

(The Revised Protocol)
[. . .]
Whereas, differences have arisen between the Manufacturers and their employees who are members of the Unions with regard to various matters, which have resulted in a strike, and it is now desired by the parties hereto to terminate said strike and to arrive at an understanding with regard to the future relations between the Manufacturers and their employees, it is therefore stipulated as follows:
[. . .]
Fourteenth: Each member of the Manufacturers Union is to maintain a union shop; a "union shop" being understood to refer to a shop where union standards as to working conditions, hours of labor and rates of wages as herein stipulated prevail, and where, when hiring help, union men are preferred; it being recognized that, since there are differences in degrees of skill among those employed in the trade, employers shall have freedom of selection as between one union man and another, and shall not be confined to any list, nor bound to follow any prescribed order whatever.

[. . .]

Sixteenth: The parties hereby establish a Board of Arbitration, to consist of three (3) members, composed of one nominee of the Manufacturers, one nominee of the Unions, and one representative of the public, the latter to be named by Meyer London, Esq. and Julius Henry Cohen, Esq. and in the event of their inability to agree, by Louis Marshall, Esq.

To such Board shall be submitted any differences hereafter arising between the parties hereto, or between any of the members of the Manufacturers and any of the members of the Unions, and the decision of such Board of Arbitration shall be accepted as final and conclusive between the parties to such controversy.

Seventeenth: In the event of any dispute arising between the Manufacturers and the Unions, or between any members of the Manufacturers and any members of the Unions, the parties to this protocol agree that there shall be no strike or lockout concerning such matters in controversy until full opportunity shall have been given for the submission of such matters to said Board of Arbitration, and in the event of a determination of said controversies by said Board of Arbitration, only in the event of a failure to accede to the determination of said Board.

Eighteenth: The parties hereby establish a committee on grievances, consisting of four (4) members, composed as follows: two to be named by the Manufacturers, and two by the Unions. To said committee shall be submitted all minor grievances arising in connection with the business relations between the Manufacturers and their employees.

Nineteenth: In the event of any vacancy in the aforesaid boards, or in the aforesaid committee, by reason of death, resignation or disability of any of the members thereof, such vacancy in respect to any appointee by the Manufacturers and Unions, respectively, shall be filled by the body originally designating the person with respect to whom such vacancy shall occur. In the event that such vacancy shall occur among the representatives of the public on such boards, such vacancy shall be filled by the remaining members representing the public in the case of the board of sanitary control, and in the case of the board of arbitration both parties shall agree on a third arbitrator, and in case of their inability to agree, said arbitrator shall be selected by the Governor of the State of New York.

Approved, Louis Marshall, Meyer London,
Julius Henry Cohen

Source: Rare document, AJA.

On March 25, 1911, fire engulfed the Triangle Shirtwaist factory building in lower Manhattan. While some of the Jewish and Italian immigrant workers, most of whom were women, managed to escape, 146 died because factory owners had blocked access to exits in order to prevent employees from stealing. Those caught in the building suffered smoke inhalation, while others leapt to their deaths trying to escape the flames on the building's upper floors. The Shirtwaist Fire tragedy provoked successful calls for improved safety measures in American factories as well as greater recognition of predominately Jewish labor unions. Two weeks after the fire, the Yiddish newspaper Der Groyser Kundes *(The Big Stick, a reference to former president Theodore Roosevelt's "big stick" policy of peaceful negotiation backed by the ever-present possibility of military action) published a cartoon image of a monstrous person named "Triangle Waist Company" leading small and nameless women to their deaths in the fire. Images of the scene appear before the cartoon, which read, "Open for Business—Help Wanted."*

Source: PC-3262, AJA.

5.16—"THE BIG STICK," REGARDING THE TRIANGLE SHIRTWAIST COMPANY FIRE, APRIL 7, 1911

Source: From the collections of the Hebraic Section, African and Middle Eastern Division, Library of Congress, Washington, D.C.

5.17—ROSE SCHNEIDERMAN, SELECTION REGARDING LABOR RELATIONS IN THE EARLY TWENTIETH CENTURY AND THE SHIRTWAIST FIRE, *All for One*, 1967

Rose Schneiderman (1882–1972) immigrated to the United States from Poland at age eight. As a factory worker in New York City, she began organizing her coworkers, eventually rising to become one of the leading labor union activists of her generation. She was particularly motivated by the tragic Triangle Shirtwaist

Fire, and reflected on the event in her 1967 autobiography, All for One.

One of the thirteen firms that succeeded in getting enough strike-breakers to defeat the Shirtwaist Makers was the Triangle Waist Company on Washington Place at Greene Street. The

League had picketed the factory, trying to get these scabs to join in the strike, but we had been hired to hang around the entrance, to say nothing been frustrated by the thugs and prostitutes who had [*sic*] of the police, from whom the pickets could expect no protection—only arrest, overt insults, and unwarranted interference when they tried to speak to the strike-breakers.

A serious problem was the strike-breakers' inability to understand our message of trade unionism. I mean literally to *understand* because language was a great problem to organizers during those years. At a mass meeting one had to have at least four interpreters—for Polish, German, Yiddish, and Italian, and sometimes a fifth one for Slovene. On the other hand, the language problem was an asset to employers like the Triangle Waist Company. By hiring newly arrived immigrants from several different countries who not only spoke no English but could not communicate with each other, they protected themselves against the union.

But the union was determined to organize the workers at Triangle and continued to campaign for over a year until March 25, 1911. Then suddenly it was all over. At five o'clock on that Saturday afternoon, when union shops were enjoying their newly won half-holiday, passersby in the neighborhood of Washington Square saw great clouds of black smoke coming from the building at Washington Place East and Greene Street. It was the Triangle factory and before the fire was out, 143 girls and women had perished. Trapped behind locked doors—locked to protect them from the union organizers—many of them died in the flames. Others, in their effort to escape, clawed their way to windows, only to plunge to their death on the pavement eight floors below. But all were victims of wanton and criminal disregard of fire and health hazards.

For a week the city was saddened by the funerals of the victims who could be identified. Then the League and Local 25 of the ILGWU [International Ladies' Garment Workers' Union] got permission from the city to hold a funeral for those who could not be claimed by anyone. More than 120,000 of us were in the funeral procession that miserable rainy April day. From ten in the morning until four in the afternoon we of the Women's Trade Union League marched in the procession with other trade-union men and women, all of us filled with anguish and regret that we had never been able to organize the Triangle workers. But in our grief and anger we, who were dedicated to the task of awakening the community to the plight of working women, would not remain silent. Already we had taken steps to make sure such a catastrophe would never be repeated.

The day after the fire, while the lifeless bodies of the women were still being gathered from the charred debris, a special joint meeting of the executive boards of the League, the Shirtwaist Makers Union, and the Hebrew Trades was called by the League at its headquarters. A relief committee to cooperate with the Red Cross in its work among the families of the victims was formed, and another committee was appointed to broaden the investigation and research on fire hazards in New York factories which was already being carried on by the League.

The League also established and played a vital part in another committee, the New York City Citizens Committee on Safety. First, it called a mass meeting on May 2 to protest the lack of safety and the inhuman conditions in the factories. Through the generosity of Anne Morgan [a philanthropist and the daughter of John Pierpont Morgan] the meeting was held at the Metropolitan Opera House. There was not an empty seat by the time it began. Jacob Schiff, the well-known financier and philanthropist, was chairman. Among the speakers were eminent civic leaders, churchmen, lawyers, labor-union officials, and representatives of women's organizations. The latter included not so eminent me.

[. . .]

. . . It was at the powerful urging of this committee that the State Factory Investigating Commission was appointed by Governor John A. Dix. . . .

The first report of the Factory Investigating Commission in 1912 contained a recommendation for a fifty-four-hour week for factories and mercantile establishments. With Frances Perkins piloting the bill through the Legislature, it was passed in 1913. This was a victory in our continuing campaign to reduce the work-week. But the most important result of the Commission's work was its recommendation for a new Industrial Code which was later enacted into law. The Code has been improved from year to year and today it is the most outstanding instrument for safeguarding the lives, health, and welfare of the millions of ware-earners in New York State and, by its far-reaching influence, in the nation at large. Indeed, the Code is a living monument to those 143 women whose lives were sacrificed in the Triangle Fire.

Source: Rose Schneiderman and Lucy Goldthwaite, *All for One* (New York: P. S. Eriksson, 1967), 97–103.

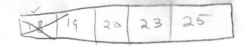

5.18—MENU, "TREFA BANQUET," JULY 11, 1883

Divisions among American Jews animated religious life. In one of the most remembered, and documented, moments in American Jewish religious history, a Reform movement rabbinic assembly meeting in Cincinnati served nonkosher food at its reception, causing more tradition-minded rabbis to bolt. The "Trefa Banquet," as it came to be known, revealed many of the religious conflicts in late nineteenth-century American Judaism. The following text retains spelling and other mistakes from the original.

Menu.

Little Neck Clams (Half Shell),
"Amontillado"
Sherry.

'POTAGES.
Consomme Royal,
"Sauternes."

POISSONS.
Fillet de Boef, aux Champignons,
Soft Shell Crabs,
a l'Amerique, Pommes Duchesse,
Salade of Shrimp,
"St. Julien."

ENTREE.
Sweet Breads, a la Monglas,
Petits Pois, a la Francaise,
"Deidesheimer."

RELEVEE.
Poulets, a la Viennoise,
Asperges Sauce, Vinaigrette Pommes
"Punch Romain."
Pate
Grenouiles a la Creme and Cauliflower,

ROTI.
Vol au Vents de Pigeons, a la Tyrolienne,
Salade de Saitue,
"G. H. Mumm Extra Dry."

HORS-D'OEUVERS.
Bouchies de Volaille, a la Regeurs,
Olives Caviv, Sardelles de Hollande,
Brissotins au Supreme Tomatoe,
Mayonaise.

SUCRES.
Ice Cream.
Assorted and Ornamented Cakes.

ENTREMENTS.
Fromages Varies, Fruits Varies,
"Martell Cognac." Cafe Noir.

Source: Rare document, AJA.

5.19—THE PITTSBURGH PLATFORM, 1885

Widely viewed as the founding document of what has come to be called classical Reform Judaism, the Pittsburgh Platform was the result of a meeting of nineteen reform-minded rabbis who gathered at the Concordia Club in

Pittsburgh, Pennsylvania, on November 16–19, 1885. The framers of this famous declaration called upon Jews to adapt Jewish practice and belief to the realities of the modern world. The platform stated that Judaism's moral precepts remained binding, while specific ritual practices had become obsolete.

In view of the wide divergence of opinion and of the conflicting ideas prevailing in Judaism today, we, as representatives of Reform Judaism in America, in continuation of the work begun at Philadelphia in 1869, unite upon the following principles:

First—We recognize in every religion an attempt to grasp the Infinite One, and in every mode, source or book of revelation held sacred in any religious system the consciousness of the indwelling of God in man. We hold that Judaism presents the highest conception of the God-idea as taught in our holy Scriptures and developed and spiritualized by the Jewish teachers in accordance with the moral and philosophical progress of their respective ages. We maintain that Judaism preserved and defended amid continual struggles and trials and under enforced isolation this God-idea as the central religious truth for the human race.

[...]

Third—We recognize in the Mosaic legislation a system of training the Jewish people for its mission during its national life in Palestine, and today we accept as binding only the moral laws and maintain only such ceremonies as elevate and sanctify our lives, but reject all such as are not adapted to the views and habits of modern civilization.

Fourth—We hold that all such Mosaic and Rabbinical laws as regulate diet, priestly purity and dress originated in ages and under the influence of ideas altogether foreign to our present mental and spiritual state. They fail to impress the modern Jew with a spirit of priestly holiness; their observance in our day is apt rather to obstruct than to further modern spiritual elevation.

We recognize, in the modern era of universal culture of heart and intellect, the approaching of the realization of Israel's great messianic hope for the establishment of the kingdom of truth, justice, and peace among all men. We consider ourselves no longer a nation, but a religious community, and therefore expect neither a return to Palestine, nor a sacrificial worship under the sons of Aaron, nor the restoration of any of the laws concerning the Jewish state.

[...]

Eighth—In full accordance with the spirit of Mosaic legislation which strives to regulate the relation between rich and poor, we deem it our duty to participate in the great task of modern times, to solve on the basis of justice and righteousness the problems presented by the contrasts and evils of the present organization of society.

Source: MS-34, AJA.

5.20—THE PREAMBLE AND ARTICLE II OF THE CONSTITUTION OF THE JEWISH THEOLOGICAL SEMINARY, MAY 9, 1886

The Jewish Theological Seminary of America was originally formed to rally traditionalists together in opposition to the Reform movement. (It was later, during the interwar years, that the seminary embraced its "Conservative" middle ground.) Written in 1886, the jts *constitution stressed the importance of tradition in American Jewish life.*

PREAMBLE:

The necessity having been made manifest for associated and organized effort on the part of the Jews of America faithful to Mosaic Law and ancestral traditions, for the purpose of keeping alive the true Judaic spirit; in particular by the establishment of a seminary where the Bible shall be impartially taught, and rabbinical literature faithfully expounded, and more especially where youths, desirous of entering the ministry, may be thoroughly grounded in Jewish knowledge and inspired by the precept and the example of their instructors with the love of the Hebrew language, and a spirit of fidelity and devotion to the Jewish law, the subscribers have, in accordance with a resolution adopted at a meeting of ministers held Shebat 25, 5646 (January 31, 1886), at the synagogue Shearith Israel, New York, agreed to organize The Jewish Theological Seminary Association, and to adopt for its government the following Constitution and By Laws:

ARTICLE II

Object

The purpose of this Association being the preservation in America of the knowledge and practice of historical Judaism, as ordained in the Law of Moses . . . and expounded by the prophets . . . and sages . . . of Israel in biblical and talmudical writings, it proposes in furtherance of its general aim, the following specific objects:

1. The establishment and maintenance of a Jewish Theological Seminary for the training of rabbis and teachers. . . .

Source: As printed in *JAW*, 243–44. From *Constitution and By-Laws of the Jewish Theological Seminary Association, etc.* (New York: n.p., 1886), 2–3.

5.21—RAY FRANK, "WHAT A JEWISH GIRL WOULD NOT DO IF SHE WERE A RABBI," MAY 23, 1890

Ray (Rachel) Frank (1861–1948), born in Gold Rush San Francisco, spent her early adult life as a public school teacher in Nevada and a religious school teacher in Oakland, California. In the fall of 1890, she traveled to Spokane, Washington, arriving on the eve of Yom Kippur. Invited by a leader of the local Jewish community, Frank delivered the sermon on the holiest day of the Jewish year, admonishing the community over its infighting and urging its members to unite and create a permanent synagogue. With that speech, Frank gained the reputation as the "Girl Rabbi of the Golden West"—the first Jewish woman to deliver a formal religious sermon in the United States. Later, Frank directed the education program at Oakland's First Hebrew Congregation. In her career, Frank pressed for the expansion of women's roles within Judaism. While she never sought rabbinic ordination, Frank inspired larger conversations about the possibility of ordaining women as rabbis. Frank's ability to create such an influential and public religious profile for herself in the western United States also affirmed the importance of regionalism in the development of American Judaism.

To the Editor:

Living in the "far West," your paper asking for replies to—"What would you do if you were a rabbi?" did not reach me in time to answer that interesting question, had I chosen to do so.

But I trust you will not think it too late to answer the question in a slightly different form, and one which is, I think, familiar to most minds. What I would not do if I were a rabbi.

First, if I were one of the elect, one who deemed myself worthy to expound the law to men created like myself with an understanding, and a small but mighty organ termed by physiologists the heart, why, then I would not, if I were a rabbi, endeavor to impress the nature of my calling by loud and shallow words, nor by a pompous bearing unbecoming the man of God. I would not say to my fancied inferiors, "*I am the rabbi*," and you must therefore do this or that; but I would reach their actions through their hearts.

I would try and remember that example is better than precept. I would not imagine myself a fixed star around which lesser lights must move.

I would try the effect of a gentle demeanor, a quiet voice, an earnest will, and a helping hand. I would learn if an unfailing courtesy and a positive sincerity were not sufficient to announce and impress my high vocation to the stranger and to the sinner.

I would not, if I were a rabbi, consider a stylish residence, fine garments, including a silk hat, not any of the jewels representing the original twelve tribes, as absolutely essential to keeping up my position as a "priest of the temple." I would not make a business matter of my calling otherwise than for the good of my congregation or for humanity in general.

I would not say my services are worthy a salary of so much per annum because I do this or that, or because I preach oftener or more learn-

edly than Mr. A. or Rev. B.; but, after satisfying my own wants in a modest way, I would use amounts expended on "high living," on cigars, cards, and other pleasantries toward enlightening the ignorant of my people—if not in my own town, where perhaps they are blessed with both intelligence and wealth, then I would use it for the poor and oppressed abroad. I would be more like Judah Asheri [(1270–1349), medieval rabbi and Talmudist]; less like one type of Hebrew satirically mentioned as "Solomon Isaacs" [a late nineteenth-century contemptuous stereotype of the Jew]. It is, indeed, difficult nowadays to note the difference between the rabbi and his friend the clothier, or the broker; his dress, his diamonds, his language, his very walk is not bookish but business; is not piety but pence.

I would not, if I were a rabbi, attempt to be a politician, for religion and politics do not and cannot under existing circumstances walk hand-in-hand. I would not degrade my holy office by assuring any ward political "boss" that for a consideration I could capture the votes of my co-religionists, "because being the rabbi, they will do as I tell them," as one rabbi of my acquaintance is said to have remarked. . . .

Source: As printed in *JAW*, 244–47. Originally published in the *Jewish Messenger*.

5.22—CYRUS ADLER, SELECTION FROM "A JEWISH RENAISSANCE," THE *American Hebrew*, NOVEMBER 9, 1894

Cyrus Adler (1863–1940), an Arkansas-born academic who taught Semitic languages at Johns Hopkins University, became the librarian for the Smithsonian Institution in 1892, where he focused on archeology and Semitics. In that capacity, he gave an 1894 speech outlining the academic development of Jewish studies in both England and the United States. Later, Adler would become chancellor of the Jewish Theological Seminary of America.

A Jewish Renaissance.

By Dr. Cyrus Adler, National Museum, Washington, D.C.

An occasion like that which the *American Hebrew* and its friends are celebrating this week affords an unusual opportunity for looking into the future in the light of the past—the recent past.

Fifteen years have witnessed a remarkable shift in Jewish activity. English Jewry has had a renaissance. The two great Universities have steadily pursued the policy of acquiring the original treasures of Jewish learning. By the painstaking work of Neubauer at Oxford and the brilliant scholarship and strong individuality of Schechter at Cambridge, these treasures are better known than ever before. The careful work of the Jews' College at London, for which most credit is due Dr. Friedlander, has given England a corps of better trained ministers than she previously enjoyed. The new college at Ramsgate, under the lead of Dr. Gaster, gives promise of the training of a race of scholars. The establishment of the *Jewish Quarterly Review*, the steady advance of the scholarly tone of the *Jewish Chronicle*, the appearance of men like Joseph Jacobs, Israel Abrahams, Claude Montefiore, S. Singer, and last, and probably first, I. Zangwill, prove that the spirit of Jewish learning has taken firm root in British soil. The Chief Rabbi, a man busy beyond conception, takes the time to assemble a great library of books and MSS., and the Maccabeans weld together all the intellectual Jews of England into an organization, where no test save that of intellect is set up. The women of England, too, do their part, and we find them translating poems of Halevi and pages from the Talmud. But the activity of England is too great to be briefly described and I must leave it with many omissions.

America has had its Jewish population doubled (to be conservative) within fifteen years, and has had unusual practical questions to meet as a result. Nevertheless this same period has witnessed the establishment of Oriental and Hebrew professorships in all of our large universities, the growth of a valuable library at the Hebrew Union College, the establishment of the Theological Seminary in New York, of the Publication Society, the Historical Society, the works of Kohut the elder, Jastrow and Mielziner, the earnest and to a degree successful endeavors of Morais towards a better knowledge of the classical Hebrew, the promise of a new college in Philadelphia, and the endowment of original research by Jacob H. Schiff and Lazarus Straus. It occasioned the Jewish activity of that unique figure, Emma Lazarus, includes the prodigious scientific activity of Richard Gottheil as well as of Morris Jastrow, Charles Gross and the remarkable suggestiveness of Charles Waldstein. It has produced the historical researches of such young men as the late Hyman P. Rosenbach, of Max J. Kohler, Herbert Friedenwald, Henry Morais and J. H. Hollander.

More significant than all these is the turning toward literary and scientific pursuits of a considerable number of Russian immigrants as soon, sometimes even before, they have earned the bare necessaries of life. In speaking of America as of England, I have made many omissions unavoidable in a summary.

Now, what does all this mean? Is it possible that the intellectual activity of the Jew in relation to Jewish learning is shifting to the English speaking world? It may be hazardous to venture an opinion, but I think it is.

It behooves us to consider well what we Americans should do towards fostering this spirit in a land as yet poor in Hebrew libraries, manuscripts, or avenues of scientific publication. In the near future, I shall make some suggestions in the *American Hebrew*, looking to the solution of this problem.

Cyrus Adler.

Source: *American Hebrew* 56, no. 1 (November 9, 1894).

5.23—PRINCIPLES ADOPTED BY THE [ORTHODOX] JEWISH CONGREGATIONAL UNION OF AMERICA, JUNE 8, 1898

The 1898 platform of the Orthodox Jewish Congregational Union of America, published as a direct response to the Reform movement's Pittsburgh Platform, insisted upon Jewish law's viability among observant American Jews.

This conference of delegates from Jewish congregations in the United States and the Dominion of Canada is convened to advance the interests of positive biblical, rabbinical, and historical Judaism.

We are assembled not as a synod, and therefore we have no legislative authority to amend religious questions, but as a representative body, which by organization and co-operation will endeavor to advance the interests of Judaism in America.

We favor the convening of a Jewish synod specifically authorized by congregations to meet, to be composed of men who must be certified rabbis, and (a) elders in official position (cf. Num. 11:16), (b) men of wisdom and understanding, and known among us (cf. Deut. 1:13), (c) able men, God-fearing men, men of truth, hating profit (cf. Ex. 18:21).

We believe in the divine revelation of the [Hebrew] Bible, and we declare that the prophets in no way discountenanced ceremonial duty, but only condemned the personal life of those who observed ceremonial law, but disregarded the moral. Ceremonial law is not optative; it is obligatory.

We affirm our adherence to the acknowledged codes of our rabbis and the thirteen principles of [the medieval philosopher-theologian] Maimonides.

We believe that in our dispersion we are to be united with our brethren of alien faith in all that devolves upon men as citizens; but that religiously, in rites, ceremonies, ideals, and doctrines, we are separate, and must remain separate in accordance with the divine declaration: "I have separated you from the nations to be mine" (Lev. 20:26).

And further, to prevent misunderstanding concerning Judaism, we reaffirm our belief in the coming of a personal Messiah, and we protest against the admission of proselytes into the fold of Judaism without milah and tebilah [circumcision and baptism].

We protest against intermarriage between Jew and Gentile; we protest against the idea that we are merely a religious sect, and maintain that we are a nation, though temporarily without a national home; and

Furthermore, that the restoration to Zion is the legitimate aspiration of scattered Israel, in no way conflicting with our loyalty to the land in which we dwell or may dwell at any time.

Source: As printed in JAW, 247–48. From Isadore Singer, ed., The Jewish Encyclopedia, vol. 4 (New York 1901–1906), 217.

5.24—ELKAN C. VOORSANGER, "PASSOVER SERVICES IN FRANCE," *Emanu-El,* MAY 3, 1918

At the U.S. entry into World War I, Elkan C. Voorsanger (1889–1963), a rabbi serving a congregation in St. Louis, enlisted as a chaplain, traveling to Europe with the first

U.S. contingent of soldiers. In the spring of 1918, he led a Passover Seder for U.S. troops, which he detailed in an article published by San Francisco's Congregation Emanu-El, where his father, Jacob Voorsanger, served as rabbi.

CHAPLAIN VOORSANGER PAYS FINE TRIBUTE TO DEVOTIONAL SPIRIT OF JEWISH BOYS "OVER THERE"

It was the most tremendously inspiring service that I have ever conducted. Nearly three hundred Jewish men came in from all parts [missing] sector to celebrate the Passover—orthodox and reform, all joined in the common service which I read. I had the little book issued by the British for the Jewish sailors and soldiers. A real spirit of devotion filled the Y.M.C.A. hut, in which the services were held. The boys really felt their Jewishness on this occasion and I could feel a thrill of pride as I looked at them. I preached what I think (be it said modestly) the best and one of the *real* sermons of my life. Any one could have preached to that crowd of sympathetic listeners—boys eager for a word of encouragement and hope, homesick lads who knew not to what fate they were going. Their spirit was fine. They were proud of their heritage of Judaism and Americanism and many told me that a feeling of loyalty to this double heritage was growing more and more with their stay in France. It was a great privilege for me to be in a position to officiate at the *first official service held for the Jews of [the] American Expeditionary Force.* One of the things that struck me during the service was the fact that all felt that they were *Jews*—neither orthodox nor reform—just plain Jews, meeting for a common cause and celebrating their day together. The question of "hats on or off," Hebrew or English, music or no, bothered no one—we just worshipped God as Jews and were happy.

I can't say too much in praise of the commanding general and officers in this section. General orders were issued allowing each Jewish man a pass for the day and in some cases two days, when the distance was too great to make the journey in one. Moreover, our efficient Quartermaster's Corps, in spite of the tremendous drains on their time and resources, had, in compliance with General Pershing's order, a stock of matzos on hand for the whole Passover week. So we strangers in a strange land are eating our matzos in the same spirit that our ancestors ate them: for the cause of liberty and democracy.

Another incident that I know will be of interest is the fact that I had telegrams from four other places where the Y.M.C.A. tried to arrange services. How I wished I could have broken myself up into five or six pieces. All praise is due the good work of the Y.M.C.A. over here, and in this case they wanted to pay my expenses to go there. How this war is breaking down prejudice, hatred and petty narrowness is indicated by just such incidents as this—a Christian organization promoting a Jewish religious service and offering to foot the bill! All hail to the new and liberal spirit which the Y.M.C.A. (and be it said all of us) is learning over here. Their work is *great* and deserves the support of all.

At present I am hard at work getting in touch with and ministering to the Jewish boys—of whom there are many thousands in France. As the one and only Jewish chaplain over here I can only make a scratch, but I am hoping that help in the shape of chaplains and welfare workers will soon be over. American Jewry can be proud of their sons; they are well thought of by the officers, make good soldiers and fighting men, and have proved true to the very best traditions of their faith. I never was prouder in my life of being a Jew than today, when I see such a large proportion of the "remnant" over here doing their bit. Thank God I've not yet had to say Kaddish for any Jewish boy—that will come, alas, too soon—but I am still glowing with the joy of having met the boys and having seen their eager, worshipful faces, following every line of the service from the first until the benediction was pronounced. When Jewish boys can participate as these boys did in a *common Jewish* service, putting aside the business of war for the moment to address themselves to their God, our faith has, in my opinion, a bigger and brighter future than ever before in the history of American Judaism.

Source: Emanu-El 45, no. 26 (May 3, 1918): cover page.

5.25 — MARTHA THAL, SELECTIONS FROM *Early Days: The Story of Sarah Thal,* ON LIFE IN A PIONEER FARMER FAMILY IN NORTH DAKOTA, CA. 1880

Sarah Thal (b. 1856) and her husband, Solomon, recent arrivals to the United States from Germany, took the advice of Solomon's brothers who were living in Milwaukee and chose the life of the pioneer farmer in North Dakota. Immediately after their 1880 marriage, the Thals settled in Nelson County in what was then the Dakota territory. The diary written by Martha Thal, Sarah's great-grandniece, reveals the challenges of Jewish life as well as the difficult lives of pioneer women as a whole.

When [I was] a child attending the religious school, the story of the sojourn of the Israelites in the Wilderness stirred my imagination. I too longed for a sojourn in the wilderness. I did not know that my dreams would become a reality, a reality covering long years of hardship and privation. I grew to womanhood in the town of Ellingen in the Saar Valley, and when I married Solomon Thal in 1880, I went to live in the picturesque village of Berg in the Mosel Valley. I remember this country as quiet and picturesque, where life was pleasant and peaceful.

My husband had brothers in Milwaukee who sent home glowing reports of conditions in America. We wished to try our luck in that wonderful land. When my daughter Elsie was fourteen months old we left to make our fortune, fully confident of our undertaking. We sailed from Antwerp and landed in Boston. I brought with me my linen chest, feather beds, pillows, bedding, etc. I have some bits of these things today. As most of the immigrants of that time were German, we reached Milwaukee without difficulty. Here my brother-in-law met us and took us to his home. I had become ill during the last part of the journey. I went to bed at once to learn I had typhoid.

My brother-in-law Sam Thal advised us to go to Dakota Territory. He had been out there and thought highly of the prospect. In fact, he had a large farm out there only twenty-eight miles from the railroad. My husband was anxious to get started and as soon as he could leave me he went out there. Six weeks later I followed. The only English I knew was "Yes" and "All right," and when my fellow passengers admired my baby and asked, "Is it a girl?" I said "Yes." And when they said "Is it a boy?" I said "Yes." I didn't know why they looked at each other and smiled.

[. . .]

. . . A newcomer must of course experience much embarrassment. My worst was one day Mr. Mendelson [who managed the Sam Thal farm] brought in a crate of pork and asked me, a piously reared Jewess, to cook it. In time I consented. However, I never forgot my religious teachings. I did, however, discard the dietary laws and practices, but to this day I observe the Passover (New Year's Day [*sic*]) and the Yon Kipper [*sic*] (the Day of Atonement).

We had few neighbors. At Harrisburg there was a little settlement and owing to the large tract of land the farm stood on, we had only one near neighbor, the Seligers, another Jewish family. We received mail rarely. A stage ran from Harrisburg to Larimore. The service was not dependable and getting mail was a big event.

[. . .]

That fall my second baby, Jacob, was born. I was attended by a Mrs. Saunders, an Englishwoman. We couldn't understand each other. It was in September. The weather turned cold and the wind blew from the north. It found its way through every crack in that poorly built house. I was so cold that during the first night they moved my bed into the living room by the stove and pinned sheets around it to keep the draft out and so I lived through the first child birth in the prairies. I like to think that God watched out for us poor lonely women when the stork came. All but two of my neighbors survived their many confinements and lived to see their children grown.

[. . .]

In the spring our baby was taken very ill. I wanted a doctor so badly. There was a terrific storm, and when it cleared the snow was ten feet deep. My husband couldn't risk a trip to Larimore. On the fourth day [t]he [baby] died unattended. I never forgave the prairies for that.

He was buried in the lot with Mrs. Seliger and a child of the Mendelsons. For many years we kept up the lonely graves. In time the wolves and elements destroyed them. They are unmarked in all save my memory. All the neighbors came to the funeral. Among them were Mr. and Mrs. Gutting. Afterwards we became fast friends. The friendships of those days lasted as long as life itself.

Source: AJAJ 23, no. 1 (1971): 47–62. Information on the relationship between Sarah Thal and Martha Thal was provided by David Epstein of the Jewish Museum of the American West.

5.26—"BINTEL BRIEF," ON INTERMARRIAGE, *Forward*, 1906

Created by Abraham Cahan in 1906, the Forward's *"Bintel Brief," which translates as "a bundle of letters," gave immigrant Jews the opportunity to ask questions about adapting to life in the United States. Among the many topics addressed on the pages of the column, this exchange on the question of intermarriage elicited a pointed response.*

Dear Editor,

For a long time I worked in a shop with a Gentile girl, and we began to go out together and fell in love. We agreed that I would remain a Jew and she a Christian. But after we had been married for a year, I realized that it would not work.

I began to notice that whenever one of my Jewish friends comes to the house, she is displeased. Worse yet, when she sees me reading a Jewish newspaper her face changes color. She says nothing, but I can see that she has changed. I feel that she is very unhappy with me, though I know she loves me. She will soon become a mother, and she is more dependent on me than ever.

She used to be quite liberal, but lately she is being drawn back to the Christian religion. She gets up early Sunday mornings, runs to church and comes home with eyes swollen from crying. When we pass a church now and then, she trembles.

Dear Editor, advise me what to do now. I could never convert, and there's no hope for me to keep her from going to church. What can we do now?

Thankfully,
A Reader

Answer:

Unfortunately, we often hear of such tragedies, which stem from marriages between people of different worlds. It's possible that if this couple were to move to a Jewish neighborhood, the young man might have more influence on his wife.

Source: This article originally appeared in the *Forward,* 1906; used by permission.

Anarchist, women's rights advocate, and labor leader Emma Goldman (1869–1940) took an early interest in birth control, rallying against the 1873 Comstock Law, which forbade individuals from disseminating literature advocating birth control. During that effort, she worked with Margaret Sanger (1879–1966), who would later become a national leader in the effort to promote birth control. In 1915, Goldman wrote to Sanger as part of their larger coordinated efforts to publicize the cause.

Chicago, Ill., 12/7/15

My dear Girl:

The enclosed money order for $40.00 represents the forty dollars collected at my Birth Control Lecture for you. I am sure it will come very handy, as you must be terribly hard pressed at the present time. It is my intention to use all other lecturers on the same subject as a means of raising some money for you. I know that it is not enough to express my affection for you and my devotion to the thing we both love so much, but in our materialistic age, the money question is very pressing indeed.

I really think it is impardonable on your part to blame yourself for the death of Peggy [Sanger's daughter, who contracted polio in 1910, before her first birthday]. I am sure that it is due only to your depressed state of mind as I cannot imagine anyone with your intelligence to hold herself responsible for something that could not possibly have been in your power.

No doubt the child would have been given better care in your home, but whether that would have saved her life is a mere speculation, which ought not to take possession of you in the way it evidently has. Please, dear, don't think me heartless. I feel deeply with your loss but I also feel that you owe it to yourself and the work you have before you to collect your strength. After all dear, it is a thing which has passed and cannot be redeemed whereas you need your vitality and unless you will take hold of yourself you will lose whatever little you have and yet not change the inexorable.

The Birth Control question has taken hold of the public as never before. That ought to be a tremendous satisfaction to you. It is this growing interest which will have no little bearing on your case and which in a measure may explain the indifference on the part of the authorities to open up your case. However, I do wish there was some decision one way or another. It would be such a wonderful thing if you could make a trip across the country. It would pull you out of yourself and at the same time give the movement an impetus of great force.

We have had interesting meetings here, but with the exception of the one on the Birth Control not so large as we had hoped. The sale of literature is phenominal [*sic*]. We leave for St. Louis to-night where you can reach me if you answer this by return mail, c/o of the Marquette Hotel. If not, write me general delivery, Indianapolis, Ind. until the 15th.

Hoping that you are feeling better and that the enclosed amount may help to give you some joy. I am devotedly and affectionately,

E. G.

Source: Library of Congress, Washington, D.C.

5.28—"A NEW SUPPLICATION FOR A WOMAN WHOSE HUSBAND HAS DESERTED HER," 1916

In 1905, the National Desertion Bureau was organized in New York in an effort to help a growing number of Jewish immigrant women who had been deserted by their husbands. In traditional Judaism, a divorce could only be granted if the husband approved, complicating the lives of women who sought legal separation. The requirement mandating a husband's consent to divorce took an even more difficult and painful turn for wives whose husbands abandoned them. Without the ability to divorce, women were unable to remarry according to Jewish law. Even if these deserted wives gained a civil divorce in a government court, Jewish law would still consider any of their subsequent offspring illegitimate. In response, prayers of supplication expressly for women, called tehinnot, *offered ways for women to communicate their frustrations through worship. In this heartfelt plea, a Jewish woman who has been abandoned by her husband makes an appeal to God, asking, among other things, for her husband's return.*

God of mercy you who dwells in the high places, merciful Father who dwells in the heavens, whose eyes are always open and who takes care of all your creatures and particularly so of all human beings who have been created in your image. Pay attention also to me your servant and see my suffering. Help me, dear God, in my need and do not turn away your love from me, even as you do not deny your love to all your creatures, and even as you show mercy to all whom you have created. Your pity extends to all whom you have created; have pity also on me. Accept my prayer and answer me when I call upon you.

O Master of the World, you have said in your Holy Law that people should marry and bring children into the world. I have hearkened to your sacred call and I married according to the Law of Moses and Israel, just as you decreed. My husband did not amount to anything and he abandoned me; he disappeared and left me a widow, a deserted woman. I know, dear God, that it is you alone who unites couples. Without your holy decree no couple can be joined. It may well be that you did not consider me worthy; perhaps it is because of my sins that I lost favor in my husband's eyes and he left me miserable and unhappy. I am now a foundering vessel adrift on the sea. There is no one to whom I can turn. I have no one to whom I can pour out the bitterness in my heart, except to you, O God, who is kind and forgiving, who is merciful and pardoning.

O God of mercy and forgiveness, God of pity and kindness, it may well be that I have sinned against you before my marriage. Perhaps after my marriage, I have not conducted myself properly as a Jewish woman should. Perhaps I have not properly observed all the commandments and the ordinances that you enjoined upon us women. Maybe I have sinned against you and against my husband, thinking evil thoughts— God forbid—and this is why you have punished me. So now I beg of you, dear merciful and gracious God, pity me, forgive my sins and turn back the heart of my husband to me. Maybe I did something to him; maybe I have not treated him with respect as a Jewish daughter ought to treat her man. O Master of the Universe, urge him to forget the evil which I have done him so that I may be acceptable in his eyes as I was when he married me and when I went under the marriage canopy. May he turn to me in love and may there be established among us, as it is written in your Holy Torah, "and they shall be one flesh"; man and woman shall be as if they were one body [Genesis 2:24]. And may there be only peace and quiet between us as long as we live.

If anyone is responsible for my misfortune, if evil men have led my husband aside from the straight road, if malicious tongues have inflamed him against me, I do not, indeed, require O Father in Heaven, that you should punish them because of this, but I do ask you to turn their hearts to good, that they no longer keep my husband from coming back to me. O Master of the World, induce him and my enemies to think no evil of me, so that I may live out my years with my husband in good fortune and in peace. Amen. Selah.

Source: As printed in *JAW*, 347–48. From *Shas Tehinnah, Rav Peninnim, etc.* (New York: Hebrew Publishing Co., 1916), 209–11.

5.29—SELECTION REGARDING AMERICAN ZIONISM
FROM ZVI HIRSCH MASLIANSKY'S MEMOIRS, CA. 1895

*Zvi Hirsch Masliansky (1856–1943), known in
Europe for his outstanding speechmaking, was
expelled from Belorussia in 1894 over his Zionist
ideology. The next year, he arrived in New York
City, where he emerged as one of the most
articulate and powerful advocates of Zionism.
Speaking in Yiddish, Masliansky became
famous for his Friday evening sermons at New
York's Educational Alliance. In the selection
that follows, Masliansky offers a transnational
perspective on the role of the police, his reactions
to life in the United States, and his efforts to
create a modern Jewish state.*

A feeling of admiration and respect for America and her institutions came over me as a result of my contact with the police. At that moment, I was reminded of my relationship with the police of Russia, who interrupted my speeches and threw me out of synagogues in Odessa, Kishinev, Lodz, etc., with savage cruelty. Tears of joy flowed from my eyes when I felt the difference between the police of New York and the gendarmes of Kishinev. The latter, wild beasts full of hateful vengeance, expelled me from the synagogue. The former, in kindness, consideration, and respect, escorted me into a synagogue. Light and darkness, slavery and freedom—what a huge distance there is between them! And my lips whispered, "Blessed are you, America, and blessed is your freedom."

[. . .]

On every street that I walked, I was distracted by the large signs with the word "Kosher" over every eating establishment, and the words "Friend of the Worker" over every saloon. Master of the Universe! Ten measures of Kashruth and "Friend of the Worker" were granted to the world. New York took nine measures, and that left the rest of the world with one measure!

[. . .]

Baltimore was the first of the many cities to invite me to come and speak. A Hovevei Zion group, young people full of devotion and enthusiasm for the ideal of Jewish nationalism, welcomed me at the railway station. Among the members of this group were: Reuben Aaronson, the President; P. F. Mirvis (Aaronson's brother-in-law); Dr. Fox; Horowitz; and Senior Abel.

I immediately felt as if I was in my natural element, among comrades. It was hard to believe that I was in America, for the spirit of national fervor was every bit as strong as it was in Vilna or in Bialystok. I visited a number of public institutions, including many synagogues and their rabbis. Everywhere there was a real spirit of Judaism; of its hallowed tradition and its finest principles. Pious Jews like the Friedenwald family, the Levy family, Rabbi Dr. Schaffer, Mr. Tanhum Silberman, and others like them rivaled even the Jews of Vilna. Great learning and civilized ways prevailed among the Jews of Baltimore. Thus, it was not without good cause that I referred to that city at the end of the 1890s as the "Bialystok of America."

Source: SC-13412, AJA. This selection is translated by Gary P. Zola, from his rabbinical thesis, "The People's Preacher: A Study of the Life and Writings of Zvi Hirsch Masliansky, 1856–1943," Hebrew Union College, 1982, 118–34.

Although American Jews of both Eastern European and Central European origin backed the Zionism movement, others viewed it as an assault on their status as patriotic Americans. Isaac Mayer Wise, who emigrated from Bohemia in 1847, helped found the Union of American Hebrew Congregations, the Hebrew Union College, and the Central Conference of American Rabbis, for which he served as president. Wise rejected Zionism, as did most Reform Jews at that time. In 1897, the same year that Theodor Herzl (1860–1904) led the First Zionist Congress in Basel, Switzerland, Wise pressed his anti-Zionist thinking on his colleagues at their annual Central Conference of American Rabbis meeting in Montreal.

. . . I consider it my duty also, Rev. colleagues, to call your attention to the political projects engaging now a considerable portion of our co-religionists in Europe and also in our country, especially in New York, Philadelphia, Chicago, and other large cities. I refer, of course, to the so-called "Friends of Zion," *Chovaveh Zion*, who revive among certain classes of people the political national sentiment of olden times, and turn the mission of Israel from the province of religion and humanity to the narrow political and national field, where Judaism loses its universal and sanctified ground and its historical signification.
[. . .]
Idealists and religious phantasts took hold upon this situation, and made of it a general restoration of the Jews and their returning to the holy land, although the greatest number of Jewish citizens in the countries where they enjoy all civil and political rights loudly disavowed any such beliefs, hopes or wishes; yet the persecuted and expatriated from Russia and such other countries preached their new doctrine loudly and emphatically, and found advocates and friends also among Christians, more so even than among Jews. At last politicians seized the situation, and one of them, called Dr. [Theodor] Herzl, proposed to establish and constitute at once the Jewish State in Palestine [although Herzl's *Judenstaat* pamphlet had never mentioned Palestine], worked the scheme, and placed it so eloquently before the Jewish communities that the utopian idea of a Jewish state took hold of many minds, and a congress of all "Friends of Zion" was convoked to the city of Munich, to meet there in August next. [Actually they met in Basel, Switzerland.]

However, all this agitation on the other side of the ocean concerned us very little. We are perfectly satisfied with our political and social position. It can make no difference to us in what form our fellow citizens worship God, or what particular spot of the earth's surface we occupy. We want freedom, equality, justice and equity to reign and govern the community in which we live. This we possess in such fullness, that no State whatever could improve on it. That new Messianic movement over the ocean does not concern us at all. But the same expatriated, persecuted and outrageously wronged people came in large numbers also to us, and they, being still imbued with their home ideas, ideals and beliefs, voiced these projects among themselves and their friends so loudly and so vehemently, that the subject was discussed rather passionately in public meetings, and some petty politicians of that class are appointed as delegates, we learn, to the Basle Congress, and in each of those meetings, as reported by the press, so and so many rabbis advocated those political schemes, and compromised in the eyes of the public the whole of American Judaism as the phantastic dupes of a thoughtless Utopia, which is to us a *fata morgana*, a momentary inebriation of morbid minds, and a prostitution of Israel's holy cause to a madman's dance of unsound politicians. . . .

Source: As printed in *JAW*, 382–83. From *Central Conference of American Rabbis Yearbook*, 7 (1897–98): x–xii.

5.31—MOSES DESCENDING WITH THE TEN COMMANDMENTS INTO YOSEMITE VALLEY, CONGREGATION SHERITH ISRAEL, SAN FRANCISCO, 1905

For many Jews, the impulse to leave their American communities and immigrate to Palestine never took hold. They considered the United States their homeland and did not respond to the Zionist movement that was gaining strength in Eastern Europe and Ottoman Palestine. In San Francisco, Sherith Israel congregants expressed their love for American Jewish life by commissioning a 1905 stained glass sanctuary window that depicted Moses descending with the Ten Commandments from Mount Sinai into California's famed Yosemite Valley.

Source: Congregation Sherith Israel, San Francisco, Calif. Autry Museum of Western Heritage, Los Angeles, Calif. Ben Ailes, photographer; used by permission of the photographer.

The American Zionist movement enjoyed dramatic growth when famed jurist and eventual U.S. Supreme Court associate justice Louis Brandeis agreed to become its leader in 1914. While Brandeis positioned Zionism as an important antidote to European antisemitism, he also crafted a version of American Zionism that addressed, and for many resolved, the dual loyalty conflict that plagued calls for Jewish nationalism in the United States. At a time when the first groups of Eastern European Jews immigrated to Palestine, American Jews worried that support for the Zionist cause would cast a shadow on their reputations as loyal Americans. Brandeis, in a 1915 speech delivered to a group of American Reform rabbis, articulated what would later be known as the Brandeisian Synthesis, combining the nationalist aspirations of Jews with the ideals of the Founding Fathers. According to Brandeis, American Jews could support the Zionist cause without leaving the United States and without compromising their civic status as loyal Americans.

ZIONISM AND PATRIOTISM.

Let no American imagine that Zionism is inconsistent with Patriotism. Multiple loyalties are objectionable only if they are inconsistent. A man is a better citizen of the United States for being also a loyal citizen of his state, and of his city; for being loyal to his family, and to his profession or trade; for being loyal to his college or his lodge. Every Irish American who contributed towards advancing home rule was a better man and a better American for the sacrifice he made. Every American Jew who aids in advancing the Jewish settlement in Palestine, though he feels that neither he nor his descendants will ever live there, will likewise be a better man and a better American for doing so.

Note what [British historian Robert] Seton-Watson says:

"America is full of nationalities which, while accepting with enthusiasm their new American citizenship, nevertheless look to some centre in the Old World as the source and inspiration of their national culture and traditions. The most typical instance is the feeling of the American Jew for Palestine which may well become a focus for his déclassé kinsmen in other parts of the world." (*The War and Democracy*, p. 290.)

There is no inconsistency between loyalty to America and loyalty to Jewry. The Jewish spirit, the product of our religion and experiences, is essentially modern and essentially American. Not since the destruction of the Temple have the Jews in spirit and in ideals been so fully in harmony with the noblest aspirations of the country in which they lived.

America's fundamental law seeks to make real the brotherhood of man. That brotherhood became the Jewish fundamental law more than twenty-five hundred years ago. America's insistent demand in the twentieth century is for social justice. That also has been the Jews' striving for ages. Their affliction as well as their religion has prepared the Jews for effective democracy. Persecution broadened their sympathies. It trained them in patient endurance, in self-control, and in sacrifice. It made them think as well as suffer. It deepened the passion for righteousness.

Indeed, loyalty to America demands rather that each American Jew become a Zionist. For only through the ennobling effect of its strivings can we develop the best that is in us and give to this country the full benefit of our great inheritance. The Jewish spirit, so long preserved, the character developed by so many centuries of sacrifice, should be preserved and developed further, so that in America as elsewhere the sons of the race may in future live lives and do deeds worthy of their ancestors.

[. . .]

OUR DUTY.

Since the Jewish Problem is single and universal, the Jews of every country should strive for its solution. But the duty resting upon us of America is especially insistent. We number about 3,000,000, which is more than one fifth of all the Jews in the world, a number larger than comprised within any other country except the Russian Empire. We are representative of all the Jews in the world; for we are composed of immigrants, or descendants of immigrants coming from every other country, or district. We include persons from every section of society, and of every shade of religious belief. We are ourselves free from civil or political disabilities; and are relatively prosperous. Our fellow-Americans are infused with a high and generous spirit, which insures approval of our struggle to ennoble, liberate, and otherwise improve the condition of an important part of the human race; and their innate manliness makes them sympathize particularly with our efforts at self-help. America's detachment from the old world problem relieves us from suspicions and embarrassments frequently attending the activities of Jews of rival European countries. And a conflict between American interests or ambitions and Jewish aims is not conceivable. Our loyalty to America can never be questioned.

Let us therefore lead, earnestly, courageously and joyously, in the struggle for liberation. Let us all recognize that we Jews are a distinctive nationality of which every Jew, whatever his country, his station or shade of belief, is necessarily a member. Let us insist that the struggle for liberty shall not cease until equality of opportunity is accorded to nationalities as to individuals. Let us insist also that full equality of opportunity cannot be obtained by Jews until we, like members of other nationalities, shall have the option of living elsewhere or of returning to the land of our forefathers.

Source: Louis D. Brandeis School of Law, Louisville, Ky. Used by permission.

5.33—SIMON WOLF, "KISHINEFF—AN APPEAL," *Jewish Criterion*, MAY 22, 1903

In April 1903, Russian newspapers carried the story of the death of a Christian child in Ukraine, accusing the local Jewish population of murder as part of an antisemitic blood libel. A pogrom, or government-sanctioned attack on Jews and Jewish businesses, followed in the town of Kishinev, where almost fifty Jews were killed and hundreds of homes and businesses destroyed. The Kishinev pogrom proved a turning point in both Russian and Jewish history, convincing thousands of Jews that they had no future in Eastern Europe and needed to emigrate. The event also sparked an international outcry. Major news outlets in the United States reported on the pogrom, while Theodore Roosevelt referenced it in his corollary to the Monroe Doctrine, arguing that the U.S. military would intervene in its sphere of influence should any other government attempt such an action. Within Russia, outrage against the czar rallied a movement to overthrow the government, leading to the failed 1905 Russian revolution.

For his part, Simon Wolf (1836–1923), the former U.S. consul-general to Egypt as well as the president of B'nai B'rith, appealed to his coreligionists in the Jewish Criterion, *which also carried news of a mass meeting in Pittsburgh held to protest the pogrom.*

The tragedy enacted on the night and succeeding day of Easter, 1903, in darkest Russia demands not vengeance, but justice. The government and the people of the Czar stand arraigned before the bar of humanity for the foulest crime of all the centuries, and the verdict of history will be "Guilty on all the counts of the indictment."

How long, oh, Lord! is this nightmare to continue? How long is the Jew to be cruelly murdered and outraged in the name of his Son, and by the offshoot of His own religion? Is Christianity only a misnomer and another name for hate, bigotry, and prejudice? It is not for the Jew to answer. Let the fair-minded, liberal, just Christian find the solution of this problem of all the ages.

The pretext for this latest outbreak and dastardly Bartholomew is the old, stale, and absurd charge of "ritual murder." A Christian boy is found murdered. "The Jews did it, to get his blood for their Passover celebration." Rigid investigations were instituted, and after three exhaustive official examinations the charge was declared false, no blood had been taken, yet this ridiculous charge was used as the reason for their hellish and frightful orgies. This "ritual" charge, invented by the cowardly priests of all ages, has been disproven each and every time, and yet is used with ghoulish glee by the spawn of the devil to satisfy their stupid fanaticism.

On its very face it bears the earmarks of the whole lie, for the Jew, of all men, is not a murderer; he is for peace, order, concord. The shedding of blood to him is revolting and contrary to every line and letter of his faith and training, and these leaders of the church know it best of all. But it does not fit into their system to proclaim the truth. The church to their thinking can only thrive by injustice and ignorance, and so the ever-slumbering embers are fanned into flame, and the midnight hour and the noonday sun bear witness to the lurid fires that unbridled passions have kindled. Neither age nor sex is spared—old and young, men and women, the gray-haired and the golden-locked, all fall victims to these brutes, these vultures of darkest Russia, and in a moment, the home and the sanctuary are alike swept away and desolation, ruin, penury, stand where thrift and Russian content were.

And all this in the name of Christ, the peacemaker, and connived at and condoned by the police and military authorities of his Christian majesty, the Czar of all the Russians. I am not drawing on my imagination, not recklessly stating conditions not warranted by facts.

The censored press of St. Petersburg, the eyewitnesses of the horrors, the correspondents of the *London Times*, all bear testimony that the half of the frightful massacres and rapine have not been told, and yet our ambassador in Russia, in answer to a cablegram of our State Department, says: "It is authoritatively denied that want or suffering exists, and all help is gratefully declined." This is the official answer to an official request. What else was to be expected? To have confessed more was to condemn itself. This request for truth and the privilege to aid was made by me as "chairman of the board of delegates of the Union of American Jewish Congregations,["] and it took Mr. McCormick two weeks to answer.

He was not to depend upon the lying answers of Russian officials, but give his unbiased opinion and the most reliable unofficial information. I know just how far our government can go. After an experience of forty years I am not a neophyte, but a past master in the devious ways of international comity. Therefore the principles so grandly proclaimed in the now famous Roumanian note of Secretary [of State John] Hay are applicable in the present status of the Jews in Russia. In 1870, when only a ukase had been issued banishing the Jews of Bessarabia, at my instance Gen. Grant cabled to our Minister, Andrew G. Curtin, to use his good offices, and that grand and patriotic American did his full duty and succeeded in preventing the expulsion.

This is the difference between a statesman and a millionaire.

These outrages in Russia will lead to increased immigration, and what was only a breeze in the case of Roumania will prove a whirlwind in the matter of Russia. Our seaboard cities are congested, our means to help and succor almost exhausted, and if the exodus is to continue, either the gates will be shut or the laws made more liberal, for the Jews, as citizens of the United States, alone cannot bear the burdens that result from the cruelties and inhumanities of Russia. Thus the whole people of our republic may be called on in time, and the Jewish problem of Europe become unfortunately a political factor in the United States.

I therefore appeal to the government of the United States to invite the great powers of Europe to cooperate on lines of civilization and common humanity and appeal to the Czar.

The reforms granted by England to Ireland have been won by the Irish in the United States; the reforms to be secured from Russia may have to be won by the Jews in the United States. I am not advocating this course, but simply . . . with conditions. This government has problems of its own to solve and ought not to be burdened with this, and the only way to avoid the political complication of the future is to deal energetically with Russia.

The Jews of the world ask nothing but justice and equal rights [that] those of the United States seek, . . . citizens of our common country, . . . prevent disaster to our institutions and demand only that recognition at home and abroad that is accord[ed] to every other American.

This horror of Kishineff concerns the Christian countries of the [entire] world—China and Japan no less. . . . If atrocities like these, that [make] even those of the Dark Ages see[m] insignificant, are to continue without stern rebuke, then the clock [of] progress will have to be set back [a] thousand years, civilization becomes a shame and mockery, and governments of the people, by the people and for the people will vanish from the earth, and the "miter, scepter[r] and censor" will rule to the infamy and disgrace of mankind.

Source: Jewish Criterion 16, no. 26 (May 22, 1903): 4.

5.34—"THE MASS MEETING," PERTAINING TO THE KISHINEV POGROM, *Jewish Criterion*, JUNE 12, 1903

On Sunday night was held the mass meeting in the Bijou Theatre [Pittsburgh]. It was a meeting which will remain in the memory of those present for years to come. Three thousand people were packed into the building from the floor to the top-most balcony. It was a most inspiring sight and every speaker of the evening felt himself called upon to do his best under the influence of such a gathering. Hundreds were turned away and the great crowd was handled with some difficulty. Many of the leading delegates occupied seats on the stage, in company with the orators of the occasion. Rabbi H. M. Lasker opened the exercises with prayer, after which Judge Cohen, Chairman of the meetings, offered a few eloquent remarks on the occasion which had attracted one of the greatest gatherings over which it had been his fortune to preside. He, said in part:

"We have with us to-night those who are more competent to tell you what Zionism is than I am. I am not sure that I myself understand it. If it is the old Zionism which means the coming of a Messiah and the establishment of the kingdom at Jerusalem, I am not sure that I concur. My Zionism is here under the stars and stripes.

"But if Zionism means the unification of the Jewish forces everywhere then I am a Zionist, heart and soul. From this meeting to-night I hope there will go forth a sentiment that will reach the shores of Europe and tell the oppressors there that if there is no physical force in the world to restrain them there is at least a moral force with which they will have to reckon."

Source: Jewish Criterion 16, no. 26 (May 22, 1903): 3.

5.35—"BINTEL BRIEF," LETTER FROM AN IMMIGRANT EXPERIENCING ANTISEMITISM, *Forward*, 1907

The rise of domestic antisemitism in the Progressive era (1890–1920) occurred largely in the urban centers of the Northeast. In New York City, the Forward*'s advice column, "Bintel Brief," published letters from immigrants facing antisemitic discrimination and the editor's suggestions for how they might respond.*

Worthy Editor,

I am eighteen years old and a machinist by trade. During the past year I suffered a great deal, just because I am a Jew.

It is common knowledge that my trade is run mainly by the Gentiles and, working among the Gentiles, I have seen things that cast a dark shadow on the American labor scene. Just listen:

I worked in a shop in a small town in New Jersey, with twenty Gentiles. There was one other Jew besides me, and both of us endured the greatest hardships. That we were insulted goes without saying. At times we were even beaten up. We work in an area where there are many factories, and once, when we were leaving the shop, a group of workers fell on us like hoodlums and beat us. To top it off, we and one of our attackers were arrested. The hoodlum was let out on bail, but we, beaten and bleeding, had to stay in jail. At the trial, they fined the hoodlum eight dollars and let him go free.

After that I went to work on a job in Brooklyn. As soon as they found out that I was a Jew they began to torment me so that I had to leave the place. I have already worked at many places, and I either have to leave, voluntarily, or they fire me because I am a Jew.

Till now, I was alone and didn't care. At this trade you can make good wages, and I had enough. But now I've brought my parents over, and of course I have to support them.

Lately I've been working on one job for three months and I would be satisfied, but the worm of anti-Semitism is beginning to eat at my bones again. I go to work in the morning as to Gehenna, and I run away at night as from a fire. It's impossible to talk to them because they are common boors, so-called "American sports." I have already tried in various ways, but the only way to deal with them is with a strong fist. But I am too weak and they are too many.

Perhaps you can help me in this matter. I know it is not an easy problem.

Your reader,
E. H.

ANSWER:

In the answer, the Jewish machinist is advised to appeal to the United Hebrew Trades and ask them to intercede for him and bring up charges before the Machinists Union about this persecution. His attention is also drawn to the fact that there are Gentile factories where Jews and Gentiles work together and get along well with each other.

Finally it is noted that people will have to work long and hard before this senseless racial hatred can be completely uprooted.

Source: This article originally appeared in the *Forward*, 1906; used by permission.

5.36—POLICE COMMISSIONER THEODORE A. BINGHAM, SELECTION FROM "FOREIGN CRIMINALS IN NEW YORK," SEPTEMBER 1908

As emigration from Eastern and Southern Europe increased in the late nineteenth and early twentieth centuries, nativists upset about the changing social fabric of American society gave voice to their concerns. In popular literature, newspapers and even some Christian religious institutions, opponents of unrestricted immigration, pressed their xenophobic attitudes into the public square. New York City's police commissioner, Theodore A. Bingham (1858–1934), carried their banner when, in September 1908, he published "Foreign Criminals in New York," accusing Jews of committing half the city's crimes. After a public outcry, Bingham reversed his report's conclusions.

When the circumstance is taken into consideration that eighty-five per cent of the population of New York City is either foreign-born or of foreign parentage, and that nearly half of the residents of the five boroughs do not speak the English language, it is only a logical condition that something like eighty-five out of one hundred of our criminals should be found to be of exotic origin. In no one police precinct on Manhattan Island does the percentage of native-born heads of families reach 50—the highest, 45.44[,] being in the West Side district lying between Forty-second and Eighty-sixth Streets and Eighth Avenue and the North River, and the lowest, 3.12, in the densely congested East Side quarter, largely peopled by Russian Hebrews, bounded by East Broadway, the Bowery and Houston and Norfolk Streets. Wherefore it is not astonishing that with a million Hebrews, mostly Russian, in the city (one-quarter of the population), perhaps half of the criminals should be of that race, when we consider that ignorance of the language, more particularly among men not physically fit for hard labor, is conducive to crime; nor is it strange that in the precinct where there are not four native-born heads of families in every hundred families, the percentage of criminality is high.

[. . .]

The crimes committed by the Russian Hebrews are generally those against property. They are burglars, firebugs, pickpockets and highway robbers—when they have the courage; but, though all crime is their province, pocket-picking is the one to which they seem to take most naturally. Indeed, pickpockets of other nationalities are beginning to recognize the superiority of the Russian Hebrew in that gentle art, and there have been several instances lately where a He-

brew and an Italian had formed a combination for theft in the streets, the former being always selected for the "tool," as the professionals term that one who does the actual reaching into the victim's pocket, while the others create a diversion to distract attention, or start a fight in case of the detection and pursuit of the thief. Central Office detectives recently arrested a Hebrew, a Greek and an Italian who were picking pockets together. Among the most expert of all the street thieves are Hebrew boys under sixteen, who are being brought up to lives of crime. Many of them are old offenders at the age of ten. The juvenile Hebrew emulates the adult in the matter of crime percentages, forty per cent of the boys at the House of Refuge and twenty-seven per cent of those arraigned in the Children's Court being of that race. The percentage of Hebrew children in the truant schools is also higher than that of any others.

Source: North American Review 188 (September 1908).

5.37—LEO FRANK TO C. P. CONNOLLY, DISCUSSING THE MURDER NOTES AND HOW THESE MIGHT DEMONSTRATE HIS INNOCENCE, MARCH 11, 1915

In one of the best-known incidents of antisemitism in U.S. history, Atlanta pencil factory supervisor Leo Frank (1884–1915) was arrested for the April 1913 murder of Mary Phagan, a thirteen-year-old employee in the company. Despite evidence that another person committed the crime, Frank, a Jew who was raised in New York, was convicted of her murder and sentenced to death. Two years later, Georgia governor John M. Slaton (1866–1955) commuted Frank's sentence to life imprisonment after he was convinced that Frank had not been treated fairly. On August 17, 1915, Frank was kidnapped from jail by several dozen armed men who lynched him for his alleged crime. The Frank case placed American antisemitism,

and Jew-hatred in the South specifically, into sharp focus. In a region where the racial boundaries between black and white typically privileged Jews over African Americans, the murder charge against Frank and the government's decision not to prosecute Jim Conley, the African American janitor believed to have been the actual murderer, stoked fear among Jews in Atlanta, in Georgia, and across the country. About half of Atlanta's Jewish population of three thousand uprooted themselves in the wake of the lynching, while B'nai B'rith, which counted Frank as one of its local leaders, created the Anti-Defamation League in September 1913 to fight against antisemitism nationally.

Atlanta, Ga.,

March eleventh,
Nineteen fifteen.

Mr. C. P. Connolly,
76 N. Munn Ave.,
E. Orange, N.J.

My dear Mr. Connolly:—

I have your kind letter of 7th inst. I have not as yet received the copy of "Jems"; however I have read the article to which you refer, and like it very much. Mr. Clark, the editor, who visited me and with whom I had a very pleasant conversation of about an hour,—he impressed me as a most intelligent and keen individual.

I desire to thank you for the letter you so kindly sent to the *N.Y. World*. The letters they published were indeed a strange "pot pourri." I expect you noted the letter from Brother Watson. Strangest of all to my mind was the letter of J. J. O'Neill, of the *World* staff, with whom, when he was here, I took so much pains. I cannot imagine what was passing through his mind when he wrote that letter.

One thing I have noted, in all of the publications on our case, and that is that the two "murder notes" have not been stressed in their true and vital significance. They are the key-stone to the whole case. They are the one fact on which the whole case can be swung. For example: two things are admitted in this case by every student of the evidence; 1st—the murder notes are the conception of the perpetrator of the crime. 2nd—Conley's hand wrote the notes. We then strike this situation: on the one hand is Conley, who admittedly and undeniably wrote the notes; he says Frank dictated them to him. On the other hand, Frank, who says he did not; he knows nothing of the notes; that they are the silly concoction of an ignorant brain, and that it is preposterous to believe that anyone of common sense would leave documentary evidence behind him. If Conley's story is true, Frank is guilty; if Frank is telling the truth and Conley is lying, Conley is guilty. There is no getting around this. It then remains to be shown which of the two, Frank or Conley did not know that handwriting is individual; that a person's handwriting can be traced surely to him. The person who conceived the notes did not know this. Conley's connection with and history in this case, proves conclusively that he did not know that one hand writing is different from another. You remember in his affidavits of May 28th and 24th and 29th Conley stated that he wrote one note and Frank the other. That Frank knew that everybody's handwriting is individual needs no discussion

If this fact is properly presented and properly stressed, with the adjacent circumstances of Conley first refusing to write at all, and then being forced to write from evidence which I gave, I cannot but believe that such presentation would be most conclusive.

With every good wish, in which Mrs. Frank joins me, I am

Cordially yours,
Leo M. Frank

Source: SC-14934, AJA.

Source: PC-1279, AJA.

Source: PC-1279, AJA.

5.40—RESOLUTION FOUNDING THE NATIONAL COUNCIL OF JEWISH WOMEN, SEPTEMBER 7, 1893

The National Council of Jewish Women (NCJW), organized in 1893 by Hannah Greenebaum Solomon (1858–1942) in Chicago following the World's Fair, emerged as a leading voice for social reform in this period. The NCJW, partnering with Jane Addams's Hull House in Chicago, advocated children's rights within the legal system, offered vocational training for girls and women, and promoted nutrition in the public school system. The NCJW also worked on behalf of Jewish immigrants and their families in the United States and reached out to support impoverished and persecuted Jews in Eastern Europe and elsewhere.

... This Congress would not be complete without some record of [what] many Jewish women have done, and are doing. Therefore, an attempt has been made to bring into a short, presentable form, the present work of Jewish women. ...

There are in existence several working girls' clubs [in New York City] for evening instruction and one—the Working Girls' Alliance—for mutual improvement and culture. This is a self-supporting institution, and is a pioneer in a field that should be actively and energetically worked.

In New York and in other cities during the past few years have been formed in the various congregations what are known as Sisterhoods. They teach the value of personal service, and practically show it in visiting the sick and poor, in providing and teaching creches [nursery schools] and kindergartens.

Their work is divided into four sections:

1. Visiting the poor;
2. Work in Kindergartens, etc.;
3. Work in Sabbath Schools and sewing classes, combining religious and practical work; and
4. Work among working girls.

Prevention is their watchword, as it must come to be that of us all. The first three of these sections are in most active operation. Work among working girls is being pushed but has assumed no such proportions as it should and will.

[...]

Miss [Sadie] American, of Chicago, then presented the following resolution:

Resolved, That we, Jewish women, sincerely believing that a closer fellowship will be encouraged, a closer unity of thought and sympathy and purpose, and a nobler accomplishment will result from a widespread organization, do therefore band ourselves together in a union of workers to further the best and highest interests of Judaism and humanity, and do call ourselves the "National Council of Jewish Women." Seconded and adopted.

Source: As printed in *JAW,* 266–70. From *Papers of the Jewish Women's Congress Held at Chicago, September 4, 5, 6, and 7, 1893* (Philadelphia: n.p., 1894), 218, 225–30, 264–65.

*Through the first decade of the twentieth
century, incidents of anti-Jewish discrimination
continued in Eastern Europe, as well as in other
regions around the world. In response to
continued pogroms, a group of Central
European American Jews, led by Louis Marshall,
organized the American Jewish Committee (AJC)
in 1906 to combat antisemitism both in the
United States and abroad. Included as follows
is a letter from Marshall to Rabbi Joseph Stolz
(1861–1941), president of the Reform
movement's rabbinic association, the Central
Conference of American Rabbis, concerning the
creation of the AJC.*

*In 1911, Jewish banker and AJC leader Jacob
Schiff (1847–1920) pressed President William
Howard Taft to punish the Russian czar for
refusing to issue Russian visas to American Jews.
Schiff wanted the president to abrogate an 1832
trade treaty on the grounds that the czar's
antisemitic policies violated the treaty's promise
to grant "the inhabitants of their respective
states" the right to "enter the ports, places, and
rivers of the territories of each party." When Taft
refused to abrogate the treaty, violating his own
campaign pledge, Schiff issued the broadside
included here, following Marshall's letter to Stolz.*

To the Rev. Dr. Joseph Stolz

I am in receipt of yours of the 9th inst., which
only reached me this morning. The notice for
the consultation, of which you have received a
copy, had already gone out, but as you will see
from the nature of the notice, that it is not a notice for a conference, but only for a meeting for
the purpose of consultation, the very thing that
your letter indicates that you are anxious to have
with some or all of the gentlemen who have
been invited to be present at the consultation.
[. . .]
I think out of a total of fifty-five who have
been asked to attend, only fifteen are residents
of New York.

I greatly appreciate everything that you have
said as to what your committee [the Reform
Rabbinical Committee on National Organiza-
tion] has done, and am very glad that you have
taken up the subject. What I am trying to accomplish is, to get order out of chaos, and to
[unite] all elements that might possibly seek
to father a national movement with the result
that discord instead of union would be the rule.
Dr. Voorsanger has attempted to organize one
movement, Dr. Magnes another, Dr. Mendes a
third, the Central Conference [of American Rab-
bis] a fourth. Mr. Kraus believes that the B'nai
B'rith affords a panacea for all ills, and the East
Side [with its Slavic newcomers] is bristling with
organizations, each national in scope and zero
in accomplishment.

It has therefore occurred to me and to my
associates, that before any scheme is launched,
those who have the welfare of Judaism at heart
should come together, merely for the purpose
of comparing notes, with a view of ascertaining
whether or not there is a possibility of promul-
gating a plan which will be generally acceptable,
and which will accomplish the objects which all
of us have sincerely at heart.

What I am trying to avoid, more than anything else, is the creation of a political organization, one which will be looked upon as indicative
of a purpose on the part of the Jews to recognize
that they have interests different from those of
other American citizens. I conceive that there
can be but two tenable theories on which the
Jews have the right to organize: first, as a religious body, and secondly, as persons interested
in the same philanthropic purposes.

Obviously, it will be an absolute impossibility
for the Jews of the country to unite as a religious
body having ecclesiastical and disciplinary powers. It could be impossible to afford to such an
organization, the authority and sanction which
are essential to successfully carry out such a
scheme.

We can, however, all unite for the purpose of aiding all Jews who are persecuted, or who are suffering from discrimination in any part of the world on account of their religious beliefs, and we can at the same time, unite for the purpose of ameliorating the condition of our brethren in faith, who are suffering from the effects of such persecution and discrimination directly or indirectly.

Whether it will be wise to go beyond this, I seriously doubt. Whether, if it were attempted, much harm would result, I strongly believe.

[. . .]

I do not believe it to be feasible to organize upon the basis of existing organizations. There would be much inequality and injustice if such a plan were adopted. We must, in some way or other, go back to the people, and organize on the theory of democracy. While the beginning would be troublesome, I think, in the end, the results accomplished would be most excellent. . . .

Source: As printed in *JAW*, 235–37. From Charles Reznikoff, ed., *Louis Marshall, Champion of Liberty, etc.* (Philadelphia: Jewish Publication Society, 1957), 21–23.

5.42—JACOB SCHIFF TO PRESIDENT TAFT ON THE MISTREATMENT OF JEWS IN RUSSIA, FEBRUARY 20, 1911

Hotel Poinciana,
Palm Beach, Florida,
February 20, 1911.

Mr. President:

I desire to take the first opportunity I can find since leaving Washington to thank you for the courteous hospitality extended to me, with others, at your family luncheon table last Wednesday and to assure you of the great pleasure it was to meet Mrs. Taft and your daughter.

[. . .]

The main reasons, which as you explained, led you to the conclusion that it was impractical to further act upon the pledges [to abrogate the 1832 trade treaty with the czar] were:

First: That Russia's failure to live up to its obligation under the treaty of 1832 to honor the American Passport, through an application of a faith test, had though constantly protested against, been permitted to continue for so long a period of time, that it was now too late to enforce the only logical remedy, the abrogation of the treaty.

Second: That special interests had in the course of time acquired rights, and that commercial relations had become established which might be jeopardized, if existing treaties with Russia were denounced.

Third: That it was moreover feared, that in case of such action on our part, pogroms and massacres of Russian Jews, such as shocked the world in 1905, might be repeated.

As to the last horrible prospect, those at the Conference undertook to assure you, that we were ready to take the responsibility upon our own shoulders; that the Russian Government having by its cruel treatment of its Jewish subjects forced the Jew all over the world into an attitude of hostility, it was recognized by our coreligionists that in such a situation, as in war, each and every man, wherever placed, must be ready to suffer, and if need be, to sacrifice his life.

The fact that certain trade interests, notably the Harvester and Sewing machine industries we assume, might be the losers from the abrogation of the treaty under which we live with Russia, but which on her part she ignores whenever this suits her, will, I believe, be hardly accepted as a good and substantial reason for the maintenance of the treaty on our part, by the gross of the American people, who not only quickly resent insult to what our flag represents—equality for and justice to all who live under it, but desire moreover their government to adopt a firm attitude in the defense of the rights of every American citizen. The fact that the denial of the rights by Russia has heretofore been permitted to continue without positive remedial action, except repeated protests, is hardly a good reason why at some time our long patience should not come to an end. Nor has Russia at any time heretofore ignored our treaty rights in such flagrant and insulting a manner, as she now does, when she goes so far as not to hesitate to publicly announce that an Ambassador of the United States, when he confesses the Jewish religion can not enter her dominions, except as an exceptional favor and by a special permit [Schiff had Oscar S. Straus in mind]. And this is the same Russia which during the past few days has actually threatened China, which it is true, is weak, with war, because the latter as Russia claims, is ignoring the rights of a few Russian traders, secured to them under an old treaty, which until recently, as is stated, had not been considered of any value.

[. . .]

Notwithstanding the present discouragement we have received, I have the unshakable belief that at some time public opinion, that most emphatic voice of the American People, will compel the government to resent the continuous insult to them which Russia has only too long been permitted to inflict by the non-observance of its treaty obligations.

Very respectfully,
Jacob H. Schiff.
To the President,
Washington, D.C.

Source: As printed in *JAW*, 299–301. From Simon Wolf, *The Presidents I Have Known from 1860–1918* (Washington, D.C.: Byron S. Adam, 1918), 310–13.

6 American Jews between the World Wars, 1918–1941

Between the First and Second World Wars, American Jews adapted to a social landscape that affirmed the United States as an exceptional locale for Jewish communal life. The 1920s, for example, witnessed an impressive growth in synagogue construction. For the first time in their history as Americans, most Jews spoke English as their native language, sought the highest levels of university education, enjoyed success as members of the American middle class, and strengthened their commitment to other Jews at home, in Europe, and in the British Mandate for Palestine.

Yet this era also included an unprecedented anti-immigrant backlash, culminating in race-based restrictive quotas imposed by the U.S. Congress in 1921 and 1924. Some of these prejudices came to America together with the Old World immigrants. But expressions of antisemitism multiplied dramatically during these years, as evidenced by the popularity of anti-Jewish critics such as Henry Ford, Father Charles Coughlin, and the American aviation hero Charles A. Lindbergh. When Adolf Hitler came to power in Germany in 1933, America had its share of antisemites eager to transplant Nazi-style bigotry on American shores. By the late 1930s, antisemites blamed Jews for dragging the United States toward a European war for their own political purposes.

These social and political changes in the larger society influenced the development of American Jewish life. With the effective end of Jewish immigration to the United States in 1924, Yiddish language and culture suffered as native speakers aged and their children learned English as their primary language. At the same time, the closing of America's golden doors accelerated an amalgamation of Jews with Central European and Eastern European ancestry. This is why the pioneering American Jewish historian Jacob Rader Marcus (1896–1995) dubbed this era "the period of the American Jew." Within the primary sources that document Jewish communal growth during these years, one finds the compelling drama of an American Jewish population, cut off from continued Old World immigration, refashioning itself in new and innovative ways.

A number of religious themes frame the era as well. Jewish denominationalism continued to evolve, and American Judaism developed along lines that often proved surprising or unexpected. Jews on the more traditional end of the religious spectrum faced tremendous challenges as the children of Eastern European Jewish immigrants became Americanized and began to lose touch with their parents' religious traditionalism. Reform Judaism began a process of transformation during these years as the descendants of Eastern European Jews entered Reform synagogues and pushed the movement toward ideological rapprochement with Zionism, liturgical reform, and engagement with traditional ritual. Also during this period, Conservative Judaism experienced a massive growth spurt that would make it the largest American Jewish denomination by the end of World War II. The birth of a uniquely American religious movement, Reconstructionism, reflected an Americanized rationale for Jewish religious practice and Jewish ideology.

The political culture of American Jews, affected by the growing conservative social climate of the nation at large, also proved a vital theme during these years. Immigrant Jews who aligned with socialist or communist ideologies in their first years on American shores reassessed their convictions, backing more mainstream liberal candidates whom they believed enjoyed a better chance of election. By 1928, a majority of American Jewish voters supported the Democratic Party's candidate for president.

The rise of Nazism spurred American Jews to look beyond their own shores. During the interwar era, Jewish organizations rallied against antisemitic actions in Germany, raising money as well as political awareness of the growing threat against European Jewry. Similarly, the Zionist movement grew stronger, with increasing numbers of American Jews offering their support for a Jewish homeland in Palestine.

6.01 — RELIEF EXPENDITURES OF FIFTY-TWO
JEWISH FAMILY WELFARE AGENCIES, 1929–1935

For more than 250 years, American Jewry raised its own funds to care for Jewish social welfare needs. Yet the ravages of the Great Depression during the 1930s called this philanthropic practice into question. A review of the chart that follows shows that relief expenditures made by fifty-two Jewish family welfare agencies between the years 1929 and 1934 literally doubled. Despite the desire to care for their own, Jewish organizations were unable to raise the funds needed to meet their obligations. Isaac M. Rubinow (1875–1936), a Russian Jewish immigrant who earned an MD as well as a PhD in economics, became one of the most influential economic theorists in the early part of the twentieth century. In a speech he gave to the National Conference of Jewish Social Service in 1930, Rubinow—one of the principal authors of the Social Security Act of 1935—insisted that the Jewish community needed government

assistance. He told his audience that the ethic of economic communal self-sufficiency could no longer meet the Jewish community's needs. Jewish communal welfare, Rubinow insisted, was tied to the welfare of the entire American nation.

Year	Relief Expenditures in Dollars	Percentage of 1929 Expenditures
1929	1.92 million	100
1930	2.12 million	110.7
1931	2.88 million	150.3
1932	3.96 million	206.5
1933	4.04 million	210.7
1934	2.38 million	124.2
1935	1.79 million	93.4

Source: Yearbook of Jewish Social Work, part 1: Service Trends in Family Welfare, Child Care, Care of the Aged, Clinics (1935): 22.

6.02 — ISAAC RUBINOW, "WHAT DO WE OWE PETER STUYVESANT?" 1930

"In 1652, Peter Stuyvesant, Governor of New Amsterdam, now New York, received a promise from the Jews who came to settle there that they (the Jews) would care for their own poor. Ever since then, the Jews of this country have prided themselves that this sacred promise which the first Jewish settlers in America made has never been broken."

The quotation (from the diminutive but influential local paper of a diminutive but influential Jewish community) may perhaps serve as well as any other to put the question bluntly before the Jewish social workers of the United States.

[. . .]

. . . Have we made a *promise*? Just what kind of a promise did we make? Have we fulfilled the pledge? And is the promise still binding? Must it control our policies and programs in the future? . . .

It would be funny if it were not so sad. For as a matter of fact, this whole misconception, supported by a curious mixture of holy tradition, race pride, and a typical Jewish sense of group guilt, has definitely colored both the theory and practice of our work, and much of the social philosophy of the American Jewish community. No more tragic illustration may be found of the truth of the statement that necessity may be made into a virtue.

Not only in my own little town of Cincinnati but in hundreds of other important Jewish communities, the case of Boston has made Jews "blush with shame." What has happened in Boston, which, I repeat, I am only using as a picturesque illustration? A very respectable non-Jewish committee has been organized (presumably not without a gentle hint from Jewish leadership) to ask for contributions from the non-Jewish community in support of the Jewish Federation. The announcement has been broadcast that the associate Jewish philanthropies need much more money than they can reasonably expect to raise within their own group. Perhaps after all it is not such an unusual situation. In many other communities non-Jewish contributions have been made to Jewish drives and campaigns. They have been diplomatically solicited in secret. Just why do we find a situation of this nature so very damaging to our pride? Is it because we are still a "chosen people"? Is it because we still live in the ghetto and must not disclose our sores to the enemy? Is it because we are so proud, or because we are afraid to admit the ugly truth?

And if we are proud, is the pride justified? Have we as a matter of fact always taken care of our poor in this country? If we have made the promise, can we really claim to have kept it? Far be it from me to deny the well known generosity of Jewish philanthropy in this country as judged by comparison with other non-Jewish groups. The facts and figures are available and surely no one could charge me with any neglect of available statistical information. The average family supported by Jewish philanthropic relief agencies receives about twice as much in relief as non-Jewish families from non-sectarian agencies. I believe that in every city where Jewish philanthropic Federations exist side by side with non-sectarian Community Chests, the per capita contribution for the Jewish population is considerably higher than for the general population. In many cities (though there are some sad exceptions) where all embracing Community Chests exist, it is again a matter of pride with leading Jews that the Jewish contributions to the Community Chest be greater than the amount required by Jewish agencies. It hardly seems necessary to overburden the audience with much statistical evidence to establish the obvious.

[. . .]

The point of the argument is just this—that the promise itself may have been not only diplomatic but fair and just in its own day and generation. It was based upon a certain definite social philosophy which, like all other social philosophies, derived its strength from a certain social structure. Two hundred and fifty years ago, and perhaps even fifty years ago, poverty may have been primarily a result of individual factors or at most group factors. Perhaps the shrewd business people who signed that blank check 250 years ago had good reasons to believe that the amount to be written in need never become a very heavy burden. But conditions have changed. Very much so! Instead of a quarter of a million of Jews scarcely a generation ago, we have four million and a quarter. Instead of being a country of small individual enterprise, we have become the greatest industrial country in all the world, and in all history. Instead of a simple society to which strong but simple minds were prone to run away from the perplexities of European civilization, we have become the most complex organization in the world. Things happen. Nobody knows how and why. Riches are accumulated and lost in a year or in a day. An excited rumor within one square block near Wall Street destroys fortunes of thousands of people scattered over hundreds of thousands of square miles. A change in an automobile model may throw hundreds of thousands of men and women out of work. Even though there be a great deal of racial, national or religious concentration in economic activity, we are nevertheless all bound together in our economic life, the 125 million of us. It may not be accurate to say that we always all stand and fall together, but in this mad rush which we call American life, no one may be responsible for his own fall, or be particularly proud of having escaped it.

[...]

... My thesis may perhaps be best summed up in the following statements:

Jewish poverty is not a result of intra-group conditions. It is a part and parcel of the whole economic and social problem of wealth production and wealth accumulation of the country as a whole.

The expectation that the problem of Jewish poverty can be met individually, may be hoped to be eliminated irrespective of those general economic forces, is an expression of excessive group pride uncontrolled by scientific research and thinking.

The sermon of independent group responsibility becomes a definite anti-social force if it destroys Jewish force—if it destroys Jewish interest, and Jewish participation in national progressive social movements.

[...]

Must then the real communal needs, the needs as a national and cultural minority, compete with the widows and orphans, and aged, and tubercular, and sick, and unemployed? Or, isn't it rather time that we draw a very clear-cut line of division between problems and needs which are distinctly ours, and problems and needs which are essentially state wide and nation wide in character. Isn't it about time that we clarified our thinking on the lines of demarcation as to what is properly a State responsibility and to what is equally properly a group responsibility. We may then be able to clarify our terminology and draw the line of distinction between what is social service for Jews as well as all others, and what may be described as distinctly "Jewish Social Service."

Source: Proceedings of the National Conference of Jewish Social Service, Jewish Communal Service Association of North America (JCSA), National Conference of Jewish Social Service (June 1930): 89–121.

6.03 — "NEW NRA COMPLIANCE DIRECTOR BLENDS EFFICIENCY AND BEAUTY," JEWISH TELEGRAPHIC AGENCY, DECEMBER 9, 1934

President Franklin D. Roosevelt, faced with unprecedented economic challenges during the Great Depression, looked for advisors and government workers who had what he called "verve"—innovative ideas that could bolster his New Deal efforts to ease the nation out of depression. High numbers of American Jews—many with Eastern European roots—joined the president's administration and eagerly lent their support to the governmental reforms. Typically, the Jews who served in Roosevelt's New Deal administrations believed that America's massive social and economic woes would need to be addressed by large communitarian solutions. In developing these social initiatives, Jewish civil servants drew on their prior experience in labor union activism or their knowledge of American

Jewry's private philanthropic machine. Anna M. Rosenberg (1902–1983), later Anna R. Hoffman, exemplified the verve Roosevelt was seeking. She held a number of key posts during the Roosevelt and Truman administrations, including serving as assistant secretary of defense from 1950 to 1953. In 1934, shortly after Rosenberg was appointed New York State's compliance director for the National Recovery Administration, the Jewish Telegraphic Agency provided its readers with the following profile.

MRS. ROSENBERG BRINGS VIGOR (AND FLOWERS) TO BIG TASKS

Imagine a huge, severe room, the walls wood-panelled, the heavy conference table, the deep chairs suggesting important board-meetings, the large desk with its green shaded lamp and its many telephones the very epitome of efficiency and you will have visualized the office of Mrs. Anna M. Rosenberg, the new State NRA Compliance Director. It is a room evidently dedicated to work, to constant, energetic, impersonal work. Yet there is one touch of beauty, one touch of femininity in all this uncompromising severity. On the dark, heavily carved mantel there stands a vase with fresh flowers, glowing in all the richest autumn hues.

Mrs. Rosenberg is just like the office she inhabits and imbues with her personality. Efficient, competent, engrossed in her work, she nevertheless possesses a distinctive feminine charm. Despite the pressure of her work, she is delightfully friendly even to those who come to interrupt her. In appearance she is petite, very pretty, brunette and hardly looking her thirty-three years. It is difficult to believe that she is the mother of a fourteen-year-old boy.

CLEVER POLITICIAN

From early youth Mrs. Rosenberg, who holds that sex makes no difference in doing work and that only personal competence ought to count, has proved herself a clever manager of political campaigns, an able reorganizer of ailing businesses. When still in school she organized the "Coming Voters' League," and even before she was actually a voter she did splendid political work in the old Seventh Assembly District. Her success as wife and mother (her husband is Julius Rosenberg of the American Rug & Carpet Co., her son a student at Horace Mann) was and is a matter of admiration and envy. She is well read, a music lover and a theatre enthusiast. Mrs. Rosenberg is reluctant to speak of herself, but as soon as her work is mentioned, she radiates enthusiasm and speaks with compelling sincerity.

DISCUSSES HER WORK

"The success of the NRA," she says, "depends not only on labor and industry, but also in a large measure on the ultimate consumer, the buyer, or in other words, the wife and mother who is usually the purchasing agent in the family. If women would only thoroughly understand for what the NRA label stands, if they would realize that the NRA has abolished child labor, has insured the worker a living wage and sanitary working conditions, they would be our most fervent supporters.

"Especially as far as the garment industry is concerned this support is needed and fully deserved. An NRA label in a coat or dress means that it can be safely bought, without fear of exposing oneself to any infection, without the feeling that the worker who fashioned it was exploited or starved. I often wonder how mothers, who are so careful with their little tots and try to guard them from every possible contamination, blithely go and buy garments which were perhaps made by a consumptive seamstress in dirt- and germ-laden rooms. An NRA label guarantees against such conditions, and if women will insist on this label and only patronize stores that comply with the NRA requirements they will help not only the New Deal but will protect themselves and their children."

With all her various activities, with all her manifold interests, Mrs. Rosenberg yet finds time for work in Jewish causes. She is a member of the National Council of Jewish Women and was executive director of the women's division of the United Palestine Appeal. She has associated in the work of the ORT [the world's largest Jewish educational and training nongovernmental organization] Reconstruction Fund and has long been a member of the Joint Distribution Committee of Jewish Charities.

Her life is brimful of interest, well rounded, intensely active. In short, she represents the modern Jewish woman at her very best.

Source: Jewish Telegraphic Agency, December 9, 1934. All rights reserved. Used with permission; more information available at www.jta.org.

6.04—JUDAH L. MAGNES, ADDRESS DELIVERED AT THE OPENING SESSION OF THE FIRST JEWISH LABOR CONGRESS, JANUARY 16, 1919

Judah L. Magnes (1877-1948), a San Francisco-born Reform rabbi, helped found and then ran the American Jewish Committee in New York City. When the United States entered World War I, Magnes protested, empathizing with many prominent labor leaders who opposed the war and criticized the U.S. government for harassing and even arresting fellow pacifists. In 1917, Magnes was invited to deliver the keynote address to a gathering of 15,000 protesters at Madison Square Garden. Two years later, the Jewish Labor Congress invited him to share his perspective at its first meeting. In 1922, Magnes immigrated to Palestine, where he served as a founder, and later president, of the Hebrew University of Jerusalem.

This first Jewish Labor Congress can become, and I hope it will become, a milestone in the progress of the Jews of America, of the Jews everywhere, of America at large, and of the world too. . . .

The first thing the organized Jewish workers will do is to declare their solidarity with the hand and head workers of all peoples and all nationalities. The organized Jewish workers will join the workers of all the world in proclaiming the need and the hope of a new world after this devastating war, a world in which there shall be no more political and industrial and spiritual slavery, a world in which complete liberty shall be proclaimed to all the inhabitants thereof. The individual man and woman shall be free, not for the purpose of heaping up possessions and property and of exploiting the dispossessed and the disinherited of the earth, but they shall be free for the purpose of using their creative energies for the benefit of their fellowmen. Nations and peoples shall be free, not in order to satisfy their lust for imperialism and for an extension of

their territories and of their dominion over colored and other so-called "inferior" races of the world, including the Jews; but nations and peoples shall be free in order that their national energies may create cultural values, in literature, in art, in science, in industry, in education, in religion. We Jews sympathize with the aspirations of the Jewish people for freedom, not only because it is our people, not only because it is our flesh and blood, but because we know that every other oppressed people must be set free together with our own, and because we know that it is only free peoples that will help to create a free world. Without free peoples and a free world, the Jewish people can never be free. The Jewish people, traditionally and through its experience, knows the meaning of internationalism, and it must apply the method of internationalism to its own national life as well, sharing the destiny of every people, free and oppressed, in freeing the world in order that it itself may be free. The Jewish people in Poland, for instance, can be free only if there be a free Polish people. . . . There will be no peace, whatever the peace treaty reads, unless, in addition to a League of Nations—that is, a League of the governments and the statesmen—there shall also be a League of Labor in the world. It is useless to cry peace, peace, when there is no peace; and there can be peace and a new social order only if those who work, if those who dream, if those who are ready to give themselves to their fellowmen, will organize their strength, and make their strength the basis of the new social order.

Those are the tasks which the organized Jewish workers have in common with the workers of all countries and of all peoples, and which are fundamental in the solution of the Jewish problem itself. But if the Jewish problem can be met in its entirety only through the creation of a new and free world of freemen, how much greater is the obligation upon the Jewish people—and particularly upon organized Jewish labor—to give their full power and wisdom to the moulding of the new and free and better world of which we all now have caught the vision. For, whatever one thinks of the Jews, it is unquestionable that Jews have intelligence, vitality, the power of concentrated devotion and self-sacrifice. . . .

Just as the Jewish labor movement gives itself to the labor and radical forces of the world, so must it pour its spirit and its strength upon the living Jewish people. The living Jewish people needs the organized Jewish workers, Jewish life needs the freedom of spirit, of outlook, that zeal for justice and righteousness which organized Jewish labor can give it. Jewish life needs the clear, direct, keen minds of the thinkers, the idealism, the vision of the poets, the singers, the enthusiasts, of the organized Jewish labor movement. Jewish life needs both the vigorous nationalism, and the generous, far-seeing internationalism of the organized Jewish labor movement. Jewish life needs the organized Jewish workers in order that Jewish life may become thoroughly democratic, broad minded, undogmatic, unprejudiced. Jewish life needs that sense of reality which the organized Jewish laborers can give it, and which brings it home to us that it is in this world, the world we live in, that justice and righteousness and peace and love must be pursued, and that the kingdom of heaven is to be established here and now upon this earth, among living, breathing men and women. From among the Jewish working masses must come positive contributions to the culture, the national life, the language, the literature, the spiritual ideals and aspirations of the whole Jewish people. The Jewish religion, too, needs contact with, needs impact with, the Jewish laboring masses. The religionists among the Jews must be ready to match their minds, their spirits, their experience, with the intellect, the spirit, and the broad experience of the spokesmen of Jewish labor. The Jewish religionists must realize that many of the best among the Jewish people, as among all peoples, have lost religion; and these, to use the words of a great thinker of this war, Bertrand Russell, have lost it because "their minds were active, not because their spirit was dead." If the Jewish religion is to have vitality and vigor and to fulfill its function in the world, as some of us believe, it must enter into the arena of the living Jewish people and there fight out its battle with all kinds of Jews, whatever be their social, their political, their spiritual outlook.

But in order that the Jewish people may do its work in the world, it must be organized—organized for its specific Jewish purposes as well as for participation in all of the cultural and spiritual movements of humanity. But the only way in which the Jewish people can be organized, the only way in which its essential unity can find vigorous expression, the only way in which its creative force can be developed to the full, is that each group and each party having its specific message and its especial work shall organize its own forces, and that then these organized forces shall come together and match mind with mind and spirit with spirit, in conflict of opinion and of aspiration that shall mirror the soul of the Jewish people as a whole.

[. . .]

Delegates to this Congress! We are met at a momentous crisis in the history of all times. What the future will bring[,] not even the wisest cannot [sic] foresee. What will transpire with the Jewish people in this maelstrom of conflicting interests and passions, only Heaven may know. But there is one thing that organized Jewish labor can do, and that is to be true to itself, true to the Jewish people, true to its international outlook. One thing at least it can do, and that is to proclaim with that great Jewish prophet of old *Likro lashevuim deror*—"to declare freedom to all the captives," to all the slaves, to all the shackled, to all the manacled, to all the disinherited,—freedom of life, freedom of expression, freedom of hope, of dreaming, of living, of serving, here and now upon this beauteous earth.

Source: AJA Biographies nearprint file, folder 3, AJA.

6.05—RABBI STEPHEN S. WISE, STATEMENT SUPPORTING ORGANIZED LABOR, SEPTEMBER 1, 1919

Due to anti-Communist raids authorized by U.S. attorney general A. Mitchell Palmer (1872–1936), the summer of 1919 was known as the Red Summer. During this period, those on the political left faced tremendous pressure not to engage in activities that might be perceived as anti-American. For Jews, Palmer's campaign created an especially difficult situation. Many Eastern European Jewish immigrants were supporters of socialism and communism— political movements that promised full equality for Jews and other oppressed minorities. The labor unions were particularly influenced by these ideologies, and some Jews feared that the government-sponsored wave of anticommunism and antisocialism would spark an upsurge in antisemitism. In September 1919, New York rabbi Stephen S. Wise (1874–1949) went on record defending the union movement on both American patriotic and Jewish grounds.

My interest in the question of unionizing the steel workers long antedates the recent resolution of the A. F. of L. For fifteen years or more, ever since I have known of the determination of the Steel Corporation to prevent the organization of their workers, I have, in addresses dealing with social industrial questions, publicly held that nothing could be more violative of the spirit of democracy than the decision of the heads of the largest financial-industrial group in the land to make impossible any organization of the workers.

That decision denied to the workers the right of collective bargaining. It seemed to me a ludicrous anachronism that the most powerful industrial-capitalistic combination should proclaim to their thousands of workers that they might not combine nor associate in order to deal collectively as employees with their employers. The thing that was far from ludicrous was that this anti-democratic determination should be tolerated by the workers and that it should be

pursued by the distinguished heads of the corporation and their indistinguishable underlings with such vigor and relentlessness as are ordinarily ascribed to organizations of employees.

Within and without my pulpit, I inveighed first against the glaring injustice of this policy— the uncomplaining acceptance of which would be the token of the moral enslavement of workers in a democracy. That men should presume to enforce this regime was bad, that it should be endured by freemen in this day and generation was worse, infinitely hurtful to the republic.

Though not unfamiliar with industrial problems, I have not been able wholly to understand why the workers have not ere this grappled more firmly with the situation. Moreover, apart from the brutally unjust attitude of the steel corporation heads, those men who thought earnestly about the problem, knew that this feudalism could not, as it should not, permanently endure, and that workers who are practically denied the right lawfully to organize, would ultimately organize under conditions making for lawlessness and violence. That the workers of the steel corporation have, up to this time, failed to organize is the measure at one and the same time of the unwisdom of the corporation heads and of the long-suffering patience of a great number of toilers in the nation.

I therefore rejoiced to learn that the A. F. of L. had finally—I think most belatedly—resolved to "enter into the iron and steel district" and at once offered such services as it lay in my power to render to the A. F. of L. and its national committee for organizing the iron and steel workers.

"I did this on two grounds. First, because I am an American, to whom democracy is as a religion, who believes the anti-union policy of the Steel Corporation to be an intolerable violation of the spirit of democracy and that this policy is if anything rendered still more execrable by a system of rewards and bounties to its wholly acquiescent workers.

For another equally compelling reason I stand ready to lend my support to the decision to unionize the iron and steel workers, yea, to arouse such among them as are indifferent to the necessity of this elementary step on the highway of industrial democracy.

I am a teacher of religion and morals, teacher of the faith of a people, which holds that men [*sic*] does not live by bread alone, nor by bonuses nor by opportunities to subscribe to stock, but by justice which is possible between man and man only when they are free. I believe that the workers in the steel and iron industry, denied the right of organization and collective bargaining, are not free men. I consider the Steel Corporation and related industrial corporations a menace to the republic, not violently not explosively menacing after the manner of the I.W.W. [Industrial Workers of the World], but silently and pervasively menacing.

The attitude of the Steel Corporation in this matter is no less hostile to the spirit of our republic than the I.W.W. I am unutterably opposed alike to Bolshevism and the reign of political and industrial despotism, which make it inevitable. I am alike opposed in my own country to the I.W.W. Bolshevism and the Steel Corporation medievalism, which seems resolved to evoke it. I shall support the iron and steel workers in every peaceable and lawful action they may take. The policies of the Steel Corporation are technically peaceable and lawful though, I concede, that morally they spell the lawlessness of war upon such workers as are resolved to live and labor as freemen.

Source: MS 49, box 5, folder 3, AJA.

6.06—LOUIS MARSHALL TO ELIAS A. COHEN, JANUARY 25, 1923

*On January 16, 1920, the Eighteenth
Amendment to the U.S. Constitution,
prohibiting the manufacture and use of
alcoholic beverages, went into effect. Prohibition
presented distinct religious challenges to
American Jews, who relied on wine for
sacramental purposes. The prominent New
York lawyer and Jewish communal leader Louis
Marshall was extremely concerned about the
unintended consequences of the Prohibition
laws. He suspected that the drafters of the law
lacked a "full understanding" of its implications
for Jews who used wine for religious purposes,
and he feared that the law's imprecision would
lead to "unpleasant insinuations" and
embarrassing problems for American Jewry. In
an attempt to avoid these difficulties, Marshall
tried to encourage Reform, Conservative, and
Orthodox rabbis to use unfermented wine—a
legal beverage—for religious purposes until
the legalities could be sorted out. In order to
achieve his goal, Marshall obtained a
responsum (legal opinion) from Professor Louis
Ginzberg (1873-1953) of the Jewish Theological
Seminary stating that it would be entirely
acceptable for Jews to use unfermented wine in
their religious rites. Marshall hoped that all Jews
would unite behind Ginzberg's responsum.
Unfortunately, as the following letter written by
Marshall to Jewish communal leader Elias A.
Cohen (1881-1952) illustrates, the Prohibition
amendment sparked a range of religious
skirmishes within the Jewish community. In this
letter, Marshall urges Cohen—president of the
Kehillah, New York City's Jewish community
organization—not to convene a public
conference of rabbis to discuss whether the
Jewish community should use unfermented
wine. Marshall was convinced that unfermented
wine was the only legal option for American
Jewry and, in explaining his position to Cohen,
cited interesting examples of rabbinical
noncompliance and waywardness.*

> Elias A. Cohen, Esq.,
> Chairman, The Kehillah,
> 114 Fifth Avenue, New York City.

My dear Mr. Cohen:

I am in receipt of yours of the 24th instant
with a copy of your letter addressed to Mr. Daniel P. Hays [1854-1923] on the subject of the use
of wine by the Jews for ritual purposes.

While I regret that the matter was taken up at
the Conference, because I prefer to have a subject of this sort dealt with by simple and unsen-
sational methods, I am nevertheless of the opinion that nothing has occurred in this country
which has so degraded the rabbinical office as
its connection with the business of distributing
wine, which, I regret to say, has to a very great
extent degenerated into bootlegging. I do not
mean to insinuate that all rabbis are consciously
engaged in any wrongdoing; they are the victims of designing men. There are, however, many
rabbis throughout the country who are deliberately engaged in a violation of the law. I have it
from good authority that in various cities there
have been organized bogus Congregations, presided over by alleged rabbis, the membership of
which consists largely of non-Jews.

I take exception to the statement made by
you that the "Orthodox rabbis are a unit in declaring that fermented wine is a part of the sacrament." The use of the word "sacrament" is most
unfortunate so far as we Jews are concerned. We
have no sacrament. Wine is used by us merely

for ritual purposes, and when you speak as an Orthodox you should be more careful in your use of terms.

The Orthodox rabbis are not a unit in declaring that fermented wine is necessary for ritual purposes. On the contrary, the only authoritative opinion that I have had access to, after much endeavor to obtain a responsum from those who claim that fermented wine is necessary, is to the effect that unfermented wine will answer every possible ritual purpose. I refer you to the elaborate responsum of Prof. Louis Ginzberg, of the Jewish Theological Seminary of America, written in Hebrew and covering some sixty printed pages. In it he reviews all of the authorities. The United Synagogue and the Rabbinic Assembly, who constitute the alumni of the Jewish Theological Seminary, are in accord with Prof. Ginzberg.

I have said that the Orthodox have never given a responsum on the subject. Immediately after the Volstead Act was passed, I learned that a small group of Orthodox rabbis had gone to Washington and had procured the formulation of a regulation which gave to them the monopoly of distributing wine for ritual purposes. That was such an outrageous act that I deemed it to be my duty to call a meeting of these rabbis and other Orthodox and conservative rabbis, as well as representatives of Reform Synagogues, for the purpose of discussing the subject and arriving at some intelligent basis for dealing with what I foresaw would prove a dreadful scandal. Among the rabbis who were in attendance representing the ultra Orthodox were Rabbis [Shalom/Solomon Elhanan] Jaffe and [Moses Z.] Margolies. Among the conservative rabbis was Dr. [Moses] Hyamson. Among the Reform rabbis were Drs. [William] Rosenau and [Samuel] Schulman. To the credit of the last named, I wish to say that he stated that he had not given the subject sufficient study to enable him to express an opinion as to whether fermented wine was necessary. He therefore suggested that Drs. Jaffe and Margolies, who were of the opinion that it was, should write a reasoned responsum on the subject maintaining their views. Dr. Hyamson was of the opinion that fermented wine was not necessary and referred to various Biblical and Talmudical passages, and to The Codes, on which he is an authority. I then asked Rabbis Jaffe and Margolies to write such a responsum. They promised to do so. I waited upwards of a month, and not having heard from them I wrote to them asking for the responsum. To the present day I have had no reply. I have seen no statement from them or any other Orthodox rabbi which would justify the statement that you have so unqualifiedly made that fermented wine is essential.

In the meantime other investigations have been made, and they all corroborate the conclusions reached by Prof. Ginzberg.

The burden of proof is on those who claim that fermented wine is necessary. Unless it be necessary and indispensable, then we as Jews owe a duty to our Government and to our fellow-citizens to conform strictly with the Constitution and the law, whether they be distasteful or not or whether we would prefer a different Constitution or a different law. We are entitled to equal rights. We are not entitled to and should not seek privileges, especially with regard to the matter of drink, a subject as to which the American people are greatly aroused. Those who have observed the dietary laws and have been able to practice self-denial should have no difficulty in suppressing the desire for strong drink. My mother was a strict conformist. In none of our family observances in which wine is employed did we ever find it necessary to use fermented wine, and I know that this practice was quite general in the community in which I lived. It would be a sad thing if those who cannot afford to purchase fermented wine would be guilty of a ritual offense because forsooth at the Seder they [d]rank a concoction of raisins which served them as wine.

It is a disgrace that the rabbinate should be placed in the humiliating position of serving as bartenders of the Jews and non-Jews who desire through their offices to satisfy their craving for drink. I took up the matter with the Department of Internal Revenue and the prohibition Director immediately after the conference to which I have referred. I prophesied just what has taken place. I asked for a revision of the regulations so that the rabbi should be kept out of the matter. There was a change in the regulations, but not to the extent that I desired. About a year ago I received information that a syndicate of newspapers was about to launch a sensational story with regard to the disgraceful abuses which had occurred in connection with the distribution of wine for ritual purposes. In anticipation of this expected outburst I wrote to Mr. [David Hunt] Blair [1868–1945], the Commissioner of Internal Revenue, informing him of what I have just said to you, protesting against this unnecessary degradation of the rabbinate, urging a revision of the regulations, and volunteering my assistance in dealing with the problem. I received a polite acknowledgment. I have since had intimations that I was to be consulted. Thus far nothing has been done. I know that there is a strong desire on the part of such men as Mr. [Julius] Rosenwald [1862–1932] to protect our good name, and they have my entire sympathy.

As one connected with the Kehillah I now protest against the holding of the conference of the rabbis which you have called for Monday next. It will only tend to the increase of the existing scandal. It is quite likely to arouse bad blood and to create an unfortunate controversy. All the resolutions that may be passed will be useless. They will only make their position and that of the Jews so much the worse. If fermented wine is necessary, why do not rabbis who are supposed to be responsible, who are urging the maintenance of the present situation, venture to put in the form of a responsum, with citation of the authorities on which they rely, the reasons which lead them to the assertion? A mere assertion is valueless. Any man in the street can make assertions. Where is the text on which they rely? Why have not Rabbis Jaffe and Margolies carried out their pledge to write such a responsum? Prof. Ginzberg has written his opinion. It has never been answered. Until it has been shown that the authorities on which he r[e]lies are not dependable, that the responsa which he cites are not reliable, that there are on the other hand decisions which overcome those to which he has called attention, there is but one course to pursue, and that is to obey the law.

I am speaking thus plainly because you say that the Kehillah is interested in the question and that we must present a united front. Let me warn you that the Kehillah must do nothing to give offense to the American people.

Very truly yours,

Louis Marshall

Source: MS 359, box 5, folder 3, AJA.

6.07 — "YESHIVA TO ERECT MODERN COLLEGE BUILDINGS," *Jewish Tribune,* SEPTEMBER 26, 1924

Yeshiva University, the flagship academic institution in America for modern Orthodoxy — a movement that emerged in Europe and the United States in the late nineteenth century — traces its inception to 1886, when Yeshivat Etz Chaim, a modest Jewish elementary school, was established in New York City. In 1915, Etz Chaim merged with the Rabbi Isaac Elchanan Theological Seminary (RIETS), the first yeshiva in America to offer advanced Talmudic instruction similar to that offered in European yeshivot. This merger, together with the appointment of a young and dynamic president that same year, Rabbi Bernard Revel

(1885–1940), laid the foundations for the school's future growth. In 1924, Yeshiva's leadership announced that it had outgrown its facilities on the Lower East Side and had acquired property in Upper Manhattan for the purpose of constructing a major campus. On this site, Yeshiva University would build its future. The following two documents exhibit the vision that would ultimately chart the school's academic expansion during the twentieth century.

New York.—An ideal Site for the modern college buildings which the Rabbi Isaac Elchanan Theological Seminary is going to erect, has just been purchased on Amsterdam Avenue in uptown New York, the Campaign Committee of the Seminary's Building Fund announces. The site, covering two and a half city blocks and continuing over sixty lots, contains ample ground for the series of college buildings which the Yeshiva is going to build, in order to provide for the hundreds of students from all over the United States and Canada, who now cannot be admitted to the present building on the lower East Side, because of its lack of facilities.

The committee is enthusiastic over the site, which contains all the desirable features, which the committee has spent months in trying to find throughout Greater New York. The site is easily accessible from all parts of the city, is close to the Columbia University and City College, and is surrounded by city parks.

Plans for the buildings which are to be constructed for America's great Orthodox Jewish institution of higher learning, include: a large Yeshiva building to accommodate 1,000 students, with classrooms, study rooms and auditorium; a senior high school building, modern in every respect to provide for a large number of students, who can later continue their studies at the Yeshiva; a college and library building for the older students; a dormitory with 200 rooms for out-of-town students, which has been one of the chief problems the Yeshiva in its present location has had to face; and a beautiful campus,

laid out with playgrounds, so that the physical development of the students will be provided for hand in hand with their ethical and cultural training.

The campaign which has the indorsement of the leading Orthodox Jews of America and is sponsored by the Union of Orthodox Rabbis, Union of Orthodox Congregations, Mizrachi [referring to a Jew with Israeli or other Middle Eastern roots] and others, will provide funds sufficient to erect these new buildings and also to establish an Endowment Fund, sufficient to bring many noted Jewish scholars from Europe to augment the present able faculty of the Yeshiva, which is under the presidency of Dr. Bernard Revel, one of America's most noted Jewish scholars. The Committee hopes that the response from American Jewry will be sufficient to realize their hope of making the Yeshiva, the largest and most important center of higher Jewish learning in the Diaspora.

The Yeshiva is now endeavoring to widen its scope by establishing branches of its preparatory schools throughout the country, so that every important Jewish community can insure its children receiving a thorough Jewish training. The Rabbinical graduates of the institution are given a wide and thorough training in Bible, Talmud, Jewish laws, history and literature, enabling them to become spiritual leaders in the most rigid Orthodox communities. They also receive a thorough secular and college education, enabling them to become real Jewish spiritual guides for the Jewish youth of America. Another of the important departments of the Yeshiva is its Hebrew Teachers' Institute which will be greatly extended by the campaign fund. In the Teachers' Institute, the students are instructed in Hebrew language and literature, Jewish history, Talmud, Pedagogy and Jewish ethics.

In a statement issued in connection with the announcement of the Yeshiva's site purchase, Dr. Revel, President of the Faculty, said:

"It is the aim of the Yeshiva (The Rabbi Isaac Elchanan Theological Seminary) to help train in this land a generation of courageous Jews, high in mind and in spirit, and conscious of its duty to Israel's heritage of spiritual and moral supremacy; Chalutzim [pioneers] of the Jewish spirit and the Renaissance of Judaism; to help create in this land—through the influence of the disciples, rabbis and teachers it sends out—a Jewish life which will draw its inspiration from and be guided by the immortal truths of our Torah—a Law of life, light and loyalty.

[. . .]

"The Yeshiva, an institution of higher learning for the education of an enlightened Jewish laity, as well as for the training of true rabbis and efficient teachers, with courses that lead to the degree of Doctor of Hebrew Literature, aims to create in this land a system of Jewish education, based upon the principle that every American Jewish child has an inalienable right to a knowledge and loving understanding of our great heritage—the Torah and Jewish idealism; an adequate system of Jewish education which will bring complete harmony into the life of the Jewish child and develop his conscience and his will to live as a true Jew; a Jewish training which will indicate the guiding laws of life, in accordance with the eternal truths of Judaism and in indissoluble union with the best thought of the age and the great humanitarian ideals of our glorious land, and which will be able to counteract the disintegrating forces which are brought to bear upon American Jewry, particularly upon our children. The light of the Torah, leading man to God and the great ideals of duty, reverance [sic] and righteousness, has at all times emanated from the Yeshiva, the most vital factor in historic Judaism.

Source: Bernard Revel nearprint file, AJA.

6.08—BERNARD REVEL, "THE VISION OF YESHIVA COLLEGE," 1926

To the great assembly of faithful sons and daughters of Israel, who on this day, sacred to God and significant to the entire House of Israel, have assembled from near and far to express their unfailing allegiance and devotion to God, and to rejoice in the fulfillment of the hope and vision of a shrine for the *Shekina* [Divine Presence], of a sanctuary on this continent, dedicated to the glory of God and the spiritual environment of our country . . . I bring the greetings and the blessings of the House of God—the Yeshiva.

This day marks the dawn of a brighter glory of the Torah on this continent and sounds a note which finds an echo in the heart of every Jew who loves God and is loyal to the Torah.

This memorable day, this rising sanctuary, this representative assembly of tens of thousands who have come distances to pay homage to the Torah, mark the resolved expression by American Israel of its inner urge to create a sanctuary in its heart and in the hearts of its children, to perpetuate Israel's spirituality and steadfastness to God and His Torah; its aspiration to a true and creative Jewish life, which rises from the sustaining strength of the Torah and its historic and abiding home; the Yeshiva. . . .

This sanctuary is consecrated to the teaching of the truths of the Torah which stand eternal in a world of changing and shifting standards and values; to the affirmations of the faith of our fathers concerning God, Israel and the Torah in their totality; . . . in union with the creative culture and humanizing forces of the time, with unshaken loyalty to our beloved country.

The Yeshiva will bring to ever-increasing numbers of American Jewish youth the true perspective of historic Judaism in the complex organization of modern life, combining with the learning of the world today those values and ideals which have been the strength of the sustaining faith of our fathers, for the enrichment of the lives of the Jewish community and of America. The Yeshiva will help span the widening chasm between intellectualism and faith in Jewish life and thought. It will imbue our Jewish youth with an active and abiding interest in, and a spirit of service to the cause of Israel.

Source: Aaron Rakefett-Rothkoff, *Bernard Revel: Builder of American Jewish Orthodoxy* (Jerusalem and New York: Feldheim, 1981), 80–83, 90–91. Used by permission of Aaron Rakefett-Rothkoff.

6.09—CONFERENCE FOR THE DISCUSSION OF THE PROBLEM OF JUDAISM, CHICAGO, FEBRUARY 21–22, 1928

Rabbi Mordecai M. Kaplan (1881–1983), a distinguished professor at the Jewish Theological Seminary and a visionary religious leader, founded the Society for the Advancement of Judaism in 1922. The society and its journal provided Kaplan with a forum for the promulgation of his ideas. In February of 1928, Kaplan and several concerned colleagues convened a Conference for the Discussion of the Problem of Judaism. The participants deliberated on a range of challenges facing American Judaism, and posed a number of possible solutions. Their analysis, outlined as follows, offered a powerful critique of denominational Judaism as it existed in the 1920s. Many of the ideas expressed at the 1928 meeting influenced the eventual development of a new and distinctly American expression of Jewish religious practice: Reconstructionism.

The following call, signed by Prof. Mordecai M. Kaplan, Dr. Felix A. Levy, Rabbi Max Kadushin, and Dr. Alexander M. Dushkin, was sent to a number of rabbis, educators, social workers and laymen in the Middle West:

Many thoughtful Jews in America are ill at ease because of the inconsistencies in their Judaism and the lack of a clear program for their life as American Jews. They find none of the existing party platforms—Orthodox, Conservative, Reform—either spiritually or intellectually satisfying. Some are struggling as individuals to organize their thoughts

and convictions, and are striving to make their daily practices as Jews conform to these convictions as best they can. This individualistic method, however, lacks the challenge, as well as the reassurance and social character of group thought and group decision. Many have felt the need for an authoritative modern program in Judaism. But we cannot wait for the meeting of authoritative synods, representing the whole Jewish people and vested with binding authority. Such synods may not meet in our lifetime.

[...]

The Conference will deal with two major problems:

1. Our own era in Judaism—the character of modern Jewish life, and the bases for reconstructing our life as Jews in America.
2. The forms in which American Jewish life should express itself:
   a. The observance of Jewish customs and folkways and the spirit and principles which should underly [*sic*] their selection and modification;
   b. The elements in a community program involving local communal undertakings, and work on behalf of Palestine and of international Jewry;
   c. An evaluation as Jews of the various questions and problems confronting our life as American citizens.

SUMMARY OF THE DISCUSSION

1. *Orthodox Judaism* is untenable for us because we cannot accept its two fundamental doctrines: first, that Judaism is immutable law, both written and oral, revealed by God to Moses at Sinai at a definite time and under definitely described conditions; second, that God miraculously interfered with the natural order of things for the sake of Israel, and brought about supernatural miraculous events at various crises in its history. According to Orthodoxy, whatever growth took place in Judaism has not been in the form of change or development, but rather as an unfolding of the Mosaic truths revealed at Sinai. According to Orthodoxy the Bible is literally true, and the miracles described in it must be viewed as actual historic events. An Orthodox Jew may be guilty of errors—sins of omission and commission—but he cannot be guilty of questioning the above fundamental doctrines and yet remain consistently Orthodox.

We cannot, therefore, hold to Orthodox Judaism, because modern scientific study discloses Judaism as a continuous development and change, responding, in its various historic epochs, to social needs, and subject to the natural conditions of human life. Every great era in Jewish history produced deep changes and new developments, both in the philosophy of Judaism and in the organization of Jewish life— Prophetic Judaism in the Bible era, Pharisaism in the Second commonwealth, Talmudic Judaism in the Diaspora. We are now at the beginning of a new era in our history, and the deep, far-reaching changes in our general life and thought must find adequate expression in a corresponding development in our Jewish living and thinking, so that our lives may be integrated wholly and honestly.

2. *Reform Judaism* is unsatisfying because, by denying the national group character of Judaism, it has so transformed Judaism that nothing remains of it but a religious philosophy, the philosophy of ethical monotheism as taught by the Prophets and Sages of Israel. The belief of Re-

form Jewish leaders that this religious philosophy can be transmitted from generation to generation without concrete social group life, has proved to be erroneous. Modern sociologic study has demonstrated that religious life is impossible unless the group living that life has other interests in common beyond that of religious ideology and practice. Moreover the modern individual Jew insists upon his duty and his privilege to integrate his religious philosophy into the rest of his own experience and thought, so that no one philosophical or ethical system can be wholly binding on all Jews. . . .

3. *Conservative Judaism* is dissatisfying because it offers no positive, systematic program. Among its adherents are persons who vary considerably in their interpretation of Judaism, and whose only bond of unity is their own dissatisfaction with present-day Orthodoxy and present-day Reform. If that dissatisfaction were expressing itself in an earnest seeking for a more satisfying formulation and system, the present lack of positive program might be commendable. But Conservative Judaism has already become too much engrossed in matters of organization and party control, so that it is fearful of any consistent seeking for truth, lest it offend some of its constituents, and it, therefore, proceeds by compromise and indirection.

[. . .]

4. *Secular nationalism*, as a system of thought, is even less satisfying to us, because it does not take into account the universalizing religious penchant or genius of the Jewish nationality. In failing to connect their thinking adequately with this unique character of Jewish group life of the past, secular nationalists merely hold out what the Jewish people may accomplish in the future. If, at least, the promise of future achievement were certain to be of a spiritual, unifying character, we might be reconciled. But nationalism, as such, is dynamite, destructive and dangerous, and it has in it the seeds of greater harm than good for the Jew and for humanity. Distinct secular nationalism may be a

necessity for groups of Jews in countries where conditions of life demand such nationalist organization. It is not a good to be sought after where conditions are such as to be favorable to minority rights.

The difficulty with the terms "nation" and "religion" as applied to Jewish thinking, is that they come out of the experience of Christian peoples, and express distinctive concepts in the development of Christendom. They do not apply to the Jews, who are neither "nation" nor "religion," in the Christian sense of these terms. The Jews are an *Am*, which Hebrew expression cannot be translated by a single word, but rather bysome such phrase as a people, folk, or nationality, having distinctive civilization, culture and ways of life, in which the universalizing spiritual ethical-religious elements are dominant. Judaism is the civilization, or way of life, of the *Am Yisrael*.

II

Dissatisfaction with the existing systems of Judaism obligates us to a positive, earnest seeking for a more constructive and more tenable formulation of Jewish principles and of forms of Jewish social organization. We cannot expect to be able to evolve a complete new system of Judaism at the present time, because we are, as yet, almost at the very beginning of the modern era in Jewish history. We shall need a much longer experience as a people living in a modern world before an adequate system of modern Judaism will fully develop. It is our task, however, carefully to lay the groundwork upon which such a system can be based. A few such ground-principles may be laid down by us now:

1. Modern Judaism must be creative. Just as the Prophets and Psalmists created ideas, attitudes and value for their day, and as the Rabbis and Sages did that for their generation, so modern Jews must create new ideas and new forms of living for themselves and their children. Unless Judaism again becomes creative, unless it becomes pro-spective rather than

retrospective, it will not be able to maintain itself in this world, which demands creation for spiritual satisfaction. Jewish creativeness must be based upon an intelligent, thorough knowledge of Jewish past achievement. It must be continuous with the Jewish past. But it may deviate considerably, both in content and in form, in order to serve the modern Jew. Jewish creativeness will express itself not only in literature and in philosophy, but also in the arts and in social organization.

2. Modern Jewry is not a uniform diaspora, living under more or less uniform conditions of exile, as were true in the centuries preceding the modern era. The Jewry of our day is an *Internationality*, living under varying conditions of national and political life. The development of Judaism as a modern religious civilization will vary in different lands. The chief variations will be in the three great zones of the Jewish diaspora today. It will develop along the lines of minor nationalism in Eastern Europe, of dominant nationalism (ultimately) in Palestine, and of communal organization in Western Europe and America. In each land the character of general life, national, political, civic, and cultural, will profoundly affect the forms of Jewish creativeness and of Jewish organization. In order that Judaism, however, may maintain its international character, and not be split up into disparate and disunited Jewries, a central Jewish Homeland in Palestine is most important. There a center can develop in which Jewish creativeness will take Hebraic forms, forms nearer to classic, pre-exilic Judaism than is possible in other lands; a center, also, in which the Jews will ultimately form a sufficiently large proportion to express their ideas and social will in all forms of organized life

and thought. The continued interest of international Jewry in such a central homeland, as well as the cultural association and interchange of achievements with it, should prove a unifying bond, very helpful and stimulating to Jewish creativeness everywhere.

3. In America the essential condition of Jewish creativeness is community life. Here, too, Jews will need a measure of social communal autonomy, if an American Jewish civilization is to develop, broader and more inclusive than the mere act of worshipping. American Jews must not satisfy themselves with synagogue activity alone, nor with charitable and educational activities alone—important as these are. They must unite all forms of their organized life and integrate their activities into Jewish Communities. To these communities will belong all Jews who feel physical or spiritual kinship with the *Am Yisrael*; all those who are interested in Jewish creativeness, no matter what their personal philosophy may be, whether they feel impelled to the activity of "worship" or not. Congregations and synagogues will be units in these communities, units consisting of groups of Jews who wish to express their Judaism through common worship. But there will be other units also, those consisting of groups and individuals who are not interested in common worship, but who wish to express their Jewishness and their creativeness through literature, the arts, social welfare, social justice activities, etc.

[. . .]

In the course of time the community will come to be vested with authority to interpret and to modify Jewish customs and practices to conform to existing conditions and needs. Thus, Sabbath observance, food regulations, form of festival observance, marriage and divorce laws, etc., will be modified or changed by the community authority so that these will again function in Jewish life positively and joyously, instead of remaining impossible, sacred laws, which the vast majority of Jews honor by entirely ignoring.

. . . The building up of the communal authority will be the *sine qua non* of continuing Jewish life in America.

[. . .]

4. As regards Jewish religion, distinction must be drawn, in our day of individual freedom of thought, between personal philosophic belief and folk religious observance. Customs, ceremonial and ritual should be viewed not as revealed Law, immutable and binding in every detail, but rather as folkways developed by our *Am* in the course of its history, and adapted to express its *mores*—its approved ways of life. These folkways have always been modified (except for the ghetto period), and should continue to be modifiable in our own day— changed and adapted when capable of being significant and valuable, abandoned when no longer of value to the Jew; just as such folkways and customs were abandoned in the past. Moreover, if the Jewish community is to be creative, new folkways and customs will be developed and sanctioned in much the same way as these have been created in former times.

Source: Mordecai Kaplan nearprint collection, box 2, folder "Articles, Reconstructionism," AJA.

In the 1930s, the Jewish Institute of Religion—a liberal rabbinical seminary founded in New York by Rabbi Stephen S. Wise—permitted a woman, Helen Hadassah Levinthal (1910–1989), to enroll in the rabbinical curriculum. Even though she completed the entire course of rabbinical study together with her male classmates, Levinthal did not receive rabbinical ordination. Many years later, in 1972, Helen's father, Rabbi Israel H. Levinthal (1888–1982), wrote a letter to Hebrew Union College–Jewish Institute of Religion professor Jacob Rader Marcus (1896–1995) challenging Marcus's assertion that Sally Priesand (b. 1946) was the first woman to complete a rabbinical curriculum. In this interesting letter, Rabbi Levinthal provides a detailed account of his daughter's rabbinical experiences, including a reference to her delivery of sermons for the High Holidays in fall 1939 at Brooklyn's Congregation B'nai Sholom.

120 Rose Hill Ave.
New Rochelle, N.Y. 10804

4-14-72

My dear Professor Marcus,

I hope that this finds you in good health; and that you will forgive me for intruding on your valuable time with this letter.

I still regard myself a Philadelphian, and I still subscribe to and read the *Jewish Exponent* of that city. In a recent issue, I read with a great deal of interest your fascinating article on "The First Woman Rabbi"—referring to the coming Rabbinical ordination of Miss Sally Priesand by the H.U.C.-J.I.R.

I was interested to learn that a woman—Regina Jonas—did study for the Rabbinate at the Berlin Academy for the Science of Judaism in the 1930s,—and that while the Professor of Talmud refused to ordain her, she was ordained by the Rev. [Max] Dienemann, of Offenbach. This was for me an interesting bit of historic news.

As you stated, there have been girl students at the H.U.C., but none went further than their Bachelor of Hebrew Lit. degree.

For the historic record, I do want to write you that there was one Jewish young woman—my daughter, Helen Hadassah (now Mrs. Lester Lyons, of above address in New Rochelle,) who did take the entire academic Rabbinic course, and completed it in full at the Jewish Inst. of Religion in 1939.

Helen and another woman—the late Prof. Dora Askowitz [Askowith], of Hunter College—entered at first as Auditors. Prof. Askowitz dropped out after a year or two, but Helen stayed on. One of the members of the faculty told her that her work was of such a high grade that she ought to apply for regular student status,—which she did, and was accepted by the faculty.

Helen, as I said, took the completed course,—and like the other graduating students wrote a graduation thesis,—under Prof. Chayim Tchernowitz ל"ז, which he praised highly. The subject of her thesis is an interesting one: "Woman Suffrage from the Halachic Aspect."

The problem of her ordination arose in her senior year, when the issue became an actual one. I used to meet the late Dr. Stephen S. Wise ז"ל quite frequently, in those days, at Zionist meetings, and I would often discuss the matter with him,—and on many occasions he told me that the faculty was seriously debating the matter.

He once told me that Prof. Tchernowitz was of the opinion that since the Hebrew title רב is a masculine term, a new title should be found which could be conferred upon a woman,—but that many in the faculty felt that while Helen did excellent work, the time was not ripe for the J.I.R. to ordain a woman.

(Incidentally, a humorous note: Dr. Wise once jestingly said to me: "If your father [Rabbi Bernard C. Levinthal (1865–1952), a prominent Orthodox rabbi in Philadelphia] will give his approval to our ordaining Helen, we will do so,"—and I, also jestingly replied to him,—which he took in good spirit.)

A compromise solution was accepted by the faculty. At the ordination service, Helen was given two diplomas,—one in English, conferring upon her the degree of Master of Hebrew Literature—signed by the entire faculty & by Judge Julian Mack [1866–1943], Chairman of the Board; and one in Hebrew, the wording of which is quite significant. I believe that Prof. Tchernowitz was responsible for the text:

בית המדרש לחכמת ישראל בניו יארק מאשרים בזה כי
תלמדתנו חוה הדסה בת הרב ישראל חיים
לבינטל שקצה על דלתי בית
מדרשנו וגמרה את חק הלימודים הקבועים בו ועמדה
למבחן בכתב ובעל פה בהתאם לדרישות
המוסד על יסוד זה הננו מחלקים לה את התואר מוסמכה
לספרות ישראל
יהי ה' עמה ותעל להפיץ רוח חכמה ודעת בקרב עמה –
ולראיה באנו וכ' . . .

[*The New York Jewish Institute of Religion confirms that our student Chavah Hadassah, the daughter of Rabbi Israel Ḥaim Levinthal, attended our school and completed successfully all the required course work and passed the written and the oral exams in accordance with the institute requirements. Thereupon we bestow upon her the degree of a Master of Israel's Literature.*]

May 28, 1939, _____
Sivan 10th 5699

The signatures in Hebrew *of entire faculty.* Judge Mack's in English.

The very word מוסמכה, I think, was used to resemble in intonation the traditional word מוסמך used in Rabbinic ordination.

The event appeared newsworthy. All the New York newspapers—English and Yiddish, as well as *Time* magazine, featured it. In Warsaw, Poland, & in Tel Aviv, papers had articles about it. A book, by a Tina Levitan, called "The Firsts in American Jewish History" published in 1954, includes this statement . . . "of a woman H. H. L. who completed a full Rabbinic course but who was denied ordination because of her sex."

Just last year, a fellow classmate at the J.I.R—Rabbi Earl Stone, of Denver, wrote to her & told her that he wrote to Dr. [Alfred] Gottschalk, after reading publicity articles about Miss Preisand [*sic*],—telling him about Helen's case. I am enclosing copies of Rabbi Stone's letter and Dr. Gottschalk's reply,—as well as a copy of [the] article which appeared in *Time* magazine.

Cong. Bnai Sholom in Brooklyn was my first Rabbinic position which I held from 1910 (date of my graduation) to 1915.

In 1939, this cong. was without a Rabbi, & they asked Helen to serve as Rabbi for the High Holy Days. She agreed to preach the sermons, on condition that they engage a Rabbi to supervise the services. This they did. They selected Rabbi Louis Hammer, who was then retired, and Helen preached on both days, Rosh Hashanah, Yom Kippur eve & morning.

I believe,—and I am sure you will agree with me, that proper cognizance, by the H.U.C.-J.I.R., of these matters, should now be taken.

Again, forgive me for taking up so much of your time, but I thought that this historic note would be of interest to you.

With high regard and all good wishes to you, I am

Respectfully & cordially yours,
Israel H. Levinthal

Source: Israel Levinthal nearprint file, AJA.

6.11—EDGAR A. GUEST, "SPEAKING OF GREENBERG," 1934

*Henry "Hank" Greenberg (1911–1986), the
Bronx-raised son of Romanian Jewish
immigrants, played professional baseball for
the Detroit Tigers between 1930 and 1946 before
ending his career in 1947 with the Pittsburgh
Pirates. In 1934, the Tigers were scheduled to
play on the Jewish High Holy Days, and pressure
mounted on Greenberg to resolve the conflict
between the Jewish traditional mandate not
to work on these days and his responsibility
to his teammates and fans. Edgar A. Guest
(1881–1959) composed a poem in the slugger's
honor, referencing both Greenberg's compromise
on Rosh Hashanah—he attended synagogue
services in the morning, then joined the
afternoon game, hitting two home runs in a
2–1 victory over the Boston Red Sox—and his
decision to sit out entirely on Yom Kippur.*

GREENBERG

The Irish didn't like it when they
heard of Greenberg's fame
For they thought a good first baseman
should possess an Irish name;
And the Murphys and Mulrooneys
said they never dreamed they'd see
A Jewish boy from Bronxville out
where Casey used to be.
In the early days of April not a
Dugan tipped his hat

Or prayed to see a "double" when
Hank Greenberg came to bat.

In July the Irish wondered
where he'd ever learned to play.
"He makes me think of Casey!" Old
Man Murphy dared to say;
And with fifty-seven doubles and a
score of homers made
The respect they had for Greenberg
was being openly displayed.
But upon the Jewish New Year
when Hank Greenberg came to bat
And made two home runs off Pitcher
Rhodes—they cheered like mad for that.

Came Yom Kippur—holy fast day
world wide over to the Jew—
And Hank Greenberg to his teaching
and the old tradition true
Spent the day among his people
and he didn't come to play.
Said Murphy to Mulrooney, "We
shall lose the game today!
We shall miss him on the infield
and shall miss him at the bat.
But he's true to his religion—and I
honor him for that!"

Source: Hank Greenberg nearprint file, AJA.

6.12—CONSTITUTION AND BY-LAWS OF THE SYNAGOGUE COUNCIL OF AMERICA, 1926

On June 9, 1925, representatives of the Reform, Conservative, and Orthodox movements met in New York City at the Harmonie Club to discuss the idea of establishing a Federal Council of Synagogues of America. As he did with the interfaith initiatives, Rabbi Abram Simon (1872–1938) played a foundational role in the creation of this council. He told his colleagues that "Despite differences among Jews, there is only one Judaism. . . . We are not divergent sects; we are only representatives of differing interpretations . . . if [we] wish to cooperate with Christian National Organizations, [then we] must be representative of all Israel and not of any reform, or orthodox, or conservative, or secular phase of thought." These representatives continued to meet over the coming months. By November 9, 1926, the representatives of "the leading Jewish religious organizations in the United States" had officially established the Synagogue Council of America and adopted the constitution reprinted here, which was conceived and drafted in St. Louis the previous winter. The vision contained in the constitution would guide the Synagogue Council until its dissolution in 1994.

ITS ORIGIN

The need for a union of the various Jewish religious forces in the United States to speak with one voice for common causes, was long felt by American Israel, and the formation of such a union was frequently advocated by the spokesmen of congregational bodies.

At the Twenty-Ninth Council of the Union of American Hebrew Congregations, held in St. Louis, January 19 to 22, 1925, the following resolution was presented on the floor of the Convention by Dr. David Philipson and Dr. Abram Simon:

Whereas, A closer religious fellowship and a practical cooperation among the national Jewish congregational organizations are eminently desirable for the advancement of Judaism and of Jewish education in the United States, and for co-operation with other national organizations interested essentially in religion and in religious education, Therefore, be it

Resolved, That the Executive Board of the Union be empowered to invite representatives of the United Synagogue of America, the Union of Jewish Orthodox Congregations, the Central Conference of American Rabbis, the Rabbinical Assembly of the Jewish Theological Seminary, and the Union of Orthodox Rabbis of the United States and Canada, to meet with a similar committee of the Union of American Hebrew Congregations to effect a conference of national Jewish Congregational bodies for the furtherance of the above aims.

[. . .]

Constitution and By-Laws of the Synagogue Council of America
Preamble
Whereas, The Synagogue is the basic and essential unit of our Jewish life, and whereas it is desirable that the representatives of the synagogues in America meet from time to time in order to take counsel together for the sacred purpose of preserving and fostering Judaism,

Be it resolved, That a Council composed of representatives of national congregational and rabbinical organizations of America be formed, for the purpose of speaking and acting unitedly in furthering such religious interests as the constituent organizations in the council have in common; it being clearly provided that the council interfere in no way with the religious and administrative autonomy of any of the constituent organizations.

Name

The name of the organization shall be "The Synagogue Council of America."

Membership

The organizations constituting this council shall be

Central Conference of American Rabbis

Rabbinical Assembly of the United Synagogue of America
Rabbinical Council of the Union of Orthodox Jewish Congregations of America
Union of American Hebrew Congregations
Union of Orthodox Jewish Congregations of America
United Synagogue of America
and such other similar national organizations as may be admitted from time to time. . . .

Source: Synagogue Council of America nearprint file, AJA.

6.13—THE STORY OF THE NATIONAL CONFERENCE OF CHRISTIANS AND JEWS, 1928

During the interwar period, when a mass emigration from Eastern Europe produced a dramatic rise in the country's Jewish population, an interest in "interfaith" or "intergroup" activities began to flourish. The beginnings of these activities can be traced to the fin de siècle. One of the first examples of this phenomenon was the remarkable Parliament of Religions, which convened during the 1893 Columbian Exposition in Chicago. Over the first two decades of the twentieth century, an array of independent initiatives aspiring to promote "better understanding" among different groups cropped up across the nation. These activities were given many labels. Efforts were dedicated to goodwill, or were described as being "intergroup," "interreligious," "tri-faith," or related to "brotherhood."

American Jews took a keen interest in these attempts to foster better understanding among the nation's different religious and ethnic groups. In 1925, for example, Rabbi Emanuel J. Jack (1889–1942) of B'nai Israel congregation in Little Rock initiated the first "Better Understanding

Week" in the state of Arkansas, as a response to the rhetoric of regional hate groups such as the Ku Klux Klan and the Knights of the White Camelia. Two years earlier, in 1923, Rabbi Abram Simon, of Washington, D.C., then president of the Central Conference of American Rabbis (CCAR), published an essay in the American Hebrew *titled "Can Jew and Christian Understand Each Other?" As a result of this article, the Federal Council of Churches of Christ in America organized a "Committee on Good-Will," and the CCAR responded by creating a Good-Will Committee of its own so that the two groups could work together. Drawing on these efforts, Rabbi Isaac Landman (1880–1946), the* American Hebrew's *editor, helped organize a "Permanent Commission on Better Understanding."*

The National Conference of Christians and Jews (NCCJ), founded in 1928, became the best known and most enduring of the many goodwill organizations that appeared during the 1920s. On December 11, 1927, the New York Times *announced the formation of a National*

Conference of Jews and Christians for the Advancement of Justice, Amity and Peace. The organizers of this conference informed the public that its program would be "to publish the fact continually before the American people that the country's best leadership is on the side of understanding and good-will between people of divergent kinds and creeds." Some of the nation's most prominent Jews joined the conference's advisory council: Benjamin N. Cardozo, Alfred M. Cohen, Edward A. Filene, Israel Goldstein, Samuel H. Goldenson, Rebekah Kohut, Louis Marshall, Henry Morgenthau, David de Sola Pool, Nathan Straus, Stephen S. Wise, and Louis Wolsey. Following is the NCCJ's first constitution, which outlines the organization's bylaws as well as its mission and vision.

ORIGIN

Some time ago a great teacher said that a community like the one in which you and I live, really is not a "community" at all unless the Catholic, Jewish and Protestant neighbors appreciate each other's highest purposes, and become interested in working together on common tasks. Otherwise isolation results in distorted prejudices, and sometimes in violent fighting.

Believing this to be true, in 1928 a number of Protestants, Catholics and Jews worked out a plan for "conference." The Hon. Charles Evans Hughes and Dr. S[amuel] Parkes Cadman signed the letter that brought the first group together.

"First," they said, "we will study to see what situations cause trouble. We will set up the machinery for consultation and understanding. Then we will ask what forms of cooperation are possible. Next we will work out techniques of cooperation and open all available channels through which they can operate."

Newton D. Baker who served as Protestant Co-Chairman until his death in 1937, was succeeded by Professor Arthur H. Compton. Professor Carlton J. H. Hayes and Mr. Roger Williams Straus are the Catholic and Jewish Co-Chairmen.

PURPOSE

At no time has this National Conference of Christians and Jews (for so it came to be called) sought uniformity. It holds that men may differ deeply in religious belief while maintaining mutual respect and working together as American citizens at common undertakings.

According to its Constitution, "The Conference is an association of individuals, not of officials commissioned by their respective religious bodies. It does not aim at any sort of union or amalgamation of religious bodies or at modifying any of the distinctive beliefs of its members.

"Believing in a spiritual interpretation of the universe and deriving its inspiration therefrom, the National Conference exists to promote justice, amity, understanding and cooperation among Jews, Catholics and Protestants in the United States, and to analyze, moderate and finally eliminate intergroup prejudices which disfigure and distort religious, business, social and political relations, with a view to the establishment of a social order in which the religious ideals of brotherhood and justice shall become the standards of human relationships."

COOPERATION

The Conference assumes that all who believe in God have much in common and are equally concerned to combat current paganisms and materialistic influences which threaten not this or that religion only, but the spiritual life of the nation.

It believes that there are wide areas of activity of common concern to Protestants, Catholics and Jews and that in these they can cooperate. In each instance religious motives prompt them to serve the best interests of man and to work for social betterment. As American citizens they acknowledge the same patriotic obligations and share a common responsibility; all cherish religious liberty and the rights of freedom in speech, assembly and press.

Recognizing that since Protestants, Roman Catholics and Jews differ on important concerns, conflicts will arise in the future as they have in the past, the American way of dealing with such situations is first to seek to understand positions that we do not ourselves hold, then to determine what is just to all the interests involved and finally by a process of friendly conference, to find a working basis of agreement.

Source: National Conference of Christians and Jews nearprint file, AJA.

6.14—BROADSIDE, ZIONIST ORGANIZATION OF AMERICA, EARLY 1920S

Until Louis Brandeis took control of the nation's leading Zionist organization in 1914, Jewish nationalism remained a small and marginalized movement in American Jewish history. Although the effort to reestablish a Jewish state in Palestine attracted a small number of ardent partisans, most American Jews were either indifferent or opposed to the cause. Yet with news spreading of the dire condition of European Jews during and after World War I, the need for a Jewish homeland resonated with a growing number of American Jews. When Great Britain defeated the Ottoman Empire, wresting control of what would become the British Mandate for Palestine, Zionist leaders pressed Arthur James Balfour (1848–1930), the United Kingdom's foreign secretary, to support the Zionist cause. In a letter to Baron Walter Rothschild (1868–1937), the British official offered an official policy statement that became known as the Balfour Declaration: "His Majesty's Government view with favour the establishment in Palestine of a national home for the Jewish people." With the explicit political support of the British Empire, Zionism in the 1920s steadily grew into a mass movement. The year after Balfour's statement, in 1918, a diverse array of American Zionist organizations joined together to create the Zionist Organization of America (ZOA), which became the official successor of the Federation of American Zionists (1897). Invigorated by the Balfour Declaration, this new organization pressed American Jews to support the Zionist cause. A ZOA broadside, reproduced as follows, sheds light on the organization's efforts during this era.

THE CALL OF PALESTINE
Listen! Palestine Is Calling You!
Palestine, the Land of our Fathers, is now being rebuilt as the Jewish National Homeland.

This is a great hour for the Jewish people, an hour for which our people has hoped and prayed almost two thousand years.

Recently, many marvelous things have come to pass.

Great Britain gave us the Balfour Declaration, a promise to do her utmost to restore to Israel the Land of Israel.

As an earnest of her good faith, she appointed Sir Herbert Samuel, the leading Jewish statesman, High Commissioner for Palestine.

France, Italy and the other World Powers gave their consent to the Balfour Declaration.

The United States has followed suit. Both Houses of Congress voted *unanimously* for the Zionist Resolution, which is now signed by President Harding.

All this culminated in the *ratification of the Palestine Mandate by the League of Nations.* Palestine as the Jewish National Homeland is now established in international law.

In the meantime, almost twenty thousand Chalutzim have flocked to the shores of Palestine, where they are building roads, erecting houses, and reclaiming barren soil for fruitful cultivation.

All this has come to pass in your day.

But this is merely the beginning.

Before the goal is reached many more struggles will have to be fought, many more victories will have to be won.

And to do that every Jew must help.

Every Jew must express his consent by joining the forces that make for the upbuilding of Palestine. He must become identified with the great cause of Zionism.

By paying $6.00 a year and becoming a member, he serves notice to the entire world that his heart is in this great work, that he wishes to see Palestine as the Jewish National Homeland.

No Jew is so poor that he cannot afford this small sum.

No Jew is so hard-hearted that he would stay away at this great hour.

Listen silently to your Jewish conscience.

Listen, and you will hear the Call of Palestine.

Palestine Needs You—Join Now!

Source: Zionist Organization of America nearprint file, AJA.

6.15—HENRIETTA SZOLD, FAMILIAR LETTERS FROM PALESTINE, DECEMBER 21, 1921

In 1921, Henrietta Szold (1860–1845), the founder of Hadassah and a leader of the Zionist movement, composed an informative letter to Hadassah chapters in the United States and Canada. Her communication provided readers with a detailed description of her experiences at the first graduation ceremonies of the Hadassah Training School for Nurses in Jerusalem. Szold recounted a debate over use of the Hebrew language, both in the graduation ceremony and in the school's curriculum. While Zionist leaders urged speakers to present their talks in Hebrew and wanted graduates to develop their Hebrew skills, school administrators faced the challenge of operating a school in a British Mandate, which also required knowledge of English.

No. 5
Jerusalem, December 21, 1921

To the Hadassah Chapters of the United States and Canada.

My dear Fellow-Workers:

The graduation exercises were finally held Wednesday, December 7. . . . To our joy the weather favored us. We had been afraid that so late a date as December 7 would land the commencement in the midst of the rainy season, when the inclemency of the weather is incalculable. In spite of our fears, the twenty-two graduates filed into the front rows of seats reserved for them, their new white uniforms and their caps with the red Mogen David uncrumpled by wind or weather. At their head walked Miss Anna Kaplan, the supervising nurse of the Rothschild Hospital, by virtue of this office the principal of the training school. After them followed the pupil nurses, with the exception of those on night duty in the hospital, to the number of twenty-three. The undergraduate nurses were in their blue uniforms, if they were full-fledged pupil nurses; in gray, if they were still in the six-months' probation stage. Standing here and there in the aisles were the American graduate nurses, also in cap and uniform. They acted as ushers, "ushering," as it were, their erstwhile pupils, colleagues about-to-become, from the school into active life. Under their marshalling and to the strains of "God Save the King," the audience rose to greet the young graduates.

Here I insert a copy of the program in English. It was distributed to the audience in Hebrew as well as in English:

Music

Address—Miss Anna Kaplan, Principal Nurses' Training School

Address—Mr. G. W. Heron, Director Department of Health

Address—Dr. M[ontague] D[avid] Eder, Member of the Palestine Zionist Executive

Address—Dr. J. Thon, Representative of the Waad Ha-Leuni [National Council]

Music

Address to the Graduates—Miss Szold, Chairman of Committee on Nurses' Training School

Conferring of the Diplomas—Lady Beatrice
   Samuel
Address on Behalf of the Graduates—Miss
   Esther Litwinovsky
Music
Address—Dr. A[braham] Ticho,
   Representative of the Medical Faculty of
   the Nurses' Training School
Closing Address—Dr. I[saac] M[ax]
   Rubinow, Director of the American
   Zionist Medical Unit. . . .

The only addresses in English were those of
Colonel Heron, the Chief of the Public Health
Department; Dr. Eder, the head of the Health
Division of the Palestine Zionist Executive; and
Dr. Rubinow, the Director of the Unit, who gave
a review of the activities of the Unit and the underlying principles of its work. The gist of these
three English addresses was given in Hebrew by
Dr. David de Sola Pool, the member of the Executive Committee of the Unit who represented
the Joint Distribution Committee upon it. The
reverse was not done. The Hebrew addresses
were permitted to go untranslated. All introductions and announcements were made in
Hebrew, and all telegrams and greetings read in
Hebrew. Lady Samuel's Hebrew address created
great enthusiasm. . . .

In my description of the audience at the Commencement, nothing was said of the part of the
audience seated on the platform; all the speakers, naturally; Sir Wyndham Deedes, the Civil
Secretary; Mr. Godfrey Samuel, one of the sons
of the High Commissioner; and the latter's aide-
de-camp, the last three having come in Lady
Samuel's party. For the rest, there were only
empty seats, a goodly number, though the capacity had been well gauged and exactly as many
tickets issued as there were seats on the platform.
The vacant seats were those which had been assigned to the Palestine Zionist Executive—not
one of whom had put in appearance. The reason
leaked out as the evening wore on. They had
absented themselves because they charged, the
Unit had selected Dr. Eder from among their
number to represent the Zionist Executive. It

was held that the Unit should have requested
the Zionist Executive to select its own representative, and it would have appointed one who
knows Hebrew and who would have spoken in
Hebrew. In that case the whole of the Zionist
Executive would have been present on the occasion which marked the consummation of nearly
ten years' effort.

This is not the whole story. It is a story of
several chapters. For reasons not necessary to
mention here, the program was not carried out
exactly in the printed order. Dr. Eder and Dr.
Thon consented to postpone their addresses
until after the conferring of the diplomas, the response of the graduate, and the address of the
member of the Faculty. Just before the latter rose
to speak, there was handed to me a note written
on the back of a card of admission, in which Mr.
[Eliezer] Ben Jehudah, the champion of Hebrew,
requested me not to profane the sanctity of the
occasion by allowing Jews to speak in a language not Hebrew. With all my respect for Mr.
Ben Jehudah's achievements, I could not heed
his request. When Dr. Eder rose to speak, Mr.
Ben Jehudah and his wife left the hall by way of
protest.

The papers of the next day's date contained
an anonymous letter of protest against the use
of English at the Commencement by a member
of the Palestine Zionist Executive. Those of the
second day after the Commencement contained
a letter by Dr. Eder in which he announced his
resignation from the Palestine Zionist Executive
to take effect on February 1. Dr. Eder has assured his friends that his resignation was not the
result of the Hadassah Commencement incident.
On one of the following days there appeared a
letter by Mr. Ben Jehudah in which he explained
the reasons for his public protest, and referred
to his request that no English addresses by Jews
be permitted, though he failed to mention the
circumstance that the request had been made
when the evening was approaching its end.

The city discussed the incident hotly.

To the Committee of Arrangements it had
seemed a foregone conclusion that Dr. Eder be

invited to address the graduates. The choice had been made for them, they thought, first, by the Carlsbad Congress [an early nineteenth-century diplomatic alliance], when it elected him a member of the Palestine Zionist Executive, with full knowledge of the fact that he speaks no Hebrew; and, second, by the Palestine Zionist Executive itself, when it appointed him to be the head of its own Health Department, again with full knowledge that he speaks no Hebrew. . . .

As for Mr. Ben Jehudah's protest, no one who knows his forty years' work and his amazing contribution to the renaissance of the national language can for a moment deny him the right of protest. Without zeal amounting to fanaticism our nation cannot reconstruct itself. But as he is the guardian of one national value, the language, so others have the right and the duty to constitute themselves equally zealous guardians of such other national values as they are fitted to promote. Can it be gainsaid that there *is* more than one national value? In all humility Hadassah may lay claim to having been such a guardian for nearly ten years. It has striven single-mindedly to establish a new profession for young Jewish women in Palestine. The Commencement was the crown of its efforts. It would seem that that might have been recognized officially through the presence of the members of the Palestine Zionist Executive.

The members of Hadassah in America must understand the situation clearly. According to the regulations of the Palestine Government on Nurses' Training Schools, the English language must henceforth be part of the equipment of any nurse who desires registry by the Government. Notice two points: The Government realizes that if a volunteer organization like the A.Z.M.U. [American Zionist Medical Unit] develops values, precautions must be taken to have the whole country profit thereby. The language of the Government Hospitals is English. If the Government desired to have the country profit by the circumstance that we have graduated nurses, it must insist that the Nurses' Training Schools which it recognizes include English in their curriculum. Colonel Heron in his address laid stress upon the fact that ours were the first women to be graduated as nurses on the soil of Palestine. The second point is that in justice to the professional women whom we prepare for the struggle with life, we must equip them with all the weapons for the battle. For better or for worse, our fate in Mandate Palestine cannot be separated from the English language. The graduates themselves—fanatics one and all for our own language—recognized that when they demanded a double diploma, in Hebrew and in English.

One thing must be admitted. With Argus eyes we must watch over the supremacy of Hebrew. Hadassah recognizes the danger ahead. Therefore the Hebrew diploma was written by a Torah scribe on parchment, the English version on ordinary paper on a typewriter. Therefore, the language of instruction is Hebrew, and the Commencement was conducted in Hebrew. Therefore, you are collecting a Text Book Fund for translations into Hebrew. Neither prudence nor courtesy has been permitted to curtail the sovereignty of Hebrew in the Hadassah Nurses' Training School, Jerusalem.

Yours sincerely,
Henrietta Szold.

P.S. 1. Study Hebrew! Learn to speak it!
P.S. 2. The needs of the Nurses' Training School:
First: Text Book Translation Fund.
Second: A Building.
Source: SC-12216, AJA.

6.16—STATEMENT ACKNOWLEDGING INCREASING SUPPORT FOR ZIONISM, CENTRAL CONFERENCE OF AMERICAN RABBIS, JUNE 1935

In the 1930s, the Reform movement was in the process of reexamining its official attitude toward Zionism and the Zionist movement. At its 1935 annual meeting in Chicago, Zionist rabbis in the Central Conference of American Rabbis secured passage of a resolution that acknowledged growing support for Zionism and, superseding the antinationalist wording found in the famed Pittsburgh Platform of 1885, adopted an official position of neutrality. Note that the resolution was adopted after the second paragraph, now in italics, was deleted. Two years later, at its annual meeting in Columbus, Ohio, the CCAR went even further, affirming that all Jews, including Reformers, had an obligation to participate in the building of a Jewish homeland in Palestine.

Your Committee offers a substitute Resolution which it recommends for your adoption:

Whereas, At certain foregoing conventions of the Central Conference of American Rabbis, resolutions have been adopted in opposition to Zionism, and

Whereas, We believe that such an attitude no longer reflects the sentiment of a very substantial section of the Conference membership, and

Whereas, We are persuaded that acceptance or rejection of the Zionist program should be left to the determination of the individual members of the Conference themselves, therefore

Be It Resolved, That the Central Conference of American Rabbis takes no official stand on the subject of Zionism; and be it further

Resolved, That in keeping with its oft-announced intentions, the Central Conference of American Rabbis will continue to co-operate in the upbuilding of Palestine, and in the economic, cultural, and particularly spiritual tasks confronting the growing and evolving Jewish community there.

Source: "The Neutrality Resolution on Zionism" from *Central Conference of American Rabbis Yearbook* XLV © 1935 by Central Conference of American Rabbis. Used by permission. All rights reserved.

6.17—EXCERPTS FROM THE "GUIDING PRINCIPLES OF REFORM JUDAISM," CENTRAL CONFERENCE OF AMERICAN RABBIS, FORTY-EIGHTH ANNUAL CONVENTION, MAY 27, 1937, COLUMBUS, OHIO

May 27, 1937

Israel. Judaism is the soul of which Israel [the Jewish people] is the body. Living in all parts of the world, Israel has been held together by the ties of a common history, and above all, by the heritage of faith. Though we recognize in the group-loyalty of Jews who have become estranged from our religious tradition, a bond which still unites them with us, we maintain that it is by its religion and for its religion that the Jewish people has lived. The non-Jew who accepts our faith is welcomed as a full member of the Jewish community.

In all lands where our people live, they assume and seek to share loyally the full duties and responsibilities of citizenship and to create seats of Jewish knowledge and religion. In the rehabilitation of Palestine, the land hallowed by memories and hopes, we behold the promise of renewed life for many of our brethren. We affirm the obligation of all Jewry to aid in its upbuilding as a Jewish homeland by endeavoring to make it not only a haven of refuge for the oppressed but also a center of Jewish culture and spiritual life.

Throughout the ages it has been Israel's mission to witness to the Divine in the face of every form of paganism and materialism. We regard it as our historic task to cooperate with all men in the establishment of the kingdom of God, of universal brotherhood, justice, truth and peace on earth. This is our Messianic goal.

Source: As printed in *JAW*, 437. Excerpts from *Central Conference of American Rabbis Yearbook*, Central Conference of American Rabbis, 48th annual convention, May 27, 1937, Columbus, Ohio. Copyright © 1937 Central Conference of American Rabbis. Used by permission. All rights reserved.

6.18—"OFFICIAL DECLARATION OF THE RABBINICAL ASSEMBLY," JUNE 7–9, 1937

As the modern Zionist movement developed, Zionist leaders and organizations pressed for differing visions of a Jewish homeland. For labor Zionists, the creation of a socialist communitarian state was most important. Religious Zionists, for their part, regarded a return to Eretz Yisrael, the land promised to the Jews by God, as their most important priority. Cultural Zionists, led by Ahad Ha'am, looked to Jewish sovereignty as an opportunity to develop an organic Jewish approach to the arts. American Jewish organizations joined this larger Zionist conversation. At its 1937 annual meeting, the Rabbinical Assembly—the rabbinical organization of Conservative Judaism—issued a "Pronouncement on Zionism" covering a variety of issues related to Jewish settlement in British Mandate Palestine, as well as asserting the growing need to create a haven for Jews suffering under increasing Nazi oppression.

For the Conservative movement leadership, the future Jewish state would provide refuge for persecuted Jews around the world, offer a source of Jewish inspiration for the diaspora, form a government based on the ethical principles of Judaism, and be achieved without "infring[ing] upon any of the inherent rights or just claims of the native Palestine population."

Pronouncement on Zionism

I.   The Zionist ideal to establish in Palestine a legally assured and publicly recognized national home for the Jewish people, has been an integral part of the religious outlook as well as of the program of practical activities sponsored by the Rabbinical Assembly of America from its very inception. Though the Assembly as such has never officially identified itself with any group or party functioning within the framework of the World Zionist Organization, it has on more than one occasion given expression to its complete and wholehearted devotion to the Zionist ideal. Its members have zealously labored in the leadership and in the rank and file of the Zionist movement and have participated in all efforts to mold public opinion into sympathy with the Zionist program and to muster the means needed for its realization.

II. We conceived of a Jewish National Home in Palestine as the place where the following conditions could obtain:

A. The maximum possible freedom of entry and residence for Jews from all countries of the world who for any reason may want to make their home there.

B. The emancipation of Jewish life from the many difficulties inherent in living everywhere as a minority group. This would make possible the free application of all aspects of Jewish religious tradition to all phases of human activity, and the untrammeled natural development of the whole of the Jewish cultural heritage with its distinct language, literature and manner of life. Such a freely developing Jewish community would then serve as a mighty centripetal force giving sorely needed strength and reality to the spiritual bonds which unite the widely dispersed Jewish communities. It would be for them an inexhaustible reservoir of inspiration, whence would flow those streams of living waters which would prevent the possible petrification or ultimate decay of the Jewish spiritual heritage in their midst.

C. A political government based upon the ethical teachings of our religion and therefore guaranteeing in the letter, spirit and administration of its law, equal political, cultural and economic rights to every inhabitant of the land irrespective of the racial, religious or cultural group to which he may belong.

[. . .]

V. We re-affirm our historic claim to Palestine, as the land where for more than a thousand years our fathers lived a national life and built a religious civilization which has profoundly and beneficently influenced the course of history. This land, further sanctified by the vision and message of the prophets, by more than eighteen centuries of unfaltering hope and tear-drenched prayer, and by the blood and sweat of the modern Jewish pioneer and martyr, has become inextricably intertwined with our religious faith and has assumed a central and all important position in every program of practical action aiming to ameliorate the present sad plight of our people and our tradition.

[. . .]

A. Our entrance into Palestine in no way infringed upon any of the inherent rights or just claims of the native Palestine population. The careful studies of the activities of the Jews in Palestine, during the past fifty years, made by both friends and foes, have not revealed any major or even minor wrong of consequence, perpetrated knowingly or unknowingly, by the Jews against the Arabs as individuals or as a group. On the contrary, the report of the British Commission itself bears eloquent testimony that benefits without number have been bestowed upon them. The land has been economically enriched, sanitation and health immeasurably improved, and culturally, the country has experienced a renaissance that has attracted the attention of the world.

B. Palestine today is an underpopulated country. The most conservative economic experts who have studied the situation agree that with the introduction of capital and modern methods in agriculture and industry, Palestine west of the Jordan has room for at least two million more people. Zionists have accepted the principle that Jewish immigration into Palestine should be dependent upon the economic absorptive capacity of the land, so that the immigrants should in no way deprive the native population of the economic positions it now holds and occupies.

[. . .]

D. Morally no less cogent than the argument based on the internationally recognized right of the Jews to enter

Palestine because of their historic association with the country is the plea based upon the present day dire needs of vast masses of the Jewish people. The unparalleled wave of anti-Semitism rising ever higher in countries of central Europe has brought indescribable physical suffering and spiritual humiliation to hundreds of thousands of Jews and is forcing them to seek new homes. The immigration laws of the countries of the world practically close all other avenues of escape to them. During the past decade Palestine alone offered hope to these thousands. We submit that neither justice nor humanity would be served by depriving these innocent victims of this hope also.

E. Palestine, moreover, is only a small fraction of the vast, sparsely inhabited territory under the political control of Arab peoples. The territories comprising the Kingdoms of Egypt, Iraq, Hedjaz, Syria, have sufficient room for the natural increase of the world Arabic population within the predictable future. Hence over against the assumed right of the Arabs of Palestine to reserve Palestine also for the future increase of the Arab people, are to be placed the moral right and the intense spiritual and physical needs of the sixteen million Jews of the world to a territory in which their spiritual heritage may find fullest expression and where millions of Jews now ruthlessly and barbarously persecuted may find a home.

F. Responsible Zionist leaders and solutions unanimously adopted at the World Zionist Congresses have repeatedly stressed the truth that Zionists look forward to a time when Jew and Arab will live side by side in peace in Palestine, the letter of the law

and the spirit in which it is administered assuring to both of them the right (1) to use whatever language they may prefer in their educational institutions as well as in their daily intercourse, from the platform and in the press; (2) to engage in whatever economic or professional pursuit the law may permit to any resident of the land; (3) to make and administer the law of the land in such a manner as in no way to infringe upon the cultural, political or economic rights of either or any racial or historic group living in the land.

[. . .]

XII. We recognize and sincerely sympathize with the legitimate national aspirations of the Arab population of Palestine and have repeatedly declared our readiness to give all possible assurances that none of these rights would be violated. We submit, however, that a portion of the Arab population has permitted itself to be led by men who were inspired either by a chauvinistic, militaristic, selfish nationalism or by personal ambition for political and economic power, or were inflamed by propaganda and promises of aid from foreign countries whose interests were at odds with those of the mandatory power. They have made no effort to understand the natures of the needs of 16,000,000 Jews of the world as contrasted with the vast opportunities open to the 14,000,000 [sic] Arabs of the world, nor to meet in any manner the hand of good-will sincerely extended them by the Jews.

It is not our intention in saying the above to impute any particular moral or intellectual retrogressiveness to the Arab people of Palestine. The manner in which the so-called advanced and civilized nations of the world are acting towards one another at the present moment has not set an example of justice, not to say generosity, which the less advanced might be urged to follow. We desire merely again to repeat that the impediments met by Zionism on its path towards realization are not of its own making but reflect the moral chaos which impedes every effort being made by men to establish a more just and more equitable human society.

Source: Proceedings of the Rabbinical Assembly of America (1937): 388–400.

6.19—LABOR ZIONIST HANDBOOK, POALE ZION/ZEIRE ZION OF AMERICA, 1939

Labor Zionism occupied the political left wing of the Zionist movement. The labor Zionists believed that the working class would reconstruct the Jewish state and create in it a progressive Jewish society. There were many factions in the labor Zionist movement, including the Poale Zion (Workers of Zion) party and the Zeire Zion Hitachduth (Union of the Youth of Zion), which in 1939 jointly published a handbook designed to give readers "the aims, activities and history of the Labor Zionist Movement in America." Excerpts included as follows reveal statistical as well as qualitative data and analysis on the strengths and challenges of labor Zionism in 1930s America.

. . . the Party membership has gradually grown and by 1939 there were 92 branches in 48 cities with an enrolled membership of about 4,000. In the smaller communities there are numerous Poale Zion groups, which for organizational convenience, are affiliated with the Jewish National Workers' Alliance. With the transfer of several older groups of the Young Poale Zion Alliance into the Party in 1936, a separate department was set up for English-speaking groups. There are 22 such groups with a membership of 500.

[. . .]

The following of the Party and the Labor Zionist movement in America may be well judged by elections to the recent Zionist Congress. In 1933 the Labor Zionist movement sold 5,000 *Shkolim* and received 9,000 votes; in 1935, 36,000 *Shkolim* and 24,744 votes; in 1937, 60,000 *Shkolim* and 36,719 votes. [The Zionist shekel— shekalim—constituted the certificate of membership individuals received after paying dues or "tax" to become members of the Zionist movement.]

[. . .]

The topic "orientation" was the main subject dealt with at the *P'gisha* (conference) at Accord, N.Y., during the Labor Day week-end 1934. The result of the lengthy discussion is expressed in the following consensus of opinion:

"The *P'gisha* recognizes in *chalutziut* [the spirit of pioneering] and *Eretz Israel* [the Land of Israel] within the confines of the *Histadrut* [the organization of trade unions in Palestine] not only a means but also an end in itself, in the realization of our Socialist Zionist ideology.

"The *P'gisha* reaffirms that both the struggle of the Jewish masses for the social, economic and cultural rehabilitation of the Jewish nation, and the struggle of the working class against capitalism, fascism, and oppression, and for the establishment of a socialist society, are integral parts of our Socialist-Zionist ideology which cannot be isolated one from the other, nor confined to any one country, and that every Young Poale Zionist must dedicate himself thereto wherever he may be."

[. . .]

A most important innovation in the life of the movement was the summer camps or *Kvutzot*, as they are called. From a modest beginning in 1932 the institution developed to embrace six *Kvutzot* throughout the country (Accord, near New York; Philadelphia; Baltimore; Chicago; Montreal; and Rochester). During the summer of 1938, close to 1,000 young people, the vast majority members of the movement, attended. The *Kvutza*, as one would expect the name to imply, is modelled after its Palestinian prototype. It is a cooperative enterprise, non-profit, enforcing the principle of self labor with all rigorousness. All campers, without exception, participate in the execution of the various menial tasks attendant upon the operation of the *Kvutza*. A major portion of the *Kvutza* program is devoted to construction of all sorts, such as building a cabin, repairing a road, or setting up large models (a *Kvutza* built in a day, etc.).

The program is in the main devoted to activity, and only in a smaller degree to study. Handicrafts, nature study, scoutcraft, photography, games and swimming, camp fires comprise the day's activities. Hebrew study circles are stressed, and reading circles are fostered. Saturday is set aside as a day of rest and recreation.

There are two sets of forces which are driving the American Jews toward recognizing the need for a more highly developed community life. The internal factors are primarily those dealing with the self-preservation of American Jewry, materially and culturally. The stoppage of large-scale immigration has cut off the source of European culture-bearers, while the prevailing means of raising the new generation to continue the cultural and communal aspects of Jewish life are totally inadequate. The inroads of assimilation and indifference among the younger generation have been scarcely offset by the blasts from Central Europe that have awakened some sections of the youth. But these internal problems have been overshadowed by far by the increasing responsibilities that American Jewry must assume toward Europe and Palestine. Despite heroic efforts on the part of various groups to meet the present Hitler-crisis, the long-harbored disease of disorganization has reduced the effectiveness of the measures that have been applied.
[...]

One of the gravest weaknesses of Jewish community life is the absence of democratic control. It is notorious that the few large donors to the Welfare Funds wield an undue influence in the determination of the policies of the agencies these Funds control or support. The capacity to give is often confused with the competence to determine allotments. The charitable, philanthropic and paternalistic attitudes of most wealthy Jews, reflect in the emphasis that a given community may place upon an orphan asylum, a Hebrew school, an overseas agency or a community center. More enlightened communities have begun to reclaim their sovereignty by placing responsibility in the hands of representative groups.

Source: Labor Zionist Organization of America nearprint file, AJA.

6.20—RABBI STEPHEN S. WISE, "HENRY FORD'S CHALLENGE AND A JEW'S REPLY," OCTOBER 10, 1920

In May of 1920, automobile mogul Henry Ford (1863–1947) began attacking Jews in his newspaper, the Dearborn Independent. *These attacks appalled and frightened American Jews, and a number of prominent Jewish leaders tried their best to combat the onslaught. One early response came from Rabbi Stephen S. Wise, whose sermon titled "Henry Ford's Challenge and a Jew's Reply" was delivered Sunday October 10, 1920, at Carnegie Hall before his congregation, the Free Synagogue.*

In the ensuing decade, Ford's paper published excerpts from the notorious antisemitic forgery The Protocols of the Elders of Zion. *The* Protocols *falsely asserted that there existed an international Jewish conspiracy that sought to control the world through the manipulation of the economy as well as the mass media and banking industries.*

Another antisemitic text published by Ford, "The Scope of Jewish Dictatorship in the U.S.," appears as follows. In 1927, Ford's paper accused Jewish bankers and merchants of seeking to gain economic control over the nation's wheat farms. The articles specifically attacked a prominent Jewish agricultural organizer, Aaron Sapiro (1884–1959), who subsequently sued Ford for defamation of character. Ultimately, Ford agreed to an out-of-court settlement with Sapiro and was also compelled to issue public apologies to various individuals and to Jews as a group. From this point on, Ford ceased publishing antisemitic materials.

It is the special shame of Christendom in America today that that tissue of lies and forgeries known as the Protocols or the "Jewish peril" is being given circulation by a confessedly nearly illiterate multi-millionaire, who has taken upon himself the onus of filing the gravest charges that have ever been uttered against Jews in this or any land. In America it is not enough for Christians to say that they have no part therein, that they place no credence in the charge. It is their business and above all in their Christian churches it is their duty to cry out against these hideous falsehoods uttered against a whole people.

[...]

Henry Ford's series of articles in "The Dearborn Independent" now reprinted in pamphlet form under the heading, "The World's Foremost Problem: The International Jew," is not so much a challenge to the Jew as an affront to public opinion, as an insult to every public decency. Before the war and the state of psychic disturbance which it has brought about, not even a Henry Ford would have dared to publish material resting for the most part upon the so-called Protocols, a forgery so clumsy, so stupid, so obvious, that none save Henry Ford could be deceived thereby.

The very title of the pamphlet, "The World's Foremost Problem: The International Jew," is a direct libel against the Jewish people at a time when the world is beset by problems national and international, and is by indirection an attempt to seize hold of the Jew as the scapegoat solvent of all its problems; the Ford screed is the most insidious of appeals to explain world-unrest by erecting the bogey of Bolshevism as an invention of Jewish capitalism and Jewish proletarianism leagued together *ad hoc.*

What Henry Ford's motives may be, it is not easy for one to determine who is unfamiliar with abnormal psychology or psychiatry. It may be that this adventure in the retailing of the contents of old garbage-pails represents a prospective Presidential candidacy. It may be nothing more serious than a publicity feat of the not unknown Ford products. Back of Henry Ford's invasion of the field of Jewish libel may lie abysmal ignorance, but that ignorance is being utilized with a skill and adroitness compact of malignity.

[. . .]

Though I must postpone the discussion of what Jews think of non-Jews in answer to the challenge of Ford, I will tell what one Jew thinks of one non-Jew. No man ought to be free to have the power which Henry Ford is exercising for evil. No man, though as rich as Ford or Croesus, ought to be suffered to libel a whole people in a land, the well-being of which depends upon the spirit of understanding and of conciliation, of tolerance and of good-will. Ford declares that the authorship of the Protocols, basic to his own challenge, is imputed by Jews to a criminal or a

madman. The reply of one Jew to Henry Ford is that his work, "The World's Greatest [sic] Problem: The International Jew," is the work of a criminal or a madman. And I do not believe, despite certain significant intimations, that Henry Ford is a madman.

Henry Ford is seeking to introduce into American life a tendency that is divisive, disruptive and morally fateful. The American people will have none of him and his ways. When once the American people, lovers of fair-play and of justice, understand that Henry Ford is seeking to introduce the spirit of or that makes for pogromism into America, they will abhor and renounce him. Henry Ford needs to be reminded that America is not a matter of *cheap engines* but of a *precious spirit*. Henry Ford shall not be suffered to cheapen the spirit of America; he shall not be permitted to vulgarize and corrupt America's soul.

Source: Stephen S. Wise nearprint file, AJA.

6.21 — "THE SCOPE OF JEWISH DICTATORSHIP IN THE U.S.,"
Dearborn Independent, DECEMBER 11, 1920

The common criticism made against President Wilson that "he played a lone hand" and would not avail himself of advice, can be made only by those who are in ignorance of the Jewish government which continually advised the President on all matters.

While the President is supposed to have been extremely jealous of his authority, this view of him can be maintained only by remaining blind to the immense authority he conferred on the members of the Jewish War Government. It is true he did not take Congress into his confidence; it is true that he made little of the members of his Cabinet; it is also true that he ignored the constitutional place of the United States Senate in the advisory work of making treaties; but it is not true that he acted without advice; it

is not true that he depended on his own mind in the conduct of the war and the negotiations at Versailles.

Just when Bernard M. Baruch, the Jewish high governor of the United States in war affairs, came to know Mr. Wilson is yet to be told; but just when he got into and out of the war are matters about which he himself has told us. He got into the war at Plattsburg, two years before there was a war; and he got out of the war when the business at Paris was ended.

"I came back on the *George Washington,*" he testified, which means that he remained at Paris until the last detail was arranged.

It is said that Mr. Baruch was normally a Republican until Woodrow Wilson began to loom up as a Presidential possibility. The Jews made much of Woodrow Wilson, far too much for his own good. They formed a solid ring around him. There was a time when he communicated to the country through no one but a Jew. The best political writers in the country were sidetracked for two years because the President chose the Jewish journalist, David Lawrence, as his unofficial mouthpiece. Lawrence had the run of the White House offices, with frequent access to the President, and for a time he was the high cockalorum of national newspaperdom, but neither that privilege nor the assiduous boosting of the Jewish ring availed to make him a favorite with the American public.

[. . .]

Now, as to Mr. Bernard M. Baruch, who for some as yet undefined reason was made head and front of the United States at war, we have his own word on several occasions that he was the most important man in the war.

"I probably had more power than perhaps any other man did in the war; doubtless that is true," he told [U.S.] Representative Albert Webb Jefferis.

And again: "We had the power of priority, which was the greatest power in the war. . . . Ex-actly; there is no question about that. I assumed that responsibility, sir, and that final determination rested within me."

And when Representative Jefferis said "What?" to that startling statement, Mr. Baruch repeated it:

"That final determination, as the President said, rested within me."

Representative [James M.] Graham said to him: "In other words, I am right about this, Mr. Baruch, that yours was the guiding mind . . ."

And Mr. Baruch replied: "That is partly correct—I think you are entirely correct . . ."

[. . .]

Mr. Baruch is but one illustration of the clustering of Jewry about the war machinery of the United States. If the Jews were the only people left in the United States who were able enough to be put in the important places of power, well and good; but if they were not, why were they there in such uniform and systematized control? It is a definite situation that is discussed. The thing is there and is unchangeably a matter of history. How can it be explained?

Source: SC-373, AJA.

6.22—A. LAWRENCE LOWELL TO JUDGE JULIAN MACK, ON JEWISH QUOTAS AT HARVARD COLLEGE, MARCH 29, 1922

During the early decades of the twentieth century, a disproportionate number of Jews—mostly children of Eastern European immigrants—began attending colleges and universities after completing their compulsory public education. Acquiring a higher education was a pathway to economic security. As the number of Jewish students matriculating at prestigious colleges and universities grew, academic administrators began worrying that their campuses would become "too Jewish." Many schools imposed quotas on the admission of Jewish students. At Harvard, President A. Lawrence Lowell (1856–1943) publicly defended a strict numerus clausus *for Jews seeking admission, insisting that the Harvard quotas were primarily intended to prevent an increase in antisemitism on the campus. In the letter that follows, President Lowell writes to Judge Julian W. Mack (1866–1943), a Harvard alumnus and Chicago-based jurist, to inquire whether or not Mack would be satisfied if approximately 15 percent of Harvard's entering classes were Jewish.*

Harvard University
Cambridge
President's Office

March 29, 1922

Dear Judge Mack:

I think we have found a way by which we can limit the Jews in Harvard College to the number that we can really benefit. As I told you, I put this at about 15%. In the present Freshman class, including the provisional Freshmen—that is, those coming from other colleges and rated as Freshmen—the proportion of Jews is about 20%. Now there are two doors into the College which we regard as discretionary. One is the transfer of students from other institutions. These we do not feel obliged to take unless they are in other ways desirable. We feel that a boy has a certain claim to enter Harvard College by the regular method of examination; that he does not have the same right to be transferred from another college without passing our entrance examinations. It appears that of the students transferring from other colleges 30% are Jews.

We have also investigated the men coming in under the new plan who have not passed all four of the sample examinations required, but who, taking their whole record together, have been admitted. These we call line cases. The admission of such boys who have not fully passed the entrance examinations is discretionary. Now it would appear that in the present Freshman class, if we excluded all but the clearly desirable Jews who came from other colleges or who had not fully passed the examinations under the new

plan, the percentage would have been reduced to 15%. It seems to us that to do this would be preferable to putting any limit upon the number of any class of boys who are admitted through the regular entrance examinations. Being an exercise of discretion already possessed by the committee, it would require no further action by any of the governing bodies; nor would it involve what Harvard cannot do,—that is, purporting to have entrance examinations open to everyone, and really excluding certain boys whom the examinations show to be intellectually qualified for admission.

I think you understand very clearly the object as we see it. It is the duty of Harvard to receive just as many boys who have come, or whose parents have come, to this country without our background as it can effectively educate; including in education the imparting not only of book knowledge, but of the ideas and traditions of our people. Experience seems to place that proportion at about 15%. That number we ought to take; but if we take more than we can bring into contact with our student body, we shall do those we do receive far less good, and to the detriment of the institution. We are trying in this to pursue the policy which, if pursued by all colleges, would be for the greatest interest of everyone concerned. What do you think of the method of accomplishing the result that we have suggested?

Very truly yours,
(Sgd.) A. Lawrence Lowell

Source: MS 359, box 5, folder 2, AJA.

6.23—"KAPLAN" PAGE IN *The Lucky Bag* YEARBOOK, UNITED STATES NAVAL ACADEMY, 1922

The U.S. Navy reported that there were nineteen Jewish midshipmen in the class of 1922 at the Naval Academy in Annapolis; one of them was Hyman G. Rickover (1900–1986), the father of *the nuclear navy. Another of the Jewish cadets in the class of 1922 was Leonard Kaplan (1900–1983), who became the subject of what was then called "cruel and unwarranted"* treatment. Kaplan was one of two midshipmen who were contending for the honor of class valedictorian. His rival, Jerauld L. Olmsted (1900-1923), was serving as editor in chief of the Naval Academy's yearbook, The Lucky Bag. Typically, each page of the yearbook contained photographs of two cadets who were roommates, accompanied by short biographical entries. Kaplan, who had no roommate, had apparently run afoul of Olmsted and some of the other midshipmen. As a prank, Olmsted placed a caricature of a large-nosed, unshaven midshipman adjacent to Kaplan's photo. Under the caricature, readers found an antisemitic parody of Kaplan's biography. In a final insult, Olmsted directed the yearbook's publisher to perforate Kaplan's page, leave it without a page number, and omit Kaplan's name from the yearbook's index. Once the perforated page was removed, no trace of Midshipman Kaplan remained. A furor broke out once the yearbook appeared. Acting secretary of the navy Theodore Roosevelt Jr. (1887-1944) conducted an official investigation and subsequently reprimanded Olmsted. The letter from Howard Sutherland (1865-1950), senator for Kaplan's home state of West Virginia—reprinted here after images

of the 1922 edition of The Lucky Bag—is representative of the many letters of complaint that were sent to President Harding and other governmental leaders in response to the event.

Source: The Lucky Bag Yearbook (1922), AJA.

6.24—LETTER FROM WEST VIRGINIA SENATOR HOWARD SUTHERLAND TO PRESIDENT HARDING, JUNE 1922

June 1922

My Dear Mr. President:

My attention has been called to an incident connected with the graduation of this year's class at the Naval Academy in the publication of The Lucky Bag, the yearbook of the academy, published, I believe, by the authorities of the graduating class, but presumably under some control by the authorities of the academy. It appears that a member of the class who graduated at or near the head of the class, Leonard Kaplan, a native of Weston, Lewis County, W. Va., of Jew-

ish extraction, but a fine product of young American manhood, was very badly treated by those responsible for the above publication.

Upon each page of the yearbook is given the portrait and a brief biography of two students. Ensign Kaplan's biography was reserved for the last page of the book and associated with him was an entirely fictitious member of the class, whose biography indicated clearly the nationality of the fictitious member of the class. The page upon which these two biographies appeared, one genuine and one spurious, was perforated near the binding, so that members of the class could tear out the page without defacing the book. No page number was given to this page, and Kaplan's name does not appear in the index.

This treatment of this young man apparently for the purpose of stigmatizing him because of his nationality and possibly to act as a deterrent to others of the same nationality from entering the school, I am sure will appeal to you as being un-American and most reprehensible, and I call your attention to the circumstances to suggest that proper and immediate steps be taken to punish those guilty of this offense and to prevent its occurrence at any time hereafter in any school controlled by the Government.

Very sincerely yours,
Howard Sutherland

Source: As printed in "Inquiry Is Ordered on Kaplan Insult," *New York Times*, June 15, 1922.

6.25 — "THE DECLARATION OF INDEPENDENCE ADDRESSED THE WORLD,"
Der Tog, JULY 4, 1924

On May 26, 1924, the U.S. Congress passed the Johnson-Reed Act, known less formally as the Immigration Act. This legislation limited the annual number of immigrants who could be admitted from any country to 2 percent of the number of people from that country who were already living in the United States in 1890. Most scholars agree that the Johnson-Reed Act was designed to restrict immigrants coming to the United States from Southern and Eastern Europe and, especially, to restrict the massive migration of Jews seeking refuge from the persecution they endured in Poland and Russia. It must also be noted that the Johnson-Reed Act severely restricted the immigration of Middle Easterners, East Asians, and South Asians. On U.S. Independence Day, July 4, 1924, Samuel Margoshes (1887–1968), the talented editor of the Yiddish newspaper Der Tog *(The Day), published a biting critique of the Johnson-Reed Act. Margoshes's editorial, excerpted as follows, ridiculed Congressman Albert Johnson's statement that the Immigration Act constituted a "new Declaration of Independence" for the United States. As far as Margoshes was concerned, the anti-immigrant spirit embodied by the new legislation was, in fact, a serious threat to America's greatness and independence.*

Independence. That has no meaning. What our independence from Europe indicated, what we have forfeited and what we may still regain.

"This," said an American politician recently [Congressman Albert Johnson of Washington State], "is America's new Declaration of Independence." And "this" was the Johnson Immigration Bill [Immigration Act of May 26, 1924].

To such strange uses may honorable terms be put, and so far may men's concepts sink.

When the American revolutionaries issued their famous document, the Declaration of Independence, they did not mean thereby simply to assert the secession of the thirteen states as a matter of political expediency. They meant a great deal more than that. They based their action on an eternal principle. And they did not address their Declaration of Independence to England: they addressed it to the world at large.

[. . .]

And herein America became independent. This was true independence, spiritual independence. It was independence of the idea that a Government is an ethnic instrument, that political institutions are the reflex of racial instincts, that to be a member of a certain country one had to have a certain ancestry.

This independence from the ideals of the old world America maintained with a remarkable degree of firmness for nearly a century and a half. The country was open to all men. To be an American meant only one thing: to subscribe to the ideals of the country and to obey its laws.

Thus arose the concept of Americanism—which was a distinct thing that other countries did not know. There is no such thing (in this particular sense) as Englishism or Germanism or Gallicism. Americanism meant not descent, but acceptance of an ideal.

Of course there were attempts to drive the country out of the historic and unique path—as for instance the Know-Nothing movement. But these attempts failed. The ideal stood firm. And toward the end of the nineteenth century [Lord James Bryce] could still write in his famous book: "The American is unique in this: that when he says he loves his country he means he loves its constitution."

And this is the independence that is threatened now, and which in the last few years has been desperately attacked and compromised. What [Congressman Albert] Johnson called "The new Declaration of Independence," was actually the return to the old racial ideal of a state. Far from being a new Declaration of Independence, it was a mortal blow struck at the old one.

Source: As printed in *JAW*, 311–12. From *Der Tog*, July 4, 1924.

6.26—ARTHUR M. KAPLAN, "ARE MEDICAL COLLEGES UNFAIR TO JEWISH STUDENTS?" *Jewish Tribune*, AUGUST 1, 1930

The Lithuanian-born physician Abraham J. Rongy (1878–1949) immigrated to America in 1893 at the age of fifteen. After earning a medical degree, Rongy became one of the country's most eminent gynecologists. In the late 1920s, Dr. Rongy conducted a nationwide investigation for the National Conference of Jews and Christians that showed only one of every three Jewish applicants was admitted to the country's medical schools. In an article published by the Jewish Tribune and Hebrew Standard *in August 1930, Rongy defended the use of quotas, noting that the enrollment of Jews was already two and a half times their proportion of the population. Since a Jewish physician's clientele was generally chiefly Jewish, Rongy insisted that restrictions on the admission of Jews would limit the excessive professional competition that would result from having too many Jewish medical practitioners.*

. . . Encountered in his West End Avenue office last Saturday morning, one of the most prominent of American medical authorities consented to an interview on a topic which has engrossed his attention for many months. The carefully assorted litter of documents and references which obscured the top of his spacious desk gave testimony to that. His picture on this page has already identified the gentleman as one who also happens to be highly esteemed for his many endeavors in American and international Jewish affairs. His wide-spread popular influence, his distinguished background and his brilliant intellect command important consideration of his views among men who are known for the importance of their own views.

At the outset Dr. [Abraham J.] Rongy . . . agreed that the methods of restriction openly violate the principle of preference to applicants most eligible on the basis of scholarship. What he denied—and quite vigorously—is that college boards who control admission are guilty of any personal desire to be unfair to Jewish applicants. No element of animus is involved. Around this point centered the most important and fascinating discussion of a fascinating interview.

"The assumption that, when Jews are most severely affected by certain restrictions, their privileges are being willfully abused," Dr. Rongy asserted, "is grossly misleading in this specific case, and is the origin of much misunderstanding and injudicious shouting. For several years, individuals not possessed of accurate facts in the matter have been jumping to superficial conclusions, and these conclusions, gained exaggerated impetus through pure hearsay. Students who knew they had been barred for valid and necessary reasons were themselves misled by the hearsay, and vindictively resorted to the plaint of anti-Semitism. Anti-Semitism, you know, can furnish a defensive alibi as well as an inferiority complex. One may possess a thousand faults justifying criticism, and yet proclaim that the faults are but mirages in the eyes of the 'antis,' if that one happens to be a weak-natured fool.

"I am anxious that the Jewish public may know the real reasons why special restrictions are imposed upon Jewish medical candidates. The truth is always to be desired, but never so much as now when it has become necessary to counteract a strong element of propaganda which, if permitted to sweep on, might commit us to action that would be both unwise and sorely regrettable.

"Whether we choose to deal in facts or theories," he went on, "we must not overlook [the] essential fact that *every Jewish student of proper competence and talent can eventually succeed in entering the doors of almost any medical school in this country*. No more important angle of the dispute can be brought out. Undeniably, Jewish applicants must exert greater effort and perseverance than the non-Jewish. Still, in a country where the Jewish population aggregates 3½ percent of the total, Jews are represented by six times their ratio percentage among the medical student body. With this score," he smiled, "can we intelligently impugn the liberal attitude of the admission boards?"

"Why may there not be a still greater proportion of Jewish students," the interviewer asked, "if students of this religious group possess a stronger inclination and aptitude for this branch of study? Shouldn't the American community be served by the very best medical talent available, regardless of religious and racial considerations?"

Source: MS 71, box 37, folder 15, AJA.

6.27 — "MEMORANDUM ON NAZI ACTIVITIES IN THE UNITED STATES," NON-SECTARIAN ANTI-NAZI LEAGUE TO CHAMPION HUMAN RIGHTS, 1936

The Non-Sectarian Anti-Nazi League to Champion Human Rights (originally known as the American League for the Defense of Jewish Rights) was founded in 1933 to urge Congress to enact an economic boycott against Nazi Germany. The prominent lawyer and Jewish communal leader Samuel Untermyer (1858–1940) founded and led the league. Reprinted here is a report wherein Untermyer outlines the extent of Nazi activities in the United States in the mid-1930s.

Organizations: The Nazis have an official organization in the United States known as the German-American Bund. This organization, after a history of internal friction is now under the leadership of Fritz Kuhn, [a] one-time chemist in the Ford Motor Company. The German-American League is a membership organization with branches in all parts of the United Bund and pursues the same ideology and tactics as the parent organization, the National Socialist party, in Germany. Membership in the German-American League is not known. Kuhn has said the membership numbers two hundred and fifty thousand but this we believe to be an exaggeration. Nazi adherents are not limited to the above organization. Other organization support for the Nazi program has been acquired by means of fraction control of seemingly unrelated organizations.

Propaganda: It has been estimated that the Nazis spend in excess of thirty million dollars a year in connection with American propaganda. This propaganda is manifold:

1. Large shipments of periodicals are mailed to the United States of original Nazi newspapers, most prominent of which is [Julius] Streicher's virulent anti-Semitic sheet "Der Stuermer" of which five thousand of each issue arrives in the United States and which is used as a source of information and illustrations for local publications. The Nazis also ship some German material in English consisting of speeches and pronouncements of [Adolf] Hitler, [Hermann] Goering, [Joseph] Goebbels, and [Alfred] Rosenberg. In addition, from Erfu[r]t, Germany, comes the "World Service," a mimeograph news service in all languages for use of editors and publicists. This is a most important part of Nazi propaganda because it develops among seemingly non-Nazi publications a unity of ideological and material subject matter. "The World Service" is issued in all languages and sent to all parts of the world.

Radio: By means of [s]hort wave broadcasting the Nazis issue from Germany regular propaganda to all parts of the world including the United States. This propaganda is particularly directed in the United States to German Nation-als and German-Americans. Local radio broadcasts on local stations supplement this original propaganda with local broadcasts. This matter has been brought to the attention of the Federal Communications Committee [Commission] by the Anti-Nazi League and by Congressman Samuel Dickstein [1885–1954], who has also aired it in the House of Representatives during the last session. Nazi propaganda in addition to radio broadcasts originating in the United States and carried on a large scale, consists briefly of the following:

The publications of the German-American League which include the official organ "The [*sic*] Deutscher Weckruf und Beobachter" [The German Wake-Up Call and Observer] a full-sized newspaper subsidized by means of shipping company ads and direct subsidy. This paper probably has a circulation of 25,000 and editorializes on American politics in behalf of Nazi policy. The paper also issues leaflets and pamphlets on such subjects as the threat of Semitism.

The menace of Nazi propaganda in the United States has become so real that in addition to the investigation already launched by the Federal Bureau of Investigation into these activities the following Senators and Congressmen are among those who have made public utterance for Federal action: [William] Borah, [Edward] Burke, [Samuel] Dickstein, [Martin] Dies, Jerry J. O'Connor, [John] McCormack, [William] Citron, etc.

Source: MS 8, box 4, folder 15, AJA.

6.28—AMERICAN NAZI PARADE, NEW YORK CITY, 1937

Of the many pro-Nazi organizations that came into existence in America after the rise of Adolf Hitler, the German American Bund (Amerikadeutscher Volksbund) was unquestionably the largest and most influential.

Officially established in March of 1936, the Bund's primary objective was to enlist American support for Nazi Germany. The Bund's leader was Fritz Julius Kuhn (1896–1951), a chemical engineer who was born in Germany, fought in the German army during World War I, and immigrated to the United States in 1928, later becoming a naturalized citizen. Kuhn, who frequently referred to himself as the "American Führer," organized the Bund's largest and most impressive rally, held in Madison Square Garden on February 20, 1939. Speaking to a crowd of more than 22,000 supporters, Kuhn said: "The Bund is fighting shoulder to shoulder with patriotic Americans to protect America from a race that is not the American race, that is not even a white race. . . . The Jews are enemies of the United States." It is difficult to overstate the fear this group instilled in American Jews during the height of its activities.

Source: MS 8, box 4, folder 2, AJA.

6.29—EXCERPTS FROM THE SPEECH OF REP. SAMUEL L. DICKSTEIN, DELIVERED BEFORE THE NATIONAL CONVENTION OF THE ANTI-NAZI LEAGUE, MAY 22, 1938

Samuel Dickstein was a member of the U.S. House of Representatives from 1923 to 1945. In 1931, Dickstein became chair of the House Committee on Naturalization and Immigration, a role in which he grew acutely aware of the many foreigners entering and residing in the United States—legally and illegally. He was also concerned about the massive amount of antisemitic literature being distributed throughout the country, which led him to investigate the activities of Nazi and other fascist groups. His investigation resulted in the establishment of the House's Special Committee on un-American Activities. In light of his efforts, *it is fascinating to note that, on the basis of Soviet documents, some historians have recently accused Dickstein of taking money from a Soviet spy agency from 1937 to early 1940. In the following speech he gave to the national convention of the Anti-Nazi League in 1938, Dickstein emphasized the universal nature of the Nazi threat by arguing that the rapid growth of antisemitism was a matter of import to all Americans.*

This is not a Jewish question or a Catholic question. It is a question of the American people versus a madman,—Hitler who is seeking to destroy the whole world through the instrumentality of secret agents. Spies are trying to undermine our government now in one form or another and are seeking to array American against American.

[...]

I am not quarreling with the many millions of American people of German blood. As a matter of fact most of my information comes from these people who hate the Bund, Hitler and the Storm Troopers and everything about them.

[...]

When Congress begins its investigation it will find two or three hundred spies running around this country under the guise of friendship, 140 organizations tied up with the Bund and other Fascist groups. They could have destroyed them two years ago if there had been any cooperation. The only symbol of cooperation or encouragement I ever received at that time was from this League who I congratulate for its fight and efforts on behalf of humanity against the tyrant who is spreading his hands all over the world.

[...]

I will fight to destroy every alien who seeks to destroy America and humanity. . . . Boats like the *Europa* and the *Bremen* [two German luxury liners] need from seven hundred to seven hundred and fifty men to run them, but you will find them with crews of 800 or 900 men. The others under the guise of sailors or seamen are spread around this country. They are the Gestapo or Secret Police. They destroy. They assault. They bring in the propaganda and when you're ready to pick them up . . . They don't need any passport. . . . They take the next boat and go right out. And if it becomes necessary, and I hope to establish that fact pretty soon, if I got to stop every German boat coming in here, I am going to do it.

[...]

There are thirty-one camps in this country where they "Heil Hitler" and drill men and women ready to take up arms for Germany. Only a few days ago in Chicago in which the Kuhn crowd, that is, the German Bund made an Anschluss with the Silver Shirts, one of the speakers told the people that if no one else killed Roosevelt, he would kill him if necessary, or words to that effect. And that is what they call free speech. If war broke out today we would have to fight the enemy within before we could reach those without. . . . Uncle Sam can take care of Communism or any other isms, we don't need any help from Hitler or Kuhn. What we need is an America for Americans despite race[,] creed or religion.

[...]

The Volksbund started off with seventy-five members in 1931 and has jumped to almost 450,000. You can turn around and find almost 200,000 who put uniforms on and are ready to use a gun. When you find them target practicing and all as I have found them, it's time to clean house on citizenship. There are 200,000 people in this country who should have their citizenship papers canceled because they are a burden and a threat to the country.

Source: MS 8, box 7, folder 3, AJA.

6.30—"PERSECUTION—JEWISH AND CHRISTIAN," BROADCAST BY REV. CHARLES E. COUGHLIN, NOVEMBER 20, 1938

Father Charles E. Coughlin (1891–1979) was a controversial Roman Catholic priest from Royal Oak, Michigan, and one of the first to use radio to reach a mass audience. In the 1930s, he had more than thirty million listeners tuned in to his weekly broadcasts. An ardent opponent of communism, Coughlin began to suggest that Jews were responsible for much of the communist activity in the United States. His rhetoric became increasingly antisemitic, and he often seemed to be rationalizing or even justifying the policies of Hitler and Mussolini. In a November 1938 radio broadcast, excerpted as follows, Coughlin argued that Jews themselves were responsible for the rise of Nazism. He minimized German antisemitism and asserted his belief that Jews controlled American mass media. This broadcast, in particular, inspired a strong negative reaction from government officials as well as from American Jewish leaders. One month after Coughlin's November 1938 broadcast, Rabbi Stephen S. Wise delivered a stinging response titled "Coughlinism, Jews and America," in which he lambasted Coughlin for his accusations and highlighted the difference between Coughlin and the more responsible voices in America's Christian community.

. . . Although cruel persecution to German-born Jews has been notorious since 1933—particularly since the loss of their citizenship—nevertheless, until last week the Nazi purge was concerned, chiefly, with foreign-born Jews. German citizen Jews were not molested officially in the conduct of their business. The property of German citizen Jews was not confiscated by the government, although a few synagogues and stores were destroyed by mob violence. The children of German citizen Jews were permitted to attend public schools with other children. The German citizen Jewish bankers pursued their business as usual. The German citizen rabbis were permitted the practice of their rites. Until this hour no German citizen Jew had been martyred for his religion by government order although restrictions were placed upon Jewish professional men. . . .

It is the belief, be it well or ill founded, of the present German government, not mine, that Jews—not as religionists but as nationals only—were responsible for the economic and social ills suffered by the Fatherland since the signing of the Treaty of Versailles.

Imbued with this idea, be it right or wrong—an idea that spread rapidly, particularly since 1923 when Communism was beginning to make substantial advances throughout Germany—a group of rebel Germans under the leadership of an Austrian-born war veteran—Adolf Hitler by name—organized for two purposes. First, to overthrow the existing German government under whose jurisdiction Communism was waxing strong and, second, to rid the Fatherland of Communists whose leaders, unfortunately, they identified with the Jewish race.

Thus, Nazism was conceived as a political defense mechanism against Communism and was ushered into existence as a result of Communism. And, Communism itself was regarded by the rising generation of Germans as a product not of Russia, but of a group of Jews who dominated the destinies of Russia. . . .

And most recently—just last week—there was no protest, no indignation aroused when Stalin, not satisfied with having paid for his Communism with the blood of (c.) 20-million martyrs—instituted a new purge against all Christians and a handful of political Jews.

Why, then, was there this silence on the radio and in the press? Ask the gentlemen who control the three national radio chains; ask those who dominate the destinies of the financially inspired press—surely these Jewish gentlemen and others must have been ignorant of the facts or they would have had a symposium in those dark days—especially when students of history recognized that Naziism is only a defense mechanism against Communism and that persecution of the Christians always begets persecution of the Jews. . . .

By all means, let us have courage to compound our sympathy not only from the tears of Jews but also from the blood of Christians—(c.) 600,000 Jews whom no government official in Germany has yet sentenced to death, and (c.) 25-million Christians, at least, whose lives have been snuffed out, whose property has been confiscated in its entirety and whose altars and Christ have been desecrated since 1917 without official protest from America—America that has extended and still extends the right hand of recognition to the murderers themselves.

Source: MS 8, box 12, folder 1, AJA.

6.31—STEPHEN S. WISE, "COUGHLINISM, JEWS AND AMERICA," DECEMBER 4, 1938

. . . Coughlinism has insisted that Jews and Jewish bankers, abroad and at home, fomented and financed the Russian Revolution. Now in the last few days dealing with the latest utterances of Coughlinism broadcast throughout America, a number of men have been heard: for example, [Alexander] Kerensky, the first President of the Russian Republic; Dr. [Pavel N.] Milyukov, Minister of Foreign Affairs under the government which came to pass after the Czarist Revolution. Now Kerensky, as every half-intelligent person knows, is the Chief of the opponents of Bolshevism. It destroyed his government. It made him an exile. Surely he hates Bolshevism and its maker. What does he say answering that extraordinary, incomparably, incredibly mendacious utterance of Coughlinism of a fortnight ago—that fifty-one or two of the first of the members of the first Bolshevist cabinet were Jews? Kerensky says there was not a single Jew in the government after the downfall of Czarism! Milyukov has made a similar statement. Of course, . . . this afternoon [Coughlin] will probably say Jews have bought Kerensky. Jews have bought Milyukov. I suppose we'll be charged next with having bought President Roosevelt because he spoke with the compassion of a man, instead of the unconcern of an inhuman monster, against the wrong done to Jews in Germany. . . .

I ask you my fellow Jews, some of you Christian men and women, I ask you fellow Americans: is there anyone in this hall today naïve enough to imagine that Coughlinism will this afternoon withdraw or modify one word that is spoken about the Jewish bankers who financed and fomented the revolution? It will be repeated a thousand times. A thousand times with never a reference to the corrections that have been offered by our governmental service, by Alexander Kerensky, by [Leon] Trotsky, by Kuhn, Loeb & Company . . .

I have this to say: Coughlinism knows as well as you and I that not one hundredth of one percent of Jews outside of the Soviet Union are communists. The vast majority of Jews are upper or lower middle class individuals opposed to every form of collectivism or communism. No man, no movement, has the right to ask us Jews, to ask Jews as Jews, or any other social and religious group to make a vow or denial of any social, political or economic theory of life. It is impossible. No one has the right to ask, no one has the right to answer and to speak for Jews. Once that right is yielded, once that right is conceded, as some Jews in New York are willing to concede it—only of course a few frenziedly, fearful Jews—tomorrow they see the attempt to extort from Jews the reputation or disavow their faith in democracy. What if Coughlinism makes such a demand upon us tomorrow, as it may?

Coughlinism lifts up its voice not to condemn, not to protest, but to explain, to argue, to extenuate. True, Coughlinism has not explicitly and frankly defended anti-Semitism or Nazism in Germany. It would if it dared, if it dared to af-front the conscience of America and mankind it would! It lacks the courage of such unpopular convictions as it has. It implies there is or there may be an excuse for Hitlerism. That excuse is Communism . . . and Jews, he adds, or implies, are [among] the Communists in Germany. For the Jew Coughlinism is a regrettable phenomenon. For the Catholic Church it is a disaster. But above all it is America's shame.

Source: Stephen S. Wise sermon collection, AJA.

6.32—CHARLES LINDBERGH, DES MOINES SPEECH, SEPTEMBER 11, 1941

Charles A. Lindbergh (1902–1974) became a national hero in 1927, when he made the first solo nonstop transatlantic flight, from Roosevelt Field on New York's Long Island to Le Bourget Field in Paris. In the 1930s, Lindbergh emerged as one of America's highest profile isolationists. In a series of speeches and publications for the America First Committee, a prominent noninterventionist lobby group in the United States prior to World War II, Lindbergh made a stark distinction between Americans and Jews. Just three months prior to the U.S. entry into World War II, Lindbergh noted this very point in a speech he delivered in Des Moines, Iowa, excerpted here.

It is now two years since this latest European war began. From that day in September, 1939, until the present moment, there has been an ever-increasing effort to force the United States into the conflict.

That effort has been carried on by foreign interests, and by a small minority of our own people; but it has been so successful that, today, our country stands on the verge of war.

[. . .]

The three most important groups who have been pressing this country toward war are the British, the Jewish and the Roosevelt administration.

[. . .]

Let us consider these groups, one at a time.

First, the British: It is obvious and perfectly understandable that Great Britain wants the United States in the war on her side. England is now in a desperate position. Her population is not large enough and her armies are not strong enough to invade the continent of Europe and win the war she declared against Germany.

[. . .]

The second major group I mentioned is the Jewish.

It is not difficult to understand why Jewish people desire the overthrow of Nazi Germany. The persecution they suffered in Germany would be sufficient to make bitter enemies of any race.

No person with a sense of the dignity of mankind can condone the persecution of the Jewish race in Germany. But no person of honesty and vision can look on their pro-war policy here today without seeing the dangers involved in such a policy both for us and for them. Instead of agitating for war, the Jewish groups in this country should be opposing it in every possible way for they will be among the first to feel its consequences.

Tolerance is a virtue that depends upon peace and strength. History shows that it cannot survive war and devastations. A few far-sighted Jewish people realize this and stand opposed to intervention. But the majority still do not.

Their greatest danger to this country lies in their large ownership and influence in our motion pictures, our press, our radio and our government.

I am not attacking either the Jewish or the British people. Both races, I admire. But I am saying that the leaders of both the British and the Jewish races, for reasons which are as understandable from their viewpoint as they are inadvisable from ours, for reasons which are not American, wish to involve us in the war.

We cannot blame them for looking out for what they believe to be their own interests, but we must look out for ours. We cannot allow the natural passions and prejudices of other peoples to lead our country to destruction.

[. . .]

In selecting these three groups as the major agitators for war, I have included only those whose support is essential to the war party. If any one of these groups—the British, the Jewish, or the administration—stops agitating for war, I believe there will be little danger of our involvement.

I do not believe that any two of them are powerful enough to carry this country to war without the support of the third [the Roosevelt administration]. . . .

The entire future rests upon our shoulders. It depends upon our action, our courage, and our intelligence. If you oppose our intervention in the war, now is the time to make your voice heard.

[. . .]

[By writing to our representatives in Washington], we can still make our will known. And if we, the American people, do that, independence and freedom will continue to live among us, and there will be no foreign war.

Source: Charles Lindbergh: An American Aviator, www .charleslindbergh.com/americanfirst/speech.asp.

6.33—LOUIS MARSHALL TO PRESIDENT WOODROW WILSON, REQUESTING SUPPORT FOR EUROPEAN JEWS AFTER WORLD WAR I, AUGUST 6, 1919

In January 1918, President Woodrow Wilson addressed a joint session of the U.S. Congress to articulate his plan for postwar Europe. While ultimately rejected by European allies and the U.S. Senate, Wilson's Fourteen Points, as they were known, called for greater democracy, more political autonomy among nation-states, as well as free trade between European countries. Wilson's postwar plans demanded greater national autonomy for the same Eastern European countries that had, in recent years, been waging antisemitic campaigns. The situation proved so dire that the organized Jewish community sent its own delegation to the Paris Peace Conference to represent the particular interests of Europe's Jewish population. In 1919, Louis Marshall appealed to President Wilson for special consideration. Days later, Wilson rejected Marshall's request.

August 6, 1919.

Dear Mr. President:

One of the most serious questions which has arisen in Eastern Europe is that which relates to East Galicia. The Poles and Ukrainians are both claiming that territory. Approximately 750,000 Jews live in that area and have suffered severely both from Polish and Ukrainian hostility. The Commission designated by the Peace Conference to report as to the future government of East Galicia, of which General La Rond, Dr. Lord and Mr. Paton are members, several weeks ago requested the Jews of East Galicia who were then in Paris, to express their views on this problem, and at their request I accompanied the delegation as their spokesman. We took the position that the Jews, as a minority, could not safely assume an attitude for or against either of the two contending nationalities, who for months have

been engaged in a bitter warfare, and that each of them resented any action that the Jews might take, as was evidenced by the series of pogroms which, ever since last November, have from time to time occurred in East Galicia in which the Poles and the Ukrainians both participated. Without undertaking to interfere with the political situation, we tentatively expressed the belief, that until conditions in East Galicia had become settled, and for a period of probably ten years, it might be desirable for the League of Nations to administer East Galicia through a High Commission, and that at the expiration of that period a plebiscite should determine the nature of the future government. That would afford a guaranty for the peaceful development of the country and give assurance of the avoidance of conflict likely to arise at any moment and to degenerate into bloodshed. The Commission intimated that a mandate over East Galicia would probably be given to Poland for a definite period, to be followed by a plebiscite, and that in the meantime the various nationalities would be enabled, by the operation of catastres or electoral colleges, to secure representation in the national and local legislative bodies. In view of the fact that the Jews of East Galicia were prepared to submit to any plan that might prove acceptable to the Peace Conference so long as they were permitted to retain their neutrality until a plebiscite had finally determined the permanent form of government, we stated that if that could be accomplished the Jews would willingly acquiesce in the plan indicated, provided (1) that they likewise were permitted to have a catastre or electoral college of their own; (2) that on account of their exceptional position they were to be exempted from conscription until after the plebiscite, and (3) that, as in the Ukraine and

Lithuania, a Jewish secretariat should be created in the provincial cabinet for the protection of the Jews of East Galicia. In addition to these provisions it was contended that the clauses protective of racial, religious and linguistic minorities, contained in the Polish treaty, should be applicable to East Galicia.

I have just received a cablegram to the effect that the Polish leaders are insisting in the Diet at Warsaw that catastres or electoral colleges should be created for the Poles and Ukrainians only, and that the Jews of East Galicia are to be forced to participate either in the Polish or Ukrainian catastres. It is also stated that Mr. Paderewski has expressed his opposition against any measure that would relieve the Jews of East Galicia from conscription and has made disagreeable comments upon the Jews, who desire to be relieved from the jeopardy in which they would find themselves of being ground between the upper and the nether millstones of Polish and Ukrainian agitation.

I am confident that a word from you would assure to these unfortunate people that protection which is essential to them in the extraordinary circumstances in which they now find themselves and would secure to them the right of remaining neutral in the bitter conflict between the two nationalities now struggling for the ultimate sovereignty over East Galicia, one or both of whom will be swift to resent as hostile and to wreak vengeance upon the Jews for any action taken that may not be in accordance with the wishes, policies or prejudices of the contending factions.

I am, with great respect and gratitude,

Cordially yours,
(Signed) Louis Marshall.

Source: Rare document, AJA.

6.34—PRESIDENT WILSON TO MARSHALL, REJECTING THE REQUEST, AUGUST 14, 1919

The White House
Washington

14 August, 1919.

My dear Mr. Marshall:

Replying to your letter of August 6th, may I not say that I am going to take pleasure in cabling the substance of it to our Commissioners in Paris, where I am sure it will be handled in the most serviceable way possible in the circumstances.

You will remember that in one of our conversations in Paris I felt obliged to express my judgment as distinctly against the creation of separate Jewish bodies or colleges, and I am sure you will remember the grounds upon which I earnestly argued my judgment in that matter. I am constrained to say that I have had no reason to change that judgment, and believe that it is in the best interest of the people we are trying to serve.

Cordially and sincerely yours,
Woodrow Wilson

Mr. Louis Marshall, 120 Broadway, New York.

Source: Rare document, AJA.

Passage of the immigration restriction laws in 1921 and 1924 focused renewed attention on the plight of Jews who remained in Eastern Europe. As we see in the Lehman report, during the 1920s the Joint Distribution Committee was deeply committed to rebuilding Jewish life in Europe. In 1924, the JDC began a special program dubbed Agro-Joint, which sought to address the severe economic crisis that befell Russian Jewry when the Soviet government outlawed businesses that supported thousands of Russian Jewish families. The Agro-Joint purchased farmland for the benefit of these Russian Jews and helped them rebuild their lives as farmers. In the report that follows, Dr. Joseph A. Rosen, director of the Agro-Joint's reconstructive work, outlined his agency's efforts and progress during its first three years.

The Agro-Joint was incorporated July 21st, 1924, in accordance with a resolution adopted at a meeting of the Executive Committee of the Joint Distribution Committee, for the purpose of carrying out in an experimental way a project of settling on the land in Southern Russia a few hundred Jewish families in order to ascertain the possibilities of Jewish colonization in Russia on a large scale. *Our project has absolutely nothing to do with the ill-famed fable of an autonomous Jewish republic in Russia. . . . It had no political aspects whatever, and was merely an effort to help along a spontaneous movement, a genuine new line of reconstructive rehabilitation originated by the Jewish masses in Russia of their own accord, as a dire necessity brought about by the post-war and post-revolutionary economic conditions of the country.*

The results have exceeded our expectations and have more than justified a continued effort in this direction on a more extensive scale. With the $400,000 originally appropriated by the Joint Distribution Committee, we expected to settle, at the most, one thousand families. Later, your committee found it possible to double this appropriation and we have succeeded in putting on the land during this period, not one thousand, but over four thousand families, a population of over 25,000 souls.

[. . .]

The general principle of our work with the settlers is to *eliminate all kinds of philanthropic and paternalistic tendencies.* We aim to put our relations on a strictly business basis, advancing all the funds in the form of loans in cash or kind. These loans must be refunded within a specified time, and bear interest at the rate of 3% per year. We make it clearly understood to the settlers that we are not assuming any responsibility or any obligations to take care of them for any length of time. We give them a start and are ready to give them competent advice and instruction, but they must then take care of themselves. We encourage them to become members of the local farmers cooperative organizations and wherever possible make use of the general government agricultural credit system. This, however, they can do only after they have been on the land not less than a year. . . .

The human material of the new settlers is of a surprisingly high quality. Not so many years ago it was my good fortune to spend a few years among the people who are settling the western prairies in the U.S.A., and I may say frankly that among these Jewish settlers in Southern Russia I was surprised to find pioneering material in no way inferior to the sturdy pioneers of the West. The spirit of the settlers is remarkable. Regardless of the very trying conditions they have to live under, without any conveniences whatever, in shanties or dugouts, often under the open sky, doing very hard work that many of them have not been accustomed to, they take it cheerfully and feel that the future is with them. . . .

Source: As printed in *JAW*, 460–61. Joseph A. Rosen, *Founding a New Life for Suffering Thousands. Report of Dr. Joseph A. Rosen on Jewish Colonization Work in Russia, etc.* (New York: United Jewish Campaign, 1925), 7, 40, 42, 47.

Since its founding in 1914, the American Jewish Joint Distribution Committee (JDC) has raised funds to provide relief for impoverished European Jews. In 1927, Herbert H. Lehman (1878–1963), who would go on to become the first Jewish governor of New York, issued a comprehensive report detailing the enormous scope of relief distributed since the JDC's founding.

HERBERT H. LEHMAN, CHAIRMAN OF
RECONSTRUCTION COMMITTEE, RENDERS
GRIPPING AND COMPREHENSIVE REPORT OF
VAST, SUCCESSFUL TASK

Sixty-seven million dollars have been spent by the Joint Distribution Committee from the beginning of its work in 1914, in forty countries and territories ranging from Abyssinia to Yokohama, according to a report rendered to the "Constructive Relief Conference" at the Standard Club, Chicago, on October 23, of the United Jewish Campaign and the Joint Distribution Committee, by Herbert H. Lehman, vice-chairman of the latter organization and chairman of its Reconstruction Committee.

Since 1921, Mr. Lehman said, with the exception of the great emergency which existed in Russia, culminating in the overwhelming famine which spread over that country in 1922, almost 90 per cent of the J.D.C.'s funds were devoted to rebuilding and rehabilitating the lives of the Jews abroad.

"The great mass of Jewish refugees, driven from their homes by war, pogrom and hunger, had to be settled, helped to new places, their homes rebuilt, their occupations regained, their health restored, their children educated, their instrumentalities for self-help reinvigorated," said Mr. Lehman.

"Of the thousands of war orphans in Poland and other European countries, as well as in Palestine, some 25,000 of the most needy had to be cared for, housed, clothed, educated, trained for productive employment. The whole structure of Jewish educational life throughout Eastern Europe and Palestine, which had broken down in the course of the war and post-war conditions, had to be reconstructed. In Eastern Europe, with some 250,000 pupils in ten countries, and with several thousand institutions representative of every type of Jewish religious and economic concept, it is the Joint Distribution Committee which has made possible their survival.

"In medical work, 121 hospitals, 160 bath houses, more than 150 other sanitary institutions, X-ray stations, the nurses' training school in Warsaw, the malaria prevention work in Palestine, the eradication of favus [a fungal disease] in Poland, had to be undertaken. What is more, there had to be stimulated and set in motion, on a national scale, permanent European organizations, directed and conducted by European Jews themselves, for the promotion of public health and medical sanitary progress. That the Joint Distribution Committee was able to encourage the growth of the TOZ [Towarzystwo Ochrony Zdrowia], the Polish Jewish medical sanitary organization, and of the OZE [Obschestvo Zdravookhraneniia Evreev; previously, Obshchestvo Okhraneniia Zdorov'ia Evreiskogo Naseleniia], the Jewish medical organization representative of the remainder of Eastern Europe, represents a notable contribution rendered by the Joint Distribution [C]ommittee in the rehabilitation of Jewish life abroad.

WHO CAVILS?
"Only the most callous, the most unsympathetic critic could close his eyes to these rehabilitative achievements, and could cavil at calling this vast range of service truly and vitally constructive.

"$5,400,000 was allocated by the J.D.C. in 1920 to the Reconstruction Committee for the purpose of developing instrumentalities for the granting of loans, to strengthen the economic position of our people, and enable hundreds of thousands who had lost their all again to win their livelihood and to rebuild their homes. Three major activities emerge from the program of the Reconstruction Committee:

1. The creation and reorganization and strengthening of a network of loan societies throughout Eastern Europe and Palestine.
2. The repair, equipment, rebuilding and maintaining of trade schools, training workshops, and the development of courses of study for productive occupations and employment.
3. Loans and assistance in the rebuilding of homes, stores, and other structures.

REPAIR OF HOMES

"Hand in hand with the assistance rendered in the development of loan and co-operative societies has been the substantial aid rendered under the supervision of the Reconstruction Committee in the rebuilding and repair of Jewish homes destroyed during the war. This activity was carried on chiefly in Poland, Lithuania, and Bukovina.

"In Poland, more than $330,000 was invested for the rebuilding of part of the 100,000 Jewish homes destroyed during the war. In Lithuania, on housing reconstruction there was expended $160,000; in Bukovina, $180,000. In all, through the instrumentality of the Reconstruction Committee and its successor, the Foundation, there has been expended approximately $750,000 in this work, with the result that some 10,000 homes have been repaired or restored in Poland. In Bukovina, 1,828 different loans were granted and resulted in the repair of 1,514 homes.

IN EASTERN EUROPE

"To summarize the activities of the Reconstruction Committee in Eastern Europe alone, there was expended by it directly, or in cooperation with other agencies, for credits, home building, and trade schools, about $3,010,000. The balance of the funds of the Reconstruction Committee was applied to activities in Russia and in

Palestine. In Russia, with the revolution, the entire network of the loan *kassas* [banks], which so materially helped the artisans and workmen, had been destroyed. This carried along with it the wiping out of all the work which the Jewish Colonization Association had been carrying on in Russia for upwards of twenty years.

"With the resumption of direct Joint Distribution Committee work in Russia in 1922, we inaugurated this work, and subsequently the ICA [Jewish Colonization Association] re-entered the field of credit activity. The ICA invested in *kassas* or loan societies in Russia about $400,000, of which some 80% was put in during the years 1925 and 1926. The Joint Distribution Committee invested in these *kassas* $286,000. There are today in Russia 233 artisan loan *kassas* in which the Joint Distribution Committee still has an investment of about $75,000, in long term loans, and about $150,000 in current account deposits. The *kassas* have a clientele of over 60,000 members, and a working capital of over $4,000,000. With this membership, Dr. [Joseph A.] Rosen [1877–1949] estimated that between 250,000 and 300,000 persons are served, and in this way that almost ten per cent of the Jewish population of Russia is benefited. In 1923 there was set aside, to be expended under the direction of Dr. Rosen, the sum of $1,240,000, $800,000 of which was applied to the initial forms of agricultural work, the balance being used for other reconstructive activities, such as assistance to the loan *kassas*, trade schools, etc.

WORK IN PALESTINE

"Mention should be made of the activities of the Reconstruction Committee in Palestine. It is noteworthy that, exclusive of substantial assets turned over under various phases of rehabilitative and general relief in Palestine, the Reconstruction Committee directly turned over to the Kupath Milveh Loan Society in Palestine approximately $90,000.

"Another institution which the Reconstruction Committee was instrumental in large measure in establishing in Palestine is the Central

Bank of Co-operative Institutions, and to which the Joint Distribution Committee loaned 50,000 pounds.

"By arrangement with the Palestine Economic Corporation, of which Mr. Bernard Flexner [1882–1946] is the chairman, the Joint Distribution Committee has assigned to that organization its interest in the Central Bank of Co-operative Institutions, in exchange for shares of stock in the Palestine Economic Corporation. In addition, the Joint Distribution Committee has transferred to the Palestine Economic Corporation the sum of approximately $230,000, which was set aside for participation in the Rutenberg Hydro-Electric project.

"It was intended that the Foundation should continue the economic help rendered theretofore by the Reconstruction Committee, and that it should be the means of securing new funds from European sources.

"The Reconstruction Committee transferred to the Foundation in free funds during May, 1924, $500,000; in cash, for the conduct of the work, $250,000; and likewise turned over the unspent balance of old appropriations, which the Foundation agreed to carry out in accordance with the original terms and purposes set by the Joint Distribution Committee. These unspent balances totaled $278,000. There was thus agreed to be turned over in cash to the Foundation by the Joint Distribution Committee a total of $1,028,000. To the Foundation, likewise, there was assigned all of the assets of the Reconstruction Department in Europe. The liquidation value of these outstanding collection and other items from various regional and co-operative groups and banks was estimated at $1,300,000.

A SUMMARY

"By way of summarizing the work of the Reconstruction Department, and its successor, the Foundation, let me submit the following figures:

"The total number of co-operatives in Eastern Europe, exclusive of Russia, is 520, with a membership of 215,670. The total gross resources of all these *kassas* amounts to $6,588,510, of which the Reconstruction Committee and Foundation credits amount to $1,841,502. The remainder represents own share capital, current deposits, and other local obligations. The total outstanding loans of these *kassas*, as of June 30, 1927, was $6,017,066.

"The Joint Distribution Committee contributed, prior to the organization of the Foundation, May 15, 1924, for credit assistance, $924,000; for housing reconstruction, $667,000; for trade schools, $420,000; for other and miscellaneous activities, $82,038, making a total of $2,093,038.

"Since the organization of the Foundation, and through the channels of the Foundation, the Joint Distribution Committee has advanced in credits $622,371, for housing reconstruction $131,500, for trade schools $21,885, and for other purposes $55,650, or a total of $831,406.

"In addition to the sums thus expended in Eastern Europe, out of the funds of the Reconstruction Committee there was expended in Russia, prior to 1925, for a reconstruction program under Dr. Rosen's direction, for agricultural assistance, credits and trade schools, the sum of $1,240,000, approximately $800,000 of which was applied to farming work. Please note that this appropriation is separate and apart from the larger scale activities subsequently developed by Dr. Rosen since the end of 1924, in the program of the 'Agro-Joint.'

"In addition, by way of credits to the Loan Bank of Palestine (Kupath Milveh), to the Central Bank of Co-operative Institutions, to a special trust fund for constructive work in Palestine, there was expended $534,000. Directly out of funds of the Reconstruction Committee, and without taking into account funds appropriated and expended by the Joint Distribution Committee, through channels other than this subcommittee, there have been expended, including the conduct of this work here and abroad, approximately $5,400,000.

"As stated before, this is exclusive of all direct appropriations made by the Joint Distribution Committee for the work of the Agro-Joint, to which there has been transmitted in 1924, $500,000;

October, 1925, to September 30, 1926, $1,500,000; October, 1926, to September 30, 1927, another sum of $1,500,000; and of the $300,000 appropriated last year for present existing operations of the ORT, more particularly in the Odessa colonies in Russia as well as for its present trade school and training work in Eastern Europe; nor does it include the sum of $1,500,000 which the Joint Distribution Committee has agreed to invest in the shares of stock of the Palestine Economic Corporation, and against which there has actually been transmitted to the latter organization the sum of $350,000.

"I feel that I ought to add one more statement which will indicate, in a concrete way, the value in physical terms of actual rebuilding, repair, of hospitals, bathhouses, sanitoria, and their equipment, which is estimated at no less than $800,000; in similar repair of orphanage, schools, workshops, trade school buildings, etc., $400,000; in building structures for housing repatriates, including communal buildings, $500,000; in repair and in renovations of other institutions, $250,000; in the application of funds intended for emergency relief, and which our European director has been able to apply to constructive purposes, such as the Gemilath Chesed *kassas*, $350,000, and in finding work for unemployed, $50,000, or the impressive total of actual physical rebuilding, equipping and renovating institutions, as well as the granting of free loans, etc., of $2,350,000."

Source: Constructive Relief Conference Special, United Jewish Campaign News (October 23, 1927): 6–7. JDC Archives, New York.

6.37 — STEPHEN S. WISE, ADDRESSING A MASS MEETING HELD AT MADISON SQUARE GARDEN, MARCH 27, 1933

As a response to growing violence against Jews in Germany after Hitler's appointment as chancellor in January 1933, Rabbi Stephen S. Wise, in March of the same year, addressed a rally in Madison Square Garden, encouraging Americans to take part in a boycott of German products. Although the anti-Nazi boycott of 1933 had no effect on Nazi policy, Rabbi Wise regarded observance of the boycott as a moral obligation.

Source: Image © Associated Press. Used by permission.

6.38—ABBA HILLEL SILVER TO SAMUEL WOHL, OPPOSING A PROPOSAL TO BRING GERMAN-JEWISH CHILDREN TO PALESTINE, NOVEMBER 26, 1934

In the early years of the Nazi regime, American Jewish leaders, unaware of events to come, understood the rising tide of German antisemitism differently from how they would by the late 1930s and early 1940s. A clear example of this occurred in 1934, when one of the nation's leading pulpit rabbis, Cleveland's Abba Hillel Silver (1893–1963), interpreted a proposal to move 250 Jewish children from Germany to British Mandate Palestine as complicity in "helping Hitler move the Jewish people out of Germany." Using sexist language that equated this humanitarian gesture with "some hysterical women in New York," Silver rejected the proposal.

Rabbi Samuel Wohl,
Wise Center,
Reading Rd. and N. Crescent Ave.,
Cincinnati, Ohio.

My dear Wohl:

I am not very enthusiastic about your plan in making a lot of noise about bringing over Ger-man-Jewish children to Palestine. You probably know from some of the editorials which I wrote in the *Jewish Daily Bulletin* that I am opposed to the project of moving Jewish children out of Germany either to Palestine or to the United States. Those that must go should be helped to go. The others should be assisted into Jewish schools and Jewish occupational opportunities in Germany. All the social workers with whom I have discussed the bringing to this country of the two hundred and fifty children from Germany are thoroughly disgusted with the whole matter. They did not favor it in the first place. Some hysterical women in New York were responsible for the idea and the social workers had to step in to avert tragic blunderings in the proceedure.

I am not in favor of helping Hitler move the Jewish people out of Germany.

With all good wishes, I remain

Very sincerely yours,
Abba Hillel Silver

Source: MS 106, box 1, folder 16, AJA.

6.39—JEWISH WAR VETERANS LADIES' AUXILIARIES, "NAZIISM IS SPREADING AND SO MUST OUR BOYCOTT ACTIVITIES," CA. 1938

Within two months of assuming power, Adolf Hitler launched a boycott of Jewish-owned businesses in Germany—one of the first antisemitic acts of the Nazi regime. While American Jewish organizational leaders would debate the wisdom of a counterboycott of German goods in the United States, it was the *Jewish War Veterans (JWV), organized in 1896 as the first veterans group in U.S. history, that took the lead. In this 1938 memo, Dorothy Kurman, the national president of the JWV's Ladies Auxiliaries, encouraged the women in her organization to raise funds in support of the boycott.*

National Headquarters
Jewish War Veterans of the U.S.
276 Fifth Avenue,
New York, N.Y.

Memo N.H.Q. #39C to the Ladies Auxiliaries

Dear Sisters:

It is a little over four years ago that Hitler came into power and with that the boycotting of German Goods and services were started by our Organization.

Since then Naziism not only spread throughout the breadth and width of Germany, but that poisonous germ spread to the various corners of the earth, and I am sorry to state that our boycott activities have not kept pace of Hitlerism. Although our organization was the originator of the boycott movement, other organizations have assumed the leadership. It is high time that our J.W.V. shall once more rise to the top where we belong in furthering the German Boycott, so that ultimate results shall be the complete break of Hitler and his form of government.

It is the intentions of National to have a paid boycott chairman, a responsible man, who shall devote his entire time to the boycott movement, and that, my sisters, requires funds, not only to pay his salary but also for incidentals for boycott activities.

Now if we women are to assist in this work, and I know that each and every one of us are ready to do so, we must help raise the necessary funds.

HERE IS A PAINLESS WAY OF DOING A GREAT PIECE OF WORK:—It is my wish that at each regular meeting, open meeting or social function, that your boycott chairman collect one penny from each member of [sic] guest present, and send his collection direct to our boycott chairman, Rebecca Lazarus, 280 Sedore Ave., Box 20, Fairview, N.J., on the first of each month. If you have a house party or a bridge or belong to other organizations, present this plan to them and ask for their cooperation in donating these pennies. In that way, your chairman will collect larger monthly contributions. If we all get together, and pennies add up very quickly, it will enable us to intensify our boycott program and will hasten the downfall of Hitlerism.

Now sisters, I want you to realize, in asking for these pennies, you will be serving a two fold purpose. Not only will you be spreading the doctrine of boycotting, but you will also be giving notice to the world that out J.W.V. is foremost in the ranks of the boycott movements—ALL THIS FOR ONE PENNY.

Loyally yours,
Dorothy Kurman
National President

Source: Jewish War Veterans of the United States nearprint file, AJA.

6.40—LETTER FROM ABRAHAM JOSHUA HESCHEL
TO DR. JULIAN MORGENSTERN, APRIL 30, 1939

Even though the United States has often been portrayed as a home for immigrants, the quota system created by the congressional restriction acts of 1921 and 1924 ended any hope of wide-scale Jewish emigration from war-torn Europe to the United States. Instead, individual

Jewish leaders tried to navigate the labyrinthine immigration system in order to rescue whomever they could. When Jewish intellectuals faced Nazi antisemitism, the Hebrew Union College, under the direction of its president, Julian Morgenstern (1881–1976), intervened in 1938 by creating a

"Jewish College in Exile." With that action, Morgenstern hoped to gain U.S. State Department visas for Jewish scholars outside the restrictive immigration quotas. Several prominent scholars received invitations to join the faculty, including Rabbi Abraham Joshua Heschel (1907-1972), whose journey across Europe and the attempts to secure him an entry visa to the United States are documented in the letters to follow.

Warszawa, April 30, 1939.
Dzika 3-103

Prof. Dr. Julian Morgenstern,
President of the Hebrew Union College,
Cincinnati, Ohio.

Dear Mister President:

I appreciate your generous kindness in communicating to me on my appointment as Research Fellow on Bible and Jewish Philosophy to the Hebrew Union College, on conditions named in your letter of April, 6th.

Highly delighted in accepting hereby your most welcome invitation I beg to thank you and all the members of the Board of Governors of the Hebrew Union College for this appointment, which is of very great importance and means a honour to me.

It was very kind of you to think of me and to help me in this sorrowful time. I respect your invitation too much to remain unmoved by your proposal. But I must be reserved to my feelings. Allow me solely to express that my gratitude for you is a cordial and deep one. I wish to render my thanks by my truthful service on the Jewish science.

I make the greatest efforts to receive the American visa, but I meet with enormous difficulties. I need assistance in this respect and wonder whether you would be good enough to undertake some steps to facilitate matters for me. As there are nearly no prospects here, I intend leaving for another country to try and get a visa there. I suppose it will be easier to get the American visa at an American consulate in another country. I shall keep you informed about my steps in this direction.

Expressing my high esteem to you, I remain with heartfelt thanks for everything you were good enough to do for me,

Very respectfully yours,
Abraham Heschel

Source: MS 30, box 5, folder 23, AJA.

6.41—LETTER FROM MORGENSTERN TO HESCHEL, JULY 5, 1939

July 5, 1939

Dr. Abraham Heschel
Dzika 3-103
Warsaw, Poland

My dear Dr. Heschel:

I have just returned from a trip to Washington where I had a conference with the Chief of the Visa Division of the State Department of our Government with regard to the "Jewish College in Exile," which the Hebrew Union College is endeavoring to establish here in Cincinnati and the call to which as Research Fellow has been extended to you.

I regret that I must inform you that we have encountered unforeseen difficulties with regard to yourself and Dr. Franz Rosenthal, to whom likewise we have extended a similar call. The immigration laws of the United States seem to be very strict in this particular ruling, that only scholars who have been actually bona fide instructors for a period of at least two full years at educational institutions of academic standing at least equal to that of the institution in America which extends the call to them—in this case, of course, the Hebrew Union College,—are eligible for non-quota visas.

Apparently neither you nor Dr. Rosenthal can comply with this requirement at the present time. I hope earnestly that I am mistaken in this opinion. It is, however, a matter upon which the American Consul will have to rule. I would earnestly advise you, therefore, to continue your negotiations with the American Consul until you receive from him a definite decision as to whether you may be granted a visa or not. Each American Consul has a great deal of personal jurisdiction in such matters and there is never, in consequence of this, any absolute assurance just how a particular Consul may rule. It is quite possible that he may decide in your favor and grant you the visa. In such case your position here at the Hebrew Union College will be waiting for you whenever you can arrive. If, however, the decision in your case be unfavorable, then the only procedure open will be for you to register your application to come in under the regular quota and await your turn. Possibly you have already made such application. I hope so. In such case it would, of course, take longer for you to be admitted to the United States. But even then, whenever you can arrive here you would find that your position here at the Hebrew Union College is still open to you.

I hope earnestly that this makes the present situation clear to you and that it will likewise convince you that the Hebrew Union College is doing its very utmost in your behalf. Should there be any further developments in your case I will, of course, inform you thereof. Meanwhile it will be well for you to keep in touch with me and let me know of any developments which may manifest themselves from your end and also keep me informed of any change of address by you.

With cordial greetings and all good wishes, I am,

Very sincerely yours,
Dr. Julian Morgenstern, President

Source: MS 30, box 5, folder 23, AJA.

7 Waging War

AMERICAN JEWS, WORLD WAR II, AND THE SHOAH, 1941–1945

The Japanese attack on Pearl Harbor and the German government's subsequent declaration of war against the United States brought instant and dramatic changes to American Jewish civic life. In the years between Hitler's rise to power in 1933 and U.S. entrance into World War II in December 1941, American Jews negotiated a difficult path. They sought to protect, aid, and then rescue their persecuted brethren in Europe while at the same time ensuring that their efforts did not compromise the official U.S. policy of neutrality in the conflict. With high-profile public figures such as Charles Lindbergh making claims that American Jews sought to drag the United States into war, and with domestic antisemitism on the rise in the late 1930s, Jewish leaders moved with caution.

Once the United States entered the war against Hitler, isolationist critics were virtually silenced, and Jewish leaders believed they could now strengthen their work on behalf of European Jews without casting doubt on their allegiance as patriotic American citizens. The country's entrance into the war promised to align the particular concerns of American Jews with the overarching goals of the U.S. government and its military. American Jews organized increasingly robust efforts to provide overseas relief, and a disproportionate number entered military service. The dual-identity conflict that sometimes challenged the civic standing of American Jews seemed to ease.

Faced with a deteriorating situation for Jews in Europe, American Jewish leaders organized an American Jewish Conference, which tried, with some success, to bring together the major American Jewish defense and advocacy organizations. The conference engaged the continuing efforts at relief and rescue of overseas Jews, and formed an important locus for debating the American Jewish organized community's position on Zionism and the eventual creation of a Jewish national homeland in Palestine. Individual Jewish organizations continued their own advocacy work as well.

Yet, as American Jews would learn, the military and political goals of the Roosevelt administration did not always mesh with the humanitarian or communal goals of American Jews. FDR's State Department took calculated steps to slow Jewish refugee assistance, and refused to fill the modest immigration quotas available for Jewish victims of Nazism. In the most infamous case, Roosevelt and his advisors refused to bomb the death camp at Auschwitz; planes carrying an extra payload of bombs near the Nazi camp were instructed to release their arsenal over the English Channel.

Among the most criticized and least understood of these Jewish organizations was the American Council for Judaism, led by a small group of Reform rabbis who opposed the Zionist movement and took high-profile steps to communicate its opposition to a Jewish homeland. The American Jewish Committee, one of the nation's leading Jewish self-defense agencies, also refused to embrace the call for a Jewish homeland. While choosing to define itself as non-Zionist rather than anti-Zionist, the AJC withdrew from the American Jewish Conference over the issue. Even within the American Zionist camp, leaders split over strategy and tactics, especially as news of the unfolding Shoah in Europe dramatized the need for a Jewish state.

On the domestic front, the U.S. entrance into World War II hastened the end of the Great Depression. Mobilization for war sparked massive growth in war industries and put Americans to work, and New Deal debates over Jewish communal self-sufficiency all but ended as American Jews joined their compatriots in the Allied effort to defeat Germany and Japan. The wartime consensus also silenced any meaningful critique of President Roosevelt's Executive Order 9066, which incarcerated 67,000 U.S. citizens of Japanese descent. Although American Jews rose to the fore on behalf of their European brethren, they, like every other American constituent group, did not protest wartime civil rights violations against their fellow U.S. citizens.

The documents to follow explore the dynamics at play between democratic principles, the basic needs of a nation at war, and the complementary (and competing) impulses felt by American Jews.

7.01—HITLER POSTER, "WANTED FOR MURDER," 1941

In April 1941, a group of politicians and civic leaders from both major political parties countered the nation's larger isolationist sentiment and organized the Fight for Freedom Committee, which advocated immediate U.S. entry into the European conflict. Harry Warner (1881–1958) and his brother, Jack Warner (1892–1978), two of Hollywood's famed Jewish moguls, joined members of the Rockefeller family as charter members. Committed to ending diplomatic relations with Germany as well as ending all U.S. neutrality laws, and, as one of its members explained, "agitat[ing] for an open declaration of war against Germany and Italy," the Fight for Freedom Committee issued a broadside demanding the arrest of Adolf Hitler for murder. The Japanese attack on Pearl Harbor ended the debate over isolationism, and the committee soon disbanded.

Source: MS 307, box 1, folder 13, AJA.

Especially for the children of Eastern European immigrants—born and raised in the United States, English speaking, and public school educated—U.S. entry into the war against Hitler and Nazi Germany resonated along both civic and Jewish lines. As they had in earlier conflicts, Jews enlisted to defend their nation. Unlike earlier conflicts, though, World War II was a fight not only against an enemy of the country in general but also of the Jews in particular.

During the war, American Jews constituted just 3.3 percent of the total U.S. population. Yet they represented 4.23 percent of women and men in the armed forces. American Jewish military service broke through class and educational lines as well. Rabbis served as chaplains, and more than half of all American Jewish physicians under the age of forty-five served in the military. By the war's end, 11,000 American Jews had lost their lives in service to their country and 40,000 were wounded.

Distribution of Jewish Servicemen by Branches and Activities

	Percent of Jewish Servicemen in the Armed Forces
Armed Forces	100.00
Army	80.59
Navy	16.46
Coast Guard	1.14
Marine Corps	1.81
*Army**	
Army Air Force	23.11
Army Ground Force	21.09
Army Service Force	36.69
*Army Activities**	
Army Air Force	
Flying Personnel	4.67
Non-Flying Personnel	5.53
Unknown	12.91
Army Ground Force	
Armored Force	2.28
Artillery	5.16
Cavalry	0.40
Infantry	12.83
Paratroops	0.42
Army Service Force	
Adjutant General	0.55
Chemical Warfare	0.68
Engineers	3.81
Finance	1.18
Medical, Dental	10.92
Military Police	1.51
Ordnance	2.60
Quartermaster	3.44
Signal Corps	4.52
Transportation	1.15
Other	6.03

Source: American Jews in World War II: The Story of 550,000 Fighters for Freedom, compiled by the Bureau of War Records of the National Jewish Welfare Board, vol. 2 (New York: Dial Press, 1947), 25.

7.03—IRVING BERLIN, LYRICS, "THIS IS THE ARMY, MR. JONES," 1942

Jewish participation in the war effort transcended organized Jewish communal life. One of the nation's most important and popular songwriters, Irving Berlin (1888–1989), who immigrated to America from Russia as a child, composed the music and lyrics to the 1942 musical This Is the Army. *Berlin, who also wrote the standards "God Bless America" and "White Christmas," offered the musical's title song, "This Is the Army, Mr. Jones," as a satire of military life for new recruits. With this tune, Berlin used American popular culture to help listeners focus on the larger wartime consensus.*

A bunch of frightened rookies were list'ning
    filled with awe.
They listened while a sergeant was laying down
    the law.
They stood there at attention,
Their faces turning red.
The sergeant looked them over and this is what
    he said:

This is the army, Mister Jones.
No private rooms or telephones.

You had your breakfast in bed before
But you won't have it there anymore.

This is the army, Mister Green.
We like the barracks nice and clean.
You had a housemaid to clean your floor
But she won't help you out anymore.

Do what the buglers command.
They're in the army and not in a band.

This is the army, Mister Brown.
You and your baby went to town.
She had you worried
But this is war and she won't worry you
    anymore.

This is the army, Mister Jones.
No private rooms or telephones.
You had your breakfast in bed before
But you won't have it there anymore.

7.04 PASSOVER OBSERVED BY ARMED FORCES, 1943

The April–May 1943 issue of the Jewish Chaplain, *a four-page magazine published by the Committee on Army and Navy Religious Activities (CANRA) of the Jewish Welfare Board, describes with enthusiasm the efforts made on behalf of Jewish members of the armed services who wished to celebrate Passover while on duty both in the United States and overseas. With the full cooperation of the U.S. Army and Navy, Jewish servicemen and women were able to observe the holiday in far-flung posts all over the world, on overseas transports, and in training camps here in the United States.*

RABBI GOLDSTEIN REPORTS ON
UNPRECEDENTED ARRANGEMENTS
In announcing the Passover report, Rabbi Herbert S. Goldstein, Chairman of the Committee on Passover Arrangements of CANRA, said that "the gigantic task of worldwide organization of the plans for the traditional observance of Passover, begun by the National Jewish Welfare Board months before, met with admirable success. No stone was left unturned to provide for the Passover needs of every Jewish member of the armed forces of the United States on land, on sea, and in the air, in practically every corner of the earth.

Both the Army and Navy cooperated magnificently in these arrangements. The Jewish and Christian chaplains, Jewish Welfare Board representatives, members of local JWB committees and the thousands of other volunteers have earned the deep gratitude of our men and women in the armed forces for their untiring efforts in making effective the proper observance of Passover."

WIDESPREAD COOPERATION
Wherever Jewish men and women in the armed services found themselves during Passover, they were able to partake in the traditional observances through arrangements made by the National Jewish Welfare Board with the cooperation of 432 local JWB Army and Navy Committees, 143 Jewish chaplains, 254 USO-JWB workers, Christian chaplains, civilian Rabbis and the military authorities.

Whether they were on the fighting fronts in Tunisia or New Guinea, or on transports going overseas, or in hundreds of Army posts on all five continents, or in training camps and colleges at home, prior arrangements had been made for them.

In the U.S. alone, 105,000 Jewish service men were the guests at over 300 community Sedarim, while thousands of others enjoyed home hospitality. Those on guard duty at lonely outposts were taken care of by the USO mobile service units. Others were able to obtain furloughs or leaves and enjoyed the festival at home. Student

members of the armed forces in 102 colleges were served.

Overseas, the cooperation of the War Department and Chaplain Corps made it possible for almost every Jewish soldier to observe the holiday.

In Palestine, Ireland, England, Australia and all the large cities of North Africa, where there are sizable Jewish communities, thousands of Jewish soldiers were invited to family Sedarim.

Community Sedarim were also held in Newfoundland (where the local Jewish women taught the Army cooks how to make gefillte fish), in Alaska, Iceland, Hawaii, Puerto Rico, Bermuda, Curacao, all the large islands of the British West Indies, and in several South American countries.

Three Passover broadcasts for service men were arranged by the JWB, with Sgt. Barney Ross, hero of Guadalcanal, as the featured speaker on one of them. The broadcasts were as follows:

The Church of the Air over CBS broadcast from Camp Grant, Ill., with Chaplain Norbert Rosenthal officiating.

CBS also broadcast the Passover services from the Sampson Naval Station with Barney Ross as guest speaker and Captain Harry Badt, commandant, Rabbi Philip S. Bernstein and Chaplain Henry Berkowitz participating.

A special Passover broadcast went out over the Mutual network with Sam Jaffe, noted actor, reading from the haggadah and Chaplain Bernard Segal officiating.

Source: SC-1390, AJA.

7.05—LT. DICK GOTTLIEB, AFFIDAVIT, RECOUNTING HIS EXPERIENCE LIBERATING THE DACHAU CONCENTRATION CAMP NEAR LANDSBERG, GERMANY, APRIL 1945

As the U.S. Army advanced across Germany at the end of World War II, Jewish soldiers participated in the liberation of Nazi concentration camps and witnessed at first

hand the horrors of the Nazis' attempted genocide of the Jewish people. When the U.S. Army's 493rd Armored Field Artillery Battalion of the Twelfth Armored Division liberated the

Dachau concentration camp near Landsberg, Germany, in April 1945, Lt. Dick Gottlieb, an American Jewish officer, provided an affidavit testimony of his experience.

This is former First Lieutenant Dick Gottlieb of the 42nd (Rainbow) Infantry Division telling about his part in the capture of Dachau and his experiences the first several days of its capture.

"This came about as follows: I was a First Lieutenant. I had been wounded and one of the policies the division had was that if possible combat officers would not be sent back to the front lines at this stage of the war unless it was absolutely necessary. Therefore, I had been assigned as a liaison officer between the 222nd Regiment and Division Headquarters. Therefore, I had no combat assignment at the time. I entered Dachau some thirty to forty-five minutes after it was originally taken and there still was a great deal of mayhem as I recall at the time that I entered. The people who had been kept in the camp had not only gone out the gates where they had been confined but had been opened by the American troops but a lot of them came through the fence by merely tearing it down. There was elation; there was a great deal of happiness; and a great deal of wildness—almost an uncontrollable crowd. Obviously they were extremely happy to see the American forces. On the other hand, they had another mission—that was to find as many of the guards, I suppose they could be classified as SS guards, that were manning the camp. Some of them did find some of those guards and it was extremely difficult for the American troops to prevent the people who had been kept in the camp for so many years under such horrible conditions to keep them from literally tearing their arms off their bodies. But order was restored before too very long and the process of dismembering the camp and doing what needed to be done just as quickly as possible began.

"I know I took a tour of the camp with some friends of mine. There were the fences—the stone fences with bullet pockmarks on them where obviously people had been lined up and shot down. There were the boxcars that had arrived there and the story that I had been told is that the people that arrived in those boxcars simply did not know where they were at and when the train stopped they merely made a mad rush out of the open boxcars and the closed ones of that long, long train and tried to make a dash for freedom, whatever that was. And, of course, immediately as they came off the boxcars they were shot down. I have submitted that the pictures I personally took and that others took of the hundreds of dead bodies that were on that train, in the train boxcars and lying all around the train—those who started to make their dash for freedom, so to speak.

"The gas chamber, when viewing that I can only say that it was a horrible thing to know what had taken place in there, but it had been kept in such a state that, as I remember seeing it, that there was no indication that so much death had happened in that one building. The two most memorable areas of Dachau for me were the ovens and the infirmary. Since I was a liaison officer at the time and not a combat officer, I was given orders to remain at Dachau and I really have forgotten now whether I stayed three, four or five days. I just know that the general had given an order, at least as I understood it, to send as many troops as they could spare back to the concentration camp so that they could view everything that was still there to be seen and once and for all get firmly embedded in their minds why we were fighting this war.

"Now the troops were moving extremely fast in those days, the German Army was in flight and, as I understand it, the general was still willing to send people back from distances that were some miles away from Dachau as the division moved on. I was one of those officers that took the troops that came back through the concentration camp. We viewed the wall; we viewed the boxcar area that had now been cleared of the bodies; we viewed the gas chamber; but when we got to the infirmary, this was where a lot of the American troops simply began to break down because still lying in those beds and still underneath at the time were people in bunks four, six, or eight to a room where there should not have been more than two bunks at the most there. Some of the bunks almost reached the ceiling. And those people were so totally emaciated, absolutely living skeletons. And these people were very weak and the people in them saying 'Comrade!' to us. It was at this moment that the people began to feel the horrors of Dachau.

"Now when we got to the ovens—one was still allowed to go, manned by a Jugoslavian refugee, a member of the camp. He was allowed to remain alive because he was doing such a good job of placing bodies into the ovens.

"As I recall on either side of the ovens were two rooms—both of them rather sizeable and with high ceilings, as I recall, in which there were stacks of human bodies: all, of course, emaciated, some blood noticeable. When I took the troops by these rooms the stench alone caused many of these big old farm boys and guys from the city to absolutely throw up (vomit) or begin to cry with such intensity that it was almost uncontrollable.

"After viewing this the two rooms on either side of the ovens, our troops went back to what they were doing with, I guess you would say, an intensity that they never had before, that no one could ever teach them or put into them, because they were so doggoned mad and so disgusted with the sights they had seen.

"While I was there, there was an American officer who gave us a deeper briefing into some of the other things that had taken place at Dachau, such as the extremely hard labor, the very little food, the crowded conditions, the huge grave site, everything about Dachau: everything about Dachau was dismal. The people were beat, almost didn't appear to be human beings. I can remember one rabbi that I had a long talk with, who had got stuck in all this mayhem. He was from Detroit, of all things. His first words to me after saying, 'hello' simply was, 'Do you have any-

thing to eat?' Unfortunately, and I don't mean to say this as a joke because I do not know what it did to him. I had to get on to other things and so did he. But the only thing I had on me at the time was a 'D' ration. But, if I remember my alphabet right it was the 'D' ration that was the rather thick heavily concentrated chocolate bar. It certainly could keep you from being hungry but at the same time it was very constipating. I really don't know what effect it had on the rabbi. All I do know is that when he took his first bite you would have thought he had taken a bite of a twelve ounce steak that had been fixed to his absolute satisfaction. He was thrilled with it.

"The Dachau that I remember, I must tell you, the faces of the people who had been interned there for so long; the emaciated bodies of the living and the oven rooms and the infirmary, the pockmarks on the walls, made me ill—the dead bodies that I saw around the train made me even sicker. Going into the gas chamber, hearing the horror stories of what went on at Dachau made me mad enough to want to whip the enemy all by myself.

"But the one thought that occurred to me the many times I went into the infirmary taking troops with me, the one thought that remains in my mind even to this day when I went by the ovens so many times and viewed the rooms on either side of the ovens with the stacks of dead bodies is that this world in all of its craziness can never let this happen again. And anyone who is so foolish as to try to impress other people with the idea that the Holocaust or the Dachau concentration camp was a hoax or a promotion and never happened, whoever that or those persons are have to be the biggest damn fools that walk the earth today. The concentration camps were very real; Dachau was very real; the people I saw were very real. While I can't remember all of the details I can never wipe those things from my mind."

Source: SC-13949, AJA.

7.06—JOHN J. MAHONEY TO CHAPLAIN S. JOSHUA KOHN, REGARDING THE
FEBRUARY 3, 1943, SINKING OF THE USS *Dorchester*, DECEMBER 7, 1944

*On February 3, 1943, the USS Dorchester, a
troop ship carrying nine hundred soldiers and
civilians, was struck by three torpedoes fired
from a German U-boat near the coast of
Greenland. Almost seven hundred enlisted
men died, including four chaplains on board,
Father John P. Washington (1908–1943), Rev.
George L. Fox (1900–1943), Rev. Clark V. Poling
(1910–1943), and Rabbi Alexander D. Goode
(1911–1943). Survivors reported that the four
chaplains, representing the three major faith
communities in the United States, took off their
own life vests and gave them to needy soldiers.
As the ship sank, the chaplains joined arms,
prayed, and together went down with the ship.
Included here is a letter from petty officer John J.
Mahoney to Chaplain S. Joshua Kohn as well as
a 1948 United States Postal Service stamp
honoring the "immortal chaplains."*

> Melvin Mills N.H.
> December 7, 1944

> Dear Chaplain
> To carry on our conversation of a few hours
> ago in regards the sinking of the S.S. *Dorchester*
> on Feb 3, 1943.
> I was in a room with two army officers, and in
> the next room directly forward to mine were the
> four chaplains, so as you can readily see, I saw
> quite a bit of them on our trip to Greenland.

> About the Chaplain Goode whom I know you
> are interested in, I would put him down as a reg-
> ular guy and a very good ship mate. In proof
> thereof I recall very well, after putting on my
> Parka and life preserver, I went out on the prom-
> enade deck, where I might say confusion reigned,
> where I found I had no gloves. Chaplain Goode
> was handy and I remarked to him of my predic-
> ament, and I added, I am going back to get them.
> Never mind, he said to me I have two pair and I
> will give you one (pair) of them. I agreed and he
> peeled a pair of gloves off and handed them to
> me, shortly after this about ten to fifteen min-
> utes I was overboard myself and after swimming
> around a while I landed in a life boat that was
> awash, that is about a foot or less of the ends of
> this boat were out of the water. Now as the offi-
> cial temperature of this water was thirty degrees,
> then I am positive that I never could of held on
> for over eight hours if my hands had not been
> covered, so I would like to credit the Chaplain
> Goode with helping to save my life. As it was
> only two of us survived out of about forty that
> was in that boat.
> Hoping to help you I am at your service

> *Your friend*
> *John J. Mahoney*
> *Lieut (jg) [Junior Grade] USCGR*
> *[U.S. Coast Guard Reserves] Ret.*

Source: SC-7668, AJA.

7.07—U.S. POSTAGE STAMP COMMEMORATING CLERGY WHO DIED IN THE SINKING OF THE USS *Dorchester*, 1948

Source: SC-9659, AJA.

7.08—"STATEMENT OF PRINCIPLES BY NON-ZIONIST RABBIS," AMERICAN COUNCIL FOR JUDAISM, AUGUST 12, 1942

The American Council for Judaism (ACJ), an anti-Zionist organization created in 1942 by a group of Reform rabbis, lobbied against the establishment of a Jewish national homeland. Claiming to be loyal American citizens and defenders of the U.S. Constitution's separation of church and state, leaders of the ACJ rejected the nationalist aspirations of Jews. They embraced the Jewish religion and advocated a form of Judaism that encouraged Jews to live side by side with non-Jews without the threat of dual-loyalty conflicts. In the summer of 1942, the ACJ issued its statement of principles.

We, Rabbis in American Israel, who believe in the universalism of Judaism's ethical and spiritual values and teachings, express our hearty agreement with the following Statement drawn up by those who convened in Atlantic City, June 1 and 2nd, 1942, for the purpose of giving voice to our convictions and to discuss ways and means of giving greater emphasis in Jewish life and thought to these doctrines and of securing wider recognition and appreciation of them among our neighbors.

The special reason for our gathering is in the growing secularism in American Jewish life, the absorption of large numbers in Jewish nationalistic endeavors and the tendency to reduce the religious basis of Jewish life to a place of secondary importance. A further reason for taking counsel together is in our realization that at this time more than ever all men for their own good and the good of mankind should give every emphasis to those moral and religious values and principles that transcend boundary lines and hold all men in a common bond of human fellowship.

1. We believe that the present tragic experiences of mankind abundantly demonstrate that no single people or group can hope to live in freedom and security when their neighbors are in the grip of evil forces either as perpetrators or sufferers. We hold, therefore, that the solution of the social, economic and political problems of one people are inextricably bound up with those of others. To this general rule the problems of our Jewish people constitute no exception, though unhappily we Jews are often the first victims of the distemper of peoples and suffer most from the maladjustments of society.

2. We declare our unwavering faith in the humane and righteous principles that underlie the democratic way of life, principles first envisaged by the Prophets of Israel and embodied in our American Bill of Rights. In keeping with these principles we hold that the Jewish people have the same right to live securely anywhere in the world and to enjoy the fruit of their labor in peace as have men of every other faith and historic background. We fervently hope and earnestly trust that in the coming peace programs that right will be fully recognized, unequivocally expressed, and inextricably woven into the texture of the new world order.

3. Realizing how dear Palestine is to the Jewish soul, and how important Palestinian rehabilitation is towards relieving the pressing problems of our distressed people, we stand ready to

render unstinted aid to our brethren in their economic, cultural and spiritual endeavors in that country. But in the light of our universalistic interpretation of Jewish history and destiny, and also because of our concern for the welfare and status of the Jewish people living in other parts of the world, we are unable to subscribe to or support the political emphasis now paramount in the Zionist program. We cannot but believe that Jewish nationalism tends to confuse our fellowmen about our place and function in society and also diverts our own attention from our historic role to live as a religious community wherever we may dwell. Such spiritual role is especially voiced by Reform Judaism in its emphasis upon the eternal prophetic principles of life and thought, principles through

which alone Judaism and the Jew can hope to endure and bear witness to the universal God.

The maladjustments of society and the consequent sufferings are at bottom due to men's forgetfulness of the elementary decencies and virtues and to the violation of moral and spiritual principles that have universal validity. It is incumbent, therefore, upon all of us, Jews and non-Jews alike, to stress to the utmost in thought, word and deed, those teachings of our own religion that are all-inclusive, if we would permanently correct the evils that so often bring suffering to mankind.

Reform Judaism, as we conceive it, is the contemporary manifestation of the eternal prophetic spirit of Israel, through which alone Judaism and the Jew live to witness to the universal God.

Source: MS 17, box 6, folder 1, AJA.

7.09—TELEGRAM FROM GERHART RIEGNER (VIA SAMUEL SILVERMAN) TO STEPHEN S. WISE, AUGUST 29, 1942

On August 29, 1942, Rabbi Stephen S. Wise received a telegram communicating a message from Geneva World Jewish Congress head Dr. Gerhart Riegner. The telegram, now considered one of the most important primary source documents in the study of American Jewish reaction to the Shoah, detailed, for the first time, Hitler's genocidal plans to gas European Jews. After the U.S. State Department refused to forward the message to Wise, it was relayed from Riegner to Samuel Silverman, a British member of Parliament, and then to Wise, who was not aware that the Roosevelt administration had already received the missive. Wise brought the telegram to State Department officials, who asked that he keep silent about its content until its veracity could be confirmed. In a much-criticized decision, Wise acceded to the State Department's demand. On November 25, 1942, the U.S. government confirmed the contents of

the telegram and released Wise from his promise of confidentiality. Included here are the Riegner telegram, a December 1942 letter from Wise to FDR requesting a meeting to discuss the unfolding atrocities in Europe, and a February 1943 letter from Undersecretary of State Sumner Welles agreeing to forward reports of Nazi atrocities but explicitly refusing to assume "any official responsibility for the information contained in [Riegner's] reports."

NV15 cable Liverpool 122 1/63 NFD
NLT Stephen Wis (care Mrs Schneeberger 250 West 94 St) World Jewish Congress NYK (330 West 42 St See SPL Instns on file (relay via SI)

Have received through Foreign Office following message from Riegner Geneva. (Received alarming report that in Fuhrers headquarters plan discussed and under consideration all Jews in countries occupied or controlled Germany number 3-1/2 to 4 million should after deportation and concentration in East at one blow exterminated to resolve once for all Jewish question in Europe

CFM 3-1/2 4.

NV15 2/59

Action reported planned for autumn methods under discussion including prussic acid. We transmit information with all necessary reservation as exactitude cannot be confirmed. Informant stated to have close connexions with highest Germen [*sic*] authorities and his reports generally reliable. Inform and consult Newyork. Foreign Office [h]as no information bearing on or confirming story

Samuel Silverman.

Source: Rare document, AJA.

7.10—LETTER FROM STEPHEN S. WISE TO FRANKLIN D. ROOSEVELT, DECEMBER 2, 1942

Office of Dr. Wise
40 West 68 Street,
December 2, 1942.

The President
The White House
Washington, D.C.

Dear Boss:

I do not wish to add an atom to the awful burden which you are bearing with magic and, as I believe, heaven-inspired strength at this time. But you do know that the most overwhelming disaster of Jewish history has befallen Jews in the form of the Hitler mass-massacres. Hitler's decision was to exterminate the Jewish people in all Hitler-ruled lands, and it is indisputable that as many as two million civilian Jews have been slain.

I have had cables and underground advices for some months, telling of these things. I succeeded, together with the heads of other Jewish organizations, in keeping these out of the press and have been in constant communication with the State Department, particularly Under Secretary Welles. The State Department has now received what it believes to be confirmation of these unspeakable horrors and has approved of my giving the facts to the press. The organizations banded together in the Conference of which I am Chairman, feel that they wish to present to you a memorandum on this situation, so terrible that this day is being observed as a day of mourning and fasting throughout the Jewish world. We hope above all that you will speak a word which may bring solace and hope to millions of Jews who mourn, and be an expression of the conscience of the American people.

I had gathered from the State Department that you were prepared to receive a small delegation, which would include representatives of the American Jewish Committee, the American Jewish Congress, the B'nai B'rith. It would be gravely misunderstood if, despite your overwhelming preoccupation, you did not make it possible to receive our delegation and to utter what I am sure will be your heartening and consoling reply.

As your old friend, I beg you will somehow arrange to do this.

Ever yours,
[Stephen S. Wise]

Source: Stephen S. Wise papers, box 68, microfilm #2367, AJA.

The Under Secretary of State
Washington

February 9. 1943

My dear Rabbi Wise:

Reference is made to the letter from this Department dated November 19, 1942 enclosing four communications addressed to you by Mr. Gerhart M. Riegner, the Secretary of the World Jewish Congress in Geneva, Switzerland, giving information he received from various private sources in Europe on the cruel persecution of Jews at the hands of the brutal Nazis.

Mr. Riegner and Mr. Richard Lichtheim recently asked the American authorities in Switzerland if they could again avail themselves of the exceptional privilege of using official channels to forward to you an additional report on the sad plight of Jews in Axis-controlled countries based on sources available to them.

You will understand that, in this case as well as in the case of the enclosures to the Department's letter of November 19, 1942, the Department of State cannot assume any official responsibility for the information contained in these reports, since the data is not based on investigations conducted by any of its representatives abroad.

I am pleased to be of assistance to you in this matter and enclose a paraphrase of this telegraphic report from the above-mentioned persons.

Sincerely yours,
Sumner Welles

Enclosure:
As stated above.

Source: Rare document, AJA.

7.12—*We Will Never Die* PROGRAM, MEMORIALIZING THE SLAUGHTERED JEWS IN EUROPE AND COMMEMORATING JEWISH CONTRIBUTIONS TO CIVILIZATION, MARCH 9, 1943

Public opinion polls in 1943 revealed that only half of the American public believed reports that the Nazis were engaged in the systematic murder of Jews, even after the Roosevelt administration confirmed the deaths of more than two million people. In order to raise public consciousness and inspire political leaders to act, Ben Hecht, a Hollywood screenwriter who wrote the screenplay for Gone with the Wind, *among other movies, wrote a pageant,* We Will Never Die. *Hecht recruited well-known Jewish celebrities such as Edward G. Robinson as well as non-Jewish icon Frank Sinatra to dramatize the plight of European Jews in a massive stage show that opened to 40,000 people at Madison Square Garden before touring to Chicago, Philadelphia, Boston, Washington, D.C., and the Hollywood Bowl in Los Angeles, where the production was broadcast on national television by NBC. While Hecht hoped that his use of Hollywood theatrics would translate into a national call for action, he closed the pageant disappointed that it had "accomplished nothing."*

We Will Never Die

"A Memorial Dedicated to Two Million
Jewish Dead of Europe"

Tuesday, March 9th, 1943
9 p.m.

Madison Square Garden

TRANSFORMED for a night into a hall of commemoration and mourning for Jewry's two million dead, Madison Square Garden on March 9th will witness, for the first time in the memory of this generation, the roll call of Jewish contribution to the sum total of man's civilization.

Written by Ben Hecht, staged by Billy Rose, with musical arrangement by Kurt Weill, this stirring spectacle will climax a day of mourning in all Jewish communities and will stand as the first call to arms sounded throughout the length and breadth of the nation, as many well-known artists, writers and musicians will appeal for an end to the slaughter of a people.

This Memorial Service to the dead Jews of Europe will bring together under one roof and before thousands of spectators the essence of Jewish determination to survive this greatest of all blows struck to an ancient nation.

"We Will Never Die"—this is the title of the gigantic Service and this too the theme of the unique pageant—an answer to Hitler's avowed extermination of the Jews. "We Will Never Die" —and in the Garden on March 9th, New York will see the saga of Jewish heroism and staunchness throughout the years.

From Moses to Einstein, from the Rabbi in the ghetto to the Jewish soldier fighting for liberty—this pageant will unfold the final reply to Nuremberg and Berchtesgaden.

A religious Service—yes! As the services held for the heroes of old who died in combat, so this Memorial will bury its dead in song and in prayer, and New York will rise from the bier of the martyrs with renewed faith and courage and a strengthened knowledge that united, we can conquer and live.

Jews—their past and their future—their place in the world when the holocaust has passed and the story of their sufferings today will be the motif for the Memorial, part which will also include a dramatization of Ben Hecht's heartbreaking story "Remember Us" appearing in the current issue of the "Reader's Digest."

Scores of rabbis, civic leaders and mass choirs will send the heralding of liberation across the seas and into the hearts of those who can still hear. This is not a gathering of the defeated and the tired, this is a gathering of all those who are sure of their will to win.

You are asked to come to Madison Square Garden on March 9th—not to give money nor to sign petitions! You are asked to come—to give and to receive courage and new heart! We are mourning our dead—but mourning is not enough. Their deaths must be avenged—and it is up to you—in your way and to the best of your ability to save and to succor those who are left in Europe's hell-holes.

Source: SC-A-86 1214, Klau Library, Hebrew Union College–Jewish Institute of Religion, Cincinnati, Ohio.

7.13—REPORT ON ATTEMPTS TO STAGE *We Will Never Die*, EARLY 1944

Even as We Will Never Die *played to thousands in New York City, Jewish leaders in other communities around the United States opposed its staging. Some feared that the public spectacle* *would spark increased antisemitism, while others disagreed with the pageant organizers' association with right-leaning Revisionist Zionist leader Peter Bergson (Hillel Kook)*

(1915–2001). In a report issued in early 1944, organizers of the pageant described the struggles they faced in promoting We Will Never Die.

Report on Attempts to Stage "We Will Never Die" in Kingston, Rochester, Buffalo, Baltimore, Gary, and Pittsburgh

On December 31, 1943, we succeeded in setting up a committee in Kingston, N.Y. for the presentation of "We Will Never Die." Everything was worked out in detail and seemed to go very well. The committee undertook to underwrite the cost. Important town's people, not only from Kingston, but also from neighbouring towns, volunteered for the committee, but all of a sudden, through the intervention of the American Jewish Congress and the Zionist Organization of America, we received a short letter from Kingston, saying: "We are not going to have 'We Will Never Die.'"

In Gary, Indiana, where Mr. Richard S. Kaplan had worked for long weeks and had succeeded in setting up a committee, (in fixing the date for the presentation) we were already preparing promotion and the printing of propaganda material when, all of a sudden, we received a letter from Mr. Kaplan, stating: "It is with considerable regret that I must advise you that the 'We Will Never Die' pageant cannot be presented in the city of Gary. I wish I could tell you something different, but circumstances make it impossible to present it. As I have hinted before, considerable agitation was started immediately after it was announced in the papers that the pageant would be presented. Typical of the American Jewish Conference's attitude, all of the Jewish organizations met, this includes the reform Temple, the orthodox Temple, the B'nai B'rith and the Jewish Welfare Board. They unanimously agreed to present a demand to the American Legion that it be stopped."

In Baltimore we engaged Rabbi A. I. Rosenberg, who, under great sacrifices and without any personal profit, succeeded in organizing a luncheon for the purpose of creating a local sponsor committee to present "We Will Never Die." There was considerable enthusiasm among prominent town's people. The Mayor of Baltimore promised to preside at that luncheon. But the Community Council there, on orders from New York, engaged in a bitter fight against us, using all the means of calumny, slander, smearing of the Emergency Committee, its members, and also Mr. [Jacob] Ben-Ami, spreading all kinds of vile rumors. The Community Council, under its executive director, Mr. Leon Sachs, organized a "telephone campaign," calling every single person liable to help us, and influencing them not to come to the luncheon. A few hours before the luncheon the Mayor decided not to come.

[. . .]

After a thorough review of the situation, we came to the following conclusion:

It appears clearly that the Jewish Conference, the Z.O.A., the American Jewish Congress and affiliated organizations are now *organized* in their fight against the Emergency Committee and, though they profess only praise for "We Will Never Die" as such, nevertheless, they are using "We Will Never Die" as the immediate target to attack. In view of this bitter opposition, the task of creating local sponsor committees to underwrite the cost of the presentation in a given city, is next to the impossible.

There is only one alternative left, to present the pageant ourselves. The opposition can exercise its power in preventing the formation of a group of leading citizens to underwrite the cost of a presentation, but they can never exercise that power to stop the general masses of people from buying tickets and attending the performance of the pageant, as they did not succeed in this effort with the previous performances in every city, though they have tried hard, indeed.

We, therefore, recommend to concentrate our efforts and to undertake the presentation of the pageant in the two large cities of Cleveland and Detroit (as far as Pittsburgh is concerned, we are not as yet free to interfere with the efforts of Rabbi [Philip D.] Bookstaber, where he still may succeed in forming a sponsors' committee). . . .

Source: Excerpt from *A Race against Death: Peter Bergson, America, and the Holocaust.* Copyright © 2002 by David S. Wyman and Rafael Medoff. Reprinted by permission of the New Press. www.thenewpress.com.

7.14—MAX LERNER, "WHAT ABOUT THE JEWS, FDR?" JULY 22, 1943

Max Lerner (1902–1992), who immigrated to the United States from Russia at age five, earned an undergraduate degree from Yale and a master's degree from Washington University in St. Louis, and emerged as a leading columnist in the 1930s, writing for the Nation, *and 1940s, when he wrote for the leftist paper* PM. *After confirmation that two million Jews had been killed in Europe, Lerner appealed in an open letter to President Roosevelt for government action to protect the remaining four million European Jews.*

Opinion

What about the Jews, FDR?

I address you with great reluctance, President Roosevelt. You are a man harried by every group in the country, every issue and every cause in the world. You carry the massive weight of the war on your shoulders. Only an issue of transcending importance can justify adding to your burden.

But I think that the fate of 4,000,000 Jews is not a trifling matter either in the war or in the conscience of Western man. That is the number of Jews who are still left in Europe. At least 2,000,000 have already been murdered by the Nazis and their satellites in the greatest mass slaughter in history.

There is no sense in pulling all the emotional stops on the theme of the massacre of the Jews. Anyone who has not already been moved to the depths of his being by the thought of the Euro-

pean earth soaked with the blood of 2,000,000 innocent and helpless people, will not be moved by rhetoric.

I can speak to you, Mr. President, in a matter-of-fact way. You know who the Nazis are, you know what they have done and are doing. You want to do everything humanly possible to rescue what Jews remain in Europe.

But you are handicapped at the very start. Neither the American nor the British government has a policy on the matter. Neither government recognizes that any Jewish problem exists. Both governments talk of the Jews as Polish nationals, or Czech nationals, or Hungarian nationals. Yet the fact remains that while Czechs are killed by the hundreds, Jews in Czechoslovakia are killed by the tens of thousands. *And they are killed as Jews, not as Czechs.*

Hitler has made out of Europe a charnel-house of the Jews. But the State Dept. and Downing St. avert their eyes from the slaughter and, with a finicky exactitude, insist on giving the Jews in their death the civic national status that Hitler denies them in life.

The problem is there, Mr. President by whatever name you call it. And it is not too late to act on it. We can stop the senseless and criminal slaughter of the remaining 4,000,000.

How? There is a conference meeting in New York—an Emergency Conference to Save the Jewish People of Europe. There are Jews and Christians in it, laymen and clergymen, Democrats and Republicans, reactionaries and liberals. The only things they have in common are a conscience and a will to action.

Several proposals are emerging. One is that the United Nations put pressure on the Axis satellite countries. Out of 4,000,000 Jews in Europe, 1,500,000 are in Hungary, Rumania, Bulgaria. Hitler is trying to crack down on them to hasten the extermination of their Jews. But Hitler can no longer give them unqualified commands.

Thanks largely to your brilliant leadership in the war, along with Churchill and Stalin, the Axis satellites know that their end is near. They will do many things to acquire even a qualified merit in our eyes. To stop the slaughter of their Jews, to send as many as possible into neutral countries, to cease the brutal discrimination against those who remain, are things they would do if we demanded it.

This is not to relent in the slightest from your Casablanca policy of unconditional surrender. It is merely to use the war power we have to save millions of innocent lives. No promises or commitments could possibly be involved.

Then there is Axis-occupied Europe. I do not include Germany itself; that is, as Hitler has put it with a beautiful irony, *Judenrein*—wholly cleansed of its Jews. But the rest of Europe which the Nazi armies occupy still has some 2,500,000

Jews. They can be saved if we act. You, Mr. President, can promise the direst retribution to the Nazi leaders unless they cease the slaughter of Jews. When it was a question of the Nazi use of poison-gas against the Russian armies, Churchill threatened to retaliate in kind. It worked. And this will work too, if the Nazis know you mean it.

Finally there are the neutral countries—Switzerland, Sweden, Turkey, even Portugal and Spain. If we give them financial aid and encouragement, they can become temporary havens for refugees from the Axis—and satellite countries.

The problem is soluble. Not by words, but by action. You, Mr. President, must take the lead in creating a United Nations agency to follow out these lines of action.

The methods are clear. Neither conscience nor policy can afford to leave them unused. And the time is now.

Max Lerner

Source: Excerpt from *A Race against Death: Peter Bergson, America, and the Holocaust.* Copyright © 2002 by David S. Wyman and Rafael Medoff. Reprinted by permission of the New Press. www.thenewpress.com.

7.15—RABBI ABBA HILLEL SILVER, SELECTION FROM "ZIONISM: WHAT IT IS—WHAT IT IS NOT," CA. 1944

During World War II, the voices of Rabbi Stephen S. Wise of New York and Cleveland's Rabbi Abba Hillel Silver predominated in the Zionist movement. Wise, a moderate with close ties to President Roosevelt, enjoyed a reputation as one of the nation's most influential Jewish leaders. His personal relationship with the president gave him important access to information as details of the atrocities in Europe reached the United States. Silver, a generation younger than Wise, emerged in the early years of the war as a strong and vocal

critic of Wise's approach. Silver, who had previously opposed the transport of German Jewish children to Palestine, now pressed for a more activist political agenda and eventually gained the support of Zionist leader David Ben-Gurion (1886–1973), who believed Silver possessed the oratorical skills and political dynamism to motivate American Jews to join in the Zionist movement. In a series of sermons delivered to his congregants during World War II, Silver outlined his defense of American Zionism.

A PEOPLE WITHOUT STATUS

We have no national status as a people. As a people we have no voice in any international conference, not even the voice of a government in exile! . . . If the League of Nations will be reconstituted after this war, every people, even the smallest—Luxembourg, Iraq or Ecuador—will have a voice in that international body. But sixteen million Jews will have no voice. They will remain excluded and anonymous as heretofore, and when Jews are again persecuted in this or that country, as they have been so often in the past, they shall again have to intercede with some government to intercede for them. The grim irony of our position was illustrated recently when intergovernmental conferences were convoked and agencies established to look after the refugee problem created by Hitlerism—a problem which so largely and so vitally involved the Jews,—but there was no room found at these conferences or on the boards of these agencies for the official representatives of the Jewish people. . . .

Zionism aims to normalize the status of the Jewish people, to give to it what all other peoples possess—an internationally recognized status in the Family of Nations.

[. . .]

THE ARGUMENT FROM FEAR

There are Jews who fear—and fear is the real reason behind most of the opposition to Zionism—that if a Jewish national home is once established, anti-Semites will say to the Jews: "Go back to Palestine!" "Go back to your own country!" They will have a good excuse for expelling the Jews. But anti-Semitic governments have never waited for such an excuse to expel the Jews. Through all the long and dreadful centuries up to these days of Adolf Hitler, Jews have been driven from one country to another in spite of the fact that they had no national home to which to go. Our enemies never waited for the establishment of a Jewish national home before they began their agitation to drive out the Jews. The contrary is probably true. Had there been a Jewish national home, many of these expulsions would never have taken place. Had there been in existence a Jewish state wherein the nationals of other states lived and with which other states carried on commerce and trade, the attitude of those other states to the Jews living in their midst would probably have been dictated by considerations of national policy, trade interests, and reciprocity. The United States is at war with Germany and with Italy today yet one never hears the cry: "You Germans go back to Germany! You Italians go back to Italy!" And precisely because there is a Germany and there is an Italy!

[. . .]

THE ARGUMENT OF DUAL ALLEGIANCE

Some Jews feel that with the establishment of a Jewish Commonwealth in Palestine, they, in the United States, or the Jews of England or of other countries will be charged with dual allegiance. Here again it should be pointed out that the enemies of our people have not waited for the establishment of a Jewish state before they began to charge the Jews with disloyalty and lack of patriotism. In fact they seized on the fact of the *absence* of a Jewish national center,—on the fact of Jewish national homelessness—as a most powerful argument in their anti-Semitic campaigns. The Jew, they clamored, has no roots anywhere. He is an internationalist. He has a secret international organization—"The Elders of Zion"—to which he owes allegiance. He, the mysterious, the sinister Jew without a country of his own, is conspiring to overthrow all governments in order to put himself in power and rule the world.

In all the anti-Semitic literature both here and abroad wherein Jews are denounced for almost every sin in the catalogue, Zionism is hardly ever mentioned as one of them. It should furthermore be borne in mind that the anti-Semite invents his lies. There is nothing which we can do or say that will satisfy him.

The right thinking American knows that the desire of the Irish in America to help in the establishment of a Free Ireland, to which they devoted themselves so energetically, or the desire of the Czechs or Poles, to help establish a Free Czechoslovakia or a Free Poland did not in any way impair their loyalty to America. No one ever accused them of dual allegiance. In fact Americans applauded their movements, in the same way as they are applauding the effort of American Jews to rebuild a free Jewish Palestine.

Every President of the United States, from Woodrow Wilson down, has endorsed Zionism. The Congress of the United States unanimously approved it. Foremost ministers, authors, writers and editors have evidenced sympathetic and helpful interest in the movement. Not a single one has ever raised the issue, which some Jews insist on raising to their and our hurt, that participation in the Zionist Movement jeopardizes the loyalty and patriotism of the American Jew.

The Jews of the United States have no other allegiance than to the United States of America. The relation of the American Jew to the Jewish homeland in Palestine will not differ in any respect from the relation of any other American towards the land of his ancestral origin. If there is any Jew in this country who will wish to give his political allegiance to a Jewish state in Palestine, he will have the privilege of emigrating to that country and of becoming a citizen of that state. That is the privilege of all free men.

In this connection the words of the late Justice Louis D. Brandeis come to mind: "Let no American imagine that Zionism is inconsistent with Patriotism. Multiple loyalties are objectionable only if they are inconsistent. A man is a better citizen of the United States for being also a loyal citizen of his state, and of his city; for being loyal to his family, and to his profession or trade; for being loyal to his college or his lodge. . . . Every American Jew who aids in advancing the Jewish settlement in Palestine, though he feels that neither he nor his descendants will ever live there, will likewise be a better man and a better American for doing so."

[. . .]

ZIONISM—SOUND AND JUST
The critics of Zionism cannot make out a valid case. Fear is behind most of their reasoning. The Jewish people has never taken counsel of fear. The Zionist movement has now entered upon its final phase of fulfillment. It is incumbent upon all faithful Jews to become acquainted with the facts and not to permit themselves to be influenced by catch-words, slogans, rumors and prejudices. There is available a substantial literature on the subject covering all phases of the movement,—political, economic, cultural and spiritual. Jews should read and become informed.

Zionism is a sound and just ideal. As such it is inevitable!

Source: Abba Hillel Silver nearprint file, AJA.

7.16—"REPORT TO THE SECRETARY ON THE ACQUIESCENCE OF THIS GOVERNMENT IN THE MURDER OF THE JEWS," TREASURY DEPARTMENT, JANUARY 13, 1944

In late 1943, U.S. Treasury Department officials learned that their colleagues in the State Department had been blocking the publication of information about Nazi atrocities as well as actively preventing the immigration of Jewish refugees from Europe to the United States. This followed a pattern of obstructionist behavior by State Department officials on the issue of aiding European Jews. Only with the intervention of Roosevelt's highest ranking Jewish officer, Treasury Secretary Henry Morgenthau, Jr. (1891–1967), were the State Department's activities brought to light. On January 13, 1944, Treasury official Josiah DuBois (1913–1983) presented a report documenting the State Department's recalcitrance and demanding that

President Roosevelt take action. In response, the president issued an executive order on January 22, 1944, creating a War Refugee Board, which was empowered to aid civilian victims of the Axis states and included three members of the president's cabinet and a staff of thirty. The board was ultimately credited with helping save some 200,000 European Jews.

One of the greatest crimes in history, the slaughter of the Jewish people in Europe, is continuing unabated.

This Government has for a long time maintained that its policy is to work out programs to save those Jews of Europe who could be saved.

I am convinced on the basis of the information which is available to me that certain officials in our State Department, which is charged with carrying out this policy, have been guilty not only of gross procrastination and wilful failure to act, but even of wilful attempts to prevent action from being taken to rescue Jews from Hitler.

I fully recognize the graveness of this statement and I make it only after having most carefully weighed the shocking facts which have come to my attention during the last several months.

Unless remedial steps of a drastic nature are taken, and taken immediately, I am certain that no effective action will be taken by this Government to prevent the complete extermination of the Jews in German controlled Europe, and that this Government will have to share for all time responsibility for this extermination.

The tragic history of this Government's handling of this matter reveals that certain State Department officials are guilty of the following:

1. They have not only failed to use the *Governmental machinery* at their disposal to rescue Jews from Hitler, but have even gone so far as to use this Government machinery to prevent the rescue of these Jews.
2. They have not only failed to cooperate with *private organizations* in the efforts of those organizations to work out

individual programs of their own, but have taken steps designed to prevent these programs from being put into effect.

3. They not only have failed to facilitate the obtaining of information concerning Hitler's plans to exterminate the Jews of Europe but in their official capacity have gone so far as to surreptitiously attempt to stop the obtaining of information concerning the murder of the Jewish population of Europe.
4. They have tried to cover up their guilt by:
   a. concealment and misrepresentation;
   b. the giving of false and misleading explanations for their failures to act and their attempts to prevent action; and
   c. the issuance of false and misleading statements concerning the "action" which they have taken to date.

Although only part of the facts relating to the activities of the State Department in this field are available to use, sufficient facts have come to my attention from various sources during the last several months to fully support the conclusions at which I have arrived.

1. *State Department officials have not only failed to use the Governmental machinery at their disposal to rescue the Jews from Hitler, but have even gone so far as to use this Governmental machinery to prevent the rescue of these Jews.*

   The public record, let alone the facts which have not as yet been made public, reveals the gross *procrastination and wilful failure to act* of those officials actively representing this Government in this field.
   a. A long time has passed since it became clear that Hitler was determined to carry out a policy of exterminating the Jews of Europe.
   b. Over a year has elapsed since this Government and other members

of the United Nations publicly acknowledged and denounced this policy of extermination; and since the President gave assurances that the United States would make every effort together with the United Nations to save those who could be saved.

c. Despite the fact that time is most precious in this matter, State Department officials have been kicking the matter around for over a year without producing results; giving all sorts of excuses for delays upon delays; advancing no specific proposals designed to rescue Jews, at the same time proposing that the whole refugee problem be "explored" by this Government and Intergovernmental Committees. While the State Department has been thus "exploring" the whole refugee problem, without distinguishing between those who are in imminent danger of death and those who are not, hundreds of thousands of Jews have been allowed to perish.

As early as August 1942 a message from the Secretary of the World Jewish Congress in Switzerland (Riegner), transmitted through the British Foreign Office, reported that Hitler had under consideration a plan to exterminate all Jews in German controlled Europe. By November 1942 sufficient evidence had been received, including substantial documentary evidence transmitted through our Legation in Switzerland, to confirm that Hitler had actually adopted and was carrying out his plan to exterminate the Jews. Sumner Welles accordingly authorized the Jewish organizations to make the facts public.

Thereupon, the Jewish organizations took the necessary steps to bring the shocking facts to the attention of the public through mass meetings, etc., and to elicit public support for governmental action. On December 17, 1942, a joint statement of the United States and the European members of the United Nations was issued calling attention to and denouncing the fact that Hitler was carrying into effect his oft-repeated intention to exterminate the Jewish people in Europe.

Since the time when this Government knew that the Jews were being murdered, our State Department has failed to take any positive steps reasonably calculated to save any of these people. Although State has used the devices of setting up inter-governmental organizations to survey the whole refugee problem, and calling conferences such as the Bermuda Conference to explore the whole refugee problem, making it appear that positive action could be expected, in fact nothing has been accomplished.

[...]

The most glaring example of the use of the machinery of this Government to *actually prevent the rescue of Jews* is the administrative restrictions which have been placed upon the granting of visas to the United States. In the note which the State Department sent to the British on February 25, 1943 it was stated:

"Since the entry of the United States into the war there have been no new restrictions placed by the Government of the United States upon the number of aliens of any nationality permitted to proceed to this country under existing laws, *except for the more intensive examination of aliens required for security reasons.*" ([Emphasis] supplied)

[...]

2. *State Department officials have not only failed to cooperate with private organizations in the efforts of these*

organizations to work out individual programs of their own, but have taken steps designed to prevent these programs from being put into effect.

The best evidence in support of this charge are the facts relating to the proposal of the World Jewish Congress to evacuate thousands of Jews from Rumania and France. The highlights relating to the efforts of State Department officials to prevent this proposal from being put into effect are the following:

a. *On March 13, 1943*, a cable was received from the World Jewish Congress representative in London stating that information reaching London indicated the possibility of rescuing Jews provided funds were put at the disposal of the World Jewish Congress representation in Switzerland.

b. *On April 10, 1943*, Sumner Welles cabled our Legation in Bern and requested them to get in touch with the World Jewish Congress representative in Switzerland, whom Welles had been informed was in possession of important information regarding the situation of the Jews.

c. *On April 20, 1943*, a cable was received from Bern relating to the proposed financial arrangements in connection with the evacuation of the Jews from Rumania and France.

d. *On May 25, 1943*, [the] State Department cabled for a clarification of these proposed financial arrangements. This matter was not called to the attention of the Treasury Department at this time.

e. This whole question of financing the evacuation of the Jews from Rumania and France was first called to the attention of the Treasury Department on *June 25, 1943*.

f. A conference was held with the State Department relating to this matter *on July 15, 1943.*

g. *One day after this conference, on July 16, 1943, the Treasury Department advised the State Department that it was prepared to issue a license in this matter.*

h. *The license was not issued until December 18, 1943.*
[. . .]

3. *State Department officials not only have failed to facilitate the obtaining of information concerning Hitler's plans to exterminate the Jews of Europe but in their official capacity have gone so far as to surreptitiously attempt to stop the obtaining of information concerning the murder of the Jewish population in Europe.*

The evidence supporting this conclusion is so shocking and so tragic that it is difficult to believe.
The facts are as follows:

a. *Sumner Welles as Acting Secretary of State requests confirmation of Hitler's plan to exterminate the Jews.* Having already received various reports on the plight of the Jews, *on October 5, 1942* Sumner Welles as Acting Secretary of State sent a cable (2314) for the personal attention of Minister [Leland B.] Harrison in Bern stating that leaders of the Jewish Congress had received reports from their representatives in Geneva and London to the effect that many thousands of Jews in Eastern Europe were being slaughtered pursuant to a policy embarked upon by the German Government for the complete extermination of the Jews in Europe. Welles added that he was trying to obtain further information from the Vatican but that other than this he was unable to secure confirmation of these stories. He stated that Rabbi Wise believed that information was available to his representatives in Switzerland but that they were in all likelihood fearful of dispatching any such reports through open cables or mail. He then stated that Riegner and Lichtheim were being requested by Wise to call upon Minister Harrison; and Welles requested Minister Harrison to advise him by telegram of all the evidence and facts which he might secure as a result of conferences with Riegner and Lichtheim.

b. *State Department receives confirmation and shocking evidence that the extermination was being rapidly and effectively carried out.* Pursuant to Welles' cable of October 5 Minister Harrison forwarded documents from Riegner confirming the fact of extermination of the Jews (in November 1942), and in a cable of January 21, 1943 (482) relayed a message from Riegner and Lichtheim which Harrison stated was for the information of the Under Secretary of State (and was to be transmitted to Rabbi Stephen Wise if the Under Secretary should so determine). *This message described a horrible situation concerning the plight of Jews in Europe.* It reported mass executions of Jews in Poland; according to one source 6,000 Jews were being killed daily; the Jews were required before execution to strip themselves of all their clothing which was then sent to Germany; the remaining Jews in Poland were confined to ghettos, etc.; in Germany deportations were continuing; many Jews were in hiding and there had been many cases of suicide; Jews were being deprived of rationed foodstuffs; no Jews would be left in Prague or Berlin by the end of March, etc.; and in Rumania 130,000 Jews were deported

to Transnistria; about 60,000 had already died and the remaining 70,000 were starving; living conditions were indescribable; Jews were deprived of all their money, foodstuffs and possessions; they were housed in deserted cellars, and occasionally twenty to thirty people slept on the floor of one unheated room; disease was prevalent, particularly fever; urgent assistance was needed.

c. *Sumner Welles furnishes this information to the Jewish organizations.* Sumner Welles furnished the documents received in November to the Jewish organizations in the United States and authorized them to make the facts public. On *February 9, 1943* Welles forwarded the horrible message contained in cable 482 of January 21 to Rabbi Stephen Wise. In his letter of February 9 Welles stated that he was pleased to be of assistance in this matter.

Immediately upon the receipt of this message, the Jewish organizations arranged for a public mass meeting in Madison Square Garden in a further effort to obtain effective action.

d. *Certain State Department officials surreptitiously attempt to stop this Government from obtaining further information from the very source from which the above evidence was received.* On February 10, the day after Welles forwarded the message contained in cable 482 of January 21 to Rabbi Wise, and in direct response to this cable, a most highly significant cable was dispatched. This cable, 354 of February 10, read as follows:

"Your 482, January 21

"In the future we would suggest that you do not accept reports submitted to you to be transmitted to private persons in the United

States unless such action is advisable because of extraordinary circumstances. Such private messages circumvent neutral countries' censorship and it is felt that by sending them we risk the possibility that steps would necessarily be taken by the neutral countries to curtail or forbid our means of communication for confidential official matter.

Hull (SW)"

Although this cable on its face is most innocent and innocuous, when read together with the previous cables I am forced to conclude it is nothing less than an attempted suppression of information requested by this Government concerning the murder of Jews by Hitler.

[...]

4. *The State Department officials have tried to cover up their guilt by:*

[...]

b. *the giving of false and misleading explanations for their failures to act and their attempts to prevent action.*

[...]

c. *the issuance of false and misleading statements concerning the "action" which they have taken to date.*

[...]

❧ "If men of the temperament and philosophy of [Breckinridge] Long continue in control of immigration administration, we may as well take down that plaque from the Statue of Liberty and black out the 'lamp beside the golden door.'"

Source: Excerpt from *A Race against Death: Peter Bergson, America, and the Holocaust.* Copyright © 2002 by David S. Wyman and Rafael Medoff. Reprinted by permission of the New Press. www.thenewpress.com.

7.17—FRANKLIN ROOSEVELT ESTABLISHES A WAR REFUGEE BOARD, JANUARY 22, 1944

Federal Register
Volume 9 Number 18
Washington, Wednesday, January 26, 1944
The President

Executive Order 9417

Establishing a War Refugee Board

WHEREAS it is the policy of this Government to take all measures within its power to rescue the victims of enemy oppression who are in imminent danger of death and otherwise to afford such victims all possible relief and assistance consistent with the successful prosecution of the war;

NOW, THEREFORE, by virtue of the authority vested in me by the Constitution and the statues of the United States, as President of the United States and as Commander in Chief of the Army and Navy, and in order to effectuate with all possible speed the rescue and relief of such victims of enemy oppression, it is hereby ordered as follows:

1. There is established in the Executive Office of the President a War Refugee Board (hereinafter referred to as the Board). The Board shall consist of the Secretary of State, the Secretary of the Treasury and the Secretary of War. The Board may request the heads of other agencies or departments to participate in its deliberations whenever matters specially affecting such agencies or departments are under consideration.

2. The Board shall be charged with the responsibility for seeing that the policy of the Government, as stated in the Preamble, is carried

out. The functions of the Board shall include without limitation the development of plans and programs and the inauguration of effective measures for (a) the rescue, transportation, maintenance and relief of the victims of enemy oppression, and (b) the establishment of havens of temporary refuge for such victims. To this end the Board, through appropriate channels, shall take the necessary steps to enlist the cooperation of foreign governments and obtain their participation in the execution of such plans and programs.

3. It shall be the duty of the State, Treasury and War Departments, within their respective spheres, to execute at the request of the Board, the plans and programs so developed and the measures so inaugurated. It shall be the duty of the heads of all agencies and departments to supply or obtain for the Board such information and to extend to the Board such supplies, shipping and other specified assistance and facilities as the Board may require in carrying out the provisions of the Order. The State Department shall appoint special attaches with diplomatic status, on the recommendation of the Board, to be stationed abroad in places where it is likely that assistance can be rendered to war refugees, the duties and responsibilities of such attaches to be defined by the Board in consultation with the State Department.

4. The Board and the State, Treasury and War Departments are authorized to accept the services or contributions of any private persons, private organizations, State agencies, or agencies of foreign governments in carrying out the purposes of this Order. The Board shall cooperate with all existing and future international organizations concerned with the problems of refugee rescue, maintenance, transportation, relief, rehabilitation, and resettlement.

5. To the extent possible the Board shall utilize the personnel, supplies, facilities and services of the State, Treasury and War Departments. In addition the Board, within the limits of funds which may be made available, may employ necessary personnel without regard for the Civil Service laws and regulations and the Classification Act of 1923, as amended, and make provisions for supplies, facilities and services necessary to discharge its responsibilities. The Board shall appoint an Executive Director who shall serve as its principal executive officer. It shall be the duty of the Executive Director to arrange for the prompt execution of the plans and programs developed and the measures inaugurated by the Board, to supervise the activities of the special attaches and to submit frequent reports to the Board on the steps taken for the rescue and relief of war refugees.

6. The Board shall be directly responsible to the President in carrying out the policy of this Government, as stated in the Preamble, and the Board shall report to him at frequent intervals concerning the steps taken for the rescue and relief of war refugees and shall make such recommendations as the Board may deem appropriate for further action to overcome any difficulties encountered in the rescue and relief of war refugees.

Franklin D Roosevelt
The White House,
Jan. 22, 1944
[F.R. Doc. 44–1274; Filed, January 24, 1944; 2:40 p.m.]

Source: Excerpt from *A Race against Death: Peter Bergson, America, and the Holocaust.* Copyright © 2002 by David S. Wyman and Rafael Medoff. Reprinted by permission of the New Press. www.thenewpress.com.

7.18—JEWISH REFUGEES AT EMERGENCY SHELTER, FORT ONTARIO, AUGUST 4, 1944

Ruth Gruber (b. 1911), a Brooklyn-born writer, studied in Cologne, Germany, at the time of Hitler's rise to power and later wrote feature articles for the New York Herald Tribune. *During World War II, Interior Secretary Harold Ickes hired Gruber as his special assistant and charged her with bringing nearly a thousand Jewish refugees from Italy to the United States on a secret rescue mission. At a time when public pressure was mounting against the U.S. government for its passivity regarding European Jewish refugees, Gruber's mission was also intended to bring much-needed positive attention to the Roosevelt administration. In August 1944, the refugees arrived and were settled at Fort Ontario, in Oswego, New York, for the duration of the war. When the war ended, Gruber joined an interfaith alliance appeal to President Truman to allow the refugees to leave the camp at Oswego and become U.S. citizens. In 1946, the refugees were permitted to apply for U.S. citizenship.*

Source: U.S. National Archives and Records Administration.

7.19—LELAND ROBINSON ET AL. TO PRESIDENT HARRY TRUMAN, REQUESTING U.S. CITIZENSHIP FOR REFUGEES HOUSED AT FORT ONTARIO, OSWEGO, NEW YORK, OCTOBER 22, 1945

The President
The White House
Washington, D.C.

Dear Mr. President:

This letter, in the interest of some 900 refugees sheltered by the United States Government at Fort Ontario, Oswego, New York, is addressed to you jointly by the Catholic, Jewish, Protestant and non-sectarian welfare agencies which have been concerned with the care of these unfortunate people during the fourteen months that they have been in this country. Many of us have made available extensive supplementary aid at the request of and in cooperation with the War Relocation Authority. Most of us have visited Oswego and we are all familiar with their circumstances and the situation in the Shelter.

As events have developed, we have all become convinced that some action should be taken by the United States Government to forestall the return of these people to the countries of their origin in Europe. This conviction has been strengthened by two considerations: First, because of the bad conditions and turmoil already existing among displaced persons in their countries of origin, and, second, because in this case, the United States can and should set a humanitarian pattern and precedent for the world at large in dealing with problems of displaced persons. In this connection, we have taken note of the recent representations by our government to friendly governments and of your recent instructions to American military authorities regarding the need for migration of the bulk of the displaced persons still in Europe who, for economic, political and psychological reasons cannot return to their places of origin.

Your action has placed the United States in a position of leadership in seeking a stable and humane solution of the problems of the masses uprooted from their homes by twelve years of persecution and war. We need hardly point out, therefore, that the reasoning underlying this policy, namely, that these people cannot be returned to the scene of their tragedy and degradation, applies with equal force to the group now at Fort Ontario.

We are fully aware of the terms under which these refugees were brought to the United States. At that time, however, neither the United States Government nor any of the interested parties was in a position to foresee that the repatriation of the group after the war would not only fail to restore them to a position of security and reasonable human decency, but would plunge most of them back into the maelstrom of hardship, uncertainty and despair which now encompasses many thousands in Europe and from which our government had rescued this handful. We respectfully submit that the repatriation of the Fort Ontario group[,] far from terminating their problem[,] would serve to increase the problem already existing in Europe.

On the other hand, it is self evident that the government cannot continue indefinitely to support these 900 persons at Fort Ontario. For fourteen months, the government has been most generous in affording them shelter and sustenance as well as safety, for which we know they will be forever grateful. However, neither they nor we, who are interested in their situation, desire that they shall continue for long to live as public charges. Moreover, they have an understandable desire now to resume a normal life as free individuals and to plan and build their own future for themselves and their families. For many years they have been living in confinement, formerly harsh and hostile, and now kindly and friendly, but still confinement.

We believe that under the existing immigration laws of the United States, it is possible for you to take action that will make possible the release of these refugees from the Fort Ontario Shelter and their resettlement in the United States. May we express the earnest hope that you will take this action at a very early date? Responsible welfare organizations are willing to assume any and all necessary guarantees which the government deems necessary, on behalf of these individuals. This is the only feasible and humane solution for this group. It is the only course of action which will serve to ameliorate rather than exacerbate the problem of displaced persons in general. It is the course which will demonstrate to all nations in a practical way the American policy for the solution of a grave international problem which you have so nobly enunciated.

Respectfully submitted

Dr. Leland Rex Robinson, President
The American Christian Committee for
    Refugees, Inc.

Miss Ruth Larned
International Migration Service, Inc.

L. Hollingsworth Wood, Chairman
International Rescue and Relief Committee

Samuel A. Telsey
Hebrew Sheltering and Immigrant Aid
    Society

Rabbi Stephen S. Wise
American Jewish Congress

Adolph Held, Chairman
Jewish Labor Committee

Louis B. Boudin, Chairman
American ORT Federation

Henry Monsky
B'nai B'rith

Mgr. Patrick A. O'Boyle
War Relief Services
N.C.W.C. [National Catholic Welfare Council]

Charles A. Riegelman, President
National Refugee Service, Inc.

Mrs. Henry A. Ingraham, President
National Board, Young Women's Christian
   Associations

Joseph M. Proskauer, President
American Jewish Committee

Mrs. Joseph N. Welt
National Council of Jewish Women

Clarence E. Pickett
American Friends Service Committee

[ ] Emerson
Unitarian Service Committee

Source: Karen J. Greenberg, ed., *Archives of the Holocaust:
An International Collection of Selected Documents*, vol. 5:
*Columbia University Library; New York. The Varian Fry
Papers; the Fort Ontario Emergency Refugee Shelter
Papers* (New York: Garland Publishing, 1990), 257–58.

7.20—POSTER URGING AMERICAN JEWS TO SUPPORT THE UNITED JEWISH APPEAL CAMPAIGN, N.D.

*In 1943, the organized Jewish community, under
its fundraising umbrella organization, the
United Jewish Appeal, mounted a national
campaign to aid European Jewish refugees
and support the creation of a Jewish national
homeland in British Mandate Palestine. As part
of its campaign, the UJA issued the following
poster, urging American Jews to give.*

Source: "Their Fight Is Our Fight: Give Today!" United
Jewish Appeal Poster (New York 1945–1946). From the
Skirball Cultural Center Museum Collection, Los
Angeles, Calif. Photograph by Susan Einstein. Reprinted
with permission of the Skirball Cultural Center Museum.

7.21—CHART, DOMESTIC ANTISEMITISM, 1940–1946

With domestic antisemitism reaching historic levels in the 1930s, Jewish leaders hoped that Nazi Germany's declaration of war against the United States would ease anti-Jewish feeling. By joining the Allied forces against Hitler, they believed, the United States would be pursuing interests more closely aligned with the particular needs of a Jewish citizenry intent on defeating Nazism. To the contrary, rates of domestic antisemitism increased as evidenced by a biennial survey asking Americans if they had "heard any criticism or talk against Jews in the last six months."

"Have you heard any criticism or talk against Jews in the last six months?"

	YES	NO
1940	46%	52%
1942	52%	44%
1944	60%	37%
1946	64%	34%

Source: Leonard Dinnerstein, *Antisemitism in America* (New York: Oxford University Press, 1994), 132. Used by permission of Oxford University Press, USA.

7.22—ACTIVITIES OF ANTISEMITIC AND ANTIDEMOCRATIC GROUPS IN THE UNITED STATES, AMERICAN JEWISH CONGRESS, APRIL 2, 1943

The American Jewish Congress, under the leadership of Stephen S. Wise, published a confidential digest summarizing the activities of the most high-profile antisemitic and antidemocratic groups in the United States. Featured in the April 2, 1943, issue are articles about Gerald L. K. Smith (1898–1976), the antisemitic minister who founded the America First Party, and John E. Rankin (1882–1960), a segregationist and antisemitic member of Congress from Mississippi.

CONFIDENTIAL
Digest of the Anti-Semitic and Anti-Democratic Press in the United States
Published Fortnightly

The American Jewish Congress publishes this Digest of the anti-Semitic and anti-Democratic Press as a public service to acquaint leaders of opinion in the United States with the agencies which are endeavoring to destroy the efforts of our country to win the war, and to establish a new world order based on freedom for all mankind. It is hoped that the information imparted in this Digest will serve as a warning and a basis of action to circumvent the purpose of these enemies of Democracy.

Volume Two, April 2nd, 1943, No. 7

AMERICA FIRST COMMITTEE
The orchestra is in the pit, the stage is all set, the locale for the first scene is in the Midwest, but there is some question backstage as to who will share the star's dressing room, and there is even some question as to who will be *the* star. The name of the production, or revival to be more accurate, is "The America First Committee."
[. . .]

During a recent trip to Washington, D.C. by the editor of the DIGEST, we learned that Congressional leaders who were heretofore ready to assume immediate leadership of the Committee, have changed their tactics and are biding their time until Gerald L. K. Smith's fast-moving, fast-growing "America First Party" has had a chance to develop in the Midwest.

Just when the America First Committee intends to make official its rebirth depends on several factors. Some of these factors include financial arrangements. Some of the factors we can list without fear of contradiction are: (1) Just, when and if the President announces his fourth term intentions. This will be the cue for a chorus-line of reactionaries to parade before the public footlights in order to pass their objections in review. They expect a storm of applause from the public and probably a concerted movement against the President; (2) The day the total casualties of our armed forces are announced. The opening of an American Riom Trial might be demanded and a movement to stimulate it begun; (3) The political offices open in the primaries which AFC'ers have the opportunity to capture thus showing the "will of the people," and (4) The number of Congressional leaders who can be counted upon to give the Committee a national flavor. Some of these leaders have given the 33 indicted [in 1942 by the U.S. government for seditious, pro-fascist views] moral support.

[. . .]

From time to time, this DIGEST will report the inside developments of the re-birth of the America First Committee. The factor to be exploited by the inner-circle of the group will be interesting to note for the future record. The opening of a second front which may be a military possibility, and the necessary loss of life which our leaders have forewarned us about which is due to follow, may be the cue for factor number 2 mentioned above.

But above all, the Jew-baiters, the alien-baiters, are not resting. The leaders are being chosen very carefully. And when the final lineup is made public they will be right up in front when the America First Committee's "Der Tag" arrives.

RANKIN'S ANTI-SEMITISM

Several years ago Representative John E. Rankin of Mississippi addressed the House of Representatives on Capitol Hill and made scurrilous and vituperative remarks against the Jews. Jumping immediately to the defense of "my brethren" was the late Representative Michael Edelstein of New York City's East Side. After Mr. Edelstein finished his speech for brotherhood, stating that the Jews were victims of persecution brought on by men of greed and intolerance, he fell dead on the floor of the House. On the contrary, from time to time he attacked the Negroes and other minorities on the floor of the House.

As recently as Friday, March 26th, 1943, Mr. Rankin arose in the House and said: "Mr. Speaker, I hesitate to use the word 'Jew' in any speech in this House, for whenever I do a little group of communistic Jews in this country howl to high heaven. They seem to think it is all right for them to abuse gentiles and stir up race trouble all over the country, but when you refer to one of them, they cry 'anti-Semitism' or accuse you of being pro-Nazi."

[. . .]

Why Mr. Rankin chose a time in the history of the Congress of [the] United States when the matters of war and post-war reconstruction are of greatest concern to issue an anti-Semitic blast, we cannot say. One can read and re-read the indictment and find that anti-Semitic utterances are the least those indicted are charged with. But one can read and re-read Mr. Rankin's speech and then recall the pre-Hitler days in the Reichstag when Nazi-inspired delegates arose and demanded to know what right Jews had or other minorities had to use free courts—courts which belonged to the Aryan: The newspapers this time gave no currency to Mr. Rankin's speech.

Source: SC-400, AJA.

The Shoah took the lives of six million Jews. A closer examination of the data reveals the particularly catastrophic impact of Hitler's attempted genocide on Jews in Poland, where just 80,000 survived from a prewar population of 3.3 million. With virtually every Jewish community in German-occupied Eastern Europe decimated, the United States emerged as the new world center for Jewish life in the postwar era, responsible for aiding survivors of the Shoah as well as helping build a Jewish national homeland in British Mandate Palestine.

Country	Jewish Population		Percentage of World Jewry		
	1939	*1945*	*1921*	*1939*	*1945*
United States of America	4,900,000	5,200,000	27.0	29.4	47.3
USSR	3,050,000	2,000,000	18.3	18.2	18.2
Palestine	475,000	592,000	0.5	2.8	5.4
Great Britain	390,000	400,000	2.1	2.3	3.7
Argentine	320,000	340,000	1.4	1.9	3.0
Rumania	850,000	335,000	6.1	5.1	3.0
Hungary	404,000	200,000	3.4	2.4	1.8
France	300,000	180,000	1.1	1.8	1.6
French Morocco	175,000	180,000	0.7	1.0	1.6
Canada	170,000	175,000	0.9	1.0	1.6
Algiers	130,000	135,000	0.7	0.8	1.2
Iraq	120,000	125,000	0.9	0.7	1.1
Iran	115,000	120,000	0.4	0.7	1.1
Brazil	110,000	115,000	0.2	0.7	1.1
South Africa	100,000	105,000	0.5	0.6	1.0
Germany	210,000	94,000	4.0	1.3	0.9
Poland	3,300,000	80,000	20.6	19.7	0.7
Czechoslovakia	354,000	65,000	2.6	2.1	0.6
Belgium	90,000	33,000	0.4	0.5	0.3
Holland	150,000	30,000	0.9	0.9	0.3
Austria	60,000	15,000	1.6	0.4	0.1
Lithuania	150,000	10,000	1.1	0.9	0.1
Latvia	95,000	10,000	0.7	0.6	0.1
Other Countries	707,000	461,000	3.9	4.2	4.2
TOTAL	16,725,000	11,000,000	100.0	100.0	100.0

Source: Center for Israel Education, http://ismi.emory.edu/home/assets/Jewish-Population-table-1939-1945-2010.pdf.

8 American Jewish Life, 1945–1965

Three major themes dominated the early postwar years: the impact of the suburbanization of American Jews, the growth of Jewish political involvement in the public square, and the emergence of the United States as a center of Jewish life in the post-Shoah world. At once, these themes dramatized competing impulses among American Jews. To begin with, suburbanization led to a weakening in traditional observance for many Jews, who chose to accommodate themselves to a more assimilationist religious lifestyle. This trend revealed itself as well in the disproportionate Jewish involvement in secular political movements such as the African American struggle for racial equality, the free speech movement, or, later, the protests against U.S. involvement in Vietnam. The loss of six million Jews in the Shoah placed American Jews front and center in the postwar Jewish world, and Jewish leaders, understanding their obligation to aid European Jewish refugees at war's end, welcomed many survivors into their own communities. When the United Nations considered the creation of a Jewish state, American Jews stepped up in support, as they did when the new State of Israel was in fact established.

In American suburbs, restrictive housing covenants eased; Jewish families were welcomed and solidified their status as full-fledged members of the white middle class. Jews adapted their modes of religious worship to this advance in their social status, and constructed synagogues that reflected the architecture of their new surroundings, permitted Shabbat travel by car in order to reach more remote houses of worship, and encouraged interfaith work to forge bonds with their new neighbors.

When African American leaders organized the modern civil rights movement, northern Jews reacted with strong support—they contributed to civil rights organizations, traveled south to participate in political actions, and, in some cases, risked their personal safety for the cause of racial equality. Strong northern Jewish support for the civil rights movement presented a triumphant moment for American Jews to demonstrate their commitment to social justice and their desire to reach across ethnic, racial, and religious lines in support of their fellow Americans. They rose to this occasion and emerged as the leading white ethnic group to enter the movement.

By adding an interracial component to their commitment to social justice in the 1950s, Jewish leaders projected an image of the United States as an open, inclusive, and diverse nation. Looking once again to the rule of law, American Jews saw in the civil rights movement an opportunity to engage the public square on minority rights and the protection of marginalized groups. In this way, involvement in the civil rights movement also served as a proxy to protect Jewish interests.

Yet the civil rights movement also revealed the limits of Jewish support for liberal causes. Southern Jews generally did not demonstrate the same strong backing of the civil rights movement as did their northern coreligionists. A decade later, when court-ordered busing to desegregate northern schools brought the civil rights movement into the backyards of urban Jews, many fled for the suburbs, strengthening claims by some recalcitrant southern Jews that northern Jewish backing of the movement proved more opportunistic than ideological.

Even among those Jews most active in the civil rights movement, few made explicit associations between their motivations for involvement and the religious precepts of Judaism. Although indirect connections existed, leftist social reformers often took special care to distance themselves and their activism from Jewish identification.

American Jews, and especially their organized leadership, devoted much of their postwar agenda to the cause of European Jews and Zionism. The relief and rescue mission of the war years evolved into massive efforts to aid Jewish refugees. Few of these refugees wished to remain in their former countries, a sentiment that inspired campaigns to provide for their material needs and find them new nations, including the United States, to call home.

American Jewish leaders who expressed ambivalence or even opposition to Zionism in the prewar years changed course after 1945, unable not to recognize the humanitarian crisis in Europe and the need for Jewish sovereignty. Although the vast majority of American Jews elected to remain in the United States after the creation of the State of Israel in 1948, they still forged strong ties to the Jewish state, raising funds as well as lobbying federal government officials on its behalf. By the mid-1960s, and especially after the 1967 Six Day War, Israel emerged as a new world center of Jewish life. In this chapter—and in the chapters that follow—the reader will find documents relating to Israel and American Jewry. One must not gauge the editors' assessment of Israel's significance from the post–World War II era to the present on the number of primary sources included in this volume. In reality, this relationship is a topic in and of itself, and this statement is validated by the existence of a documentary volume dedicated exclusively to Zionism and Israel (see Itamar Rabinovich and Jehuda Reinharz, eds., *Israel in the Middle East: Documents and Readings on Society, Politics, and Foreign Relations, Pre-1948 to the Present* [Brandeis University Press, 2007]).

8.01—LEVITTOWN (PA.) RESIDENT REFLECTS ON HIS COMMUNITY, 1950S

In July 1947, Levitt and Sons construction company broke ground on Levittown in Long Island. Widely regarded as the nation's original suburban planned community, Levittown benefited from the navy wartime experience of William Levitt, a Jewish builder who learned how to create housing units with interchangeable parts. For Jews who faced restrictive housing covenants keeping them out of many popular middle-class neighborhoods in the prewar years, the construction of Levittown and other suburban communities offered a chance to achieve the American middle-class goal of home ownership. But despite this success in overcoming antisemitic restrictions, race-based discrimination persisted, even in Levittown, where African Americans could not purchase homes until the late 1950s. Included as follows is a selection from the oral history of Holocaust survivor David Wisnia, recorded January 29, 2014. Wisnia, who settled in Levittown, Pennsylvania, which was built in the 1950s, served for twenty-two years as cantor at Har Sinai Temple in Trenton, New Jersey.

We moved [to Levittown] in 1950 from Philadelphia. I worked for a publishing company. I was a general sales manager for Pennsylvania and we heard the story about Levittown.

It was the talk of the Jewish community in Philadelphia because who would think of buying a house with $1,000 dollars down, or $500 dollars down? We've lived here and never moved. But we moved from one house to another within the community because we outgrew the little house. Levittown really was the talk of Philadelphia. We knew there was one on Long Island, but who ever thought in terms of having a Levittown in Pennsylvania? We had been living in an apartment in northwest Philly. . . . And it was rather expensive. I mean, at the time. And we had only one child. But then, in 1955, we had our second son.

They were advertising the houses for $9,900.00. Would you believe it? The advertising was geared mostly not to Jews but to the veterans who came home from the war who could not afford to buy a home and who were middle or lower middle class. You could not dream of buying a home in Philadelphia, really. Levittown was a new community and they promised all kinds of churches and synagogues. The advertising was good. I had the pleasure of meeting Mr. Levitt. I should say the honor; he accomplished something that nobody else did. Beautiful. He was quite active in our Reform community.

Ours was a single-family house with a carport. Not even a garage; a carport. A living room, a kitchen; it was a small house. It was geared, I would say, to a family just like ours—husband, wife, children; father, mother and kids. That's about it. They're all private homes, of course.

Another Jewish fellow who was working for me at the time mentioned he was going to move to Levittown, and I thought, "okay, we'll find out." Everybody wanted to buy a house, and that was in 1950, '51, '52. We lived in a different section then, called Birch Valley, because the house we live in now wasn't built until 1957. And by 1957 we had another child; we had our second son, Michael. In 1957 we added the upstairs and that cost another $5,000. So the whole house cost between $25 and $26,000. . . . It's got 6 bedrooms, 3½ bathrooms, a little office—unbelievable. They built what they called "country clubbers," and I want you to know, in the "country clubber" everyone added an upstairs. Remember, we had four children.

Levittown became a heavily "Jewish-seeking" area because immediately Levitt gave a beautiful piece of property to the Conservative congregation. Eventually, they gave ground to the Reform congregation, too. In other words, Temple Shalom in Levittown was not built at the same time as the Conservative congregation, Beth El.

The Reform congregation got a rabbi [Herbert] Hendel—may he rest in peace. When they found out I was a cantor I became quite instrumental in helping build the building because I tried to gather people. They wanted to hear me. See, I'm known as "the singer." And I speak, read, and write Hebrew and I knew the liturgy. Remember, I learned from the best. I don't know if you've ever heard of the two cantors: Sirota—Gershon Sirota—that's the Caruso of Jewish music—and then Moshe Koussevitzky at the Tlomacka synagogue [in Warsaw, Poland]. I learned their whole business, the High Holiday pieces, too. And I, to date, still use their compositions, the whole bit.

Now, you don't have the Conservative and Reform congregations anymore. The Conservative congregation slowly deteriorated. It moved out something like ten or fifteen years ago. The Reform congregation was just sold, and merged with Shir Ami in Newtown. As a matter of fact, I had a wall there, a memorial to my family. The problem with the Levittown area now is that Jews don't move in here. The neighborhood has changed . . . slowly. Most of the children, the second generation, went away to school, and of course, after they grew up, and got married, would never stay here. We have now—out of the 22 [houses on the street]—two Jewish families here.

As long as we can, we will stay here. The house is paid off. And it's a beautiful home. People told us, "Oh, it's going to last about 25, 50 years at most." It's a gorgeous home, I'm telling you. It's just unbelievable. I have in my living room a beautiful Steinway piano. It's not a small place.

It's been an absolutely positive experience living in Levittown. Absolutely. You cannot take Levittown as one entity. Why? Because there are many sections and the sections that have the country clubbers were sort of, you know, "the nose up." The average person could not afford to buy a house like ours. First of all it was air-conditioned, and that was the greatest incentive for us at the time. You see, this was sold for $20,000 fully air-conditioned.

I never experienced any discrimination in Levittown because I'm a proud Jew. But, as a matter of fact, my mission is to educate not only the Jews, but the Christians. Most of my friends who are Christian, I teach them Bible. So I don't hide the fact that I'm Jewish. Wisnia is not a Jewish name, you know. Wisnia is Polish. It means "cherry."

Levittown is still the best value for the money. No matter what it costs now. These homes are pretty good in our area, particularly the country club area. There are three country club sections and they have about a couple of hundred homes, maybe not even that. It's sort of spacious; it has all sorts of yards. It's beautiful. It's really beautiful. It's not what you call rich, but it's quite good.

Source: Interview with David Wisnia, January 29, 2014.

Levittown Family Income, 1959

Dollar range of income	No. of families	Percentage
0–$4,999	1,837	12.1
$5,000–5,999	1,996	13.1
6,000–6,999	2,606	17.1
7,000–7,999	2,513	16.5
8,000–8,999	2,003	13.2
9,000–9,999	1,173	7.7
10,000–14,999	2,489	16.3
15,000 and over	607	4.0

Source: "Income in 1959 of Families and Persons and Weeks Worked in 1959 for Standard Metropolitan Statistical Areas, Urban Areas, and Urban Places of 10,000 or More," in *The Eighteenth Decennial Census of the United States. Census of the Population 1960,* vol. 1: *General Social and Economic Characteristics: New York.*

Religious Composition of Levittown, 1958

Religious denomination	Percentage of population
Catholic	45
Jewish	20
Protestant	35

Source: Harold L. Wattel, "Levittown: A Suburban Community," in *The Suburban Community,* ed. William M. Dobriner (New York: G. P. Putnam's Sons, 1958).

8.03—"NCRAC DISCUSSES DECLINE IN JEWISH POPULATION IN CITIES," JEWISH TELEGRAPHIC AGENCY, JUNE 22, 1955

At the 1955 meeting of the organized Jewish community's national umbrella group, the National Community Relations Advisory Council, organizers devoted their plenary session to the dynamics at play in the urban to suburban migration. New Jewish suburban residents often faced a challenge as they moved into neighborhoods with few Jews, struggling to build Jewish institutions and develop the infrastructure necessary to Jewish life. Those left behind in the migration, including elderly, Orthodox, and less affluent Jews, worried about their future in neighborhoods that had changed from being predominantly Jewish to having African American, Puerto Rican, or other non-Jewish majorities.

Atlantic City—

Some cities in the United States have lost more than half of their Jewish population within recent decades in the mass movement to the suburbs, it was established here at the plenary session of the National Community Relations Advisory Council. A discussion of this subject at the session established the following facts.

1. In recent years the Jewish populations of metropolitan centers have been moving away from the central city neighborhoods in which they have lived into new and growing suburban communities. As a result of this exodus, which has been characteristic of middle class population groups generally, the percentage of Jews in many major cities has declined sharply.

2. This has markedly affected the extent of Jewish participation in community-wide enterprises, reducing it within the cities and greatly increasing it in the suburban communities.

3. Many of the suburban communities into which Jewish families have moved were formerly wholly or almost wholly non-Jewish in composition. Older residents thus find themselves with Jewish neighbors for the first time. Similarly, in many cases, the Jewish families for the first time find themselves in neighborhoods that are predominantly non-Jewish in character. This creates a new and fruitful basis for the bettering of relationships and the furtherance of mutual acceptance and appreciation. It also creates new sources of hostility where prejudices are at work.

4. Meanwhile, new groups have moved into the neighborhoods formerly occupied by the Jewish families that have moved to the outlying suburbs. These newcomers generally are of lower income levels and often comprise groups that have been the victims of discrimination in housing. Frequently they are Negroes, or Puerto Ricans, or other racial minority groups. The disparities in income level between them and the remaining Jewish families are sometimes quite striking and constitute a source of friction.

5. Jewish-supported welfare, health and recreational facilities and institutions such as community centers in these neighborhoods in many cases have for years offered their services to residents without regard to religion or race. They now find themselves serving a clientele which includes a constantly diminishing proportion of Jews. At the same time, the Jewish populations in the suburbs continue to demand the services they have been accustomed to receiving from the Jewish institutions and agencies that they support through their contributions. A multiplicity of problems flow from these trends. Some of the speakers at the session deplored the growth in some places of predominantly Jewish neighborhoods in new suburban communities, expressing the fear that "middle class ghettoes" may be in the making. This was coupled with the recognition, however, that Jewish religious practices and observances made it necessary for Jewish families to live in reasonable proximity to temples and synagogues. Considerable stress was placed on the "plural culture" of the United States, which gives equal status and acceptance to all religious, ethnic and cultural groups, in the belief that from the friendly interaction among them the greatest good for the whole society is derived.

Source: Jewish Telegraphic Agency (June 22, 1955), http://archive.jta.org/article/1955/06/22/3044423/ncrac-discusses-decline-in-jewish-population-in-cities.

8.04—PHINEAS J. BIRON, "PORTRAIT OF AN INFORMER," *Israel Light*,
DECEMBER 31, 1947

*The Cold War anticommunist climate of the
early postwar years caught Jewish communal
leaders in a bind. While relatively few American
Jews espoused communist beliefs, a
disproportionate number of vocal Communists
were Jews. This led some American Jews to fear
that their community's historic affinity for
left-leaning politics in the United States would
smear them with the anticommunist brush.
Postwar American Jews also particularly valued
the constitutional protections afforded to free
speech, even when it was unpopular. This
affinity led some Jewish leaders to push back
against the more extreme expressions of
anticommunism, especially those of Wisconsin
senator Joseph McCarthy (1908-1957) and his
supporters. Several of these themes coalesced in
late 1947, when Rabbi Benjamin Schultz
(1906-1978) of the Reform congregation
Emanuel-El in Yonkers, New York, published an
anticommunist screed in the* New York World-
Telegram. *In a sensationalistic style that drew
comparisons to William Randolph Hearst's
infamous yellow journalism, Schultz accused
revered rabbi Stephen S. Wise of complicity with
the Communists in their attempts "to soften
America for Soviet aggression." In response, the
Israel Light columnist Phineas J. Biron (pen
name for the leftist writer and Zionist leader
Joseph Brainin [1895-1970]) offered a critical
reply. Schultz resigned his pulpit as a
consequence of the controversy.*

Strictly Confidential
By Phineas J. Biron

PORTRAIT OF AN INFORMER
The Association of Reform Rabbis, the New York
Board of Rabbis and the Alumni Association of
the Jewish Institute of Religion are in an up-
roar . . . These bodies are terribly incensed—
and rightly so—because one of their number,
Rabbi Benjamin Schultz, has behaved in what
they term a most unethical manner, unbecoming a religious leader . . . Speculation is running high as to what these rabbinical groups will
do to save the honor of the rabbinical profession . . .

A RABBINICAL FINGERMAN
Benjamin Schultz, who still holds the job of
Rabbi at Temple Emanu-El in Yonkers, N.Y., wrote
three articles for the *New York World-Telegram*
last week under the title "Commies Invade the
Churches" . . . In these articles Schultz pur-
ported to show "the penetration of religion by
Communists" . . . An ignoramus of the first
water, Schultz, in sensational Hearst style (last
year he wrote a series of articles on Judaism in
Russia for the Hearst papers) clumsily warns
Protestants, Jews and Catholics that "the Communists are working hard on the three faiths to
soften America for Soviet Aggression" . . . And
who, in Schultz's view, are the credulous fellow
travelers who are "ensnared by red crocodile
tears"? . . . First of all, Rabbi Stephen S. Wise,
who, Schultz asserts, defends Soviet expansion
and committed the crime of speaking at a rally
under the auspices of the Jewish People's Fraternal Order, which Schultz labels a Communist
front organization. . . . And the proof that the
JPFO is red? . . . Well, it gave more than $40,000
to the Hadassah Hospital in Palestine and helps
the Jews of Poland and supports Jewish cultural projects . . . What a red front organization
it must be! . . . Schultz must be terribly afraid of
Jewish culture, because it might reveal his abysmal ignorance . . .

DR. WISE'S CRIME

And—please don't tremble—Schultz actually reveals that Dr. Stephen S. Wise "sincerely believes that liberals and Communists can work together against Fascism, as certain Protestant bishops and ministers also believe" . . . Can you imagine how dangerous Dr. Wise is to the cause of democracy? . . . He is ready to fight Fascism without demanding a "loyalty test" of his co-workers . . . Now, really, Dr. Wise—what is this country coming to?" . . .

Among the other "reds" who menace the Jewish religion Schultz cites Joseph Brainin, who, he discovered, writes "Strictly Confidential" under the pseudonym Phineas J. Biron . . . What an earth-shaking revelation! . . . Biron, Schultz says, follows the party line . . . Proof? . . . "He boosts the American Youth for Democracy," which Schultz labels Communistic . . . Others who share the spotlight with Dr. Wise are Rabbi Abraham Bick, Rabbi Joshua Block, Professor Abraham Cronbach and journalist B. Z. Goldberg . . . The major crime of these dangerous men is their sponsorship of the School for Jewish Studies, which, Schultz says, "cleverly sandwiches a Bible class in between courses on Marxism" . . .

WHO IS SCHULTZ?

This great crusader for the purity of religion has a rather shabby reputation among his rabbinical colleagues . . . From 1938 to 1942 he masqueraded under the title of Doctor of Philosophy . . . Only when caught and exposed did he withdraw his listing of this degree beside his name in the Yearbook of the Central Conference of American Rabbis . . . We happen to know that Charles Schnall, president of Schultz's congregation, is very unhappy about his rabbi . . . He has prohibited Schultz from referring to his rabbinical connection with Temple Emanu-El in his extra-curricular activities . . . Schultz has no compunction against using lies in his career as informer . . . Last year he wrote that Jews are not qualified to become officers in the Russian army,

knowing full well that he was using a lie . . . We could go on enumerating Schultz's mendacious statements, but no purpose would be served . . .

DISGRACES PULPIT

Schultz is too notorious a character to require unveiling in the Jewish press[.] Dr. Wise, commenting on Schultz's articles, declared his statements on rabbis and the Communist line to be "not only mendacious but utterly and inexcusably vicious." Rabbi Louis I. Newman, one of the most distinguished graduates of the Jewish Institute of Religion, wrote: "Rabbi Wise, Professor Cronbach, Dr. Joshua Block and others mentioned in the (Shultz) article need no defense as loyal Americans . . . To those non-Jews and Jews who have been grievously wronged by Schultz in his vicious articles, I, as one rabbi, wish to extend my apology for my Rabbinical colleagues, and to say we are ashamed that such a vilifier has arisen in our midst" . . .

MORAL

Dr. Wise, America's most beloved and courageous Jewish leader, does not need protection . . . His words and deeds speak for themselves . . . Schultz would never have merited so much space in our column were it not for the lamentable fact that he is using his rabbinical status to join with the un-American hordes who smear every liberal expression as Communist . . . But the real reason for Schultz's role of informer and paid espionage agent in the synagogue is this: There may soon be a job open in Hearst's *American Weekly*, a job held for many years by Rabbi Clifton Harby Levy, a venerable gentleman who writes on Biblical subjects and ancient history in a popular style . . . Schultz apparently is putting forth his candidacy for the Hearst job, although his scholarship does not entitle him to teach history even to a kindergarten class . . . And that is the story of Benjamin Schultz, the rabbinical Bilbo and Hearst's fingerman . . .

Source: Rabbi Benjamin Schultz nearprint file, AJA.

In March of 1951, Julius Rosenberg (1918–1953) and his wife, Ethel (1915–1953), along with codefendant Morton Sobell (b. 1917), went to trial on charges of espionage, accused of, among other offenses, passing top-secret information about the atomic bomb to the Soviet Union. The Rosenberg case highlighted political fears within the American Jewish community. As Jews and Communists, the Rosenbergs embodied the strong historic commitment of many Jews of Eastern European descent to leftist politics. Amid a strong Cold War anticommunist culture, Jews feared that a left-leaning political past would spark antisemitic claims challenging American Jewish patriotism. While evidence against Ethel Rosenberg proved far less convincing than the charges against Julius, both were convicted and sentenced to death in a courtroom where Jewish attorneys represented both sides and a Jewish judge presided. A national outcry by civil libertarians, death penalty opponents, and anti–Cold War activists failed to overturn their sentence. On June 19, 1953, Julius and Ethel Rosenberg were sent to the electric chair, the only Americans ever executed for Cold War espionage.

Fear that antisemitism might have played a role in the Rosenbergs' arrests and in the severity of their sentences is exemplified as follows in the National Committee to Secure Justice in the Rosenberg Case preface to a transcript of the trial proceedings, as well as in a flyer calling for clemency that includes a handwritten letter from the Rosenbergs' sons to President Eisenhower and an editorial critical of the verdict published in Jewish Life. *In 1995, the U.S. Central Intelligence Agency released previously classified documents from the Venona project, an anti-Soviet intelligence effort started in 1943 by the Army Signal Intelligence Service. In one cable deciphered by the CIA and included here, Soviet agents discuss Julius Rosenberg's attempt*

to recruit Ethel Rosenberg's sister-in-law, Ruth Greenglass (and later her husband—and Ethel's brother—David Greenglass), to his spy ring. At the Rosenbergs' trial, it was the testimony of Ruth and David Greenglass that provided key evidence for conviction. In an interview conducted in 2001, David Greenglass admitted to lying about his sister Ethel Rosenberg's role in the espionage ring in order to secure lighter sentences for himself and his wife.

To the Reader:

In response to widespread and growing requests for the facts in the Rosenberg Case, we have taken the unprecedented step of making available to the public the complete transcript of the trial proceedings. We are pleased to perform this service and are confident that the dispassionate reader will perceive the gross miscarriage of justice that cries out for redress.

We think it is not amiss to add a note of caution to the lay readers of this legal document. This is not a mystery novel whose solution is supplied by the author in the last chapter. Each reader will be compelled to find the correct answer for himself out of the maze of the conflict of testimony.

To tell the true story from the false one, it is necessary to look beneath the surface. Therefore, the Committee suggests that attention be directed to the following: (1) By testifying for the Government, the main witnesses—the Greenglasses—who faced a death penalty for their own confessed crimes, were given a chance to save themselves and did receive lenient treatment, David Greenglass being sentenced to fifteen years and Ruth Greenglass being permitted to go free; Max Elitcher, who faced a five year perjury charge was never indicted; (2) the absence of any documentary evidence tending to connect the defendants with the crime; (3) flimsy corroboration; (4) the injection of the alleged Communist affiliations and beliefs of the defendants, exploited by the prosecutor and acquiesced in by the trial judge, that only served to prejudice the jury against the defendants; (5) the barbaric sentence of death on the Rosenbergs.

And finally, we suggest that you ask, as you come to each point of testimony and exhibit, this simple question: "How does this link the Rosenbergs and Sobell to espionage?"

National Committee to Secure Justice
in Rosenberg Case
1050 Sixth Avenue
New York 18, N.Y.

Source: Julius and Ethel Rosenberg nearprint file, AJA.

8.06—FLYER FOR CLEMENCY, ROSENBERG CASE, MAY 30, 1953

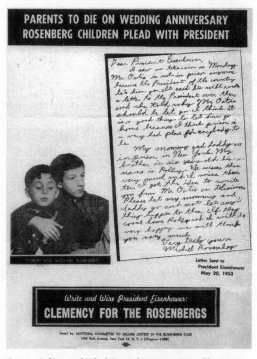

Source: Julius and Ethel Rosenberg nearprint file, AJA.

An evaluation of the significance of the murder of the Rosenbergs and perspectives in the continuing struggle

An Editorial Article

At the short distance of a month from the murder of Ethel and Julius Rosenberg the significance of that event for the American people takes shape. It has the broadest and deepest ramifications and affects the life of every American. Nor has the case ended with the death that the Rosenbergs met with a dignity and courage rare in the annals of mankind.

The ruthless actions of the government in the last weeks of the fight to save the Rosenbergs reveal much about the intentions and policy of the Eisenhower administration. Why did the government brush aside new evidence, evidence of perjury, of denial of credibility to Greenglass' testimony by atomic scientists like Dr. Harold Urey? Why the indecent haste into which the Supreme Court was pushed, a haste recorded in the remarkable dissents printed elsewhere in this issue? And why did President Eisenhower ignore the world demand, unprecedented since the Sacco-Vanzetti case, to grant clemency to the Rosenbergs, a demand attesting to the recognition by the peoples of the world of Washington's aggressive intentions?

The conclusion is inescapable that the government regarded the murder of the Rosenbergs to be necessary. By this hasty, cold-blooded murder, the Big Business government of Eisenhower served notice that it would let nothing stand in the way of striking fear into all opposition to the cold war, that the McCarthyite elements are trying to hasten the descent into fascism and that the government sought a diversion from the unpopularity of the Korean war. The flouting of millions of protesting voices at home and abroad signifies an advanced state of pro-fascist policy in the highest places and of a desperate stage of the "go it alone" policy in foreign affairs. For, as

Alice Citron shows in her article in this issue, Europe was united against the execution and is more suspicious than ever of any "alliance" with Washington.

[...]

THE JEWISH ASPECT

Although the basic issues involved in this case were most emphatically the concern of the whole American people and of common people all over the world, the Jewish people of our country irresistibly felt that the case touched them quite particularly. That the case had a Jewish aspect was felt by the Jewish masses from the start and was indeed reflected in expressions to this effect in the entire Yiddish and some of the English-Jewish press from the outset. That press stated quite frankly that Judge Irving Kaufman had imposed the death sentence in order to appease the anti-Semites in a futile effort to gain immunity from anti-Semitism. Many Jews were impelled into the case by the justified feeling that the death sentence would never have been imposed, let alone carried out, if Jews had not been involved. This feeling was again reflected in the English-Jewish press after the execution, as reported in this issue.

The reactionary leadership of many major Jewish organizations played a shameful role in trying to hold back the tide of Jewish protest. Midway in the campaign the American Jewish Committee led in issuing blasts echoed by the major Jewish organizations and in the press against any suggestions that anti-Semitism had operated in any way in the death sentence. Many Jews were intimidated into silence by this hush-hush tactic. But the mass sentiment among the Jews was too great to be suppressed. A number of columnists and editorial expressions appeared throughout the campaign in the English-Jewish press urging clemency, from Rabbi George E. Fox in the Chicago *Sentinel* to Samuel Gach, editor and publisher of the *California Jewish Voice*, to Rabbi Louis Gross of the Brooklyn *Jewish Ex-*

aminer and many others. Memberships of national organizations tried to break through the top leaders who were sitting on the lid of protest. Many rabbis throughout the land, including many eminent ones like Rabbi Abba Hillel Silver and Rabbi Joseph Fink, president of the Central Conference of American Rabbis, and rabbis in New York, Los Angeles, Boston and many other places came out for clemency. But above all, there was a great outpouring of Jewish rank and file sentiment for clemency, despite the official boycott.

THEY COULD HAVE BEEN SAVED
This pressure, both Jewish and non-Jewish, increased as the last weeks approached. A massive growth in strength of the clemency forces developed. The many thousands who crowded the unprecedented mass demonstrations that marked the last weeks were only a token of the shocked awareness that at last seized the people as to the grave implications of the case and the enormity of the injustice that impended. But even this proved too little and too late. The American people had not awakened to the danger in sufficient numbers to avert the execution. This would have been possible if our people at home had had as keen an awareness as, for instance, the French people. A measure of responsibility for this inadequacy rests with the labor and pro-

gressive movement. Even the most advanced elements, influenced by the "atom spy" hysteria, started too late and did too little.

Jewish Life was among the first to recognize the true significance of the case and brought it to its readers in three articles beginning with November 1951. The effectiveness with which we raised the issue, including the Jewish aspect of the case, brought down upon us the unbridled denunciation of the Jewish oligarchy. Yet, *Jewish Life* did not by any means do everything it could have done.

Most serious of all, however, was the pitifully small participation in the campaign of labor leaders and of the labor movement as a whole. Labor should have realized that the spy hysteria has as one of its main purposes the softening up of mass opinion in preparation for an attack on the labor movement. By its virtual silence the labor movement did injury to its own cause.

No estimate of the Rosenberg case up to now would be complete without recognition of the heroic battle put up by Emanuel H. Bloch, the Rosenbergs' attorney, or of the tremendous, persistent and militant campaign conducted by the National Committee to Secure Justice in the Rosenberg Case. Great courage was demanded of both the attorney and the Committee to carry on under the prevailing hysterical atmosphere.

Source: Julius and Ethel Rosenberg nearprint file, AJA.

8.08—SOVIET CABLE INCRIMINATING JULIUS ROSENBERG, SEPTEMBER 21, 1944

VENONA
Reissue(T1362)
From: NEW YORK
To: MOSCOW
No: 134C
                    21 September 1944
To VIKTOR[i].
Lately the development of new people [D% has been in progress]. LIBERAL [ii] recommended the wife of his wife's brother, Ruth GREENGLASS, with a safe flat in view. She is 21

years old, a TOWNSWOMAN [GOROZhANKA] [iii], a GYMNAST [FIZKUL'TURNITsA] [iv] since 1942. She lives on Stanton [STANTAUN] Street. LIBERAL and his wife recommend her as an intelligent and clever girl.

[15 groups unrecoverable]

[C% Ruth] learned that her husband [v] was called up by the army but he was not sent to the front. He is a mechanical engineer and is now working at the ENORMOUS [ENORMOZ] [vi] plant in SANTA FE, New Mexico.

[45 groups unrecoverable]

detain VOLOK [vii] who is working in a plant on ENORMOUS. He is a FELLOWCOUNTRY-MAN [ZEMLYaK] [viii]. Yesterday he learned that they had dismissed him from his work. His active work in progressive organizations in the past was the cause of his dismissal.

In the FELLOWCOUNTRYMAN line LIBERAL is in touch with CHESTER [ix]. They meet once a month for the payment of dues. CHESTER is interested in whether we are satisfied with the collaboration and whether there are not any misunderstandings. He does not inquire about specific items of work [KONKRETNAYa RABOTA]. In as much as CHESTER knows about the role of LIBERAL's group we beg consent to ask C. through LIBERAL about leads from among people who are working on ENORMOUS and in other technical fields.

Your no. 4256[a]. On making further enquiries and checking on LARIN[x] we received from the FELLOWCOUNTRYMEN through EKhO [xi] a character sketch which says that they do not entirely vouch for him. They base this statement on the fact that in the Federation LARIN does not carry out all the orders received from the leadership. He is stubborn and self-willed. On the strength of this we have decided to refrain from approaching LARIN and intend to find another candidate in FAECT [FAKhIT] [xii].

No 751   MAJ [xiii]
20 September

Notes: [a]   Not available.

Comments:

[i]	VIKTOR:	Lt. Gen. P. M. FITIN.
[ii]	LIBERAL:	Julius ROSENBERG.
[iii]	GOROZhANKA:	American citizen.
[iv]	FIZKUL'TURNITsA:	Probably a Member of the Young Communist League.
[v]	i.e. David GREENGLASS.	
[vi]	ENORMOZ:	Atomic Energy Project.
[vii]	VOLOK:	
[viii]	ZEMLYaK:	Member of the Communist Party.
[ix]	CHESTER:	Communist Party name of Bernard SCHUSTER.
[x]	LARIN:	Unidentified.
[xi]	EKhO:	i.e. ECHO, Bernard SCHUSTER.
[xii]	FAKhIT:	Federation of Architects, Chemists, Engineers and Technicians. See also NEW YORK's message no. 911 of 27 June 1944.
[xiii]	MAJ:	i.e. MAY, Stepan APRESYaN.

Source: U.S. National Security Agency.

8.09—MAURICE L. ZIGMOND, SELECTION FROM "BRANDEIS UNIVERSITY IS ONE YEAR OLD," 1949

In the fall of 1948, 107 students entered the first freshman class at Brandeis University in Waltham, Massachusetts. The university, named after Supreme Court associate justice and American Zionist leader Louis Brandeis, sought to reflect "the ideals of academic excellence and social justice he personified." Designed as a Jewish-sponsored yet nonsectarian school, Brandeis embodied an attempt to bridge the secular and religious worlds of American Jewry in the postwar years. In many ways, the founding of Brandeis in the postwar suburbs offers an excellent comparison to Yeshiva University's founding a generation earlier in an urban setting. On Brandeis's first anniversary, Rabbi Maurice L. Zigmond (1904–1998), director of the Harvard Radcliffe Hillel, reflected on the school's progress and purpose.

America's first Jewish-sponsored, non-sectarian university has completed its initial academic year. After a difficult and critical period of preparation—there were times when the very life of the institution hung in the balance—Brandeis was formally dedicated on October 7, 1948, with Dr. Abram Leon Sachar, for 15 years National Director of the B'nai B'rith Hillel Foundations, and now Chairman of the National Hillel Commission, as its President. Two weeks later its doors were opened to a small "pilot" class of incoming students. . . .

Last fall, 107 students gathered to form a Freshman class which, in the opinion of the faculty members, was not qualitatively below the average of similar classes of colleges of the first rank. Once the University started to function and became better known through nationwide publicity, applications came in a steady stream.

Thus, the second Freshman class, numbering about 150, which matriculates this fall, represents a selection from more than 900 young people who expressed a desire to attend.

The most frequent question asked about Brandeis—at least by Jews—concerns its "Jewishness." What is Jewish about the institution? How does Jewish sponsorship influence its operation, its character, or the content of its curriculum? When it is recalled that Brandeis is officially described as both "Jewish sponsored" and "non-sectarian," it will be apparent that the problem is not a simple one. Under Jewish sponsorship the initial steps were taken by Jews and, with a few exceptions, the subsequent supporters of the project have been Jewish. On the other hand, its non-sectarian complexion implies not only that people of all creeds (and races, too) are welcome as students and as members of faculty, staff, and Board of Trustees, but also that there will be no denominational emphasis in official activities or in the classroom. . . .

This policy of non-sectarianism is pursued with consistency and thoroughness at Brandeis. In its application blanks for the admission of students, the University goes beyond the precaution of seeking no information about religious and racial backgrounds. It refrains also from asking invidious questions relative to the maiden name of one's mother and the occupation of one's father. While it is known that a majority of the student body is Jewish, the administrative staff is not interested in statistics of this type. "Those institutions concerned with quotas and percentages must of necessity be preoccupied with such facts and figures," explains the Director of Admissions [who happens to be a non-Jew]. "They are of no importance to us here." The University Calendar respects the major Jewish as well as the major Christian holy days. Courses are geared to a five-day week schedule—there are no sessions on either Saturday or Sunday. A similar indifference to origins and creeds characterizes the selection of members of the faculty and staff. As the Board of Trustees reaches its full strength (21 members are authorized by the Massachusetts legislature), emphasis is being laid upon diversity rather than upon uniformity.

On the other hand, Brandeis gives to Jewish learning a rightful place in its curriculum. Thus Hebrew is to be found alongside of French, Spanish, and German in fulfillment of the "Language and Literature Requirement." Among the "Fields of Concentration" (to be developed in the upper classes) there is one entitled "Semitic Languages and Civilization." The University Library, whose first function is to serve classroom needs, is beginning to build what is expected to be an outstanding Judaica collection. But perhaps most significant of all, Brandeis does not hesitate to challenge age-old academic judgments. In those courses considering such mat-

ters, there is a conscious effort to revaluate the role of the Jew in the history of civilization. Without erring in the opposite direction, an attempt is made to correct the bias of textbooks which would limit the participation of the Jewish people in world culture to a paragraph on the "Old Testament," or of historians who would submerge the Jewish contribution within the anonymity of "Syrian" culture.

The "Jewishness" of Brandeis cannot be measured in quantitative terms. It is to be discerned not so much in tangibles as in intangibles. It is not a label; it is an attitude, a *weltanschauung*, an awareness of the wrongs done in the name of education and a determination not to tolerate them. Perhaps there is nothing Jewish about the pledge of the University that it "is open to all students who meet academic standards without reference to race, color, or religious affiliations," but is not any deviation from this principle justifiably regarded as anti-Jewish? . . .

Source: As printed in *JAW*, 453–54. Originally appeared in *National Jewish Monthly*, September 1949.

8.10—RABBI ABBA HILLEL SILVER, SELECTION FROM "LIVING JUDAISM," DELIVERED AT THE DEDICATION OF THE NEW UAHC HEADQUARTERS, OCTOBER 27, 1951

The growing affluence of American Jews in the postwar years, the continuing importance of mass media, and the increasing integration of Jews into American life coalesced in 1951 when Cleveland's Rabbi Abba Hillel Silver delivered the keynote address at the dedication of the Reform movement's new headquarters on Fifth Avenue in New York City. For Silver, a fiery orator, the opportunity to offer his perspectives on the major themes of postwar American Jewish life became even more compelling when NBC Radio deemed the event, and his speech, important enough to broadcast across the entire country.

Living Judaism
By
Dr. Abba Hillel Silver, Rabbi of the Temple, Cleveland, Ohio
Address Delivered at the Dedication of the House of Living Judaism

Hotel Statler
New York City
October 27, 1951
By
Dr. Abba Hillel Silver
The Temple
Cleveland, Ohio

The House of Living Judaism which the Union of American Hebrew Congregations is dedicating this weekend bears a very appropriate and auspicious name. "Nomen est omen." The accent here is on *living* Judaism. This House is dedicated to the living faith of a life-enchanted people whose God is a God of life, whose Torah is a Tree of Life, and whose ethical doctrines are a supreme affirmation of life.

Our people and our faith have long lived in the deep shadows. They were sore beset in our day and the cords of death encompassed them. But they have now come away from the shadows. They have emerged into the light of a new and more hopeful day. They are again walking free in the land of the living.

Great forces converged time and again to destroy both Judaism and the Jewish people. Assimilation threatened the one; anti-Semitism the other. In our day these forces reached their cataclysmic climax. They took a frightful toll. We suffered millions of casualties. But both Judaism and the Jewish people emerged, scathed and scarred to be sure, by the most brutal onslaught in their history, but unbeaten and undefeated. They have now recoiled from weakness to strength, and as so often in the past, following changes of fortune and dangerous experiences, they have resumed their historic march again with greater confidence than ever before.

In the newly established State of Israel, the millennial hope of our people for national restoration found, in our day, its blessed anchorage. Everywhere our people are buoyed up with a new-found pride and dignity, and with the prospect of exciting new beginnings.

Judaism, too, has experienced a marked revival which is reflected in increased congregational membership, in new synagogues and schools, and in general expansion.

Thus, the prophets of doom who foretold the extinction of Judaism with the disappearance of the sheltering ghetto walls and the physical and spiritual collapse of the Jewish people as a result of the monstrous Nazi carnage have again been proven to have seen empty visions and to have divined falsely. The Psalmist's paean of triumphant life is echoing in our hearts "I shall not die but live to declare the deeds of the Lord." There is deathlessness in the faith which is Judaism, and as long as our people remain loyal to it, they share in its immortality.

It is with a clearer vision that we now can see the road ahead, now that so many of its roadblocks have been removed.

We are now convinced, for example, that there is no refuge for our people in assimilation. The friendly world does not ask for it; the hostile world spurns it. This is a bitter lesson from our credulous past which we are not likely to forget. There is no appeasing the enemy through self-effacement and self-denial. His purpose is not to absorb us but to destroy us. He hates the modern, thoroughly Westernized Jew even more than other Jews. Dr. Walter Frank, who was Director of the Reich Institute for the History of the New Germany, declared: "It will always remain a task of paramount importance to unveil the so-called 'noble,' educated, 'German' Jew and to expose him as the most dangerous type of alien parasite. It is easy to show a Galician Jew as a member of the 'Asiatic horde' on European soil. This is harder when the 'Asiatic' meets us in the civilized form of a Baruch Spinoza, a Moses Mendelssohn, or a Friedrich Gundolf, or an Albert Einstein, a Maximilian Harden, Walter Rathenau or a Benjamin Disraeli."

Anti-Semites of this type cannot be appeased or answered. They can only be destroyed, and they attend to their own destruction. The free world does not call for the physical amalgamation of peoples, only for their voluntary cooperation for their common good. The free world does not ask of men to surrender their historic faiths—only to live up to them. Freedom of faith and worship is one of the basic rights of civilized society. Black, brown and red dictatorships dread it and suppress it.

Nor is there security for us or meaning or dignity in fighting anti-Semitism as such or in hectically defending our loyalty or proclaiming our patriotism from the housetops. No fair-minded man questions our loyalty and no bigot will ever be persuaded of it.

Our security lies in uniting with all right-minded men, to defend our society against all demagogues and political adventurers and against the conditions which give these enemies of the free society their opportunity. Our security lies in fighting poverty, injustice, inequality, and above all, war and the things which lead to war. It is in the championing of the great ethical and spiritual traditions of Judaism which we have shared with the rest of the world—for our faith was born not for ourselves alone but for the whole world—and in our loyal carrying out of its mandates and commitments that our fundamental security lies.

Again we have learned, I believe, that there is no security for our people and, for that matter, for any people in scientific progress alone, for more knowledge does not mean more goodness, more tolerance or more brotherhood in the world.

The great slaughtering of our people took place in the most scientifically advanced country in the world—Germany, and the progress of the centuries did not attenuate the virulence of intolerance. In the middle of the 17th century one-third of the Jews of Europe were massacred. In the middle of the 20th century two-thirds were massacred.

[. . .]

We have also come to understand that there is no survival for our people in the Diaspora except in and through Judaism. I mean, of course, a dignified and purposeful survival, for a people can drag out an inglorious and meaningless existence almost indefinitely. We shall not be able to survive as a secular nationality group in the Diaspora, especially in those countries, like the United States, where there are no minority nationality groups determined to preserve their cultural identities. Freedom will accelerate the process of disintegration, and persecution may retard it, but the process is inevitable.

The establishment of the State of Israel is undoubtedly one of the most significant and mag-nificent events in Jewish history. With it we have reached one of the great stages in our history. Its importance will not be isolated in time nor limited to Israel. It is too early for us to foresee all its spreading and deepening influences in the future. It will undoubtedly affect all Jewish life in the Diaspora, and no attempts to isolate it from the rest of world Jewry will succeed. The contacts and the influences will be continuous and increasing. They will, of course, be non-political. We shall not belabor this point just because others are inclined to distort it. But it would be a mistake to assume that the State of Israel will preserve Judaism either inside or outside of Israel. This is a task all of its own which the Jews of the world must carry on in the future as in the past. This applies also to the Jews of the State of Israel. They need Judaism quite as much as we do. A political state cannot be counted upon to preserve our spiritual heritage. There was danger of the extinction of Judaism even within ancient Palestine, and the seers and prophets and the spiritually faithful had to fight desperately hard for its preservation against powerful assimilationist tendencies there.

It is good for our clear confronting of this universal task of vitalizing and preserving Judaism that the State of Israel has been established and that the controversy which raged around its establishment has finally been resolved. Liberal Judaism unfortunately spent too much time and energy in fighting Zionism. It took it too long a time to arrive at the conclusion that opposition to Zionism was not an integral part of the philosophy or the purposes of Liberal Judaism. This issue fortunately is now closed. There are, of course, the intransigent few who are still flogging the horse of this dead controversy, out of habit, I presume, or out of dudgeon, but where their efforts are not mischievous, they are quite silly and futile. The State of Israel is there and will, by the grace of God, continue. The Jews of the world will continue to take pride in it and to support it. Jews from all parts of the world who in the days to come will wish to migrate there or who may have to—for who can forecast the future or foresee the course of events in our people's history distinguished for its unpredictability—will find a welcoming home there. But it is clear that the majority of the Jewish people will, in the foreseeable future, live outside the borders of Israel, and the majority of these will live in the United States. These Jews will continue in the future as in the past to be loyal and patriotic citizens and to participate fully and eagerly in the total life of their country. But the problem and the duty of preserving Judaism, the faith of our fathers, and the great traditions of our people which were moulded both inside and outside of Palestine through the long centuries will remain the challenge and the opportunity of the Jewish people everywhere—here, in Israel, and throughout the world. To see all this clearly is to serve the best interests of the State of Israel, the Jewish communities of the world and of Judaism.

[...]

I am afraid that many of our people have turned to Liberal Judaism not for the maximum challenge which it offers, but for the minimum demands which it makes—minimum education, minimum worship, minimum observances, few renunciations and fewer commitments. Most everything seems to be optional. The opinion is widespread that Liberal Judaism does not require of us ever to row against the tide. What-

ever is difficult may be abandoned. But convenience has never been the way of a conquering faith. Nor is it the way of spiritual growth nor yet of survival. A dynamic faith cannot be tucked away in a corner of one's life. If ones' [sic] religion is incidental, it is no religion at all.

I am afraid, too, that we have not made the synagogue central in our Jewish community life, which is today more secular than at any time in Jewish history. The synagogue is on the periphery, tolerated, at times even indulged, but the real diligent and central activity in our communal life has to do with charity and relief which, in themselves, are undoubtedly noble and necessary activities, but which in Jewish life were always looked upon as derivatives from a deeper source, as spokes radiating from a central hub which was always the synagogue and the religious school.

[...]

This House of Living Judaism which we are now dedicating is earnest of all these resolves. It is a banner raised high for a forward-moving, upward-mounting army of the faithful, advancing in the name of God, with a new hope in their hearts for the progress of man, the destiny of the people of Israel, and the salvation of mankind.

Source: MS 745, box 2, folder 1, AJA.

8.11—BETH SHOLOM SYNAGOGUE, DESIGNED BY FRANK LLOYD WRIGHT, ELKINS PARK, PENNSYLVANIA, 1953

In their new suburban environs, American Jews of the 1950s constructed synagogues whose architecture aligned with the styles that surrounded them. Leaders of Beth Sholom congregation, founded in 1918 within the city limits of Philadelphia but moved to suburban Elkins Park in 1951, enlisted the talents of one of the postwar era's most famed architects, Frank Lloyd Wright (1867–1959), to design their new synagogue building. Completed in September 1959, just five months after the death of its architect, Beth Sholom stands as Frank Lloyd Wright's only synagogue project. The American Institute of Architects determined the synagogue building to be one of Wright's best works.

Source: Synagogue Architecture nearprint file, AJA.

8.12—IMAGE FROM THE AMERICAN JEWISH TERCENTENARY FILMSTRIP, UNION OF AMERICAN HEBREW CONGREGATIONS, 1954

The year 1954 marked the tercentenary of American Jewish life, which had begun with the arrival of Jews to Dutch colonial New Amsterdam from Recife, Brazil, in 1654. To commemorate the milestone, Jewish organizations across the country staged events, promoted educational opportunities, and sought to capitalize on the anniversary to strengthen Jewish identity and demonstrate the inherent symmetry between Judaism and American life. The Reform movement's synagogue arm, the Union of American Hebrew Congregations, produced a filmstrip with images of American Jews over the centuries. A close examination reveals the depiction of Jews as pilgrims, as Founding Fathers, and as westerners. Yet none of the images show any distinctive Jewish dress—a reflection of the assimilationist religious tendencies of early postwar Reform Jews.

Source: PC-116, AJA.

8.13—MENACHEM SCHNEERSON, "IN ORTHODOXY THE WOMAN IS NOT INFERIOR," MAY 27, 1957

On January 17, 1951 (10 Shevat 5711), Menachem Mendel Schneerson (1902–1994) formally accepted the leadership of Chabad-Lubavitch, a Hasidic sect of Judaism with origins in late eighteenth-century Eastern Europe. Menachem Mendel was the son-in-law of Chabad's sixth "Rebbe" (Yiddish for "rabbi"), Yosef Yitzchak Schneerson (1880–1950), who had died the previous year. As a result of the Nazi upheaval, the Lubavitch court relocated to Brooklyn in 1940. The new Rebbe would transform the entire character of Chabad by calling for a much broader conceptualization of educational shlichut *(Jewish outreach). The* shlichut *he envisioned involved an ambitious program that would transform Chabad into*

what historian Jonathan D. Sarna has called "the most successful Jewish religious story of the post–World War II era." By focusing specifically on nonobservant or less observant Jews, including those who had assimilated almost completely, and by welcoming them into Jewish life and introducing them to traditional ritual observance, Schneerson inspired the development of a national, and then international, system of emissaries (shlichim) *who were implacably committed to increasing commitment to traditional Jewish practice and belief. Schneerson promoted his missionary program with a verse from Genesis (28:14): "Ufaratzta yamah va-kedmah ve-tsafonah va-negbah" (And you shall spread forth to the west, to the east, to the north, and to the south). The results have been astounding. In pursuit of Schneerson's vision, Chabad has creatively appropriated aspects of modern American culture to further its own objectives. Women, for example, played an important role in the new Rebbe's battle against Jewish assimilation. In contrast to the long-standing Orthodox custom of reserving high-level Torah learning for men and boys only, Schneerson insisted that men and women were equally obligated to study Torah and Hasidic teachings. Women also played a vital role in Chabad's ambitious new program of educational outreach.*

As the first document to follow demonstrates, Schneerson, in 1957, defended traditional Judaism's attitude toward women from its critics. Two years later, as Chabad expanded its outreach efforts in Israel, the Rebbe used the occasion to underscore his desire to have both genders involved in shlichut. Once again, he stressed the mitzvah of "ufaratzta," a slogan that had become synonymous with Chabad's dynamic new mission and radiated throughout the world from its postwar Brooklyn headquarters.

As for the remarks that were made to you in respect of the place of the Jewish woman in Jewish life that it was "undemocratic," etc.—needless to say such charges are absurd.

The attitude of the Torah in so far as the place of the Jewish woman is concerned is clear. Suffice it to quote our Sages on the duty of the husband to respect his wife more than himself . . .

And another: When G-d was about to give His Torah to the Jewish people, the Torah which is the very life and existence of our people, He told Moses to approach the women first, as our Rabbis commented: "Thus shalt thou say to the 'house of Jacob'—i.e. the women—and (then) tell the children of Israel—the men."

The charges that the Jewish woman is placed in an "inferior" category are claimed to be based on the fact that the Jewish woman is relieved of those Mitzvoth [obligations] which have a time-element. This is nothing but a complete misunderstanding of the real issue. To mention but one explanation: Everything in the world has its specific functions and purposes. For example, the brain and heart are the two most vital organs in the human body. Would it make sense to say that the brain is inferior to the heart, because the former lacks emotional quality; or the brain is superior to the heart, because the latter lacks the power of reasoning? It is precisely upon the proper functioning of each that the existence of the organism is dependent.

Similarly, man and woman, each has a specific function to fulfill. The woman's function is to be a mother and to care for, and bring up the infants, when they require the mother's utmost attention. Hence, G-d has freed her from certain obligations which He has imposed on the man. What is not less important is the woman's duty to take care of the household and create the right Jewish atmosphere, etc. Thus, it is for reasons of priority rather than her inferiority that the Jewish woman has been relieved from certain Mitzvoth, which are connected with a time-element, so that they would not interfere with her vital specific functions.

As for the argument that a woman is deemed legally unfit in cases of evidence and certain other legal matters—the explanation is to be found in the fact (which is a necessary result of the above matter) that a woman has been gifted with an extra measure of natural emotion, for having to take care of infants and children in their early years requires extraordinary love, patience and softness of character. But an overly measure of emotionalism is a hindrance in legal matters, where strict and completely impartial judgment and reason are of essence. Therefore, as the Torah deals with average persons, and the average woman is obviously more emotional, the woman had to be disqualified from judgeship and similar legal matters, which have been placed on the shoulders of the man, who is less emotional and can be more objective. Clearly, there is no reflection here on the woman, as in the case of an analogy from the brain and heart, mentioned above.

Needless to say, that there are women who are more rational than men, and men who are more emotional than women. But, obviously, when the Torah lays down the Law, it must be based on the majority and average, not on the exception, or it would not be practicable.

It is difficult to enlarge in a letter on such matters, but I trust that the above principles will suffice to refute the baseless charges, and you will be able to find many more points in support of the truth that G-d's Law is perfect, and the ways of the Torah are pleasant and peace-full.

Wishing you success in strengthening Yiddishkeit [traditional Jewish life] and disseminating its practice and observance, and wishing you also a kosher and happy Pesach.

With blessing,

Menachem Schneerson

Source: As printed in *JAW*, 441–43. From *Illustrated Bulletin of the Second National Convention of the Agudas Neshei Ubenois Chabad of the United States and Canada, 26th of Iyar, 5717* (Brooklyn: n.p., 1958), 6–7. Reprinted with permission of the Central Organization for Jewish Education.

8.14—"UFARATZTA!" A PROGRAMMATIC STATEMENT DELIVERED BY THE LUBAVITCHER REBBE, MENACHEM M. SCHNEERSON, 1959

"Ufaratzta yamah va-kedmah ve-tsafonah va-negbah" (And you shall spread forth to the west, to the east, to the north, and to the south) (Genesis 28:14):

A timeless slogan was promulgated a few months ago by the leader of our generation through the scriptural passage: "And you shall spread forth to the west, to the east, to the north, and to the south." And the inner meaning of this verse is to disseminate the wellsprings, meaning [to disseminate] all that pertains to Torah and mitzvot so as to fulfill [the biblical injunction] and its promise: "And you shall spread forth . . ."

And it is for this reason that the Chabad Hasidim throughout the world have internalized the meaning of this slogan and intensified their efforts to disseminate the wellsprings [viz., Torah and mitzvot] by broadening the reach of authentically Jewish educational institutions and strengthening Judaism in every way they can.

This enhanced activity became particularly prominent in our Holy Land [Israel] through the expansion of educational institutions for the boys and for girls within the [educational] network known as "Ohelei Yosef Yitzchak" [the Chabad school system], which were established throughout the world in [honor of] the Rebbe Yosef Yitzchak Schneerson, the [sixth] Lubavitcher [Rebbe]. . . .

In accordance with the instruction given by the leader of our generation, groups of male and female teachers from the Chabad community left their homes and places of work, and assumed responsibility for teaching and administering in educational institutions that enrolled hundreds of boy and girl students. . . .

The youth of the Chabad Hasidim in the United States of America came together in the Rebbe's Bet Midrash in Brooklyn [770 Eastern Parkway] for a farewell party . . . on the ninth day of Elul (August 25), 1958. The Rebbe graciously took part in this gathering and delivered a special talk for those who were heading off to the Holy Land, which we are publishing for you now (in [a Hebrew] translation from the [original] Yiddish). This holy talk [to follow] created a deep impression among those who had assembled, and many subsequently volunteered to participate in the [Rebbe's] holy mission, which engendered a spirit of admiration throughout the [Chabad] community:

1. The *shaliach*'s [emissary's] mission in our Holy Land is to act both personally and, also, to instill this same spirit of action within others so that (in addition to the virtue that is already present) in the mission of *schlichut* [outreach] he will teach pure holiness in the educational institutions that have been named after the [the sixth] Rebbe, which is the primary reason we have gathered together . . .

4. When [the *shaliach*] experiences the inner feeling that this is the mission of the Rebbe, it will become clear to him that [this undertaking] is for his own spiritual and material good, and he will do [this mission] joyfully and with a willing heart. And it is up to the [*shaliach*] to arouse this very same feeling in those whom he will find in the place to which he is being sent. . . .

There is a need to act—not because of the benefit that will come to [the *shaliach*] nor because of any reward that he will receive, but because it is the fulfillment of [the biblical teaching] "*bakshu panai*" [to seek the face of God—cf. Psalms 27:8]. And in acting for this purpose, it is certain that he will meet with both material and spiritual success; indeed [the *shaliach* will be successful] in both the public as well as the private realms. . . .

8. The *shaliach* will take all of these concepts in their totality with him, he will bring them to [his destination] in their totality, and he will put all of them into practice among those to whom he has been sent. Let [these *shlichim*] go wherever they are needed with diligence, joyously and with a willing heart because that is the will of the one who has sent them. As said before, [the *shlichim*] must act not to receive a reward, but because this [endeavor] will benefit them by bringing them true happiness both in the material and spiritual realms. . . .

11. With regard to our entire topic, concerning [*shlichut* to] the educational institutions, there are those who might set the conditions and select the places that are close to where we dwell—places wherein there is already a God-fearing spirit. To this we say: when there is a possibility of taking action in a faraway place and in a materially and spiritually remote corner [of the world], then there is a genuine opportunity to fulfill the mitzvah of "*hakeym takim*" [you must help to lift . . . —cf. Deuteronomy 22:4]. Not only is it forbidden that [the fulfillment of this mitzvah in remote locations] be lacking in diligence and joy, but to the contrary, [carrying *shlichut* to remote locations] will actually strengthen the diligence and the joy [that come through the fulfillment of this mitzvah]. . . .

12. Therefore, it should be clear that all we have thus far said applies not only to the education of boys but also to the education of the girls; it applies not only to the male teachers but also to the female teachers. As a matter of fact, [that which has been said] applies to the women even more than it does to the men, with more diligence, with more vitality.

13. May it be God's will that the *shaliach* will undertake [to fulfill] every aspect of *shlichut* completely in bringing [*shlichut*] to our Holy Land, and may it also be that "words that come from the heart will enter the heart" [a famous expression in *Shirat Yisrael* often attributed to Moses ibn Ezra] of all who are listening, and influence the young yeshiva students—the male and female teachers alike—so that every single one of them will act with diligence, with vitality and with joy to bring God's word to any place they are assigned. . . . And this will bring ample success to their own personal efforts as well as God's rewards, in like measure, yet multiplied over and over, in [their homes and family life]. . . .

Source: Excerpts from *Bitaon*, no. 19 (10th of Shevat 5719/January 19, 1959): 30–36. Translation of Hebrew text by Margalit Tal.

8.15—RABBI MENACHEM M. SCHNEERSON, "LETTER ON THE QUESTION OF PRAYER IN THE PUBLIC SCHOOLS," 1964

In the postwar years, American Jews approached the constitutional question of church-state separation in sometimes surprising ways. Most American Jews were politically liberal and tended to vote Democratic, a pattern established by the 1928 presidential election, if not even earlier, by left-leaning Eastern European Jews. As immigrant Jews and their children acculturated to American life in the early decades of the twentieth century, they saw that public schools were critically important to their economic and social mobility. Yet when postwar Jews entered suburban schools, they would sometimes encounter the recitation of religious prayers as part of the school day. Most Jewish organizations embarked on campaigns to halt the practice, calling it a violation of the U.S. Constitution and a threat to Jewish students. In many districts, though, there were Jewish parents who embraced Christian practices in the school setting, arguing that their children should know and understand Christian America and that inclusion in such activities reflected a growing acceptance of Jews in suburban American life. In addition, some within the American Orthodox Jewish community supported the recitation of prayer in public schools because they viewed it as an opportunity to promote the students' belief in God. In 1964, Chabad Rebbe Menachem Mendel Schneerson offered his perspective on this salient issue.

By the Grace of G-d
26th of Nissan [April 8], 5724
Brooklyn, N.Y.

Greeting and Blessing:

. . . In reply to your inquiry as to whether or not there has been a change in my views on the question of prayer in the public schools, inasmuch as this issue has again become a topic of the day in connection with congressional efforts to introduce a constitutional amendment to permit certain religious exercises in the public schools,

Let me assure you at once that my views, as outlined in my letter of the 24th of Cheshvan, 5723 [November 21, 1962], have not changed. As I stated then, my views are firmly anchored in the Torah, *Torath Chayim* [the living Torah]. Their validity could therefore not have been affected by the passing of time. On the contrary, if there could have been any change at all, it was to reinforce my conviction of the vital need that the children in the public schools should be allowed to begin their day at school with the recitation of a non-denominational prayer, acknowledging the existence of a Creator and Master of the Universe, and our dependence upon Him. In my opinion, this acknowledgment is absolutely necessary in order to impress upon the minds of our growing-up generation that the world in which they live is not a jungle, where brute force, cunning and unbridled passion rule supreme, but that it has a Master Who is not an abstraction, but a personal G-d; that this Supreme Being takes a "personal interest" in the affairs of each and every individual, and to Him everyone is accountable for one's daily conduct.

[. . .]

Children have to be "trained" from their earliest youth to be constantly aware of "the Eye that seeth and the Ear that heareth." We cannot leave it to the law-*enforcing* agencies to be the keepers of the ethics and morals of our young generation. The boy or girl who has embarked upon a course of truancy will not be intimidated by the policeman, teacher or parent, whom he or she thinks fair game to "outsmart." Furthermore, the crux of the problem lies in the success or failure of bringing up the children to an awareness of a Supreme Authority, Who is not only to be feared, but also loved. Under existing conditions in this country, a daily prayer in the public schools is for a *vast* number of boys and girls the *only* opportunity of cultivating such an awareness.

On the other hand, as I have emphasized on more than one occasion, only a *strictly non-denominational* prayer, and no other, should be introduced into the public schools. Any denominational prayer or religious exercise in the public schools must be resolutely opposed on various grounds, including also the fact that these would create divisiveness and ill-feeling. Likewise must Bible reading in the public schools be resolutely opposed for various reasons, including the obvious reason that the reading of the Koran and the New Testament will arouse dissension and strife. Moreover, the essential objective is a religious expression that would cultivate reverence and love for G-d, and this can best be accomplished by prayer, while Bible reading is not so important in this instance.

During the time that has elapsed since my previous letter on this subject was published, my attention was called to several objections which have been voiced by opponents to my views. I will take this opportunity to explain here, within the limitations of a letter, why these objections have not convinced me to change my position on this vital issue.

1. It has been argued that the child attending public school is in the category of a "captive," since his refusal to participate in a prayer would "stigmatize" him. His participation would therefore be involuntary and an encroachment on his freedom.

In my opinion, the notion of "captivity" as applied in this case should lead to a conclusion which is quite the reverse, for the following reasons:

The child attending public school knows that his attendance is compulsory, because his parents and the government consider his education of the utmost importance. Together with this comes the recognition that what is really important and essential to his education is taken care of in the school. The child's instinctive feeling and inference from this is that anything that is not included in the school curriculum is of secondary importance if, indeed, of any importance at all. Hence, if religion (prayer) is excluded from the school, the child would inevitably regard it in the same category as an extra foreign language, or dancing, or music lessons, which are not required by the school but are left to the parents' free choice, and which the child, not illogically, considers a burden or even a nuisance. In other words, the present system of the public school education is such that it *impresses* upon the pupil the belief that everything connected with religion, such as knowledge of G-d's existence, etc., is of little consequence, or of no importance whatever.

It will neither interest nor impress the child if he were told that the exclusion of prayer from the school is due to the principle of the separation of State and Church, or to a constitutional technicality. These reasons or explanations, even if they be actually conveyed to the child from time to time, will not nearly impress him as much as the plain fact itself, which reasserts itself *each and every day*, that nothing can be very important to his education if it is not included in the school program. Such a situation can only reinforce the child's attitude of indifference, or even disdain, to any religious beliefs.

[. . .]

2. To oppose non-denominational prayer "on constitutional grounds" is, in my opinion, altogether a misunderstanding or misrepresentation of the problem.

The issue is: Whether a non-denominational prayer wherewith to inaugurate the school day is, or is not, in the best interests of the children. If the answer is "yes," then obviously it should be made constitutional, for there can be no difference of opinion as to the fact that the Constitution has been created to serve the people, not vice versa.

[. . .]

3. It is argued that the principle of separation of Church and State is the only safeguard for freedom of religion, equal rights for minorities, etc.

Without going into the question whether there actually exists a strict separation between State and Church in this country (for there are undeniable facts to the contrary, e.g. the institution of Chaplaincy in the armed forces; the opening of Congress with a prayer; the motto "In G-d we trust" on American currency, the emphasis on Divine Providence in the Declaration of Independence; etc., etc.), I submit that the validity of the argument is contingent upon the question *who is behind* this principle, and how is it to be interpreted and applied? Suffice it to cite an illustration from two representative States now in existence, in one of which the said principle is in full operational force, while in the other it is not. In the first, as the *daily* press reports, there is a calculated war on religion and religious practices, with the suppression of *all* religious freedom, etc. Incidentally (and perhaps it is quite relevant to our discussion), it all started there [in the Soviet Union] with a ban on religious instruction to young children. In other countries, for example England, there is no separation of Church and State, there is religious instruction in the public schools, yet you find there *complete religious freedom* for *all* religious denominations.

4. Some argue further that the principle of separation of State and Church must be maintained at all costs, in order to prevent a resurgence of religious persecution so prevalent in the Middle Ages, when an established state-religion denied equal, or any, rights to other religions, etc. The fallacy of this argument should be quite obvious. By way of illustration: Suppose a person was ill at one time and doctors prescribed certain medication and treatment. Suppose that years later the same person became ill again, but with an entirely different, in fact quite *contrary*, malady. Would it be reasonable to recommend the same medication and treatment as formerly?

[. . .]

5. It has also been argued that if a non-denominational prayer were permitted and left to the discretion of every school board in the country, this practice could lead to abuse.

I do not consider this a valid argument. Firstly, we are talking here about a strictly *non-denominational* prayer, and agreement should not be difficult on this point. Nor could there be room for any undercover abuse, since the prayer would be recited openly in the school. Besides, a proviso could be made which would require the unanimous approval by the representatives of religious denominations before the particular non-denominational prayer is introduced into the school. Moreover, there is no need to compose new non-denominational prayers, as there are already such.

6. The argument that a short non-denominational prayer would have no effect on the child reciting it, could not be considered as a serious argument by anyone who has knowledge or experience in child education. On the contrary, the fact that prayer will be recited in the school and classroom, and day after day, will *inevitably* become an integral part of the child's thinking and is bound to be a factor which could be further cultivated to the child's advantage in terms of spiritual and psychological development.

[. . .]

Certainly a non-denominational prayer in the public schools will not, in itself, provide an adequate basis for the right and complete world-outlook, but it is an *indispensable first step* in this direction, considering the state of our society as it is *at present*, and as it is likely to remain for quite a long time, insofar as it can be judged from the prevailing conditions and factors.

With blessing
Menachem Mendel Schneerson

P.S. Not being a politician, I did not wish to include in the body of the letter the remarks that follow hereunder, which have to do not with principles but with method and good policy. However, as a citizen who has taken a keen interest in the issue and its repercussions, I cannot refrain from making the following observations:

a. The vehement opposition to any kind of prayer and to the mention of G-d's Name in the public schools, which, in my opinion, is unjustified and ill-conceived, and which has placed the proponents of this view in league with the atheistic and anti-religious elements in this country, has inevitably called forth a correspondingly strong counter reaction. As a result, we are now faced with a concerted effort to introduce a constitutional amendment which would permit sectarian prayers and Bible readings in the public schools. I am convinced that had there been taken a more practical position in the first place, it would have been possible to bring about a peaceful solution of the controversy on the basis of a non-denominational prayer which would have been acceptable to everybody (except a few fanatical anti-religionists), since such a prayer would be voluntary, and any conscientious objector would be excused from participating in it. . . .

Source: SC-1011 ("Bible Reading in the Public Schools"), AJA.

8.16—MRS. ALLEN I. EDLES, SELECTION FROM "THE AMERICAN JEWISH WOMAN OF TOMORROW," 1958

Even as the postwar years brought dramatic change for suburban non-Orthodox Jews, this period also hastened new approaches to Orthodox Jewish life in urban environments. When Yeshiva University opened its Rabbi Isaac Elchanan Theological Seminary in 1928, it did not include a course of study for women. Later, in 1954, YU opened the Stern College for Women, also in New York City, offering a Jewish and secular education to observant Jewish women. In 1958, on the occasion of the college's first graduating class, Helen Hurowitz Edles (1914–2002), the national president of the women's branch of the Union of Orthodox Jewish Congregations, offered an address reflecting on the role of Jewish women in postwar America.

Never before in history have women been given such opportunity to assume leadership, and color the destiny of future generations of the American Jewish community. Never before have women risen so admirably to the occasion.

Women have emerged from their places in the kitchen, to their rightful places beside their fathers, brothers, husbands, and indeed, their sons. The past three decades have witnessed the opening of newer and wider avenues of education for women. The bedrock reality is that the world has finally recognized the immense influences exerted by women in the past. We have every reason to believe these influences will become even more intensive and extensive.

History is the inventory of human experiences, and who can gainsay that women have been an integral part of that history, having felt the pains of progress equally? These experiences have necessarily served as the proving grounds for living, living in this great complex web called "world." And so, through the ages, the participation of women in every phase of endeavor presents a balanced picture today, not one of unrealistic fantasy.

A woman no longer lives a passive existence, content merely to nod in assent to situations that affect her vitally; her voice is heard from every direction. Not only has she pursued the classic professions as law, medicine, education, and politics, but has valiantly pioneered in the newer professions including the specialized areas of medicine, as psychiatry, etc. There were many contributing factors to this so-called "coming of age," not the least important of which is the mechanized kitchen and prepared foods. This innovation has afforded the distaff side leisure time for use in furthering her education and increasing her skills. The result has produced a unique effort [*sic*] on present-day society. Women have produced a magnetic influence in many areas of living by their perception and innate abilities to coordinate efforts into useful and meaningful action. They encourage positive endeavors and gracefully accept challenges presented to them.

What does all this add up to? How impressive are these facts in relation to the future of the American woman? To me, this spells out continued development and intensified education for a far greater segment of women. Stern College [of Yeshiva University] is a cogent force in fostering and encouraging that development. Stern College represents foresight, courage, talent, generosity, and hard work. It now stands on the threshold of far-reaching successes through the training of its students, who will find their ultimate paths leading them to diverse parts of the world. These graduates will take with them the reinforced religious patterns strengthened at Stern College.

Heretofore, women's opinions were barely tolerated; today our enlightened society not only accepts, but invites comments and opinions from women. This is further encouragement to those reticent females who feared to tread in fields overrun and monopolized by males; those retarded females who subscribed to the theory that women should not and cannot compete with men. They even stressed the risks involved. These were our timid sisters who are now gleaning new strength from the successes of their more courageous co-workers. These over-cautious ones have now realized that the risks of inaction are infinitely greater.

Today, 6 out of 10 married women are gainfully employed. This is our barometer for tomorrow. Women have learned the art of balancing their home lives proportionately with their business or professional lives. Their homes are happier and their families have fuller lives because of the wider experience of the mother, who has ceased to live in a vacuum. Because of these extended opportunities for women, security has evolved into a family project, and is no longer a one-man job. Despite all this, we women do not seek to supplant the man's position, merely to supplement it.

Source: As printed in *JAW*, 455–56. From Mrs. Allen I. Edles, "America's Leaders Look at Woman's Role Today," commencement address, Yeshiva University, New York, 1958. Used with permission.

8.17—BESS MYERSON, "MISS AMERICA SPEAKS TO YOUNG AMERICA,"
Jewish Veteran, 1945

The acculturation of American Jews over the first half of the twentieth century centered largely on business, and then educational, success. In the postwar years, American Jews enjoyed the opportunity to expand their interests into arenas of American popular culture once off-limits to them. For Bess Myerson (b. 1924), such an opportunity arrived early. In 1945, she became the first Jewish contestant to win the Miss America beauty pageant. Myerson's victory announced that the nation was willing to acknowledge a Jew as its representation of an idealized woman. In a 1945 article in the Jewish Veteran, *Myerson reflected on her experience.*

Being chosen Miss America of 1945 has meant more to me than winning the beauty contest in Atlantic City. Perhaps, for the first time, I have come to realize what a wonderful thing democracy is.

I had never given much thought to democracy, but like most people, I had taken it for granted. Here was I—an ordinary girl who lives in the Bronx—setting out on an adventure which every girl dreams about—being selected by a group of judges as representing all of American womanhood. Naturally, no one in my family, least of all I, expected that I would be No. 1 among the best that the land had to offer.

[. . .]

When I came to Atlantic City I found that my concept of what Miss America of 1945 should be like was entirely changed. I expected to find that all of these girls would just be beautiful, perhaps show girls or night club entertainers. But let me tell you something about some of those girls. Twenty out of 40 girls were college students. They knew the score and they could talk intelligently on most of the important current issues. They

knew a lot about what the war was being fought for and a great majority of them could tell all of us about the things that matter and the things that don't.

And one of the things that didn't matter, at least the thing that stood out in my mind, was that nobody cared about your religion or your ancestry, or whether your parents spoke with an accent. It seemed so unimportant at the time. And after living with those girls for days, I began to think of some of the things they said and some of the things they really believed in. And now that I have been chosen Miss America, I realize more than ever, the tremendous responsibility I now have in representing American womanhood.

First of all, I became a representative of my generation—the way we dress, act and think. Let's not underestimate the importance of the way we think, because the way we think is the way we are going to treat our neighbors—yours and mine. I feel it a much greater compliment when somebody says about me, "Isn't she sweet and sincere?" than when someone says, "Isn't she beautiful?" because I represent the American woman. Bear this in mind—I wasn't chosen as the most beautiful girl in the United States.

Speaking of beauty, let me relate some of my experiences when down in Atlantic City for the contest. This may sound like vanity but please don't interpret it as such. I feel that I have become much more beautiful, not because I hold the title today, but because I have become a better American out of my experiences. Being Miss America has naturally opened the door to adventures which I would never have experienced. It has given me a better understanding of women around the country, whether they be Negro or Protestant or Catholic or Jewish.

[...]

The scholarship offered in Atlantic City was one of the most discussed subjects between my roommate at the contest—Miss Birmingham and me. She was taking singing lessons and she kept repeating that if she won, she would get the best music teacher in America. And I equally told her, although I had my tongue in my cheek at the time, that I would use the money to continue my piano and flute lessons.

When we weren't talking about music, we were discussing prejudice, and since she came from the South, she confided that she couldn't quite understand the reasons for such intolerance on the part of different groups in the area from which she came.

"It is so matter-of-fact," she said, "that people in the South accept discrimination, and this discrimination passes from one generation to another." She admitted that she found such a lack of sincere understanding in those people who considered themselves superior; and the more I think of it, the more I have come to realize that hate is a corroding disease which affects everything you do. It will show up in your work, in your personality, in your appearance. It will warp your soul. Prejudice is out of date.

If you're going to question a person's religion or color before you like him, you'll find that your views will become distorted and your thoughts and your actions will be reflected in your face.

I had never done any serious thinking about this subject until I went through some of the hospitals. And when I saw a Negro boy lying next to a white, and a Jewish boy among Gentiles, and all of them accepted as buddies, I kept asking myself over and over again—If these boys fought and bled together, why couldn't all of them live together? Why did there have to be such a tremendous experience to make them realize that they were dependent on each other?

These experiences have made me more anxious to go on and do more and learn more. Learning to live together—that's our job. It is a challenge which we must meet every day.

Source: Bess Myerson nearprint file, AJA.

8.18—SELECTION FROM "A STATEMENT BY STEPHEN S. WISE TO A U.S. SENATE EDUCATION SUB-COMMITTEE," APRIL 1947

At the end of World War II, the federal government initiated a massive program to fund public education. While responsibility for public education belongs to each of the individual states, the Cold War encouraged Congress to augment state funding so that the United States could better compete against the communist superpower. The organized Jewish community supported these efforts, convinced that a strong public education system would benefit American Jews as well as the nation at large. Yet on an April 1947 lobbying venture to Washington, D.C., in support of government funding for public schools, Rabbi Stephen S. Wise, then head of the American Jewish Congress, experienced the complexities involved with greater federal funding. Southern senators feared that the new education windfall would come with strings attached—challenges to the system of racial segregation in southern schools. When these southern senators threatened a

filibuster unless the legislation promised not to interfere with segregated schools, Wise found himself in the middle of a basic civil rights question: do separate educational facilities offer an equal education to African Americans? Wise's response offered a tacit defense of the 1896 Plessy v. Ferguson *case, which gave legal sanction to racial segregation.*

"A segregated system is not merely an unfair system but it is a wasteful and inefficient system. Nevertheless, we do not believe that a federal law to equalize educational opportunities by public subsidy should be used as means to attack the segregated school system. So long as the law guarantees that States having segregated school systems do not discriminate financially against children in the minority schools, we believe that the bill should be supported."

Source: Papers of Stephen S. Wise, box 64, AJHS.

8.19—RABBI JULIAN B. FEIBELMAN, "PETITION TO THE ORLEANS PARISH SCHOOL BOARD," SEPTEMBER 12, 1955

For southern Jews, the civil rights movement pitted the ethical imperatives of racial equality against the economic, social, and even physical safety of a Jewish minority in the white South. While some native-born southern Jews offered public support for segregation, a far greater number opted for quiet, behind-the-scenes civil rights work intended to bring gradual change. Rabbi Julian B. Feibelman (1904–1980), a Mississippi native serving a Reform congregation in New Orleans, emerged in the

1950s as one of the few rabbis willing to take a public stand in favor of civil rights. In 1955, he organized a petition drive to pressure the local school district to comply with the Supreme Court's 1954 Brown v. Board of Education *decision to desegregate schools. His comments to the board of education are included as follows.*

Petition to the Orleans Parish School Board
September 12, 1955

(Preliminary remarks by Rabbi Julian B. Feibelman)

Mr. President and Members of the Board of Education of Orleans Parish:

First of all, and in behalf of my friends and colleagues, I wish to thank you for the privilege of appearing before you this evening.

I shall present to you a petition, signed by at least 180 citizens of New Orleans. This petition represents our feeling and studied position on the delicate and moot question of segregation in our public schools. The burden of this petition is to ask you to study and to evolve a plan, which will, in the fairest and most comprehensive way, show a positive attitude to the recent decision of the Supreme Court of the United States in re the question of segregation in our public schools.

In no sense do we come before you in a militant or antagonistic attitude. We are positive that you are as deeply concerned with this question as we are. We take for granted that you are anxious to perform your official duty and to live up to the high requirements of your responsible office. You are also aware, as are we, that there are always inevitable usual differences of opinions, and extremes of conviction, by which all serious issues are met, and, that in due democratic process, usually resolved.

Even so, certain statements have been forthcoming by representatives of the School Board and certain action already taken which in no wise can be said to have taken into consideration all the segments of our community. Nor have the normal differences involved been considered in even a consultative manner—so far as we know.

There has appeared in the local press a report that the School Board has engaged an attorney at a stipulated compensation of $25,000 per annum and $150.00 per diem if the attorney must function out of the city, for the specific purpose of defending the School Board in its position on segregation.

Some of us feel that this is a usuage [sic] of the tax payers money designated to circumvent and defy the law, as now written in the decision of the Supreme Court of the United States in the matter of segregation. In this sense it would appear to be a mis-usage of public monies.

Our primary purpose however is to urge you gentlemen of the School Board to face the issue of segregation in a more realistic sense than that which would specifically imply your determination to defy it or to ignore both its existence and its validity.

We are quite aware, as well as deeply conscious, of the vast implications which make up the component parts of this issue. We know that in heavy [sic] populated mixed racial areas, such as our community and State represent, that there is no single road to the solution of this problem. Its ramifications stretch into every category of our social, economic, spiritual and moral relations.

However, as conscious as we are of these difficulties, we are also aware of the fact that many states have gone seriously to work to overcome the problem, to begin to iron out the differences, and at least to evidence the fact that they are aware that the law exists and must be carried out. Respect for the law would warrant the further study we ask you to make.

It is no mark of pride to us that our State is one of the five remaining of the forty-eight which defiantly would protect the status quo without so much as formulating a plan to integrate or desegregate, and to face this living issue with a positive attitude determined to solve instead of to defy.

There are many plans now satisfactorily working in other States to the best interest of all, and in compliance with the law.

Nor need we inform intelligent men and worthy public-spirited servants that there is too much at stake for our City and State merely to close its eyes, harden its heart and ostrich-like pretend that no such issue faces us.

We have all seen what has happened in the state of Mississippi, where men stubbornly refused to believe that the world has moved forward and that all children, black and white, are the children of God. The entire Nation has been aroused by the wanton act of disregard for law and order [likely a reference to the social and political unrest that preceded the August 1956 decision by the New Orleans archdiocese to postpone integration in the public schools]. Fortunately, that State is endeavoring to restore the due process of law. Unfortunately it cannot restore the life which has been sacrificed on the false altar of prejudice, hatred, and unforgivable violence.

We are chagrined to call attention to the fact that children applying for admission into our schools in New Orleans today must present a notarized statement that they are white. This would hardly appear, in the light of the proud history of public education, which is one of the keystones in the American Republic, to be consistent with a democratic spirit or even of a humane policy. Such a practice we have never countenanced before, and to be brutally frank, we are ashamed to add that it now prevails in New Orleans.

Reducing the issue to its basic elements, we must admit that when the highest law of the land is pronounced in unanimous decision, the compliance and obedience of the people, the State and most positively the officials of the State, is implicit in such decisions. Certainly, it is no man's, nor any official's prerogative to offer defiant resistence [sic]. Such resistance is equivalent to anarchy and anarchy inevitably leads to violence and horror—to say nothing of the bad example it sets.

I do not feel that I am overstating the case nor do we wish it to be under-estimated by men in such responsible positions as you hold.

There is a segment of our community—we have no way of knowing what proportion it represents—who definitely feel that neither you nor ourselves can close our eyes nor harden our hearts to the basic principles involved. We represent only ourselves. We are not an organization nor do we wish to become one. We know that you have had petitions presented to you before by responsible groups and it is our conviction that all such people, who are citizens of New Orleans, have not only a right to be heard but also that their earnest petition should be considered. This, we are happy and thankful to say, is a fundamental American principle.

Finally, when the School Board decides to act in accordance with the Supreme Court ruling, as I am certain the board will want to do in time, we want you to know that the board will have the support of at least the number of persons whose names are signed to this petition.

It is in this spirit, and with appreciation for the privilege of appearing before you, that I present now, in behalf of my colleagues, the following petition to which we have some 180 names attached.

Source: MS 94, box 29, folder 5, AJA.

8.20—RABBI JACOB ROTHSCHILD, "NO PLACE TO HIDE," *Southern Israelite*, AUGUST 1963

Rabbi Jacob Rothschild (1911–1973) of Atlanta's largest synagogue, the Hebrew Benevolent Congregation, better known as The Temple, emerged as another of the handful of southern rabbis willing to take a public stand against segregation and in support of the civil rights movement. Rothschild, a native of Pittsburgh, *completed his service as an army chaplain in World War II before moving to Atlanta in 1946. While his 1947 Rosh Hashanah sermon on racial injustice in the South announced his intention to use his rabbinate to fight for civil rights, it was not until the 1954* Brown *decision that Rothschild, as a member of several Atlanta*

*interfaith and interracial organizations, took
even stronger public stands. Reflecting on
President Eisenhower's commitment to civil
rights in 1957, Rothschild offered his thoughts
on the relationship between legal change
and social change. On October 12, 1958, his
synagogue endured a bombing, which he
attributed, in part, to his willingness to make
civil rights a high-profile issue.*

Since 1954, the tempo of the Negro's march
toward equality has quickened, his demands
have become more insistent and his patience
less majestic. The foot-dragging reluctance of
the white majority to pay more than lip service
to the clearly stated principles of "one nation,
under God, with liberty and justice for all" has
forced him constantly to dramatize himself as
the object of injustice—lest otherwise his very
real second class status lie buried and conveniently forgotten.

No white American can evade any longer his
personal involvement in the Negro's struggle for
full citizenship. Indeed, he has already been involved by no act of his own: The law guarantees
equality—so he is involved as an American citizen. Every major religious organization has clearly
stated its moral commitment to equality—so he
is involved as Christian or Jew. It is in this latter
area that the Southern Jew finds himself most
discomfitted. How he wishes that Judaism didn't
really say that. Or, since it does, that his national
body or his own rabbi would stop reminding
non-Jews of the fact. To paraphrase an old joke
—doesn't he have enough tzores just being a
Jew! Yet deep down inside himself, he knows
what is right and what isn't. As a member of
a minority group who has long struggled for
equality for himself, he can empathize with the
members of another minority group. But still, he
is white, and he lives among a white majority
and, after all, there are local customs and he
can't stick his neck out—and, and, and . . .

So the Southern Jew—not only he, to be sure,
but still he more than all other decent, God-
fearing "moderates"—squirms and rationalizes.

Above all, he joins with his Christian friends
(whose religion has also compromised them with
uncompromising statements on the subject) in
seeking to separate religion from life itself. To do
so, he has maintained that the Negro drive for
equal rights falls into the area of politics—and
the synagogue ought to keep out of politics. Or,
he says that religion must eschew controversial
issues altogether. In recent days, however, he
himself seems to have become less enamored of
arguments such as these. They no longer sound
quite so convincing even to him. Perhaps the
stubborn importunings of his religious leaders
have begun to convince him that religion—
specifically Judaism—is involved. Perhaps the
recent National Conference on Religion and Race
helped him see the light. Perhaps even the open
acknowledgement on the part of some political
figures that we are indeed faced with a moral
crisis has helped him to change his mind.

Whatever the reasons, the Southern Jew
seems ready to admit that this is an area in
which religion cannot keep silent. Admittedly,
he is a Jew. Now, Judaism is involved. How, then,
can he escape that feeling of Southern exposure
that he wants so desperately to avoid? Well, he is
nothing if not "ingenious and ingenuous." He
has devised a new philosophy which he hopes
will provide him with the protective coloration
he so desperately seeks. He now takes the stand
that the struggle to achieve a desegregated society in America doesn't really involve him as a
Jew at all—it involves him only as an American!
This position must be reckoned as one of the
most startling pieces of evasion—and the most
potentially dangerous escape hatch he has yet
conjured up.

Does the Southern Jew really want to establish a dichotomy between his patriotism and his
religion? Is this what he really wants to say—the
Jew who has bitterly fought anyone who dares
accuse him of dual loyalty? Who has proclaimes
[*sic*] himself an "American of the Jewish faith"?
Who maintains—and rightly—that because he
is a good Jew he can become a better American?
Who with pride has asserted that the greatness

of American democracy rests upon the Judeo-Christian tradition, part of which he shares? And now in order to avoid embarrassment and discomfiture does he seriously intend to present this new and damaging self image?

For what is he saying? That there are two separate compartments of his life—one Jewish and the other American. That what concerns him in one area need not concern him in the other. That when his fellow-citizens look at him, they must distinguish between him as a Jew and him as an American. He would have them blame his Americanism if he does anything they don't like —and credit his Judaism when they are pleased. But what if they come to the opposite conclusion —as well they may?

No, my fellow Southern Jews—this way lies. We cannot—we dare not—make second class citizens out of ourselves just to ease the pain and anguish of a given moment in time. We can never separate our spiritual heritage from our place in the society which we have helped to create. Whatever involves us involves us as Americans who are Jews. We are involved because our religious heritage has led us to a concept of morality which democracy has taken as its own. That heritage had something to say—and we have always prided ourselves on that indisputable fact—in setting the standards of our republic. How then can we deny its involvement—and ours—when the tarnished ideals of that republic need repair and burnishing?

In this—as in every struggle which challenges the fulfillment of our American democracy—we are involved because we are citizens of a potentially noble land. And we are involved all the more because we are of that ancient people who first taught the world the concept of the fatherhood of God and the brotherhood of man. We cannot escape our heritage as American Jews.

Source: Jacob Rothschild nearprint file, AJA.

8.21—RABBI WILLIAM MALEV, "THE JEW OF THE SOUTH IN THE CONFLICT ON SEGREGATION," *Conservative Judaism,* 1958

In contrast to Rabbi Rothschild of Atlanta, Rabbi William Malev (1898-1973), spiritual leader of Houston's largest Conservative synagogue, opposed the civil rights movement and considered it antithetical to Jewish interests as well as to Judaism, even though he professed to support integration. Malev, who immigrated to the United States from Russia at age ten, earned degrees from the City College of New York and the Jewish Theological Seminary before devoting his first twenty years of professional life to serving congregations in New York City. In 1946, he accepted the pulpit at Congregation Beth Yeshurun in Houston, where he emerged as a leading voice in American Zionism and the founder of the southwestern United States' first Jewish day school. Drawing from his perspective as a former New Yorker,

Malev published the following article in a 1958 edition of the journal Conservative Judaism.

The aim of this article is not to present an exhaustive study of the attitude of the Jewish community in the South in the segregation conflict. Nor do I intend to concentrate on its anti-Semitic overtones in recent months—such evidence of them as has been recorded in the well-known book by John Bartlow Martin, *The Deep South Says Never,* or in the bombing, or attempts at bombing, of Jewish synagogues and centers in Southern cities, in Gastonia, Charlotte, Miami, Jacksonville and Birmingham.

It is rather my hope to present a proposal which may prove helpful in this present crisis, and, perhaps, in the future similar emergencies, which may face our Jewish communities.

Before presenting my views on the strategy and methodology of the Jewish community in this critical issue, let me say that I do not intend to straddle the issue itself. I am, needless to say, on the side of integration. Morally and religiously it can be the only way of solving the problem ultimately and permanently. Judaism teaches— and upon that teaching our American tradition is based—that man was created in the image of God and that therefore all human beings are equal whatever their race, color or creed. They are entitled to the privileges and rights which our Constitution grants them.

American tradition teaches "that all men are created equal; that they have been endowed by their Creator with certain inalienable rights, that among these are life, liberty and the pursuit of happiness." This implies that every child in our country deserves the right to the best education available, without any discrimination because of race, or color or creed. That is my stand, and it leads inevitably to complete desegregation, not only in our school system but in every department of our public life.

My proposal is based upon the following premises:

1. The status of the conflict on this issue of segregation is different in each community, and it cannot be treated, therefore, according to one uniform pattern.

Thus one Rabbi writes: "In my community the Jews generally recognize the justice of de-segregation. There are a few who have expressed their fears of Jews speaking forth on the question, but no one has voiced any racial views whatsoever. I have spoken from the pulpit and have written letters to the Press; no one has criticized my views. On the contrary, I think most of our Jews concur." On the other hand, a Rabbi in Georgia writes that opinion in his congregation is divided, and some are definitely opposed to desegregation. In his community there are quite a number of Jews who are members of the White Citizens' Council. In such communities the rabbis have not spoken out, and to have done so would have been to invite resentment and an-

ti-Semitism, if not, indeed, violence towards the Jewish community.

Obviously, the strategy must be left to each individual community to work out at its own discretion and in accordance with the decision of the local people themselves.

2. To the non-Jew the Jews are not an ethnic minority, but representatives of one of the three great faiths of America. I need hardly add that that is the way we wish to be regarded. In many of our Southern communities where we constitute one or two percent of the population we would not count at all in any social issue were it not that we are looked upon religiously as one-third of the community, as one of the three great faiths. It isn't according to the size of our population but in our representative capacity that we count on the American scene.

3. When the Jew is represented by his spiritual leaders, he takes his place normally with the forces which make for social progress and liberal thought in every community.

Thus, for example, when the desegregation issue came up before the School Board in my own city of Houston, three clergymen were asked to speak on the issue—one Catholic priest, one Protestant minister and myself. Regardless of the fact that the Jews constitute less than 2% of the population of Houston, I was one of the three spokesmen of the spiritual forces of our city. Thus, also, both in the city of Houston and in Dallas when the ministers and the rabbis spoke out on the issue of segregation and law and order, it was expected and taken as the normal state of affairs in both of these communities. In Dallas, a few days later, a counter-statement for segregation was made by a number of ministers. It was not directed against the Jews, but against all religious leaders who were on the side of seg-regation [sic in the original, but it appears clear from the context that this should read "desegre-gation"]. The issue was not between the Jew and the non-Jew, not between one ethnic minority and the rest of the community, but between religious leaders of all faiths on one side, and those on the other side of the issue.

4. On the other hand the so-called "defense" organizations in Jewish life are an anomaly to the non-Jew. Whom do they represent? Are the Jews an ethnic group as well as a religious one? If so, who is properly their spokesman, the Anti-Defamation League or the rabbis of their communities? It is not to be wondered at that the Anti-Defamation League as the best represented "defense" group in the South and other such "defense" organizations are nasty words in Southern communities, considered in the same class with NAACP and even the Communist groups. The reason for this is that these other groups are also non-religious, but radical or ideological in character. The participation of our "defense" organizations, therefore, in the conflict on segregation is not an advantage but a liability to the Jewish communities in the South.

5. Most important, these so-called "defense" organizations do not command the respect that religious spokesmen usually do. Ordinarily, they come from the North, and speak, primarily, for a large Northern constituency. Since that is so, Southern Jews do not feel any particular pangs of conscience in threatening to secede from the Anti-Defamation League, especially when they speak with arrogance, looking down their noses at the backward and timid Southern Jews and sometimes commit blunders because of their incomplete knowledge of the situation.

[. . .]

While the Jew may secede from the ADL or the American Jewish Congress, he cannot, in the nature of things, secede from his religion. To that extent, the religious spokesmen of the Southern Jewish communities have an advantage which the Jewish "defense" organizations do not have. They have the sanction of the Jewish religion, and can cite with authority the religious traditions of our faith. Then, also, they are the representative [sic] of the local communities rather than emissaries from the distant North which in this struggle does not command the affection of Southern communities. These local Rabbis understand and sympathize with the tenor and caliber of their own Jewish communities and the general communities in which they live and can speak with due regard for local conditions and situations.

[. . .]

What would be my proposal?

a. First, I would suggest that national defense organizations in Jewish life abandon their unfortunate habit of beating the drum on every possible occasion. A high ranking official, for example, of one of them came to Houston some months ago and delivered a talk, the tenor of which was that Southern Jews should have more courage and face the enemies of desegregation without fear or timidity. The impression he left was that if the Jews had a little more fortitude, the entire issue of desegregation would be more readily and satisfactorily settled for the better. To add insult to injury, these spokesmen get considerable notice in the general press, and their words are not calculated to smooth the ruffled feelings of the non-Jewish community.

Indeed, the national "defense" organizations have gone far beyond their sponsorship of the Supreme Court decision for desegregation. Thus Will Maslow, general counsel for the American Jewish Congress, recommends in his recent speech in Miami Beach that cities establish new schools in fringe areas between the centers of white and colored populations and adopt integration as one of the key criteria in school zoning. The purpose would be *to make sure* that white and colored children attend the same schools. Thus, desegregation is not to take place naturally and normally in the community in which white and colored children live, but they are actually to be compelled by city ordinance to go to the same schools, even where the natural centers of population do not indicate it.

I submit that in view of the present difficulties in the struggle for desegregation in the South, such propaganda published widely in our Southern cities has not helped the cause of desegregation, and certainly has not made the Jew more popular among his neighbors. Apparently diplomacy and statesmanship are not the strong points of some of our "defense" organizations.

[. . .]

Yet we can have no quarrel with the law decreeing desegregation, because it is based upon the Constitution which is sacred to all Americans. However, there is no constitutional principle which decrees that integration must be compulsory for white and colored people. It only stipulates that there can be no compulsory segregation, but certainly no one can argue that we must, by law, compel white and colored children who live in different neighborhoods and who could ordinarily attend their own schools to go to integrated schools, despite the fact that they do not live in the neighborhood and are not interested in attending such integrated schools. That certainly is a law which will not be acceptable to many white and colored people, and the enforcement of it will certainly confront no end of difficulties, because it is not based neither on constitutional principle nor on the acceptance of the vast masses of the American people.

[. . .]

c. I would suggest also that the Jewish religious leaders in each community make their pronouncement as a part of the *American* religious community, both nationally and locally. For, after all, desegregation is not a Jewish issue but an *American* issue, and in solving it we must take our place *with* our fellow-Americans in fighting for equal rights for those who do not at present enjoy them.

[. . .]

I certainly agree that martyrdom is perhaps the noblest service which anyone can render to a great cause. My only contention is that no one has the right to martyr somebody else for the cause he believes in. Certainly, the Jews of the South have the sovereign and unalienable right to become martyrs in the cause of desegregation if they so wish. I reject however any claim on the part of the national "defense" organizations to impose martyrdom upon the unwilling Jews of the South and to bask in their reflected glory

of their self sacrifice. It would seem to me that if they think so much of martyrdom they ought to come down South and try it for themselves.

[. . .]

Why does Dr. King single out the Jews in his accusation against their apparent silence and complacency? Why doesn't he accuse the Protestants or the Catholics of their reluctance to take side with the Negro in this conflict?

The answer is obvious. There is a glaring inconsistency between the constant and vociferous speech-making on the part of the national leaders of the "defense" organizations and the discreet and necessary silence on the part of the Jews whose position in the small towns of the deep South is far from enviable. On the one hand, there is the constant beating of drums in Washington and New York by the national executives of our "defense" organizations, proclaiming the righteousness of the cause of desegregation, and, on the other, there are the Jews of the deep South, a very small minority, caught in the vise between the Negroes who demand that they side with them, and the white population who threaten them with violence if they do. I submit that, under such circumstances, the excessive and aggressive propaganda of the national organizations is a distinct and tragic disservice to the Jew of the South.

[. . .]

Will the course of action I recommend ensure us against anti-Semitism and bombing? Perhaps not, but, at least, we shall not be recklessly baiting those who need only a pretext to rouse the sleeping dogs of hate and violence. Is it essential that we flaunt before the poor, perplexed and embattled Southerners, the spread-eagle oratory of travelling spell-binders from the so-called "defense" organizations, who tour the Southern states, and harangue their fellow Jews to rise up against their benighted neighbors and liberate the Negro from his under-privileged status? Would it not be better if each community were permitted to go forward in accordance with its own needs, its own problems, its own understanding and its own leadership? It may not be the panacea for a problem which is too complex and too crucial to be easily solved, but I believe that it points, at least, in the right direction.

Source: Reprinted with permission from *Conservative Judaism*, a publication of the Rabbinical Assembly, vol. 13, no. 1 (1958): 35–46.

8.22—SELECTION FROM AN ADDRESS BY SOUTH CAROLINA SPEAKER OF THE HOUSE SOLOMON BLATT TO THE HEBREW BENEVOLENT SOCIETY OF CHARLESTON, APRIL 6, 1959

Solomon Blatt (1895–1986), the Blackville, South Carolina–born son of Russian Jewish immigrants, earned both his undergraduate and law degrees from the University of South Carolina before heading to France to serve as a supply sergeant in World War I. After winning election to the South Carolina House of Representatives in 1932, Blatt became speaker in 1937, a position he held for twenty-nine years. At the height of the civil rights movement, Speaker Blatt offered his optimistic assessment, no doubt jarring to some, of the status of blacks in South Carolina at a meeting of the Hebrew Benevolent Society of Charleston.

No occasion could give me greater pleasure than to participate in this, the 175th Anniversary Celebration of the Hebrew Benevolent Society.

The distinguished record of this organization, coupled with the whole history of the Jewish race in America's most historic city, makes me proud to be included among you.

[. . .]

There are dangerous inclinations among some of the Jewish people in America today, out of the goodness of their hearts, to establish themselves as a minority force in the tragically exaggerated storm of political propaganda which surrounds and confuses the Negro question in the South.

Let it be clearly understood that if there were indeed conditions anything similar to those which prevailed during the Hitler persecutions of Jews in Germany—if there were any such persecutions against any particular race in America, I think that all good Americans should and would rally to defend the oppressed, whomever they might be.

But let us examine the status of the Negro race in South Carolina. We all know about our own problems better than we do about the problems elsewhere in the nation, and by the same token we know better about our own problems than do people who live elsewhere in the nation.

The fact is that nowhere else on the face of the earth are Negroes happier, more prosperous, more contented, more a part of the general way of life than in South Carolina.

During the last twenty-five years especially, the Negroes have made tremendous strides in this State politically, economically, professionally and otherwise.

Never before in any other part of the world has so much relative progress been made by the Negro race as has been enjoyed in the South during the present generation.

Where else in America are such a large proportion of Negroes actively participating as respected ministers, teachers, lawyers, doctors, businessmen, and citizens in general?

About 40% of the school teachers in South Carolina are Negroes, teaching school in the most modern buildings, receiving the same State aid salaries as white teachers in their classifications, and otherwise becoming more and more a large and constructive force in our way of life.

314 | CHAPTER 8: AMERICAN JEWISH LIFE

Where else in America, outside of the South, are Negroes able to afford to become such extensive and prosperous participants in all phases of life?

There are more Negro teachers in the schools of South Carolina today than there are in any five or six states combined, outside of the South —and in that respect this includes such States as New York, Michigan, California and others where political propaganda is rampant, where the South is being used as a whipping boy for ambitious propagandists who have no genuine interest in the real progress of the Negro.

We know that in South Carolina the already excellent relations between the races have been so sound and friendly that all of the misrepresentations in national newspapers, magazines and over television and radio have not so much as dented the good will existing down here.

That, to me, is the finest evidence available that our good relationships are based on proper understanding, proper treatment, a proper and rapid rate of progress, and a proper perspective for the future.

If our relationships were not based on strong and deep-rooted good will, we would be in a state of utter chaos because of the unwise, unfriendly and generally deplorable and deliberate misrepresentations which have been heaped upon us.

Make no mistake about it—our racial relationships in the South have been put to the acid test, and we have not been found wanting.

Still another strong evidence is the fact that, as we have good reason to believe, the truly thoughtful and sincere people over the rest of the nation are beginning to understand, despite the false and tragic curtain of propaganda, that the South does indeed live in a much more healthy and promising atmosphere of racial good will than any other section of the country.

We do not have in South Carolina the kind of gangs, and mobs, and misunderstanding, and social conflict, and teen-age terrorism which prevails in States like New York, Pennsylvania, Michigan and California—the very states from which have come the most abuse against the South.

[. . .]

No, my friends, the Negro race, nor any other race, is oppressed in the South Carolina way of life today, and I am a living example of the tolerance of the people of this great State.

People of all races in South Carolina can look forward with confidence to the future, knowing full well that if they have character, talents and abilities, and if they exert themselves intelligently and constructively, they will be recognized and appreciated.

[. . .]

Let me thank you again from the bottom of my heart for this opportunity to be with you tonight. It is truly one of the highlights of my lifetime. I will never forget your kindness in inviting me and I assure you that everything I do, I will do as a South Carolinian, as one of your faith interested in the welfare of all of our people and I believe I will be a better man because of this experience. May God bless and keep you, each and every one.

Source: Solomon Blatt nearprint file, AJA.

8.23—SELECTION FROM AN OPEN LETTER FROM RABBI RICHARD W. WINOGRAD TO THE NATIONAL DIRECTOR OF B'NAI B'RITH, 1963

At the 1963 annual meeting of Conservative movement rabbis, a group broke off from the convention to journey to Birmingham, Alabama, in support of Dr. King and the civil rights movement. Among those who believed that support for racial equality demanded more than mere resolutions passed at the assembly, Rabbi Richard W. Winograd (1936–1974), interim director of the University of Chicago Hillel, chronicled his experiences in an open letter to Hillel's national director. While Winograd certainly understood the moral imperatives of his civil rights work, his experience with Birmingham's Jews increased his understanding of and compassion for their relative lack of public involvement in the struggle for racial equality.

Birmingham—A Personal Statement
Rabbi Richard W. Winograd

BEGINNINGS

I approached the possibility of going to Birmingham with mixed feelings. I very much wanted to volunteer as a "witness" for the Negro struggle. During the past year I had worked closely with the CORE [Congress of Racial Equality] group at the University of Chicago (the student leaders of which have been closely identified with Hillel). I had followed with admiration, and with envy, the participation of rabbis and ministers in other freedom actions—the rides and sit-ins. I felt that the involvement in the Negro struggle of a significant number of whites, and especially of Jews, was important. And above all, I have held in my memory the experiences of the Jews of Europe when nobody came to help . . .

The very mixture of my motivations caused my hesitation. I did not see this as requiring any sacrifice on my part (the possibility of physical danger was never a real one to me). I feared that my motives were too selfish, that I would gain much more than I could possibly give, that I had not made a significant enough contribution to civil rights in my own community to make me worthy of the endeavor.

Furthermore, I was not fully convinced that we had a right to place the Jewish community of Birmingham in a more dangerous position than we were willing, and able, to place ourselves. In weighing the morality of this particular aspect the scales were very even.

[. . .]

Though I now firmly believe that it was proper of the Rabbinical Assembly to have sent the delegation to Birmingham, and though I am glad that I was part of that delegation, I have not fully resolved some of the above concerns.

ARRIVAL

. . . The Jews of Birmingham approached us as petitioners, which made me very uncomfortable. . . . I had the feeling that we somehow were the Hamans and Torquemadas to these *sh'tadlanim* [emissaries, in the medieval period, between the Jewish community and the civil government]. . . . I felt ashamed for them . . . ashamed for having put them in this position . . . but most of all ashamed for the circumstances which had led to pitting Jew against Jew. . . .

RANDOM REACTIONS

. . . The young people have a faith and determination reminiscent of our own Zionist youth . . . of an earlier period. . . . I was too young in those days to take an active role in the struggle for Israel. . . . I envied the opportunity which these youngsters have. . . . Their goals are clear . . . they have something to live for . . . but what will happen to all this energy and idealism when the goals are achieved and life in all its complexities confronts these young people. . . . They will be exchanging the collective anguish of the Negro for the individual anguish of the human dilemma. . . . They will look back on these good old days . . . like old Palmachnikim [members of the Palmach, the underground Jewish army that fought for an independent Israel].

[. . .]

A question asked by a Negro girl of fifteen: "Do you really think that we are equal to white people, that we are as intelligent?". . . Is she testing me, or seeking reassurance? . . . I would prefer to think it is the former, but I have the feeling that it is the latter. . . . The words of James Baldwin come to me: "From my own point of view, the fact of the Third Reich alone makes obsolete forever any question of Christian superiority, except in technological terms." . . .

A good antidote to prejudice: When seeing a gang of black hoodlums, picture white Germans shoveling Jews into an oven.

[. . .]

A Jewish teenager called the motel and asked to speak to "a rabbi." . . . I answered the phone. . . . He established his credentials by saying that he was familiar with the Seminary in New York, and was going to Israel this summer. . . . He said:

"We are glad that you are doing what we would like to do but do not have the courage to do. But, please, do not endanger us. Do not get our synagogue bombed." . . . I asked for his telephone number and tried to reach him later in order to invite him to come with us to a church meeting, but he wasn't home. . . .

Source: SC-2846, AJA.

8.24—SELECTION FROM A SPEECH DELIVERED BY RABBI JOACHIM PRINZ AT THE MARCH ON WASHINGTON, AUGUST 28, 1963

Martin Luther King Jr.'s (1929–1968) famed "I Have a Dream" speech, delivered at the August 1963 March on Washington, remains one of the most important orations in U.S. history. Standing on the steps of the Lincoln Memorial with Dr. King that day was the American Jewish Congress leader Joachim Prinz (1902–1988), an immigrant from Nazi Germany, who had earlier served as a rabbi in Berlin. Organizers of the march invited Prinz to give a speech, which he delivered just before King spoke. Prinz drew connections between Jewish suffering in World War II Europe and his own impetus for joining the civil rights movement in the United States.

. . . When I was the rabbi of the Jewish community in Berlin under the Hitler regime, I learned many things. The most important thing that I learned under those tragic circumstances was that bigotry and hatred are not the most urgent problem. The most urgent, the most disgraceful, the most shameful and the most tragic problem is silence.

A great people which had created a great civilization had become a nation of silent onlookers. They remained silent in the face of hate, in the face of brutality and in the face of mass murder.

America must not become a nation of onlookers. America must not remain silent. Not merely black America, but all of America. It must speak up and act, from the President down to the humblest of us, and not for the sake of the Negro, not for the sake of the black community but for the sake of the image, the idea and the aspiration of America itself. . . .

Source: Michael Staub, ed., *The Jewish 1960s: An American Sourcebook* (Hanover, N.H.: University Press of New England, 2004), 90–91. Used by permission of the publisher.

8.25—MARCH ON WASHINGTON, AUGUST 28, 1963

Source: Library of Congress, Washington, D.C.

8.26—SEARCH FOR CIVIL RIGHTS WORKERS JAMES CHANEY, ANDREW GOODMAN, AND MICHAEL SCHWERNER, 1964

In 1964, a coalition of leading civil rights groups organized the Mississippi Summer Project, better known as "Freedom Summer"—an attempt by local African American activists as well as white northern volunteers to promote black voter registration. When three civil rights workers, James Chaney (1943-1964), an African American from Meridian, Mississippi, Andrew Goodman (1943-1964), a Jewish civil rights worker from New York, and Michael Schwerner (1939-1964), a Jewish New York City social worker, went missing in June 1964, the FBI, under pressure from civil rights leaders, launched an investigation. Two months later, the bodies of the three men were located in an earthen dam, having been beaten and shot to death by KKK members in conspiracy with local law enforcement officials. The deaths of these three men came to symbolize the black-Jewish alliance and the risks American Jews were willing to take in support of racial equality.

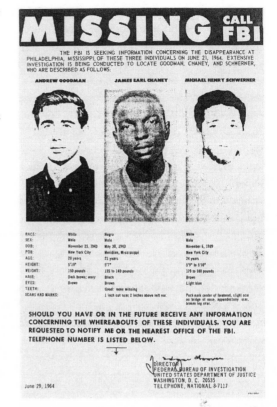

Source: PC-748, AJA.

8.27—SELECTION FROM ORAL HISTORY INTERVIEW WITH KIVIE KAPLAN, REGARDING HIS ENTRANCE INTO CIVIL RIGHTS WORK AND HIS ELECTION AS PRESIDENT OF THE NAACP, 1970

Boston-born Jewish businessman Kivie Kaplan (1904-1975) joined the National Association for the Advancement of Colored People (NAACP) in 1932 and devoted most of his life to civil rights work. By 1954, the year the NAACP successfully argued the Brown case before the U.S. Supreme Court, Kaplan joined the organization's national board, a move that reflected the strong alliance between blacks and Jews in this period. Twelve years later, he became the NAACP's president, serving until his death in 1975.

Kaplan, who was also a member of the national board of Judaism's Reform movement, reflected in an interview on why he chose to devote much of his philanthropic career to a non-Jewish communal organization.

Kivie Kaplan Interview, Terrace Hilton Hotel Cincinnati, June 28, 1970

. . . Dr. [Jacob Rader] Marcus wants to know how I got into the Civil Rights work, particularly the NAACP. Thirty-eight years ago—we are now in June, 1970, I am sixty-six years old, I turned sixty-six on April 1, 1970, I was born in 1904—when I was twenty-eight years old, thirty-eight years ago, I was on a business trip to Central America for two weeks and in those days my wife did not drive and I left my wife and my mother at Miami Beach for two weeks. I hired a Negro gentleman to take them around to see the sights and take them out for drives during the two weeks I was on business. When I got back, my mother and my wife wanted, in the four hours that we had before we were leaving for Boston, to show me some of the gardens, the estates where the rich people lived and other things of interest. Not being a sight-seer I suffered for the cause and went around, and during the course of the afternoon we saw a sign on a hotel that said "no dogs or Jews allowed." The Negro gentleman stopped the car. He thought that I was visibly perturbed by my facial expression, but I didn't react that way. I was glad to see the sign on that hotel because I wouldn't want to spend my money there because I knew that there were ninety-nine other hotels in the Miami Beach area that did accept Jews and dogs and that's the place where I would want to spend my money. But he thought I was hurt so he took out his wallet and he said, "Mr. Kaplan, you know we Negroes cannot go out after eight p.m. in Miami Beach without a permit." He took this permit out and showed me where he had a permit to go after eight p.m. Evidently he wasn't satisfied that this consoled me and I still had this serious face on, and he said, "You know, Mr. Kaplan, we Negroes cannot go swimming in the ocean." Well, being twenty-eight years of age, knowing that we Jews have suffered for 5,000 years, having had experiences of anti-Semitism all of my life since I was a kid, I compared the problems of the Jew in the United States with the problems of the Negro and I said, "Gee, they really have a problem." I went home and I thought about this and I immediately joined up with the NAACP and started to work with them in a small way and continued for

thirty-eight years until I finished up as president of the NAACP.

Dr. Marcus wants to know something about the preceding president in the NAACP before me. Arthur Spingarn had been president for twenty-six years before I was. One Sunday night—we have our fellowship annual dinner the night before the annual meeting which is in January, and then after the annual meeting we have our elections of the board and officers—well this Sunday night at the fellowship dinner, Arthur Spingarn surprised everybody and said he was not going to run for president again. The next day I was approached by two groups, the Old Guards and the Young Turks, and it was evidenced that each wanted to know whether I would accept the presidency because I seemed to be the man that there was no doubt as to my dedication to the cause, and I said to each one, and both of these approaches were unbeknown to the other, that if I could serve the cause and I could save a fight, I'd be honored to be president, although I had never dreamt of it up until that time. I was unanimously elected at that time as president of the NAACP.

Dr. Marcus wants to know why they didn't choose a Negro. Well, I'll elaborate on this a little. At an all-day meeting in Boston, at a college career youth meeting, all college seniors, all black—one of the professors who was conducting the meeting who I had been very friendly with for many many years came up to me and practically put his finger in my eye and he said, "Kivie, why do you, a white Jew, be president of the NAACP, I don't see a black man president of the B'nai B'rith." When I was eighteen years of age, my dear friend and lawyer, Lee M. Friedman, of blessed memory, took me aside and said, "Kivie, I want to give you a little lesson which will pay big dividends in the years to come, if you take it, and if you listen to me. Kivie, remember 'the man who keeps cool, has the advantage.'" So I've tried to follow this in my life and being human I slip every once in a while and get off the beam, but when I have something as violent as this that I am faced with, I not only slow down, but I start talking very very slowly so that I will choose my words and not say anything that I will be sorry that I said. So when this gentleman asked me that question, I said, "Well you know, Joe, the B'nai B'rith, I feel if we found a qualified black Jew, and as you know we have many thousands of black Jews in the United States, I'm sure that he would be elected president of the B'nai B'rith." Of course I knew that this wasn't what he was driving at and then I went on to say, "Well listen Joe, if after thirty-eight years of dedicated service I have the Young Turks and the Old Guards come to me and [*sic*] when Mr. Spingarn resigned and ask me if I would accept the presidency of the NAACP, on account of my thirty-eight years of dedicated service, and amongst the many things that I have done, I took over the life membership of the National Association of the Advancement of Colored People when they only had 221 life members and life membership is $500. I felt that this was a good way of raising funds for the association as they were always short of money and for the first forty-five years we had 221 and now we have over 39,000 life members which represents over $19,500,000 when all the money is collected. Do you think that I should say no, I will not accept the presidency of the NAACP, you should give it to a less qualified black man just because he is black."

[. . .]

Dr. Marcus asked me about the attitude of the southern Jew towards legal civil rights in the South. It's a sad situation. Basically our Jewish brothers and sisters in the South, recognizing that they are Jews, are sympathetic, but from a practical point of view with the violent action of the white bigots, the white Citizens Council and the Ku Klux Klan over the years, they are afraid, and I couldn't tell my friend, Jake Goldberg, who runs a family business in any southern city, his

father before him ran it, they make their living, and this is their only form of livelihood, I can't tell him to stand up and be counted and the next morning he goes to his store and it's burnt to the ground. The white southern bigots are vicious and violent. In Mississippi they have a record of over 4,300 blacks that have been murdered in cold blood and they are all positive that there are at least ten that they have no record of that have been killed because the families of those who have been killed are afraid to report it to the police. When I said we have a record of over 4,300 that have been killed, we are positive that there is at least 43,000 that haven't been reported because the families of those who have been killed are afraid to report it because they know if they do that they will come in and they will clean the whole family out and nobody is willing to get killed. When I spent eight days there in 1964 as one of a volunteer committee of seven of the national board of the NAACP, on the eighth night that I was there I stopped at this retired railroad man's house in Clarksdale, Mississippi and it was about 115 in the shade and I couldn't sleep all night and I was down in the living room with Mr. Stone, the retired railroad man, and we got very very friendly and he told me confidentially, and he insisted that I wouldn't repeat it in Mississippi, because he said he wanted to live. He said when he was on the railroad that the white conductors and the white trainmen used to carry these revolvers and just the same as a person would shoot at a rat in the railroad yard, they would shoot Negroes and kill them either in the back of the train, or in the yard, or going by, and at the end of the run, at the barroom, when they were having their drinks, they would compare their score as to how many niggers they killed on this trip. . . .

Source: SC-6092, AJA.

8.28—PRESIDENT HARRY S. TRUMAN, RECOGNITION OF THE STATE OF ISRAEL, MAY 14, 1948

On May 14, 1948, British forces withdrew from the Mandate for Palestine, prompting the Zionist leadership under the direction of David Ben-Gurion to declare an independent State of Israel. Much of the new country's diplomatic success would depend on whether it enjoyed legitimacy in the international community, and recognition by the United States was especially crucial. Hours after Ben-Gurion proclaimed Israel's independence, President Harry S. Truman recognized the new state, helping solidify its standing. A copy of the original document, which includes Truman's edits, is included here.

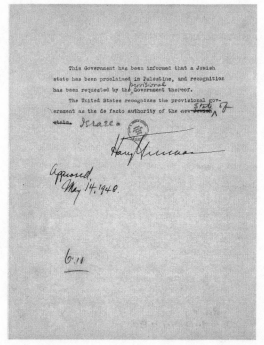

Source: Charles Ross Papers, 1904–1967, Alphabetical correspondence file: "Handwriting of the President," Harry S. Truman Library, U.S. National Archives and Records Administration.

8.29—EXCHANGE BETWEEN DAVID BEN-GURION AND JACOB BLAUSTEIN ON THE RELATIONSHIP BETWEEN AMERICAN JEWS AND THE STATE OF ISRAEL, AUGUST 1950

While most Jewish organizations came to embrace Zionism in the wake of the Shoah and the creation of the State of Israel, the American Jewish Committee still clung to its non-Zionist inclinations. In 1950, AJC head Jacob Blaustein (1892–1970) traveled to Jerusalem to meet with Israeli prime minister David Ben-Gurion.

Worried that the existence of a Jewish national homeland would open American Jews to charges of dual loyalty, Blaustein wanted Ben-Gurion to offer public assurances that the Jewish state would not make a claim on the political allegiances of America's Jews. Ben-Gurion, for his part, sought support from American Jews and especially their organizational leadership. In a famous exchange at Jerusalem's King David Hotel, the two figures offered perspectives that have become known as the "Blaustein and Ben-Gurion Agreement."

Ben Gurion, the Israeli Prime Minister, Addresses the American Notable, Jacob Blaustein

We are very happy to welcome you [Jacob Blaustein] here in our midst as a representative of the great Jewry of the United States to whom Israel owes so much. No other community abroad has so great a stake in what has been achieved in this country during the present generation as have the Jews in America. Their material and political support, their warm-hearted and practical idealism, has been one of the principal sources of our strength and our success. In supporting our effort, American Jewry has developed, on a new plane, the noble conception, maintained for more than half a century, of extending its help for the protection of Jewish rights throughout the world and of rendering economic aid wherever it was needed. We are deeply conscious of the help which America has given to us here in our great effort of reconstruction and during our struggle for independence. This great tradition has been continued since the establishment of the State of Israel. You, Mr. Blaustein, are one of the finest examples of that tradition, and as an American and as a Jew you have made many and significant contributions to the Jewish cause and to the cause of democracy. We are therefore happy on this occasion of your visit here as our guest, to discuss with you matters of mutual interest and to clarify some of the problems which have arisen in regard to the relationship between the people of Israel and the Jewish communities abroad, in particular the Jewish community of the United States.

It is our great pride that our newly gained independence has enabled us in this small country to undertake the major share of the great and urgent task of providing permanent homes under conditions of full equality to hundreds of thousands of our brethren who cannot remain where they are and whose heart is set on rebuilding their lives in Israel. In this great task you and we are engaged in a close partnership. Without the readiness for sacrifice of the people of Israel and without the help of America this urgent task can hardly be achieved.

It is most unfortunate that since our State came into being some confusion and misunderstanding should have arisen as regards the relationship between Israel and the Jewish communities abroad, in particular that of the United States. These misunderstandings are likely to alienate sympathies and create disharmony where friendship and close understanding are of vital necessity. To my mind the position is perfectly clear. The Jews of the United States, as a community and as individuals, have only one political attachment and that is to the United States of America. They owe no political allegiance to Israel. In the first statement which the representative of Israel made before the United Nations after her admission to that international organization, he [the Israeli UN ambassador] clearly stated, without any reservation, that the State of Israel represents and speaks only on behalf of its own citizens and in no way presumes to represent or speak in the name of the Jews who are citizens of any other country. We, the people of Israel, have no desire and no intention to interfere in any way with the internal affairs of Jewish communities abroad. The Government and the people of Israel fully respect the right and integrity of the Jewish communities in other countries to develop their own mode of life and their indigenous social, economic and cultural institutions in accordance with their own needs and aspirations. Any weakening of American Jewry, any disruption of its communal life, any lowering of its sense of security, any diminution of its status, is a definite loss to Jews everywhere and to Israel in particular.

We are happy to know of the deep and growing interest which American Jews of all shades and convictions take in what it has fallen to us to achieve in this country. Were we, God forbid, to fail in what we have undertaken on our own behalf and on behalf of our suffering brethren, that failure would cause grievous pain to Jews everywhere and nowhere more than in your community. Our success or failure depends in a large measure on our cooperation with, and on the strength of, the great Jewish community of the United States, and, we, therefore, are anxious that nothing should be said or done which could in the slightest degree undermine the sense of security and stability of American Jewry.

In this connection let me say a word about immigration. We should like to see American Jews come and take part in our effort. We need their technical knowledge, their unrivaled experience, their spirit of enterprise, their bold vision, their "know-how." We need engineers, chemists, builders, work managers and technicians. The tasks which face us in this country are eminently such as would appeal to the American genius for technical development and social progress. But the decision as to whether they wish to come—permanently or temporarily—rests with the free discretion of each American Jew himself. It is entirely a matter of his own volition. We need halutzim, pioneers too. Halutzim have come to us—and we believe more will come, not only from those countries where the Jews are oppressed and in "exile" but also from countries where the Jews live a life of freedom and are equal in status to all other citizens in their country. But the essence of halutziuth is free choice. They will come from among those who believe that their aspirations as human beings and as Jews can best be fulfilled by life and work in Israel.

I believe I know something of the spirit of American Jewry among whom I lived for some years. I am convinced that it will continue to make a major contribution towards our great effort of reconstruction, and I hope that the talks we have had with you during these last few days will make for even closer cooperation between our two communities.

Response of Jacob Blaustein

I am very happy, Mr. Prime Minister, to have come here at your invitation and to have discussed with you and other leaders of Israel the various important problems of mutual interest.

But more than [your impressive efforts to conquer the Negev and your use of American know-how in this work], what you are doing and creating in this corner of the Middle East is of vital importance not only to you and to Jews, but to humanity in general. For I believe that the free and peace-loving peoples in the world can look upon Israel as a stronghold of democracy in an area where liberal democracy is practically unknown and where the prevailing social and political conditions may be potential dangers to the security and stability of the world. What President Truman is intending to do under his Four Point Program, in assisting underdeveloped peoples to improve their conditions and raise their standards of living, you here to a large extent have been doing right along under most difficult conditions and at great sacrifice.

Important to your future, as you recognize, is the United States of America and American Jewry. Israel, of course, is also important to them.

[. . .]

I thought I knew it even before I came to this country on this trip, but my visit has made it still more clear to me—and as an American citizen and a Jew I am gratified—that the Israeli people want democracy and, in my opinion, will not accept any dictatorship or totalitarianism from within or from without.

Democracy, like all other human institutions, has its faults; and abuses are possible. But the strength of a democratic regime is that these faults and those abuses can be corrected without the destruction of human rights and freedoms which alone make life worth living.

There is no question in my mind that a Jew who wants to remain loyal to the fundamental basis of Judaism and his cultural heritage, will be in the forefront of the struggle for democracy against totalitarianism.

The American Jewish community sees its fortunes tied to the fate of liberal democracy in the United States, sustained by its heritage, as Americans and as Jews. We seek to strengthen both of these vital links to the past and to all of humanity by enhancing the American democratic and political system, American cultural diversity and American well-being.

As to Israel, the vast majority of American Jewry recognizes the necessity and desirability of helping to make it a strong, viable, self-supporting state. This, for the sake of Israel itself, and the good of the world.

The American Jewish Committee has been active, as have other Jewish organizations in the United States, in rendering, within the framework of their American citizenship, every possible support to Israel; and I am sure that this support will continue and that we shall do all we can to increase further our share in the great historic task of helping Israel to solve its problems and develop as a free, independent and flourishing democracy.

[. . .]

Israel's rebirth and progress, coming after the tragedy of European Jewry in the 1930s and in World War II, has done much to raise Jewish morale. Jews in America and everywhere can be more proud than ever of their Jewishness.

But we must, in a true spirit of friendliness, sound a note of caution to Israel and its leaders. Now that the birth pains are over, and even though Israel is undergoing growing pains, it must recognize that the matter of good-will between its citizens and those of other countries is a two-way street; that Israel also has a responsibility in this situation—a responsibility in terms of not affecting adversely the sensibilities of Jews who are citizens of other states by what it says or does.

In this connection, you are realists and want facts and I would be less than frank if I did not point out to you that American Jews vigorously

repudiate any suggestion or implication that they are in exile. American Jews—young and old alike, Zionists and non-Zionists alike—are profoundly attached to America. America welcomed their immigrant parents in their need. Under America's free institutions, they and their children have achieved that freedom and sense of security unknown for long centuries of travail. American Jews have truly become Americans; just as have all other oppressed groups that have ever come to America's shores.

To American Jews, America is home. There, exist their thriving roots; there, is the country which they have helped to build; and there, they share its fruits and its destiny. They believe in the future of a democratic society in the United States under which all citizens, irrespective of creed or race, can live on terms of equality. They further believe that, if democracy should fail in America, there would be no future for democracy anywhere in the world, and that the very existence of an independent State of Israel would be problematic. Further, they feel that a world in which it would be possible for Jews to be driven by persecution from America would not be a world safe for Israel either; indeed it is hard to conceive how it would be a world safe for any human being.

The American Jewish community, as you, Mr. Prime Minister, have so eloquently pointed out, has assumed a major part of the responsibility of securing equality of rights and providing generous material help to Jews in other countries. American Jews feel themselves bound to Jews the world over by ties of religion, common historical traditions and in certain respects, by a sense of common destiny. We fully realize that persecution and discrimination against Jews in any country will sooner or later have its impact on the situation of the Jews in other countries, but these problems must be dealt with by each Jewish community itself in accordance with its own wishes, traditions, needs and aspirations.

Jewish communities, particularly American Jewry in view of its influence and its strength, can offer advice, cooperation and help, but should not attempt to speak in the name of other communities or in any way interfere in their internal affairs.

I am happy to note from your statement, Mr. Prime Minister, that the State of Israel takes a similar position. Any other position on the part of the State of Israel would only weaken the American and other Jewish communities of the free, democratic countries and be contrary to the basic interests of Israel itself. The future development of Israel, spiritual, social as well as economic, will largely depend upon a strong and healthy Jewish community in the United States and other free democracies.

We have been greatly distressed that at the very hour when so much has been achieved, harmful and futile discussions and misunderstandings have arisen as to the relations between the people and the State of Israel and the Jews in other countries, particularly in the United States. Harm has been done to the morale and to some extent to the sense of security of the American Jewish community through unwise and unwarranted statements and appeals which ignore the feelings and aspirations of American Jewry.

Even greater harm has been done to the State of Israel itself by weakening the readiness of American Jews to do their full share in the rebuilding of Israel which faces such enormous political, social and economic problems.

Your statement today, Mr. Prime Minister, will, I trust, be followed by unmistakable evidence that the responsible leaders of Israel, and the organizations connected with it, fully understand that future relations between the American Jewish community and the State of Israel must be based on mutual respect for one another's feelings and needs, and on the preservation of the integrity of the two communities and their institutions.

I believe that in your statement today, you have taken a fundamental and historic position which will redound to the best interest not only of Israel, but of the Jews of America and of the world. I am confident that this statement and the spirit in which it has been made, by eliminating the misunderstandings and futile discussions between our two communities, will strengthen them both and will lay the foundation for even closer cooperation.

In closing, permit me to express my deep gratitude for the magnificent reception you and your colleagues have afforded my colleague and me during our stay in this country.

Source: As printed in *JAW*, 489–94. From *American Jewish Year Book*, 58 (1952): 565–68. Adapted and reprinted with permission from *American Jewish Year Book*, New York: American Jewish Committee, ©1952. www.AJC.org. All rights reserved.

8.30—"MAJOR U.S. JEWISH GROUPS APPEAL FOR EQUAL RIGHTS FOR SOVIET JEWS," JEWISH TELEGRAPHIC AGENCY, SEPTEMBER 29, 1960

The emergence of the Cold War offered American Jews a strong political platform upon which to articulate their concerns about the mistreatment of Jews in the Soviet Union. As early as 1960, leading American Jewish organizations from across the denominational and political spectrum issued a joint appeal to raise awareness for the plight of Soviet Jews. Months later, representatives from Jewish communities in the United States, Great Britain, and South Africa appealed to the United Nations for support.

New York—

Seventeen major American Jewish organizations today issued a Joint appeal to "men of good-will everywhere" to help secure equal rights for Soviet Jewry. The Jewish groups expressed "deep sorrow and ever-mounting concern" over the "tragic" position of the Jewish population of the Soviet Union.

The statement was accompanied by a fact sheet detailing the disabilities Soviet Jews face both as a cultural group and a religious community as a result of official Soviet policy. This policy, it was asserted, stands in "sharp contrast" to the treatment of other ethnic and religious groups in the Soviet Union. The appeal called for bringing "the full weight of responsible public opinion to bear so that the tragic position of Soviet Jews may be alleviated."

"We find it difficult to believe," the Jewish organizations declared, "that the Soviet authorities can refuse to take note of the collective concern of mankind." Copies of the statement have been sent to the headquarters of all United Nations delegations here.

The organizations signing the appeal included the major American Jewish religious bodies—Orthodox, Conservative and Reform—plus national Jewish civic and communal groups representing the great majority of American Jews. Signers were:

American-Israel Public Affairs Committee; American Jewish Congress; American Trade Union Council for Labor Israel; American Zionist Council; B'nai B'rith; Hadassah; Jewish Agency for Israel; Jewish Labor Committee; Jewish War Veterans of the U.S.; Labor Zionist Movement; Mizrachi-Hapoel Hamizrachi; National Community Relations Advisory Council; National Council of Young Israel; Union of American Hebrew Congregations; Union of Orthodox Jewish Congregations of America; United Synagogue of America; Zionist Organization of America.

The USSR's discrimination policy, according to the statement, includes a "persistent refusal to restore their cultural institutions to Soviet Jews after years of forcible deprivations; the continued removal of Jews from most leading positions in Soviet political life; and a campaign of incitement in Russia and the Ukraine against Judaism."

CHARGE SOVIET AUTHORITIES WITH STIMULATING ANTI-JEWISH INCITEMENT

The statement charges that "not only have the Soviet authorities ceased for many years now to enforce the penal clause against anti-Semitic incitement, but the Soviet press has been guided into publishing a vast number of scurrilous attacks upon Judaism as a religion and upon individual Jews as anti-social elements—publications which not only have an unmistakably anti-Semitic flavor but also act as incitement in a country where the public regards every publication as officially inspired."

Asserting that this policy "contradicts the very principles of equality which the Soviet authorities have professed," the Jewish organizations urged a "major change in policy towards Soviet Jewry," including:

1. The granting of full cultural and religious group rights and institutions in Yiddish and Hebrew to Soviet Jews, including the right to organize a nationwide federation of Jewish communities.
2. Permission to emigrate for purposes such as the reunion of dispersed families, "in accordance with international obligations assumed by the Soviet Union under the United Nations Charter."
3. The resumption of organizational contact between Soviet Jews and Jewish groups in other parts of the world.

Soviet Premier Nikita Khrushchev, when asked today by newsmen in front of the Soviet Embassy to comment on a statement issued a week ago by Walter Reuther, president of the United Auto Workers, and other Americans, denouncing "cultural anti-Semitism" in the Soviet Union, replied: "One should not pay attention to dogs that howl and bark. Any reasonable person would walk away when he hears them."

Source: Jewish Telegraphic Agency, September 29, 1960, http://archive.jta.org/article/1960/09/29/3064051/major-us-jewish-groups-appeal-for-equal-rights-for-soviet-jews. All rights reserved. Used by permission.

8.31—"UN TOLD RUSSIA DENIES UNIVERSAL DECLARATION OF HUMAN RIGHTS TO JEWS," *Jewish Criterion*, NOVEMBER 18, 1960

New York—A report filed with the United Nations by three major Jewish organizations charges the Soviet Union with discriminating against Jewish citizens in its emigration policies for reuniting families separated by war and political turmoil.

Documented with quoted statements of Premier Khrushchev and other Kremlin leaders, and with news accounts of cases in which the reunion of families and even of ethnic groups have been authorized, the report stresses that the U.S.S.R. has been "sympathetically disposed" to the practice "except in the case of Soviet Jews."

The 24-page memorandum, prepared by B'nai B'rith, the Board of Jewish Deputies of Great Britain and the South African Board of Jewish Deputies, also surveys emigration policies towards Jews in other East European countries and in North Africa.

Among Communist satellite states, the report finds that permission for Jews to emigrate is "more liberal" than in the U.S.S.R. but is "subject to the vagaries of administrative arbitrariness."

In the North African countries of Morocco, Tunis [*sic*], Libya and Egypt, varying forms of restriction exist that hinder the right of Jews to emigrate voluntarily or to return to their own countries, the report says.

The three Jewish organizations jointly maintain consultative status with the United Nations through the Coordinating Board of Jewish Organizations. The CBJO submitted the survey to the United Nations Subcommission on Prevention of Discrimination and Protection of Minorities.

Philip M. Klutznick, chairman of B'nai B'rith's International Council, who this week made public the study's contents, said "there is further evidence of the Soviet Union's pattern of anti-Jewish discrimination that openly violates the U.S.S.R.'s own constitutional guarantees of equality among its multiple nationalities."

"The tragedy of the Soviet Jew," Mr. Klutznick added, "is that he is denied the right to live as a

Jew in his homeland and denied the right to emigrate where he would be free to do so."

Mr. Klutznick said the study was submitted to the United Nations "as documentation of the Soviet Union's disregard for a cardinal principle in the U.N.'s Universal Declaration of Human Rights." This, he said, was a section of Article 13 of the Declaration which affirms that "everyone has the right to leave any country, including his own, and return to his country."

The study observes that Soviet policy makes a distinction between an absolute right to leave, which the Soviets reject, and a specific right for the purpose of reuniting dispersed families. It then makes a further distinction by denying Jews the specific right granted other Soviet citizens.

This "inconsistency . . . creates an obvious embarrassment" for the Soviet Union which it seeks to hide by denying that Soviet Jews want to emigrate, the report declares.

It quotes Khrushchev at a July 8 press conference in Vienna that the Soviet Ministry of Foreign Affairs had had "no requests of Jews wishing to go to Israel."

In contradiction to Khrushchev's statement, the report notes:

An August 8 statement to the Foreign Minister Golda Meir that 9,236 members of Jewish families in the U.S.S.R. have asked relatives in Israel to furnish documents to support emigration applications.

The Soviet Red Cross, replying to inquiries and petitions for assistance from Israelis seeking passports for relatives in the Soviet Union, invariably answers that U.S.S.R. authorities find no adequate basis for granting such exit permits.

Source: Jewish Telegraphic Agency, November 18, 1960.

8.32—"KHRUSHCHEV TALKS ABOUT SOVIET JEWS," *Jewish Criterion,* MARCH 31, 1961

When Soviet leader Nikita Khrushchev (1894–1971) hosted a dinner party at his country's United Nations office in New York City in October 1960, he invited the singer Frank Mercer to entertain the attending dignitaries. Mercer, who did not speak Russian, invited his twenty-three-year-old Russian-speaking Jewish secretary, Juliet Grosse, to help with translation. During the dinner, Grosse pressed the Soviet leader on the plight of Jews in his country. Later, the Anti-Defamation League published a transcript of the conversation.

 . . . The facts about the plight of Soviet Jews are well enough known, documented by ADL (The *Anti-Defamation League Bulletin,* September 1958 and September 1960) and scores of other sources. But the following exchange is sig-

nificant in the way it presents the official party line of evasion and half-truth about the position of Jews in the Soviet Union, uttered by the very top man in the Soviet hierarchy.

The questions and answers given here were exchanged intermittently between courses, between the songs of Mr. Mercer. Miss Grosse, who is hardly a full-fledged Soviet expert, was prevented by her position as a guest from following up the obvious rebuttals to Mr. Khrushchev.

The fact that Mr. Mercer is a Negro led to Khrushchev's observation that there is no prejudice in the Soviet Union and that all minorities are happy there.

MISS G: And the Jews—are they as happy as
  other minority groups?

MR. K: Yes. There is no prejudice at all against
  Jews in the Soviet Union.

MISS G: How come there is no Yiddish or Hebrew publishing house in the U.S.S.R.?

MR. K: But there is. In Birobidjan there is a Yiddish language newspaper and books and periodicals in Yiddish are available there.

MISS G: Well, that doesn't seem to be very much. Is Hebrew or Yiddish culture maintained throughout the Soviet Union?

MR. K: You must understand. Jews in the Soviet Union are thoroughly integrated. They speak the same language and go to the same schools as other people of the Soviet Union. Only the older people care about the past culture and there are not enough of them left to make it worthwhile to sustain it.

MISS G: Jews contributed a great deal to the military defense of Russia during World War II and there were many Jewish "Heroes of the Soviet Union." Yet today, I understand that there are no Jewish officers in the Soviet armed forces.

MR. K: That is a terrible exaggeration. Why in the Central Eastern sector there is even a Jewish general.

MISS G: There have been reports that Jews are denied advancement generally in Soviet cultural life. Are they true?

MR. K: You have only to look at the facts, the record of achievement. We have such men as [Emil] Gilels, [David] Oistrakh, and [Ilya] Ehrenburg and many others, Jews who are prominent in the Soviet Union today.

MISS G: But those men are artists and uniquely gifted. How about other Jews, ordinary people?

MR. K: Look, I have nothing at all against Jews. During the revolution, my closest friend was a Jew. I ate at his table, his mother gave me *Matzohs*. Tell your friend that the Jews in the Soviet Union are free and there's no need to be concerned about their welfare.

MISS G: I've also read that Jews are subject to discrimination in the other Communist countries.

MR. K: (Absolutely and with a wave of relief) Look—why don't you ask [János] Kadar over there about that?

The interview on the "Jewish question" was over. There will be no effort to rebut Mr. Khrushchev here, except to point up a few of his more significant evasions. There is a Yiddish language newspaper published in Birobidjan as Mr. Khrushchev says. It is a two page affair, published twice a week, with a circulation of about 1,000. (There are an estimated 3,000,000 Jews in the Soviet Union.) Some books in Yiddish are still available in the Soviet Union—but no new ones have been published in more than a decade. There is a Soviet general who is Jewish; there are a few more Jewish officers too, remnants of the promotion system of World War II. But, as a matter of state policy, no Jews are accepted in Soviet military schools today. And Mr. Khrushchev avoided the general question about discrimination against Jews in the Soviet Union by giving, in effect, the weariest dodge of all, "Some of my best friends, etc., etc."

from the ADL Bulletin
published by B'nai B'rith

Source: *Jewish Criterion* (March 31, 1961): 75–76.
Pittsburgh Jewish Newspaper Project, Carnegie Mellon University Libraries.

8.33—"SOVIET MISTREATMENT OF JEWS ATTACKED IN BOTH HOUSES OF U.S. CONGRESS," JEWISH TELEGRAPHIC AGENCY, JANUARY 25, 1962

Organizers of the Soviet Jewry movement enjoyed the political alignment of their cause with the larger Cold War political imperatives of the federal government, especially Congress. In the early 1960s, members of the U.S. Senate and House of Representatives embraced the cause of Soviet Jewry and included the mistreatment of Soviet Jews in their larger critiques of the Soviet Union. In 1961, New York senator Jacob Javits (1904–1986) traveled to the Soviet Union, reporting back to his colleagues in the Senate on his findings.

Washington—

Grave concern over the continued pressures by the Soviet Government on the Jews in the Soviet Union was expressed today in a lengthy report on the situation of Soviet Jewry presented to the U.S. Senate by Senator Jacob K. Javits, New York Republican, who recently visited the USSR. At the same time, Soviet discriminations against Jews were condemned in the House of Representatives by Congressman Abraham Multer, New York Democrat.

In his report, prepared for delivery today on the floor of the Senate, Sen. Javits called for a "world scale protest against the anti-Jewish persecutions in the Soviet Union." Rep. Multer, addressing the House, said that the Soviet Government is using anti-Semitism for "political ends." He said that the present regime in Moscow is sanctioning anti-Jewish action "in the manner of the Czarist regimes."

Senator Javits told the Senate in his report that "the continued existence of the Jews in the Soviet Union may be in danger" unless the free world "makes known its strong disapproval" of the Soviet measures against Jews. Declaring that "all signs indicate a steadily deteriorating situation that was signaled by the prosecution of Jewish community and religious leaders in Leningrad and Moscow, last October," Sen. Javits stated:

"The immediate intent of Soviet authorities in taking these measures is apparently to warn Jews that it will not tolerate any emigration of Jews to Israel or any pro-Israel agitation toward that end—the long-range purpose is quite clearly the liquidation of Judaism and Jewish consciousness in the USSR."

"All the rigid Soviet protestations that there is no Jewish problem in the Soviet Union and that anti-Semitism is against the law cannot disguise the fact that the plight of its Jewish citizens is grave and complex," Senator Javits continued. "Developments this past weekend indicate that the pressure of the attack on Jews in the Soviet Union is continuing. The obviously trumped-up accusations of spying in synagogues create new elements of danger in addition to those that have already existed."

Senator Javits said that Jews in the Soviet Union are recognized as a nationality in the Soviet Union but are not given the rights accorded other nationalities in the USSR. Despite more than 40 years of pressures and restrictions of all kinds to discourage religious identification and to isolate them from other Jewish communities throughout the world, 2,268,000 persons voluntarily declared themselves to be Jews in the January 1959 census, of whom 472,000 gave Yiddish as their native tongue," he pointed out.

(Tourists just returned from the Soviet Union have reported the closing of the only kosher public dining room in Moscow, located in the Moscow Yeshiva, according to the *Jewish Day-Morning Journal*, New York Yiddish daily newspaper.)

Source: Jewish Telegraphic Agency, January 25, 1962, http://archive.jta.org/article/1962/01/25/3068175/soviet-mistreatment-of-jews-attacked-in-both-houses-of-us-congress. All rights reserved. Used with permission.

8.34—AMERICAN JEWISH COMMITTEE, 1945, 1950–1959, CHART, ANTISEMITISM IN THE UNITED STATES DURING THE 1940S AND 1950S

As we saw, domestic antisemitism strengthened in the 1930s with the rise of Hitler in Germany and a growing isolationist attitude among Americans. During World War II, public opinion polls revealed an even greater level of anti-Jewish feeling. In the postwar period, though, antisemitism in the United States dropped significantly as awareness of the horrors of the Holocaust deepened and more efforts were made toward interfaith work aimed at weakening prejudicial thinking. A study of postwar admissions to New York colleges showed a similar decrease in bias, although a 1964 study of anti-Jewish discrimination at New York law firms found continued bias.

AJC Polls, 1945, 1950–1959

A Nov. 1945 poll asked "American high school students which of the following groups, if any, would be their last choice as a roommate."

Swedes	5%
Protestants	4%
Negroes	78%
Catholics	9%
Jews	45%
Irish	3%
Chinese	9%
Makes no difference	5%
Don't know	3%

[. . .]

. . . Polls commissioned by the American Jewish Committee in 1950, 1951, 1953, and 1954 revealed increasingly favorable attitudes toward Jews. To the question "Have you heard any criticism or talk against the Jews in the last six months?" the responses in different years highlighted the decline. . . .

	Yes	No
1940	46%	52%
1942	52	44
1944	60	37
1946	64	34
1950	24	75
1951	16	84
1953	21	79
1954	14	86
1955	13	87
1956	11	89
1957	16	84
1959	12	88

Source: Leonard Dinnerstein, *Antisemitism in America* (New York: Oxford University Press, 1994), 132. Used by permission of Oxford University Press, USA.

New York—

A survey of the experiences of 1,235 top-ranking New York high school seniors in seeking college admission has revealed "no significant evidence" of religious discrimination, the American Jewish Congress disclosed today in a report transmitted to State Education Commissioner James E. Allen, Jr.

The study by the American Jewish Congress shows a marked decline in religious bias encountered by college-bound students compared with similar surveys undertaken in 1949 and 1952. The latest study was based on a sampling of high school seniors throughout New York State who applied for scholarships awarded annually by the New York Board of Regents. A two-page questionnaire was mailed to 4,641 members of the June 1958 graduating class—every seventh name from a list of 32,876 male and female applicants for Regents Scholarships. The sample was compiled by the New York State Department of Education, which also helped to prepare the questionnaire. A total of 1,235 completed questionnaires were returned. Nearly 70 percent of the respondents were in the top quarter of their graduating classes and 35 percent were actually granted scholarships.

Of the 1,235 completed questionnaires, 37.1 percent came from Jewish students; 30.8 percent from Protestants; 29.1 percent from Catholics and 3.0 percent from those of other religions or with no religion. Nearly half—43.6 percent—of the questionnaires came from New York City students. The rest came from other parts of the state. The survey disclosed that Jewish students tended to file more applications to various colleges than their Christian classmates.

An analysis of the comparative acceptance rate for Jewish and Protestant students by the college of their first choice showed that the Jewish rate of acceptance was 74.0 percent, compared with 84.7 percent for Protestants. This difference is held not significant, since the first choices of each group were not comparable. Thus, 38.4 percent of the Jewish students in the survey applied to "Ivy League" schools—generally agreed to have the highest admission standards—as compared with 26.8 percent of the Protestant students.

A comparison of the rate of acceptance by the "Ivy League" schools according to religion showed that 67.5 percent of the Jewish students and 73.5 percent of the Protestants who applied were accepted. The small difference is considered not statistically significant and may be due to chance.

Results of the study, indicating that no measurable religious discrimination is encountered in college entrance by top-ranking Jewish students, were attributed by the American Jewish Congress to the operation of state fair education laws prohibiting religious discrimination by schools in New York and Massachusetts, in which the largest number of colleges covered in the survey are located. The AJC also cited a "general lessening of racial and religious prejudice in the North during the last decade."

Source: Jewish Telegraphic Agency, July 27, 1959, http://archive.jta.org/article/1959/07/27/3059635/no-anti jewish-bias-exists-in-new-york-college-admission -study-shows. All rights reserved. Used with permission.

9 Turning Inward
JEWS AND AMERICAN LIFE, 1965–1980

In the late 1960s and early 1970s, "identity" emerged as the dominant theme in American Jewish life. Ever since Jews had begun to enjoy the promise of civil equality in the eighteenth century, they had faced the challenge of deciding how much they wanted to accommodate themselves to the non-Jewish societies around them and how much they wanted to preserve distinctive traits and traditions as Jews. In the 1950s, American Jews typically took a universalist tack, favoring a political alliance with African Americans while they also reached out to white Christian America in a massive demographic shift to the suburbs. By the mid-1960s, though, a new generation of American Jews sought to preserve their ethnic identities. They embraced Zionism in ways that their parents never did and adopted many of the religious rituals discarded by their parents and grandparents.

Liberalism, espoused by a majority of American Jews since the Gilded Age and Progressive era, encountered a significant challenge in this period. While most American Jews supported affirmative action as the next step in the struggle for civil rights, many Jewish organizations balked when those efforts included mandatory quotas in higher education, government service, and business. A few American Jews rejected liberalism and helped found the neoconservative movement. Jewish neocons, as they came to be known, supported right-leaning grassroots organizations such as the Jewish Defense League and its critique of mainstream Jewish leadership for its apparent apathy toward the plight of Soviet Jews and the challenges of urban Jewish life.

Antisemitism reappeared as a theme in the 1960s, though in a far different form by comparison with earlier eras. Although Jews in the early and mid-twentieth century faced the specter of an antisemitic U.S. Congress and the rise of popular antisemitic personalities, American Jews in the 1960s experienced prejudice from a seemingly unlikely source: the African American community. Compared with state-sponsored antisemitism, the rise of black antisemitism proved far less consequential. Yet its presence challenged the strength of the black-Jewish alliance and the larger ability of Jews, or of any American group, to build alliances across ethnic, racial, or religious divides.

Gender also emerged as a major theme in this period with the rise of second-wave feminism. Within the Jewish communal world, women challenged the male-dominated hierarchy, pressed for an egalitarian approach to Jewish ritual life, and, within the Reconstructionist, Reform, and Conservative movements, succeeded in their call for the ordination of women as rabbis. Within Orthodoxy, small groups of women pressed for more expansive roles as teachers and experts in Jewish law.

GOVERNMENT, POLITICS, AND CIVIC STATUS

9.01—BETTY FRIEDAN, "A COMFORTABLE CONCENTRATION CAMP?" 1963

The publication of Betty Friedan's (1921–2006) The Feminine Mystique in 1963 is credited with launching the second-wave feminist movement, which culminated in a wide-ranging call for gender equality in the 1970s. The book, based on interviews Friedan conducted with women college graduates, offered a stinging indictment of postwar suburban life. In her most controversial and well-known citation, Friedman wrote that suburban housewives lived in "comfortable concentration camps."

It is not an exaggeration to call the stagnating state of millions of American housewives a sickness, a disease in the shape of a progressively weaker core of human self that is being handed down to their sons and daughters at a time when the dehumanizing aspects of modern mass culture make it necessary for men and women to have a strong core of self, strong enough to retain human individuality through the frightening, unpredictable pressures of our changing environment. The strength of women is not the cause, but the cure for this sickness. Only when women are permitted to use their full strength, to grow to their full capacities, can the feminine mystique be shattered and the progressive dehumanization of their children be stopped. And most women can no longer use their full strength, grow to their full human capacity, as housewives.

It is urgent to understand how the very condition of being a housewife can create a sense of emptiness, non-existence, nothingness, in women. There are aspects of the housewife role that make it almost impossible for a woman of adult intelligence to retain a sense of human identity, the firm core of self or "I" without which a human being, man or woman, is not truly alive. For women of ability, in America today, I am con-

vinced there is something about the housewife state itself that is dangerous. In a sense that is not as far-fetched as it sounds, the women who "adjust" as housewives, who grow up wanting to be "just a housewife," are in as much danger as the millions who walked to their own death in the concentration camps—and the millions more who refused to believe that the concentration camps existed.

In fact, there is an uncanny, uncomfortable insight into why a woman can so easily lose her sense of self as a housewife in certain psychological observations made of the behavior of prisoners in Nazi concentration camps. In these settings, purposely contrived for the dehumanization of man, the prisoners literally became "walking corpses." Those who "adjusted" to the conditions of the camps surrendered their human identity and went almost indifferently to their deaths. Strangely enough, the conditions which destroyed the human identity of so many prisoners were not the torture and the brutality, but conditions similar to those which destroy the identity of the American housewife.

In the concentration camps the prisoners were forced to adopt childlike behavior, forced to give up their individuality and merge themselves into an amorphous mass. Their capacity for self-determination, their ability to predict the future and to prepare for it, was systematically destroyed. It was a gradual process which occurred in virtually imperceptible states—but at the end, with the destruction of adult self-respect, of an adult frame of reference, the dehumanizing process was complete. This was the process as observed by Bruno Bettelheim, psychoanalyst and educational psychologist, when he was a prisoner at Dachau and Buchenwald in 1939.

[…]

It was said, finally, that not the SS but the prisoners themselves became their own worst enemy. Because they could not bear to see their situation as it really was—because they denied the very reality of their problem, and finally "adjusted" to the camp itself as if it were the only reality—they were caught in the prison of their own minds. The guns of the SS were not powerful enough to keep all those prisoners subdued. They were manipulated to trap themselves; they imprisoned themselves by making the concentration camp the whole world, by blinding themselves to the larger world of the past, their responsibility for the present, and their possibilities for the future. The ones who survived, who neither died nor were exterminated, were the ones who retained in some essential degree the adult values and interests which had been the essence of their past identity.

All this seems terribly remote from the easy life of the American suburban housewife. But is her house in reality a comfortable concentration camp? Have not women who live in the image of the feminine mystique trapped themselves within the narrow walls of their homes? They have learned to "adjust" to their biological role. They have become dependent, passive, childlike; they have given up their adult frame of reference to live at the lower human level of food and things. The work they do does not require adult capabilities; it is endless, monotonous, unrewarding. American women are not, of course, being readied for mass extermination, but they are suffering a slow death of mind and spirit. Just as with the prisoners in the concentration camps, there are American women who have resisted that death, who have managed to retain a core of self, who have not lost touch with the outside world, who use their abilities to some creative purpose. They are women of spirit and intelligence who have refused to "adjust" as housewives.

It has been said time and time again that education has kept American women from "adjusting" to their role as housewives. But if education, which serves human growth, which distills what the human mind has discovered and created in the past, and gives man the ability to create his own future—if education has made more and more American women feel trapped, frustrated, guilty as housewives, surely this should be seen as a clear signal that *women have outgrown the housewife role.*

It is not possible to preserve one's identity by adjusting for any length of time to a frame of reference that is in itself destructive to it. It is very hard indeed for a human being to sustain such an "inner" split—conforming outwardly to one reality, while trying to maintain inwardly the value it denies. The comfortable concentration camp that American women have walked into, or have been talked into by others, is just such a reality, a frame of reference that denies woman's adult human identity. By adjusting to it, a woman stunts her intelligence to become childlike, turns away from individual identity to become an anonymous biological robot in a docile mass. She becomes less than human, preyed upon by outside pressures, and herself preying upon her husband and children. And the longer she conforms, the less she feels as if she really exists. She looks for her security in things, she hides the fear of losing her human potency by testing her sexual potency, she lives a vicarious life through mass daydreams or through her husband and children. She does not want to be reminded of the outside world; she becomes convinced there is nothing she can do about her own life or the world that would make a difference. But no matter how often she tries to tell herself that this giving up of personal identity is a necessary sacrifice for her children and husband, it serves no real purpose. So the aggressive energy she should be using in the world becomes instead the terrible anger that she dare not turn against her husband, is ashamed of turning against her children, and finally turns against herself, until she feels as if she does not exist. And yet in the comfortable concentration camp as in the real one, something very strong in a woman resists the death of herself.

[. . .]

The suburban house is not a German concentration camp, nor are American housewives on their way to the gas chamber. But they are in a trap, and to escape they must, like the dancer, finally exercise their human freedom, and recapture their sense of self. They must refuse to be nameless, depersonalized, manipulated, and live their own lives again according to a self-chosen purpose. They must begin to grow.

Source: Michael Staub, ed., *The Jewish 1960s: An American Sourcebook* (Hanover, N.H.: University Press of New England, 2004), 321–24. Used by permission of the publisher.

9.02—NORMAN PODHORETZ, "MY NEGRO PROBLEM—AND OURS," *Commentary,* FEBRUARY 1963

Norman Podhoretz, born in Brooklyn in 1930 and raised in a leftist family, became, in the 1960s, one of the intellectual leaders of Jewish neoconservatism. After earning degrees from Columbia University, the Jewish Theological Seminary, and the University of Cambridge, Podhoretz took editorial control of the American Jewish Committee's Commentary *magazine in 1960. Three years thereafter, Podhoretz wrote "My Negro Problem—and Ours," an article that detailed his troubled relations with African Americans in his youth, his thoughts about racial equality and the civil rights movement, and, because of the considerable attention it received, solidified his reputation as a leading neoconservative writer. Under his stewardship,* Commentary *developed into the most important right-wing voice of American Jewry.*

Two ideas puzzled me deeply as a child growing up in Brooklyn during the 1930's in what today would be called an integrated neighborhood. One of them was that all Jews were rich; the other was that all Negroes were persecuted. These ideas had appeared in print; therefore they must be true. My own experience and the evidence of my senses told me they were not true, but that only confirmed what a day-dreaming boy in the provinces—for the lower-class neighborhoods of New York belong as surely to the provinces as any rural town in North Dakota—

discovers very early: *his* experience is unreal and the evidence of his senses is not to be trusted. . . .

And so for a long time I was puzzled to think that Jews were supposed to be rich when the only Jews I knew were poor, and that Negroes were supposed to be persecuted when it was the Negroes who were doing the only persecuting I knew about—and doing it, moreover, to *me.* During the early years of the war, when my older sister joined a left-wing youth organization, I remember my astonishment at hearing her passionately denounce my father for thinking that Jews were worse off than Negroes. To me, at the age of twelve, it seemed very clear that Negroes were better off than Jews—indeed, than *all* whites. A city boy's world is contained within three or four square blocks, and in my world it was the whites, the Italians and Jews, who feared the Negroes, not the other way around. The Negroes were tougher than we were, more ruthless, and on the whole they were better athletes. What could it mean, then, to say that they were badly off and that we were more fortunate? Yet my sister's opinions, like print, were sacred, and when she told me about exploitation and economic forces I believed her. I believed her, but I was still afraid of Negroes. And I still hated them with all my heart.

[. . .]

In my own neighborhood, a good deal of animosity existed between the Italian kids (most of whose parents were immigrants from Sicily) and the Jewish kids (who came largely from East European immigrant families). Yet everyone had friends, sometimes close friends, in the other "camp," and we often visited one another's strange-smelling houses, if not for meals, then for glasses of milk, and occasionally for some special event like a wedding or a wake. If it happened that we divided into warring factions and did battle, it would invariably be half-hearted and soon patched up. Our parents, to be sure, had nothing to do with one another and were mutually suspicious and hostile. But we, the kids, who all spoke Yiddish or Italian at home, were Americans, or New Yorkers, or Brooklyn boys: we shared a culture, the culture of the street, and at least for a while this culture proved to be more powerful than the opposing cultures of the home.

Why, *why* should it have been so different as between the Negroes and us? How was it borne in upon us so early, white and black alike, that we were enemies beyond any possibility of reconciliation? Why did we hate one another so?

. . . What happened to me, from Brooklyn, who grew up fearing and envying and hating Negroes? Now that Brooklyn is behind me, do I fear them and envy them and hate them still? The answer is yes, but not in the same proportions and certainly not in the same way. I now live on the upper west side of Manhattan, where there are many Negroes and many Puerto Ricans, and there are nights when I experience the old apprehensiveness again, and there are streets that I avoid when I am walking in the dark, as there were streets that I avoided when I was a child. . . .

The hatred I still feel for Negroes is the hardest of all the old feelings to face or admit, and it is the most hidden and the most overlarded by the conscious attitudes into which I have succeeded in willing myself. It no longer has, as for me it once did, any cause or justification. . . .

How, then, do I know that this hatred has never entirely disappeared? I know it from the insane rage that can stir in me at the thought of Negro anti-Semitism; I know it from the disgusting prurience that can stir in me at the sight of a mixed couple; and I know it from the violence that can stir in me whenever I encounter that special brand of paranoid touchiness to which many Negroes are prone.

This, then, is where I am; it is not exactly where I think all other white liberals are, but it cannot be so very far away either. And it is because I am convinced that we white Americans are . . . so twisted and sick in our feelings about Negroes that I despair of the present push toward integration. . . .

. . . [The Negro's] past is a stigma, his color is a stigma, and his vision of the future is the hope of erasing the stigma by making color irrelevant, by making it disappear as a fact of consciousness.

I share this hope, but I cannot see how it will ever be realized unless color does *in fact* disappear: and that means not integration, it means assimilation, it means—let the brutal word come out—miscegenation. The Black Muslims, like their racist counterparts in the white world, accuse the "so-called Negro leaders" of secretly pursuing miscegenation as a goal. The racists are wrong, but I wish they were right, for I believe that the wholesale merging of the two races is the most desirable alternative for everyone concerned. I am not claiming that this alternative can be pursued programmatically or that it is immediately feasible as a solution; obviously there are even greater barriers to its achievement than to the achievement of integration. What I am saying, however, is that in my opinion the Negro problem can be solved in this country in no other way. . . .

Source: Reprinted from *Commentary*, February 1963, by permission; copyright © 1963 by Commentary, Inc.

In the late 1960s, most American Jews, and many national Jewish organizations, opposed U.S. involvement in Southeast Asia. Aligning themselves with the larger liberal critique of the Cold War, American Jews joined antiwar protests in disproportionate numbers. Within the world of American Orthodoxy, though, questions of Cold War politics and U.S. foreign policy proved more complex. For Berlin-born philosopher Michael Wyschogrod (b. 1928), a former yeshiva student who eventually earned his PhD at Columbia University, the war in Vietnam aligned with the interests of Jews. In a 1966 article published by Tradition, *a journal of Orthodox Jewish thought, Wyschogrod offered a Jewish defense of U.S. interventionism.*

Among the oldest jokes told in Jewish circles is the one whose punchline is some variation of the "Is it good for Jews or bad for Jews?" theme. Stanley discovers Livingstone in central Africa, Bannister runs the four-minute mile, and the other side of the moon is photographed for the first time. To all of these revelations, Tevyeh the Milkman, or his American equivalent, responds with the age-old Jewish question—is it good or bad for Jews? We smile at the provincialism, we are amused by the one-sided obsession with concern for the fate of the Jews that these stories reflect and we feel superior because we are cosmopolitan and citizens of the world, concerned with issues that affect all mankind and not just the Jews. We would be more than embarrassed to pass judgment on events, particularly when serious moral questions are involved, with an eye to the Jewish interest. If there is a Jewish interest involved we will lean over backwards to be fair and impartial so that no one can accuse us of special pleading. For many of us, the meaning of our Jewishness is precisely this concern with the suffering of all mankind and for injustice wherever it occurs. To take up the cudgels for Jewish interests seems almost a betrayal of the lofty moral ideals of the prophets and the best in the Jewish tradition. Our cause is justice, not self-interest. . . .

II

What is the Jewish interest in the Vietnamese situation? There are two aspects to this problem, one general, the other more specific. The general aspect concerns Jews and Communism as such and the effects of a Vietcong victory on European stability. The other is more specific in that it revolves around the parallel that must be drawn between the situation of Israel and South Vietnam.

. . . While it is true that conditions in other European Communist countries, such as Poland and Hungary, are better for Jews, the much larger number of Jews in the Soviet Union makes that the focal problem. From this point of view it is to the interest of the Jewish people that Soviet power not be extended, quite apart from all other legitimate objections one might justifiably have to the totalitarianism of the Soviet variety. In fact, this is largely an academic issue because a certain stabilization has occurred in Europe safeguarding the non-Communist portion of that continent from Communist encroachment. Since the fall of China to Communism and the Korean war, the major area of instability has been the Far East and there, as already noted, there are no major Jewish communities. Nevertheless, it is not at all unreasonable to assume that should Communism score a series of major successes in the Far East, the stability of Europe and even the United States would very likely be affected and to this extent Jewish existence would be placed in jeopardy. This is particularly true in view of the deep Soviet involvement in the Vietnamese war and the inevitable prestige that would accrue to the Soviet Union in case of a Vietcong victory. Whether this would be enough to upset the precarious European balance is hard to say; that it might is a distinct possibility. . . .

. . . In the nuclear age, no rational person can consider war of an offensive variety as anything but the greatest calamity. But it does mean that the Soviet Union must be taught what in fact she seems to have learned: that borders cannot be changed by force, be it in the guise of national wars of liberation, externally supported guerrilla operations, etc. In Europe, this lesson seems to have sunk in, a fact to which we owe the peace of that continent.

Asian Communism has, however, not yet learned this fact. As a result, there is no peace there. In any direct way, there is little Jewish interest as such in the Far East except to the extent that the interests of the State of Israel are involved. And here we come to the crux of our argument.

Israel is an Asian country. It stands to reason that Asian events will therefore not leave Israel unaffected. But being Asian is only the first of the similarities between Vietnam and Israel. Both are countries that have been split artificially into two components. Both have long borders separating one segment from the other. In both cases nobody likes the split but one side is willing to abide by the status quo while the other is not and resorts to force to unify the country. In both cases the theme of national liberation is heard: the Arab infiltrators, often of Palestinian origin, who spread death and destruction in Israeli villages, like to think of themselves as liberating their country just as the Vietcong see themselves liberating their country from the American invaders and their local supporters. In both cases the sympathy of the world Communist movement is on one side, while the Western world by and large supports the other. And in both cases, the only hope for peace rests on the aggressors resigning themselves to the existence of borders they do not like and devoting their energies to building the part of the country they control and leaving their neighbor alone.

[. . .]

All historic parallels have their limits, of course. No two historic situations are exactly alike as no two events or objects in the universe are exactly alike. Thus one can point out that the Jewish population of Israel is united and determined to resist Arab aggression while the population of South Vietnam is much less clearly united. . . . If the United States with the magnitude of its military effort on behalf of South Vietnam is defeated, no small nation surrounded by hostile neighbors such as Israel can put any trust in American guarantees. The issue here is simply the credibility of American commitments. Given the fact that Israel can expect no support from the Communist countries, it is of vital significance for its national survival that American support command the respect of its foes. While the Israeli spirit likes to look to itself for its defense, it would be foolhardy in the extreme to overlook the support the Arab cause receives from the Communist world. This support must be balanced by a countervailing support from another major power whose support is not seen as that of a paper tiger. The American commitment to the security of Israel, some of it on the record and much of it undoubtedly off the record, must therefore retain its credibility or one of the most crucial factors contributing to the precarious peace of the Middle East will have been destroyed. American repudiation of its commitment to South Vietnam would cast a deep shadow over all of its commitments, a prospect which Israeli diplomats in private conversation view with the profoundest anxiety. This, in short, is the Jewish stake in the events of Vietnam.

There is one other point that must be made with some emphasis. While the security of Israel is a matter of legitimate concern to Jews, it is not the only matter of concern to Jews. If the war in Vietnam were inherently immoral, it would be proper for American Jews to condemn that war whatever the consequences of such a condemnation for the Israeli national interest may be. But such is not the case. Because the Vietnamese situation has been so thoroughly debated so many times from so many different points of view, there is no point in going over that territory here except in regard to the parallel with the Israeli situation. From the moral point of view, it is the question of the reunification of divided states by force that is the issue. . . . In view of this it is my conviction that by supporting the U.S. effort in Vietnam the American Jew is supporting a cause that is not only in the interests of Israel and the U.S. but, even more important, of justice itself. It must finally be added that nothing I have said implies that only total victory for the Allies is an acceptable solution to the Vietnamese conflict. The U.S. should be ever ready to negotiate with the enemy and to come to reasonable terms, even well short of total victory. It is only withdrawal under conditions of the surrender of South Vietnam to Communist rule, the course recently advocated by the Catholic Journal *Commonweal*, that would be catastrophic to Jewish interests.

III

Why has all this gone so largely unnoticed by the bulk of the American Jewish community? Why did it come as such a shock when in the fall of 1966 the press carried reports about President Johnson's allusions to the Jewish interest in Vietnam? Whatever the exact content or propriety of those remarks may have been, the fact remains, as I have tried to demonstrate, that there is a Jewish interest in Vietnam, even if it would have been preferable for American Jews rather than President Johnson to discover this fact. What prevented this discovery?

It is here that the situation is a bit alarming. It is true that American Jews are not only Jews but they are, by and large, also liberals and that to the extent that liberals have been critical of the U.S. effort in Vietnam, Jews, as liberals, have simply reflected this fact. But while all this is understandable, it also means that large segments of the American Jewish community lack the almost instinctual reflexes that come into play when vital interests of a group are threatened. If such reflexes were missing in this case, it may be because large segments of the American Jewish community no longer identify as Jews on this visceral level. If that is the case, we have something to worry about that extends far beyond any individual issue, be it Vietnam or anything else. . . .

Source: Vietnam War nearprint file, AJA.

9.04—RABBI ABRAHAM JOSHUA HESCHEL, SELECTION FROM "THE MORAL OUTRAGE OF VIETNAM," JANUARY 31, 1967

Rabbi Abraham Joshua Heschel, born in Poland and educated in Berlin, escaped first to London and then moved to New York City after Hitler came to power in Europe. As a faculty member first at the Reform movement's Hebrew Union College, then at the Conservative movement's Jewish Theological Seminary, Heschel took political stands on the larger issues of the day. He embodied, and helped define, a progressive Jewish politics that linked liberal and Democratic positions with the prophetic impulse of Judaism. Heschel is perhaps best known for marching side by side with Dr. Martin Luther King Jr. to Selma, Alabama, in 1965. Two years later, on January 31, he offered his textual opposition to U.S. involvement in Vietnam at a Washington, D.C., worship service attended by sympathetic clergy and laymen. His talk was based on the words of the prophet Ezekiel (34:25–31).

Ours is an assembly of shock, contrition, and dismay. Who would have believed that we life-loving Americans are capable of bringing death and destruction to so many innocent people? We are startled to discover how unmerciful, how beastly we ourselves can be.

So we implore Thee, our Father in heaven, help us to banish the beast from our hearts, the beast of cruelty, the beast of callousness.

Since the beginning of history evil has been going forth from nation to nation. The lords of the flocks issue proclamations, and the sheep of all nations indulge in devastations.

But who would have believed that our own nation at the height of its career as the leader of free nations, the hope for peace in the world, whose unprecedented greatness was achieved through "liberty and justice for all," should abdicate its wisdom, suppress its compassion and permit guns to become its symbols?

America's resources, moral and material, are immense. We have the means and know the ways of dispelling prejudice and lies, of overcoming poverty and disease. We have the capacity to lead the world in seeking to overcome international hostility.

Must napalm stand in the way of our power to aid and to inspire the world?

To be sure, just as we feel deeply the citizen's dilemma, we are equally sensitive to the dilemma confronting the leaders of our government. Our government seems to recognize the tragic error and futility of the escalation of our involvement but feels that we cannot extricate ourselves without public embarrassment of such dimension as to cause damage to America's prestige.

But the mire in which we flounder threatens us with an even greater danger. It is the dilemma of either losing face or losing our soul.

At this hour Vietnam is our most urgent, our most disturbing religious problem, a challenge to the whole nation as well as a challenge to every one of us [as] an individual.

When a person is sick, in danger or in misery, all religious duties recede, all rituals are suspended, except one: to save life and relieve pain.

Vietnam is a personal problem. To speak about God and remain silent on Vietnam is blasphemous.

When you spread forth your hands
I will hide my eyes from you;
Yea when you make many prayers,
I will not hear—
Your hands are not clean. [Isa 1:15]

In the sight of so many thousands of civilians and soldiers slain, injured, crippled, of bodies emaciated, of forests destroyed by fire, God confronts us with this question:
Where art thou?
Is there no compassion in the world? No sense of discernment to realize that this is a war that refutes any conceivable justification of war?

The sword is the pride of man; arsenals, military bases, nuclear weapons lend supremacy to nations. War is the climax of ingenuity, the object of supreme dedication.

Men slaughtering each other, cities battered into ruins: such insanity has plunged many nations into an abyss of disgrace. Will America, the promise of peace to the world, fail to uphold its magnificent destiny?

The most basic way in which all men may be divided is between those who believe that war is unnecessary and those who believe that war is inevitable; between those to whom the sword is the symbol of honor and those to whom seeking to convert swords into plowshares is the only way to keep our civilization from disaster.

Most of us prefer to disregard the dreadful deeds we do over there. The atrocities committed in our name are too horrible to be credible. It is beyond our power to react vividly to the ongoing nightmare, day after day, night after night. So we bear graciously other people's suffering.

O Lord, we confess our sins, we are ashamed of the inadequacy of our anguish, of how faint and slight is our mercy. We are a generation that has lost the capacity for outrage.

We must continue to remind ourselves that in a free society, all are involved in what some are doing. *Some are guilty, all are responsible.*

Prayer is our greatest privilege. To pray is to stake our very existence, our right to live, on the truth and on the supreme importance of that which we pray for. Prayer, then, is radical commitment, a dangerous involvement in the life of God.

In such awareness we pray . . .

We do not stand alone. Millions of Americans, millions of people all over the world are with us.

At this moment praying for peace in Vietnam we are spiritually Vietnamese. Their agony is our affliction, their hope is our commitment.

God is present wherever men are afflicted.

Where is God present now?

We do not know how to cry, we do not know how to pray!

Our conscience is so timid, our words so faint, our mercy so feeble.

O Father, have mercy upon us.

Our God, add our cries uttered here to the cries of the bereaved, crippled, and dying over there.

Have mercy upon all of us.

Help us to overcome the arrogance of power. Guide and inspire the President of the United States in finding a speedy, generous, and peaceful end to the war in Vietnam.

The intensity of the agony is high, the hour is late, the outrage may reach a stage where repentance will be too late, repair beyond any nation's power.

We call for a covenant of peace, for reconciliation of America and all of Vietnam. To paraphrase the words of the prophet Isaiah (62:1):

For Vietnam's sake I will not keep silent,
For America's sake I will not rest,
Until the vindication of humanity goes forth
   as brightness,
And peace for all men is a burning torch.

Here is the experience of a child of seven who was reading in school the chapter which tells of the sacrifice of Isaac:

Isaac was on the way to Mount Moriah with his father; then he lay on the altar, bound, waiting to be sacrificed. My heart began to beat even faster; it actually sobbed with pity for Isaac. Behold, Abraham now lifted the knife. And now my heart froze within me with fright. Suddenly, the voice of the angel was heard: "Abraham, lay not thine hand upon the lad, for now I know that thou fearest God." And here I broke out in tears and wept aloud. "Why are you crying?" asked the Rabbi. "You know that Isaac was not killed."

And I said to him, still weeping, "But, Rabbi, supposing the angel had come a second too late?"

The Rabbi comforted me and calmed me by telling me that an angel cannot come late.

An angel cannot be late, but man, made of flesh and blood, may be.

Source: Robert McAfee Brown, Abraham J. Heschel, Michael Novak, *Vietnam: Crisis of Conscience* (New York: Association Press, Behrman House, Herder and Herder, 1967), 48–51. Copyright © Susannah Heschel. Used by permission.

9.05 — "RADICAL SAUL ALINSKY: PROPHET OF POWER TO THE PEOPLE," *Time*, MARCH 2, 1970

Labor activist and organizer Saul Alinsky (1909–1972), a Chicago native and the son of Russian Jewish immigrants, spent his career organizing disenfranchised groups. Alinsky formed the Industrial Areas Foundation as a training school for labor organizers. Later he helped mobilize Irish Americans in Chicago, African Americans in Rochester, and Chicanos in California. A 1970 Time *magazine essay reflected on his activism.*

Saul Alinsky has possibly antagonized more people—regardless of race, color or creed—than any other living American. From his point of view, that adds up to an eminently successful career: his aim in life is to make people mad enough to fight for their own interests. "The only place you really have consensus is where you have totalitarianism," he says, as he organizes conflict as the only route to true progress. Like Machiavelli, whom he has studied and admires, Alinsky teaches how power may be used. Unlike Machiavelli, his pupil is not the prince but the people.

It is not too much to argue that American democracy is being altered by Alinsky's ideas. In an age of dissolving political labels, he is a radical—but not in the usual sense, and he is certainly a long way removed from New Left extremists. He has instructed white slums and black ghettos in organizing to improve their living and working conditions; he inspired Cesar Chavez's effort to organize California's grape pickers. His strategy was emulated by the Federal Government in its antipoverty and model-cities programs: the poor have been encouraged to participate in measures for their relief instead of just accepting handouts.

A sharing of power, thinks Alinsky, is what democracy is all about. Where power is lacking, so are hope and happiness. Alinsky seeks power for others, not for himself. His goal is to build the kind of organization that can dispense with his services as soon as possible. Nor does he confine his tactics to the traditionally underprivileged. Although he has largely helped the very poor, he has begun to teach members of the alienated middle classes how to use power to combat increasingly burdensome taxes and pollution.

In his view, the end of achieving power justifies a wide range of means. "To get anywhere," Alinsky teaches, "you've got to know how to communicate. With city hall, the language is

votes, just as with a corporation it's stock power. This means that they never hear with their ears but only through their rears." He knows how to kick. To force slumlords, corporations or city officials to clean up buildings, provide jobs or stop cheating consumers, he resorts to picketing, boycotts, rent strikes and some imaginative dramatic stunts. He had garbage dumped on an alderman's driveway to make the point that collections were inadequate in the slums; ghetto rats were ceremoniously deposited on the steps of city hall. If the occasion requires, Alinsky's forces will not refrain from spreading rumors about an antagonist or indulging in something that comes very close to blackmail. "Our organizers," he says, "look for the wrong reasons to get the right things done." He has only contempt for liberals who appeal to the altruism of their opponents: "A liberal is the kind of guy who walks out of a room when the argument turns into a fight."

HELP FROM THE ESTABLISHMENT
. . . Even Alinsky's everyday habits and gestures are intended to demonstrate the uses of power. Once, while addressing students at an Eastern college in the campus chapel, he lit up a cigarette. The college president rose to tell him that smoking was not allowed, whereupon Alinsky started to leave. "No smoking, no speech," he announced. The embarrassed president at once relented: though having made his point, Alinsky refrained from smoking. He upholds the public's right to good service in restaurants: to get attention, he will throw a glass on the floor or bellow insults at the waiter.

[. . .]

Alinsky grew up in Chicago, experiencing many of the same frustrations that now embitter the city's blacks. The son of a Jewish tailor from Russia, he burned as a youth with the need to compensate for his own lack of power. "I never thought of walking on the grass," he recalls, "until I saw a sign saying 'Keep off the grass.' Then I would stomp all over it." He studied archaeology at the University of Chicago, but what really excited him was spending a summer helping dissident miners in their revolt against John L. Lewis' United Mine Workers. Later he wrote a biography of Lewis, who became a close friend and mentor. After graduation, he received his first lesson in the realities of power when, as a graduate fellow in criminology, he studied Al Capone's gang. He learned that in the Chicago of the 1930s, crime was the Establishment. "When one of those guys got knocked off, there wasn't any court. Most of the judges were at the funeral, and some were pallbearers."

It was hatred of Hitler that first impelled Alinsky to try his hand at organization. In the so-called Back of the Yards section of Chicago in the late '30s, fascism was making many converts among the jobless, bitterly frustrated slum-dwellers. "This was not the slum across the tracks," recalls Alinsky. "This was the slum across the tracks from across the tracks." By organizing a series of sitdowns and boycotts, he forced the neighborhood meat packers and slumlords to meet the demands of the community for a better life. Alien ideologies lost their force, and Back of the Yards became the model of a stable neighborhood.

. . . Alinsky has a keen sense of mortality and seems to find more satisfaction in the pursuit than in the attainment of a goal. No ultimate utopia lies over the horizon for him. "Every time you resolve a problem," he says, "you create another. My life is a quest for the unexpected." After life? "They'll send me to hell, and I'll organize it."

Source: Saul Alinsky nearprint file, AJA.

9.06—JEWISH DEFENSE LEAGUE TEN-POINT PROGRAM, N.D.

In the mid-1960s, Jews joined other ethnic Americans who focused their political activism on the particular needs of their own communities. When most urban Jews retreated to the suburbs, they left a population of working class and elderly Jews behind in what became majority African American communities. Growing antagonism between the African American and Jewish communities led to charges of black antisemitism and Jewish racism alike. In 1968, Meir Kahane (1932–1990), a Brooklyn-born Orthodox rabbi and admirer of the Revisionist Zionist leader Ze'ev Jabotinsky (1880–1940) as well as Peter Bergson, responded by creating the Jewish Defense League, a vigilante group focused on protecting Jews from antisemitism. Membership in the JDL swelled to an estimated 15,000 people when it took the national lead in the emerging struggle to save Soviet Jewry. Included as follows are a document that outlines the principles of the JDL, an interview with Kahane, and a JDL promotional flyer.

We, of the Jewish Defense League, offer the following *Ten Point Program* originated by Rabbi Meier Kahane, toward the resolving of the imprisonment and cultural extermination of Soviet Jewry:

1. An immediate end to all Western talks with the USSR including Disarmament, Space, Cultural and Trade talks.
2. Embargo on trade with the Soviet Union and a world-wide boycott on all firms dealing with the USSR.
3. An end to all tourism to the Soviet Union, except for selected individuals who go on behalf of Soviet Jewry.
4. A cessation of all cultural, entertainment and sports exchanges.
5. The banning of the Soviet Union from the Olympics and from all International organizations.
6. Legal harassment of Soviet officials, including picketing of private residences and mass telephone calls to embassies, consulates, etc.

7. Political wooing of anti-Soviet politicians and prominent business and social figures.
8. Non-violent Civil Disobedience, i.e., sit-downs, chainings, etc. to pressure world governments to suspend contact with the Soviet Union.
9. Compulsory courses in all Jewish schools on the Soviet Jewish question and optional courses in public schools.
10. Non-stop day-by-day demonstrations at all official Soviet installations.

Source: Jewish Defense League nearprint file, AJA.

9.07—ZVI LOWENTHAL AND JONATHAN BRAUN, "AN INTERVIEW WITH MEIR KAHANE," 1971

Do you think that the activist program of the J.D.L. has been the decisive factor in attracting so many youth to the J.D.L.?

I think that's probably the key to everything that we have done. The bankruptcy of Jewish leadership is manifested most clearly in the results that we see with Jewish youth. I don't always like to use the term "Establishment" but the fact is that it does exist. Our Jewish leaders carry the sin and the crime of negligence when it comes to Jewish youth.

How do you think they've failed the Jewish youth community?

They have not given the young Jew any reason to feel Jewish. When I speak in synagogues and temples out in the suburbs, the adults come there expecting me to agree with them when someone gets up and attacks the Jewish New Left youth as lousy kids with long hair, and so on. They're usually very stunned when I say—and all our people say—that, on the contrary, our great hope is not so much the apathetic youth, but the radical leftist who at least marches for something and feels something. If someone feels something he's alive.

And now, of course, you have to change them to the right way. How do you resurrect the dead? Both the dead Jews, the apathetic young Jews, and those who have gone into foreign fields, into strange fields, and marched with all sorts of non-Jewish and anti-Jewish causes—they have all done so because they've never received any reason for being proud to be Jewish. Everyone knows the incredible kind of training the young Jews get. A kid of eleven or twelve is brought to Hebrew school, not to be Jewish but for a *bar mitzvah*. If I had my way, I'd bury this entire ritual because it has buried us. A *bar mitzvah*, my God! That's not the beginning. That's it; that's the end of everything.

Judaism in this country is hypocrisy. It's a fraud. And when we come, we say to young people, "We don't want to give you anything; we demand of you something. You've got to help. You've got to march. You may even get arrested; you may have to fight police—but for something Jewish."

So you would say that the activism of the J.D.L. presents a viable alternative to the so-called Portnoy Judaism or the bagels-and-lox Judaism of the Jewish Establishment?

No question about it. I believe that there are only two meaningful Jewish trends at this moment on campus. They are the J.D.L. and the radical Zionist trends. These are two groups which offer sacrifices, which offer substance, not form. I feel very close in many ways to the Radical Zionist Alliance and to the Jewish Liberation Project. I differ with them strongly on certain issues. But I know there is substance there, and meaning and sincerity which young Jews sense both in them and in us.

You have indicated that you feel a closeness to the Radical Zionist Alliance and to the Jewish Liberation Project. Do you also feel a possible closeness toward other militant ethnic groups, such as the Puerto Rican Young Lords and the Black Panthers?

There is no question that despite the effort to paint us as racists—which is incredible nothingness—we certainly do feel and understand a great many of the things that, for example, the Panthers say. We differ with them on a number of things—for example, branding all police as pigs. But there are pigs. No one has to teach me that. I've seen cops charging and shouting, "Lousy kikes!" I've seen and heard those things. I myself, in the 90th precinct in Queens, when I was arrested last June, saw one of our people handcuffed, both hands cuffed to a chair as he was beaten by a cop. I've seen the anti-Semitism. So there are pigs, and if they can do this to us you can imagine what they can do to some poor black guy.

So we don't differ with the Panthers on that. And we don't differ with the Panthers in the sense that if after asking for 300 years for things from the government—federal or local—it becomes necessary to use unorthodox or outrageous ways. There is no question. On this we don't differ. We don't differ on their wanting to instill in their young people ethnic pride. Not at all. Where we do differ with them is where we think that nationalism crosses the boundary line and becomes Nazism; instead of just love of our own people, hatred of others.

What I believe is clear evidence of anti-Semitism on the part of Panthers is not just anti-Zionism. This is a cop-out. This is nothing. I remember reading the April 25, 1970 issue of the Panther paper where they attack those three well-known Zionists— Abbie Hoffman, Jerry Rubin, and William Kunstler. They're not Zionists. They're Jews. This is a code name, the kind of thing the Poles used two years ago to expel their Zionists when they meant Jews. So we empathize with the Panthers and sympathize with them; but we get turned off when they suddenly deviate from what we feel to be a legitimate nationalism and go on to hatred of other people. . . .

Does that mean that you feel that the American Jewish community may be endangered in the near future?

There is no hope for the Jews in this country. I'm going to say that quite clearly. I've said this over and over again to adults in the suburbs. I'd go for 40 minutes and they'd eat it up and love it, and then I'd say, "Remember, the only place for a Jew to live is in Israel." That's it. Goodbye. But again, I'm not out to score points with people. I'm out to deal with what I honestly believe to be a serious, physical crisis for Jews arising in this country.

I think that I love Jews enough to say things to them for what I think is their benefit, without having to make points. This is why we did take the stand that we took on Vietnam. We didn't have to say that. We could have gotten—I know we could have had at this moment—thousands and thousands of new members on campuses if we didn't take that stand [in favor of the war]. I believed then and I believe to this day that any time there is a conflict between what I think is good for Jews and for J.D.L. there is no conflict. Jews come first. . . .

Source: Michael Staub, ed., *The Jewish 1960s: An American Sourcebook* (Hanover, N.H.: University Press of New England, 2004), 264–67. Used by permission of the publisher.

JEWS בד"ה

The time for waking up has already passed. The storm is here. Due to the fact that Nazis have achieved electoral successes in the U.S., the J.DL. is offering extensive self-defense and firearms training for anyone with a sincere interest. Learn how to defend yourself, your loved ones, and your property. There are 90 million handguns in America, and Jews are'nt the ones who own them. CLASSES ARE HELD EVERY SUNDAY. CALL FOR MORE INFO and to find out how you can help to weather the storm.

658-6087

JEWISH DEFENSE LEAGUE "NEVER AGAIN"

Source: Jewish Defense League nearprint file, AJA.

9.09—JO ANN LEVINE, "A WOMAN'S PLACE IS IN THE HOUSE," *Christian Science Monitor*, JUNE 28, 1972

Social activist Bella Abzug (1920–1998), who represented New York City in the U.S. Congress from 1973 to 1977, was the first Jewish woman elected to Congress from the Democratic Party, following Republican Florence Prag Kahn (1866–1948) of San Francisco in the 1920s and 1930s. Abzug, after helping found the National Women's Political Caucus in 1971 with Betty Friedan and Gloria Steinem (b. 1934), led President Jimmy Carter's (b. 1924) commission on women. The Christian Science Monitor *offered a review of her 1972 book,* Bella! Ms. Abzug Goes to Washington.

Everytime Rep. Bella Abzug lost a crucial vote in Congress, was thwarted back home in Manhattan, or was trampled upon by an unthinking male chauvinist in either place, she bounced back very high, according to this account of her first year in Congress.

She leaves little doubt that her pattern will not change now that Rep. William F. Ryan has resoundingly defeated her in the new Democratic primary. In this race, Rep. Abzug didn't even carry her own Greenwich Village voting district. Why not? Maybe she had her sledgehammer into too many pies.

Her diary-form book, dictated into a tape recorder, is a stream of anecdotal insights into Rep. Abzug as congresswoman, wife, mother, speaker, steam-roller, and women's libber.

She delights in the reactions of the "men on the hill" to the most visible, outspoken, freshman "congressperson" they had probably ever seen.

"They don't understand me," she writes, "because they see I'm multi-dimensional. I confuse them. They see that I'm a perfectly reasonable human being when they'd like to be able to call me a wild nut. One moment they see me outside with the demonstrators and the next moment I'm inside diligently working with the legislative process. And I don't allow myself to be intimidated by them. I'm as friendly as can be; I talk about the weather, about how I feel, about how they feel, about the problems of being mothers and fathers. I go to committee meetings, do my homework, question witnesses and have a very good attendance record on the floor. I never lose my cool in debate, I'm consistent, and I'm very responsible about not missing votes and so on. This drives them up the wall! They expect me to be totally iconoclastic, without relief, totally scornful, unable or unwilling to function within the arena of legislation—and I'm not."

Rep. Abzug reveals problems which men never have, such as her first meeting with fellow freshman Congresswoman, Mrs. Louise Day Hicks of Boston. It took place under hairdryers in the House beauty parlor.

"What are you going to wear tomorrow? Long or short?" Mrs. Hicks asks her. And at her first meeting with the First Lady, which took place in a White House reception line, Mrs. Nixon said, "Oh, I've been looking forward to meeting you. . . . I've read all about you and your cute little bonnets."

Rep. Abzug's stance is consistent: she is always against every facet of the Vietnam war, she always puts her frame of reference as a liberated woman around her view of legislation and she keeps watch on the shape of everybody else's frame too.

She writes: "We could have a universal child care program in this country for what it costs to maintain the military for a month and a half . . . this movement [moment] in history requires women to lead the movement for radical change. First, because we have the potential of becoming the largest individual movement; second because our major interests are in common with other oppressed groups; and third, because we've never had a chance to make mistakes in government and so we have no mistakes to defend. Men have made the world the way it is."

Rep. Abzug admits that she has often been lonely while in Congress. The continuous march of constituents into her office, innumerable meetings with congressional committees, speaking engagements around the country allow her little time for depth of contact with members of the public, much less with her own husband, Martin, and her two college-age daughters.

But, looking back over her first year, she writes " . . . is there anything I would have done differently? No, if anything, I should have done more of it."

Source: Bella Abzug nearprint file, AJA.

In 1984, the Los Angeles Times *featured a debate on the future of American Jewish politics between Rabbi Arthur Hertzberg (1921–2006), a Polish-born Conservative movement rabbi and academic historian who was active in the civil rights struggle of the 1960s, and David G. Epstein, a right-leaning Jewish member of the Santa Monica, California, city council.*

IS IT LIBERALISM?

ARTHUR HERTZBERG

The accepted wisdom among American politicians is that the way to court "the Jewish vote" is to outbid each other in proclaiming their devotion to the cause of Israel. For example, in the Democratic primaries Walter F. Mondale and Gary Hart have squabbled in the states where there are large Jewish populations over who is more committed to Israel and, from an earlier date, over who is more committed to moving the American Embassy from Tel Aviv to Jerusalem.

It is equally the accepted wisdom of the leaders of the American Jewish establishment that it is politic to deny that there is such a thing as a "Jewish vote." So, for example, when Mondale and Hart were trying to outbid each other on the Israel issue, the Washington representative of the American Jewish Committee, Hyman Bookbinder, published a short essay in the *New York Times* in which he insisted that Jews vote as individuals, just as do all other Americans (which of course they do), and that there is no such thing as a recognizable Jewish vote.

Neither of these propositions is true. It is beyond doubt that since the creation of Israel the American Jewish community has trusted both major parties to be for Israel. But Jews have believed, on occasion, that both major parties will try to be more "evenhanded" between Israel and the Arabs than the most ardent supporters of Israel would want.

It is statistically demonstrable that in election after election Jews have voted heavily for the Democratic candidate, even when he has been suspected of being somewhat less ardently Zionist than was his Republican competitor. So in 1980 Ronald Reagan was known to be the most hard-line supporter of Israel, yet he received only 40% of the Jewish vote. Jimmy Carter got 40%, and 20% went to independent John Anderson, even though his public pronouncements were less pro-Israel than were Carter's.

Something comparable happened 12 years ago in the Richard M. Nixon–George McGovern election. McGovern had a majority among only two groups in the American electorate—blacks and Jews. This happened among Jews despite the fact that McGovern was known even then to harbor thoughts of American "evenhandedness"— the code word for some tilt toward the Arabs. This pattern was present as early as 1952, in the Dwight D. Eisenhower–Adlai E. Stevenson election, though Stevenson was the less pro-Zionist of the two. There is some present polling evidence that this voting behavior still holds between Reagan and any of his probable Democratic opponents.

Thus there is a recognizable Jewish vote: All the other largely "have" groups in America vote Republican. The Jews are the only ones of the "haves" to remain Democrats or, at the very least, liberals. Why? The explanation is to be found in domestic considerations. Many centuries of persecution in Europe and a marked amount of anti-Semitism in the United States in the first half of the 20th Century have persuaded Jews that they are safest in a society that is nonconfrontational. One hundred years ago, when the muzhiks—the landless peasants—became hungry under the Czar of Russia, they carried out pogroms against Jews for a number of decades before they finally made the revolution against the czar.

Such traditional Jewish fear of social conflict reinforces a social conscience, which comes naturally to a people whose ancestors wrote the Bible.

Like all other recognizable groups in America, Jews are concerned about their interests. Perhaps more than for any other group in America, Jewish self-interest includes concern that all contending forces in the country should be less angry, more satisfied and civil. That is why Jews are prepared to vote in their majority for the welfare state, even if such votes increase their taxes.

The problem for Jewish voters in the present election campaign is that they are less certain of where to go. Reagan's vision of America is one that largely excludes the dispossessed. Jesse Jackson, at the other end, despite his talk of a rainbow coalition, is essentially the expression of the anger of the dispossessed. He is not perceived as a builder of bridges between this class and the rest of America. Mondale and Hart, for all their supposed differences, are both speaking the language of the old Democratic coalition that included the majority of Jews. Neither as yet has ignited Jewish hearts by finding a way of bringing Jackson and his supporters into the reformist political center.

Nor has Mondale or Hart ignited the Jewish community with the kind of passion that will make Jews reject Reagan, even as he is good for their pockets because they fear that he is bad for their souls.

The politician who will galvanize the Jewish conscience in this election had best forget about where the American Embassy in Israel is to be placed. He had best try to remember that American Jews want to vote for someone who can lead this country toward inner cohesion. Then, in the dominant Jewish view, both Israeli and American Jews will be better off—and so will America.

. . . OR IS IT AN EMERGING CONSERVATISM?
DAVID G. EPSTEIN

Since the days of Franklin D. Roosevelt, American Jews have voted heavily for Democratic candidates. Jews also have been disproportionate supporters of such issue groups as the American Civil Liberties Union. They provided the margin of victory for such liberal black candidates as Mayor Wilson Goode in Philadelphia and Mayor Harold Washington in Chicago.

However, there are signs that this pattern is changing—and it is high time. The condition of Jews in America has changed for the better, and liberal politics have changed for the worse. The issues that divide liberals from conservatives also have changed.

Jewish liberalism grew out of a concern for basic democratic rights that had often been denied Jews in their countries of origin. It was reinforced by the open anti-Semitism that Jews frequently encountered in the America of a generation ago, and by the poverty that Jews (like other immigrants) experienced in their first years on these shores.

When Roosevelt became the leader of the democracies' struggle against Nazi Germany, the loyalties of the American Jewish voter to F.D.R.'s party were further cemented. And, because of their own experience of ethnic discrimination, Jews became active supporters of civil liberties and the civil-rights struggles against racial discrimination and segregation by law.

None of these motivations for Jewish liberalism are salient parts of today's American political scene.

Now the focus of Jews' concerns about the survival of their people is the state of Israel. Meanwhile, American liberals have increasingly abandoned their internationalist commitment to America's role as a world power. The anticommunist consensus of the postwar era has been replaced by a generalized hostility toward both American military strength and the use of force under almost any circumstances—along with a sympathy for Third World tyranny.

The politics of the late Sen. Henry M. Jackson, who supported a strong America *and* a liberal domestic agenda, have been all but replaced by the politics of Jesse Jackson, who embraces the Nicaraguan tyrants and Yasser Arafat, the leader of the Palestine Liberation Organization. Jews are realizing that if America proves unable to protect its strategic interests as close to home as

Central America, it can hardly afford much protection to faraway Israel.

The United Nations—born in hope, the darling of a generation of suburban trick-or-treaters—has become a cartel for tin-pot tyrants, and has officially embraced the Soviet disinformation campaign whose slogan is "Zionism is racism."

The civil-rights issues that aroused Jewish sympathies a generation ago have radically changed form. The struggle against official segregation and overt discrimination has largely been won. Minorities increasingly demand not legal equality and the elimination of barriers to free competition but redress for subtle and "institutional" forms of discrimination. Their demands often amount to political intervention to secure the results that they cannot achieve under the existing rules of competition.

Because of their history and cultural predispositions, Jews have historically thrived on free competition, and their concern has always been to eliminate artificial barriers to such competition—numerical quotas, for example. Accordingly, the insistent demand of black and other minority spokesmen for such schemes does not fall on the same sympathetic Jewish ears as the demand to end legal segregation.

Nor does the current economic status of American Jews coincide with the liberal penchant to throw tax money at social problems. Jews now have an educational and economic level comparable to the Episcopal elite; their new prosperity is more likely to lead them to a concern over excessive taxation and government waste than to finding new reasons to levy taxes.

Although fueled partly by self-interest, this instinct is sound. The prosperity and security of Jews (and other minorities the world over) have always been best guaranteed by a government of laws and an economy of free competition. The heavy-handed political management of the economy generally leads to unequal privilege, and economic and cultural stagnation.

Finally, although Jews torn loose from their traditional moorings often have been involved in countercultural movements, they also have been a family-oriented people. While they remain suspicious of some of the religious aspects of the cultural New Right, they also are becoming aware that the destruction of family values, standards of social decorum and social order has caused tremendous problems. These include streets that are unsafe for children, women and old people, and the decay of our educational institutions.

What passes today for liberalism in America seems not to offer solutions to these problems, but to promote the kind of cultural changes and the decline of social discipline that have brought them about. Especially among religiously observant Jews, and those who are concerned about the state of family life, these concerns find resonance. A program of sodomy, abortion and Miranda warnings meets no one's spiritual needs.

A generation ago none of these issues took the form that they take now. Every one of them leads to the conclusion that American liberalism and the American Jewish community have arrived at a parting of the ways. It is time to make the divorce final. Perhaps a new political leadership will do just that.

Source: MS 294, box 26, folder 6, AJA.

9.11—PROPOSED MISSION STATEMENT OF NEW JEWISH AGENDA, 1987

Gaining much of their inspiration from the late 1960s Jewish New Leftists led by Mark Rudd, Abbie Hoffman, and Jerry Rubin, progressive-minded Jews in the 1980s sought organizational ways to promote a political agenda that

reflected left-leaning politics while still protecting Jewish interests. The leading voice of progressive American Jewry in this period, the New Jewish Agenda, organized Jews in fifty local chapters across the country. NJA strove to be "a Jewish voice among progressives and a progressive voice among Jews." The NJA engaged a variety of left-leaning causes including Palestinian rights, nuclear disarmament, feminism, and discrimination. Included here is its mission statement as well as a promotional flyer sampling its political work.

New Jewish Agenda is a Jewish organization with members across the United States who are dedicated to furthering peace and social justice and challenging oppression in all its forms. The Jewish precept of Tikkun Olam, the "repair of the world," guides us to work toward a society free of exploitation and inequity and a world that values co-operation and dialogue over weaponry and militarism. We believe that the positive development of Jewish communal life depends upon commitment to both the particular and the universal; that is, to both the specific concerns of Jewish peoplehood and the liberation from oppression of all human beings.

Through education, activism, and community building, New Jewish Agenda embodies a specifically Jewish presence in movements for peace and social justice while speaking as a progressive voice within the organized Jewish community. Among non-Jews, we work in coalition on issues of common ground, challenging anti-Semitism and engendering support for Jewish concerns. Within the Jewish community, we

demonstrate the strength that Jewish and progressive values have when melded together, constructively criticizing policies and actions that counterpose these values.

Nationally and through local chapters, New Jewish Agenda is creating a political home for Jewish-identified progressives. Our members find their inspiration in different aspects of Jewish history and culture, including interpretations of Jewish theology, the heritage of Jewish secular radicalism, and the insights of Jewish feminism. We welcome diversity among our membership, recognizing the need to overcome the influence of all forms of prejudice and discrimination. We affirm the development of a more inclusive Jewish community through respect for both traditional and non-traditional lifestyles, families and households. We are committed to an organization in which all members are free to participate fully, within a framework that incorporates the principles of inclusiveness and accountability we seek to foster in the Jewish community and the world at large.

Respectfully submitted by:
Laurie Kauffman
Adrienne Rich
Ellen Stone
Jon Weisberger
1/10/87

9.12—NEW JEWISH AGENDA PROMOTIONAL FLYER: SOME EXAMPLES OF OUR WORK, N.D.

THE MIDDLE EAST
- From the point of view of our commitment to Israel and deep concern for its survival and well-being, New Jewish Agenda joins with hundreds of thousands of Israelis in opposing the policies of the Begin government in Lebanon and in the West Bank and Gaza—and in calling for negotiation and compromise with the Palestinian people.
- Agenda chapters across the country have promoted our views on the Middle East crisis with a wide range of activities: in educational forums, vigils and rallies;

in letters and articles in the press; in appearances on radio and television; and by sponsoring talks by representatives of the Israeli peace movement before American Jewish audiences.

- Agenda's Middle East Program includes a Speakers' Bureau, the Shalom network Newsletter, Educational Resources, the Jewish Committee for Relief in Lebanon, and a national Petition for Israeli-Palestinian Co-Existence.

DISARMAMENT

- As one of the sponsors of the disarmament rally of June 12, 1982, in New York City, Agenda brought several hundred members to march under our banner at that historic event. On the evening before the rally, Agenda sponsored a "Peace Sabbath" celebration with the Jewish Peace Fellowship and the Stephen Wise Free Synagogue.
- In Spring 1982, Agenda chapters organized Rainbow Sign commemorations in synagogues— linking the Biblical story of The Flood to the present day danger of nuclear disaster.
- Northampton Agenda (Khevre) made presentations of the disarmament issue at synagogues in Northampton and Springfield [Massachusetts], and before the Springfield Jewish Community Relations Council—and subsequently these organizations endorsed the nuclear freeze campaign.
- New Jewish Agenda is a member of the coalition for a New Foreign and Military Policy.

REAGANOMICS

- In March 1982, Agenda organized a press conference at the Stephen Wise Free Synagogue in New York City. Twenty Christian and Jewish clergy, including Rabbi Balfour Brickner, Rev. Robert Polk,

Rev. Ben Chavis, and Sister Mary Hegarty, gathered to denounce the choice of Ronald Reagan to receive an award from the National Conference of Christians and Jews, for "courageous leadership in governmental, civic and humanitarian affairs." At this event, Rabbi Arnold J. Wolf returned an award he had been given by the NCCJ in 1962 for his activities in the civil rights movement. All participants spoke out against the Reagan Administration's cuts in social programs and increases in military spending.

WOMEN'S ISSUES

- Boston Agenda sponsored a day-long Jewish Women's Conference. A video-tape of the event has been produced for use in educational outreach.
- Philadelphia Agenda joined in a rally in July, 1982, in Cherry Hill, New Jersey, at the site of an anti-abortion convention.
- Los Angeles Agenda greeted Jerry Falwell with a picket line when he was [sic] arrived to speak before a Jewish organization in L.A.
- New Jewish Agenda is a member of the Reproductive Rights National Network.

HUMAN RIGHTS

- Agenda chapters have adopted political prisoners in Argentina and worked for their release in an effort to combat anti-Semitism and rights' violations in that country.
- At the Soviet Mission to the U.N., Agenda joined other organizations protesting repression of Soviet citizens working to build an independent movement for nuclear disarmament.

ANTI-SEMITISM

- Chapters in Ann Arbor, Chicago, Los Angeles, and Washington D.C. participate in anti-racist and anti-Klan coalitions.

- Northampton Agenda (Khevre) conducts workshops on anti-Semitism for left and progressive organizations.
- Seattle Agenda (Kadima) produced "They Fought Back," a dramatic enactment of stories about Jewish resistance during World War II.

JEWISH CULTURE

- Agenda held the conference, *Toward a Progressive Jewish World View*, at Fellowship Farm, in Pottstown, PA, in June 1982. Agenda members, writers, rabbis, and academics, religious and secular, gathered to explore the meanings of Jewish identity today.
- Agenda chapters celebrate Jewish culture in activities such as: a Shabat [*sic*] retreat in Minneapolis, a coffeehouse for musicians and poets in Washington D.C., a Seder in Boston, and an art exhibit in San Francisco.
- San Francisco Agenda sponsored, with an Argentine group, a Purim party to benefit support work for Argentine political prisoners. The Megillah was read in Hebrew, English, and Spanish.

9.13—"DEPAUL UNIVERSITY, A CATHOLIC INSTITUTION, OPENS FULL DEPARTMENT OF JEWISH STUDIES," JEWISH TELEGRAPHIC AGENCY, SEPTEMBER 4, 1968

Prior to World War II, there were no "Judaic studies" programs in any major American colleges or universities. Students interested in postsecondary study of Jews and Judaism would have to matriculate either to Jewish seminaries or a handful of private colleges that offered courses in Jewish subjects. All this began to change after World War II. Courses on antisemitism, the Holocaust, as well as the study of Hebrew as a modern language both reflected and contributed to a growing interest in Jewish studies. In the late 1960s, a number of colleges and universities began to establish programs dedicated to the academic study of Jews and Judaism.

It is interesting to note that in 1968 Depaul University, a Catholic institution in Chicago, announced plans to open a department of Jewish studies, the first time a Catholic school backed such an effort. Two years later, Jewish students within New York's CUNY system pressed for independent departments of Jewish studies at City College, Queens College, and Brooklyn College.

Chicago—

DePaul University here has become the first Catholic educational institution in the United States to open a complete department of Jewish studies, it was announced today. The department will be inaugurated at the beginning of the 1968–69 academic year under a reciprocal agreement with the College of Jewish Studies which will offer a program of Judaic studies to students enrolled at DePaul. The College of Jewish Studies is an undergraduate institution specializing in four year degree programs of Judaic and Hebraic subjects.

Source: Jewish Telegraphic Agency, September 4, 1968: JTA online (http://archive.jta.org/article/1968/09/04/2945210/depaul-university-a-catholic-institution-opens-full-department-of-jewish-studies). All rights reserved. Used with permission.

9.14—"JEWISH STUDENTS LAUNCH DRIVE FOR JUDAIC STUDIES DEPARTMENTS IN CITY UNIVERSITY SYSTEM," JEWISH TELEGRAPHIC AGENCY, DECEMBER 9, 1970

New York—

A city-wide campaign to institute Judaic Studies Departments in all branches of the City University (CUNY) system is being launched by a group of Jewish students here. The effort is spearheaded by the Jewish Student Union of City College and coordinated by the New York Union of Jewish Students. According to Jonathan Braun, president of the New York Union of Jewish Stu-

dents, the purpose of the campaign is to "alert students to the power they possess in making Judaic studies a reality and to pressure the various college administrations into establishing permanent Judaic Studies Departments." During the present fall semester, Judaic studies courses are available at City College, Queens College and Brooklyn College on an inter-disciplinary basis.

However, due to student and faculty efforts at Brooklyn College, the Board of Education last week authorized the institution to establish a separate Judaic Studies Department next fall, offering a major and a degree in this field. According to reports there is a strong possibility that Queens College may soon be authorized to establish a similar department. Campaign efforts therefore will be directed mainly at City College. As part of the campaign, 20,000 stickers declaring, "Work for Jewish Studies" are being distributed at all branches of CUNY. Leaders of the drive are also urging students to join student-faculty committees on Judaic Studies at their respective colleges where they can work from within to have the Department instituted.

Source: Jewish Telegraphic Agency, December 9, 1970: JTA online (http://archive.jta.org/article/1970/12/09/2955212/jewish-students-launch-drive-for-judaic-studies-departments-in-city-university-system). All rights reserved. Used with permission.

9.15—SYLVIA ROTHCHILD, "HAVURAT SHALOM: COMMUNITY WITHOUT CONFORMITY," *Hadassah*, JUNE 1970

As part of the larger counterculture of the 1960s, young American Jews, dissatisfied with the confines and structure of the synagogue, sought ways to express their Judaism that combined a desire for meaningful Jewish life with the larger social and political climate of the era. The havurah movement emerged, bringing a new generation of Jewish worshipers together to learn and pray in a home setting, most often with lay leadership. In 1970, Hadassah magazine featured Boston's Havurat Shalom. In 1978, a decade after Havurat Shalom's formation, Brandeis University professor Bernard Reisman (1926–2011) offered his analysis of the movement.

Amidst the turmoil of a changing society, the Havurat Shalom thinks of itself as "a still, small voice," crying out to be heard in a Jewish community too big and impersonal to respond to small voices.

Founded in Cambridge, Massachusetts by a few rabbis and graduate students, the Havurah is attempting to create a religious community that combines the spirit of the ancient Jewish academies of Yavneh and Safed with the concerns of contemporary dissenters. They seek a personal encounter with the sources of Judaism, not out of an academic interest in the past, but as part of their search for a meaningful way of life. They are concerned not so much with preserving Judaism as with preserving themselves as Jews and human beings.

In its two short years the Havurah has been praised for its responsiveness to the needs of Jewish youth and denounced for its willingness to tamper with tradition. It has earned the support of distinguished rabbis and scholars, the affection of Elie Wiesel and the hostility of many who misunderstand its goals and its criticisms of organized Jewish life. Orthodox and Conservative rabbis find them too ready to change the liturgy. Reform rabbis complain that they are too hasidic. Educators find them too eager for innovation. Those who can't stand the sight of beards and long hair simply denounce them as a bunch of "Jewish hippies." Their still, small voice, however, has been heard in New York, Philadelphia, and San Francisco, where there are other attempts to create religious fellowships. Jewish students in Houston and Dallas speak of the Havurah in Boston with admiration and envy.

One Saturday, early in 1969, I decided to discover the Havurah for myself. I drove through the warren of one-way streets in Cambridge, a few minutes from Harvard Square, looking for a small Hebrew sign that distinguished the Havurah from other substandard student housing. I finally found the narrow house tightly wedged between its neighbors.

The door was open. My welcome was a small note, hung at eye-level: "Today something is happening to the whole structure of human consciousness. A fresh kind of life is starting." (Teilhard de Chardin.) There was a bulletin board with notices of draft resistance rallies and letters from Jewish students in other cities, including some from Cuba.

The room was empty. I heard music from a loudspeaker—sacred music, but not Jewish. I thought it might be a Gregorian chant but there was no one to ask. There were a few folding chairs at the back of the room. Most of the floor was covered with old sofa pillows. A childish mobile hung from the ceiling and a light behind a sheet of plastic flickered on and off, casting shadows on a picture of a dove that hung behind it. The room looked more like the headquarters of a day camp or nursery school than a seminary.

A few minutes later, however, young people began to straggle in. There were thirty or forty college-age men and women. The girls were conventionally dressed. Some of the men wore suits and shoes. Others wore jeans, sandals, ponchos. There was every variety of hair length and beards, plus a few smooth-shaven cheeks, and the downy fuzz of those too young to shave. The variety of attire and appearance seemed to express the Havurah's philosophy of individual freedom, its tolerance for idiosyncracies [sic], and its wish for a community that did not demand conformity. There were skull caps and uncovered heads, conventional prayer shawls and some with multicolored stripes. For some, unconventional dress seemed a declaration of a moral stance. For others, it seemed only a sign of indifference to the importance of outward appearance.

What was important was the service they had come together to share. The young men wrapped themselves in their prayer shawls, some pulling them over their heads. The congregation settled down on the pillows on the floor and began to *daven* [pray]. The prayers were chanted in beautiful Sephardic Hebrew with no English repetition. There were familiar hasidic and Israeli tunes and occasionally some new rhythms and melodies borrowed from contemporary folk rock music. I sat in the back of the room on a folding chair and couldn't see who was leading the service but I was moved by the sensitivity of those who followed. The prayers seemed to be passed around the room from one voice to another. Every now and then an English phrase was added for emphasis. "God is," came from a corner, like an amen. There was a Torah reading after the *Shaharis* (morning prayer), with one member of the Havurah chanting the Hebrew while another softly read the English translation like a musical obligato. There was a *Haftora* reading with comments on the weekly portion and a report on the Jews in Cuba by someone who had just returned from there.

[. . .]

Over a period of many months, I came to know a little about the members of the Havurat Shalom. There were only sixteen members in the beginning. Six were ordained rabbis. Ten were graduate students. The rabbis had been influenced by the teachings of Abraham Heschel and the writings of Martin Buber. They were critical of the divisions in American Jewry, the failures of Jewish education and the unrealistic priorities of the organized Jewish community. They saw a greater challenge in working with troubled college-age youth than in the placid suburbs. The other members of the Havurah came from both religious and secular families. Some had no Jewish training until they prepared to join the Havurah. They spoke of being, "turned on" during a visit to Israel, of moving experiences in Mea Shearim [an ultra-Orthodox neighborhood in Jerusalem] and in religious kibbutzim. Some discovered their Jewishness in Germany and others in Hebrew-speaking summer camps in America. They were members of a generation that was repudiating the materialism and superficiality of American (and Jewish-American) culture and were hoping to find alternatives by dedicating themselves to the idealistic and prophetic aspects of Jewish tradition.

At the Havurah, they hoped to create a community in which spiritual search would be of central importance. There was concern for the connection between religion and personal relationships. Their walls were decorated with quotations from Erich Fromm and Theodore Roszak along with posters about Soviet Jewry and modern illustrations of the Song of Songs. The Havurah's educational programs and its experiments with liturgy all attempted in some way to create bridges, to connect the past and the present, secular and religious knowledge, contemporary and Jewish music.

[. . .]

Committed to flexibility and change, the Havurah's members engage in endless discussions and evaluations of their educational program and their personal problems. Their image is not fixed, and new members create new challenges. Pressures on the part of a few to turn the Havurah into a commune have been resisted. Drugs of any kind are absolutely forbidden.

[. . .]

Now grown to over twice its original size, the Havurah has begun to turn away many applicants. The group has moved to larger and more comfortable quarters in Somerville, Massachusetts, but its space is still limited and its funds are low. They had originally received a grant from the Danforth Foundation, but the organized Jewish community is too suspicious of dissent to support them.

[. . .]

Like other concerned Jewish students, the members of the Havurah study the Torah and the Prophets for support for their idealism and radicalism. They are asking embarrassing questions of their fellow Jews, but the questions are not raised in mockery. They reject Jewish institutions but not Judaism. They reject the divisions within the Jewish community and the separation of the wisdom of traditional and modern thinkers, as if they were not part of the same search. They are trying to reconcile a rich tradition with spontaneity, creativity, and the conviction that Judaism is alive and growing; that it must be discovered and created anew.

Source: Havurah nearprint file, AJA.

9.16—BERNARD REISMAN, "THE IMPACT OF THE HAVURAH," *Jewish Digest,* SUMMER 1978

Almost a decade has passed since the concept of the *havurah* first appeared as a popular religious phenomenon in the American Jewish community. The havurah has been seen by its supporters as a much needed innovative reform in Jewish institutional life: offsetting the bureaucratization and impersonality of Jewish life. Others have viewed the havurah with more skepticism. Some dismiss it as one of the many fads which periodically attract popular support in Jewish life and soon fade into oblivion. Still others suggest that the Havurah may indeed be a negative development, deflecting people from

serious Jewish study and celebration with a program which is essentially social, and which generates divisiveness in synagogue and communal life.

The havurah has become a fairly wide-spread phenomenon in Jewish life today. A recently completed survey indicates that at least 25 percent of Reform and Conservative synagogues now have some type of havurah program. It is difficult to determine the number of havurot which have been organized as independent entities, outside of the synagogue, partly because of their lack of connection to the organized Jewish community and partly because of problems of definition. There are many groups, with diverse programs and objectives, which identify themselves as havurot, and yet others which have many of the same features, but do not use the term "havurah" to define themselves.

The establishment in Fall 1968, of Havurat Shalom, an independent religious community of young adults in Somerville, Mass., represents the popularization of the havurah idea in the current period. Since then a number of groups have emerged which share many common objectives and principles and which bear the title of havurah. The term, havurah, best defined as "fellowship," describes a range of approaches in which relatively small groups of Jews meet together regularly for programs which include Jewish study, worship, celebration and personal association.

[. . .]

Among the modern havurot two general types can be identified: *independent havurot* and *synagogue-based havurot*. The former are those groups which have no ties to synagogues or other Jewish communal organizations; the latter are groups which have been organized by, or have some association with, a synagogue. Havurot Shalom is the prototype of the independent havurot. The independent havurot are comprised mainly of young people who feel alienated from traditional Jewish institutions and form alternative structures to pursue collectively their Jewish interests. Examples include:

- *Batim*—university-based living arrangements, with Jewish purposes.
- *Commune-Type Havurot*—like Havurat Shalom, geared primarily to young adults, most of whom are single but some married, usually without children.
- *Educational Havurot*—Groups of young families who assume responsibility for organizing their own Jewish educational programs for their children as well as for themselves.

The impetus for the development of the havurah within the synagogue was provided by the pioneering work of Harold M. Schulweis, rabbi of Valley Beth Shalom, a Conservative synagogue in Encino, California. Schulweis recognized that the principle of intimate community, inherent in the idea of the havurah, enabled the synagogue to be responsive to a generation of essentially lonely and rootless individuals. . . .

The havurah primarily attracts synagogue members whose personal Jewish background and commitment, as measured by level of Jewish education, Jewish attitudes and Jewish practices, are above the average for their synagogue. Further, the havurah members are neither marginal in their involvement in the synagogue nor are they primarily the newly arrived or transient members of the community. The predominant distinction between members of a synagogue who choose to join a havurah and those who do not, is the greater salience Jewishness has for the former group. This distinction is reflected in the high priority afforded to Jewish purposes and programs in the functioning of the havurot. The informal, personalized flavor of the havurot answers social needs of its members, while providing a supportive atmosphere for their quest in defining a meaningful Jewish life style.

The evidence, emerging from studying members after almost two years of participation in the havurah, indicates that the experience does have a positive impact on those involved. On a general level, the high rate of survival of the havurot suggests fulfillment of some basic needs of the members. More specifically, there is tangible evidence of positive change in the Jewish attitudes and behaviors of havurah members. To be sure these are not major changes, nor do they apply to all participants, but the changes indicate that the havurah has the potential to be responsive to the interests and concerns of a significant segment of contemporary Jews.

[. . .]

A basic feature of the havurah which contributes significantly to its appeal is its autonomy. At the same time the absence of any formal pattern of leadership in the havurah may limit its effectiveness. Program planning and follow-through in some havurot seem to suffer from the absence of leadership. Similarly, initiatives which might enhance group morale and stability are not forthcoming. A matter to be further explored is whether a pattern of havurah leadership can be fostered which respects the principle of autonomy and still provides the benefits of direction and delegation of responsibility. Two possibilities suggest themselves: 1) a program to provide leadership training to a selected member of each of the havurot; and 2) introducing into the synagogue's professional staff complement a person to work with the havurot.

[. . .]

As with any innovative venture, there are apt to be risks and uncertainties in introducing a program of havurot in the synagogue. In view of the statistics reported earlier, indicating that almost two out of three synagogue members characterize their involvement in the institution as "passive," it would seem, on balance, that the risks of establishing havurot are likely to be significantly offset by the advantages. Moreover, considering the values and expectations of the generation now coming of age, it would appear to be particularly appropriate for the synagogue to have available the option of the havurah.

Source: Havurah nearprint file, AJA.

9.17—EZRAT NASHIM, "JEWISH WOMEN CALL FOR CHANGE," 1972

In 1972, ten Conservative-movement-educated women formed Ezrat Nashim (literally "women's help" but also a reference to the women's section of a traditional synagogue) to press for gender equality within their denomination. They launched their efforts by attending the annual meeting of the Rabbinic Assembly, urging the rabbis' wives, and any other women in attendance, to join them in an organizing meeting. Ezrat Nashim leaders presented their "Jewish Women Call for Change" to the rabbinic leadership, demanding, among other priorities, the counting of women in a prayer quorum, the ability for women to initiate divorce, and the right of women to become rabbis and cantors.

The Jewish tradition regarding women, once far ahead of other cultures, has now fallen disgracefully behind in failing to come to terms with developments of the past century.

Accepting the age-old concept of role differentiation on the basis of sex, Judaism saw woman's role as that of wife, mother, and homemaker. Her ritual obligations were domestic and familial: *nerot* [candle lighting], *challah*, and *taharat hamishpachah* [family purity]. Although

the woman was extolled for her domestic achievements, and respected as the foundation of the Jewish family, she was never permitted an active role in the synagogue, court, or house of study. These limitations on the life-patterns open to women, appropriate or even progressive for the rabbinic and medieval periods, are entirely unacceptable to us today.

The social position and self-image of women have changed radically in recent years. It is now universally accepted that women are equal to men in intellectual capacity, leadership ability and spiritual depth. The Conservative movement has tacitly acknowledged this fact by demanding that their female children be educated alongside the males—up to the level of rabbinical school. To educate women and deny them the opportunity to act from this knowledge is an affront to their intelligence, talents and integrity.

As products of Conservative congregations, religious schools, the Ramah Camps, LTF [Leaders Training Fellowship], USY [United Synagogue Youth], and the [Jewish Theological] Seminary, we feel this tension acutely. We are deeply committed to Judaism, but cannot find adequate expression for our total needs and concerns in existing women's social and charitable organizations, such as Sisterhood, Hadassah, etc. Furthermore, the single woman—a new reality in Jewish life—is almost totally excluded from the organized Jewish community, which views women solely as daughters, wives, and mothers. The educational institutions of the Conservative movement have helped women recognize their intellectual, social and spiritual potential. If the movement then denies women opportunities to demonstrate these capacities as adults, it will force them to turn from the synagogue, and to find fulfillment elsewhere.

It is not enough to say that Judaism views women as separate but equal, nor to point to Judaism's past superiority over other cultures in its treatment of women. We've had enough of apologetics: enough of Bruria, Dvorah, and Esther; enough of *eshet hayil*.

It is time that:

women be granted membership in
    synagogues
women be counted in the minyan
women be allowed full participation in
    religious observances—*aliyot* [Torah
    blessing], *baalot keriah* [Torah reading],
    shelihot zibbur [prayer service leading]

women be recognized as witnesses before
    Jewish law
women be allowed to initiate divorce
women be permitted and encouraged to
    attend Rabbinical and Cantorial schools,
    and to perform Rabbinical and Cantorial
    functions in synagogues
women be encouraged to join decision-
    making bodies, and to assume
    professional leadership roles, in
    synagogues and in the general Jewish
    community
women be considered as bound to fulfill all
    mitzvot equally with men.

For three thousand years, one-half the Jewish people have been excluded from full participation in Jewish communal life. We call for an end to the second-class status of women in Jewish life.

Ezrat Nashim
411 Avenue N
Brooklyn, New York 11230

Source: Ezrat Nashim nearprint file, AJA.

9.18—"THE FIRST AMERICAN WOMAN RABBI," REFLECTIONS BY RABBI SALLY PRIESAND, 1972–1975

While there were women in America who had earlier completed rabbinic training, and Regina Jonas (1902-1944) had acquired private ordination in Germany in 1935, Sally Priesand became the first woman to receive rabbinical ordination from the faculty of a rabbinical seminary. She graduated from the Reform movement's Hebrew Union College-Jewish Institute of Religion in 1972 and was ordained in Cincinnati by Rabbi Alfred Gottschalk (1930-2009) HUC-JIR's president, on behalf

of the school's faculty. In 1964, Priesand, who first thought of pursuing the rabbinate during her high school years, enrolled in a joint undergraduate program at the University of Cincinnati and HUC-JIR, located just across the street. After her graduation in 1968, Priesand began rabbinic studies, though without the stated intention of gaining ordination. With the support of HUC-JIR president Nelson Glueck (1900-1971), Priesand earned ordination after completion of her studies. In "The First American

Woman Rabbi," Priesand reflects on her experiences in rabbinical school and shares her thoughts about becoming the nation's first ordained woman rabbi.

On June 3, 1972 I was ordained rabbi by Hebrew Union College–Jewish Institute of Religion in Cincinnati, Ohio. As I sat in the historic Plum Street Temple, waiting to accept the ancient rite of *s'micha* (ordination), I couldn't help but reflect on the implications of what was about to happen. For thousands of years women in Judaism had been second-class citizens. They were not permitted to own property. They could not serve as witnesses. They did not have the right to initiate divorce proceedings. They were not counted in the *minyan* [quorum]. Even in Reform Judaism, they were not permitted to participate fully in the life of the synagogue. With my ordination all that was going to change; one more barrier was about to be broken.

When I entered HUC-JIR, I did not think very much about being a pioneer. I knew only that I wanted to be a rabbi. With the encouragement and support of my parents, I was ready to spend eight years of my life studying for a profession that no woman had yet entered. My decision was an affirmation of my belief in God, in the words of each individual, and in Judaism as a way of life. It was a tangible action declaring my commitment to the preservation and renewal of our tradition.

As one would expect, there were problems even as I worked toward ordination. Though Reform Judaism had long before declared an official religious equality between men and women, Reform Jews still believed that a woman's place was in the home. They no longer insisted that men and women sit separately during worship services. They allowed women to be counted in the *minyan* to conduct the service, to serve as witnesses on ritual matters. They demanded that girls receive a religious education equivalent to that provided for boys. They allowed women to become members of the congregation with the privilege of voting and they even permitted them to be elected to offices on synagogue boards. But they were not yet ready for the spiritual leadership of a woman.

Undoubtedly, many believed that I was studying at HUC-JIR to become a *rebbetzin* rather than a rabbi, to marry rather than to officiate. Four years passed (while I concentrated on my studies at the University of Cincinnati) before people began to realize that I was serious about entering the rabbinate. During that time, I felt that I had to do better than my classmates so that my academic ability would not be questioned. Professors were fair, but occasionally I sensed that some of them would not be overly upset if I failed. And when, in my fifth year, I was ready to serve my first congregation as student rabbi, some congregations refused to accept my services. Still the members of Sinai Temple in Champaign, Illinois, received me warmly.

My sixth year of study brought the beginning of a tremendous amount of publicity. When you are a "first," you are expected to be an expert in everything. Personal appearances, interviews, statements on contemporary issues—all are expected. Surprisingly enough, though I have always considered myself an introvert, I somehow managed to cope with these new pressures. It helped to know that by this time I had the support, or at least the respect, of most of the members of the college community. Dr. Nelson Glueck, the late president of HUC-JIR, was a particular source of strength. His courage in accepting me as a rabbinic student made possible my eventual ordination.

As my eighth and final year drew to a close, I was faced with finding a job. Some congregations refused to interview me. I was disappointed and somewhat discouraged by these refusals. But since I had not expected everyone to welcome me with open arms, I had prepared myself for this possibility. I knew that I needed only one acceptance and I never really doubted that I would find one synagogue ready to accept me.

The offer of a position as assistant rabbi at the Stephen Wise Free Synagogue in New York

City was a blessing in the true sense of the word. I have been extremely well-received by the members of the congregation, and it has been my privilege to work with and to learn from Rabbi Edward E. Klein, the senior rabbi. My activities have not been limited to one area of the Synagogue. My duties include conducting worship services, preaching on Shabbat, teaching both in the Adult Institute and in the Religious School, supervising the youth program, advising a biweekly study group, lecturing to the Golden Age Club, counseling, officiating at life-cycle events, and attending all committee meetings. The only area in which people have shown any real hesitancy has been that of my officiating at funerals.

In addition to my congregational responsibilities, I have lectured extensively throughout the country—an activity which has shown me that congregations and rabbis are ready for change. Ten years ago, women were much more opposed to the idea of a woman rabbi than were men. Since then, however, the feminist movement has made a tremendous contribution in terms of consciousness-raising, and women now demand complete and full participation in synagogue life. This is a significant development because changes will not be made until we change the attitudes of people.

Men and women must learn to overcome their own psychological and emotional objections and regard every human being as a real person with talents and skills and with the option of fulfilling his or her creative potential in any way he or she finds meaningful. Women can aid this process—not by arguing but by doing and becoming, for accomplishments bring respect and respect leads to acceptance. Women must now take the initiative. They should seek and willingly accept new positions of authority in synagogue life.

It is still too soon to assess the impact of my ordination, but I would hope that it would at least mark a transition in our congregations, that sole involvement on the part of women in the synagogue kitchen and the classroom should move toward complete and full participation on the pulpit and in the boardroom as well.

When I accepted ordination on June 3, 1972, I affirmed my belief in Judaism and publicly committed myself to the survival of Jewish tradition. I did so knowing that Judaism had traditionally discriminated against women; that it had not always been sensitive to the problems of total equality. I know that there has been a tremendous flexibility in our tradition—it enabled our survival. Therefore, I chose to work for change through constructive criticism. The principles and ideals for which our ancestors have lived and died are much too important to be cast aside. Instead we must accept the responsibilities of the covenant upon ourselves, learn as much as possible of our heritage, and make the necessary changes which will grant women total equality within the Jewish community.

Source: As printed in *JAW*, 550–52. Reprinted with permission of the author.

9.19—"JEWISH WOMEN'S MAG *Lilith* HITS THE STANDS," *Jewish Chronicle,* JULY 15, 1976

A variety of traditional Jewish texts describe a female demon named Lilith. Appearing first in the Babylonian Talmud and later included in medieval Jewish folklore and the Zohar, Lilith typically recalled a figure who, according to one midrash, served as Adam's first wife until she was banished to the Sea of Reeds for refusing to be subservient to him. While traditional Jewish literature characterizes Lilith in negative terms, modern Jewish women have reclaimed her as an example of early feminism. They interpreted her rejection by Adam as an affirmation of women's equality. When a group of Jewish feminists sought, in 1976, to launch a magazine that would "foster discussion of Jewish women's issues and put them on the agenda of the Jewish community," they titled it Lilith.

New York. (JTA)—*Lilith Magazine*, a new quarterly dedicated to "exploring the world of the Jewish woman" has published its first issue here. The magazine, the only independent Jewish women's magazine in North America, is named for Adam's legendary first companion and co-equal, originally "the embodiment of independent womanhood."

Lilith is a non-profit venture started by a group of Jewish women journalists headquartered at 500 East 63 Street. It is sold by subscription at $6 a year and on selected newsstands. The executive editor is Susan Weidman Schneider, originally from Winnipeg.

Lilith's goal, its editors state, "is to foster discussion of Jewish women's issues and put them on the agenda of the Jewish community."

The magazine intends to serve as an "ongoing forum" for exploring Jewish women's concerns, conflicts, experiences and history and plans to devote special issues to the Jewish family, the Holocaust, and Israeli women. Among the articles in the 48-page first issue are:

An interview in which Betty Friedan, founder of the National Organization for Women, calls upon Jewish women to stop raising money for Jewish organizations which discriminate against them or exclude them from membership and decision-making;

An analysis of "The Lilith Question," discussing how and why the story of Lilith, the first independent woman, was changed to make her demonic;

An article by a psychiatric social worker on the toll on lower-class Jewish women and men of the American Jewish drive for success;

A scholarly piece by Blu Greenberg on how halacha can and must be changed so that the Jewish woman is equal in privileges and obligations.

Source: Reprinted with permission of the *Jewish Chronicle* (Pittsburgh, Pa.).

9.20—"SHARP DECLINE REPORTED IN ANTI-JEWISH BIAS IN WINTER RESORTS," JEWISH TELEGRAPHIC AGENCY, AUGUST 6, 1965

The sort of anti-Jewish discrimination that typified the early postwar years had all but vanished by the late 1960s. Little evidence remained of university-based restrictions against Jewish students or housing covenants banning Jews from suburban neighborhoods. In 1964, Congress passed the Civil Rights Act, which ended legal discrimination against African Americans and helped create a political culture resistant to those early forms of government-sponsored discrimination that affected Jews. By the time the Anti-Defamation League conducted a survey of anti-Jewish discrimination at winter resorts between November 1964 and March 1965, levels of prejudicial activity had dropped dramatically.

New York—

Discrimination against Jews in the leading winter resort hotels and motels in the United States had gone down in the last year to 2.1 percent, as against 14.8 percent of those surveyed in 1963, the B'nai B'rith Anti-Defamation League reported here today on the basis of a fresh survey conducted between November, 1964, and March, 1965.

Noting that the new survey was conducted after the Civil Rights Act of 1964 had become law, specifically barring racial and religious discriminations in places of public accommodation, the ADL revealed it had used the "dual letter test" in evaluating winter resorts in Florida, Arizona, California, Alabama, Mississippi, Arkansas, Colorado and Idaho.

In each case, applications for reservations were sent by three pairs of applicants. In each pair, one was signed with a name that sounded distinctly Jewish, the other apparently non-Jewish. In each set, the letter bearing the Jewish-sounding name preceded the non-Jewish signer by at least 24 or 48 hours, so there would be no question of priority.

The report showed that, among 595 winter resorts from which definitive replies were obtained, 13 were identified as discriminatory. All of these, stated the report, were in Florida and Arizona, the two states recognized as the winter playgrounds of America. Eight of the discriminators were in Florida, five in Arizona.

The ADL noted that, in both states, there have been drops in discrimination since a previous survey conducted in 1963. The Florida group had been diminished from 14.7 percent to 1.9 percent. In Arizona, the drop was from 23.9 percent in 1963 to 5.4 percent in the last test.

No evidence of discriminatory practices were found among California hotels where, in 1963, 9 percent discriminated against Jews. In the South, where racial turmoil is still boiling over, there was almost no religious discrimination as far back as 1963, the ADL found. There was none at all in Mississippi and Alabama, and only two of 15 winter resorts in Arkansas were found to be discriminatory against Jews in 1963. Since then, the ADL reported, these Arkansas resorts have dropped the practice as far as Jewish applicants were concerned.

The responses to the tests showed, the ADL declared, that, despite the 1964 Civil Rights Act, the discriminating resorts still find various formulas for rejecting applicants whose names seemed Jewish. Some emphasized that, for many years, their clientele was "entirely Gentile." Others still use in their brochures certain terms easily recognized as discriminatory, like "selected clientele," "discriminating clientele," or "churches near by." Some try to evade the law by terming themselves as "private clubs," which are exempt from the provisions of the Civil Rights Act.

"Although pockets of discrimination remain," the ADL report concluded, "the 1964-65 study of winter resorts discloses remarkable improvement in the acceptance of Jewish guests. Giant strides toward the elimination of religious discrimination were made in all areas under study."

Passage of the Civil Rights legislation in 1964 and a continuing educational campaign were the main factors which brought about the reduction in winter resort discriminations, Dore Schary, national chairman of the ADL, noted in releasing the report.

Source: Jewish Telegraphic Agency, August 6, 1965: JTA online (http://archive.jta.org/article/1965/08/06/ 3081476/sharp-decline-reported-in-antijewish-bias -in-winter-resorts). All rights reserved. Used with permission.

9.21—STATEMENT FOR RELEASE BY BLACK AND JEWISH ORGANIZATIONS, AUGUST 28, 1979

In July 1979, U.S. ambassador to the United Nations Andrew Young (b. 1932) met secretly with representatives of the Palestine Liberation Organization in violation of U.S. law. Under pressure from President Jimmy Carter, Young resigned. The affair stoked black-Jewish tensions, as it focused attention on the differences between American Jewish support for the State of Israel and the African American community's growing sympathy for the Palestinian cause. In the wake of the Young affair, Chicago-area Jewish and black organizations came together and issued a joint statement outlining their respective positions on a series of issues confronting their communities. In October 1979, NAACP executive director Benjamin L. Hooks (1925–2010) offered his comments on the controversy at a forum titled A Social Justice Agenda for the 1980s sponsored by the UAHC in Washington, D.C.

In these times of frustration and uncertainty, it is all too easy for suspicion and enmity to take [the] place of trust and understanding. As Jews and as Blacks, therefore, we are determined to deal with the problems that confront us as well as our society at large without resorting to the stereotypes and generalized fears that lead to increased tension and hostility. We are committed to build and not to tear down. We are well aware that we share a common background schooled in the prejudices and disabilities which have victimized and continued [*sic*] to victimize both of our communities. We are also aware that, while there are problems between us, what we share together is much greater than what keeps us apart. We see this as an occasion to talk honestly and dialogue at a level where effective solutions are forthcoming to the problems that have exacerbated tensions within our communities.

In this spirit, we propose the following program:

I. Statement of Positions—Jewish and Black Communities

   A. Jewish Community

    1. Andrew Young is a capable and dedicated servant to the American people. Any pressure which was exerted for his resignation is deplored. Many contributions he made as Ambassador of the U.N. are recognized. While we differ in perspective on a very critical issue of policy in the Middle East, we believe that Andrew Young has generally pursued the interests of this nation, thus

we do not challenge his integrity and we express appreciation for his outstanding contributions.

2. The Jewish community has in the past and will continue to aggressively fight racism. We recognize that racism today leads to anti-semitism tomorrow. Jews and the Blacks are both targets of forces of hatred exemplified by the KKK and the Nazis and it is not surprising that these hate groups have historically turned their wrath against both Blacks and Jews.

3. We must work to achieve a stronger Jewish commitment supporting affirmative action. The historic opposition of the Jewish community to quotas used to systematically exclude them in the past is understandable. In light of the present context, we do believe that such quotas should be distinguished from attempts to bring about equality through affirmative action, compensatory goals and timetables. These seek to overcome the corrosive effects of past acts of racial and ethnic discrimination in employment and admissions to universities and professional schools.

4. We are committed to expand current programs in the area of urban affairs and to initiate new programs with the Jewish community to promote education, and involvement in urban issues, such as employment, housing, and education, which affect the Black community and the Jewish community as well.

5. We disassociate ourselves from neo-reactionary intellectual movements including those undertaken in our own community and represented by magazines such as *Commentary* which call for the abandonment by whites of the civil rights causes and which have the effect of disengaging Jews from the Black struggle for civil rights.

6. The Jewish community understands and supports the opposition of Blacks

and Third World people to the hideous system of apartheid in South Africa and is strenuously opposed to this system which destroys the dignity of human beings. Specifically, within the Jewish community we will support the current campaign to cancel the pending prize fight in South Africa.

B. Black Community

1. The Black community abhors anti-semitism and will initiate a program to fight it. We specifically reject stereotypes or group generalizations which cast Jews in an unfavorable light. We recognize that anti-semitism operates to the detriment of Blacks and Jews.

2. Israel's existence and security is firmly and unequivocally supported. This support has been enunciated by Black leadership both here and throughout the United States.

3. The long-standing important contributions and support by members of the Jewish community for the furtherance of issues important to the Black community, such as affirmative action, open housing, and full and equal employment, is recognized.

4. It is acknowledged that a vast majority of Jewish persons did not seek Andrew Young's resignation. At the same time, we recognize that the immediate reactions and furor led to misunderstandings which both acknowledge contributed to creating a further wedge between the Black and Jewish communities.

II. Differences between the Black and Jewish communities which we will continue to address:

A. Our major area of difference is in regards to what the United States' response would be in the Middle East regarding Israel and the Palestinians. The Black position remains that the U.S. should speak at this time to the PLO. The Jewish community remains firmly opposed to conversations with a group that refuses to recognize Israel's very right to exist.

B. While the Jewish community supports the goals of affirmative action, our differences have arisen over the means of accomplishing these goals, thus the actions taken by some Jewish organizations in specific cases puts in question its views on the central issue. We are prepared to face the existent differences over such matters. We are prepared for example, to interpret the use of compensatory goals and timetables with more clarity so as to properly focus their role in gaining equity and parity for blacks, minorities, and females in our society. . . .

We are pledged to create a climate together where people can openly deal with each other and each other's problems rather than build stereotypical images of one another. We are aware that we have much to learn from one another. We are determined that our differences will be handled with amity and understanding and what we share in common will be used to build a stronger and more just society for all people.

Source: MS 294, box 27, folder 1, AJA.

9.22—NAACP HEAD BENJAMIN HOOKS, SPEECH ON CIVIL RIGHTS, AMERICAN JEWS, AND THE PALESTINE LIBERATION ORGANIZATION, 1979

. . . It is the disagreement over the use of *inclusive* quotas that have increased tensions between blacks and many Jews. We understand the historic dimensions of the controversy. Quotas were used to restrict the number of Jews in colleges and universities. But Jews should know and appreciate the fact that quotas have also been used to restrict blacks. Blacks have been "quota'd out." Indeed, the Jewish population is not monolithic in their attitude toward affirmative action and numerical remedies to societal discrimination. While some self-styled Jewish groups helped finance and support the Alan Bakke case up to the Supreme Court, other Jews supported the NAACP's amicus brief and backed our affirmative action work through contributions and other assistance. Still, it cannot be ignored that erstwhile allies in the civil rights movement within the established Jewish organizations have directly challenged black people's interests before the highest court of the land—in *De Funis,* in *Bakke,* and to a lesser degree, in the *Weber* case. They have done so on the basis of defending "merit" and opposing "reverse discrimination." But in so doing they have sided with the reactionary movements of white militants who would discard or weaken all affirmative action programs because of its color-conscious elements.

The all-commanding question is, whether blacks and Jews can be effective allies in the civil rights movement without candidly facing up to and addressing this pivotal philosophical policy dispute. This is a central issue that surfaced from the four statements from the recent meeting of black leaders in New York City convened to assess the implications of Ambassador Andy Young's resignation. That group said, rather matter of factly, that:

"Realism demands that the burden of resolving the black/Jewish tensions . . . cannot be placed disproportionately on the backs of already overburdened blacks; . . . (and) realism demands . . . that all discussions seeking to ameliorate or resolve fundamental differences between American blacks and Jews be conducted in terms of specific issues and problems rather than in terms of emotions, supplication, subtle or flagrant threats and coercion or arrogance."

This contemplates a recognition of the wide spectrum of views of black people and Jews, and the reality that established civil rights organizations and Jewish organizations have a responsibility to each other to be candid, forthright, and diligent in communicating the high priorities of their respective memberships and of avoiding, whenever possible, the open, public rancor of two friends fighting. Should we disagree nothing is solved by threats of an across-the-board withdrawal of support for one another's mutual objectives. Responsible black leadership will have no truck for ugly anti-Semitism. And we will expect our Jewish allies never to abandon us on a crest of anti-black sentiment, whereas their interests as whites become more paramount than their identification with the plight of the poor, the powerless, and the oppressed.

The black people and the Jewish people are on the threshold of a great-regeneration of cooperation. The fall-out from the Andy Young resignation—over the issue of meeting with the PLO—has served notice on both communities that we must be candid with each other before the newswriters arrive. We have got to spell out what is rationally the best course to defend the interests of our country, to secure and protect the state of Israel, and to gain human and political rights for the Palestinian. To do this, we have got to be specific and not just generic in our prescription for peace in the Middle East. This, no doubt, will have to entail compromise from the warring parties. But it cannot, must not, will not mean the destruction of the Israeli state. It will have to include recognition of the legitimate rights of the Palestinian people to a homeland, and it cannot, must not, will not mean the violation of territorial borders established in the interest of securing the peace. The stark realities, born of Israeli's [sic] existence, is that Jew and Arab must live in the same region, and so we have to move beyond the headlines and dissolve the battlelines.

The peace-making process, if it is to be fruitful and lasting, will have to include both sides of the combat, talking to each other. The NAACP believes that the U.S. policy of not talking directly with the PLO is shortsided [sic]. If the U.S.

is going to be an effective mediator, then it will speak directly with the PLO and the Israelis in an effort to produce changes in the positions of each side. A no-talk, no compromise policy is a destructive and dangerous course to pursue and is detrimental to the security of Israel, to any legitimate demands of the Palestinians, and to the national interests of the United States.

Armies will not change ideas on the Israeli or the Palestinian. Not even secure borders and the most sophisticated military hardware can do that. Armies are not sociological in their structure or mission. The armies, when they are mobilized, cause death and destruction and that's the reason there must be a bilateral and immediate ceasefire, an immediate end to wanton acts of violence and terrorism, and a cessation of territorial acquisitions. The responsibility is upon the political leaders, not the armies, to end Israeli-Arab friction and clashes.

A change in the affairs of men is occurring. We ought not fear it because change, on the domestic and international fronts, will test our commitment to certain basic values. Freedom, equality, justice are not only words to recite; they are concepts to put into practice. To the extent that the black man in America is yet struggling for common rights of citizenship, we must look for and welcome change in the affairs of this nation. To the extent that Israelis are yet struggling to secure their existence and to win peace, they will welcome a change toward stability and coexistence with their Arab neighbors.

No genuine settlement will be imposed on the state of Israel. No legitimate settlement will compromise the security of the Israeli people. The word of God as set forth in Leviticus 26:13:

"I am the Lord your God which brought you forth out of the land of Egypt, that you should not be their bondsmen; and I have broken the bonds of your yoke, and made you go upright."

Our task for this time is to go forward, and to go upright.

I believe there is every reason to be hopeful about the future, and to be optimistic about improving black/Jewish relations. Black people are not going to abandon their allies or shirk their moral principles over a barrel of oil. Nor will black Americans be willing or content to stand on the shoulder of the American society to allow the traffic of progress and superior privileges to go unabated for white Americans.

It is left to us—leaders in the black American and Jewish community—to devise the mature strategies that will reckon with the new emerging world economic order and intergroup tensions. This is our larger and greatest challenge. It is important that calm reasonableness prevail, that the difficulties of adjustment be realized, and that without any sacrifice of basic principles,

the spirit of sharing and cooperation characterize our future civil and human rights campaigns. Let it not be said of us that we failed to take advantage of a challenge posed, to emerge from a dark period into a better climate for all. And let it not be said that we imposed unnecessary hardships either upon those responsible for working out the details of the adjustment, or those who have traditionally born [sic] the brunt of sacrifice and deprivation.

Thank you for inviting me and listening. God bless you.

Source: MS 630, box 2, folder 9, AJA.

9.23—ADVERTISEMENT, "JEWS AGAINST JACKSON," *New York Times*, NOVEMBER 11, 1983

Jesse Jackson (b. 1941) emerged in the 1960s as one of the civil rights movement's leading spokespeople. A onetime confidant of Dr. Martin Luther King Jr., Jackson followed his civil rights work with political aspirations, including a run for the Democratic nomination in the 1984 presidential contest. After a series of anti-Israel comments, as well as calls to embrace PLO chairman Yasser Arafat (1929–2004), Jackson came under fire from American Jews who believed he threatened Israeli, Jewish, and American interests. One group of critics organized themselves into "Jews against Jackson" and published an ad in the New York Times *to make their case.*

Do you believe that any Jew should support this man?
Should *any* decent American?

We believe that Jesse Jackson is a danger to American Jews, to the State of Israel and to America itself. *And we are appalled at the absolute silence of the liberal community and, most importantly, of Jewish leaders and organizations!*

Consider this:

- "When it came to the division of power we did not get from the Jews the slice of cake we deserved . . . the Jews do not share with us control of wealth, broadcasting stations and other centers of power."
  (Jesse Jackson on CBS' *Sixty Minutes*, Sep. 16, 1979)

- "The conflict (with the Jews) began when we started our quest for power. Jews were willing to share decency but not power."
  (Jesse Jackson in *The N.Y. Times*, Aug. 19, 1979)

- "One who does not think (Yasir) Arafat is a true hero does not read the situation correctly."
  (Jesse Jackson in Israel, as quoted in Israel's largest newspaper, *Maariv*, September 27, 1979)

- "Arafat is educated, urbane, reasonable. I think his commitment to justice is an absolute one."
  (Jesse Jackson in *Penthouse* magazine, Feb. 1981)

- "Jesse Jackson blames Israel for tying the hands of the U.S. and endangering her national and economic interests . . . He warned against a development of anti-Semitism if Israel continued to erode American interests."
  (*Maariv*, September 25, 1979)

In light of these outrageous statements against Jews and Israel, and in view of Jackson's support of the PLO architects of murder of women and children, we ask?

How can Jewish leadership be so utterly silent? Had Jesse Jackson been white, would the liberal establishment and Jewish leadership be so cravenly timid?

We believe that Jesse Jackson is far more powerful than most think. We believe that he is successfully building a coalition of malcontents who will be a disaster for Jews, for Israel, for America, for the free world. We believe that he is successfully moving to a position of power within the Democratic party. *We are afraid and we intend to act.*

We are forming chapters of Jews against Jackson in every community for the purpose of alerting Jews and non Jews, alike, to the very real threat this man represents. We intend to pressure national and local political leaders to openly condemn Jesse Jackson and cut all political ties and funds to him. We will expose Jesse Jackson for the danger he really is: *ruin, Jesse, ruin.*

As Jews and as Americans you have a deep obligation to join us and DO. The Jackson machine is more powerful than you know and we must stop it. You *can* stop it. . . .

Jesse Jackson is no good for Jews, for Israel or for America. Stop him. *Ruin Jesse, now.*

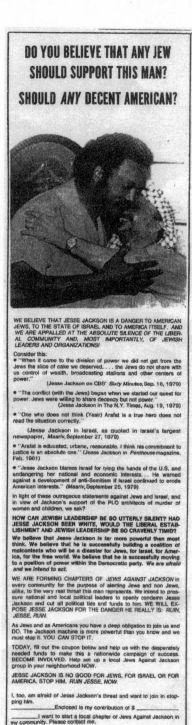

DO YOU BELIEVE THAT ANY JEW SHOULD SUPPORT THIS MAN? SHOULD *ANY* DECENT AMERICAN?

WE BELIEVE THAT JESSE JACKSON IS A DANGER TO AMERICAN JEWS, TO THE STATE OF ISRAEL AND TO AMERICA ITSELF. *AND WE ARE APPALLED AT THE ABSOLUTE SILENCE OF THE LIBERAL COMMUNITY AND, MOST IMPORTANTLY, OF JEWISH LEADERS AND ORGANIZATIONS!*

Consider this:

● "When it came to the division of power we did not get from the Jews the slice of cake we deserved. . . . the Jews do not share with us control of wealth, broadcasting stations and other centers of power."
(Jesse Jackson on CBS' *Sixty Minutes*, Sep. 16, 1979)

● "The conflict (with the Jews) began when we started our quest for power. Jews were willing to share decency but not power."
(Jesse Jackson in The N.Y. Times, Aug. 19, 1979)

● "One who does not think (Yasir) Arafat is a true hero does not read the situation correctly."
(Jesse Jackson in Israel's largest newspaper, *Maariv*, September 27, 1979)

● "Arafat is educated, urbane, reasonable. I think his commitment to justice is an absolute one." (Jesse Jackson in *Penthouse* magazine, Feb. 1981)

● "Jesse Jackson blames Israel for tying the hands of the U.S. and endangering her national and economic interests. . . He warned against a development of anti-Semitism if Israel continued to erode American interests." (*Maariv*, September 25, 1979)

In light of these outrageous statements against Jews and Israel, and in view of Jackson's support of the PLO architects of murder of women and children, we ask?

HOW CAN JEWISH LEADERSHIP BE SO UTTERLY SILENT? HAD JESSE JACKSON BEEN WHITE, WOULD THE LIBERAL ESTABLISHMENT AND JEWISH LEADERSHIP BE SO CRAVENLY TIMID?

We believe that Jesse Jackson is far more powerful than most think. We believe that he is successfully building a coalition of malcontents who will be a disaster for Jews, for Israel, for America, for the free world. We believe that he is successfully moving to a position of power within the Democratic party. *We are afraid and we intend to act.*

WE ARE FORMING CHAPTERS OF *JEWS AGAINST JACKSON* in every community for the purpose of alerting Jews and non Jews, alike, to the very real threat this man represents. We intend to pressure national and local political leaders to openly condemn Jesse Jackson and cut all political ties and funds to him. WE WILL EXPOSE JESSE JACKSON FOR THE DANGER HE REALLY IS: *RUIN, JESSE, RUIN.*

As Jews and as Americans you have a deep obligation to join us and DO. The Jackson machine is more powerful than you know and we must stop it. YOU *CAN* STOP IT.

TODAY, fill out the coupon below and help us with the desperately needed funds to make this a nationwide campaign of success. BECOME INVOLVED. Help set up a local Jews Against Jackson group in your neighborhood NOW.

JESSE JACKSON IS NO GOOD FOR JEWS, FOR ISRAEL OR FOR AMERICA. STOP HIM. *RUIN JESSE, NOW.*

I, too, am afraid of Jesse Jackson's threat and want to join in stopping him.

_____Enclosed is my contribution of $ _____

_____I want to start a local chapter of Jews Against Jackson in my community. Please contact me.

NAME _____ PHONE_____

ADDRESS _____

Please make checks payable to: Jews Against Jackson and mail to:
1916 Kings Highway, Brooklyn, N.Y. 11229. Attn: Fern Rosenblatt-Director

9.24—PHILIP ROTH, SELECTION FROM "WRITING ABOUT JEWS," 1963

Philip Roth (b. 1933) rose to literary fame with the 1959 publication of his novella Goodbye, Columbus, *a critique of middle-class American Jews. Ten years later, Roth's publication of* Portnoy's Complaint, *with its explicit sexual themes, brought him even more popularity, and eventual acknowledgment as the author of one of* Time *magazine's best one hundred novels written between 1923 and 2005. More recently,* American Pastoral, *a novel reflecting on American and Jewish themes of the 1960s, won the 1998 Pulitzer Prize for fiction. In 2010, Roth published* Nemesis, *the last of his thirty-one books, and, two years later, announced his retirement. In a 1963 publication, "Writing about Jews," Roth responded to those who criticized his depiction of Jews and Judaism in his work.*

Ever since some of my first stories were published in 1959 in a volume called *Goodbye, Columbus,* my work has been attacked from certain pulpits and in certain periodicals as dangerous, dishonest, and irresponsible. I have read editorials and articles in Jewish community newspapers condemning these stories for ignoring the accomplishments of Jewish life, or, as Rabbi Emanuel Rackman recently told a convention of the Rabbinical Council of America, for creating a "distorted image of the basic values of Orthodox Judaism," and even, he went on, for denying the non-Jewish world the opportunity of appreciating "the overwhelming contributions which Orthodox Jews are making in every avenue of modern endeavor. . . . " Among the letters I receive from readers, there have been a number written by Jews accusing me of being anti-Semitic and "self-hating," or, at the least, tasteless; they argue or imply that the sufferings of the Jews throughout history, culminating in the murder of six million by the Nazis, have made certain criticisms of Jewish life insulting and trivial. Furthermore, it is charged that such criticism as I make of Jews—or apparent criticism—is taken by anti-Semites as justification for their attitudes, as "fuel" for their fires, particularly as it is a Jew himself who seemingly admits to habits and behavior that are not exemplary, or even normal and acceptable. When I speak before Jewish audiences, invariably there have been people who have come up to me afterward to ask, "Why don't you leave us alone? Why don't you write about the Gentiles?"—"Why must you be so critical?"—"Why do you disapprove of us so?"—this last question asked as often with incredulity as with anger; and often when asked by people a good deal older than myself, asked as of an erring child by a loving but misunderstood parent.

It is difficult, if not impossible, to explain to some of the people claiming to have felt my teeth sinking in, that in many instances they haven't been bitten at all. Not always, but frequently, what readers have taken to be my disapproval of the lives lived by Jews seems to have to do more with their own moral perspective than with the one they would ascribe to me: at times they see wickedness where I myself had seen energy or courage or spontaneity; they are ashamed of what I see no reason to be ashamed of, and defensive where there is no cause for defense.

Not only do they seem to me often to have cramped and untenable notions of right and wrong, but looking at fiction as they do—in terms of "approval" and "disapproval" of Jews, "positive" and "negative" attitudes toward Jewish life —they are likely not to see what it is that the story is really about.

[. . .]

I do not care to go at length here into what a good many readers take for granted are the purposes and possibilities of fiction. I do want to make clear, however, to those whose interests may not lead them to speculate much on the subject, a few of the assumptions a writer may hold—assumptions such as lead me to say that I do not write a story to make evident whatever disapproval I may feel for adulterous men. I write a story of a man who is adulterous to reveal the condition of such a man. If the adulterous man is a Jew, then I am revealing the condition of an adulterous man who is a Jew. Why tell that story? Because I seem to be interested in how—and why and when—a man acts counter to what he considers to be his "best self," or what others assume it to be, or would like for it to be. The subject is hardly "mine"; it interested readers and writers for a long time before it became my turn to be engaged by it, too.

[. . .]

The chances are that there will always be some people who will despise Jews, just so long as they continue to call themselves Jews; and, of course, we must keep an eye on them. But if some Jews are dreaming of a time when they will be accepted by Christians as Christians accept one another—if *this* is why certain Jewish writers should be silent—it may be that they are dreaming of a time that cannot be, and of a condition that does not exist, this side of one's dreams. Perhaps even the Christians don't accept one another as they are imagined to in that world from which Jews may believe themselves excluded solely because they are Jews. Nor are the Christians going to feel toward Jews what one Jew may feel toward another. The upbringing of the alien does not always alert him to the whole range of human connections which exists between the liaisons that arise out of clannishness, and those that arise—or fail to—out of deliberate exclusion. Like those of most men, the lives of Jews no longer take place in a world that is just *landsmen* and enemies. The cry "Watch out for the *goyim*!" at times seems more the ex-

pression of an unconscious wish than of a warning: Oh that they were out there, so that we could be together in here! A rumor of persecution, a taste of exile, might even bring with it that old world of feelings and habits—something to replace the new world of social accessibility and moral indifference, the world which tempts all our promiscuous instincts, and where one cannot always figure out what a Jew is that a Christian is not.

Jews are people who are not what anti-Semites say they are. That was once a statement out of which a man might begin to construct an identity for himself; now it does not work so well, for it is difficult to act counter to the ways people expect you to act when fewer and fewer people define you by such expectations. The success of the struggle against the defamation of Jewish character in this country has itself made more pressing the need for a Jewish self-consciousness that is relevant to this time and place, where neither defamation nor persecution are what they were elsewhere in the past. Surely, for those Jews who choose to continue to call themselves Jews, and find reason to do so, there are courses to follow to prevent it from ever being 1933 again that are more direct, reasonable, and dignified than beginning to act as though it already is 1933—*or as though it always is.* But the death of all those Jews seems to have taught my correspondent, a rabbi and a teacher [who complained to the Anti-Defamation League and later corresponded with Roth personally], little more than to be discreet, to be foxy, to say this but not that. It has taught him nothing other than how to remain a victim in a country where he does not have to live like one if he chooses. How pathetic. And what an insult to the dead. Imagine: sitting in New York in the 1960's and piously summoning up "the six million" to justify one's own timidity. . . .

Source: Michael Staub, ed., *The Jewish 1960s: An American Sourcebook* (Hanover, N.H.: University Press of New England, 2004), 196–208.

*A winner of the Pulitzer Prize and two National
Jewish Book Awards, Bernard Malamud
(1914–1986) emerged as one of the most
important writers in twentieth-century Jewish
America. His first novel,* The Natural, *published
in 1952, recounts the life of baseball player
Roy Hobbs and was made into a major 1984
Hollywood motion picture with Robert Redford
in the lead role. His Pulitzer-winning novel,* The
Fixer, *published in 1966, tells of antisemitism
in czarist Russia. Scholar Robert Alter reflected
on Malamud's work in an article published in*
Commentary *magazine.*

From his earliest stories in the 50's, the relationship between Bernard Malamud's literary
imagination and his Jewish background has been
a peculiar one. For the most part, it has proved
to be a remarkably creative relationship, though
there are a few points in his work where the
wedding of Jewish materials and fictional invention seems largely a shotgun affair, performed
to legitimize imaginative offspring that ought
to have validated themselves without benefit of
skull-capped clergy. Now, American Jewish novelists, from Abraham Cahan and Ludwig Lew-
isohn to Philip Roth, have, quite understandably,
often written about Jews, as the kind of people
they have known best; and since the novel as
a rule tries to reconstruct the social matrices of
individual character, this has generally meant
writing about Jewish milieux, first in the ghetto,
more recently in suburbia. The concentration
on Jewish social environments has not, however, led to anything like a distinctively Jewish
mode of imaginative writing. Henry Roth's *Call
It Sleep*, for example, still probably the most fully
achieved work of fiction by an American writer
of Jewish descent, is a novel of immigrant experience, using Joycean methods for the lyric rendering of consciousness; the principal characters happen to be Jews, but I see nothing in the
conception or execution of this extraordinary

book that could not be readily transferred to a
novel about a family from some other immigrant group.

In Malamud's work, on the other hand, the
immigrant experience is at once more periph-
eral and more central than in writers of comparable background. Although most of his protagonists are avowedly Jewish, he has never really
written *about* Jews, in the manner of other American Jewish novelists. Especially revealing in this
connection is the fact that nowhere does he attempt to represent a Jewish milieu, that a Jewish
community never enters into his books, except
as the shadow of a vestige of a specter. What literary sense, then, does Malamud make of the
emphatic, vividly elaborated ethnic identity of
his characters—those whitefish-eating, Yiddish-
accented isolates in a bleak, generalized world
of harsh necessity? He clearly means Jewishness
to function as an ethical symbol; it is, as Theodore Solotaroff has written, "a type of metaphor . . . both for the tragic dimension of anyone's life and for a code of personal morality."
Last year in these pages ("Sentimentalizing the
Jews," September 1965), I had occasion to observe that such symbolism (as in the relationship between Morris Bober and Frank Alpine
in Malamud's *The Assistant*) can become uncomfortable; when a writer assigns a set of abstract moral values to the representatives of a
particular group, the connection thus insisted
on may strike a reader as arbitrary, an artistic
confusion of actualities and ideals. The symbolic use Malamud makes of Jewishness deserves more detailed attention, but before we
consider that, it is worth noting another, more
organic, way in which Jewish experience enters
into his writing.

Malamud is, to the best of my knowledge, the
first important American writer to shape out of
his early experiences in the immigrant milieu a
whole distinctive style of imagination and, to a
lesser degree, a distinctive technique of fiction

as well. He is by no means a "folk" artist, but his ear for the rhythms of speech and the tonalities of implication, his eye for the shadings of attitude and feeling, of Jewish folk culture, have helped make the fictional world he has created uniquely his own. Though such influences are hard to prove, I suspect that the piquant juxtaposition in his fiction of tough, ground-gripping realism and high-flying fantasy ultimately derives from the paradoxical conjoining of those same qualities that has often characterized Jewish folklore.

To put this another way, it would seem as though the homespun Jewishness of Malamud's characters affords him a means of anchoring his brilliant fantasies in reality, for the dreariness of daily privation and frustration familiar to him through the ghetto are his indicators of what the real world is like, reminding him of the gritty, harsh-grained texture of ordinary human experience. It is significant that the only book he has written in which there are no identifiable Jews, his first novel, *The Natural*, is also the only one in which the underpinnings of reality are finally pulled away by the powerful tug of fantasy. *The Natural* is a spectacular performance, a sort of *Parzival* on the ball field that combines serious moral fable with pointed comedy, superbly sustained suspense, and sheer wish-fulfillment, zestfully imagined; but in the end the novel entertains more than it convinces because too much of the world as we know it has been rearranged in the service of imaginative play.

The Jewish folk figure on which Malamud has modeled most of his protagonists is, of course, the *shlemiel*, the well-meaning bungler, compounded with the *schlimazel*, the hapless soul who is invariably at the wrong end of the bungling. The way he handles this doubly ill-starred figure illuminates his whole artistic relationship to his Jewishness. The *shlemiel* is, we hardly need to be reminded, often an engaging kind of character, and Malamud treats him—most memorably, in the Fidelman stories—with a very special quality of amused sympathy modified by satiric awareness. The spirit of wry folk humor that

Malamud has caught in his personages is nicely expressed in the Yiddish joke about the man who comes to a doctor to complain that he talks to himself all the time: when the doctor answers that he, too, talks to himself and that it is really nothing to worry about, the man objects, "But, Doctor, you have no idea what a *nudnik* I am!" Malamud's protagonists are frequently just this: *shlemiel*s who talk to themselves, who repeatedly engage in self-confrontation, shrewdly but futilely aware of their own limitations, like Fidelman, "self-confessed failures" caught in the trap of themselves and rankling over their predicament, though just a little amused by it, too.

. . . Malamud's new novel, *The Fixer* (Farrar, Straus & Giroux, 352 pp., $5.75), emerges as a far less radical departure from his earlier fiction than one might initially conclude. The surface differences, to be sure, between this book and his previous work are abundant and striking. Malamud has always written about spheres of experience with which he was personally familiar; here he sets his novel in Kiev, toward the end of the Czarist regime. Except in a few of his comic fantasies, he has always written about everyday people in a world whose most basic quality is uneventfulness; here his subject is a lurid murder case and an incredible conspiracy against justice. Suffering in his novels and stories has generally been a matter of humiliated egos or the gnawing fears of poverty; in *The Fixer* the central action is a process of suffering through violence, torture by inches, complete with the obscene inventions of a jailer's sadism, an attempted poisoning, a suicide, even Dostoevskian hallucinations including one where a frantic-eyed horse is beaten over the head with a log. Malamud has always known the art of counterpointing a flat, understated style with flights of whimsy and poetic invention, but never before has he written such taut, muscular prose—as, for example, in this prisoner's nightmare, with its stacatto [*sic*] parade of short declarative sentences and sharply-etched physical images that give fantasy the weight and tactile hardness of palpable fact:

The wind wailed mutely in the prison yard. His heart was like a rusted chain, his muscles taut, as though each had been bound with wire. Even in the cold he sweated. Amid the darkly luminous prisoners he saw spies waiting to kill him. One was the grayhaired warden with a gleaming two-headed ax. He tried to hide his crossed eye behind his hand but it shone like a jewel through his fingers. The Deputy Warden, his fly open, held a black bullwhip behind his back. And though the Tsar wore a white mask over his face and another on the back of his head, Yakov recognized him standing in the far corner of the cell, dropping green drops into a glass of hot milk.

[. . .]

The Fixer is clearly Malamud's most powerful novel—and, it seems to me, his first wholly suc-cessful one. An important reason for its tight artistic unity is the identity in it between cen-tral metaphor and literal fact: the Malamudian prison is here not merely an analogy, a moral and metaphysical state, but has real, clammy, stone walls, excretory stenches, heavy-fisted jailers, dank unheated cells, lice. Similarly, Malamud's symbolic Jew is much more believable here than in his last two novels because the character's symbolic implications flow naturally from the literal fact of his Jewishness which is, after all, the real reason for his arrest. Though to be a Jew in this novel does imply a general moral stance, it also means being involved in the fate of a particular people, actively identifying with its history—in contrast, for example, to Morris Bober, for whom the meaning of Jewishness is exhausted in "to do what is right, to be honest, to be good." . . .

Source: Barnard Malamud nearprint file, AJA.

9.26—SAUL BELLOW, "I SAID THAT I WAS AN AMERICAN, A JEW, A WRITER BY TRADE," NOVEMBER 14, 1976

Saul Bellow (1915–2005), a writer born in Canada and raised in Chicago, earned the Pulitzer Prize, a National Medal of Arts, and the 1976 Nobel Prize in literature. A professor at the University of Chicago, Bellow is credited with influencing generations of writers, many of whom studied with him as part of the university's interdisciplinary graduate program. In a 1976 speech, he reflected on the influence of his Jewish identity on his work.

How enviable it sometimes seems to have a brief and simple history. Ours is neither simple nor brief. You have honored me with an award, and my part in acknowledging this distinction with gratitude, is to make a short speech about America and its Jews, the Jews and their Amer-ica. The difficulty of this obligation is consider-able, for the history we share is full of intricate, cunning and gloomy passages; it is also illu-minating and it is noble—it is a large piece of the history of mankind. Many have tried to rid themselves in one way or another of this dread-ful historic load by assimilation or other means. I have, myself, never been tempted by the hope of waking from the nightmare of history in a higher state of consciousness and freedom. As much as the next man, I enjoy meditating on such things, but my instincts have attached me to what is actually here, and among the choices that were actually open to me, I have always pre-ferred the liberal and democratic ones—not al-ways in the popular sense of these terms.

When I read last summer in the *American Scholar* an article by Professor Sidney Hook on the great teacher and philosopher Morris R. Cohen, I was stirred by Cohen's belief that "the future of liberal civilization" was "bound up with America's survival and its ability to make use of the heritage of human rights formulated by Jefferson and Lincoln." Professor Cohen was no sentimentalist. He was a tough-minded man, not a patriotic rhetorician.

He arrived on the Lower East Side at the age of 12. He knew the slums and the sweatshops. His knowledge of the evils of American life was extensive and unsparing—the history of the Indians and of the Negroes, cruelty, prejudice, mob violence, hysteria, injustice. Acidulous is Hook's word for Cohen's criticism of the U.S.A. Cohen, says Hook, was not a nationalist. He knew that no one chooses the land of his birth. He placed his hopes in the rule of enlightened world law. But Cohen was in some ways piously American. Now piety has become one of our very worst words. It used to be one of the best— think of Wordsworth's desire for "natural piety." Maybe we can do something to rehabilitate the term. Cohen accepted Santayana's definition of piety as "reverence for the sources of one's being." This emotion, says Hook, was naturally acquired by Cohen without ideological indoctrination or blinding.

I understand this without effort. Most of us do. There *are* people for whom it is entirely natural to despise the life that they were born in to. There are others, like myself, who suspect that if we dismiss the life that is waiting for us at birth, we will find ourselves in a void. I was born in Eastern Canada and grew up in Chicago. My parents were Jewish immigrants from Russia. They sent me to a *heder* [Jewish afternoon religious school]. They didn't want me out in the sandlots or playing pool in the poolroom. All these matters were discussed or disputed by us in Yiddish. But when I went to the public library, the books I borrowed were by [American writers] Poe and Melville, Dreiser and Sherwood Anderson. I did not bring home volumes of the Babylonian Talmud to read. I took myself as I was—a kid from the Chicago streets and the child of Jewish parents. I was powerfully stirred by the books brought home from the library, I was moved myself to write something.—These

are some of the sources of my being. One could have better sources, undoubtedly. I could make a list of those more desirable sources, but they are not mine, and I cannot revere them. The only life I can love, or hate, is the life that I—that we— have found here, this American life of the Twentieth Century, the life of Americans who are also Jews. Which of these sources, the American or the Jewish, should elicit the greater piety? Are the two exclusive? Must a choice be made? The essence of freedom is that one makes the choice, if choices must be made, for the most profound of personal reasons. It is at this very point that one begins to feel how intensely enviable it is to have a brief and simple history. (But is there any such thing?)

In Israel, I was often and sometimes impatiently asked what sort of Jew I was and how I defined myself and explained my existence. I said that I was an American, a Jew, a writer by trade. I was not insensitive to the Jewish question, I was painfully conscious of the Holocaust, I longed for peace and security in the Jewish State. I added, however, that I had lived in America all my life, that American English was my language, and that (in an oddly universalist way) I was attached to my country and the civilization of which it was a part. But my Israeli questioners or examiners were not satisfied. They were trying to make me justify myself. It was their conviction that the life of a Jew in what they call the Diaspora must inevitably be "inauthentic." Only as a Jew in Israel, some of them told me, could I enter history again and prove the necessity and authenticity of my existence. I refused to agree with them that my life had been illusion and dust. I do not accept any interpretation of history that declares the deepest experience of any person to be superfluous. To me that smells of totalitarianism. Nor could I accept the suggestion that I repudiate some six decades of life, to dismiss my feelings for some of the sources of my being *because I am a Jew or nothing.* That would wipe out me totally. It would be not only impiety and irreverences, but also self-destruction.

But one need not hold long arguments with views that are so obviously wrong. What underlies the position that I have just rejected is the assumption that America is bound to go the way of other Christian countries and expel or destroy its Jewish population. But *is* it a Christian country like the others? The question almost answers itself as soon as it is asked—this nation is not, in the European sense, a recognizably Christian country. One could write many volumes on what America is *not*. However, there is no need, in a brief talk on an occasion such as this to make grandiose statements about liberal democracy. It is sufficient to say in the most matter of fact way what is or should be obvious to everyone. In spite of the vastness and oppressiveness of corporate and governmental powers

the principle of the moral equality of all human beings has not been rejected in the United States. Not yet, at any rate. Sigmund Freud, I remember reading, once observed that America was an interesting experiment, but that he did not believe that it would succeed. Well, maybe not. But it would be base to abandon it. To do so would destroy our reverence for the sources of our being. We would inflict on ourselves a mutilation from which we might never recover. And if Cohen is right, and the future of liberal civilization is bound up with America's survival, the damage would be universal and irreparable.

Source: As printed in *JAW*, 520–22. Copyright © 1976 by Saul Bellow. Originally delivered as a speech upon receiving the America's Democratic Legacy Award. Used by permission of The Wylie Agency LLC.

9.27—ALLAN SHERMAN, LYRICS, "IF I WERE A TISHMAN," 1967

On his 1962 album, My Son, the Folk Singer, *Hollywood writer and television producer Allan Sherman (1924–1973) translated traditional folk tunes into parodies that included Jewish themes and content. The album eventually went gold, selling more than a million copies. On his 1967 album,* Togetherness, *Sherman parodied the song "If I Were a Rich Man" from the hit Broadway musical* Fiddler on the Roof. *Referencing the Jewish real estate developer Robert Tishman, whose grandfather Julius Tishman started the family business on the Lower East Side in 1898, Sherman moved the song from the fictional shtetl of nineteenth-century Anatevka to twentieth-century New York City.*

Oh, New York is changing.
Wherever you look,
Big tall buildings by Tishman
Tishman, ahh . . .

If I were a Tishman,
Yum di diddle didle doody didle diddy didy di

(Yum di didle)
All day long I'd buildy buildy build,
If I were a building man.

I'd build a lot of buildings,
Yum di didle doody deedle didle deedle didle
    dumb
(Yum di didle)
Building buildings anywhere I wish,
If I were a Tishy Tishy Tish.

I'd build the 666 Fifth Avenue building
Right in the middle of the town,
One block wide and forty-eight stories high.
And I'd have eighteen elevators going up
And twenty-seven more going down,
All of them express to pass you by.
(Di diddle di)

I'd build a ladies' room and also a men's
    room,
Right there on each and every floor,
Each one in a style that is apropos.

And like the restrooms in the best office
   buildings,
You'd need a key to open up the door,
Though who would steal a bathroom, I dunno!

Oh, if I were a Tishman,
Yum di diddle doidle didle dadle doodle deedle
   dumb
(Yum di didle)
All day long I'd buildy buildy build,
If I were a building man.

I'd build a lot of buildings,
Yum di doodle dadle didle deedle didle dodle
   dumb
(Yum di didle)
I could realize my life's ambish,
Raising rents whenever I would wish,
Telling tenants, "You can call me pish."
If I were a rich Tishman

Source: "If I Were a Tishman," by Allan Sherman,
© Curtain Call Productions, 1967. Used by permission
of the publisher.

9.28—"HALF OF ALL AMERICANS REGISTER SUPPORT FOR ISRAEL; NO AMERICAN BACKS ARABS," JEWISH TELEGRAPHIC AGENCY, JUNE 12, 1967

Throughout May 1967, tensions rose between Israel and its Arab neighbors, especially Egypt. Intelligence reports indicated that Syria, Egypt, and Jordan were massing troops on their respective borders with Israel. On May 19, Egyptian leader Gamal Abdel Nasser ordered the removal of United Nations forces from the Sinai Peninsula and Gaza Strip. Three days later, he closed the important Straits of Tiran and called for "the destruction of Israel." With more than a hundred thousand Egyptian troops prepared for war, Israel formed a National Unity Government on June 1. Four days later, the Israeli military launched a preemptive strike against the Egyptian air force. After just six days, the State of Israel emerged triumphant, scoring victories against Egypt to the south, Jordan to the east, and Syria to the north. Public opinion polls, conducted immediately after the fighting began in the Mideast, revealed strong support for the State of Israel among Americans at large. While half of those polled expressed little interest in the conflict, those who did care sided overwhelmingly with Israel. Respondents believed that Israel had acted in self-defense while the Arab states "have wanted to attack Israel for a long time."

New York—

The first poll of American public opinion since the start of the third Arab-Israel war on June 5 indicated today that about half of all Americans registered substantial sympathy and support for Israel. Almost no Americans expressed sympathy for the Arabs and about half of all Americans reported they did not have strong feelings on either side of the conflict.

The Harris Poll survey, conducted soon after the fighting started showed that suspicion about the aggressive intentions of the Arab countries was high among those reporting strong feelings on the conflict. By a 12 to 1 ratio, such respondents agreed with the statement that the Arab countries "have wanted to attack Israel for a long time."

Suspicions about Israeli intentions were correspondingly low. The respondents by a three to one ratio rejected Arab charges that Israel wanted to start the fighting. The American public was shown to believe by about two to one that the Soviets encouraged the start of the war as a way to divert attention from the United States effort in Vietnam.

Most Americans endorsed the United States effort to bring a halt to the fighting through the United Nations, but doubts about the effectiveness of the U.N. in the Middle East crisis outweighed confidence in the U.N. by a two to one margin.

Israel's dramatic victory in the Six Day War energized American Jews with a newfound sense of pride in the State of Israel and, by extension, in their own Jewish identity. At a time when many different American groups expressed pride in their ethnic heritage, Jews trumpeted Israel's status as a strong nation willing and able to defend itself against its enemies. Fund-raising for Israel-related causes nearly doubled in the year after the war, while 7,500 Jewish college students traveled to Israel to support the Jewish state. In the documents that follow, American Jews reflect on the Six Day War's impact on Jewish identity and American Zionism.

ODDMENTS AND REMAINDERS:

Today Jews, whatever their stripe or attitude, can be deeply proud to be Jews. Despite their hatred of war, when they were confronted with war, the Israelis waged it courageously and with the scientific smoothness of a well-lubricated machine. And what no generation will ever be permitted to forget, they went it alone, against a foe that was presumed to be formidable, if not unbeatable, but which turned out to be tissue paper.

Because from Nasser and Shukairy up and down the Arab line, they were more fury than power, more noise than sober judgment. And the entire Arab fiasco, especially as it centered in Cairo, revealed an old axiom: that he who is motivated by hatred alone falls by the weight of his own rancor.

🐟 Israel is bigger today in the eyes of the world than it ever dreamed of being so early in its infancy. The reason must be the way it discharged itself on the battlefield and the way its spokesmen in the UN comported themselves. With humility and forbearance by contrast, [the Israelis] shamed their Arab adversaries, the angry voice of Soviet Russia and its carefully instructed satellites.

[...]

Because of Israel's incredible performance, the United States came off smelling like the proverbial rose. Though this Government played no part in Israel's victories, despite the mountain of Arab accusations to the contrary, the U.S. image brightened while that of Russia became tarnished and worn. Because Israel demonstrated the toughness of her mettle under fire, the status of the U.S. as a world power has recovered some of its lost luster and much of her bite as a global peacekeeper has returned.

This could be a good augur for an early conclusion of the Vietnam fiasco.

🐟 And didn't your heart leap with admiration every time [Israeli foreign minister] Abba Eban appeared on the small screen or came through your radio? This master of shaped speech with the voice and inflection of Churchill offered a devastating contrast to the flat and fumbling presentations of the Arab and Communist representatives who, as they faithfully echoed the forlorn instructions of their governments, made empty and pathetic sounds.

[...]

The news just came over the air that hostilities in the Middle East have ended and to all intents the shooting is over. As we all pray that the days ahead will be the bearers of peace, over the dusty horizon looms the very big question, what of her gains will Israel keep, what will she summarily release and what will she use for bargaining purposes?

Already you can hear the issue joined on practically any street corner, but on one decision you can make book now: Israel will not surrender Jordanian Jerusalem with its Western Wall, not after nearly twenty years denial of this sacred bastion of prayer. Otherwise, Israel could be holding the key to world peace in her firm, young hands. It is hoped that in her eagerness she does not jam the lock. ...

Source: Reprinted with permission of the *Jewish Chronicle* (Pittsburgh, Pa.).

9.30—"THE PORTRAIT OF COURAGE:
THE PEOPLE MADE ISRAEL
VICTORIOUS," *Jewish Chronicle,*
JUNE 16, 1967

9.31—"THE WEEK THAT ROCKED THE
WORLD," JUNE 5–11, *Jewish Chronicle,*
JUNE 16, 1967

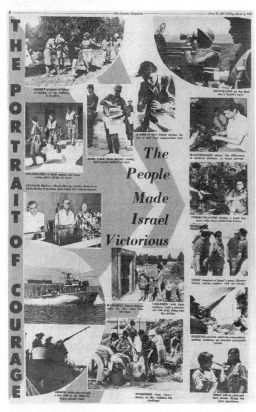

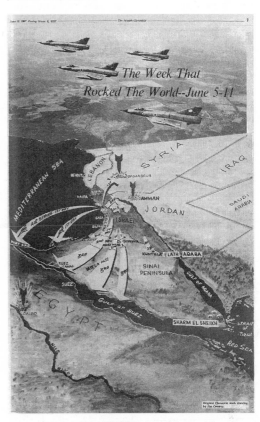

Source: Reprinted with permission of the *Jewish Chronicle* (Pittsburgh, Pa.).

Source: Reprinted with permission of the *Jewish Chronicle* (Pittsburgh, Pa.).

9.32—BREIRA'S NATIONAL PLATFORM, FEBRUARY 21, 1977

Israel's victory in the Six Day War brought a military occupation of Palestinians in the West Bank and Gaza Strip. For many left-leaning American Jews, the Israeli occupation violated the rights of Palestinians and stood as an obstacle to eventual peace. In 1973, a group of progressive Zionist American Jews met at Rutgers University and formed an organization called Breira, Hebrew for "alternative" and a play on the popular Hebrew expression "ain breira" (there is no alternative). Breira's

founders, many of whom participated in the creation of the havurah movement, sought a means to "break the 'taboo' on public criticism of Israel within the American Jewish community." In 1977, Breira offered a national platform articulating its views; the following excerpt is pulled from the middle of the document.

DIASPORA-ISRAEL RELATIONS

We are committed to Jewish life—its resilient ethical principles, its moving spiritual and aesthetic achievements, its cultural heritage, its inspiring, evolving history. We affirm that Jews throughout the world and throughout the ages constitute one people. The State of Israel is a particular manifestation of this peoplehood; the communities of the Diaspora form an equally vital element. We believe that the continuity of Jewish life now rests on the interdependence of the Jewish people in both Israel and the Diaspora.

We love Israel. We cherish the cultural treasures and the many moral examples it has given us. And we similarly affirm the richness of the Jewish experience in North America and are eager to explore and extend its possibilities.

The primary decisions of Israel's life and policy must be made by the Israelis, as the many decisions of Diaspora life must be made by each Jewish community for itself. Nonetheless, we must communicate our feelings to each other, as a reflection of our mutual responsibility, support, and concern. Israel and the communities of the Diaspora are strong enough to accept or reject the others' suggestions on their merits; neither should attempt to manipulate or intimidate the other.

We affirm *aliyah* as a positive act, but we also affirm the right of Israelis to take up residence elsewhere. We similarly reject any move to make it difficult or impossible for those Soviet Jews who exercize their right to resettle and rebuild their lives outside Israel. We do not believe that Israelis living outside Israel, or Soviet Jews who choose to emigrate to North America have, merely by that choice, betrayed a special Jewish imperative.

In light of the above, it is resolved that Breira:

1. Emphasize its support for the existence and development of a secure State of Israel as an expression of Jewish national self-determination.

2. Advocate direct political, moral, and financial support of those forces within Israeli society which promote the principles of peace, social equality, democracy, civil rights, and other values consistent with the Jewish prophetic tradition. An important expression of this tradition includes safeguarding the rights of Arab and other non-Jewish minorities within the State of Israel.

3. Demand that in all matters concerning the relations of Jews in Israel to those of the Diaspora, a climate of free and candid exchange shall prevail.

4. Support and create programs which strengthen the knowledge of Jewish history and the diversity of Jewish culture in Israel and the Diaspora. To facilitate the mutual understanding of Israeli and Diaspora communities, we call for the promotion of Hebrew language education.

5. Strongly advocate communal fundraising for the development of all Jewish life in Israel and the Diaspora and call for accountability in the disbursement of those funds. We deplore the wasteful, corrupting, and anachronistic practice of diverting such funds to any political party. We call for the constitution of a commission to explore the ways that these kinds of inequalities be eliminated; and that more responsible, just procedures be initiated.

6. Defend the rights of Jews everywhere to live freely as Jews in their country of residence or to emigrate.

Source: Breira nearprint file, AJA.

9.33—JACKSON-VANIK AMENDMENT, 1974

*In the mid-1960s, following earlier efforts to
draw international attention to the plight of
Jews in the Soviet Union, American Jews
coalesced in a national movement to secure the
free emigration of Soviet Jews. Several existing
Jewish organizations devoted resources to the
cause, while others were formed explicitly to
press the communist government to "let my
people go." Soviet Jewry activists focused their
political pressure on the U.S. Congress, hoping to
translate the larger Cold War antipathy toward
the Soviet Union into legislation that would help
Soviet Jews. In 1974, with the sponsorship of
Senator Henry "Scoop" Jackson (1912–1983)
and Congressman Charles Vanik (1913–2007),
the Jackson-Vanik Amendment, removing
most-favored-nation status from communist
countries that limited emigration, passed
unanimously.*

Section 2432. Freedom of emigration in East-
West trade

(a) Actions of nonmarket economy countries making them ineligible for normal trade
relations, programs of credits, credit guarantees, or investment guarantees, or commercial
agreements

To assure the continued dedication of the
United States to fundamental human rights, and
notwithstanding any other provision of law, on
or after January 3, 1975, products from any nonmarket economy country shall not be eligible
to receive nondiscriminatory treatment (normal
trade relations), such country shall not participate in any program of the Government of the
United States which extends credits or credit
guarantees or investment guarantees, directly
or indirectly, and the President of the United
States shall not conclude any commercial agreement with any such country, during the period
beginning with the date on which the President
determines that such country—

1. denies its citizens the right or opportunity
   to emigrate;
2. imposes more than a nominal tax on
   emigration or on the visas or other
   documents required for emigration, for
   any purpose or cause whatsoever; or
3. imposes more than a nominal tax, levy,
   fine, fee, or other charge on any citizen
   as a consequence of the desire of such
   citizen to emigrate to the country of his
   choice,

and ending on the date on which the President determines that such country is no longer
in violation of paragraph (1), (2), or (3).

In 1973, Anatoly Sharansky (b. 1948) was denied an exit visa by the Soviet Union and subsequently became one of the best-known Soviet refusenik Jews. He was arrested on charges of spying for the United States in March 1977, and the following year was convicted and sentenced to thirteen years of hard labor. The New York–based Student Struggle for Soviet Jewry focused on bringing international pressure against the Soviet Union in its efforts to gain the release of Sharansky, who would later adopt the name Natan after immigrating to Israel.

Source: FF cabinet 5, drawer 12, AJA. Copyright Center for Russian Jewry with Student Struggle for Soviet Jewry. Used by permission.

IO Contemporary America
JEWISH LIFE SINCE 1980

The final chapter of this book focuses on Jewish identity and Jewish demography in the final years of the twentieth century and the first decade of the twenty-first century. Jewish sociologists, anthropologists, and historians continue to predict where current trends will lead. As we have seen in previous chapters, students of American Jewry have long been discussing the consequences of decreasing ritual observance among American Jews as well as the powerful influence exerted by general American culture on Jewish identity. Since World War II, the rate of intermarriage in America has surged. Community leaders and researchers continue to debate how exogamy—"marrying out"—will influence American Jewish life in the coming years.

For many Jews, America's open society translated into increasing rates of assimilation and lower levels of Jewish identification, whether expressed in synagogue affiliation, membership in Jewish organizations, or family observance of Jewish holidays and rituals. By the end of the twentieth century, most sociological surveys indicated that the rate of intermarriage among American Jews was hovering around 50 percent.

The current debate over the meaning and import of these trends has spawned a number of possible interpretations. According to one overarching view, American Jews have become a highly assimilated, marginally identified population. They lack formal Jewish education and resist Jewish ritual practices. These analyses assert that there is a pronounced decline in all markers used to measure Jewish identification in America.

Proponents of a second view, however, assert that American Jewish identity patterns are now in transformation. These commentators suggest that a bustling and creative population of American Jews, broadly defined, will emerge from the influx of non-Jewish spouses and the expanded reach of American Jewish life beyond its historic boundaries. Intermarriage, they say, far from being the death knell of American Jewish life, may very well lead to an increase in the number of American Jews. Similarly, new religious trends may present an unprecedented opportunity for community outreach that will attract interest in Judaism and strengthen Jewish life.

IMMIGRATION AND ADAPTATION

10.01 — KEVIN WEST, "THE PERSIAN CONQUEST," *W*, JULY 2009

Under the rule of Iran's Shah Mohammad Reza Pahlavi (1919–1980), Jews enjoyed a large measure of religious freedom and social opportunity. But in early 1979, radical Muslim clerics and other revolutionaries overthrew the shah, and the new Iranian regime persecuted its Jewish population, which sought emigration en masse. After the early arrival of several wealthy and influential Persian Jewish families to Beverly Hills, the city of Los Angeles grew, within a decade, to be a new center of Persian Jewish life. A 2009 article in W *magazine and an essay by Saba Soomekh, a young Persian academic, chronicle the immigration of Persian Jews to Los Angeles.*

. . . In his office above Wilshire Boulevard, architect Hamid Gabbay, 66, traces the dazzling success of the Persian community in Beverly Hills back to Tehran before the revolution. The Sixties and Seventies saw a full-tilt economic expansion, fueled by the Shah's dream of westernization and financed by vast oil reserves. "The real-estate boom was incredible," explains Gabbay, who founded an architecture firm with his brother in Tehran. "We got to design a city— projects I can't even dream of now."

The country's Jewish minority thrived, at least in Tehran's educated quarters, thanks to the Shah's official policy of religious tolerance and cultural openness. But radical Muslim clerics gained strength during the late Seventies, and in January 1979 they overthrew the ailing monarch. Gabbay left in November 1978, landing a job with an L.A. firm that he had been interviewing to work for him just four months earlier. "I went to the firm," he recalls, "and said, 'I'm sorry, I can't hire you. But would you hire me?'"

Even before the revolution, a few Iranian Jews had already decamped to California. Jimmy Del-

shad, who made local history in 2007 by becoming the first Iranian-American mayor of Beverly Hills, left modest origins in Shiraz in 1959 and attended California State University at Northridge with his brothers. "I don't think there were more than 10 or 12 [Persian] families we knew in Los Angeles," he says.

The present-day elite Persian community in Beverly Hills, though, really got its start in the early Seventies, when four brothers of the Mahboubi clan—who had grown rich at home from their virtual monopoly on chewing gum—moved to Los Angeles and sank their money into real estate on Rodeo Drive. One of the brothers, Dar Mahboubi, backed haberdasher Bijan during the Eighties, and younger Mahboubis continue to manage the family's considerable property holdings. Another group of brothers, the Yadegars, also arrived in Beverly Hills before the revolution and began snapping up real estate. Today so many Persians own stakes in Beverly Hills' Golden Triangle, the prime streets between Wilshire and Santa Monica boulevards, that the area is known to some as "Tehrangeles." (Another Persian shopping district in Westwood has also earned that moniker.)

The area's attractions were obvious: Beverly Hills was synonymous with wealth and status, plus it delivered a beautiful climate, safe residential neighborhoods and a well-established Jewish community. But perhaps the key asset was the then top-notch school system. [Entrepreneur and real-estate magnate] Sam Nazarian's sister-in-law, former psychology professor Angella Nazarian, recalls that her father bought a house here in the early Seventies so her brother could attend Beverly Hills High School. "My father had no plans of coming to the U.S.," she says over a lunch of tuna tartare in Westwood. "It was more 'This way my son can go to a really good school.'"

Later in the decade, as Ayatollah Khomeini's followers denounced the freedoms that had enabled Jewish prosperity, some in Tehran began to worry, says prominent hostess Mahroo Moghavem, whose husband was a successful appliance distributor at that time. "We thought investment in other countries would be good," she says during a brunch with friends at her home in the hills above Sunset Boulevard. "We were happy, but we thought that one day the Shah would pass away and what would happen then?"

As armed students took to the streets of Tehran in late 1978, the Moghavems whisked their children off to Los Angeles for a vacation. Events unfolding on television made clear that they would not be returning home. The Moghavems were among the lucky ones, however. Thanks to their investments outside of Iran, they were able to buy a house in Beverly Hills from billionaire John Kluge and then sink money into a development project parceling the estate of silent-screen star Harold Lloyd into a 16-home subdivision.

Although dispossessed, the thousands of Iranian Jews who flocked to Beverly Hills in the coming years had assets most immigrants lack: advanced education, business experience and, in the majority of cases, some cash in overseas accounts. Iranian Jews also landed in Israel and New York, and it's worth noting that the mass flight away from theocracy included Muslims and members of other religious minorities. But entire neighborhoods of Tehran's Jewish elite settled in Beverly Hills—something like a wholesale transplant of a social community. Initially the shell-shocked refugees found solace in local synagogues, where older members remembered the influx from Europe after World War II and welcomed them. Sympathies grew strained, however, by the differences in language and custom between the Ashkenazi Jewish community and the Sephardic newcomers. By American standards, Persian decorum at synagogue was freewheeling, even disruptive, as family members rose to greet one another and chat during services. In addition, says Delshad, Persians didn't understand that American-style membership in a prestigious synagogue like Sinai Temple meant paying annual dues and getting involved with fundraising. "The other members looked at them as freeloaders coming and taking but never contributing," he explains.

[. . .]

Generational shift, slow though it may be, has pushed the Persian community toward the American mainstream—or at least the Beverly Hills version of it. Still, the community clings tightly to its core values of respect for family, faith, education and success, and some age-old customs remain. Friday-night Shabbat dinners are sacrosanct, and the meal can easily include 60 people. (Persians often cite such gatherings as a reason they need large houses.) Likewise, a majority in the younger generation choose to marry fellow Persians—much to their parents' relief. "They don't have to marry Persian," says Jasmine Yadegar, in a tone suggesting that she hopes her two twentysomething daughters—both of whom still live at home—eventually will. "All I want for them is to be happy and find people with the same background."

"For me," says daughter Sabrina, an aspiring fashion designer, "I think it's a lot easier to fall in love with someone who has the same ideas and experiences."

"I need to love their family, and they need to love mine," adds older sister Jessica, a documentary filmmaker. "Some of my American friends have told me that you're not dating the parents. They say you don't need to meet the parents on the first, second or third date. That's not my view. I think the longer you postpone the introduction to the family, the longer it takes you to get to know if this is someone you want to spend the rest of your life with."

Among much older women, the Iranian custom of the *doreh*—a semiformal circle of women who meet to eat home-cooked Persian fare, play cards and gossip in Farsi—has also proved resilient enough to make it to the 21st century. But whether the tradition survives two generations in America is an open question as women's roles change. "The younger generation works more," says grandmother Jacqueline Moradi during the brunch gathering at Moghavem's house. "In our generation in Iran, that was unheard of."

The Baradarans represent this new face of the Persian upper-middle class. Natasha [an interior designer], who has a busy career, doesn't attend a *doreh*, and Bob [a lawyer] shares the job of raising their two young daughters. The Baradarans' circle not only includes Persian friends but also his colleagues, her clients and other parents from the girls' prestigious private schools. "I am raising kids in a city in which I was raised," says Natasha. "This is my home. I don't feel like a transplant." And why should she? After 30 years in Beverly Hills, few, if any, Persians still hope to return to Tehran. "It's a reality," says Gabbay of his community's new life in California, as he gazes out his office window at the Golden Triangle. "We are a reality."

Source: © Kevin West, *W* magazine, Condé Nast Publications.

10.02—SABA SOOMEKH, AMERICAN JEWISH UNIVERSITY, "THE POLITICAL EMERGENCE OF THE LOS ANGELES PERSIAN COMMUNITY," 2010

Today, many civic leaders, Jewish scholars, Israeli politicians, and heads of organizations reach out to the Iranian community because they are aware of the tremendous economic resources that this group provides. They also know that if this community believes in a cause, especially when it is relevant to helping other Jews and the State of Israel, they will do everything they can to support it.

I believe that the Palestinian Intifada of 2000 and the numerous suicide bombings in Israel heightened the Iranian Jewish community's consciousness and their religious identity. The state of Israel is important to many Jews, but more so to the Iranian Jewish community because they are a dislocated people and they know how important it is to have a Jewish state. Thus, Iranian Jews feel it is significant to support Israel; unlike many American Jews, Iranians do not question the Israeli government and are more conservative in regards to Israeli politics. Traditionally, Iranians supported Israel through Jewish charitable organizations. Yet, within the last ten years, with the rallying of some very influential Iranian businessmen, a top priority for the community has been to give financial support to politicians who support the state of Israel.

There is a lot of criticism of the community for excluding local politics in favor of Israeli politics. For example, more than half [likely an overstatement] of the residents of Beverly Hills are Iranian Jews, yet when the city asks for support for their fire, police, and school funds, Iranian Jews barely donate their time or money. Yet, if there is an affair to raise money for Israel more Iranians will attend than any other people in the Jewish community. However, in the last couple of years, this pattern has begun to change as Iranian Jews also recognize the importance of getting involved in local civic life.

[. . .]

Iranian Jews' involvement in global politics made them recognize that they make a difference in their local community. This is the reverse strategy of immigrant communities that first get involved on a local level and then move on to Washington and global politics. Once the community accepted that it would not be returning to Iran, and it became aware of its influence in the American political system, the people were encouraged and felt comfortable enough to get involved in local community politics.

[. . .]

Although the Iranian community will be accused of being insular, it is developing its own civic identity, which is helping their acculturation with American Jews. Slowly the people have been able to relinquish the mentality that they had while living under a corrupt political regime and recognize that they no longer have to be fearful of being Jewish. Once this fear was gone and Iranians accepted their life in America, they began to embrace the democratic system that allowed them to be successful and practice their religion openly and proudly.

. . . First, second, and third generation Iranians have formed a civic identity based on their Jewishness and have now moved on to deal with other issues that affect their daily lives. It will only be a matter of time before more Iranian Jews get involved in local and state politics because the drive and passion has now been engrained in the community.

Source: American Jewish University e-zine. Used by permission.

10.03—VISION AND MISSION STATEMENTS, UNITED STATES HOLOCAUST MEMORIAL MUSEUM, 1993

In 1978, Holocaust survivor and writer Elie Wiesel (b. 1928) chaired the President's Commission on the Holocaust, which was charged by Jimmy Carter to formulate plans for the creation of a memorial to the victims of the Holocaust. The report, issued in September 1979, called for a museum located on the National Mall in Washington, D.C. With unanimous support from the U.S. Congress and a gift from the federal government of a parcel of land near the Washington Monument, the museum opened April 22, 1993. Its vision and mission statements, as approved by the United States Holocaust Memorial Council on June 24, 1993, are included here.

VISION

As a living memorial to the Holocaust, the United States Holocaust Memorial Museum envisions a world in which people confront hatred, prevent genocide, and promote human dignity.

MISSION

The United States Holocaust Memorial Museum is America's national institution for the documentation, study, and interpretation of Holocaust history, and serves as this country's memorial to the millions of people murdered during the Holocaust.

The Holocaust was the state-sponsored, systematic persecution and annihilation of European Jewry by Nazi Germany and its collaborators between 1933 and 1945. Jews were the primary victims—six million were murdered;

Gypsies, the handicapped, and Poles were also targeted for destruction or decimation for racial, ethnic, or national reasons. Millions more, including homosexuals, Jehovah's Witnesses, Soviet prisoners of war, and political dissidents, also suffered grievous oppression and death under Nazi tyranny.

The Museum's primary mission is to advance and disseminate knowledge about this unprecedented tragedy, to preserve the memory of those who suffered, and to encourage its visitors to reflect upon the moral and spiritual questions raised by the events of the Holocaust as well as their own responsibilities as citizens of a democracy.

Chartered by a unanimous Act of Congress in 1980 and opened on April 26, 1993, adjacent to the National Mall in Washington, D.C., the Museum strives to broaden public understanding of the history of the Holocaust through multifaceted programs: exhibitions; research and publication; collecting and preserving material evidence, art, and artifacts related to the Holocaust; annual Holocaust commemorations known as Days of Remembrance; distribution of educational materials and teacher resources; and a variety of public programming designed to enhance understanding of the Holocaust and related issues, including those of contemporary significance.

Source: United States Holocaust Memorial Museum, www.ushmm.org/museum/mission. Used with permission.

In August 2000, Democratic presidential candidate Al Gore (b. 1948) selected Joseph Lieberman (b. 1942), an observant Jew and the U.S. senator from Connecticut, as his vice presidential running mate. Lieberman was the first American Jew to run on a national major party presidential ticket. While his nomination excited Jews across the country, several Jewish groups remained wary. Left-leaning Jews opposed Lieberman's support for school vouchers, while right-leaning Jews criticized his stand favoring abortion. Still others feared that such a high-profile Jewish politician would provoke antisemitism. Included here is a news story from the Forward, *followed by Lieberman's address to the 2000 Democratic National Convention.*

New York—Even as an ebullient American Jewish community brims with pride at Vice President Gore's choice of Senator Lieberman as his running mate, some on both the right and left are questioning a number of the lawmaker's stances on issues of importance to Jews.

While praise for Mr. Lieberman's character, honesty and conscience was nearly universal, some Orthodox groups criticized Mr. Lieberman for his stance on clemency for Jonathan Pollard, an American Jew convicted of spying for Israel, and for his support of late-term abortion. At the same time, some liberal Jews expressed concern about his support of school vouchers, including those for religious schools, and his strongly pro–free trade and pro-defense record.

The praise Mr. Lieberman is getting from some Orthodox groups, whose members are traditionally on the right of the political spectrum, could raise concerns among centrist and left-leaning Jewish voters.

Orthodox groups in favor of releasing Pollard have criticized Mr. Lieberman for his opposition, rare among Jewish politicians, to granting the spy clemency. "I would welcome his taking the opportunity in his new position to go back and dig firsthand into Jonathan's file and see what he did do and what he didn't do," the executive vice president of the National Council of Young Israel, an Orthodox group, Rabbi Pesach Lerner, said. "My thoughts are, he was briefed by the CIA, but so was Chuck Schumer and he says 'enough is enough,'" Rabbi Lerner said about the New York senator, who is in favor of Pollard's release.

Some countered that Mr. Lieberman's stance on the Pollard issue was an asset. "It's helpful to the ticket. It doesn't give the other side an issue on national security on which [then vice president Dick] Cheney's an expert," a Democratic pundit, Hank Sheinkopf, said.

The director of public affairs of Agudath Israel of America, Rabbi Avi Shafran, said Mr. Lieberman was "in line" with Orthodox voters on many issues such as "his targeting of violence and sex in films and video and television" and "his censure of President Clinton." . . .

Source: This article originally appeared in the *Forward,* 1906; used by permission.

Is America a great country, or what?

Ten days ago, with courage and friendship, Al Gore asked me to be his running mate.

This has been an extraordinary week for my family and me.

There's an old saying that behind every successful man . . . there is a surprised mother-in-law.

I am here tonight to tell you . . . it's true.

I want to thank the daughter of my mother-in-law, the woman who just introduced me.

Hadassah—even before Al Gore made me his running mate, you made me the luckiest guy in the world.

I am fortunate to have you by my side on this journey and I thank you sweetheart.

That miraculous journey begins here and now. Tonight, I am so proud to stand as your candidate for Vice President of the United States.

Only in America.

I am humbled by this nomination and so grateful to Al Gore for choosing me.

And I want you to know . . . I will work my heart out to make sure Al Gore is the next President of the United States.

We have become the America that so many of our parents dreamed for us.

But the great question this year, is what will we dream for our country . . . and how will we make it come true?

We who gather here tonight believe, as Al Gore has said, that it's not just the size of our national feast that is important . . . but the number of people we can fit around the table. There must be room for everybody.

As every faith teaches us—and as Presidents from Lincoln to Roosevelt to Reagan to Clinton have reminded us—we must as Americans, try to see our nation not just through our own eyes . . . but through the eyes of others.

In my life, I have seen the goodness of this country through many sets of eyes.

I have seen it through the eyes of my grandmother.

She was raised in Central Europe, in a village where she was often harassed because of the way she worshiped God.

Then, she immigrated to America.

On Saturdays, she used to walk to synagogue, and often, her Christian neighbors would pass her and say, "Good Sabbath, Mrs. Manger."

It was a source of endless delight and gratitude for her that here in this country, she was accepted for who she was.

I have seen America through the eyes of my parents, Henry and Marcia Lieberman.

My father lived in an orphanage when he was a child.

He went on to drive a bakery truck and own a package store in Stamford, Connecticut.

He taught my sisters and me the importance of work and responsibility.

With my mother by his side, he saw me become the first person in my family to graduate from college.

My mom is here tonight.

She's 85 years old, and never felt younger than she does today.

Mom—thank you, I love you—and you and I know how proud dad would be tonight.

And I have tried to see America through the eyes of people I have been privileged to know.

In the early 1960s, when I was a college student, I walked with Martin Luther King in the March on Washington.

Later that fall, I went to Mississippi, where we worked to register African-Americans to vote.

The people I met never forgot that in America . . . every time a barrier is broken . . . the doors of opportunity open wider for everyone.

And I have tried to see America through the eyes of families who had the deck stacked against them . . . but fought back.

As Connecticut's Attorney General, I worked to be the people's lawyer.

I went after polluters who were spoiling our water and our air.

I stood with single moms to go after deadbeat dads.

We even sued big oil companies who were trying to gouge consumers at the pump.

And I have seen America through the eyes of my wife and her parents.

By now, most of you know Hadassah's story.

Her family was literally saved by American GI's who liberated the concentration camps.

Then her parents escaped Communism and were welcomed as immigrants to America and given a new life.

The fact that a half century later, their daughter would be standing on this stage is a testament to the power of the American Dream.

In my life I have tried to see this world through the eyes of those who have suffered discrimination.

And that's why I believe that the time has come to tear down the remaining walls of discrimination in this nation based on race, gender, nationality or sexual orientation. And that's why I continue to say, when it comes to affirmative action . . . mend it, don't end it.

When you try to see the world through other people's eyes . . . you understand that the smallest changes can make the biggest differences in all our lives.

That's something I'm sorry to say I don't think our Republican friends really understand.

They're fond of dismissing the achievements of the past eight years. But at the end of the day the people I talk with tell me that their lives are better than they were eight years ago.

Our opponents are decent and likable men.

I am proud to call many in their party my friends.

But America must understand: there are very real differences between us in this election.

Two weeks ago, our Republican friends tried to walk and talk a lot like us.

But let's be honest . . . we may be near Hollywood . . . But not since Tom Hanks won an Oscar has there been that much acting in Philadelphia.

I am glad the GOP has changed their rhetoric . . . but I wish they would also change their policies.

As my friend John McCain might say . . . and let me say that John is in our thoughts and prayers tonight [over health concerns]—let me now do some straight talking.

I think it's a good thing that our opponent talks about the environment.

But I'm sad to say that in Texas, the quality of the air and water is some of the worst in America.

We see the environment through a different set of eyes.

For more than 20 years Al Gore has been a leader on the environment.

He and I will continue the work we have done together to keep our air, water and land clean. We are going to continue to work to make sure that a child can drink a glass of water, or a father can fish in a stream, or a family can go to a park, without having to worry that their health and safety is at risk.

And it's a good thing that our opponent is talking about health care.

But I'm sad to say that Texas is also falling behind on that. Texas led the nation in the percentage of residents who were uninsured.

Today, it ranks next to last for health insurance for both women and kids.

We see health care through a different set of eyes.

We know that health care is one of the most important problems facing families today. We believe that medical decisions should be made by doctors, not bureaucrats. We believe that senior citizens shouldn't be stopped from filling a prescription because they can't afford to pay for it. And Al Gore and I are the only candidates in this race who will extend access to health care coverage to every single child in America.

And, I think it's a good thing that our opponent talks about education.

Schools need to be held to the highest standards of performance and accountability.

But I'm sad to say their plan doesn't provide the resources our schools need to meet those high standards.

Sometimes it seems to me like their idea of school modernization means buying a new calendar for every building.

We see education through a different set of eyes.

We're committed to making America's public schools the best in the world.

We are going to target more education funding to the schools that need it most . . . to rebuild and modernize our crumbling classrooms . . . and to provide all children with the skills they need to succeed in the 21st Century . . . And we're going to do one other thing that our Republican friends will not: we are going to treat the people who teach our children like the professionals that they are.

This is a question of priorities.

Our opponents want to use America's hard-earned surplus to give a tax break to those who need it least . . . at the expense of all our other needs.

Under their plan, the middle class gets a little . . . and the wealthy get a lot.

Their tax plan operates under that old theory that the best way to feed the birds . . . is to give more oats to the horse.

We see the surplus through a different set of eyes . . . the eyes of working middle class families.

We want to use America's hard-earned success to preserve the future of Social Security and Medicare, to pay off our national debt, and cut the taxes of middle class families. We want to make the investments that will keep our economy moving forward. It's this simple—we Democrats will expand the prosperity—they will squander it.

And this party will reform campaign finance, because it is only Al Gore and not George W. Bush who will send the McCain-Feingold bill to Congress and sign it when it's passed.

For those of you at home who haven't made up your mind if you want to build on our prosperity . . . if you want progress not partisanship in Washington . . . if you want to reform the system and not retreat from the problems . . . then your choice is clear . . . Al Gore is the best man for the job.

I have known Al for 15 years.

I know his record and I know his heart.

I know him as a public servant and I know what it is like to sit with him around the dining room table.

We have discussed—sometimes even debated—policy issues, and we have shared private moments of prayer.

I can tell you that Al Gore is a man of family and faith—a father, and now a grandfather.

When my daughter was six, after spending time with Al, she looked at me and said . . . "he must be a daddy."

Al Gore is a man of courage and conviction.

He believes in service to America.

He volunteered for Vietnam.

Together, we crossed party lines to support the Gulf War.

I was there in the room when he forcefully argued that America's principles and interests were at stake in Bosnia and Kosovo.

Two weeks ago . . . our opponent claimed that America has a hollow military.

I must tell you, that made me angry.

America . . . we know better than that—our fighting men and women are the best-trained, best-equipped, most potent fighting force in the history of the world, and they will stay that way when Al Gore and I are elected.

And Al Gore is also a man of vision and values.

Long before it became popular, Al and Tipper led a crusade to renew the moral center of this nation, to call America to live by its highest ideals.

He knows that in many Americans, there is a swelling sense that our standards of decency and civility have eroded.

No parent should be forced to compete with popular culture to raise their children.

For his entire career, Al Gore's values have guided the way he meets the challenges that lie ahead.

That's why I hope you will conclude—as I have—that for his honesty—for his strength—for his integrity—and for his character—Al Gore must become the next President of the United States.

Forty years ago, we came to this city and crossed a new frontier with a leader who inspired me . . . and so many in my generation . . . into public service.

Today, we return with prosperity at home and freedom throughout the world that John F. Kennedy could have only dreamed about.

We may wonder where the next frontier really is.

Tonight I believe that the next frontier isn't just in front of us . . . but inside of us . . . to overcome the differences that are still between us . . . to break down the barriers that remain . . . and to help every American claim the limitless possibilities of their own lives.

Sometimes, I try to see this world as my dad saw it from his bakery truck.

About this time, he'd be getting ready for the all-night run.

And I know that somewhere in America right now . . . there is another father loading a bakery truck . . . or a young woman programming a computer . . . or a parent dreaming of a better future for their daughter or their son.

If we keep the faith, then 40 years from now, one of their children will stand before a gathering like this . . . with a chance to serve and lead this country that we love.

So, let them look back to this time, and this place, and this stage and say of us: they kept the faith.

Let them say that we helped them realize their hopes and their dreams.

And let them look around at this great and good nation that we are all so blessed to share, and say: Only in America.

10.06—GLOBAL ANTI-SEMITISM REVIEW ACT, OCTOBER 8, 2004

With incidents of antisemitism on the rise throughout Europe in the early twenty-first century, U.S. congressman Tom Lantos (1928–2008), a Holocaust survivor, introduced legislation requiring the government to track and report incidents of antisemitism and report them to Congress. While the State Department opposed the bill, arguing that it had already collected data on antisemitism, President George W. Bush (b. 1946) signed the bill on October 16, 2004.

108th Congress
2d. Session
S. 2292
An Act

To require a report on acts of anti-Semitism around the world.

Be it enacted by the Senate and House of Representatives of the United States of America in Congress assembled,

SECTION 1. SHORT TITLE.
This Act may be cited as the "Global Anti-Semitism Review Act of 2004."

SEC. 2. FINDINGS.
Congress makes the following findings:
1. Acts of anti-Semitism in countries throughout the world, including some of the world's strongest democracies, have increased significantly in frequency and scope over the last several years.
[. . .]
3. Anti-Semitism in old and new forms is also increasingly emanating from the Arab and Muslim world on a sustained

basis, including through books published by government-owned publishing houses in Egypt and other Arab countries. . . .

SEC. 3. SENSE OF CONGRESS.

It is the sense of Congress that—

1. the United States Government should continue to strongly support efforts to combat anti-Semitism worldwide through bilateral relationships and interaction with international organizations such as the OSCE [Organisation for Security and Co-operation in Europe], the European Union, and the United Nations; and

2. the Department of State should thoroughly document acts of anti-Semitism that occur around the world.

SEC. 4. REPORTS.

Not later than November 15, 2004, the Secretary of State shall submit to the Committee on Foreign Relations of the Senate and the Committee on International Relations of the House of Representatives a one-time report on acts of anti-Semitism around the world, including a description of—

1. acts of physical violence against, or harassment of, Jewish people, and acts of violence against, or vandalism of, Jewish community institutions, such as schools, synagogues, or cemeteries, that occurred in each country;

2. the responses of the governments of those countries to such actions;

3. the actions taken by such governments to enact and enforce laws relating to the protection of the right to religious freedom of Jewish people;

4. the efforts by such governments to promote anti-bias and tolerance education; and

5. instances of propaganda in government and nongovernment media that attempt to justify or promote racial hatred or incite acts of violence against Jewish people.

lok

10.07—SELECTIONS, MANDELL L. BERMAN INSTITUTE—NORTH AMERICAN JEWISH DATA BANK, N.D.

In the last quarter of the twentieth century, as American Jews came to enjoy a high level of general social acceptance, rates of Jewish intermarriage rose steeply. Jewish communal leaders, concerned about the negative impact of intermarriage on Jewish identity and continuity, *commissioned demographic studies to determine the levels of intermarriage in their respective communities. Researchers at the North American Jewish Data Bank compiled a series of these demographic studies.*

Table 1: Intermarriage: Community Comparisons
Communities Organized by the Percentage of Intermarried Couples

Community	Year	Individual Rate: % of Married Jews Who Are Married to non-Jews	Couples Rate: % of Couples Who Are Intermarried[1]	Couples Rate: % of In-Married[2] Couples Comprising Two Born/ Raised Jews	Couples Rate: % of Conversionary[3] In-Married Couples	Couples Conversion Rate[4]
Portland (ME)	2007	44	61	33	6	9%
Seattle	2000	38	55	35	10	15%
San Francisco	2004	38	55	40	5	8%
Denver	2007	36	53	33	14	21%
Atlanta	2006	33	50	40	10	17%
Las Vegas	2005	32	48	46	6	12%
Charlotte	1997	30	47	44	10	18%
York	1999	29	46	41	14	24%
Tucson	2002	30	46	46	8	15%
Boston	2005	30	46	50	4	9%
Columbus	2001	29	45	43	13	23%
San Diego	2003	28	44	45	11	20%
Jacksonville	2002	28	44	45	11	20%
Tidewater	2001	28	43	45	12	22%
Washington	2003	26	41	52	6	13%
Phoenix	2002	25	40	51	9	18%
St. Paul	2004	25	39	49	12	24%
San Antonio	2007	23	37	50	13	25%
Pittsburgh	2002	22	36	51	13	27%
Lehigh Valley	2007	22	36	55	9	21%
Cincinnati	2008	20	34	53	13	27%

Community	Year	Individual Rate: % of Married Jews Who Are Married to non-Jews	Couples Rate: % of Couples Who Are Intermarried[1]	Couples Rate: % of In-Married[2] Couples Comprising Two Born/Raised Jews	Couples Rate: % of Conversionary[3] In-Married Couples	Couples Conversion Rate[4]
Richmond	1994	21	34	56	10	23%
Rhode Island	2002	21	34	59	7	18%
New Haven	2010	21	34	60	6	16%
Harrisburg	1994	20	33	56	11	26%
Chicago	2010	20	33	57	10	23%
Minneapolis	2004	20	33	59	8	20%
Wilmington	1995	19	33	60	7	18%
Westport	2000	20	33	61	6	16%
Orlando	1993	19	32	59	9	22%
Rochester	1999	17	30	62	8	22%
Howard County (MD)	2010	17	29	52	19	40%
St. Petersburg	1994	17	29	58	14	32%
Milwaukee	1996	16	28	68	4	12%
Philadelphia	2009	16	28		72	NA
Martin–St. Lucie	1999	15	27	62	12	30%
Atlantic County (NJ)	2004	15	26	68	6	19%
Buffalo	1995	15	26	71	3	10%
St. Louis	1995	14	25	64	11	32%
Hartford	2000	13	23	69	8	27%
Los Angeles	1997	13	23	71	6	20%
Cleveland	1996	13	23	74	3	11%
New York	2002	12	22	72	7	24%
Baltimore	2010	11	20	71	9	31%
Sarasota	2001	11	20	76	4	17%
Palm Springs	1998	10	19		81	NA
Broward	1997	10	18	78	4	19%
Bergen	2001	10	17	78	5	23%
Monmouth	1997	9	17	81	3	15%
Miami	2004	9	16	75	9	38%
Detroit	2005	9	16	76	8	33%
W. Palm Beach	2005	9	16	79	5	22%
Middlesex	2008	7	14	84	2	14%
S. Palm Beach	2005	5	9	88	3	24%
NJPS (National Jewish Population Survey)	2000	31	48		52	NA

1. An *intermarriage* is a marriage in which one spouse currently considers himself/herself Jewish and the other spouse does not currently consider himself/herself Jewish.

2. An *in-marriage* is a marriage in which both spouses were born or raised Jewish and currently consider themselves Jewish.

3. A *conversionary in-marriage* is a marriage in which one spouse was born or raised Jewish and currently considers himself/herself Jewish and the other spouse was not born or raised Jewish but currently considers himself/herself Jewish (no question about formal conversion was asked in some studies).

4. The *couples conversion rate* is calculated by dividing the percentage of conversionary in-married couples by the total percentage of married couples involving marriages between Jewish persons and persons not born or raised Jewish (conversionary in-married couples and intermarried couples).

Source: Berman Jewish DataBank at The Jewish Federations of North America, "FAQ on American Jews—#2 Intermarriage," Table 2-a, compiled by Ron Miller, Arnold Dashefsky, Ira M. Sheskin and Laurence Kotler-Berkowitz. Used with permission.

10.08—RABBI ALEXANDER M. SCHINDLER, "TO THE BOARD OF DIRECTORS OF THE NEW YORK FEDERATION OF REFORM SYNAGOGUES," MARCH 3, 1983

Rabbi Alexander Schindler (1925–2000), head of the Union of American Hebrew Congregations— the synagogue arm of the Reform movement— urged a reappraisal of intermarriage and its impact on the future of American Jewish life. Rather than marginalize Jews who marry outside Judaism, Schindler advocated an embrace of the non-Jewish spouse in order to encourage conversion and increase the number of active and engaged American Jews.

. . . First of all, very briefly, what is the Outreach Program? It is in effect the Reform Jewish community's, the American Jewish community's, determination to come to grips in some comprehensive positive manner with the problem of intermarriage. That problem has been persistently perplexing for a great many years. And it is not diminishing, not in the slightest degree. At the time that I spoke five years ago, we estimated the rate of intermarriages to have been in the neighborhood of 30%. There have been no national studies since then, but local studies confirmed the continuing extent of this perplexity. In Denver, for instance, a survey was taken of some 20,000 Jewish families; telephone calls were actually made. This is not a narrow base of study, but is a wide base of study, which revealed that while the overall community intermarriage rate was, in fact, 30%, in the crucial 20 to 40 year age period, it had approached 50%. Now that does not mean that it is a 50% intermarriage rate. (50% of the marriages: Jew, Jew, Jew, Non-Jew. It is still only about 30 to 35%. 25 out of 75.) But it does indicate that no less than 1 out of 3 of our children chooses a non-Jew as a life mate. And our internal studies of the Union of American Hebrew Congregations have enabled us to predict without any hesitation that within five years at the most, over 50%, if not as many as 60% of our children, the children in our religious schools, and I'm talking about hundreds of thousands of children, will have at least one parent who was born a non-Jew. Now this is going to have a dramatic impact on our education program. Many of those things that we were taught when we were young, as for instance, that you can't have a Christmas tree on Christmas, cannot be taught so glibly when these kids will have at least one grandparent or two grandparents who will have Christmas trees, if not crucifixes in their home.

Be it as it may, intermarriage continues to increase, and there is precious little we can do to stop it. Education helps some, that we know, in preventing it. An intensive Jewish education is a preventative; it is an antibiotic, if you will. As a matter of fact, it helps in a way even when an intermarriage takes place, because studies show that where the Jewish partner is insistent on the conversion of the non-Jewish partner, the Jewish education of the children, then that conversion and that Jewish education is more likely to occur. Intermarriage is the sting that comes to us with the honey of our freedom, and the only way of preventing intermarriage is to place ourselves into a safe, self-contained ghetto, no matter how gilded it might be. Since no one wants this, there is little we can do in preventing intermarriage.

Once an intermarriage has taken place, there is something we can do. We can either do what our fathers and mothers did, sit shiva over our children, or, we can do just the opposite; draw them closer to us, in the hope that the non-Jewish partner will be attracted to Judaism, or that at the very least, the children issuing from such intermarriages will, in fact, be reared as Jews.

The Reform Jewish community determines to do the latter, and established a five prong effort in order to translate that program into reality. And I will list them in the order of our priorities, for this is the manner in which we have approached this problem.

1. We felt that we must raise the standards and improve the education of those who want to be Jews. In the past, these Introduction to Judaism courses, these conversion courses were approached from a cognitive point of view exclusively, from a cerebral point of view. Judaism was presented much in the manner of Abba Hillel Silver's "Where Judaism Differed," primarily as a system of thought, or as a system of practice. As we all know, Judaism is something more than that. And to become a Jew does not mean just to accept a certain way of thinking, but also to accept a way of doing and to become part of a people. It

is therefore not a conversion process in the classical sense, but rather a process of naturalization. Hence it has to include something which is not just cognitive, but which helps introduce the prospective convert to Judaism[,] to the Jewish people and to the Jewish community.

2. An effort to more successfully integrate the Jew-by-choice into the life of the congregation. When I spoke to converts, to Jews-by-choice—this term is really Reform Judaism's contribution. Traditionally we're not supposed to call a converted person a convert. Conversion is a process that ends with the moment of conversion, and once a person converts, he's a Jew. It is a sin, even in Orthodoxy, to remind a person that they were born a non-Jew. We therefore determined not to call them Converts, but rather to call them Jews-by-choice. I suppose in a sense, living in an open society as we do, every Jew is a Jew-by-choice, because they all choose not to opt out. Be that as it may, when I spoke to many of these Jews-by-choice they told me they were suffering from what they called a post-conversion depression. People would get excited as they went along to the moment of conversion; then they forgot about them. But as newcomers to Judaism, they had particular problems, and they needed some program which would help them during the initial year of their involvement in the Jewish community. And we established supportive groups in various congregations under regional and national levels, and a system of adoption whereby members of the congregation would adopt individual newcomers to Judaism, and so on and so forth. This is prong number 2 of our Outreach effort.

3. A special outreach to the non-Jewish partner of the intermarriage, in the hope that he (she) will be attracted to Judaism.

4. An effort to bring Jewish education, either formal or informal, to the children issuing from such marriages whether or not their parents belong to a congregation.

5. And, finally, this is the item that caught the fancy of the media: An Outreach Program for the many Americans, many, many Americans, who are seekers after truth, and who are searching for a religion that will be meaningful to them. You have to know in this connection, that *the* best as we can establish it, 10% of those who convert to Judaism in America, do so for reasons other than for an intermarriage. This is the statistic which we can glean from those who attend our own courses and from the information which we receive from many places. As a matter of fact, there is some evidence to show that intermarriage may actually be the consequence of an inclination towards Judaism by the non-Jewish partner. A number of Jews-by-choice have told us that they are drawn to Judaism early in life and that they sought a Jewish partner precisely because they had this inclination towards Judaism. . . .

We have so very much to offer. Judaism celebrates life, not death. It insists on freedom, and the capacity of the individual to determine his fate. Judaism is a religion of hope and not of despair. It insists that humankind and society are perfectable. Moreover, we offer something more than a disembodied faith system. We are a people of faith. A caring community of Jews. In other words, we have an enormous amount of wisdom and experience, warmth and love to offer to our troubled world. And we Jews ought to be proud to speak about it . . . frankly, freely and with dignity.

Source: MS 630, box 15, folder 1, AJA.

10.09—REPORT OF THE COMMITTEE ON PATRILINEAL DESCENT, CENTRAL CONFERENCE OF AMERICAN RABBIS, MARCH 15, 1983

Jewish law stipulates that it is the mother, not the father, who transmits a child's status as a member of the Jewish community. When rates of intermarriage began to rise in the 1970s, leaders of the Reform movement observed that some children of a Jewish father and a non-Jewish mother were raised as Jews, even though they were not considered Jewish by tradition. In an effort to enfranchise these practicing offspring, as well as to increase the number of Jews in general, the Reform movement determined in 1983 that children of Jewish fathers and non-Jewish mothers, if raised as Jews, would be considered Jewish. The movement's final report on the subject, "The Status of Children of Mixed Marriages," is included as follows. In 1986, the Conservative movement's Rabbinical Assembly debated the question as well, ultimately rejecting the embrace of patrilineal descent.

The Status of Children of Mixed Marriages
Following is the final text of the Report of the Committee on Patrilineal Descent adopted on March 15, 1983

The purpose of this document is to establish the Jewish status of the children of mixed marriages in the Reform Jewish community of North America.

One of the most pressing human issues for the North American Jewish community is mixed marriage, with all its attendant implications. For our purpose, mixed marriage is defined as a union between a Jew and a non-Jew. A non-Jew who joins the Jewish people through conversion is recognized as a Jew in every respect. We deal here only with the Jewish identity of children [for] which one parent is Jewish and the other parent is non-Jewish.

[. . .]

According to the Halacha as interpreted by traditional Jews over many centuries, the offspring of a Jewish mother and a non-Jewish father is recognized as a Jew, while the offspring of a non-Jewish mother and a Jewish father must undergo conversion.

As a Reform community, the process of determining an appropriate response has taken us to an examination of the tradition, our own earlier responses, and the most current considerations. In doing so, we seek to be sensitive to the human dimensions of this issue.

Both the Biblical and the Rabbinical traditions take for granted that ordinarily the paternal line is decisive in the tracing of descent within the Jewish people. The Biblical genealogies in Genesis and elsewhere in the Bible attest to this point. In intertribal marriage in ancient Israel, paternal descent was decisive. Numbers 1:2, etc., says: "By their families, by their fathers' houses" (*lemishpechotam leveit avotam*), which for the Rabbis means, "The line [literally: 'family'] of the father is recognized; the line of the mother is not" (*Mishpachat av keruya mishpacha; mishpachat em einah keruya mishpacha*; Bava Batra 109b, Yevamot 54b; cf. *Yad*, Nachalot 1.6).

In the Rabbinic tradition, this tradition remains in force. The offspring of a male *Kohen* who marries a Levite or Israelite is considered a *Kohen*, and the child of an Israelite who marries a *Kohenet* is an Israelite. Thus: *yichus*, lineage, regards the male line as absolutely dominant. This ruling is stated succinctly in Mishna Kiddushin 3.12 that when *kiddushin* (marriage) is licit and no transgression (*ein avera*) is involved, the line follows the father. Furthermore, the most important *parental* responsibility to teach Torah rested with the father (Kiddushin 29a; ch. *Shulchan Aruch*, Yoreh De-a 245.1).

When, in the tradition, the marriage was considered not to be licit, the child of that marriage followed the status of the mother (Mishna Kiddushin 3.12, *havalad kemotah*). The decision of our ancestors thus to link the child inseparably to the mother, which makes the child of a Jewish mother Jewish and the child of a non-Jewish mother non-Jewish, regardless of the father, was based upon the fact that the woman with her child had no recourse but to return to her own people. A Jewish woman could not marry a non-Jewish man (cf. *Shulchan Aruch*, Even Ha-ezer 4.19, *la tafsei kiddushin*). A Jewish man could not marry a non-Jewish woman. The only recourse in Rabbinic law for the woman in either case was to return to her own community and people.

[. . .]

We face today an unprecedented situation due to the changed conditions in which decisions concerning the status of the child of a mixed marriage are to be made.

There are tens of thousands of mixed marriages. In a vast majority of these cases the non-Jewish extended family is a functioning part of the child's world, and may be decisive in shaping the life of the child. It can no longer be assumed *a priori*, therefore, that the child of a Jewish mother will be Jewish any more than that the child of a non-Jewish mother will not be.

This leads us to the conclusion that the same requirements must be applied to establish the status of a child of a mixed marriage, regardless of whether the mother or the father is Jewish.

Therefore:

The Central Conference of American Rabbis declares that the child of one Jewish parent is under the presumption of Jewish descent. This presumption of the Jewish status of the offspring of any mixed marriage is to be established through appropriate and timely public and formal acts of identification with the Jewish faith and people. The performance of these *mitzvot* serves to commit those who participate in them, both parent and child, to Jewish life.

Depending on circumstances,[1] *mitzvot* leading toward a positive and exclusive Jewish identity will include entry into the covenant, acquisition of a Hebrew name, Torah study, Bar/Bat Mitzvah, and *Kabbalat Torah* (Confirmation).[2] For those beyond childhood claiming Jewish identity, other public acts or declarations may be added or substituted after consultation with their rabbi.

NOTES

1. According to the age or setting, parents should consult a rabbi to determine the specific mitzvot which are necessary.

2. A full description of these and other mitzvot can be found in *Sharrei* [*sic*] *Mitzvot*.

Source: Excerpts from Report of the Committee on Patrilineal Descent, Central Conference of American Rabbis, March 15, 1983, © 1937 Central Conference of American Rabbis. Used by permission. All rights reserved.

10.10—RABBIS JOEL ROTH AND AKIBA LUBOW, A STANDARD OF RABBINIC PRACTICE REGARDING DETERMINATION OF JEWISH IDENTITY, 1986

This Standard of Rabbinic Practice was approved by the Committee on Jewish Law and Standards in a two-stage process, as required by the rules of the Rabbinical Assembly adopted in Convention assembled in 1972. First, it was adopted at a meeting of the committee held on May 1, 1985, by a vote of 15-1. It was then adopted by mail ballot by a vote of 21-2-1. Members voting in favor: Rabbis Kassel Abelson, Jacob B. Agus, Isidoro Aizenberg, Ben Zion Bergman, Elliot N. Dorff, David M. Feldman, Morris Feldman, David Gordis, Robert Gordis, Benjamin Z. Kreitman, David H. Lincoln, Judah Nadich, George Pollak, Mayer E. Rabinowitz, Barry S. Rosen, Joel Roth, Morris M. Shapiro, David Wolf Silverman, Israel N. Silverman, Henry A. Sosland and Gordon Tucker. Members voting in opposition: Rabbis Seymour Siegel and Phillip Sigal. Abstaining: Rabbi Alan J. Yuter.

The Standard was then formally adopted by the Rabbinical Assembly at the 1986 Rabbinical Assembly Convention by a vote of 235-92.

WHEREAS Jewishness is defined either through lineage or through conversion to Judaism; and

WHEREAS the Committee on Jewish Law and Standards has on several occasions reaffirmed its commitment to matrilineal descent, which has been authoritative in normative Judaism for many centuries as the sole determinant of Jewish lineage; and

WHEREAS rulings of the Committee on Jewish Law and Standards which govern procedures for conversions supervised by Rabbinical Assembly members, require *tevilah* in the case of females, and *tevilah* and *brit milah* in the case of males; and

WHEREAS the Committee on Jewish Law and Standards has long advocated that members of the Rabbinical Assembly welcome and assist those who wish to approach Judaism in a serious fashion and to convert to Judaism in a manner which fulfills the requirements for conversion, including those steps outlined above;

THEREFORE, BE IT RESOLVED that the Committee on Jewish Law and Standards recommends to the Convention of the Rabbinical Assembly that

a. ascription of Jewish lineage through a legal instrument or ceremonial act on the basis of anything other than matrilineal descent; or

b. supervision of a conversion which omits *tevilah* in the case of females, or *tevilah* and *brit milah* in the case of males

shall continue to be regarded as violations of the halakhah of Conservative Judaism. They shall henceforth be violations of a Standard of Rabbinic Practice and be inconsistent with membership in the Rabbinical Assembly, it being understood that any member of the Rabbinical Assembly shall continue to possess the right to petition the Committee on Jewish Law and Standards for an opinion on any case of extraordinary circumstances.

Source: Joel Roth and Akiba Lubow, "A Standard of Rabbinic Practice Regarding Determination of Jewish Identity," in *Proceedings of the Committee on Jewish Law and Standards, 1980–1985* (New York: Rabbinical Assembly, 1988), 177–80. Reprinted with permission of the publisher.

10.11—PRESS RELEASE, EZRAT NASHIM, OCTOBER 24, 1983

Eleven years after the Hebrew Union College–Jewish Institute of Religion ordained Sally Priesand as the first female Reform rabbi, the Jewish Theological Seminary voted to ordain women as rabbis within the Conservative movement. This 1983 resolution led to a press release by the Conservative movement's feminist group, Ezrat Nashim, hailing the decision. Two years later, the Jewish Theological Seminary ordained Amy Eilberg (b. 1954) as its first woman rabbi.

In March, 1972 Ezrat Nashim, the first Jewish feminist organization, publicly called upon the Conservative movement to ordain women as rabbis. Today we salute the faculty of the Jewish Theological Seminary for voting to accept women as candidates for ordination in the Rabbinical School. This act recognizes the compelling moral claim of women's equality as well as the changed status of women in the modern world. It is consonant with Conservative interpretation of the development of *halakha* (Jewish law). It also follows logically from earlier decisions of the Conservative movement to reject the sexual segregation characteristic of the Jewish past by providing equal education for Jewish daughters, introducing mixed seating in the synagogue, counting women in the *minyan* (prayer quorum), and calling them to the Torah.

This important step forward enables the Conservative movement, the largest denomination within American Jewry, to draw upon the talents of all Jews for religious leadership and prepares the way for including women, and women's sensibilities, in the ongoing interpretation of Torah which has ensured the survival of Judaism.

Ezrat Nashim was established in 1971 as a study group and lobby to attain equality for women in the Jewish community. Its members occupy leadership positions in religious, educational, and communal organizations.

Members have included

Martha Ackelsberg	Paula Hyman
Leora Fishman	Judith Samuels
Judith Plaskow	Elaine Shizgal Cohen
Arlene Agus	Elizabeth Koltun
Gilda Flashman	Leslie Shanken
Toby Reifman	Flora Davidson
Toby Brandriss	Maureen McLeod
Judith Hauptman	Susan Shevitz
Dina Rosenfeld	Phyllis Sperling
Edith Cohen	

Source: Ezrat Nashim nearprint file, AJA.

The decision by the Jewish Theological Seminary to ordain women precipitated a split in its faculty. Rabbi David Weiss Halivni (b. 1927), a professor of Talmud and a leading authority on Jewish law, protested both the substance of the decision, arguing that it violated Jewish law, as well as the way it was decided—by a faculty vote rather than a ruling of a rabbinic court. He published an open letter to his colleagues explaining his position. After the vote, he resigned his position at the seminary and went on to found the Union for Traditional Judaism with other similarly minded Conservative Jews.

To the members of the Faculty Assembly:

My position concerning women's ordination is by now, I take it, well known to all of you assembled here. I am against it. It is in violation of halakhah which to me is sufficient grounds to reject it.

I am cognizant of the enormous pressure exerted upon us from different quarters to ordain women. But, a religious Jew, when faced with a confrontation between sociology and religion, must choose religion. . . .

That is not to say that there were no changes in Halakhah; that Halakhah remained monolithic throughout the ages. Changes did take place, *but they were not done consciously.* The scholars who legalized them did not perceive of themselves as innovators. The changes were integrated into community life long before they sought—and received—legal sanction. They originally came about imperceptibly, unnoticed; the result of a gradual evolutionary process. By the time they demanded legal justification, they were ripe, overgrown, as it were. So much so, that in many an instance, whoever opposed the changes was considered a breaker of tradition, adopting a "holier than thou" attitude.

A Jew knows no way of reaching out to God other than through Halakhah. (The latter taken in the widest possible sense). He knows no way

to penetrate the highest recesses of spirituality other than through a structured pattern of behavior. In the course of that engagement he may experience a sense of elevation, a touch of ecstasy, a feeling of being near to God. That is his greatest reward. While it lasts, he is desirous of nothing more. Indeed, nothing else exists.

How does a mitzvah catapult one into such religious heights? What is its power? Nobody knows, any more than we know when looking at the sunset, or at a smiling child, how and why we are gripped, riveted to the scene, transformed "in a foretaste of the world to come" [Hebrew in original]. Our religious and aesthetic experiences are shrouded in mystery. *We are put on fire, but do not know how the fire is being kindled.* The mistake of Reform is that it claims that it knows how the fire is being kindled; that, as a result, it can control the flame. When it actually tried to control the flame, alas, there was no fire; everything was so cold!

The truly religious Jew is awe-stricken both by the mystery of God and by the efficacy of the mitzvot to bring man closer to God. He dares not tamper with the mitzvot for he humbly acknowledges that he knows not their secret, or secrets. He is grateful to tradition for having kept alive through the ages the connection between God and the performance of the mitzvot, so that he can *now* relive it, re-experience it and bequeath it to his children. Without tradition, he would not have found his way to God; it is his religious lifeline. He cannot part from it.

In the light of the above, I hope you will understand why I cannot participate in the vote on women's ordination scheduled for October 24, 1983. I am committed to Jewish tradition in all of its various aspects. I cannot, therefore, participate in a debate on a religious issue of major historical significance where the traditional decision making process is not sufficiently honored; its specific instructions as to who is qualified to pass judgment not sufficiently reckoned with. Even to strengthen tradition, one must proceed traditionally. Otherwise it is a *mitzvah haba'ah ba'aveirah*—a mitzvah performed by means of a transgression.

It is my personal tragedy that the people I *daven* with, I cannot talk to, and the people I talk to, I cannot daven with. However, when the chips are down, I will always side with the people I daven with; for I can live without talking. I cannot live without davening.

David Halivni

Source: SC-4479, AJA.

10.13—JUDITH S. ANTONELLI, "JEWISH FEMINISMS EXPLORE TORAH, GOD, AND SEXUALITY," *Jewish Advocate*, JANUARY 25, 1991

As part of the larger second-wave feminist movement that inspired Jewish women to challenge the patriarchy of Jewish life, Judith Plaskow (b. 1947), a religious studies professor at Manhattan College, published the pathbreaking book Standing Again at Sinai: Judaism from a Feminist Perspective *in 1990. Plaskow's treatise, regarded as one of the most important works of feminist Jewish literature, called for the reclamation of Torah by rendering "visible the presence, experience, and deeds of women erased in traditional sources." In a 1991 interview published in the* Jewish Advocate, *Plaskow reflected on her work.*

Q: You say in your book right from the start that you "do not believe there is some nonsexist 'essence' of Judaism" in the name of which you struggle, that Judaism is an inherently patriarchal tradition. So why do you bother with it?

A: I am a Jew. I don't think there's anything in the tradition that's pure, but there's a lot that I love: the social justice, the holiday cycle. I always loved Passover, but that was ruined when I was married [15 years to a Conservative rabbi] and had to clean the house. Then Rosh Hashana became my favorite holiday.

As a student of Christian theology, I love the realism of Judaism, its this-worldliness, the rituals for lifecycle events, such as death.

My son's bar mitzvah was very profound for me. I love the Jewish view that one's purpose in this world is to live a holy life, contrasted to the otherworldliness nature of Christianity. The more I study Christianity, the more I love that I'm a Jew.

Q: You take for granted that the Torah was written by man (which means men), and have even advocated the writing of a new "women's Torah." This certainly puts you in a different camp from feminists who believe that the Torah itself was given by God, that it is *emet* (truth). Is there a possibility for common work between liberal Jewish feminists and halachically observant Jewish feminists?

A: There are issues in common. The Orthodox woman's struggle is every woman's struggle. I want to see everything that Orthodox women want. For instance, the *agunah* issue [referring to a "chained wife," whose husband has either deserted her or disappeared and who thus cannot be released from her marriage] is absolutely crucial. But I also want a lot of things that they *don't* want, like a new Torah.

Women need to write midrashim which, like traditional rabbinic midrashim, must come to be thought of as Torah. It's irrelevant if the stories are true. Is it true when the rabbis say the patriarchs had Torah academies? Midrash works as an expression of the collective sense of a people. A lot of feminist midrash is horrible, though—it's bad writing, preachy, or not coming out of a deep wrestling with the text.

But we must honor women's words as Torah. I know women who put on tefillin in the morning and read Adrienne Rich. At women's rituals in which I participate we have read the words of contemporary women, or have had older women share their wisdom and we make the Torah blessings before and after that.

Torah is our history, it has shaped us for good and for bad. I would like to see it relativized, to become a larger corpus. But, to get back to your original question, there are a lot of issues that liberal and halachic feminists can work on together. The real issue is: Can we pray together?

I'm not sure what the answer is, and there hasn't been a lot of exploration of it. But I think that the "wilder" the service—the more original it is, rather than changing the already existing prayer service—then the more we *can* pray together. I'd like to see more effort and conversations between Orthodox and non-Orthodox women.

Q: You place a great deal of emphasis on the importance of women's experience in a feminist Judaism, yet in your characterization of Jewish attitudes towards sexuality, you have not interviewed any women who observe the laws of *niddah* (menstrual taboos) and *tzniut* (modesty). Criticism of these practices comes from women who do *not* observe them. Isn't it important for a feminist view of these practices to be based on the testimony of those women who experience them?

A: I don't make any claim that I'm speaking for all Jewish women, or all Jewish women's experiences. But from the perspective I do speak from, *niddah* is part of a system oppressive to women. Women may possibly transform the meaning of that practice in their own consciousness. I'm not saying that women can't resolve or rework it, but if it leaves the whole system intact, there is no change.

I would be happy if my book generated other books. I am aware that we can understand menstrual taboos totally differently. But it must be part of challenging the whole male-centeredness of the system.

[. . .]

Q: Some Orthodox feminists have a more separatist kind of spirituality, which those who disparage it call segregation. Do you see any positive feminist action in women's halachic prayer groups, Simchat Torah dancing, leyning [chanting Scripture in the synagogue], etc., rather than trying to do this in mixed groups?

A: I advocate a combination. We can't have an articulation of women's spirituality, prayer, and theology unless we have women's groups. A certain amount of separation is essential. But we cannot leave the male system intact. We need women's spaces, but to challenge male groups, too, simultaneously.

Q: You criticize rabbinic Judaism for viewing men's sexual impulses as "powerful (evil) inclinations in need of firm control." Given the level of sexual exploitation and violence in our society, don't you, as a feminist, agree with this? What is wrong with controlling sexuality through the Torah's means, laws which are mostly directed at men?

A: I do not believe that male sexual aggression is natural, or due to testosterone. Men are socialized to believe their sexuality is uncontrollable and that they are *entitled* to believe they don't have to control it. The subject is deeply ambiguous, for it is women's "fault" that men are aroused. I can't help but believe that it is bad to teach men to be so controlled and guarded about their sexuality or else it will seize them from behind.

Source: Judith Plaskow nearprint file, AJA.

10.14—MISSION STATEMENT OF THE SOCIETY FOR HUMANISTIC JUDAISM, OCTOBER 8, 1999

In 1963, Reform-educated Rabbi Sherwin Wine (1928–2007) founded the Birmingham Temple near Detroit. Wine removed references to God in his services and focused on secular Jewish concepts such as ethics and culture. Humanistic Judaism would develop rapidly as a movement, emerging as a distinct branch of Judaism by fall of 1964, with theistic language, God references, and Reform practices and prayers deleted from the services. Encompassing three synagogues by 1969, the movement would eventually grow to include more than thirty congregations. Included as follows are the Society for Humanistic Judaism's mission statement, affirmations, and core principles.

The Society for Humanistic Judaism mobilizes people to celebrate Jewish identity and culture consistent with a humanistic philosophy of life independent of supernatural authority. As the central body for the Humanistic Jewish Movement in North America, the Society assists in organizing and supporting congregations and in providing a worldwide voice for its members.

[. . .]

Humanistic Jews Affirm That . . .

- A Jew is someone who identifies with the history, culture and future of the Jewish people.
- Jewish identity is best preserved in a free, pluralistic environment.
- Jewish history is a human saga, a testament to the significance of human power and human responsibility.
- Judaism is the historic culture of the Jewish people.
- We possess the power and responsibility to shape our own lives independent of supernatural authority.
- Ethics and morality should serve human needs.

- The freedom and dignity of the Jewish people must go hand in hand with the freedom and dignity of every human being.

CORE PRINCIPLES

As members of the Society for Humanistic Judaism:

- We affirm our identity as members of the Jewish People. We draw strength from the history, culture, and achievements of our people. We see Jewish history as testimony to the continuing struggle for human dignity and, like the history of other peoples, as a product of human decisions and actions.
- We demonstrate our bond to the Jewish people through humanistic celebrations of Jewish holidays and life-cycle events. We create and use non-theistic Jewish rituals, services, and celebrations that invoke the ethical core of Jewish history, literature, and culture. Our aim is to foster a positive Jewish identity, intellectual integrity, and ethical behavior among celebrants.
- We affirm the value of study and discussion of Jewish and universal human issues. We rely on such sources as reason, observation, experimentation, creativity, and artistic expression to address questions about the world and in seeking to understand our experiences.
- We seek solutions to human conflicts that respect the freedom, dignity, and self-esteem of every human being. We make ethical decisions based on our assessment of the consequences of our actions.
- We believe that it is human beings who have the responsibility for solving human problems. We are committed, in the

enduring Jewish tradition of support for social action and social progress, to community service and actions for social justice. We each take responsibility for our own behavior, and all of us take collective responsibility for the state of our world.

We are committed to passing these values on to present and future generations through education and by our example.

10.15—CHARLES PASSY, "DEBBIE FRIEDMAN IS A TROUBADOUR OF FAITH; SYNAGOGUES RING WITH FOLK," *Palm Beach Post*, DECEMBER 6, 2004

Inspired by American folk singers such as Joan Baez and Peter, Paul, and Mary, Debbie Friedman (1951–2011) crafted a new form of Jewish music that combined elements of traditional Jewish text with melodies that resonated with a generation of young Jews. As a song leader at the Reform movement's Olin-Sang-Ruby Union Institute in Wisconsin and Camp Swig in California, Friedman wrote and played music that would, by the end of her career, fill twenty-two albums. Her folksy, camp-style songs alienated many cantors concerned that her popularity would undermine traditional musical forms. In 2007, though, she was invited to become a teacher in HUC-JIR's cantorial program. Three weeks after her death in 2011, the school was named in her honor.

Debbie Friedman insists that she never intended to start a revolution.

And yet, this sweet-voiced, 53-year-old Jewish folk singer has done just that over the past three decades, challenging the ways Jews consider religious music to the point that change became inevitable.

Before Friedman, the melodies heard inside synagogues—even in contemporary-minded Reform congregations—revolved around centuries-old prayer melodies. But once Friedman broke onto the scene in the early '70s with her land-

mark album, *Sing unto God*, the idea of incorporating contemporary music into Jewish worship became increasingly acceptable as a way to welcome a broader swath of congregants.

"Ultimately, in a service, you want people to feel comfortable so that they can make a connection to God," says Friedman, speaking by phone from her New York apartment in advance of her concert Tuesday (the first night of Hanukkah) at Palm Beach Community College's Eissey Campus Theatre in Palm Beach Gardens.

Which is not to say that Friedman's music, from her popular setting of a prayer for healing (Mi Shebeirach) to her beloved children's songs (The Alef Bet Song, The Latke Song), has been universally welcomed. As a documentary about the singer-songwriter, *A Journey of Spirit* (recently seen as part of the Palm Beach Jewish Film Festival), demonstrates, Friedman has faced continual challenges from die-hard traditionalists. They say her secular style should play no part in a religious setting.

Friedman says she never intended for her music to replace the standard prayer melodies, otherwise known as nussach (pronounced noosahk). She simply sees it as a complement to traditional music.

"You can't have a full diet of contemporary music. It doesn't work for me. I need to be able to connect to my ancestors, too," says Friedman, who has worked as a cantorial soloist in synagogues, even though she lacks the formal training and title.

Friedman's musical path started after her family—her father was a kosher butcher—moved from upstate New York to St. Paul, Minn. In the process, they started to lose some of their Jewish identity, particularly because they were no longer living close to religious relatives. Friedman relied on music to rekindle that connection.

But as a child of the '60s, Friedman was as much interested in Peter, Paul and Mary, Joan Baez, Judy Collins and Joni Mitchell as she was in traditional Jewish music. So, she went about writing songs—or settings of prayers and other religious texts—that reflected her world. When she saw how young people responded to them—Friedman was teaching music in various Jewish settings—she knew she had found her calling.

"It happened slowly. It started in the (summer) camps," she says of the response. And from there, her albums—she's released 19 to date—started finding their way into more and more Jewish homes.

Still, Friedman never expected that her works would one day become part of the services in countless synagogues. Or that her Alef Bet Song —the Hebrew alphabet set to music—would become such a kiddie favorite that it would find its way onto a Barney concert video.

Or that her lyrics would become the basis of a Jewish-themed line of Hallmark greeting cards.

"Who knew?" Friedman says.

In recent years, Friedman has expanded her mission beyond just music. Partly as a result of contending with her own illness—Friedman suffers from a neurological disorder that often makes it difficult for her to walk—she has focused increasingly on the healing process, creating a "healing service" that has been embraced by many synagogues as a different form of prayer.

Friedman insists it's not just for those who are physically sick, but for those who experience "pain and frustrations" on an emotional level as well. "We concentrate on the healing of the soul," she says.

Not that Friedman has forsaken music. Last year, she came out with a jazz and reggae-influenced album of Hanukkah favorites, including some of her own songs.

"Why not?" she says of the approach. "It's the same songs with a little bit of rhythm. It's fun."

But as much as Friedman has become a household name in the Jewish community, she has yet to enjoy the crossover success that, say, many Christian pop stars have found. She remains largely indifferent about the matter—"If it happens, it's going to happen"—saying her focus is faith, not fame.

In that regard, she recalls a meeting with a music executive who once chided her for being a big fish in a little pond—as opposed to a big fish in a big pond. Friedman's response? "I'm not a fish."

Instead, she's a woman of religious resolve—with a song to sing for the people.

Source: Palm Beach Post, December 6, 2004.

10.16—OREN LEE-PARRITZ, "SYNAPLEX: A CREATIVE RESPONSE TO A DECLINE IN SYNAGOGUE IDENTIFICATION," *Jewish Post*, CA. 2007

As synagogue affiliation rates dropped in the late twentieth century—especially among younger Jews, intermarried families, single parents, and gay and lesbian Jews—several leading Jewish philanthropists, including Edgar

Bronfman (1929–2013), Charles Schusterman (1935–2000) and Lynn Schusterman (b. 1939), and Michael Steinhardt (b. 1940), funded the creation of Synagogues: Transformation and Renewal (STAR) in order to find new ways of

attracting Jews to worship. STAR's leading
initiative, Synaplex, went beyond the prayer
focus of synagogue services by including classes
in Jewish learning and expanding organized
social interaction, especially for Jewish singles.
These efforts proved successful, as synagogues
participating in Synaplex noted marked
increases in attendance. Included here is
a news story published in the Jewish Post
describing the Synaplex initiative.

According to this year's National Rabbinic Survey, declining involvement in Jewish activities was cited as the most pressing issue. Whereas Israel-related topics were at the forefront in previous years, a recent lull in the conflict has cleared the way for a focus on community concerns.

This survey also concluded that a great many Rabbis (92% of participants) found it necessary to reach out to previously under-included segments of the Jewish community such as gays, lesbians, interfaith couples, singles, and single parents.

STAR (Synagogues: Transformation and Renewal) is a project designed to help temples cope with changing trends in society, maintain professional growth among their leaders and Rabbis, and to help boost membership and attendance. According to their website, "STAR works with synagogues to bridge the chasm between the American Jewish Community and the synagogue."

Synaplex is [a] STAR initiative that focuses on a three pronged approach to reestablishing the synagogue as the center for a Jewish community. According to their website: "While most Jews think of a synagogue as Beit Tefilah—a house of prayer, a synagogue is also Beit Midrash—a house of learning, and Beit Knesset—a house of gathering." By re-affirming these other roles that the synagogue is to play, it is believed that more people will be drawn to one of these aspects and thus further identify with it.

According to Rabbi Hayim Herring, it is essential to focus on the "synagogue as a commu-

nal center" as the main goal. While it is desirable that people become more religious, reinforcing the community is viewed as the crucial first step. Furthermore, Synaplex strives to include the groups mentioned above that have previously been overlooked.

The movement is multi-denominational, though most of its adherents are reform. A smaller portion of participants are conservative with a handful of participating congregations describing themselves as Orthodox.

Much of this community building is accomplished by "casting a wider net" to the diverse American Jewish population via offering an array of temple activities. These include but are not limited to expanded social events and study groups. Some alternatives include meditation workshops and yoga. One interesting development is "Rosh Chodesh: It's a Girl Thing." This was established as a way for mothers and adolescent daughters to have a forum to discuss contemporary family issues and to provide support in a Jewish setting during these difficult formative years.

In order to address the issue of lacking a sense of community among the congregants, some of the participating temples have initiated "a speed schmooze" in order to have members get to know each other better and thus feel more at home at the synagogue.

Temples participate by gaining access to resources that provide ideas and networking tools. The guidelines set forth by the program are by no means rigid and give the Rabbi suggestions, as opposed to a strict program, allowing the leader to act within the comfort level of the current congregants. Another important resource is the inter-congregational communication network established by STAR and Synaplex that helps Rabbis to work together on the ground level to address pressing issues.

The central pillar of Synaplex is the Shabbat Initiative, a project designed to re-establish the Sabbath as a gathering time for Jews. According to Rabbi Herring, it conveniently falls at a time when most secular Jews would have the time to participate in temple activities, contributing to the potential efficacy of the program.

Initially, there was some resistance to Synaplex as some viewed it as possibly detracting from traditional worship. According to Rabbi Herring, not only were these not the intentions of the program, but they were very carefully designed not to interfere with the traditional services utilized by the original active members. As a result, he contends that many of these initial fears have long since abated.

Other features of Synaplex include PEER (Professional Education for Excellence in Rabbis) to enrich professional practice and "Storahtelling" as an effort "to bring the Torah to life" for those who were not previously interested in bible study. In addition to these features, Synaplex and STAR include a great many other organizational partners that help to augment the experience. Rabbi Herring was also proud to announce that STAR and Synaplex have helped to nurture social action programs evolving from the synagogues.

One interesting aspect of their literature includes their use of the term "marketing." While many might find such a term distasteful in a religious context, the website is careful to explain that "marketing" does not need to take on a commercial connotation and that advocating participation in any organization is a form of marketing, whether or not we feel comfortable thinking of it in that way.

According to Rabbi Herring, it has been a phenomenal success as they have seen positive results (attendance-wise) for over 100 temples and are still growing. . . .

Source: Reprinted with permission of the publisher.

10.17—HAVIVA NER-DAVID, "BREAKING THE GLASS MEHITZA," *Hadassah*, MAY 2004

While the Reform, Reconstructionist, and Conservative movements ordained women as rabbis in the 1970s and 1980s, the Orthodox movement refused, claiming that Jewish law forbids the practice. In the early twenty-first century, several Orthodox rabbis and communal leaders began to explore the possibility of women's ordination. In 2004, Haviva Ner-David (b. 1969), an Orthodox student engaged in rabbinic study, offered her defense of women's ordination in Hadassah *magazine. Two years later, she received ordination in Israel and became a pioneering female rabbi in the Orthodox movement.*

Sara Hurwitz (b. 1977), a South African–born graduate of Columbia University, completed five years of rabbinic training under Rabbi Avi Weiss, founder of Orthodoxy's most progressive rabbinic school, Chovevei Torah. Rabbi Weiss ordained Hurwitz with the title "maharat," a Hebrew acronym for a leader in Torah, spirituality, and Jewish law. Later he changed that designation to "rabba," the feminine form of rabbi. After several Orthodox organizations protested, Rabbi Weiss agreed not to confer the title "rabba" on any other women.

In New York City, Kehilat Orach Eliezer, an Orthodox practicing congregation founded by former Jewish Theological Seminary professor Rabbi David Halivni, offered a leadership position in 2006 to Dina Najman (b. 1968), a scholar of Jewish law and ancient Jewish texts. She was not considered a rabbi, nor was she permitted to lead regular worship services or read from the Torah. But, as the synagogue's "head of the congregation," she delivered sermons and answered questions on Jewish law. In a 2010 article from the Jewish Week, *"Beyond the Rabba-Rousing," Tamar Snyder offers an overview of the controversy.*

A man is under the obligation to teach his daughter Torah . . . —Ben Azzai in Mishna Sota 3:4

Whoever teaches his daughter Torah teaches her frivolity. —Rabbi Eliezer in Mishna Sota 3:4.

I grew up in a Modern Orthodox home in the States where the messages I received about a woman studying Torah were often conflicting. On the one hand, the Jewish day schools I attended were coed; I was on the honors track in Talmud through high school. My father and I even had a regular Talmud study date on Friday nights after our Shabbat meal.

On the other hand, as much as I found Torah learning an exciting journey, it was understood I could go just so far with Jewish legal study. As a woman, I could not aspire to the highest levels or *smikha,* rabbinic ordination, despite the barriers being sociological and not halakhic. Being a disseminator of Torah and a spiritual and religious counselor appealed to me—but I knew it was not an option. This was a difficult reality for me to swallow at a time when other careers seemed to be opening equally to men and women.

So why do I continue my quest for *smikha* after having been told again and again that an Orthodox woman rabbi is an oxymoron?

I do it because once I became hooked on Torah—which connects me to generations past, to my roots and ancestors and feeds my Jewish soul—I wanted to share that love with others. That is the way I see the rabbi's role.

With no halakhic barrier, why not follow that dream? Though there are those who resist, I know the time has come for *smikha* to be granted to women in the Orthodox world; and I am pushing this agenda—not only for myself, and not only for justice's sake, but for what I believe to be the greater good.

Women rabbis will serve and benefit the entire community, men and women. They will bring new voices with fresh perspectives into religious leadership and scholarship. There will be a balance, a new *shleimut,* wholeness, that has too long been missing—this is part of *tikkun olam,* repairing of the world. Of this I am certain.

Despite the setbacks—and there have been many—I am getting closer to my goal. For the past seven years I have been studying toward private *smikha* with an Orthodox rabbi while working on a doctorate in the philosophy of *halakha* at Bar-Ilan University. I have been writing, teaching, delivering *divrei Torah,* leading *tefilot,* reading from the Torah and acting in many ways like a rabbinical figure.

Recently, I have even found a few more rabbis willing to sit on a *beit din* (Jewish court of law) when I am tested (which I plan to be within the next two years) and sign their approval of my ordination if I pass.

I have also learned of two other women who have already received Orthodox *smikha.* It seems then that I am not alone, and I will not be the first. The question is: Will the fever spread? I think it will, especially after the positive discussions on the topic at the Jewish Orthodox Feminist Alliance conference, held in February in New York.

And even if my *smikha* is not accepted by mainstream Orthodoxy, it is only a matter of time before a woman rabbi will be no more radical than a bat mitzvah or a married woman covering her hair with a *sheitl* (wig), both ideas resisted initially by the Orthodox rabbinic establishment —until women persisted and the rabbis came around.

Source: Reprinted with permission of *Hadassah* and the author.

The news that the leading Orthodox advocate for female spiritual leadership reversed his decision to embrace the title *"rabba"* seemed at first a major setback for Orthodox feminists.

But supporters of the expansion of women's roles in the Orthodox community have found cause for celebration in what they see as an unprecedented nod to women's leadership by the Modern Orthodox establishment in the course of a debate over the term. In a statement, the Rabbinical Council of America, the organization of centrist Orthodox rabbis, referred to its commitment to "the assumption of appropriate leadership roles within the Jewish community" by women.

"I think it bodes very well," said Blu Greenberg, founding president of the Jewish Orthodox Feminist Alliance and a leading figure in the movement. "The fact that it was a recognition by the RCA of women's leadership roles and talents in synagogues means a step forward, and in a certain sense a breakthrough."

The controversy didn't start out looking well for Greenberg and her allies. In late January, Rabbi Avi Weiss of the Hebrew Institute of Riverdale and founder and president of Yeshivat Chovevei Torah, the left-leaning Modern Orthodox rabbinical school, announced that Sara Hurwitz, a spiritual leader at the Hebrew Institute, would use the title "rabba." That title is widely used in Israel by Reform and Conservative rabbis as a feminine form of the Hebrew word *"rav,"* or rabbi.

A representative for Weiss said the rabbi was traveling and unavailable to be interviewed for this story.

Previously, Hurwitz bore the title *"maharat,"* an acronym denoting a leader in Halacha, spirituality and Torah. She is the dean of Yeshivat Maharat, a new institution founded by Weiss to train more female spiritual leaders.

"We thought ['rabba'] would be a better description of what I actually do, and a more respectful description of what my functions are," Hurwitz said.

The new term raised objections throughout the Orthodox Jewish community, eliciting condemnations by the ultra-Orthodox Council of Torah Sages and more moderate figures.

"To confer ordination on women is a breach of our *mesorah*, of our tradition, and it is unacceptable within an Orthodox synagogue," said Rabbi Moshe Kletenik, president of the RCA. "The title 'rabba' seems to say rabbi, and it certainly gives the indication of ordination."

Critics refrained from pointing to specific halachic issues with Weiss's decision, but some saw the term as crossing a boundary.

"The ordination of women as rabbis is distinctively identified as elements that are present within the Conservative and Reform movements," said Rabbi Saul Berman, a professor at Yeshiva University's Stern College for Women who is close to Weiss. "Anything that sounds like the ordination of women, even if it takes cognizance of all of the halachic constraints, is going to raise a lot of questions as to whether a barrier then is not being broken."

On March 5, Weiss announced that following a series of conversations with the RCA, he would not bestow the title "rabba" on any other women.

"He wisely said that peace in the community is more important to me than fighting for this word right now," said Rabbi Marc Angel, another close ally of Weiss and a former president of the RCA.

In a letter to Kletenik that was distributed by the RCA, Weiss wrote, "It is not my intention or the intention of Yeshivat Maharat to confer the title of 'rabba' upon its graduates." He did not use the term "ordain" in his letter, although the term has been used in the past by Yeshivat Maharat to describe what happens upon the completion of studies there.

Hurwitz said that she will continue to use the title *"rabba,"* but that her synagogue is debating that usage. She also said that Yeshivat Maharat would amend its materials and exclusively use the term "confer" rather than "ordain." She maintained that there is no practical difference between the terms.

In Weiss's letter, which was distributed with the RCA statement referring to "appropriate leadership roles" for Orthodox women, Weiss listed the roles for which graduates of Yeshivat Maharat had been trained, including pastoral counseling and answering questions of Halacha. Kletenik said that the RCA planned to discuss at its conference in April which leadership roles it considers appropriate for women.

That discussion comes at a time when Yeshivat Maharat is one of a growing number of Orthodox institutions of higher Jewish learning for women. Others include the Drisha Institute

for Jewish Education and Yeshiva University's Graduate Program for Women in Advanced Talmudic Studies.

"At this point in time, the quality and quantity of Jewish education available to Jewish women far exceeds anything that has been available to Jewish women in the whole of Jewish history," Berman said.

With that expansion comes heightened expectations. "On the one hand, I do feel the disappointment [of] women who have worked for a title and a certain certification," Greenberg said. "But I also feel, in the context of this entire enterprise, it's going to work in their favor. . . . Ultimately we have to keep our eye down the road, as well as on today."

Source: This article originally appeared in the *Forward,* 2010; used by permission.

10.19—TAMAR SNYDER, "BEYOND THE RABBA-ROUSING," *Jewish Week,* MARCH 24, 2010

Dina Najman, *rosh kehilah* (head of the congregation) at Kehilat Orach Eliezer on the Upper West Side, spends a majority of her day answering halachic questions, teaching classes expounding upon Jewish texts and counseling couples and individuals who are having personal difficulties. Her male rabbinic colleagues often consult with her on questions of bioethics, her area of expertise.

The bulk of the work that she does, she says, is not gender specific—and shouldn't be viewed that way.

"The Orthodox community needs men and women who are skilled and can help guide their communities through education, leadership and pastoral counseling," she told *The Jewish Week.*

The recent controversy surrounding Riverdale Rabbi Avi Weiss' decision to change Sara Hurwitz's title from *maharat* to rabba "has been more about the title than really about what we're doing," Najman says. And in debating titles, the

issue of Orthodox spiritual leadership "gets gender-fied," she says.

"The bigger picture here is that we really just want to do the work" of building and shaping Orthodox communities, she says. "It needs to be understood that [Orthodox women] are doing this in the spirit of learning, for the sake of heaven. These women, regardless of title, have remained true to their *mesorah* [tradition], the process of halacha and halachic observances."

Originally called "*maharat*," an acronym for halachic, spiritual and Torah leader, Hurwitz has been "a full member of the rabbinic staff" at Rabbi Weiss' Hebrew Institute of Riverdale since last spring and had attracted surprisingly little controversy until January, when her title switched to "rabba."

That change invoked the wrath of the *haredi* Agudath Israel, whose spokesman last week made clear that if Hurwitz maintains her rabbinic role the group will no longer consider the Hebrew

Institute to be Orthodox. Of greater concern to Modern Orthodox congregations that, like the Hebrew Institute, are bringing women into the clergy is the opinion of the centrist Rabbinical Council of America, of which Rabbi Weiss is a member. At its convention next month, the RCA will be discussing the broader issue of appropriate leadership roles for women.

For the half-dozen Orthodox women in spiritual leadership roles in New York and beyond, lost amid the squabble over titles has been a true understanding of the day-to-day work they have been doing and continue to undertake on behalf of the communities they serve.

Whether referred to as rabba, assistant congregational leader or *rosh kehilah*, these Orthodox women say that they are acting in accordance with halacha and that their public involvement "won't destroy the rabbinate; it will enhance the rabbinate," Najman says.

In an indication of how sensitive this issue is, several of the women *The Jewish Week* reached out to declined to be interviewed for this story, as they worried that the increased attention would kindle the ire of the RCA and lead to the possible dissolution of the significant inroads they have made as spiritual leaders and *yoatzot halacha*—halachic counselors.

"We just want to continue doing the work we're doing," one woman said, on the condition of anonymity.

Among those who agreed to be interviewed, many felt that focusing on the "5 to 10 percent" of rabbinic duties that they, as Orthodox women, cannot perform is shrouding the real issue, namely the fact that a growing number of Modern Orthodox women feel disenfranchised by religious life.

"Many Orthodox women do not feel that they are essential members of the community," says Malka Adatto, a Washington Heights resident who is currently the Zusman Visiting Scholar at Ohev Sholom, The National Synagogue in Washington, D.C. Adatto spends one weekend a month at the Orthodox synagogue, where she organizes *ymei iyun* (days of learning), delivers a se-

ries of *shiurim* (lectures) and gives 15-minute *drashot* (textual analyses) from the bima in the "*drasha* slot"—the time during the service when a male Orthodox rabbi would typically deliver his sermon.

When she previously served as a Sanford Lurie Fellow at The Jewish Center on the Upper West Side, she and other women spoke at the end of the service, once the men had already removed their prayer shawls.

Adatto credits the shul's rabbi, Rabbi Shmuel Herzfeld, for "going above and beyond to make me feel welcome and make women feel that they are full members of the community," while acting in accordance with halacha. In addition to offering a women's prayer group, the synagogue allows the Torah to be passed to both the men's and the women's sides during the main service.

"I feel like we are at a critical juncture within the Orthodox world," says Adatto, a 26-year-old graduate of Stern College and a fifth-year student at the Graduate Program for Women in Advanced Talmudic Studies at Yeshiva University (GPATS). Debates revolving around women's role within the broader Orthodox community have been going on for decades, she says, "but now we're at the climax of this discussion."

"Title or not, rabbi or not—that's not the real issue," Adatto says. "The real issue is that Orthodox women are searching [for a place within the Jewish community] and we need to address that."

Orthodox women like herself who are taking on spiritual leadership roles serve as role models for the communities in which they live. "Even if individual women don't feel the need or desire to be in spiritual leadership positions, they see that there are options for the broader community."

At a symposium on the topic hosted by the Jewish Women's Foundation of New York last week, Rabba Sara Hurwitz said that the change in title—intended to provide more respect and "not require an entire paragraph to explain"—created "a firestorm that we did not expect."

While difficult to bear, a firestorm is a "necessary step in making the change I'm very optimistic is going to happen," commented fellow panelist Shifra Bronznick, a noted Jewish feminist who runs a change-management consulting firm and is the founder of Advancing Women Professionals and the Jewish Community. "Those who support the opportunity that has been created by Rabba Sara and Rabbi Avi Weiss should step in with volumes of support—both moral and financial," she said.

The brouhaha takes the conversation focused on Orthodox women leadership out of the private sphere. "Suddenly, people are asking, 'Where do you stand?' 'What do you think?'" Bronznick said. "Everyone becomes part of that conversation as we wrestle with the deep challenges that these issues pose to our tradition, to our narrative."

Many in the Orthodox community suffer from a "level of amnesia" when it comes to recalling the historic precedent of women's ability to answer halachic questions, Najman says. "There were many well-known women who were learned, who taught Torah, and [ruled on halachic questions] . . . and this was not something that was challenged in terms of their abilities," she says. "And I'm not talking just about Bruriah or Deborah."

She cites the examples of Asnat Barzani, the 17th-century widow of Rav Yaakov Mizrahi, who wrote a commentary on Rashi and headed her husband's yeshiva after his death; the Dulcie of Worms, who gave public discourses on Shabbat in the 13th century; and Pearl, the wife of the 16th-century Maharal of Prague, among others. "Communities saw the need for women to function in this capacity," she says.

It pains Najman when people say that she is not Orthodox because she is leading a congregation.

"They're wrong. I'm a Michlalah, Drisha, Nishmat, YU person," she says, referring to the Orthodox institutions where she has studied. She was given the ability to answer halachic questions by three Orthodox rabbis, she says, and would not have taken the *rosh kehilah* position in 2006 had she not had their support.

"We will make progress only if we will be honest about what [within halacha] is possible," she says. "If we hide behind what we think is *pas nisht* [not appropriate], as they say, and not recognize *kavod habriut* [human dignity]—and that involves respect for people who are committed to halacha—this will do a disservice to *klal yisrael.*"

For Adatto, despite the swirl of negativity surrounding the rabba controversy, she is hopeful that "while the women of my generation are fighting the battles, it will be a bit easier for my children's generation."

And at Yeshivat Maharat, the institution for training Orthodox women clergy, which Rabbi Weiss founded last year and where Hurwitz serves as dean, Hurwitz says that her students are not retreating or waning in their commitment to taking on women's spiritual leadership roles within the Orthodox community.

"They are hitting the books harder," she says. "It's made them more committed and more directed in terms of what's important—the learning."

Source: Reprinted with permission of the author.

With the rise of the gay rights movement in the late 1960s and 1970s, activists in the lesbian, gay, bisexual, and transgender community challenged Jewish norms regarding homosexuality. In 1977, San Francisco's Congregation Sha'ar Zahav opened as a spiritual center for Bay Area LGBTQ Jews. To give voice to its community's perspective on Jewish life, theology, and worship, the synagogue embarked on a decades-long effort to produce its own prayer book. The result, Siddur Sha'ar Zahav, *published in 2009, gathered the contributions of both clergy and membership from more than thirty years of synagogue history. The prayer book begins with Rabbi Camille Shira Angel's "Rabbi's Welcome." A selection of prayers from the volume is also included in the documents to follow.*

RABBI'S WELCOME

Sha'ar Zahav, the Golden Gate, is one name for the Eastern gate of Jerusalem. Located close to the Temple Mount, the Golden Gate was sealed shut in the sixteenth century.

We LGBTQ Jews know how it feels to have gateways blocked and doors closed. How many of us have been blocked from entering a synagogue as our own, out selves? Even in the many congregations we are now welcome to enter, most of us cannot open our prayer books and find our lives reflected there.

The sages knew that we need not wait for the Temple to be rebuilt to adapt and evolve our practice. Like them, we can open the Golden Gate ourselves, making our liturgy relevant and compelling to our lives.

A prayer book captures the time and place in which it is put together. When I first came to Congregation Sha'ar Zahav, I found a diversity of Jews I had never seen before: motorcycle dykes with helmets still on, transfolks of all genders and orientations, multiracial couples and families, gorgeous gay men decked in leather, a woman in a wheelchair on the bimah, giving the drash—here, finally, I had found what the words *ahavah rabbah*, God's great love, really mean.

We are each made *b'tzelem Elohim*, in the image of God. This book is not afraid to name the deepest human experiences. It invites us, all of us, to stand naked before God, to see—and to be seen.

Based as we are in San Francisco, our name, Sha'ar Zahav, the Golden Gate, also refers to our famous bridge. We pray that this book can become a bridge between isolation and community, connecting LGBTQ Jews and our allies everywhere to the Jewish tradition.

We pray that this book can become a bridge over time, from the past when we were made to feel marginalized and excluded to a future when we can be in honest dialogue with God, with our full selves, and with the world in which we live.

Kein Y'hi Ratzon, May it be so,
Rabbi Camille Shira Angel

FOR COMING INTO OUR SEXUALITY

For his proud femininity, for her matter-of-fact androgyny, for wherever she may or may not fall on the butch-femme scale, for his blessed path of transitioning . . . we praise You for the queerness of our being.

For the subversive beauty of drag royalty, for all stubborn refusals to diminish the power of our queer nation, we praise You for creating us in Your many beautiful images.

FOR COMING OUT

I praise You, Source of Life, who said *Lech l'cha* to our ancestors Abraham and Sarah: "Go forth. Go to yourself. Go find yourself." And they left their home, the only world they knew, to begin again in a new land, in a new way.

God of creation, who renews Your work each day, be with me now as I step out into the world in my own new way.

God of revelation, be with me as I affirm that I will move proudly through life as the strong, loving, wise, beautiful person You made me to be.

God of redemption, in coming out today in community, I fulfill the command You gave to our ancestors. *"Lech l'cha.* Go forth. Go to yourself. Go find yourself." And so I have, for life and health, for joy and blessing.

And together in celebration, let us all say, Amen.

FOR TRANSGENDER TRANSITIONING

To be recited before any moment of transition:

Ba-ruch a-tah A-do-nai,
E-lo-hei-nu me-lech ha-o-lam,
ha-ma-a-vir et ha-ov-rim.
Blessed are You, Eternal One, our God,
Ruler of time and space, the Transforming
    One to those
who transition/transform/cross over.

To be recited afterwards:

Ba-ruch a-tah A-do-nai,
E-lo-hei-nu me-lech ha-o-lam,
she-a-sa-ni b'tzal-mo kir-tzo-nah.
Blessed are You, Eternal One, our God, Ruler
    of time and space, who has made me in
    His image and according to Her will.

Ba-ruch a-tah A-do-nai,
E-lo-hei-nu me-lech ha-o-lam,
she-he-che-ya-nu v'ki-y'ma-nu
v'hi-gi-ya-nu, laz-man ha-zeh.
Praised are You, God, who created the
    world, who grants us life, who sustains
    us, and who brought us to arrive at this
    moment.

ON HOLINESS

We are your gay, lesbian, bisexual, transgender children:

You must not seek vengeance, nor bear a grudge against the children of your people. (Leviticus 19:18)

We are your bi, trans, lesbian, and gay parents:
Revere your mother and father, each one of you. (Leviticus 19:3)

We are elderly lesbians, bisexuals, gay men, and transgender people:
You shall rise before the aged and show deference to the old. (Leviticus 19:32)

We are the stranger:
You must not oppress the stranger.
You shall love the stranger as yourself, for you were strangers in the land of Egypt. (Leviticus 19:34)

We are lesbian, gay, trans, and bi Jews:
You must not go about slandering your kin. (Leviticus 19:16)

We are your trans, gay, bi, and lesbian siblings:
You shall not hate your brother or sister in your heart. (Leviticus 19:17)

We are lesbian, gay, trans, and bi victims of gay-bashing and murder:
You may not stand idly when your neighbor's blood is being shed. (Leviticus 19:16)

We are your bi, gay, trans, and lesbian neighbors:
You must not oppress your neighbor. (Leviticus 19:13)

You must judge your neighbor justly. (Leviticus 19:15)

You shall love your neighbor as you love yourself. (Leviticus 19:18) [. . .]

Source: "Rabbi's Welcome" authored by Rabbi Camille Shira Angel; "For Coming into Our Sexuality," copyright © 2009 by Anna Lichtenberg; "For Coming Out," copyright © 2008 by Andrew Ramer; "For Transgender Transitioning," copyright © 2008 by Rabbi Elliot Kukla; "On Holiness," copyright © 2008 by Rabbi Lisa Edwards. Excerpted from *Siddur Sha'ar Zahav*, copyright ©2009, Congregation Sha'ar Zahav, San Francisco, Calif. Reprinted with permission. All rights reserved. http://shaarzahav.org.

10.21—AMANDA CARPENTER, "J STREET PRO-ISRAEL LOBBY TAKES ON AIPAC, ALIENATES BACKERS," *Washington Times*, OCTOBER 21, 2009

Founded by former Clinton administration official Jeremy Ben-Ami, J Street emerged in 2008 as a left-leaning pro-Israel advocacy group in Washington, D.C. Deriving its name from a missing lettered street in the grid of the nation's capital, and suggesting the word "Jewish," the organization offers itself as an alternative voice to the American Israel Public Affairs Committee (AIPAC) and other lobby groups, many of which are located on K Street. J Street has attracted support from progressive Zionists openly critical of Israel's occupation of the West Bank, just as it has faced tough scrutiny from other Zionists who either reject its conciliatory views or do not believe it is the place of American Jews to dictate Israeli policy.

An upstart group trying to displace the powerful American Israel lobby has attracted President Obama's national security adviser to its first big meeting next week, but the event is also being shunned by Israel's U.S. ambassador and several members of Congress because of its views and ties to controversial figures.

J Street was formed a year and a half ago as a more liberal alternative to the nation's main pro-Israel lobbying organization, the American Israel Public Affairs Committee, better known as AIPAC. J Street's executive director has said that he wants his group to be the "blocking back" for Mr. Obama's efforts to bring peace to the Middle East.

But by taking on the long-established AIPAC and the hawkish Israeli government, and by embracing individuals who have expressed hostility to Israel, J Street also has alienated some veteran Israel supporters in Washington. For example, one of next week's speakers is a Muslim activist who has said that Israel should be considered a suspect in the Sept. 11, 2001, terrorist attacks.

[. . .]

One key difference between J Street and AIPAC is that the latter calibrates its public positions to reflect the current government in Israel, but J Street is liberal-leaning and has been critical of the center-right governing coalition of Prime Minister Benjamin Netanyahu.

The Israeli Embassy said in a statement Tuesday about Ambassador Michael Oren's invitation to address J Street's meeting next week that it would send an observer and "will follow [J Street's] proceedings with interest."

[. . .]

Earlier this year [the group] supported a Washington Jewish theater company's decision to show Caryl Churchill's "Seven Jewish Children," a play that depicts in its final scene a monologue of a parent explaining that Jews must rationalize the killings of Palestinian children in Gaza.

On Monday, J Street's organizers canceled a panel at the conference after some bloggers posted a video on the Internet of one of its poets, Josh Healey, reciting a poem in which Jews were compared to Nazis writing "numbers on the wrists of babies born in the ghetto called Gaza." . . .

In July 2005, a group of 171 different organizations called for a coordinated movement to boycott, divest, and sanction the State of Israel. The BDS movement, as it came to be known, sought an end of the Israeli army's occupation of land claimed by Palestinians, the elevation of Israeli Arab citizens to full civil equality, and the right of Palestinian refugees and their descendants to return to their ancestral homes within the current borders of the State of Israel. In December 2013, BDS supporters within the ranks of the American Studies Association, a professional guild for scholars of the Americas, passed a resolution calling for the academic boycott of Israel. In this op-ed published in the Israeli newspaper Haaretz, *Harvard law professor Alan M. Dershowitz offered his critique not only of the ASA vote but also of the BDS movement's ongoing efforts.*

The American Studies Association has just issued its first ever call for an academic boycott. No, it wasn't against China, which imprisons dissenting academics. It wasn't against Iran, which executes dissenting academics. It wasn't against Russia, whose universities fire dissenting academics. It wasn't against Cuba, whose universities have no dissenting academics. It wasn't against Saudi Arabia, whose academic institutions refuse to hire women, gay or Christian academics. Nor was it against the Palestinian Authority, whose colleges refuse to allow open discourse regarding the Israeli-Palestinian conflict. No, it was against only academic institutions in the Jewish State of Israel, whose universities have affirmative action programs for Palestinian students and who boast a higher level of academic freedom than almost any country in the world.

When the association was considering this boycott I issued a challenge to its members, many of whom are historians. I asked them to name a single country in the history of the world faced with threats comparable to those Israel faces that has had a better record of human rights, a higher degree of compliance with the rule of law, a more demanding judiciary, more concern for the lives of enemy civilians, or more freedom to criticize the government, than the State of Israel.

Not a single member of the association came up with a name of a single country. That is because there are none. Israel is not perfect, but neither is any other country, and Israel is far better than most. If an academic group chooses to engage in the unacademic exercise of boycotting the academic institutions of another country, it should do it in order of the seriousness of the human rights violations and of the inability of those within the country to seek redress against those violations.

By these standards, Israeli academic institutions should be among the last to be boycotted.

I myself disagree with Israel's settlement policy and have long urged an end to the occupation. But Israel offered to end the occupation twice in the last 13 years. They did so in 2000–2001 when Prime Minister Ehud Barak offered the Palestinians a state on approximately 95% of the occupied territories. Then it did so again in 2008 when former Prime Minister Ehud Olmert offered an even more generous deal. The Palestinians accepted neither offer and certainly share the blame for the continuing occupation. Efforts are apparently underway once again to try to end the occupation, as peace talks continue. The Palestinian Authority's President Mahmoud Abbas himself opposes academic boycotts of Israeli institutions.

China occupies Tibet, Russia occupies Chechnya and several other countries occupy Kurdish lands. In those cases no offers have been made to end the occupation. Yet no boycotts have been directed against the academic institutions of those occupying countries.

When the President of the American Studies Association, Curtis Marez, an associate professor of ethnic studies at The University of California, was advised that many nations, including all of Israel's neighbors, behave far worse than Israel, he responded, "One has to start somewhere." This boycott, however, has not only started with Israel. It will end with Israel. Marez's absurd comment reminds me of the bigoted response made by Harvard's notorious anti-Semitic president A. [Lawrence] Lowell, when he imposed anti-Jewish quotas near the beginning of the twentieth century. When asked why he singled out Jews for quotas, he replied, "Jews cheat." When the great Judge Learned Hand reminded him that Christians cheat too, Lowell responded, "You're changing the subject. We are talking about Jews now."

You would think that historians and others who belong to the American Studies Association would understand that in light of the history of discrimination against Jews, you can't just pick the Jewish State and Jewish universities as the place to "start" and stop.

The American Studies Association claims that it is not boycotting individual Israeli professors, but only the universities at which they teach. That is a nonsensical word game, since no self-respecting Israeli professor would associate with an organization that singled out Israeli colleges and universities for a boycott. Indeed, no self-respecting American professor should in any way support the bigoted actions of this association.

Several years ago, when a similar boycott was being considered, a group of American academics circulated a counter-petition drafted by Nobel Prize Physicist Steven Weinberg and I that read as follows:

"We are academics, scholars, researchers and professionals of differing religious and political perspectives. We all agree that singling out Israelis for an academic boycott is wrong. To show our solidarity with our Israeli academics in this matter, we, the undersigned, hereby declare ourselves to be Israeli academics for purposes of any academic boycott. We will regard ourselves as Israeli academics and decline to participate in any activity from which Israeli academics are excluded."

More than 10,000 academics signed this petition including many Nobel Prize winners, presidents of universities and leading scholars from around the world.

Shame on those members of the American Studies Association for singling out the Jew among nations. Shame on them for applying a double standard to Jewish universities. Israeli academic institutions are strong enough to survive this exercise in bigotry. The real question is will this association survive its complicity with the oldest and most enduring prejudice?

Source: Reprinted with permission of the author and publisher. All rights reserved.

10.23—MISSION STATEMENT, JDATE, 1997

With the advent of the Internet, Jewish entrepreneurs searched for ways to leverage modern technology to deepen American Jewish life. In the social media arena, JDate, an online service, sought to modernize the traditional Jewish matchmaker for the digital age. Launched in 1997, JDate claims more than five hundred thousand users. It seeks to "strengthen the Jewish community" and "ensure that Jewish traditions are sustained for generations to come." With features such as "secret admirer," which permits JDate members to express anonymous interest in each other, the website boasts a strong record in Jewish matchmaking. When members noted that many non-Jews had joined, JDate officials added a "willing to convert" question to the site. In the article to follow, Dr. Paulette Kouffman Sherman employs the story of Hanukkah to give JDate clients advice on dating.

Building the Jewish Community for Over a Decade

JDate's mission is to strengthen the Jewish community and ensure that Jewish traditions are sustained for generations to come. To accomplish this we provide a global network where Jewish singles find friendship, romance and lifelong partners within their faith.

While deeply committed to Israel and Jewish cultural programs, we provide support for numerous non-profit organizations of all faiths. These efforts honor our proud Jewish tradition and values.

Source: Reprinted with permission.

10.24—PAULETTE KOUFFMAN SHERMAN, "EIGHT LOVE LESSONS FROM THE FESTIVAL OF LIGHT," DECEMBER 8, 2013

Most of you probably know the story of Hanukkah, but here's a quick version: During the time of the 2nd Temple, the Holy Land was ruled by cruel Greeks. A Jew named Mattityahu and his sons fought them and won. Afterwards, the Maccabees found one jar with enough oil for just one day, and yet that oil burned for eight days! This was a miracle!

So, what can this story about those eight miraculous nights teach us about dating? Plenty! Here are eight lessons we can apply to dating:

1. When Things Seem Tough, Keep the Faith
Dating can feel challenging at times. It's tempting to give up or take a break. Remember, it only takes one great date!

2. Hold Off before Cutting a Prospect Loose after Just One Date
On an ego level in the physical world, we have many requirements and judgments. On a spiritual level, however, we're willing to be surprised by the good. Sometimes it takes time to see the miracle of who a date really is, so be willing to wait a bit (unless there are red flags).

3. Be a Fighter: Never Give Up on Yourself
You may feel you've been through a battleground with dating, and you may even think about tak-

ing yourself off the market. Don't. You're a miracle to that special someone and, more importantly, remember your own worth. You may experience some rejection by others, but that doesn't mean you should reject yourself!

4. Creatively Make the Most of What You *Do* Have
When the Maccabees found oil for one night, they decided to make the most of it. Too often I see singles comparing themselves to others, thinking: "Why don't I have a better job?" or "Why aren't I taller?" Choose to embrace all that you are now and remember that it is more than enough or G-d wouldn't have made you that way. You are a gift.

5. Look for the Light in Everyone & Everything
In dating, we can be judgmental. We don't want to settle, but even if we aren't a match with a date, we can be kind. It makes dating more enjoyable for everyone when we look for the light in our dates and in the situation. Good things happen when we do this.

6. Believe in Miracles, Not Scarcity
When your environment is full of strife and scar-

city, it's easy to think that portends a bad ending. But, like the Maccabees, remember that it's not over till it's over. Look within instead of without, to the source of your love. Do what you need to do to move forward in dating. It's most important to stay in the vibration of love and faith, not fear.

7. Remember You Aren't Alone
The Maccabees were helped by G-d to achieve their goals. Dating can feel lonely when it isn't going well. But remember that you are unconditionally loved by the Source and are never alone.

8. Be Proud of Who You Are
The Maccabees chose to fight to defend their Jewish people. Many dating experts advise playing games to attract a mate, but the moral here is to be yourself and to always be proud of who you are. The right mate will stick around and will join you.

Source: Originally published by *Jmag*, the online magazine for JDate.com. Reprinted with permission of the author and publisher.

10.25—JONATHAN MILLER, "HOW ADAM SANDLER'S 'CHANUKAH SONG' HELPED SAVE THE JEWS," *Huffington Post*, DECEMBER 23, 2011

The "December dilemma" refers to the discomfort many Jews face during the Christmas season. As historian Andrew Heinze (b. 1955) has chronicled in a study of early twentieth-century American Jewish history, Chanukah has emerged as a powerful and important Jewish antidote to widespread Christmas celebrations. When comedian Adam Sandler (b. 1966) performed "The Chanukah Song" on the December 3, 1994, broadcast of Saturday Night Live, *he created an instant sensation. By naming celebrities with Jewish roots, Sandler at once celebrated Jewish heritage amid the December dilemma and ascribed Jewish identity to individuals who oftentimes did all they could*

to minimize their Jewish backgrounds. "The Chanukah Song" captured a lingering sense of American Jewish marginality while reflecting enough comfort in America to tout the sometimes unknown accomplishments of many famous, and not so famous, Jews. In this December 2011 blog post, which appeared in the Huffington Post, *Jonathan Miller reflects on the cultural resonance of Sandler's song for American Jews.*

The Last American Jew.

It was an alarming image for a Jewish adolescent.

Yet, in the 1980s, it was a common theme of our temple youth group gatherings.

Jewish teens in Generation X were admonished regularly about demographic trends and intermarriage rates that suggested our community could soon splinter into the dustbin of history—as early as the end of the 21st century.

At the same time, our rabbis began to share a darker take on the holiday of Hanukkah, at variance with the bright and fanciful miracle of our childhood celebrations. (You know the legend: how the day's supply of the Great Temple's oil lasted eight crazy nights, yadda, yadda, yadda.)

As teens, we were old enough to process the back story—how Judah Maccabee and his brothers successfully revolted against the Greek King Antiochus' oppressive regime that was exploiting Jewish assimilation, poised to destroy our religion from within. We were warned gravely that 20th century assimilation similarly could lead to our own extinction.

The '80s indeed were a challenging time for American Jewry. Overt, sometimes violent anti-Semitism had almost entirely vanished, the horrors of the Holocaust still fresh in the minds of our parents' generation. And yet, in many areas of middle America, such as my old Kentucky home, we were still the "other": There were social clubs my family couldn't join, classmates' parties to which I wasn't invited, civic organizations that excluded my parents—all because of our separate faith. Anti-Zionism coincidentally peaked during the decade, as Israel's war in Lebanon provoked unbalanced, disproportional coverage of the Jewish State from much of the American media.

It was easy to understand why so many Jews—particularly our youngest—took comfort by fading into the multi-colored fabric of secularized Christianity that enveloped American culture. With Gentile discrimination so diffuse and subtle, the only remaining strident enemy in the 3,000-year battle for Jewish survival was, in fact, ourselves.

But then the 1990s brought forth a modern-day Judah Maccabee: Adam Sandler.

OK, *I exaggerate a little.*

What the '90s did bring was an army of modern Maccabees, in the form of prominent, familiar, likable Jews thrust into the pop media spotlight: Jews that were both clearly identifiable and proud of their heritage.

This helped produce a dramatic sea change in Christian Americans' acceptance of their Jewish neighbors. In the vast center of the country where few Jews lived, ignorance previously had bred distrust and suspicion. Now, through the magic of television—and shows such as *Northern Exposure*, *Beverly Hills 90210*, *Friends*, and most prominently, *Seinfeld*—Jewish comedians, actors, and characters entered the living rooms of middle America. Rural citizens who'd never met a Jew before now "knew" dozens, and understood that "they were just like us"—maybe a bit wackier.

Just as significant was the impact on Jewish Americans. We could now hold our heads up a bit higher, feel a little more comfortable to publicly pronounce our faith. We were now the tellers of Jewish jokes, alternatively wry and self-deprecating, instead of divisive and mean-spirited.

It was a phenomenon that Jonathan Alter—in his famous 2000 *Newsweek* cover piece heralding Joe Lieberman's history-making Vice-Presidential candidacy—labeled the "Seinfeldizing of America."

And at its epicenter in 1994 was a hastily produced, three-and-a-half minute musical segment on *Saturday Night Live*'s "Weekend Update."

It's a nostalgic treat to revisit Sandler's premier performance of his now-classic "The Chanukah Song": The comedian's now all-too-familiar, man-child vocal affectations are, on the old video, refreshingly charming—emanating from the self-mocking smile of the skinny Gen Xer, struggling to read his cue cards.

But as silly as his lyrics were on the surface, Sandler's sing-songy outing of pop culture icons with Jewish blood was sort of revelatory to his fellow Chosen People. Who knew that James Caan—*Sonny Corleone!*—lit the Hanukkah menorah? And while the Jewish-ness of Mr. Spock (Leonard Nimoy) was well-known (we all learned in Hebrew School that the Vulcan hand salute was a tribute to a rabbinic blessing gesture), the Hebraic faith of Captain Kirk (William Shatner) was a welcome surprise. And Harrison Ford being a quarter Jewish? Not too shabby.

(Actually, Harrison Ford is fully half-Jewish. And contrary to another Sandlerian stanza, baseball Hall-of-Famer Rod Carew—whose wife and children were Jewish—did not convert: The former California Angel and Minnesota Twin was never a Member of the Tribe. But who's kvetching?)

I remember picturing myself as a child in the '70s, literally the only kid on my block (with my sis) without a Christmas tree. What I would have given to have known at the time that the epitome of coolness—The Fonz himself (Henry Winkler)—had a Bar Mitzvah! I imagined millions of other children learning the same way that many of their celebrity idols spun the Hanukkah dreidel, just like they did.

After near saturation of holiday radio play rotations (station managers must have determined it both a popular and politically correct inclusion), as well as through its subsequent sequels—the risqué Part 2 in 1999; the NSFW Part 3 in 2002—the song intended as a filler comedy sketch emerged as a holiday icon. And with its central, irresistible prophecy—that . . . "so many Jews are in the show biz"—there was one simple conclusion to be drawn:

It's cool to be Jewish.

Of course, "The Chanukah Song" does very little to educate or inspire its listeners about the central principles of the faith that make me and so many others so proud to be Jewish. Nor did it ameliorate the same demographic trends, intermarriage rates and anti-Zionist propaganda that were a concern in the 1980s. And as long as humankind remains an imperfect species, anti-Semitism will continue to fester, albeit under the societally accepted surface here in the U.S.

Yet in this, the most wonderful time of the year, when modern-day Antiochian mad men exploit naked consumerism to suck out the spirituality of the winter holidays, when attention-hungry Chicken Littles conspire to manipulate public sentiment by alleging phony wars on multi-denominationally embraced holidays, it's comforting to realize that a silly, little comic ditty has played a small role in revitalizing the true meaning of the season.

So the next time you hear "The Chanukah Song"—whether you're a Jew, Jew-ish or Gentile —take a cue from the Maccabees and make an appointment to spend a little time culturally and spiritually enriching the lives of your children and/or grandchildren.

Oh, and also try out the latkes—they're really tasty. And have a happy, happy, happy, happy Hanukkah.

Source: Copyright © Jonathan Miller. Reprinted with permission of the author.

10.26—TRI-FAITH INITIATIVE OF OMAHA, NEBRASKA, MAY 2010

Faced with a synagogue too small to meet the needs of its congregants, leaders from Omaha, Nebraska's Temple Israel initiated a search for a new, larger home. They reached out to a local Muslim group in the hope that a coordinated building effort might ease some of the practical issues involved in such a big undertaking. Finally, the partnership moved beyond practical issues, and the Jewish and Muslim leaders germinated a plan to build a tri-faith campus that would include a synagogue, a mosque, and a church. Temple Israel and the American Institute of Islamic Studies and Culture were joined by the Episcopal Diocese of Nebraska and incorporated in 2006. Four years later, the group found a thirty-five-acre property where it is collocating Jewish, Christian, and Muslim houses of worship and an interfaith center. The mission statement, vision statement, and goals of the initiative are included as follows.

MISSION STATEMENT

Initially, to facilitate the creation of a dynamic Neighborhood or Campus which intentionally co-locates Jewish, Christian and Muslim places of Worship and Study; and

Once those three Faiths commit their presence, thereafter to establish and sustain an acclaimed Tri-Faith Center for Abrahamic Faith Learning and Collaboration.

VISION STATEMENT

Our vision is to build bridges of Respect, Acceptance, and Trust among people of the Abrahamic Faiths; to challenge the stereotype of each other and to learn from and about each other; to celebrate our common histories and respect our different approaches to finding God; and to share God's most basic humanitarian principle—treating others as you wish to be treated.

GOALS

The Tri-Faith Initiative of Omaha, Nebraska ("TFI") has helped to create the unique opportunity presented by a Jewish Temple, a Christian Church and a Muslim Mosque intentionally co-locating their places of worship. The proposed site is on a beautiful acreage which has been a golf country club. Each Faith Group must and will rightfully focus on creating a single purpose religious building dedicated solely to serving its own members. On the other hand, the (long-term) commitment to this site by Jews, Christians and Muslims creates an unprecedented opportunity for Interfaith Collaboration and shared learning. (Numerous interfaith dialogues exist, many of which are academia based; none are rooted in an investment of millions of dollars in religious buildings that connote a permanence of proximity and relationships.)

The "4th Building" will be a Tri-Faith Center. It will emphasize People, Place and Programs to develop a one-of-a-kind environment for learning about Abrahamic history, traditions and beliefs, commonalities and differences. TFI will own a 4 acre site, and have access to (or possibly own) an adjacent 8 acre Green Space. The Tri-Faith Center will be Spiritual, inside and out. Indoor meeting, gathering, study and exhibition space will be complemented by outdoor contemplative space where individuals or groups can reflect, meditate or pray. The Tri-Faith Center will be open to people of all faiths. As visitors seek further learning, social interaction or connections to God, they will find welcome from each of the 3 congregations surrounding the Center.

In short, a never-before opportunity exists to facilitate Jewish–Christian–Muslim learning, acceptance, respect and ultimately collaboration. TFI exists to maximize the possibilities that arise from this opportunity.

Source: Reprinted with permission of the Tri-Faith Initiative.

10.27—THE ADVENTURE RABBI PROGRAM, 2012

American Jews coming of age in the twenty-first century have challenged traditional models in organized Jewish life. Synagogue affiliation, for example, once a mainstay for American Jews, has dropped precipitously; the 2001 National Jewish Population Survey revealed that only 40 percent of American Jews were affiliated with a synagogue. Later community studies have shown synagogue affiliation rates as low as 14 percent in Las Vegas, Nevada, and 10 percent in Sonoma County, California (forty miles north of San Francisco). In Boulder, Colorado, Rabbi Jamie Korngold responded to this trend by forming the Adventure Rabbi Program, which focuses on reinventing the synagogue-centered model of observance for a younger generation of postdenominational (or nondenominational) Jews. Among other innovations, Korngold's effort eliminated mandatory synagogue dues and moved Jewish worship and learning out of the synagogue building. Korngold initiated a nature-based program that promoted Shabbat morning mountain hikes and even skiing expeditions as powerful and meaningful ways to connect to Judaism. The following article appears on the Adventure Rabbi home page.

LOCATIONS:
Boulder, Colorado
Lake Tahoe, California

A NEW KIND OF SYNAGOGUE:
The Adventure Rabbi Program is a cutting edge model of synagogue life appropriate for 21st century Judaism. Gone are the days when Jews felt obligated to belong to a synagogue. Today, 70% of American Jews do not belong to a congregation.

In fact, many Jews today don't feel obliged by Judaism at all. *Judaism has become a choice and if the religion does not enhance and enrich our lives, if Judaism is not relevant, meaningful and accessible, many of us opt out completely.*

The Adventure Rabbi Program puts meaning back into Judaism. We meet people where they are (often literally hiking or skiing) and show them how Judaism can enhance their lives, without having to give up their weekends or making big pledges. *Through our activities and community, adults and kids come to love Judaism.*

We teach age-old Jewish concepts like taking some time off each week and stop[ping] trying to be perfect, but we teach them in a modern context. We climb mountains, go skiing, play the guitar and sing around a campfire. We have thoughtful discussions and debates based on a scientific and rational view of the world. (We have lots of physicists and rocket scientists in our congregation.)

We don't simply teach Bar and Bat Mitzvah students Hebrew; we teach them the relationship skills, based on Jewish teachings, that they need to become responsible and happy teenagers. *We present Judaism in a way that fits into modern American life.*

OUR PROGRAMS ARE IN SYNC WITH WHAT JEWS IN AMERICA ARE LOOKING FOR:
Membership:
We do not require yearly membership dues (although we offer them for those who prefer a traditional model). Rather, we offer [a] pay as you

go fee for services. Gone are the days when Jews would willingly pay 3% of their income for synagogue dues even when they only attended High Holiday services. *Today's Jews ask, "What am I getting for my money?" and only wish to pay for what they use.*

At the Adventure Rabbi Program, you become part of our community just by showing up.

Services:

We do not offer weekly Shabbat Services. Our constituency doesn't want to go to weekly services. (Do you? Lots of synagogues offer them so we can recommend one to you.)

Adventure Rabbi people are busy with full lives and on weekends we ski, hike, party, hang out, go dancing and relax. When the weekend arrives, we don't want to get dressed up to come to synagogue to count pages and have the rabbi preach at us and tell us how we should be more Jewish.

[. . .]

Rather we offer one Friday night and one Saturday a month. On Fridays we enjoy brief joyful services. (We have no interest in long, boring, sad services.) On Saturdays we offer hikes or services on skis. Our Shabbat hikes and ski days are great examples of how we meet our participants where they are. "OK so you are going skiing on Shabbat? Let me come with you and I will show you how to make it Jewish."

Participant Involvement & Power to Create:

Many of our most popular programs were created at the suggestion of our participants. For example, Passover in Moab was dreamed up by Kara and Steve Mertz.

Unlike large synagogues, with institutional traditions, chains of command and committee charts, we are a nimble and flexible program. We have few committees and fewer meetings. New program ideas, or at least ones that can support themselves financially, can easily and quickly be brought to fruition.

Prayer:

We do not believe that prayer changes the will of a divine being. Therefore, we feel liberated to expand and contract our liturgical choices to create a service that is meaningful. We do believe that communal prayers offer an opportunity to connect with others in our community, our families and the Jewish people all over the world as well as to look within ourselves.

Origins of the Program:

. . . Adventure Rabbi Program was envisioned by Rabbi Jamie S. Korngold, who has experienced her most vibrant Jewish experiences in the outdoors. From scaling mountains to running ultra-marathons, she has found that the spirituality of the wilderness awakens Judaism.

Surrounded by the raw wonder of creation, Rabbi Korngold helps people experience an inner peace and an abiding connection to That Which is Greater Than Ourselves. In the wilderness, she believes, it is possible to distance ourselves from politics and protocol and allow the awareness of the connectedness of all things to permeate our souls.

Come join us; let the wilderness awaken your Judaism.

Location:

The Adventure Rabbi Headquarters is located in Boulder Colorado and is managed by Rabbi Jamie Korngold. We have a large office building in which we teach classes, lead smaller services, and hold meetings and conferences. For larger services we rent space.

In 2011, we opened our first AR branch in South Lake Tahoe, California in partnership with Temple Bat Yam and managed by Rabbi Evon Yakar. Our South Lake Tahoe location provides easy access to extraordinary winter and summer outdoor sports.

Source: Reprinted with permission of the Adventure Rabbi Program.

Organized in 2006 to bolster Jewish life for people in their twenties, Moishe House, which is based in Oakland, California, sponsors Jewish social and religious events in more than fifty homes throughout the United States and worldwide. In exchange for agreeing to serve as hosts, participants gain funding support from Moishe House as well as from local Jewish philanthropies. Moishe House does not own any of the homes it supports, believing that nonownership encourages a more rapid and dynamic proliferation of these Jewish meeting places. By encouraging residents to determine their own programming, Moishe House seeks to strengthen connections between its houses and their surrounding communities. When residents of a home in West Hollywood, California, joined the Moishe House consortium, the Los Angeles Jewish Journal *covered the story.*

Before they discovered Moishe House L.A. (MoHoLa), Rodrigo Rodarte had never led a Shabbat dinner, Jon Shoer was looking to solidify his Jewish identity, and Joshua Nathan Finn was searching for a way to create a home away from home for his Jewish peers.

All three found a place to belong at MoHoLa in West Hollywood at 1003 N. Crescent Heights Blvd., one of 54 houses in 14 countries established by Moishe House.

Started in 2006, the nondenominational organization aspires to bring Jews in their 20s together to celebrate their heritage through social events, Shabbat dinners, volunteer opportunities and holiday gatherings. Its model employs "houses" in which three to five young adults plan and host a wide range of events.

Moishe House boasts serving 60,000 program attendees around the world every year. Locally, there are other houses in the San Fernando Valley and West Los Angeles.

MoHoLa, which has a total of five residents, puts together seven events every month. It hosts Shabbat meals every two weeks for an average of 50 people, held a Chanukah quiz night and put together a singles event at a local bar around Valentine's Day. During the second night of Passover, they are co-sponsoring a seder at Sinai Temple that will focus on social justice.

Ariela Emery, 24, who worked at her local Jewish community center in Houston and moved here this past July, joined to stay involved in the Jewish community.

She said that what Moishe House does is important because, "Everyone feels Jewish a different way. Some people have memories of grandmas, and others remember Chanukah parties. The good thing about Moishe House is we try to give people a huge variety of ways they can connect to Judaism. If they just like to meet other Jews and that makes them feel Jewish, we have purely social activities. We do two Shabbats a month if they like Shabbat. If they like social justice, we volunteer at a food pantry. It's a great platform for young people to come and [experience] many ways to feel Jewish and connect with people their own age."

[. . .]

Tamar Raucher, marketing and development associate for Moishe House, which is headquartered in Oakland, said a new house can be approved at any time. If a group of devoted friends is willing to hold a certain number of Jewish-themed events per month and there is a need in a community, they have the chance to receive funding. What they are looking for in a candidate is someone who is an outgoing leader and passionate about building a Jewish community.

Dave Cygielman, CEO and founder of Moishe House, said that having houses in Los Angeles is important for two reasons: There are many young adults who want to be part of a community, and there are transplants "who are brand-new to the area and have to figure out who they are and what kind of life they are going to live. Moishe House gives that opportunity for Jewish life."

Cygielman said the model of his organization is effective in its outreach efforts because it relies on its young residents.

"By doing it peer-to-peer rather than staff person-to-the-program recipient, we find that a lot more people come. Recruitment and engagement is easier and much more simple," he said. "It becomes very cost effective, and it takes on the personality, interests and needs of the generation taking on the programming, which is key. We don't have to continually figure out what young people want because it's being planned and created by young people."

Rodarte, 26, said for the first one and a half years that he lived in Los Angeles, he didn't feel like he belonged to any Jewish community. When he attended Moishe House events, though, he started to feel the bond to his religion and heritage once again.

"There were people my own age that I recognized," he said. "It's kind of like going to friends' or friends of friends' houses at first. That grows and builds. We feel like we're part of our own community."

Because of the house, he said he's had the chance to get in touch with his Judaism. Growing up, Rodarte never led services or dinners, which he now does regularly at the house. He also never had a bar mitzvah, and felt like he was missing out. He applied to the organization's scholarship fund, received $500 and was able to take classes leading up to a bar mitzvah last summer.

"The experience with Moishe House has been really great," he said. "I've been able to do things I never would have done." . . .

Source: Reprinted with permission of the author.

10.29—PRESIDENTIAL PROCLAMATION—JEWISH AMERICAN HERITAGE MONTH, MAY 2013

After a yearlong commemoration in 2004 marking the 350th year of American Jewish life, Congresswoman Debbie Wasserman Schultz and Senator Arlen Specter drafted a resolution calling for the creation of a Jewish American Heritage Month. In December 2005, Congress passed the resolution unanimously. Two months later, the Senate concurred without an opposing vote, and President George W. Bush declared that the first such month would be observed in May 2006. In the following passage, President Barack Obama reflects on the role of Jews in American society in his 2013 Jewish American Heritage Month proclamation.

In his second year in office, President George Washington wrote a letter to the Touro Synagogue in Newport, Rhode Island—one of our Nation's first Jewish houses of worship—and re-affirmed our country's commitment to religious freedom. He noted that the Government of the United States would give "to bigotry no sanction [and] to persecution no assistance," and that all Americans are entitled to "liberty of conscience and immunities of citizenship." Those words ring as true today as they did then, and they speak to a principle as old as America itself: that no matter who you are, where you come from, or what faith you practice, all of us have an equal share in America's promise.

It was such a belief that drew generations of Jewish immigrants to our shores. It is what brought Jewish families westward when pogroms and persecution cast a shadow over Europe in the last century. It is what led Holocaust survivors and Jews trapped behind the Iron Curtain to rebuild their lives across the Atlantic. And with every group that arrived here, the Jewish

American community grew stronger. Our Nation grew stronger. Jewish immigrants from all over the world wove new threads into our cultural fabric with rich traditions and indomitable faith, and their descendants pioneered incredible advances in science and the arts. Teachings from the Torah lit the way toward a more perfect Union, from women's rights to workers' rights to the end of segregation.

That story is still unfolding today. Jewish Americans continue to guide our country's progress as scientists and teachers, public servants and private citizens, wise leaders and loving parents. We see their accomplishments in every neighborhood, and we see them abroad in our unbreakable bond with Israel that Jewish Americans helped forge. More than 350 years have passed since Jewish refugees first made landfall on American shores. We take this month to celebrate the progress that followed, and the bright future that lies ahead.

Now, therefore, I, Barack Obama, President of the United States of America, by virtue of the authority vested in me by the Constitution and the laws of the United States, do hereby proclaim May 2013 as Jewish American Heritage Month. I call upon all Americans to visit www .JewishHeritageMonth.gov to learn more about the heritage and contributions of Jewish Americans and to observe this month with appropriate programs, activities, and ceremonies.

In witness whereof, I have hereunto set my hand this thirtieth day of April, in the year two thousand thirteen, and of the Independence of the United States of America the two hundred and thirty-seventh.

Barack Obama

Aaronson, Reuben, 165

Abbas, Mahmoud, 425

Aboab de Fonseca, Isaac, 9, 9

abolitionism, Jewish opposition to, 104–7

Abrams, Emanuel, 18

Abzug, Bella, 350–51

Adams, Hannah, 58–61

adaptation. *See* assimilation and acculturation

Adatto, Malka, 420–21

Addams, Jane, 177

Adler, Cyrus, 156–57

Adventure Rabbi Program, 432–33

African Americans: antisemitism among, 335, 373–74; Jewish relations with, 65–66, 275–76, 306–21, 339–40, 369–74; in Reconstruction era, 113–16; school desegregation, 306; violence against, 114–16

agricultural settlements, 133–34

Agro-Joint program (JDC), 234, 237–38

Agus, Jacob B., 407

AJC (American Jewish Committee), 178–79, 244, 285, 339–40

Alinsky, Saul, 345–47

Alpert, Abraham, 141

Alter, Robert, 377–79

America First Committee, 230–31, 272–73

American Council for Judaism, 244, 253–54

American Jewish Committee (AJC), 178–79, 244, 285, 339–40

American Jewish Conference, 243–44, 258

American Jewish Congress, 258, 272–73, 333

American Jewish Joint Distribution Committee (JDC), 234–38

American League for the Defense of Jewish Rights, 224

American Revolution and early national era: business activities, 52–55; civic status, 36–39, 40–51; family life, 64–66; immigration and adaptation, 33–35; politics and government, 31, 36–51; religious life, 56–63

American Society for Evangelizing the Jew, 61–63

American Studies Association, 425–26

Angel, Camille Shira, 422–23

antebellum period: antisemitism in, 68, 91–92; business participation, 75–78; civic status, 73–74; education of American Jews, 82–86; immigration and adaptation in, 69–72; labor participation, 75–78; politics and government, 73–74, 108; religious life, 79–86; social life, 79–86

anticommunism, 189–90, 281–87

Anti-Defamation League, 329–30

anti-immigrant movement, 130, 181–82, 222–23, 240–42

Antin, Mary, 135–38

antisemitism: in antebellum period, 68, 91–92; in Civil War era, 127–28; in colonial era, 18; decline of, 368–69; in early national period, 34–35, 37–38, 43–44; Global Anti-Semitism Review Act, 399–400; in interwar period, 181–82, 217–31, 238–42; Iranian Revolution and, 390–93; Jewish writers on, 375–81; in mid-twentieth century, 283–86, 332–33, 335; in Progressive era, 170–76; violence, 114–16, 174–75, *176*; in World War II, 272–74. *See also* Shoah (Holocaust)

Antonelli, Judith S., 410–11

Arafat, Yasser, 373–74, *374*

Ararat, 87–88

Ashkenazi liturgical rituals, 1, 391

Askowitz, Dora, 200

assimilation and acculturation: in antebellum period, 69–72, 85–86; in colonial period, 7–30; in contemporary America, 389–93; declining synagogue affiliation rates, 414–16; in early national period, 33–35; of Eastern European Jews, 1–2; historic trends in, 2–4; immigrants' advice on, 131–32; intermarriage, 3–4, 8, 89–90, 161, 389, 401–7, 403n1; in interwar period, 181–82; post–World War II acceleration of, 275–80; World War II refugees, 3, 269–74. *See also* Gilded Age and Progressive era; Jewish identity

Atlantic City, New Jersey, 279–80

Balfour, Arthur James, 207

Balfour Declaration, 207–8

Baron, Salo W., 5

Baron de Hirsch Fund, 133–34

Baruch, Bernard, 2, 219

baseball, 138, *138*, 202

BDS movement, 425–26

Bellow, Saul, 379–81

Ben-Ami, Jacob, 258

Ben-Ami, Jeremy, 424

Ben-Gurion, David, 260, 322–26

Benjamin, Israel Joseph, 85–86

Benjamin, Judah P., 99, 111

Bergson, Peter (Hillel Kook), 257

Berlin, Irving, 247

Beth Sholom Synagogue (Elkins Park), 293, *293*

Bettelheim, Bruno, 337–38

Bierfield, S. A., 114–16

Bill of Rights, 40, 49

Bingham, Theodore A., 173–74

Birmingham, Alabama, 310–14

Biron, Phineas I., 281–82

birth control, 162

Black Power movement, 3

Blatt, Solomon, 314–15

Blau, Joseph L., 5

Blaustein, Jacob, 322–26

blood libel, 91–92, 170–71

B'nai B'rith, 103, 116, 123, 174, 315–17

Board of Delegates of American Israelites, 107, 123, 125–26

Bookstaber, Philip D., 259

Bosch, Justus, 17–18

Bowman, Lawrence, 114–16

boycotts of Nazi Germany's goods, 2, 238–40

Brainin, Joseph, 281–82

Brandeis, Louis, 147, 168–69, 207, 288

Brandeis University, 288–89

Braun, Jonathan, 348–49

Breira organization, 385–86

British colonialism, 1, 7, 18–30

British Naturalization Act, 12, 16

Bronfman, Edgar, 414

Bronznick, Shifra, 421

Brownlow, William Gannaway, 106, 107n1

Brown v. Board of Education, 306–8

Bruckman, Henrietta, 145

Buchanan, James, 118

Bush, George W., 399

business, Jewish participation in, 17–19, 52–55, 75–78, 187–90

Cadman, Samuel Parkes, 204

Cahan, Abraham, 131–32, 144, 161

California, 1, 67, 77–78, 167, 390–93

Campanall, Valentin, 23

Carigal, Haim Isaac, 56–57

Carleton, Guy (Sir), 39

Carter, Jimmy, 369, 394

Central Conference of American Rabbis (CCAR), 166, 178–79, 205–6, 211–12, 282, 285–86, 405–7

Central Europe: Jewish emigration from, 1, 67, 93, 141, 146–47; pogroms in, 170–72, 178–79

Chabad-Lubavitch, 294–301

Chaney, James, 319, *319*

Chanukah, in contemporary Jewish life, 427–30

"The Chanukah Song" (Sandler), 428–30

chaplains, Jewish Americans as, 122–28, 158–59, 247–48, 251, *252*

Charleston, South Carolina, 36, 45–48, 69, 79–80, 91, 110–11, 314–15

Chicago, Illinois, 97

Chisolm, Edward, 91

Christian organizations, 61–63, 205–6

Cincinnati, Ohio, 71–72, 153

citizenship status, 12, 16, 31–32, 129

civic status: during American Revolution, 36–39, 40–51; in antebellum period, 73–74; of colonial period, 15–16; in contemporary American Jewish life, 394, 399–400; during interwar period, 183–86; 1960s to 1970s, 337–40, 345–47, 355–57; in post–World War II period, 283–86; in Progressive era and Gilded Age, 141; during World War II, 245–50

Civil Rights Act of 1964, 368

civil rights movement, 3, 275–76, 306–21, 339–40, 369–74

Civil War: antisemitism, 103–4, 127–28; Confederacy, Jewish relationship to, 93–94, 100–101, 109–12, *111–12*; conflicted loyalties, 94–101; military chaplaincy issue, 122–28; overview, 93; religion and slavery, 118–22; Union, Jewish relationship to, 93–94, 102–8

Cohen, Abraham Hyam, 53–55

Cohen, Eleanor H., 100–101

Cohen, Elias A., 191–93

Cohen, G. P., 91

Cohen, J. I., 50–51

Cohen, Julius Henry, 147–48

Cohen, Philip, 58–61

Cohen, Samuel, 29

Cold War, 3, 283–87, *284*, 306, 327–33, 341–45

colonial period: business activities of Jewish communities, 17–19; civic status, 15–16; Dutch colonies, 1, 10–12; family life for Jews in, 26–30; immigration experience, 1, 13–14; overview, 7; politics and government, 15–16; religious life, 7–9, 20–25

Columbus Platform, 211

Communism in U.S., 189, 281–87

Confederacy, 93–94, 100–101, 109–12, *111–12*

Congregation Saar Asamaim (Gate of Heaven) (London), 29

Congress, U.S., 122–28, 181–82, 222–23, 226, 240–42, 331, 387, 394, 399–400

Congress of Racial Equality (CORE), 315–17

Conley, Jim, 174–75

Connolly, C. P., 174–75

Conservative Judaism: civil rights movement, 310–14; emergence of, 154–55; feminist movement, 336, 408; interfaith and intergroup relations, 203–6; in interwar period, 181–82, 196–99; patrilineal descent issue, 405–7; post–World War II changes to, 278; Prohibition, 191–93; Vietnam war, 343–45; women's issues, 363–64, 418; Zionism, 212–15

Constitutional Convention, 31–32, 40

Constitution of the United States, 49, 134, *134*

contemporary America (since 1980): civic status, 394, 399–400; immigration and adaptation, 390–93; overview, 389; politics and government, 395–99; popular culture, 427–30; religious life, 401–23; twenty-first century developments, 431–36; Zionism in, 424–26

Continental Congress, 31–32

conversionary in-marriage, defined, 403n3

CORE (Congress of Racial Equality), 315–17

Coughlin, Charles, 2, 181, 228–30

couples conversion rate, defined, 403n4

Cygielman, Dave, 434–35

Dachau concentration camp, 248–50

Davis, Jefferson, 110–11

Dearborn Independent, 2, 217–19

Declaration of Independence, 37, 134, *134*

De la Motta, Jacob, 48–49

Delancey, Oliver, 26

DeLucena, Abraham Haim, 17

Democratic Party, 183, 352–54, 394–99

Depaul University, 358

Der Groyser Kundes (The Big Stick), 149, *150*

Dershowitz, Alan M., 425–26

Dickstein, Samuel L., 226–27

Dillingham Commission, 139

Dittenhoefer, Abram J., 102–3

divorce, in American Jewish communities, 163–64

Dorchester, sinking of, 251, *252*

Drayton, William H., 36–37

DuBois, Josiah, 262–67

dueling, 91

Dutch colonialism, 1, 10–12, 294

Eastern Europe: Jewish emigration from, 67, 129, 131, 133–34, 142–44, 181–82, 189, 234; pogroms in, 170–72, 178–79

Edgeworth, Maria, 89–90

Edles, Mrs. Allen I., 302–3

education: in antebellum era, 82–86; antisemitism in colleges and universities, 333, 368; Jewish identity and, 288–89; Jewish quotas at colleges and universities, 219–20; Judaic studies programs at colleges and universities, 358–61; post-World

War II public education funding increases, 306; *shlichut* programs, 294–301

Eighteenth Amendment, 191–93

Eilberg, Amy, 408

Einhorn, David, 97, 118–22

Elizer (Eliezer), Isaac, 16, 19

emissaries *(shlichim)*, 294–301

Epstein, David G., 352–54

European Enlightenment, 31

European Jewish refugees, post–World War II, 275–76

evangelization of American Jews, 61–63

Ezekiel, Jacob, 73–74

Ezrat Nashim, 363–64, 408

family life: colonial era, 26–30; early national period, 64–66; Gilded Age, 160–64; mid-twentieth century, 302–3

Federal Council of Churches of Christ, 204–6

Federal Council of Synagogues of America, 203–4

Feibelman, Julian B., 306–8

Felsenthal, Bernhard, 93, 97–99

Female Hebrew Benevolent Society, 82–84

feminism, 335–39, 350–51, 410–11. *See also* women

Fight for Freedom Committee, 245

First Amendment, 40

Fischel, Arnold, 122–26

The Fixer (Malamud), 378–79

folk music, 413–14

Ford, Henry, 2, 181, 217–19

Forsyth, John, 92

Forward (Der Forverts), 131–32, 138, *138*, 144

Fourteen Points Plan, 232–33

Fox, George L., 251, *252*

Frank, Leo, 174–75, *176*

Frank, Ray (Rachel), 155–56

Frankel, Jacob, 123

Franks, Bilhah Abigaill, 26–27

Franks, Jacob, 26–27

Franks, Naphthali (Heartsey), 26–27

Friedan, Betty, 337–39, 350

Friedman, Debbie, 413–14

Friends of Zion *(Chovaveh Zion)*, 166

gay rights movement, 422–23

gender issues, 335–39, 350–51, 363–64, 410–11. *See also* women

Georgia, 7, 127, 174–75, *176*, 308–10

Gettysburg address, Jewish parody of, 141

Gilded Age and Progressive era: antisemitism in, 170–76; civic status, 141; factory work by women, 142–44, 145–52; family life, 160–64; immigrant life, 131–40; overview, 129–30; philanthropy, 139–40, 145, 177–80; politics and government, 141, 144–45; religious life, 153–59; Zionism in, 165–69

Ginzberg, Louis, 191–93

Gliddon, John, 92

Glueck, Nelson, 364

Goldman, Emma, 162

Gold Rush, 67, 77–78

Goldstein, Eric, xxiii

Goldstein, Herbert S., 247–48

Gomez, Daniel, 22, 24–25

Gomez, Isaac, 24–25

Gomez, Moses, 22–25

Goode, Alexander D., 251, *252*

Goodman, Andrew, 319, *319*

Gore, Albert, 395

Gottlieb, Dick, 248–50

Gottschalk, Alfred, 201, 364

government. *See* politics and government

Grant, Ulysses S., 103–4, 116–17

Gratz, Bernard, 13–14

Gratz, Michael, 13–14, 27–28

Gratz, Rebecca, 82–84

Great War. *See* World War I

Greenberg, Henry (Hank), 202

Greenleaf, Thomas, 43–44

Grosse, Juliet, 329–30

Gruber, Ruth, 269

Guest, Edgar A., 202

"Guiding Principles of Reform Judaism," 211–12

Hadassah, 208–10

Halivni, David Weiss, 409, 416

Hall, Sarah, 89–90

Halleck, Gen. Henry Wager, 103, 104

Hammer, Louis, 201

Hand, Learned, 426

Harby, Isaac, 45–47, 79

Harding, Warren G., 222

Harrington (Edgeworth), 89–90

Harrison, Peter, 20

Hart, Henry, 123–24, 125–26

Harvard College, 219–20

Hasidism, 294–301

havurah movement, 359–62, 385–86

Hayman, Nepthali, 24–25

Hays, Gitlah, 24–25

Hays, Solomon, 24–25

Hebrew Benevolent Congregation (Atlanta), 308–10

Hebrew Benevolent Society (Charleston), 314–15

Hebrew Benevolent Society (Cincinnati), 72

Hebrew Congregation of Shreveport, 109

Hebrew Immigrant Aid Society (HIAS), 139, *139*, 141

Hebrew language, 79, 154–55, 195–96, 208, 358

Hebrew School in antebellum era, 82–84

Hebrew Union College (later HUC-JIR), 166, 200–201, 240–42, 343–45, 364

Hebrew University of Jerusalem, 187

Hecht, Ben, 256

Heinze, Andrew, 428

Hendel, Herbert, 278

Hertzberg, Arthur, 352–54

Herzl, Theodor, 166

Heschel, Abraham Joshua, 240–42, 343–45

HIAS (Hebrew Immigrant Aid Society), 139, *139*, 141

Hillel organization, 288, 315–17

Hitler, Adolf, 2, 181, 224–25, 239–40, 243, 245, *245*, 254

Hoffman, Anna (née Rosenberg), 185–86

Holocaust. *See* Shoah (Holocaust)

Hooks, Benjamin L., 369–73

housing covenants, easing of restrictions on Jews, 275

HUC-JIR (Hebrew Union College-Jewish Institute of Religion), 343–45, 364. *See also* Hebrew Union College (later HUC-JIR); Jewish Institute of Religion (later HUC-JIR)

Hughes, Charles Evans, 205

Hull House, 177

Humanistic Judaism, 412–13

humor, by American Jewish writers, 381–82

Hunter, Robert, 17

Hurwitz, Sara, 416, 419–21

Ickes, Harold, 269

ILGWU (International Ladies' Garment Workers' Union), 150–52

immigration: antebellum period, 69–72; anti-immigrant movement, 69–72, 181–82, 222–23, 240–42; antisemitism and, 172–73; from Central Europe, 1, 67, 93, 141, 146–47; in colonial period, 1, 13–14; in contemporary America, 390–93; in early national period, 33–35; from Eastern Europe, 67, 129, 131, 133–34, 142–44, 181–82, 189, 234; Gilded Age and Progressive era, 131–40; interwar quotas, 181–82; post–World War II trends in, 277–80

Independent Order of True Sisters (later UOTS), 145–46

in-marriage, defined, 403n2

interfaith and intergroup relations, 203–6, 251, *252*, 306–21, 368–74, 431–36

intermarriage, 3–4, 8, 65–66, 89–90, 161, 389, 401–7, 403n1

International Ladies' Garment Workers' Union (ILGWU), 150–52

Internet, Jewish identity on, 427–30

interwar period: antisemitism, 217–31; civic status, 183–86; interfaith and intergroup relations, 203–6; labor activism, 187–90; overview, 181–82; philanthropy, 183, 232–42; politics and government, 183–86; popular culture, 202; religious life, 191–201; Zionism, 207–16

Iranian Revolution, 390–93

Isaacs, Myer S., 107–8, 124

Isaacs, Samuel Myer, 107, 109

Israel: American Jewish criticism of, 385–86, 424–26; American Jewish support for, 275–76, 322–26, 368; Arab threats to state of, 383; Chabad expansion in, 294–301; U.S. recognition of, 322, 322

Jackson, Jesse, 373–74, *374*

Jackson-Vanik Amendment (1974), 387

Jacobs, Jacob, 52–53

Jalonick, Isaac, 84

Javits, Jacob, 331

JDate, 427

JDC (American Jewish Joint Distribution Committee), 234–38

Jefferson, Thomas, 48–49, 53–55

Jewish aid programs, 177–80, 232–42, 327–33, 387–88

Jewish American Heritage Month, 435–36

Jewish Defense League, 335, 347–49, *350*

Jewish identity: civic status, 337–40, 345–47, 355–57; in contemporary America, 389; declining synagogue affiliation rates, 414–16; feminist movement and, 337–39; interfaith and intergroup relations, 368–74; Jewish American Heritage Month, 435–36; Moishe House project, 434–35; philanthropy, 387–88; politics and government, 347–57; in popular culture, 375–81, 427–30; religious life, 358–67;

twenty-first century issues,
431–36; Zionism and, 383–86.
See also assimilation and
acculturation
Jewish Immigrant (pamphlet), 139,
139
Jewish Institute of Religion (later
HUC-JIR), 200–201, 281, 343–45,
364
Jewish Labor Congress, 187–88
Jewish Theological Seminary of
America, 154, 191, 196, 343,
408–9
Jewish War Veterans Ladies'
Auxiliaries, 239–40
Johnson-Reed Act, 222–23
Jonas, Joseph, 71–72
Jonas, Regina, 200, 364
Jones, Emanuel, 65–66
Jones, Samuel, 65–66
Josephson, Meir, 27–28
J Street, 424
Judaic studies programs, 358–61

Kahal Kadosh Beth Elohim
congregation (Charleston),
79–80
Kahane, Meir, 348–49
Kahn, Florence Prag, 350–51
Kalisch, Isidor, 123–24
Kalm, Peter, 15
Kaplan, Arthur M., 223–24
Kaplan, Kivie, 319–21
Kaplan, Leonard, 220–22, *221*
Kaplan, Mordecai M., 196–99
Kaplan, Richard S., 258
Kaskel, Cesar J., 103
Kauffman, Laurie, 354–55
Kaufman, Irving, 285
Kehilat Orach Eliezer congregation
(NYC), 416
Khrushchev, Nikita, 329–30
King, Martin Luther, 315–17, 343,
373
Kishinev pogrom, 170–72
Kluge, John, 391
Kohn, Abraham, 76–77
Kohn, S. Joshua, 251
Korngold, Jamie, 432–33

Kuhn, Fritz Julius, 225–26
Ku Klux Klan, 114–16
Kurman, Dorothy, 239
Kursheedt, Israel B., 91–92

Labatt, Henry J., 77–78
labor: in antebellum period, 75–78;
colonial period, 17–19; in early
national period, 52–55; factory
work in Gilded Age, 142–44,
145–52; in interwar period,
187–90; union activity, 147–52,
187–90
Labor Zionism, 215–16
Lantos, Tom, 399
Lazarus, Emma, 132–33
Lee-Parritz, Oren, 414–16
Leeser, Isaac, 71–72, 81–82, 84, 123,
126–27
leftism in Jewish politics, 131–32,
259–60, 281–83, 354–57
Lehman, Herbert H., 235–38
Lerner, Max, 259–60
Levi, Hayman, 24–25
Levine, Jo Ann, 350–51
Levinthal, Bernard C., 200–201
Levinthal, Helen Hadassah, 200–201
Levinthal, Israel H., 200–201
Levitt, William, 277–78
Levittown, Pennsylvania, 277–78
Levy, Aaron, 75
Levy, Clifton Harby, 282
Levy, Ezekiel, 112
Levy, Isaac, 130
Levy, Leonora, 112
LGBTQ community, 422–23
liberalism, 335, 352–54. *See also*
leftism in Jewish politics
Lieberman, Joseph, 395–99
Lilith Magazine, 366–67
Lincoln, Abraham, 93, 101–4, 107–8,
123, 126–28, 141
Lindbergh, Charles A., 181, 230–31,
243
literature, American Jewish
contributions to, 132–33,
144–45, 375–81
London, Meyer, 147–48
Lopez, Aaron, 12, 16, 28

Lopez, Isaac, 7
Lopez, Moses, 12–13
Lowell, A. Lawrence, 219–20, 426
Lowenthal, Zvi, 348–49
Lubavitch, 294–301
Lubow, Akiba, 407–8
Lucky Bag Yearbook (U.S. Naval
Academy), 220–22, *221*

Mack, Julian, 219–20
Madison, James, 45–47
Magnes, Judah L., 187–88
Mahoney, John J., 251
Mailert, August, 69
Mailert, Charles Lucius, 69
Malamud, Bernard, 377–79
Malev, William, 310–14
Mandell Berman Institute, 401–3
Marcus, Jacob Rader, xxii, 181,
200–201, 319–20
Marez, Curtis, 426
Margoshes, Samuel, 222–23
Marshall, Louis, 147–48, 178–79,
191–93, 232–33
Maryland, 37–38, 49–51
Masliansky, Zvi Hirsch, 165
Melville, Allan, 18
Mendes da Costa, Emanuel, 33–34
mid-twentieth century. *See*
post–World War II American
Jewish life
Mikve Israel congregation
(Philadelphia), 53–55, 57–58
military service, 94, 122–28, 158–59,
246–50
Milledoler, Phillip, 61–63
Miller, Jonathan, 428–30
mitzvot, patrilineal descent issue
and, 407nn1–2
modern Orthodoxy. *See* Orthodox
Judaism
Moïse, Abraham, 79–80
Moïse, Penina, 69
Moishe House, 434–35
Monroe, James, 45–47
Mordecai, Alfred, 94–97
Mordecai, Alfred Jr., 94
Mordecai, George Washington,
94–96

Mordecai, Jacob, 94

Mordecai, Moses, 106

Mordecai, Rosa, 82–84

Morgan, Anne, 151–52

Morgenstern, Julian, 240–42

Morgenthau, Henry, 262–67

Moses, Samuel, 19

music, Jewish contributions to,
413–14

Myers, Asher, 24–25

Myerson, Bess, 304–5

Najman, Dina, 416, 419–20

Nasser, Gamal Abdel, 383

Nathan-Kazis, Josh, 418–19

National Association for the
Advancement of Colored
People (NAACP), 319–21,
369–74

National Committee to Secure
Justice, 283–87, 284

National Community Relations
Advisory Council (NCRAC),
279–80

National Conference of Christians
and Jews, 204–6, 223

National Conference of Jews and
Christians for the Advancement
of Justice, Amity and Peace, 205,
223

National Council of Jewish Women
(NCJW), 142–44, 177

National Hillel Commission, 288

nationalism, Jewish, 129–30. See
also Zionism

National Recovery Administration
(NRA), 185–86

National Unity Government (Israel),
383

Native Americans, 36–37, 87–88

nativism, 2, 130, 173–74

The Natural (Malamud), 378

Nazi Germany, 224–27, 226, 238–42.
See also Shoah (Holocaust)

NCJW (National Council of Jewish
Women), 142–44, 177

NCRAC (National Community
Relations Advisory Council),
279–80

neoconservative movement, 335,
339–40, 352–54

Ner-David, Haviva, 416–17

New Amsterdam, 7, 10–12, 294, 294

New Deal policies, 2, 185–86, 244

New Jewish Agenda, 354–57

New York Jewish Federation, 139–40

New York State Constitution,
emancipation of Jews in, 38–39

Noah, Mordecai Manuel, 45–49,
87–88

Nobel Prize, 379

nonsectarianism, Jewish identity
and, 288–89

North Dakota, 160–61

NRA (National Recovery
Administration), 185–86

Obama, Barack, 435–36

Olmsted, Jerauld, 221

Orthodox Judaism: feminist
movement and, 336; interfaith
and intergroup relations, 203–6;
in interwar period, 196–99; in
post–World War II period,
279–80; in Progressive era, 158;
Prohibition, 191–93; Vietnam
War, 341–45; women in, 294–96,
336, 416–21

Palestine, 29, 129–30, 207–16, 239,
260, 271, 271

Palestine Liberation Organization,
369–72, 374

Palestinian Authority, 425

Palestinian refugees, 425–26

Palmer, A. Mitchell, 189–90

Passover, 112, 158–59, 247–48

Passy, Charles, 413–14

patrilineal descent issue, 405–7

Paysaddon, Hannah, 28

Peck, John, 19

Peixotto, Benjamin F., 116–17

Pennsylvania, 7, 40

Perkins, Frances, 151–52

Perley, Thomas F., 127

Persian Jewish immigrants, 390–93

Phagan, Mary, 174–75

Philadelphia, 13–14, 57–58

philanthropy: colonial period,
28–29; Gilded Age and
Progressive era, 139–40, 145,
177–80; in interwar period, 183,
232–42; in mid-twentieth
century, 387–88; in post–World
War II era, 327–33

Philipson, David, 203–4

Phillips, Eugenia Levy, 110–11

Phillips, Jonas, 40–41

Phillips, Philip, 110–11

Pittsburgh Platform, 153–54, 211

Plaskow, Judith S., 410–11

Plessy v. Ferguson, 306

Poale Zion (Workers of Zion),
215–16

Podhoretz, Norman, 339–40

Poling, Clark V., 251, 252

politics and government: American
Revolution, 31, 36–51; in
antebellum period, 73–74, 108;
civil rights movement, 3, 275–76,
306–21, 339–40, 369–74; colonial
period, 15–16; contemporary
America, 395–99; in Gilded Age
and Progressive Era, 141, 144–45;
in interwar period, 183–86;
Jewish conservative trend,
352–54; labor activism (1970s),
345–47; leftism in Jewish politics,
131–32, 259–60, 281–83, 354–57;
liberalism, 335, 352–54; 1960s to
1970s, 345–57; in post–World
War II period, 275–76, 281–87;
socialism, 131–32, 144–45,
189–90, 212–15; State
Department's stonewalling on
rescue immigration, 254–56,
262–67; Treasury Department
and Shoah, 262–67; Vietnam
war, 341–45; World War II, 245.
See also Congress, U.S.

popular culture: in interwar period,
202; Jewish contributions to,
375–81, 427–30; in post–World
War II era, 304–5; during World
War II, 247

post–World War II American Jewish
life: antisemitism in, 333; family

life in, 302–3; immigration and adaptation, 277–80; interfaith and intergroup relations, 306–21; overview, 275–76; philanthropy, 327–33; politics and government, 275–76, 281–87; popular culture, 304–5; religious life, 288–301; Zionism, 322–26

prayer in public schools, 298–301

Priesand, Sally, 200–201, 364–66, 408–9

Prinz, Joachim, 317

Progressive era. *See* Gilded Age and Progressive era

Prohibition, 191–93

The Protocols of the Elders of Zion, 2, 217–19

Pulitzer, Joseph, 132

Pulitzer Prize, 375, 377, 379

Pye, Henry James, 43–44

Rabbi Isaac Elchanan Theological Seminary (RIETS), 193–95

Rabbinical Assembly, 212–15, 363, 407

racial equality, 3, 275–76, 306. *See also* civil rights movement

Rankin, John E., 272–73

Raphall, Morris, 118–22

Raucher, Tamar, 434–35

Recife, Brazil, 7, 9, *10*, 294

Reconstruction era, 113–17

Reconstructionism, 181–82

Reform Judaism: in antebellum period, 79–81; anticommunism and, 281–82; chaplaincy issue, 122–23; civil rights movement, 306–8; in Civil War, 97; feminist movement and, 336; folk music and, 413–14; interfaith and intergroup relations, 203–6; intermarriage, 403–5; in interwar period, 181–82, 196–99; patrilineal descent issue, 405–7; philanthropy and relief, 178–79; post–World War II changes in, 278, 289–92; in Progressive era, 153–59; Prohibition, 191–93; tercentenary filmstrip of Jewish

life, 294; Vietnam war and, 343–45; women rabbis in, 364–66, 418; World War II and the Shoah, 244; Zionism, 166, 211–12, 253–54

Reisman, Barnard, 359, 361–62

relief programs, 177–80, 183, 232–42, 327–33, 387–88

religion: in antebellum period, 79–86; colonial American Jewish experience, 20–25; in contemporary American Jewish life, 401–23; in early national period, 56–63; freedom of, 40, 45–49; impact of suburbanization on, 275–76; in interwar period, 181, 191–201; Jewish chaplaincy issue, 122–28; for mid-twentieth century Jews, 358–67; post–World War II issues for American Jews in, 288–301; slavery, 118–22

Republican Party, 352–54

resort industry, 368–69

Revel, Bernard, 195–96

Rhode Island, 7, 12, 16, 41–43, 56–57

Rice, Abraham, 81–82

Rich, Adrienne, 354

Richman, Julia, 142–44

Rickover, Hyman G., 220

Riegner, Gerhart, 254

RIETS (Rabbi Isaac Elchanan Theological Seminary), 193–95

Ripley, James Wolfe, 94, 96–97

Rivera, Jacob Rodriguez, 56

Rivington, James, 43–44

Robinson, Leland, 270–71

Rockefeller family, 245

Rongy, Abraham J., 223–24

Roosevelt, Franklin Delano, 2, 185–86, 243, 254–56, 259–60

Roosevelt, Theodore Jr., 220

Rosen, Joseph A., 234

Rosenberg, Abraham, 147–48

Rosenberg, Anna M. (Mrs. Hoffman), 185–86

Rosenberg, Ethel, 283–87, *284*

Rosenberg, Julius, 283–87, *284*

rosh kehilah (congregational leader), women as, 419–21

Roth, Joel, 407–8

Roth, Philip, 375–76

Rothchild, Sylvia, 359–61

Rothschild, Jacob, 308–10

Rothschild, Baron Walter, 207

Rubinow, Isaac M., 183–85

Russian Jews, 234

Sabsovich, H. L., 133–34

Salomon, Haym, 52

Salvador, Francis, 33, 36–37

Salvador, Joseph, 33–34

Samuel, Rebecca Alexander, 34–35

Sandler, Adam, 428–30

Sanger, Margaret, 162

Sapiro, Aaron, 217

Sarasohn, Kasriel, 134

Sarna, Jonathan D., 4

Schappes, Morris U., xxi

Schiff, Jacob, 179–80

Schindler, Alexander M., 403–5

Schnall, Charles, 282

Schneerson, Menachem Mendel, 294–301

Schneerson, Yosef Yitzchak, 294

Schneiderman, Rose, 150–52

school desegregation, 306

School for Jewish Studies, 282

Schultz, Benjamin, 281–82

Schusterman, Charles, 414

Schusterman, Lynn, 414

Schwerner, Michael, 319, *319*

secular nationalism, 196–99

Seixas, Gershom Mendes, 44–45, 58–61

Seixas, Moses, 41–42

Seixas, Theodore J., 91–92

Sephardic Jewish community, 11, 69, 391

Sha'ar Zahav Congregation (San Francisco), 422–23

Sharansky, Anatoly, 388, *388*

Shearith Israel synagogue (NYC), 15, 22–25, 48–49

Sheftall, Frances, 64–65

Sheftall, Mordecai, 64–65

Sheftall, Sheftall, 64–65

Sherman, Allan, 381–82

Sherman, Paulette Koufman, 427–28

Shoah (Holocaust): American government and, 255–56, 259–60, 262–68; American Jewish identity following, 275; Dachau concentration camp, 248–50; Fight for Freedom Committee, 245; Jewish refugees from, 269, 269–71; Judaic studies programs, 358; overview, 243–44; Riegner's details of Nazi plans for genocide, 254–55; U.S. Holocaust Memorial Museum, 394; *We Will Never Die* program, 256–59; world Jewish population before and after World War II, 274

Shreveport, Louisiana, 109

Silver, Abba Hillel, 239, 260–62, 289–92

Silverman, Samuel, 254

Simon, Abram, 203, 204

Simson, Sampson, 44–45

Six Day War, 383–86, *385*

Slaton, John M., 174–75

slavery, 19, 27–28, 52–53, 65–66, 68, 93, 97–101, 104–7, 118–22

Smith, Gerald L. K., 272–73

Snyder, Tamar, 419–21

Sobell, Morton, 283

socialism, 131–32, 144–45, 189–90, 212–15

social life and acceptance, 87–90, 93, 181. *See also* antisemitism; assimilation and acculturation

social media, Jewish identity on, 427

Social Security Act of 1935, 183

Society for Humanistic Judaism, 412–13

Society for the Advancement of Judaism, 196–99

Solomon, Hannah Greenebaum, 177

Soomekh, Saba, 392–93

South Carolina, 7, 36–37, 69, 112

Soviet Union, 283–87, 327–33, 335, 387–88, *388*

Spanish-Portuguese liturgical rite, 1, 29

Standing Again at Sinai (Plaskow), 410–11

State Department (U.S.), 254–56, 262–67

states' rights, 1, 93

Statue of Liberty, 132

Steinem, Gloria, 350

Steinhardt, Michael, 414

Stiles, Ezra, 56–57

Stolz, Joseph, 178–79

Stone, Earl, 201

Stone, Ellen, 354

Straus, Isidor, 127–28

Straus, Lazarus, 127

strike activity, 147–52

Stuyvesant, Peter, 10–12

suburbanization, post–World War II, 275–76

Susman, Milton K., 384

Sutherland, Howard, 220–22

synagogues: in colonial era, 7–8; declining affiliation rates in, 414–16, 431–34; folk music in, 413–14; havurah movement, 359–62; non-Jewish observations on, 15; post–World War II construction of, 278, 293, *293*, 329; Touro Synagogue, *20–21*, 39. See also *individual congregations*

Synaplex initiative, 414–16

Szold, Henrietta, 208–10

Taft, William Howard, 179–80

Talmudic instruction, 193–95

Temple Israel (Omaha), 431–32

The Temple (Atlanta), 308–10

Ten Commandments, 144–45, *167*

Tennessee, 114–16

territorialism, 87–88

Texas, 84

textile industry, 147–52

Thal, Martha, 160–61

Thal, Sarah, 160–61

Thal, Solomon, 160–61

"This Is the Army, Mr. Jones" (Berlin), 247

Thomas, E. S., 50–51

Torah, women's study of, 294–301

Touro, Isaac, 39

Touro Synagogue (Exterior, N.D.), *20–21*, 39

Treasury Department, U.S., 262–67

"Trefa Banquet," 153

Triangle Shirtwaist Company Fire, *149–50*, 149–52

Tri-Faith Initiative, Omaha, Nebraska, 431–32

Truman, Harry S., 270–71, 322, 326

Trumbull, Lyman, 123

Tunis, Kingdom of, 45–47, 87–88

twenty-first century Jewish American life, 431–36

Tyler, John, 73–74

Union, Jewish relationship to during Civil War, 93–94, 107–8

union activity, Jewish involvement in, 147–52, 187–90

Union of American Hebrew Congregations (UAHC), 166, 203–4, 294, 369, 403–5

United Jewish Appeal, 271, *271*

United Nations, 275–76

United Order of True Sisters (UOTS), 145–46

United States Holocaust Memorial Council, 394

United States Holocaust Memorial Museum, 394

United States Military Academy (West Point), 94

United States Naval Academy (Annapolis), 220–22

Universal Declaration of Human Rights, 328

Untermeyer, Samuel, 224–25

UOTS (United Order of True Sisters), 145–46

U.S. Congress. *See* Congress, U.S.

Van Buren, Martin, 91–92

Vietnam War, 3, 341–45

violence against Jews, 114–16, 174–75, *176*. *See also* Shoah (Holocaust)

Virginia, 34–35

Voorsanger, Elkan C., 158–59

Wagenaer, Zacharias, 9
Warburg, Felix, 139
Warner, Harry, 245
Warner, Jack, 245
War Refugee Board, 263, 267–68
Washington, George, 41–43
Washington, John P., 251, *252*
Weisberger, Jon, 354
Weiss, Avi, 416, 418–19
West, Kevin, 390–91
westward migration in U.S., 1,
    67–92, 160–61
We Will Never Die memorial
    program, 256–58
Wiesel, Elie, 359, 394
Wilson, Woodrow, 232–33
Winchevsky, Morris, 144–45
Wine, Sherwin, 412–13
Winograd, Richard W., 315–17
Wise, Isaac Mayer, 81, 113–14, 166
Wise, Stephen S.: anticommunism
    campaign, 281–82; anti-
    semitism, 217–19, 228–30,
    272–73; interfaith relations, 306;
    Shoah, 238, *238*, 254–56, 260–62,
    265–67; support of organized
    labor, 189–90; women's
    rabbinical training, 200–201
Wohl, Samuel, 239

Wolf, Simon, 170–71
women: antebellum education of,
    82–86; birth control for, 162;
    divorce, 163–64; *doreh* (Iranian
    circle of women), 391–92; Ezrat
    Nashim, 363–64; as factory
    workers, 142–44, 145–52,
    149–50; feminism, 335–39,
    350–51, 410–11; magazines for,
    366–67; in Orthodox Judaism,
    294–96, 416–21; post–World
    War II Jewish life, 302–3; as
    rabbis, 155–56, 200–201, 364–66,
    408–10, 416–21; relief and
    philanthropy by, 177; religious
    studies by, 294–301
Women's Trade Union League,
    150–52
Woodbine Colony, 133–34
World War I, 2, 129, 158–59
World War II: American Jewish
    community, 2–3, 243–74;
    antisemitism in, 272–74; civic
    status, 246–50; global Jewish
    population before and after,
    274; interfaith and intergroup
    relations, 251, *252*; politics and
    government, 245; Zionism
    during, 244, 253–71

Wright, Frank Lloyd, 293
Wyschogrod, Michael, 341–43

Yadegar, Jasmine, 391
Yeshivat Chovevei Torah Rabbinic
    School, 416, 418
Yeshiva University, 193–96
Yiddish-language writing and
    publications, 131–32, 138, 144,
    149, *150*, 181, 222–23
Young, Andrew, 369
Yulee, David Levy, 99

Zeire Zion Hitachduth, 215–16
Zigmond, Maurice L., 288–89
Zionism: American Zionist
    movement, 2, 165–69; in
    contemporary period, 424–26;
    in interwar period, 183, 207–16;
    Labor Zionism, 215–16; in
    mid-twentieth century, 335,
    383–86; nineteenth-century
    emergence of, 129–30;
    post–World War II, 275–76,
    322–26; Religious versus Cultural
    Zionists, 212–15; during World
    War II, 244, 253–71
Zionist Organization of America,
    207–8, 258